Accessibility and Diversity in Education:

Breakthroughs in Research and Practice

Information Resources Management Association
USA

Volume II

Published in the United States of America by
IGI Global
Information Science Reference (an imprint of IGI Global)
701 E. Chocolate Avenue
Hershey PA, USA 17033
Tel: 717-533-8845
Fax: 717-533-8661
E-mail: cust@igi-global.com
Web site: http://www.igi-global.com

Copyright © 2020 by IGI Global. All rights reserved. No part of this publication may be reproduced, stored or distributed in any form or by any means, electronic or mechanical, including photocopying, without written permission from the publisher. Product or company names used in this set are for identification purposes only. Inclusion of the names of the products or companies does not indicate a claim of ownership by IGI Global of the trademark or registered trademark.

Library of Congress Cataloging-in-Publication Data

Names: Information Resources Management Association, editor.
Title: Accessibility and diversity in education : breakthroughs in research
 and practice / Information Resources Management Association.
Description: Hershey, PA : Information Science Reference (an imprint of IGI
 Global), [2020] | Includes bibliographical references and index. |
 Summary: ""This book examines emerging methods and trends for creating
 accessible and inclusive educational environments and examines the
 latest teaching strategies and methods for promoting learning for all
 students. It also addresses equal opportunity and diversity requirements
 in schools"--Provided by publisher"-- Provided by publisher.
Identifiers: LCCN 2019026518 (print) | LCCN 2019026519 (ebook) | ISBN
 9781799812135 (hardcover) | ISBN 9781799812142 (ebook)
Subjects: LCSH: Educational equalization. | Inclusive education. |
 Multicultural education.
Classification: LCC LC213 .A336 2020 (print) | LCC LC213 (ebook) | DDC
 379.2/6--dc23
LC record available at https://lccn.loc.gov/2019026518
LC ebook record available at https://lccn.loc.gov/2019026519

British Cataloguing in Publication Data
A Cataloguing in Publication record for this book is available from the British Library.

The views expressed in this book are those of the authors, but not necessarily of the publisher.

For electronic access to this publication, please contact: eresources@igi-global.com.

Editor-in-Chief

Mehdi Khosrow-Pour, DBA
Information Resources Management Association, USA

Associate Editors

Steve Clarke, *University of Hull, UK*
Murray E. Jennex, *San Diego State University, USA*
Ari-Veikko Anttiroiko, *University of Tampere, Finland*

Editorial Advisory Board

Sherif Kamel, *American University in Cairo, Egypt*
In Lee, *Western Illinois University, USA*
Jerzy Kisielnicki, *Warsaw University, Poland*
Amar Gupta, *Arizona University, USA*
Craig van Slyke, *University of Central Florida, USA*
John Wang, *Montclair State University, USA*
Vishanth Weerakkody, *Brunel University, UK*

List of Contributors

Addison, Mark Antony / *Western Michigan University, USA* 390
Alegre de la Rosa, Olga M. / *University of La Laguna, Spain* 599
Aleshina, Ekaterina / *Penza State University, Russia* 291, 296
Alisat, Laurie / *University of Calgary, Canada* 995
Amaral, Maryan / *Aero, Inc., USA* 509
Angulo, Luis M. Villar / *University of Seville, Spain* 599
Ash, Anthony / *University of North Carolina Charlotte, USA* 782
Bagnato, Karin / *University of Messina, Italy* 356
Bateman, David F. / *Shippensburg University, USA* 550
Benedict, Amber Elizabeth / *University of Florida, USA* 143
Bowman, Nicky / *University of Missouri, USA* 102
Brookfield, Stephen / *St. Thomas University, USA* 738
Brownell, Mary T. / *University of Florida, USA* 143
Bruyere, Susanne / *Cornell University, USA* 215
Chamblin, Michelle / *Molloy College, USA* 972
Clarke, Veronika Bohac / *University of Calgary, Canada* 995
Cline, Jenifer / *Great Falls Public Schools, USA* 550
Coffey, Heather / *University of North Carolina at Charlotte, USA* 782
Cooley, Derek / *Godwin Heights Public Schools, USA* 121
Crosby-Cooper, Tricia / *National University, USA* 163
Curran, Christina M. / *University of Northern Iowa, USA* 906
Ehlinger, Emily / *University of Minnesota, USA* 34
Epler, Pam / *Grand Canyon University, USA* 940
Ford, Theron N. / *John Carroll University, USA* 1022
Foster, Monika / *Edinburgh Napier University, UK* 822
Gaona, Alma Rosa García / *Universidad Veracruzana, México* 535
Gibbon, Thomas C. / *Shippensburg University, USA* 550
Gilic, Lina / *St. John's University, USA* 972
Glimps, Blanche Jackson / *Tennessee State University, USA* 1022
Golden, Thomas / *Cornell University, USA* 215
González, Alfredo Mendoza / *Universidad Juárez Autónoma de Tabasco, México* 535
Gower, Wendy Strobel / *Cornell University, USA* 215
Griffin, Cynthia C. / *University of Florida, USA* 143
Gulley, Ann / *Auburn University at Montgomery, USA* 495
Gupta, Sanjeev Kumar / *All India Institute of Speech and Hearing, India* 431
Hadley, Wanda / *Western Michigan University, USA* 390

Hagelkruys, Dominik / *University of Vienna, Austria* 272
Hawbaker, Becky Wilson / *University of Northern Iowa, USA* 906
Heineke, Amy J. / *Loyola University, USA* 757
Hosfelt, Patricia D. / *Frederick County Maryland Public Schools, USA* 550
Hsu, Jennifer / *Grand Valley State University, USA* 390
Hu, Luanjiao / *University of Maryland at College Park, USA* 197
Huang, Liujuan / *Guangming Experimental School, China* 865
Huang, Ying / *Changzhen Elementary School of Guangming District, China* 865
Ikuta, Shigeru / *Otsuma Women's University, Japan* 464
Ishitobi, Ryoichi / *University of Tsukuba, Japan* 464
Jackson, Keonta N. / *Texas A&M University – Commerce, USA* 446
Jackson, Nykela H. / *University of Central Arkansas, USA* 666
Johnson, Ronn / *Creighton University Medical School, USA & VA Nebraska-Western Iowa
    Health Care System, USA* 680
Kennedy, Adam S. / *Loyola University, USA* 757
Keough, Penelope Debs / *National University, USA* 179
Kim, Ji Youn Cindy / *University of Iowa, USA* 680
Lee, JoJo Yanki / *University of San Diego, USA* 680
Li, Jiacheng / *East China Normal University, China* 865
Li, Yan / *East China Normal University, China* 865
Lin, Jing / *University of Maryland at College Park, USA* 197
Lopez, Ann E. / *University of Toronto, Canada* 613
Luján-Mora, Sergio / *University of Alicante, Spain* 52
Mary, Latisha / *Université de Lorraine, France* 630
Mkrttchian, Vardan / *HHH University, Australia* 291, 296
Motschnig, Renate / *University of Vienna, Austria* 272
Myers, Jonte A / *University of Florida, USA* 143
Nakui, Haruka / *Abiko Special Needs Education School for the Mentally Challenged, Japan* 464
Nemoto, Fumio / *University of Tsukuba, Japan* 464
Nkabinde, Zandile P. / *New Jersey City University, USA* 806
O'Connor Jr., Johnny R. / *Lamar University, USA* 446
Odia, Agnes Anuoluwapo / *University of Benin, Nigeria* 80
Odia, James Osabuohien / *University of Benin, Nigeria* 80
Olan, Elsie L. / *University of Central Florida, USA* 613
Pacis, Dina / *National University, USA* 163, 179
Pendergast, Mark O. / *Florida Gulf Coast University, USA* 19
Perez, Luis / *Eye on Access, USA* 495
Pfannenstiel, Kathleen Hughes / *American Institutes for Research, USA* 240
Pluta, Rebecca Magee / *Special Education Advocate, USA* 578
Preast, June L. / *University of Missouri, USA* 102
Prickett, Logan / *Auburn University at Montgomery, USA* 495
Raasch, Jennifer / *Clemson University, USA* 1
Raghunandan-Jack, Nadira / *Charter School Sector, USA* 649
Rankin, Jenny Grant / *University of Cambridge, UK* 843
Ritter, Zachary S. / *University of Redlands, USA* 712
Robles, Teresita de Jesús Álvarez / *Universidad Veracruzana, México* 535

Rodríguez, Francisco Alvarez / *Universidad Autónoma de Aguascalientes, México* 535
Rose, Chad A. / *University of Missouri, USA* 102
Roth, Kenneth Robert / *California State University, USA* 712
Rudstam, Hannah / *Cornell University, USA* 215
Ruffin, Tiece / *University of North Carolina – Asheville, USA* 891
Russell, Carol / *Emporia State University, USA* 404
Sanchez-Gordon, Sandra / *National Polytechnic School of Ecuador, Ecuador* 52
Sanders, Jennifer "JC" / *Independent Researcher, USA* 240
Schwilk, Christopher L. / *Shippensburg University, USA* 550
Talbot, Donna / *Western Michigan University, USA* 390
Tseng, Margaret / *Marymount University, USA* 578
Uduigwome, George / *Los Angeles Unified School District, USA* 320
Urushihata, Chiho / *University of Tsukuba, Japan* 464
Van Looy, Sara / *Cornell University, USA* 215
Wang, Jun / *University of Florida, USA* 143
Webster, Nicole / *Pennsylvania State University, USA* 782
Whitten, Elizabeth / *Western Michigan University, USA* 121
Wright, Michelle F. / *Masaryk University, Czech Republic* 368
Yamaguchi, Kyoko / *Abiko Special Needs Education School for the Mentally Challenged, Japan* 464
Young, Andrea / *Université de Strasbourg, France* 630
Zheng, Binyao / *Kennesaw State University, USA* 865

Table of Contents

Preface xv

Volume I

Section 1
Accessibility Laws and Frameworks

Chapter 1
Laws, Finance, and Policies of Higher Education Accessibility 1
Jennifer Raasch, Clemson University, USA

Chapter 2
Evaluating the Accessibility of Online University Education 19
Mark O. Pendergast, Florida Gulf Coast University, USA

Chapter 3
Expanding Notions of Access: Opportunities and Future Directions for Universal Design 34
Emily Ehlinger, University of Minnesota, USA

Chapter 4
Design, Implementation and Evaluation of MOOCs to Improve Inclusion of Diverse Learners 52
Sandra Sanchez-Gordon, National Polytechnic School of Ecuador, Ecuador
Sergio Luján-Mora, University of Alicante, Spain

Chapter 5
Accessibility to Higher Education in Nigeria: The Pains, Problems, and Prospects 80
James Osabuohien Odia, University of Benin, Nigeria
Agnes Anuoluwapo Odia, University of Benin, Nigeria

Section 2
Disabilities: General

Chapter 6
Creating Inclusive Classroom Communities Through Social and Emotional Learning to Reduce Social Marginalization Among Students 102
    June L. Preast, University of Missouri, USA
    Nicky Bowman, University of Missouri, USA
    Chad A. Rose, University of Missouri, USA

Chapter 7
Special Education Leadership and the Implementation of Response to Intervention 121
    Derek Cooley, Godwin Heights Public Schools, USA
    Elizabeth Whitten, Western Michigan University, USA

Chapter 8
Leveraging Professional Development to Prepare General and Special Education Teachers to Teach within Response to Intervention Frameworks 143
    Amber Elizabeth Benedict, University of Florida, USA
    Mary T. Brownell, University of Florida, USA
    Cynthia C. Griffin, University of Florida, USA
    Jun Wang, University of Florida, USA
    Jonte A Myers, University of Florida, USA

Chapter 9
Implementing Effective Student Support Teams 163
    Tricia Crosby-Cooper, National University, USA
    Dina Pacis, National University, USA

Chapter 10
Best Practices Implementing Special Education Curriculum and Common Core State Standards using UDL 179
    Penelope Debs Keough, National University, USA
    Dina Pacis, National University, USA

Chapter 11
Access to Higher Education for People with Disabilities: A Chinese Perspective 197
    Luanjiao Hu, University of Maryland at College Park, USA
    Jing Lin, University of Maryland at College Park, USA

Chapter 12
Beyond Handicap, Pity, and Inspiration: Disability and Diversity in Workforce Development
Education and Practice 215
    Hannah Rudstam, Cornell University, USA
    Thomas Golden, Cornell University, USA
    Susanne Bruyere, Cornell University, USA
    Sara Van Looy, Cornell University, USA
    Wendy Strobel Gower, Cornell University, USA

Chapter 13
Characteristics and Instructional Strategies for Students With Mathematical Difficulties: In the
Inclusive Classroom 240
    Kathleen Hughes Pfannenstiel, American Institutes for Research, USA
    Jennifer "JC" Sanders, Independent Researcher, USA

Chapter 14
Inclusion of Users with Special Needs in the Human-Centered Design of a Web-Portal 272
    Renate Motschnig, University of Vienna, Austria
    Dominik Hagelkruys, University of Vienna, Austria

Chapter 15
Providing Quality Education for Persons With Disabilities Through the Implementation of
Individual Educational Programs Managed by the Intelligent Agents in the Sliding Mode 291
    Vardan Mkrttchian, HHH University, Australia
    Ekaterina Aleshina, Penza State University, Russia

Chapter 16
Digital Control Models of Continuous Education of Persons with Disabilities Act (IDEA) and
Agents in Sliding Mode 296
    Vardan Mkrttchian, HHH University, Australia
    Ekaterina Aleshina, Penza State University, Russia

Section 3
Disabilities: Learning and Developmental

Chapter 17
Specific Learning Disabilities: Reading, Spelling, and Writing Strategies 320
    George Uduigwome, Los Angeles Unified School District, USA

Chapter 18
Coping Strategies of Primary School Students With Specific Learning Disabilities 356
    Karin Bagnato, University of Messina, Italy

Chapter 19
School Bullying and Students with Intellectual Disabilities 368
    Michelle F. Wright, Masaryk University, Czech Republic

Chapter 20
Marginality and Mattering: The Experiences of Students With Learning Disabilities on the College Campus 390
    Wanda Hadley, Western Michigan University, USA
    Jennifer Hsu, Grand Valley State University, USA
    Mark Antony Addison, Western Michigan University, USA
    Donna Talbot, Western Michigan University, USA

Chapter 21
Understanding Nonverbal Learning Disabilities in Postsecondary Students with Spina Bifida 404
    Carol Russell, Emporia State University, USA

Chapter 22
Use of Assistive Technology to Empower Persons with Intellectual Disabilities 431
    Sanjeev Kumar Gupta, All India Institute of Speech and Hearing, India

Chapter 23
The Use of iPad® Devices and "Apps" for ASD Students in Special Education and Speech Therapy 446
    Johnny R. O'Connor Jr., Lamar University, USA
    Keonta N. Jackson, Texas A&M University – Commerce, USA

Chapter 24
Handmade Content and School Activities for Autistic Children with Expressive Language Disabilities 464
    Shigeru Ikuta, Otsuma Women's University, Japan
    Ryoichi Ishitobi, University of Tsukuba, Japan
    Fumio Nemoto, University of Tsukuba, Japan
    Chiho Urushihata, University of Tsukuba, Japan
    Kyoko Yamaguchi, Abiko Special Needs Education School for the Mentally Challenged, Japan
    Haruka Nakui, Abiko Special Needs Education School for the Mentally Challenged, Japan

Section 4
Disabilities: Physical

Chapter 25
Improving Access to Higher Education With UDL and Switch Access Technology: A Case Study 495
    Luis Perez, Eye on Access, USA
    Ann Gulley, Auburn University at Montgomery, USA
    Logan Prickett, Auburn University at Montgomery, USA

Volume II

Chapter 26
Wheelchair Access and Inclusion Barriers on Campus: Exploring Universal Design Models in Higher Education 509
Maryan Amaral, Aero, Inc., USA

Chapter 27
Addressing Accessibility of MOOCs for Blind Users Hearing Aid for Screen Orientation 535
Teresita de Jesús Álvarez Robles, Universidad Veracruzana, México
Alfredo Mendoza González, Universidad Juárez Autónoma de Tabasco, México
Alma Rosa García Gaona, Universidad Veracruzana, México
Francisco Alvarez Rodríguez, Universidad Autónoma de Aguascalientes, México

Chapter 28
The Educational Rights of Students with Chronic Disease 550
Thomas C. Gibbon, Shippensburg University, USA
Jenifer Cline, Great Falls Public Schools, USA
Christopher L. Schwilk, Shippensburg University, USA
Patricia D. Hosfelt, Frederick County Maryland Public Schools, USA
David F. Bateman, Shippensburg University, USA

Chapter 29
Educating Students with Chronic Illness: How the Old Service Model Fails 578
Margaret Tseng, Marymount University, USA
Rebecca Magee Pluta, Special Education Advocate, USA

Section 5
Diversity and Culturally Responsive Teaching

Chapter 30
Social Inclusion and Intercultural Values in a School of Education 599
Olga M. Alegre de la Rosa, University of La Laguna, Spain
Luis M. Villar Angulo, University of Seville, Spain

Chapter 31
Critical Practices for Teaching and Learning in Global Contexts: Building Bridges for Action 613
Ann E. Lopez, University of Toronto, Canada
Elsie L. Olan, University of Central Florida, USA

Chapter 32
The Role of Multi-Media in Expanding Pre-Service Teachers' Understanding of Culturally and Linguistically Diverse Classrooms and Furthering Their Professional Identities 630
Latisha Mary, Université de Lorraine, France
Andrea Young, Université de Strasbourg, France

Chapter 33
Teacher Preparatory Programs and Culturally Responsive Teaching 649
    Nadira Raghunandan-Jack, Charter School Sector, USA

Chapter 34
Fusing Culturally Responsive Teaching, Place Conscious Education, and Problem-Based
Learning With Mobile Technologies: Sparking Change 666
    Nykela H. Jackson, University of Central Arkansas, USA

Chapter 35
A Forensic Psychological Perspective on Racism in Schools of Educational Leadership: Impact
on Organizational Culture 680
    Ronn Johnson, Creighton University Medical School, USA & VA Nebraska-Western Iowa
        Health Care System, USA
    JoJo Yanki Lee, University of San Diego, USA
    Ji Youn Cindy Kim, University of Iowa, USA

Chapter 36
Channeling Race: Media Representations and International Student Perceptions 712
    Kenneth Robert Roth, California State University, USA
    Zachary S. Ritter, University of Redlands, USA

Chapter 37
Using Narrative and Team-Teaching to Address Teaching About Racial Dynamics 738
    Stephen Brookfield, St. Thomas University, USA

Chapter 38
Preparing Urban Educators to Address Diversity and Equity through Field-Based Teacher
Education: Implications for Program Design and Implementation 757
    Adam S. Kennedy, Loyola University, USA
    Amy J. Heineke, Loyola University, USA

Chapter 39
#UrbanLivesMatter: Empowering Learners through Transformative Teaching 782
    Nicole Webster, Pennsylvania State University, USA
    Heather Coffey, University of North Carolina at Charlotte, USA
    Anthony Ash, University of North Carolina Charlotte, USA

Chapter 40
Multiculturalism in Special Education: Perspectives of Minority Children in Urban Schools 806
    Zandile P. Nkabinde, New Jersey City University, USA

Chapter 41
Exploring Intercultural Awareness: International Student Mobility in China and the UK through a
Non-Essentialist Lens 822
    Monika Foster, Edinburgh Napier University, UK

Chapter 42
Data System-Embedded Analysis Support's Implications for Latino Students and Diverse Classrooms 843
Jenny Grant Rankin, University of Cambridge, UK

Section 6
Inclusive Classrooms and Campuses

Chapter 43
Creating Inclusive Classroom: Innovative Practices by Chinese Banzhurens 865
Jiacheng Li, East China Normal University, China
Yan Li, East China Normal University, China
Ying Huang, Changzhen Elementary School of Guangming District, China
Liujuan Huang, Guangming Experimental School, China
Binyao Zheng, Kennesaw State University, USA

Chapter 44
Equity and Inclusion in Today's Diverse and Inclusive 21st Century Classroom: Fostering Culturally Responsive Pre-Service Teachers with the Tools to Provide Culturally Responsive Instruction 891
Tiece Ruffin, University of North Carolina – Asheville, USA

Chapter 45
Cultivating Communities of Inclusive Practice: Professional Development for Educators – Research and Practice 906
Christina M. Curran, University of Northern Iowa, USA
Becky Wilson Hawbaker, University of Northern Iowa, USA

Chapter 46
Supporting Secondary Students with Disabilities in an Inclusive Environment 940
Pam Epler, Grand Canyon University, USA

Chapter 47
Assessing the Functions of Behavior for Students with Autism in the Inclusive Classroom Environment 972
Lina Gilic, St. John's University, USA
Michelle Chamblin, Molloy College, USA

Chapter 48
An Integral Analysis of Labeling, Inclusion, and the Impact of the K-12 School Experience on Gifted Boys 995
Laurie Alisat, University of Calgary, Canada
Veronika Bohac Clarke, University of Calgary, Canada

Chapter 49
A Comparison of "Inclusiveness" in Two Liberal Arts Catholic Universities: What Nurtures an
Inclusive Campus Climate? 1022
    Theron N. Ford, John Carroll University, USA
    Blanche Jackson Glimps, Tennessee State University, USA

Index xx

Preface

Providing an inclusive educational environment is rapidly becoming critical for pre-service teachers as many students now come from diverse economic and racial backgrounds, and/or present different learning abilities and behavioral challenges. Educators, including teachers, administrators, and academicians, now require a set of dispositions, skills, and practices that honor students' differences, are representative of deep content knowledge, and result in the delivery of high quality, rigorous instruction. An inclusive education centers on creating a classroom community that is comprised of diverse students, including those with varying abilities, from differing races and ethnicities, and bringing with them a variety of cultural and familial backgrounds.

The cultural composition of American public schools has changed over recent years, and as such, it is vital that educators become equipped with the appropriate cross-cultural competencies required to effectively teach and meet the needs of diverse students. Today's inclusive classrooms require educators to understand differences in culture, language, and ability and how these differences can affect a child's aptitude for learning.

However, the vast majority of educators are unprepared for the diversity that they will ultimately face in schools. Therefore, it is critical for teachers to acknowledge that diversity is an important element in education and can have a massive impact on the classroom atmosphere as well as student achievement. Teacher education programs must endeavor to prepare educators to interact more effectively with diverse populations and enhance students' achievement at the same time.

Additionally, it is critical for teachers to model the knowledge, skills, and attitudes of culturally competent professionals as without that it will be difficult for students to apply the knowledge, skills, and attitudes that foster cross-cultural competence. The challenge that educators face today is clear as they strive to differentiate learning environments and academic achievement for all students.

The everchanging scene surrounding the varied applications of different educational areas can make it very challenging to stay on the frontline of ground-breaking research trends. That is why IGI Global is pleased to offer this two-volume comprehensive reference that will empower teachers, administrators, principals, higher education faculty, curriculum developers, instructional designers, policymakers, students, researchers, and academicians with a vigorous understanding of education policies and inclusion barriers.

This compilation is designed to act as a single reference source on conceptual, methodological, and technical aspects, and will offer insight into emerging topics including but not limited to educational technology, differentiated learning, inclusive pedagogy, special education, and online learning. The chapters included in this publication will provide readers with the tools that are necessary for future research and discovery within education.

Accessibility and Diversity in Education: Breakthroughs in Research and Practice is organized into six sections that provide comprehensive coverage of important topics. The sections are:

1. Accessibility Laws and Frameworks;
2. Disabilities: General;
3. Disabilities: Learning and Developmental;
4. Disabilities: Physical;
5. Diversity and Culturally Responsive Teaching; and
6. Inclusive Classrooms and Campuses.

The following paragraphs contain a summary of what to expect from this invaluable reference source:

Section 1, "Accessibility Laws and Frameworks," opens this wide-ranging reference source by highlighting the latest trends in educational policy and special educational laws. The first chapter in the section, "Laws, Finance, and Policies of Higher Education Accessibility," by Prof. Jennifer Raasch of Clemson University, USA, explores and explains the complex interconnections of laws, finances, and policies in supporting accessibility on campuses and offers potential guidelines for further institutional policies and procedures related to students with disabilities. The next chapter is titled "Evaluating the Accessibility of Online University Education," by Prof. Mark O. Pendergast of Florida Gulf Coast University, USA, and examines the requirements of accessibility laws, the formation of the accessibility initiative, and the resulting WCAG 2.0 standard. Chapter 3 in this section is titled "Expanding Notions of Access: Opportunities and Future Directions for Universal Design," by Prof. Emily Ehlinger from University of Minnesota, USA, and studies several different frameworks of universal design that are specific to the context of instruction and learning, as well as the scholarship and theory related to implementation of these frameworks in postsecondary classroom environments. The next chapter, "Design, Implementation, and Evaluation of MOOCs to Improve Inclusion of Diverse Learners," by Prof. Sandra Sanchez-Gordon from National Polytechnic School of Ecuador, Ecuador and Prof. Sergio Luján-Mora from the University of Alicante, Spain, presents accessibility requirements that need to be considered in the design, implementation, and evaluation of massive open online courses (MOOCs) to ensure they are inclusive of all students. The last chapter in this section, "Accessibility to Higher Education in Nigeria: The Pains, Problems, and Prospects," by Profs. James Osabuohien Odia and Agnes Anuoluwapo Odia of the University of Benin, Nigeria, considers the issues and challenges that are associated with low accessibility to university education in Nigeria and also suggests ways to address these issues and challenges for the future.

Section 2, "Disabilities: General," discusses emerging research on disabilities and how they create diversity within educators' classrooms. The first chapter in this section, "Creating Inclusive Classroom Communities Through Social and Emotional Learning to Reduce Social Marginalization Among Students," by Profs. June L. Preast, Nicky Bowman, and Chad A. Rose from University of Missouri, USA, looks at how we can identity the key components of social and emotional learning (SEL), provide guidance in implementation, and describe how SEL can help reduce the social marginalization among youth with disabilities and those at-risk for disability identification. Another chapter in this section titled "Implementing Effective Student Support Teams," by Profs. Tricia Crosby-Cooper and Dina Pacis from the National University, USA, discusses the historical aspects, purpose and processes, and challenges of student support teams (SST) and also presents strategies for teachers and educators to effectively implement and work within the SST process. Another significant chapter within this section is titled "Best

Preface

Practices Implementing Special Education Curriculum and Common Core State Standards using UDL," by Profs. Penelope D. Keough and Dina Pacis of the National University, USA, which provides a model for collaboration between general education and special education teachers using universal design for learning (UDL) and shows how the curriculum can be accessed by students with special needs. Also included in this section is "Beyond Handicap, Pity, and Inspiration: Disability and Diversity in Workforce Development Education and Practice," by Profs. Hannah Rudstam, Thomas Golden, Susanne Bruyere, Sara Van Looy, and Wendy Strobel Gower from Cornell University, USA, focuses on 10 misconceptions that have fueled the marginalization of disability in diversity and inclusion efforts. The final chapter in this section, "Digital Control Models of Continuous Education of Persons With Disabilities Act (IDEA) and Agents in Sliding Mode," by Prof. Vardan Mkrttchian from HHH University, Australia and Prof. Ekaterina Aleshina from Penza State University, Russia, covers models of continuous education and how they will affect persons with disabilities and what this will mean for the future of education.

Section 3, "Disabilities: Learning and Developmental," presents chapters that examine challenges for students with intellectual and developmental disabilities including nonverbal learning disabilities and students with autism. The first chapter included in this section, "Specific Learning Disabilities: Reading, Spelling, and Writing Strategies," by Prof. George Uduigwome from the Los Angeles Unified School District, USA, discusses best practices in providing support for students diagnosed with reading (dyslexia), writing (dysgraphia), and spelling (dysorthographia) deficits and explains that early intervention is key to providing students with learning disabilities a meaningful learning experience. Another important chapter contained in this section, "School Bullying and Students with Intellectual Disabilities," by Prof. Michelle F. Wright from Masaryk University, Czech Republic, aims to explore multidisciplinary research concerning school bullying among students with intellectual disabilities and to make recommendations for public policy and prevention programs as well as future research. Also included within this section is a chapter titled "Marginality and Mattering: The Experiences of Students With Learning Disabilities on the College Campus," by Prof. Wanda Hadley from Western Michigan University, USA; Prof. Jennifer Hsu of Grand Valley State University, USA; and Profs. Mark Antony Addison and Donna Talbot from Western Michigan University, USA, which discusses students' access and adjustment to the campus culture and how this experience influences their identity development. One of the closing chapters included in this section, "The Use of iPad® Devices and 'Apps' for ASD Students in Special Education and Speech Therapy," by Prof. Johnny R. O'Connor Jr. of Lamar University, USA and Prof. Keonta N. Jackson from Texas A&M University – Commerce, USA, examines the various uses of iPads and other applications ("apps") for students with autism spectrum disorders (ASD) in special education and speech therapy settings. The final chapter in this section, "Handmade Content and School Activities for Autistic Children With Expressive Language Disabilities," by Prof. Shigeru Ikuta from Otsuma Women's University, Japan; Profs. Ryoichi Ishitobi, Fumio Nemoto, and Chiho Urushihata of University of Tsukuba, Japan; and Profs. Kyoko Yamaguchi and Aruka Nakui of Abiko Special Needs Education School for the Mentally Challenged, Japan, considers how different multimedia such as audio, movies, web pages, HTML files, and PowerPoint files can be used to help children with expressive language disabilities and autism spectrum disorders (ASD) learn more effectively.

Section 4, "Disabilities: Physical," includes chapters on improving access to education for students with physical handicaps, including blind students and those restricted to wheelchairs, and how to help educate students with chronic illnesses. The first chapter in this section, "Improving Access to Higher Education With UDL and Switch Access Technology: A Case Study," by Prof. Luis Perez from Eye on Access, USA and Profs. Ann Gulley and Logan Prickett of Auburn University at Montgomery, USA, presents an in-depth case study of the creative use of a mobile technology system by a diverse learner who is blind and has significant fine and gross motor impairments. The next chapter, "Wheelchair Access and Inclusion Barriers on Campus: Exploring Universal Design Models in Higher Education," by Prof. Maryan Amaral from Aero, Inc., USA, explores the barriers to inclusive education that students with disabilities face and propose solutions to create more inclusive and welcoming campuses that facilitate the success of all students. Also included in this section is "Addressing Accessibility of MOOCs for Blind Users: Hearing Aid for Screen Orientation," by Prof. Teresita de Jesús Álvarez Robles from Universidad Veracruzana, Mexico; Prof. Alfredo Mendoza González of Universidad Juárez Autónoma de Tabasco, México; Prof. Alma Rosa García Gaona from Universidad Veracruzana, México; and Prof. Francisco Alvarez Rodríguez of Universidad Autónoma de Aguascalientes, México, which examines a set of guidelines for designing hearing messages that help blind students to maneuver a massive online open course's (MOOC's) interface. This chapter is followed by "The Educational Rights of Students With Chronic Disease," by Prof. Thomas C. Gibbon from Shippensburg University, USA; Prof. Jenifer Cline of Great Falls Public Schools, USA; Prof. Christopher L. Schwilk from Shippensburg University, USA; Prof. Patricia D. Hosfelt of Frederick County Maryland Public Schools, USA; and Prof. David F. Bateman from Shippensburg University, USA, which discusses the consideration for education in the least restrictive environment, and key components in the development of both IEP's and Section 504 plans, issues related to providing a free appropriate public education, and the Family and Educational Rights Privacy Act. The final chapter in this section, "Educating Students With Chronic Illness: How the Old Service Model Fails," by Prof. Margaret Tseng from Marymount University, USA and Prof. Rebecca Magee Pluta of Special Education Advocate, USA, illuminates the need for schools to break away from the traditional administrative special education mold when responding to the challenges of educating frequently absent students with chronic illness.

Section 5, "Diversity and Culturally Responsive Teaching," discusses current perspectives on multiculturalism in education and tackles the challenge of addressing race and racism in the classroom. The first chapter in this section, "Social Inclusion and Intercultural Values in a School of Education," by Prof. Olga M. Alegre de la Rosa of University of La Laguna, Spain and Prof. Luis M. Villar Angulo from University of Seville, Spain, aims to analyze the contextual and personal factors associated with student teachers' inclusive and intercultural values to minimize barriers to learning and participation for students. Another chapter included in this section, "Teacher Preparatory Programs and Culturally Responsive Teaching," by Prof. Nadira Raghunandan-Jack from Charter School Sector, USA, focuses on culturally responsive educational programs within higher education institutions and also includes a framework for recommendation and improvements for higher education institutions to implement in order to further refine and strengthen teacher preparatory programs. Also included in this section is "Channeling Race: Media Representations and International Student Perceptions," by Prof. Kenneth Robert Roth of California State University, USA and Prof. Zachary S. Ritter from University of Redlands, USA, which examines how media representations can flavor cross-cultural interactions, and the implications these interactions may have for campus climate, diversity initiatives, and the increasingly multicultural and globalized work place. Another important chapter in this section, "#UrbanLivesMatter: Empowering Learners Through Transformative Teaching," by Prof. Nicole Webster of Pennsylvania State University, USA and Profs. Heather Coffey and Anthony Ash from University of North Carolina at Charlotte, USA, discusses the need for professional development embedded in culturally responsive teaching, multicultural education, and critical literacy, all of which have the power to incite social action. The final chapter within this section, "Data System-Embedded Analysis Support's Implications for

Preface

Latino Students and Diverse Classrooms," by Prof. Jenny Grant Rankin from University of Cambridge, UK, highlights study findings that can significantly improve teachers' ability to use data to help Latino students thrive in diverse classrooms.

Section 6, "Inclusive Classrooms and Campuses," explores strategies for educators of all levels of education who are looking to make their classrooms more diverse and inclusive. The first chapter in this section, "Creating Inclusive Classroom: Innovative Practices by Chinese Banzhurens," by Prof. Jiacheng Li from East China Normal University, China; Prof. Yan Li of East China Normal University, China; Prof. Ying Huang from Changzhen Elementary School of Guangming District, China; Prof. Liujuan Huang of Guangming Experimental School, China; and Prof. Binyao Zheng from Kennesaw State University, USA, discusses inclusive education throughout China and offers practical applications, limitations on research, and future research directions. Another chapter included in this section is "Equity and Inclusion in Today's Diverse and Inclusive 21st Century Classroom: Fostering Culturally Responsive Pre-Service Teachers With the Tools to Provide Culturally Responsive Instruction," by Prof. Tiece Rufin from the University of North Carolina – Asheville, USA. It shares the odyssey of one African American teacher educator at a predominately white institution in a diverse learner's course fostering culturally responsive pre-service teachers with the tools to provide culturally responsive instruction for today's diverse and inclusive 21st century classroom. A noteworthy chapter included in this section, "Supporting Secondary Students With Disabilities in an Inclusive Environment," by Prof. Pam L. Epler from Grand Canyon University, USA, informs and educates secondary (Grades 6-12) pre-service teachers on how to provide content and design assignments for students within the special education curriculum. Finally, the last chapter included in this section, "A Comparison of 'Inclusiveness' in Two Liberal Arts Catholic Universities: What Nurtures an Inclusive Campus Climate?" by Prof. Theron N. Ford, Independent Researcher, USA and Prof. Blanche Jackson Glimps from Tennessee State University, USA, looks retrospectively at Madonna University and compares it to John Carroll University to highlight differences in how each has dealt with the issue of inclusiveness.

Although the primary organization of the contents in this work is based on its six sections, offering a progression of coverage of the significant concepts, practices, technologies, applications, social issues, and emerging trends, the reader can also find specific contents by utilizing the extensive indexing system listed at the end of the publication.

Chapter 26
Wheelchair Access and Inclusion Barriers on Campus:
Exploring Universal Design Models in Higher Education

Maryan Amaral
Aero, Inc., USA

ABSTRACT

Students with disabilities are achieving greater success in high school and attending post-secondary institutions at higher rates than ever before. However, disabled students are graduating at a lower rate than their able-bodied peers. Federally legislated mandates on accessibility have strengthened over the past decades, yet statistics suggest that inclusion, access, and support services for students are inadequate. Universal Design principles and barrier-free concepts are beginning to trend as possible solutions to higher education inclusion barriers. The universal design paradigm shifts the focus from providing accommodations for individual students to removing barriers in the environment and thus promoting universal access. This chapter will explore the barriers to inclusive education that students with disabilities face and propose solutions to create more inclusive and welcoming campuses that facilitate the success of all students.

INTRODUCTION

No otherwise qualified individual with a disability in the United States shall, solely by reason of her or his disability, be excluded from the participation in, be denied the benefits of, or be subjected to discrimination under any program or activity receiving Federal financial assistance... (§ 504 of the Rehabilitation Act of 1973, 29 U.S.C. §794, ED, 2010)

DOI: 10.4018/978-1-7998-1213-5.ch026

A student wheelchair user at a private Jesuit University is unable to access the campus quadrangle because all wheelchair ramps have been removed and replaced with flights of stairs. A student who is deaf finds that there is no American Sign Language (ALS) interpreter or assistive listening system (ALS) available during his *First Year* orientation. A student who is blind is unable to access the computers in his college library due to the absence of accessible screen readers. A wheelchair user feels great fear of injury while wheeling down the extremely steep, slippery path to her classroom that the university map identifies as a "wheelchair negotiable path."

What do these students have in common? They are persons from diverse backgrounds and abilities who encountered architectural and access barriers on campus that prevented them from participating equally with their peers at their institutions of higher education (IHE).

According to federal statistics, people with disabilities (PWD) who are denied opportunities to obtain certificates or degrees from post-secondary education institutions (PSI) are at increased risk of living in poverty and unemployment, and with a decreased standard of living than their able-bodied (AB) peers (DOL, 2016, para. 4-7). In 2015, statistics reported only 17.5% percent of persons with disabilities (PWD) were employed compared to 65% percent of AB persons were employed (DOL, 2015, para.1).

The statistics provided by the U.S. Department of Education (ED), the U.S. Department of Justice (DOJ) and Department of Labor (DOL) suggest that despite the substantial increases in the number of students with disabilities (SWD) enrolled in programs at IHE, the number of SWD graduating from these IHE is far lower than the graduation rates of their able-bodied (AB) peers (DOL, 2016, para.7). At the same time, the IHE incidents of disability discrimination cases reported by ED and DOJ under the title "Enforcement Activities" are increasing over the last several years (DOJ, 2016b, para.1-210). According to a 2016 report, "…Nearly 6,000 complaints of disability discrimination were submitted to the Education Department's Office for Civil Rights during fiscal year 2016, which concluded in September. That's up from 4,800 the year prior"(Heasley, 2016). These statistics suggest that the disability service providers (DSP) at institutes of higher education (IHE) may be failing to remove access barriers on campus or adequate accommodations to enable SWD to succeed with their AB peers (Rothstein, 2010).

All IHE are required to follow the practices of nondiscrimination in all of their programs and services under the Americans with Disabilities Act (ADA) and Section 504 of the Rehabilitation Act of 1974 (Section 504) (HECA, para.1). The goal of the ADA is to "assure equality of opportunity, full participation, independent living, and economic self-sufficiency for such individuals" (35 42 U.S.C. § 12101(a)(7) (2012) (Rothstein, 2014, p.1271)

The utilization of Universal Design in Higher Education (UDHE) paradigms and Barrier-Free (BF) concepts are trending in many institutes of higher education (IHE) (Burgstahler, 2016). The UDHE paradigm focuses on the removal of access barriers in the environment or in classrooms with a design to accommodate the most number of persons with diverse body types and abilities. This paradigm differs from the current ADA accommodation model where SWD request accommodations from the DSP at their IHE, usually at a time after they have met campus access barriers.

UDHE paradigms may effectively address the needs of IHE to provide accessible technology, access to older campus buildings, and meet the needs for the growing population of SWD seeking HE. According to the statement from the Office for Students with Disabilities (OSD) at McGill University (MU) "…With the number of users exploding in an unprecedented way, the traditional 'accommodation approach' begins to be inadequate"(MU, 2016, para. 2).

The UDHE paradigms discussed in this chapter include Universal Design in Learning (UDL), Universal Design in Public Spaces (UDPS), and Universal Design in Technology (UDIT) (Burgstahler, 2008).

The goals of this chapter are to:

- *Examine* incidents of physical architectural access and technology barriers for students with disabilities (SWD) attending United States (U.S.) institutes of higher education (IHE):
- *Review* current (U.S.) federal and state legislated mandates for inclusion of SWD in IHE, along with examples of recent court cases involving failures of IHE to provide accessible physical access and digital technologies;
- *Explore* the current practices of the paradigm for Universal Design in Higher Education (UDHE) and Barrier-Free (BF) principles as models of inclusive practices in HE, including Universal Design in Physical Spaces (UDPS), Universal Design for Learning (UDL) and Universal Design in Information Technology (UDIT), and
- *Discuss* some of the current problems of implementation of UDHE at IHE along with discussion of future trends.

Two research questions explored in this chapter:

- What are some of the current cases and incidence of architectural access barriers, web-access, and attitudinal barriers to inclusion for persons with disabilities (PWD) on US college campuses?
- How might the information from the current IHE disability discrimination lawsuits be used to support the paradigm switch from the current "reasonable accommodations" approach to the UDHE social model on campus?

BACKGROUND: ACCESS BARRIERS TO EDUCATION

Every person-child, youth and adult-shall be able to benefit from educational opportunities designed to meet their basic learning needs (WCEFA, 1990, para.1).

Many children around the world are unable to attend school due to the prevalence of physical and social barriers to inclusion in their countries (WCEFA, 1990, para.1-3). It may be assumed that SWD who attend North American IHE would benefit from the abundant resources and inclusion in all IHE programs. However, statistics are suggesting that this is not the case (DOL, 2015). The 2010 U.S. census reports that 19% of Americans, or 56.7 million Americans are living with a disability (Census, 2012; para.1). Many of the persons with disabilities (PWD) returning to post-secondary institutions (PSI) are veterans (DOL, 2016). In 2014-15, approximately 2 million SWD were being served by 4,207 PSI throughout the U.S. (NCES, 2016, para.1). Statistics in 2011 reported that 60% of students who graduate from high school continue to PSI. Of these, approximately 17% of the 2 million SWD attending these IHE were undergraduate students attending two-year and four-year colleges (NCSER, 2011, para.2). In 2007-8, approximately 8% of the enrolled SWD were master's candidate students and an additional 7% of SWD were doctoral candidate students (DSDRRTC, 2014). In 2012, it was reported that 20,000 students in higher education (HE) were students who were deaf or hard of hearing (NCES, 2012).

The U.S. Department of Labor (DOL) statistics indicate that PWDs are less likely to have obtained a bachelor's degree or advanced degree at PSI than their able-bodied (AB) peers (DOL, 2016, para.7). Although there is an exponential growth of SWD attending PSI in the last decade, only 34% of these students complete their degree or certificate (NCES, 2016). This statistic suggests a failure of disability service providers (DSP) to provide SWD the supports, accommodations and removal of architectural access barriers that might enable them to successfully graduate with their peers.

EVOLVING BARRIER-FREE AND DISABILITY RIGHTS LEGISLATION

We are trying to construct a more inclusive society. We are going to make a country in which no one is left out (Franklin D. Roosevelt 1944, AZ Quotes, 2016).

The U. S. Disability Rights Movement gained its first momentum in the 1920's after World War I at a time when soldiers with disabilities, returned to their PSI to find the presence of architectural and other access barriers prevented them inclusion and success. Further momentum was gained with the birth of the Barrier-Free (BF) Movement after World War II. These WWII Veterans found they were met with both physical access and attitudinal barriers at their PSI (DRES, 2016).

President Franklin D. Roosevelt, a wheelchair-user, proposed a vision for an inclusive American society where "…no one is left out" (A.Z. Quote, 2016). The U.S. GI bill allocated funds for the rehabilitation and education for WWII Veterans. In 1947, Dr. Tim Nugent at the University of Illinois pioneered the first program to provide physical access to WWII wheelchair-users. This DRES program has provided a national model for inclusion (DRES, 2016).

In 1960's, the BF Movement gained momentum as a result of the issuance of the first access building code standards by the American National Standards Institute (ANSI). Although these standards were not enforceable, they set the precedent for the birth of the following enforceable access code standards.

In 1965, President Lyndon B. Johnson signed the Elementary and Secondary Education Act (ESEA) into law. ESEA was the first legal mandate to educate and provide extra resources for students in elementary and secondary education (ESE) who were at an educational disadvantage due to factors such as low economic status. The ESEA was later amended in 1966 to include services to SWD in elementary and secondary education (ESE) institutions (ED, 2015).

In 1968, President Lyndon B. Johnson passed the Architectural Barriers Act (ABA) enforced by the United States Access Board (Access Board). The ABA, still in effect today, requires for the construction of all buildings, altered or leased using federal funds to be "accessible to and usable by" persons with disabilities (PWD)((42 U.S.C. §§ 4151 *et seq.* 1968, Access Board, 2016). President Johnson considered the presence of physical access barriers in the built environment as "cruel discrimination." Access Board, 2016, para. 2).

In 1970, the U.S. Congress enacted the Education of the Handicapped Act (EHA), (P.L. 91-230) later renamed the Individuals with Disabilities Education Act" (IDEA) of 1990 (20 U.S.C. § 1401, 1990) (Karger, 2016). The Federal Bureau of Education for the Handicapped (BEH) was founded to enforce the IDEA provisions promoting nondiscrimination of SWD by ESE institutions (ED, 2016).

In 1973, the U.S. Congress passed Section 504 of the Rehabilitation Act (Section 504). This was one of the most notable federal non-discrimination statutes guaranteeing the rights of PWD to be included in all federally funded programs (ED, 2016; Rothstein, 2016). The U.S. Department of Education, (ED) Office of Civil Rights (OCR) enforces Section 504 mandates in ESE and IHE (ED, 2016a, para. 2). Section 504 still in effect today, requires all school districts to provide a "free and appropriate public education" (FAPE) in the "least restrictive environment" (LRE) to all SWD (ED, 2016, para.3).

In 1984, the U.S. Congress passed the Uniform Federal Accessibility Standards (UFAS) (49 FR 31528). These UFAS regulations were the first enforceable federal accessibility laws for the built environment including public housing, transportation and other built environment facilities (Access Board, 2016, para.1).

In 1988, U.S. Congress passed the "Technology-Related Assistance Act for Individuals with Disabilities" (Tech Act,) (29 U.S.C.§ 2201 *et seq.*,1988). The Tech Act, renamed the Assistive Technology Act (AT Act) was re-authorized in 1994, 1998 and 2004. The Tech Act defined Assistive Technology (AT) as "technology devices which assisted or improved the daily activities or functional tasks of individuals with disabilities"(Rothstein, 2016). Some of the current AT devices available for SWD in ESE and IHE include screen reading software such as JAWS (F.S., 2016), electronic tablets with software to allow for voice output, enlarged keyboard keys, keyboards with Braille, patient lifts, orthotics and prosthetics such as braces, prosthetic limbs, and wheelchairs (NCAEM, 2016).

Substantive rights for SWD expanded from 1990 to 1999 (Rothstein, 2016, p.10-11) with the 1990 Americans with Disabilities Act (ADA) (42 U.S.C. § 12101, 1990) being the most significant legislated mandate. President George H. W. Bush signed the ADA into law with the promise, that "…With today's signing of the landmark Americans with Disabilities Act (ADA), every man, woman and child with a disability can pass through once-closed doors into a bright new era of equality, independence and freedom"(DOJ, 2016; Rothstein, 2016). All public and private IHE are mandated under Title II and Title III of the ADA to provide SWD "reasonable accommodations" to access all programs and services (DOJ, 2016; Rothstein, 2016, p.361). The ADA provided increased coverage of programs and services for students in HE including mandates for communication, transportation, and housing and technology (Rothstein, 2016, pp.317-326). The ADA Standards of Accessible Design provide legislated mandates requiring for the removal of physical access barriers in ESE and HE (DOJ, 2010; Rothstein, 2016, p.317).

In 1997, U.S. Congress passed the IDEA Amendment and No Child Left Behind (NCLB) Act. The NCLB Act met less favorable reviews. In 2015, Congress replaced NCLB Act with the Every Student Succeeds Act (ESSA) act in 2015. It is suggested that IDEA and Section 504 raised the expectation for inclusive services for all SWD in ESE, which provided a future path to success for SWD to graduate from high school and attend PSI (Rothstein, 2016; ED 2016a).

The ADA Amendment of 2008 (ADAAA) (P.L.110-325) and amendment to Section 504 broadened the definition of disability. This Act effectively increased the number of PWD who were eligible to be covered by the Act (ED, 2016, para.1-2). The ADA Accessibility Guidelines (ADAAG) provided technical requirements for facilities, transportation and the removal of barriers in the built environment (Access Board, 2016). An additional amendment of Section 504 increased OCR's enforcement of the rights for PWD by providing a mechanism for increased litigation remedies while preserving the student's rights under Title VI of the Civil Rights Laws (Rothstein, 2016).

The Higher Education Opportunity Act (HEOA) of 2008 mandated for all federally funded entities to provide funding for students who are often marginalized, students with intellectual disabilities (ID). One of the significant mandates of this Act mandated funding of inclusion of students with intellectual disabilities (ID) to attend PSI (ED, 2010), effectively spurring the development of nonprofit programs such as *ThinkCollege* (UMB, 2016).

The growth of computers and the Internet led to exponential growth in digital technologies (ED, 2016b). In 2008, the U.S. Congress amended the Rehabilitation Act of 1973 under § 508 to mandate that the federal agencies that develops, procures or maintains information technology must make it accessible by following the "Electronic and Information Technology Accessibility Standards" (EITAS) (29 U.S.C.

§ 794 (d)) (Access Board, 2015, para.1-3). The EITAS have been utilized by PSI's as excellent guides to meet the ADA mandates and utilize accessibility options in computer labs for SWD (Rothstein, 2016).

From 2010-2011, the DOJ increased federal legislated mandates at IHE to require service animals to be allowed on campus, increase provisions for accessible technology and accessible housing, and increased educational funding for veterans (Rothstein, 2010). The ADA was amended in 2010 to include "housing in a place of education" (Luskin, 2015, para. 5). This Act mandates equal access and allowance for service animals in campus housing. Wheelchair users, and SWD using service animals who feel their rights have been violated in other discriminatory acts by their PSI can file a "disparate impact claim" under the federal Fair Housing Act (FHA) (Luskin, 2015, para.1-15).

In 2013, the U.S. Department of Education (ED) issued a "landmark" directive to ESE schools and IHE that schools are bound by federal mandates to ensure that SWD are provided equal opportunities to compete in school athletics (ED, 2013, para.1-4). IHE are required to provide auxiliary aids and services are used for people who have hearing or vision loss or speech and communication disabilities. On November 21, 2016, the DOJ revised a rule from Title III of the ADA that requires for movie theaters and Title III entities to provide assistive listening devices, captioning on films, auxiliary aids and services for PWD, including IHE (DOJ, 2016).

ADA, SECTION 504, ACCESS BARRIERS, AND LITIGATION

Abelism... the devaluation of disability that results in societal attitudes that uncritically assert that it is better for a child to walk than roll, speak than sign, read print than read Braille, spell independently than use a spell-check, and hang out with nondisabled kids as opposed to other disabled kids (Hehir,T. 2005).

Access for PWD to attend PSI is important due to the significance of HE for future participation in employment and life. PWD denied access to PSE are at a distinct disadvantage in employment, future income, and quality of life (ED, 2016).

The ADA defines a person with a disability covered in a protected class under the law if their disability "...substantially limits major life activities such as seeing, hearing, speaking, walking, breathing, performing manual tasks, caring for oneself, or working"(DOJ 2008,Q&A, para.2; Rothstein, 2016, para.39). Disability service providers (DSP) at IHE traditionally provide accommodations for SWD including arranging the services of an American Sign Language (ASL) interpreter for a student who is deaf, arranging for extended time on tests for a student who may have a learning disability, providing access to a computer equipped with screen readers such as JAWS (F.S. 2016) for a student who is blind, and moving a class from an inaccessible location to an accessible location for a student who uses a wheelchair (NE ADA Center, 2016; DOJ, 2010).

The late 1980's and early 1990's saw a significant increase in litigation by students against their PSI when they were met with disability discrimination (Rothstein, 2010). Disability discrimination against SWD at IHE may occur at all levels of education from the initial application stage, to access to programs, to access to videos or inaccessible computers, or exclusion from sports and recreation activities to graduation (DOJ, 2016; ED, 2016). Attitudinal barriers including "abelism" negatively impact a student's access to inclusive education (Hehir, 2005).

The ADA and Section 504 laws and requirements for institutions and protections for SWD can be confusing. In response to the need to educate the public on the ADA, the DOJ and U.S. Congress created 10 regional ADA centers across the country to offer technical support and resources about the ADA for members of the public (IHCD, 2016).

In December 2016, the US Department of Education Office of Civil Rights (OCR) found the greatest increase of SWD reporting disability discrimination and retaliation at their ESE schools and IHE in 2016 (Heasley, 2016, para. 2). These OCR, ADA and AAB statistics indicate that the current accommodation paradigms at IHE are not sufficient to support SWD to equal access and successful inclusion.

Boston College, OCR, and AAB

Boston College (BC) is a private Jesuit University in Massachusetts with the expressed mission of "promoting social justice and equity"(BC, 2016). BC's "$800 million 10 Year Master Plan" involved the acquisition of the Boston Archdiocese land, and paved the way for many new buildings and reconstruction of most of the existing campus including the Gasson Quad (BC Chronicle, 2008; Paulson, 2004). A BC spokesperson stated "…Once the (Gasson) Quad is redone, you will have a continuous path from the front of O'Neill to Stokes creating a more unified campus"(Smith, 2013, para. 6). However, the newly reconstructed main campus route removed wheelchair access ramps and replaced the area with stairs, rendering it inaccessible to wheelchair users (Rocheleau, 2015).

According to a 2015 report, "As of December (2014,) BC was the only college in Massachusetts facing such a federal (OCR) investigation and one of just 23 nationally, according to the US Education Department"(Rocheleau, 2015, p.1).

The OCR investigations and complaints included the absence of a student grievance procedure and absence of an ADA/Section 504 Coordinator whose primary mission would be to provide SWD and employees campus access and accommodations under the federal ADA and Section 504 as mandated (Care2, 2016; Rocheleau, 2015). In May 2015, the BC architect was brought to court for having falsified his architecture license, according to the court settlement agreement by the Massachusetts Division of Professional Licensure (DPL), Board of Registration of Architects (AR-15-001, DPL, 2015;DAC-BC, 2016, video#1). The two Stokes Hall buildings and Amphitheater stairs constructed at a cost of $78 million were under investigation. Other reported complaints included removal of the wheelchair lift at O'Neill Atrium without replacement, construction of wheelchair ramps that lead to stairs, door with excessive door opening pressure, absence of handrails on stairs or ramps, absence of accessible wheelchair seating at BC Alumni Stadium, and absence of other required accessibility features. Newly constructed auditoriums were cited for failing to provide mandated assistive listening system (ALS) for persons who were deaf or hard of hearing (521cmr regulations, Section 14.00) (AAB, 2016; A.J., 2016; DAC-BC, 2016a).

On July 17, 2015, a Massachusetts Commission Against Discrimination (MCAD) hearing officer ordered BC President William Leahy and BC Board of Trustees to pay $125,000 to a faculty member for restitution of damages for ongoing disability discrimination and unlawful retaliation acts that were called "highly irregular, hostile and isolating"(Krantz, 2015).

A sports media reporter uncovered what appears to be another discriminatory practice at BC of carrying people instead of providing accommodations. Dick Kelley, an employee and wheelchair user developed ALS while employed with the BC sports program. According to Gregg Doyle, "When (Dick Kelley) could no longer walk, co-workers carried him up the stairs to his office. Nineteen months after his diagnosis, he cannot work at the office anymore" (Doyle, 2013, para.29).

BC students and Alumni advocated for the construction of inclusive wheelchair routes, handrails to be placed on stairs and ramps, auxiliary services made available to students, and petitioned against the lack of required wheelchair inclusive seating at Alumni stadium (Care2, 2016; DAC-BC, 2016; Rocheleau, 2015). A wheelchair user graduate student at BC spoke about the absence of wheelchair ramps after the construction of stairs behind McGuinn Hall (DAC-BC Video#2). The state Architectural Access Board (AAB) was investigating dozens of new BC 521cmr regulation complaints as of September 2016 with stipulated orders of violations of the cited 521cmr regulations after new construction (AAB, 2016; DAC-BC, 2016).

Harvard, MIT, and NAD

Harvard University (Harvard) and the Massachusetts Institute of Technology (MIT) are private universities located in Cambridge, Massachusetts. Harvard, a private ivy league research university and MIT, a top engineering university offer open online courses with thousands of videos and audio tracks under the program, *Massive Open Online Courses (MOOC)*. In February 12, 2015, the National Association of the Deaf (NAD) filed punitive class action lawsuits against Harvard and MIT in the Massachusetts Federal Court (US District Court briefs DOJ, 2016) alleging absence of captioned videos for the thousands of free online videos and audio tracks (DOJ, 2016d; NAD, 2016). The CEO of NAD, Howard Rosenblum states, "Online content represent the next frontier for learning and life-long education." Recently, the Massachusetts court judge moved the lawsuits forward to trial (,DOJ, 2016d; NAD, 2016).

All IHE receiving federal funding are required under the ADA and Section 504 to provide access to auxiliary services for SWD. As of November 21, 2016, theaters are required to provide captioning on all movies and auditory captioning and other auxiliary options.

McNeese State University and DOJ

In 2008, McNeese State University (MSU), a public university that is part of Louisiana University (LU) was cited by DOJ for ADA violations under the Title II regulations. The ADA violations included failure to admit students with disabilities, failure to maintain an ADA Coordinator responsible for ADA and Section 504 compliance, and failure to provide accessible routes to campus buildings (DOJ, 2016c).

DOJ found that "in the absence of alternative measures to achieve programmatic access… programs were not readily accessible to and usable by individuals with disabilities"(DOJ, 2016). They were ordered to address the removal of architectural access barriers, as well as to designate an ADA Coordinator whose primary authority and responsibility was to ensure that the University meets requirements of the ADA, specifically 28 C.F.R. § 35.107(a) (DOJ, 2016c).

University of California, Berkeley and DRA

The University of California Berkeley is a public research university located in Berkeley California. It is also home of the disability rights movement with the pioneer Ed Roberts. In 2005, the Disability Rights Advocates (DRA) brought a Class Action Lawsuit against the University of California Berkeley (UC Berkeley) citing thousands of physical and access barriers at the university that prevented them from participation under the ADA. The Plaintiffs represented a class of UC Berkeley students with mobility and vision disabilities. This landmark case brought by DRA sets in motion a precedent that IHE may be held accountable by for the removal of inclusion barriers for PWD, whether these were structural architectural access barriers or programmatic barriers (DRA, 2005).

Under the settlement, administrators at UC Berkeley were ordered to remove thousands of access barriers throughout its facilities (DRA, 2005; DOJ, 2016). The Executive Director of DRA, Laurence Paradis stated that as a result this court order to remove the campus architectural access barriers,"… Students with disabilities will be able to focus on being students without the frustration and aggravation of unnecessary barriers to participation" (DRA, 2005, para 1-6).

These ADA noncompliant access barriers and lack of captioning on videos at IHE are in stark comparison the architectural access designs and accessible digital access that employ the principles of Universal Design in Higher Education (UDHE) and Barrier-Free (BF) concepts both satisfy the federal legislated mandates of the ADA and Section 504 and accommodate the maximum number of persons at their IHE.

UNIVERSAL DESIGN IN HIGHER EDUCATION

The design of products and environments to be usable by all people, to the greatest extend possible, without the need for adaptation or specialized design (Center for Universal Design, 1997, p.1; Mace, 1997).

The IHE are required by mandates to provide minimum standards of physical accessibility, often thought of as wheelchair access. However, a BF campus must take into consideration the great diversity of students that both physically and virtually attend their IHE, need for AT, multi-modal education and access to all programs. The Universal Design in Higher Education (UDHE) paradigm is evolving to address these architectural access and technology barriers in education environments.

The UDHE is a subset under the Universal Design (UD) framework. UD is considered an inclusive paradigm. UD is sometimes called Inclusive Design, Lifespan Design, Human Centered Design or Design for All (IHCD, 2016, para. 2). UD was founded in the 1970's by Ronald Mace, an architect and wheelchair user who later founded the Center for Universal Design (CUD) at North Carolina State University, (Burgstahler, 2008, p.6).

The UDHE paradigm includes UD for physical spaces (UDPS), UD for learning (UDL), and UD for information technology (UDIT) (Burgstahler, 2008, p.14). In 1997, CUD at NCSU established seven UD principles for the universal design (UD) of all products and environments (CUD, 1997). These seven UD principles are:

1. **Equitable Use:** The design is useful and marketable to people with diverse abilities.
2. **Flexibility in Use:** The design accommodates a wide range of individual preferences and abilities.
3. **Simple and Intuitive Use:** Use of the design is easy to understand, regardless of the user's experience, knowledge, language skills, or current concentration level.
4. **Perceptible Information:** The design communicates necessary information effectively to the user, regardless of ambient conditions or the user's sensory abilities.
5. **Tolerance for Error:** The design minimizes hazards and the adverse consequences of accidental or unintended actions.
6. **Low Physical Effort:** The design can be used efficiently and comfortably and with a minimum of fatigue.

7. **Size and Space for Approach and Use:** Appropriate size and space is provided for approach, reach, manipulation, and use regardless of user's body size, posture, or mobility (CUD, 1997).

The UD principles emerged after WWII alongside the birth of the Barrier-Free (BF) Movement. Some of the examples of UD principles in practice in the environment include the construction of curbcuts on sidewalks that both provide access for wheelchair users as well as strollers, audio voice announcement systems on buses, and wheelchair lifts on buses that kneel for users to wheel or walk onto the platform. Accessible single stall "Gender Neutral" restrooms may accommodate PWD but also may provide access for people who are transgender, provide privacy for families with infants, and more (ACUI, 2007). Flip lever door handles provide access for persons who cannot grip a door handle, but also usable for small children and people of all abilities (DOJ, 2010).

UDHE paradigms are grounded in the value of diversity and inclusion in HE. The UDHE paradigm differs from ADA compliant standards that typically require for an entity to meet minimum standards for accessibility for a PWD that may not be inclusive for all PWD. For example, an entity may be allowed under the ADA to retrofit the building with separate ramps or a wheelchair lift leading to a campus building. This retrofit may not be accessible to all persons on the campus. A UDHE example would be to provide the same entrance for wheelchair users as members of the general public (NDA, 2016).

The use of UDHE differs from the ADA "reasonable accommodation" paradigm (HECA, 2016). The UDHE framework provides a paradigm to be used to create inclusive and accessible campus environment for all people. If college campus utilizes UDHE principles by maximizing inclusion of the number of persons on all ends of a spectrum, they may additionally benefit the DSP by shifting some of the load by focusing on single student accommodations to creating an inclusive and usable educational environment for all (CAST, 2016).

UNIVERSAL DESIGN IN PHYSICAL SPACES

Universal Design in public spaces (UDPS) is a paradigm under UDHE with designs for physical accessibility of the campus including access to buildings, parking lots, access to campus residences, and around other areas of the built environment. The construction of UDPS at an IHE may include building a wheelchair ramp that serves as the entrance for all members of the public, designing an automatic door opener on the floor for wheelchair-users to press to open the door with their wheelchairs (ERC, 2016) and designing a lecture hall with swivel seats and tables to accommodate many different body types and allow for interaction in groups (Burgstahler, 2008, pp.203-204; NDA, 2016).

University of Virginia

The University of Virginia (UVA) is a public university located in Charlottesville, Virginia. The 1980's reconstruction of historical buildings utilized the UD principles to address both the physical needs of access to the buildings and grounds, and preservation of the historical buildings and landscape (CUD, 1994, pp.88-93).

The original campus designs by Thomas Jefferson included the "quadrangle" or vast lawn as the centerpiece of the campus. These historic buildings housed student residences and campus classrooms. Many of the UVA facilities and grounds were originally designed without wheelchair accessible entrances. Some of the new designs using UDHE principles included installing wheelchair accessible ramps alongside the building entrances at points abutting but not touching the historical buildings and creating aesthetically pleasing landscaping to augment the accessible features (CUD, 2016, pp.92-93). An electrically powered wheelchair lift was installed below ground and the exterior was covered with identical bricks of the abutting building, so as to preserve the character of the building while providing equitable access (CUD, 2016, pp.92-93).

Access to another campus residential building was accomplished with the installation of a concealed elevator within a new outbuilding designed to reflect the 1820's era architecture. To minimize intrusion, the outbuilding was nestled into the hillside and behind trees. Accessibility maps are used to guide students to the location of these access points. According to NCSU, "Designing for the integration of historical details with modern accessibility technology resulted in more equitable use for all students"(NCSU, 2016).

It is of note that although the UVA design provides for unobtrusive access ramps to the buildings on their historic campus, a traditional UD paradigm would typically support that the same route for wheelchair users and members of the public is the same (NDA, 2016, para. 5-74).

Ed Roberts Campus

Ed Roberts Campus (ERC) is a unique model building for UD built transit oriented campus at the Ashby BART station in Berkeley, California (ERC, 2016, para.1). ERC was named in honor of Ed Verne Roberts, the first student wheelchair user to graduate from UC Berkeley. Ed Roberts confronted the architectural access and attitudinal barriers at his university and later pioneered the disability rights movement, the Independent Living Center (CIL) movement, and co-founded the World Institute on Disability (WID) (ERC, 2016).

Disability rights activists and other leaders at UC Berkeley, CIL, and WID decided to memorialize Ed Roberts with constructing one of the best UD models in the country. Architects, engineers and users describe it as a building that was designed for the diverse characteristics of people who are using it, as opposed to a building where people need to adapt to it. "Ed Roberts Center is a national and international model dedicated to disability rights and universal access"(ERC, 2016). William Leddy, an ERC architect described the importance of effective UD as "a social justice issue"(Leddy, et.al, 2016).

McGill University

McGill University (MU) is private university founded in 1821 and located in Montreal, Quebec, Canada. This model IHE campus uses UD principals and BF design concepts on a large scale (MU, 2016).

MU's standards for a barrier-free university include physical access in all campus buildings and across the campus. MU published public guidelines for all of its campus on their MU website (MU, 2016). The website also employs UDL principles with multiple color-coding and other UD designs for ease of web navigation (CAST, 2008; MU, 2016).

The MU UD guidelines require for the same entrance to be accessible to wheelchair users and all members of the university public (MU, 2016). Their policies include implementation of UD principles in their washrooms and theaters. The classrooms, stadiums and auditoriums are required to have integrated wheelchair seating on all levels, and designed wheelchair accessible paths of travel to all campus buildings and parking lots (MU, 2016).

Two of the IHE models for BF and UDHE practices include the Disability Resource and Education Services (DRES) at the University of Illinois Urbana Champaign campus and *DeafSpace* Architectural Design architecture and guidelines at Gallaudet University (Hurley, 2016; Sirvage, et al., 2016).

DRES Program at the University of Illinois

The University of Illinois Urbana-Champaign (UICU) is a public university founded in 1868 in Illinois. The (DRES) program, originally called the Division of Rehabilitation Education Services, boasts of being the first and oldest post-secondary disability support program in the world (DRES, 2011).

DRES was founded in 1947 at a time when WWII Veterans attended the rehabilitation programs housed on the UIUC campus with the financial support of the U.S. GI bill. UIUC initially shuttered the DRES program in 1947 but later reopened it in 1948 due to student protests and the advocacy of Dr. Nugent. He advocated based on the belief that all Veterans should be able to attend college, and the university should be responsible to remove the architectural access barriers on the campus to allow for full inclusion (DRES, 2011).

In 2012, Mark Lichter, the Executive Director of Paralysed Veterans of America (PVA) presented the "Barrier-Free America Award" to DRES for the exemplary UDHE practices at Nugent Residence Hall with the statement, "…Accessible Design benefits not only people with disabilities, but everyone in the community—something exemplified by the DRES Program and the UI"(PVA, 2012, para.5).

Most of the DRES students who are staying at the Beckwith Residential Hall at Nugent Hall residence are wheelchair-users. All of the bedrooms at Nugent Hall are furnished with hospital beds and accessible furniture designed to resemble typical residence hall furniture (DRES, 2016). The rooms at Nugent Hall are installed with push button room darkening blinds, and a wireless paging system for calling an assistant personal aid "floater" available to all students 24 hours a day. The SWD use a proximity card to open doors without requiring the use of a key and have full access to hydraulic physical lifting systems provided for students who might not otherwise be able to independently access the bedroom or bathrooms (DRES, 2016, BSS, para. 2).

The DRES program today is considered a model for accessibility with many programmatic innovations including the first wheelchair accessible fixed route bus system, the first accessible residence halls, and the first service fraternity and advocacy group comprised of students with disabilities (Delta Sigma Omicron) (DRES, 2016, DSO, para.1-3). Additionally, UIUC offers the oldest wheelchair sports and national *Paralympic* training program in the country, coaching top athletes such as Tatyana McFadden, a national and *Paralympic* Marathon Champion (DRES, 2016; Athletics, para.1). The UI sports motto, "To exercise our abilities to a maximum so as to minimize our disabilities, that we may live most and serve best" exemplifies UI's commitment to enabling students of all abilities to succeed (DRES, 2016, DSO, para.1).

UD Design Concepts for Blind, Deaf and Hard of Hearing PWD

Some of the principles of UDHE are universal with the paradigm to provide the maximum accessibility to the most number of people. Barrier-Free designs on the contrary, may design BF spaces specific for the population of SWD they serve. For example, a Barrier-Free (BF) college campus designed for students who are deaf may provide specific designs that incorporate visual cues, and a campus that primarily serves students who are blind may provide additional tactile and auditory cues. Designers using the UDHE principles or BF concepts need to consider the disability, economic, engineering, cultural, gender, and environmental concerns in all of their designs and in particular, designs serving students with mobility and sensory disabilities (NAD, 2016).

Martine Abel-Williamson from the Universal Design (UD) project of the World Blind Union (WBU) in Toronto, Canada expressed that the BF access needs for persons who are blind may not always be incorporated in the built environment (Abel-Williamson, 2016, p.2). The presence of adequate lighting may be one of the most essential elements of BF design for persons who are blind. At an IHE, lighting options could be incorporated in the physical spaces and computer labs with individually adjusted blinds and low glare lights, along with computers and electronic tablets with screens that adjust for color contrast and glare (Abel-Williamson, 2016, p.3). Sounds, colors, and physical structures in the built environment could be designed to aid navigation. For example, ambient noise may cause navigation confusion for students who are blind. The strategic use of a certain placed sound, such as a fountain near an entrance or the sound of an elevator, can assist in navigation (Abel-Williamson, 2016, p. 5-6). If an IHE space is confusing to navigate, the use of color-coding floors, walls and corridors with thoughtful contrasts can aid in navigation (Wilson, 2016, para.7-12). Detectable warnings or tactile warning strips on sidewalk curbcuts can aid in identifying the end of a curb or street corner. The directional signage should include Braille opposed to raised letters (Abel-Williamson, 2016, p.6).

The federal legislated mandates of the ADA and state building codes require for IHE to provide students who are deaf with auxiliary aids, American Sign Language (ASL) interpreters, access to assistive listening systems (ALS), real-time captioning, and telecommunication relay services, or video relay services (DOJ, 2016e, para. 5-13). A well-designed space will take into account environmental acoustics in quiet study areas and public spaces with strategically designed spaces using BF concepts or UDHE principles.

Gallaudet University

The world's only university designed to be barrier-free for deaf and hard of hearing students (GU, 2016, para.1).

Gallaudet University (Gallaudet) is a private university located in Washington, DC. For more than 150 years, Gallaudet has led advances in education of students who are deaf and hard of hearing and promoted deaf rights worldwide (GU, 2016, para.1-2). In the 1800's, Gallaudet provided access for students who were deaf by creating interesting adaptations. One of the most original accessibility features in a residence hall at Gallaudet was the feature of a doorbell that was linked to a coffin door. When someone rang the doorbell, a heavy ball would drop into a box and the vibrations would alert deaf residents that the doorbell rang. This box has since been replaced with an ADA code compliant doorbell with flashing lights to alert people who are deaf or hard of hearing (Hurley, 2016, para.1-2).

Students at Gallaudet advocated for a representative university through protests and activism. In 1988, deaf students protested for the removal of the "hearing" president to be replaced with a Deaf President. They stormed Gallaudet demanding a "Deaf President Now!" with a protest that was nicknamed "deaf Selma"(GU, 2016, DPN, para.1).

In 2015, the "*DeafSpace* Design Guidelines" won an award under "Regional Planning" by the International Association of Universal Design (IAUD) (IAUD, 2015; IHCD, 2016). Architects at Gallaudet pioneered the award winning BF guidelines to benefit students who are deaf called the *DeafSpace* paradigm (Hurley, 2016). The *DeafSpace* researchers explain that the designs may best be described as using barrier-free concepts rather than the UD paradigm. Robert Sirvage, the *DeafSpace* design researcher, explained that "...*DeafSpace* incorporates Universal Design principles, though with a difference. Rather than a general absence of barriers, *DeafSpace* favors the presence of certain design elements...*DeafSpace* is particular and culturally expressive where Universal Design is general and passive"(Sirvage, et al., 2016).

These *DeafSpace* guidelines were composed by and for people who were deaf and hearing and translated into BF guidelines to meet the needs of students who are deaf or hard of hearing (Hurley, 2016). For example, persons who are deaf primarily use vision and touch for spatial awareness and orientation and sign language for communication (Sirvage, 2015; Wilson, 2015). The *DeafSpace* founders incorporated guidelines for sensory and physical dimensions for the designs of all campus classrooms and physical spaces. Their designs include wide corridor spaces to support deaf individuals who depend on close proximity to communicate with another person through sign or other expressive means (Wilson, 2015). Since hearing aids and Cochlear Implants amplify sounds, the *DeafSpace* designs include physical spaces to mediate the acoustics so the spaces are quiet without interference of excessive ambient noise (Lee, 2015; Hurley, 2016). Other *DeafSpace* guidelines include use of low-glare reflective surfaces, corridors with ample lighting and viewing, and details of colors, specifically muted blues and greens to provide color and light contrast for ease of communication (Hurley, 2016; Wilson, 2015).

Universal Design for Learning

The UDL framework began as a project of the National Center on Accessing the General Curriculum (NCAC, 2016), the Center for Applied Special Technology (CAST, 2016) and the U.S. Department of Education (ED), Office of Special Education Programs (OSEP). The 2004 IDEA reauthorization, and HEOA of 2008 refers to UDL by name (P.L.110-315, ED, 2016b, para.1). The principles of the Universal Design for Learning (UDL) are considered a subset of the UDHE principles (CAST, 2016b; ED, 2004).

UDL is based on the research findings that people learn in different ways. UDL provides an educational framework for educators to provide multi-modal instruction for all types of learners so they may best access the curriculum. The three main principles of UDL are "representation, expression and engagement" (NCUDL, 2016, para.3; CAST, 2008, para.1). Some of the UDL practices in these classrooms may include providing written material and content by use of videos, interactive computer interfaces, group collaborative projects, dance, art, and different modalities for students who may learn differently through vision, or touch, or hearing. The options for SWD with sensory disabilities should include alternative options for auditory and visual materials, such as use of close captioning (c.c.) on videos, audio description, digital books, speech to text (voice recognition) or text to speech for spoken language (CAST, 2016a). UDL examples of expression may include online mapping or speech to text options. UDL examples of engagement might include use of expression with collaboration or scaffolding of learned lessons (ED, 2016b, p.19).

Universal Design of Information Technology

The Universal Design for Information Technology (UDIT) is a subset of UDHE and sometimes considered a subset of UDL. UDIT principles incorporate the requirements from the 1994 Assistive Technology Act, and may provide maximum access to technology for a diverse population including students from

Wheelchair Access and Inclusion Barriers on Campus

diverse cultures, languages, sensory disabilities, and intellectual disabilities (Burgstahler, 2008). The UDIT paradigm supports the use of accessible apps, electronic tablets, computers and other electronic devices designed to serve the learning needs for the greatest and most diverse number of students, with a focus on multi-modal instruction and SWD who may require AT or alternative augmentative communication (AAC) devices to access the curriculum (CAST, 2016a; ED, 2016b).

Close captioning (c.c.) on a video are text words on the screen that translate the exact spoken words on the screen or translate words from music for each frame. "Voice-over" and "video descriptions" are either typed or spoken words on the video to narrate a description of the action of the video (ED, 2016b). Audio descriptions may be added to movies to describe the content in real time to a viewer who may be blind or visually impaired. Many Windows and Mac computers, iPads, are readily equipped with UD screen readers with voice output (NCUDL, 2016).

The Assistive Technology Act requires for the use of AT to be provided to students who might require AT to gain inclusive access to physical spaces and the curriculum (NCAEM, 2016). The legislative mandates for accessibility under the 1990 ADA, the 1994 Assistive Technology Act (A.T. Act) and amendments prompted the expansion of inclusive designs in computer labs, LMS and digital labs (ED, 2016b; Rothstein, 2016).

Some examples of UDIT may be as simple as touch screens, accessible to everyone. Touch screens as AAC are often essential for SWD who may be unable to use their hands, or voice for communication (NDA, 2016). SWD may use augmentative communication devices (AAC) such as a picture board or *Eye-Gaze* technology.

The *Eye-Gaze* technology allows for those who are unable to speak or type to gain access to AT by use of moving their eyes, caught on camera and translated to a cursor on their computer (Gips, 2011). The *BC Eagle Eyes* technology, engineered by Dr. James Gips is designed for PWD who are unable to use their voice or typical means for communication. A camera and electrodes are configured so eye movement replaces a hand movement with a computer mouse. Dr. Gips also designed the *CameraMouse*, a universally available program for all users that provides access for people to use their head movement to move a mouse cursor (Gips, 2011; Inkley, 2012).

Students attending IHE are increasingly expected to access and process large amounts of information from online sources including research of online catalogues and large databases and videos. Universities are increasingly dependent on the IT department to enable full access to all students who use the IHE Learning Management Systems (LMS) platform. The IHE are increasingly using LMS (ie. *Blackboard, Canvas*, or *Moodle*) as they expand their technology resources and reach to students around the world with Distance Learning (ie. *e-learning*) courses (ED, 2016). The benefit of LMS for *Distance Learning* for SWD is access to HE without requiring access to the campus. However, the drawback is that the LMS and videos may present further access barriers for students who are unable to read print, deaf, or blind (CAST, 2016b; Karger, 2016).

Computers with raised tactile keys can assist students with to identifying keys. Accessible software, screen readers, text to voice, voice to text, or voice to Braille programs provide accessibility options that may not only benefit SWD, but might also benefit all students, including those who may not choose to access services from a DSP. (CAST, 2016; ED. 2016).

The potential use of UDIT may address the needs as illustrated in the current lawsuits pending against Harvard and MIT alleging the absence of captions on online videos (DOJ, 2016d; NAD, 2016). The principles of Universal Design for Information Technology (UDIT) may provide design options for captioning to be provided on all videos, and other multi-modal formats (CAST, 2016b). The most current ADA regulations regarding auxiliary aids, movie captions and accessible accommodations for persons who are deaf, suggests there will be a measurable shift towards accessibility for film and digital media in the future at IHE (DOJ, 2016e).

UDIT practices and technology at an IHE are constantly evolving. Computers available to each student with software that allows for print size and graphics to be adjusted on the screen with a toggle or touch screens, computers or tablets that can adjust color contrast and glare, voice programs, screen readers such as JAWS (F.S, 2016), and video with captioning along with audio description availability are UDIT practices (Karger, 2016; ED, 2016b).

PROMOTERS AND INHIBITORS OF UDHE AND BF CONCEPTS

In 1978, Supreme Justice Powell stated, "Diversity in our colleges and universities improves the learning process for everyone . . . the nation's future depends upon leaders trained through wide exposure to the ideas and mores of students as diverse as this nation of many peoples"(Powell, 1978; AffirmativeAction16, 2016, para.1).

It may be suggested that some of the model IHE using UDHE were prompted by federal ADA complaints, and student activism on campus. The IHE that seek to provide the least amount of access to pass the ADA requirements may not be open to hiring UDHE consultants and engineers to exceed the minimum mandates of the federal regulations. (Burghstaler, 2008). Although there are mandates for ADA, Section 504, and building code regulation compliance, presently the UDHE Guidelines in the U.S. are not enforced through legislated mandate. At present, the voluntary use of accessible design principles needs to be encouraged by means of education of administrators, staff and faculty along with evidence based research (Burghstaler, 2008, pp.279-283;UW, 2016b).

It has been reported that some university administrators express that they are unable to build ramps or remove the architectural access barriers on campus due to the obstructions in natural topography, such as a university built on a hill (Hildebrandt, 2014; A.J., 2016; Rocheleau, 2015). Some IHE express that due to low enrollment of SWD, that they do not need to provide wheelchair accessible ramps, or providing access for students who are deaf such as ASL interpreters and assistive listening systems (Hildebrandt, 2014). The federal legislated mandates of the ADA and Section 504 specify that all institutions receiving federal funds are required to practice nondiscrimination and equal access for all SWD, as well as nondiscrimination in employment of faculty and staff (DOJ, 2010; ED, 2016). The cost of technology for UDIT may appear to exceed budget. However given that computer software and technology quickly become obsolete over time, the technology costs at an IHE is an ongoing line item expense (ED, 2016b, p.48).

Some of other possible inhibitors for the adoption of UDHE principles are the associated costs for hiring qualified professionals (Burgstahler, 2008, p.281). Gallaudet found a solution by utilizing the expertise of SWD along with hearing and deaf professionals to instrument the new *DeafSpace* guidelines. As a result of this collaboration Gallaudet is a model institution of BF inclusion for students who are deaf and hard of hearing (GU, 2016; Hurley, 2016).

The initial cost for UD designs for older and larger college campuses could be a major capital improvement expense. However, UDL, UDIT or UDPS paradigms could be utilized in smaller projects in classrooms and computer labs to provide exceptional access benefits and sustainable designs. An example of an effective small UDPS project was the Hemenway Labs Science at FSU that won a UD award from the Boston Society of Architects (BSA) (FSU, 2016, para.1-4; BSA, 2016).

The federal ADA requires for IHE to conduct a self-audit of all of their campus programs and services to meet ADA compliance (DOJ, 2016c). A well-prepared IHE might benefit from utilizing the checklist for UDHE on campus, create and analysis of the costs associated with renovating aging campus buildings, removal of the access barriers, and implementing UD principles at all programs at their institute (Burgstahler, 2016; UW, 2016b). The future benefit of a campus that is accessible to all students, employees and visitors, may have the benefit of leading to sustainable future cost savings.

METHODOLOGY

Research on the chapter included reviews of the utilization of UDHE paradigms, BF concepts and incidents of DOJ, OCR, DRA and NAD lawsuits and findings (DOJ, 2016b; ED, 2016; DRA, 2016; NAD, 2016). The research on BC access barriers was gained from newspaper articles including the Boston Globe, Heights; from an online petition, websites, and YouTube DAC-BC videos (A.J, 2016; Care2Petitions, 2016; DAC-BC, 2016; Hildebrandt, 2014; Rocheleau, 2016). The reports of UDHE paradigms and BF concepts were found through nonprofit and government organization websites including CAST, DO_IT, DOJ, ED, IAUD, IHCD, NDA, news articles, books by Attorney Laura Rothstein, Sheryl E. Burgstahler (Burgstahler, 2008; Burgstahler, 2016; CAST, 2016b; ED 2016; IAUD; 2016; IHCD, 2016; NDA, 2016; Rothstein, 2016; UW, 2016).

FUTURE RESEARCH DIRECTIONS

One of the things I do when I go to teach my classes, I bring every one who has ever been kind to me with me... black, white, Native American, gay, straight... I have rainbows in my clouds... Prepare yourself so you can be a rainbow in someone else's cloud. (Excerpt of Maya Angelou video interview, 'Be a Rainbow In Someone Else's Cloud,' Angelou, 2014)

IHE typically seek to diversify their enrollment and faculty with persons from different social, economic, and cultural backgrounds and abilities. The legislative mandates for inclusion have set a path for increased population of SWD accessing disability services at IHE. Some of students come through programs, such as *"ThinkCollege, TCT Model"* where SWD have opportunities to attend college during their high school transition year (UMB, 2016). Other collaborations include placing ESE students at colleges, such as a model of SWD at the Boston College Campus School (Campus School) housed at the Campion Building at Boston College (Campus School, 2016).

Enrolled SWD at IHE may be confronted with many barriers when they are met with discrimination at their IHE. These barriers may include physical access and safety issues on an inaccessible campus, attitudinal barriers on campus where they feel marginalized, and incur insurmountable debt while attempting to succeed at their IHE. The IHE and ESE that fail to provide inclusion for SWD, and instead create physical and technology barriers to education combined with institutional attitudes of "ableism," serve to create oppressive educational systems (Hehir, 2005).

The recent explosion of disability discrimination complaints received by the U.S Department of Education, Office of Civil Rights against IHE are generally due to physical access barriers and technology (Healey, 2016). The state regulatory commissions, OCR and DOJ may issue stipulated orders against

IHE demanding the removal of architectural or other access barriers to inclusion (Rothstein, 2016, para. 39-42). As IHE open their campuses to increased numbers of SWD including veterans and a growing population of older students, there will be a future need for additional access barrier removal to make the campus accessible to everyone (Burgstahler, 2008).

It was found that although there currently appears to be limited data available regarding the efficacy of UDHE paradigms on IHE campuses, the new award winning UD guidelines developed at Gallaudet University, McGill University, and the University of Washington may lead the way to UD becoming a legislated mandate (Hurley, 2016; MU, 2016, para.1-10; UW, 2016). The IHE campuses globally provide a fertile ground for the growth of UDHE. For example, "Georgia Tech Center for Assistive Technology and Environmental Access" (CATEA) is an IHE in Georgia, US with students and faculty invested in extensive cutting-edge research in exploring the use of assistive technology (AT), UDIT and accessible web designs in educational settings (CATEA, 2016 para.1-6).

The IHE that are involved in cutting-edge research and utilizing BF concepts or UDHE principles across their campus facilities and programs may have the additional benefit of providing access for all students as well as visitors, utilizing DSP resources more efficiently and planning for a sustainable future.

CONCLUSION

The DOJ, NAD, and OCR investigations and lawsuits against IHE across the U.S. appear to support findings that the most typical complaints against IHE involve physical barriers and inaccessible web and technology. As important as computers and AT may be in providing access, if they are inaccessible to SWD, then a barrier is created to learning.

The statistics suggest that SWD are graduating at a decreased rate compared to their AB peers, suggesting that IHE may need to change the paradigm model from DSP offering accommodations for SWD, to IHE using UDHE principles and BF concepts to create inclusive environments (MU, 2016; NDA, 2016).

This research on UDHE and BF campuses found the use of Universal Design in learning (UDL) paradigms in classrooms are trending in the U.S. (CAST, 2016) and UD concepts are being employed at public spaces and universities around the world (IAUD, 2016). The UD paradigm and BF concepts appear to support the fabric of campus diversity. UDL included guidelines of multi-modal formats for people who may learn best through the use of other senses such as touch, smell, and hearing. The inclusive practices in UDL allow for all students to build skills with multi-modal instruction in inclusive and collaborative classrooms (CAST, 2016a).

The implementation of the UDHE paradigm removes the DSP focus from passively waiting for a SWD to request accommodations to actively providing an accessible environment that incorporates inclusion for SWD and all members of the public. The UDHE paradigm allows for access to the physical and virtual campuses including to LMS, AAC and computer technology (CAST, 2016b, para.1). IHE that design BF access to computer labs, IT, and wheelchair access to all public spaces and transportation will apparently accommodate more students resulting in less SWD seeking accommodations. Conversely, the IHE that are expanding without creating BF campuses may find that they are not keeping pace with the advances in technology and influx of SWD on their campus, or preparing for the future (Burgstahler, 2008, p.282).

This UDHE and BF research suggests the need for a national and international dialogue regarding the current ADA "reasonable accommodation" paradigm as compared to the future use of the UDHE paradigm and BF concepts in all IHE (IAUD, 2016). Students should be provided access to their peers in inclusive physical spaces, provided access to all technology, and provided the support to grow as leaders. The IHE need to address the future expansion of students with disabilities, diversity and plan for future accessibility in new and creative ways. UDHE principles and BF concepts on campus are at the helm of the future.

REFERENCES

Abel-Williamson, M. (2015). *Universal Design.* World Blind Union Paper. Retrieved from http://www.worldblindunion.org/English/Pages/default.aspx

AffirmativeAction16. (2016). *Diversity in our colleges and universities improves the learning process for everyone…peoples.* Retrieved from https://affirmativeaction16.wordpress.com/2016/04/08/diversity-please/

Amaral, M. (2016). *Access Inclusion in Higher Education- NewTV draft.* Retrieved from https://www.youtube.com/watch?v=A2ONoP44jXw

American National Standards Institute. (2016). *Access Standards.* Retrieved from https://ansi.org/

Angelou, M. (2014). *One of the things I do when I go to teach my classes… cloud.* Retrieved from www.youtube.com/watch?v=0nYXFletWH4

Architectural Access Board. (2016). *521cmr Regulations, Most Recent Edition.* Massachusetts Department of Public Safety (DPS). Retrieved from http://www.mass.gov/eopss/architectural-access-board.html

Association of College Unions International. (2007). *Campus Restroom Roles in Universal Design.* Retrieved from www.acui.org/publications/bulletin/article.aspx?issue=448&id=2300

Boston College, Advanced Journalism. (2016). BC Cited by State Agency for Disability Discrimination. *The BC Heights Newspaper.* Retrieved from http://bcheights.com/author/journalism-class/

Boston College. (2016). *Disability Services.* Office of Disability Services, Dean of Students. Retrieved from http://www.bc.edu/offices/dos/subsidiary_offices/disabilityservices.html

Boston College Chronicle. (2008). *Boston College Submits 10 year Institutional Plan: Master Plan Calls for $800 Million in Construction and Renovation for Academic Buildings, Student Housing, Recreation Complex, University Center, Playing Fields and Arts District in Support of University's Strategic Plan.* Retrieved from http://www.bc.edu/content/dam/files/top/alumni/connections/connx0108/masterplan_map.pdf

Boston Society of Architects. (2016). *Accessible Design.* Retrieved from http://www.architects.org/awards/accessible-design-0

Burgstahler, S. (2016). *Equal Access: Universal Design of Physical Spaces: A checklist of designing spaces that are welcoming, accessible, and usable.* University of Washington College of Engineering Information Technology, College of Education. Retrieved from http://www.washington.edu/doit/sites/default/files/atoms/files/EA_Spaces_06_08_12.pdf

Burgstahler, S., & Cory, R. (2008). *Universal Design in Higher Education: From Principles to Practice.* Cambridge, MA: Harvard Education Press.

Campus School at Boston College. (2016). *Welcome to the Campus School at Boston College.* Retrieved from http://www.bc.edu/schools/lsoe/campsch

Care2Petition. (2016). *Demand Compliance with the American with Disabilities Act at Boston College.* Disability Awareness Committee of Boston College (DAC-BC). Retrieved from http://www.thepetition-site.com/770/652/882/demand-compliance-with-the-americans-with-disabilities-act-at-boston-college/

Center for Applied Special Technology. (2016a). *About Universal Design for Learning.* Retrieved from http://www.cast.org/our-work/about-udl.html

Center for Applied Special Technology. (2016b). *Universal Design in Learning (UDL) on Campus.* Retrieved from http://udloncampus.cast.org/home#.WEionmQrLZs

Disability Awareness Committee of Boston College. (2016a). *BC Access Barriers.* Retrieved from http://bc-dac-g.weebly.com/list-of-buildings-campus-grounds-and-access-barriers.html

Disability Awareness Committee of Boston College. (2016b). *Boston College Campus, Wheelchair Access Barriers,#RampUpBC.* DAC-BC YouTube video #1-14. Retrieved from https://www.youtube.com/watch?v=KAPsqQX2_l0

Disability Awareness Committee of Boston College. (2016c). *Facebook: Disability Access Project of DAC-BC.* Retrieved from https://www.facebook.com/DACatBC/

Disability Resources and Education Services. (2016). *Disability Services, DRES.* College of Applied Health Sciences, University of Illinois, Urbana-Champaign (UIUC). Retrieved from http://disability.illinois.edu/

Disability Rights Advocates (2005). *Gustafson v. U.C. Berkeley, Landmark Settlement of Class Action Lawsuit to Improve Disability Access at University of California, Berkeley.* Retrieved from dralegal.org/case/Gustafson-v-u-c-berkeley

Disability Statistics & Demographics Rehabilitation Research & Training Center. (2015). *Disability Statistics Annual Report.* Retrieved from https://www.disabilitycompendium.org/docs/default-source/2015-compendium/annualreport_2015_final.pdf

Division of Rehabilitation and Education Services. (2011). *Breaking ground in 1948.* Retrieved from disability.illinois.edu/history-firsts/Breaking%20ground%20in%201948

Doyel, G. (2013). *Boston College publicist Kelley inspires as he battles ALS.* NCAABB, CBSSports.com. Retrieved from http://www.cbssports.com/collegebasketball/story/22206627/boston-college-publicist-kelley-inspires-as-he-battles-als

Framingham State University. (2016). *Hemenway Labs Recognized With Accessible Design Award by the Boston Society of Architects* (BSA). Retrieved from https://www.framingham.edu/about-fsu/news-and-events/articles/hemenway-labs-recognized-with-accessible-design-award-by-the-boston-society-of-architects

Freedom Scientific. (2016). *JAWS Headquarters, world's leading screen reader...* Retrieved from http://www.freedomscientific.com

Gallaudet University. (n.d.). *Equal Opportunity/Non-Discrimination.* Retrieved from https://www.gallaudet.edu/academic-catalog/admissions/undergraduate/eeonon-discrimination.html

Georgia Tech Center for Assistive Technology and Environmental Access. (2016). *About CATEA.* Retrieved from http://www.barrier-free.arch.gatech.edu

Gips, J. (2011). *EagleEyes.* Retrieved from http://www.bc.edu/schools/csom/eagleeyes/

Harvard University. (2016). *Statement of Equal Opportunity Laws and Policies.* Office of the Assistant to the President, Department of Institutional Diversity and Equity. Retrieved from https://diversity.harvard.edu/pages/statement-equal-opportunity-laws-and-policies

Heasley, S. (2016). *Education Department Sees a Rise in Disability Complaints.* Retrieved from https://www.disabilityscoop.com/2016/12/08/education-rise-disability/23103/

Hehir, T. (2005). *New Directions in Special Education, Eliminating Abelism in Policy and Practice.* Cambridge, MA: Harvard Education Press.

Higher Education Compliance Alliance. (2016). *Disabilities and Accommodations.* Retrieved from http://higheredcompliance.org/resources/disabilities-accommodations.html

Hildebrandt, E. (2014). *Students See Need For Expanded Disability Access At BC.* Retrieved from http://bcheights.com/news/2014/students-see-need-for-expanded-disability-access-at-bc/

Hurley, A. K. (2016). *How Gallaudet Architects are Redefining Deaf Space.* Retrieved from http://www.yahoo.com/news/news/gallaudet-university-architects-redefining-deaf-150003425.htm

Inkley, D. (2012). *Alternative Access: Eagle Eyes and Camera Mouse.* Retrieved from http://hnmny-6tyytu876yt/stories/alternative-acess-eagleeyes-and-camera-mouse/

Institute for Human Centered Design. (2016). *What is Universal Design?.* Retrieved from http://www.humancentereddesign.org/universal-design

International Association of Universal Design. (2015). *Gold Awards: In the category of regional planning, DeafSpace Project receives a Gold Awards for it's DeafSpace Design Guidelines.* Retrieved from https://www.iaud.net/global/dayori-f/archives/1512/22-000001.php

Jones, A. (2016). *Disability Unemployment Rate Drops Below 10 Percent.* Rooted in Rights. Retrieved from http://www.rootedinrights.org/disability-unemployment-rate-drops-below-10-percent/

Karger, J. (2016). *Access to the General Curriculum for Students with Disabilities: A Brief Legal Interpretation.* National Center on Accessible Educational Materials. Retrieved from http://aem.cast.org/about/publications/2003/ncac-curriculum-access-legal-interpretation.html

Krantz, L. (2015). BC Ordered to Pay Professor Over Retaliation. *Boston Globe.* Retrieved from https://bostonglobe.com/metro/2015

LC Technologies. (2016). *Eye Gaze.* Retrieved from http://www.eyegaze.com/

Leddy, W., & Leddy, Maytum, Stacy Architects. (2016). *Ed Roberts Campus, Building Community*. Retrieved from YouTube video, http:// www.edrobertscampus.org, https://www.youtube.com/watch?v=7THtXFm_954

Luskin, E. D. (2015). *The Fair Housing Act: Update For Campus Housing*. Retrieved from http://thesciongroup.com/wpcontent/uploads/2012/02/Fair_Housing_Update_2015.pdf

Massachusetts Division of Professional Licensure, Board of Registration of Architects. (2015). *Lewis AR-100-1*. Retrieved from http://www.mass.gov/ocabr/licensee/dpl-boards/ar/

Massachusetts Institute of Technology. (2016). *Nondiscrimination Policy Commitment to Equal Opportunity*. Retrieved from https://referencepubs.mit.edu/what-we-do/nondiscrimination-policy

McGill University. (2016). *Universal Design Paradigm Shift*. MU Office for Students with Disabilities, Montreal, Quebec, Canada. Retrieved from https://www.mcgill.ca/osd/facultyinfo/universal-design

McNeese State University. (2016). *Diversity Awareness Policy*. Retrieved from http://www.mcneese.edu/policy/diversity_awareness

National Association for the Deaf. (2016). *NAD Sues Harvard and MIT for Discrimination in Public Online Content*. Retrieved from http://www.nad.org

National Center for Education Statistics. (2016). *Characteristics of Degree Granting Post-Secondary Institutions*. Retrieved from nces.ed.gov/pubsearch/pubsinfo.asp?pubid=2016144

National Center for Special Education Research. (2011). *The Post High School Outcomes of Young Adults with Disabilities up to 8 Years After High School*. Retrieved from ie.ed.gov/ncser/pubs/20113005

National Center on Accessible Educational Materials. (2016). *Assistive Technology*. Retrieved from http://www.aem.cast.org/navigating/assistive-technology.html#.WEVy4GQRLZt

National Center on Universal Design in Learning. (2015). *UDL Guidelines-Version 2.0 Examples and Resources*. Retrieved from http://www.udlcenter.org/aboutudl/udlguidelines

National Disability Authority. (2016). *Buildings for Everyone: A Universal Design Approach; Entrances and Horizontal Circulation 2*. Center of Excellence in Universal Design. Retrieved from http://universaldesign.ie/Built-Environment/Building-for-Everyone/2-Entrances%20and%20Horizontal%20Circulation.pdf

New England American with Disabilities Act Center. (2016). *NE ADA Center, a Project of the Institute of Human Centered Design*. Retrieved from http://www.newenglandada.org/

North Carolina State University Center for Universal Design. (1997). *The Principles of Universal Design*. Retrieved from http://www.ncsu.edu/ncsu/design/cud/about_ud/udprinciplestext.htm

North Carolina State University Center for Universal Design. (2016). *Case Studies on Universal Design (UD): Case 1, Principle 1: Equitable Use: University of Virginia (UVA); Promoting Equality While Preserving History At the University of Virginia (UVA), Academical Village*. Retrieved from https://www.ncsu.edu/ncsu/design/cud/pubs_p/docs/udffile/case_1.pdf

Paralysed Veterans of America. (2012). *Barrier-Free America Award*. Retrieved from http://www.pva.org/site/c.ajIRK9NJLcJ2E/b.6305457/k.49C6/BarrierFree_America_Award.htm

Paulson, M. (2004). *Diocesan Headquarters Sold to BC: Brighton Land Nets $107.4M: The Boston Globe Spotlight Investigation; Abuse in the Catholic Church, the financial cost.* Retrieved from http://www.archive.boston.com/globe/spotlight/abuse/stories5/042104_sale.htm

Quotes, A. Z. (2016). *We are trying to construct a more inclusive society. We are going to make a country in which no one is left out. Franklin D. Roosevelt.* Retrieved from http://www.azquotes.com/quote/250917

Rocheleau, M. (2015). BC Faces Inquiry Over Accessibility On Campus. *Boston Globe.* Retrieved from https://www.bostonglobe.com/metro/2015/02/18/boston-college-faces-criticism-investigations-over-accessibility-campus/AJyW1ZUYHVQSjqtCJcVmIL/story.html

Rooted in Rights. (2016). *Ed Roberts Activist.* Retrieved from http://www.rootedinrights.org/ed-roberts-disability-rights-activist/

Rothstein, L. (2014). Disability Discrimination Statutes or Tort Law: Which Provides the Best Means to Ensure an Accessible Environment? *Ohio State Law Journal, 75*(06), 1264–1287.

Rothstein, L., & Irzyk, J. (2016). *Disabilities and the Law.* Louisville, KY: Thomas Reuters.

Sirvage, R., & Bauman, H. (2016). *Campus Design and Planning: What is DeafSpace?* Retrieved from http://www.curbed.com/2016/3/2/11140210/gallaudet-deafspace-washington-dc

Smith, S. (2013). New Look Coming for Gasson Quad: Work on St. Mary's, Merkert, Conte Also To Take Place This Summer. *Boston College Chronicle.* Retrieved from http://www.bc.edu/publications/chronicle/FeaturesNewsTopstories/2013/features/gassonquad050913.html

United States Access Board. (2015). *About the Section 508 Standards.* Retrieved from https://www.access-board.gov/guidelines-and-standards/communications-and-it/about-the-section-508-standards

United States Access Board. (2016). *Advancing Full Access and Inclusion For All: Uniform Federal Accessibility Standards.* Retrieved from https://www.access-board.gov/guidelines-and-standards/buildings-and-sites/about-the-aba-standards/ufas

United States Census Bureau. (2012). *Newsroom Archive: Nearly 1 in 5 People Have A Disability in the U.S.: Report Released to Coincide with 22nd Anniversary of the ADA, Census Bureau Reports.* Retrieved from https://www.census.gov/newsroom/releases/archives/miscellaneous/cb12-134.html

United States Department of Education. (2008). *Higher Education Opportunity Act, Laws and Guidance.* Retrieved from http://www2.ed.gov/policy/highered/leg/hea08/index.html

United States Department of Education. (2010). *No otherwise qualified person with a disability...* 29 U.S.C. § 794. Excerpt from § 504, Rehabilitation Act of 1973. Retrieved from http://www2.ed.gov/about/offices/list/ocr/docs/edlite-FAPE504.html

United States Department of Education. (2013). *We Must Provide Equal Opportunity in Sports to Students With Disabilities.* Retrieved from http://www.blog.ed.gov/2013/01/we-must-provide-equal-opportunity-in-sports-to-students-with-disabilities/

United States Department of Education. (2015). *A New Education Law.* Retrieved from https://www.ed.gov/essa?src=rn

United States Department of Education, Office of Civil Rights. (2016a). *OCR: Protecting Students with Disabilities. Frequently Asked Questions About Section 504 and the Education of Children with Disabilities.* Retrieved from http://www2.ed.gov/about/offices/list/ocr/504faq.html

United States Department of Education, Office of Educational Technology. (2016b). *Future Ready Learning: Reimagining the Role of Technology in Education: 2016 National Education Technology Plan.* Retrieved from http://tech.ed.gov/files/2015/12/NETP16.pdf

United States Department of Education, Office of Special Education Programs. (2004). *IDEA's That Work: UDL Toolkit Home.* Retrieved from https://www.osepideasthatwork.org/federal-resources-stakeholders/tool-kits/tool-kit-universal-design-learning-udl

United States Department of Justice. (2005). *A guide to disability rights laws.* United States Department of Justice Civil Rights Division. Retrieved from https://www.ada.gov/cguide.htm

United States Department of Justice. (2010a). *Americans with Disabilities Act, ADA Amendment of 2010: Standards of Accessible Design* (P.L.110325). Retrieved from https://www.ada.gov/2010ADAstandards_index.htm

United States Department of Justice. (2010b). *Information and Technical Assistance on the Americans with Disabilities Act: ADA Standards for Accessible Design 2010.* Retrieved from https://www.ada.gov/2010ADAstandards_index.htm

United States Department of Justice. (2010c). *Settlement Agreement Between the United States of America, McNeese State University and the Board of Supervisors of the University of Louisiana System Under Title II of the American with Disabilities Act.* Retrieved from https://www.ada.gov/mcneese.htm

United States Department of Justice. (2016a). *Americans With Disabilities Act, ADA Requirements: Effective Communication.* Retrieved from http://www.ada.gov/effective-comm.htm

United States Department of Justice. (2016b). *American with Disabilities Act: Information and Technical Assistance ADA Enforcement: Cases from 2006 to present.* Retrieved from https://www.ada.gov/enforce_current.htm

United States Department of Justice. (2016c). *Checklist for Existing Facilities.* Retrieved from https://www.ada.gov/racheck.pdf

United States Department of Justice. (2016d). *National Association of the Deaf et al. v. Harvard University et al Case Number 3:15-cv-30023.* US District Court briefs Harvard University, Massachusetts, Retrieved from https://www.ada.gov/briefs/harvard_soi.pdf

United States Department of Justice. (2016e). *Notice of Proposed Rule Making Under Title III of the ADA to Require Movie Theaters to Provide Closed Movie Captioning and Audio Description.* Retrieved from https://www.ada.gov/regs2014/movie_nprm_index.htm

United States Department of Labor. (2016). *Persons with a Disability: Labor Force Characteristics, 2015 Summary.* Bureau of Labor Statistics (BLS). Retrieved from http://www.bls.gov/news.release/disabl.nr0.htm

University of California Berkeley. (2016). *Nondiscrimination Policy Statement- Student-Related Matters.* Retrieved from http://sa.berkeley.edu/nondiscrimination

University of Illinois Urbana Champaign. (2016). *World-changing achievements, discoveries, and creations are realized at Illinois.* Retrieved from http://illinois.edu/about/research.html

University of Massachusetts Boston, Institute for Community Inclusion. (2016). *The Think College Transition Model Project; College Options for People with Intellectual Disabilities.* Retrieved from http://www.thinkcollege.net/

University of Virginia. (2016). *Notice of Nondiscrimination and Civil Rights.* Office for Equal Opportunity and Civil Rights. Retrieved from http://eocr.virginia.edu/notice-non-discrimination-and-equal-opportunity

University of Washington, Disabilities, Opportunities, Internetworking, and Technology Program. (2016a). *AccessCollege: Helping post-secondary faculty, administrators, students and service units increase the success of all students.* AccessCollege Center, University of Washington. Retrieved from http://www.washington.edu/doit/programs/accesscollege

University of Washington, Disabilities, Opportunities, Internetworking, and Technology Program. (2016b). *DO-IT Admin: A Project to Help Post-Secondary Student Service Administrators Work Successfully With Students Who Have Disabilities.* Retrieved from http://www.washington.edu/doit/do-it-admin-project-help-postsecondary-student-services-administrators-work-successfully-students

University of Washington, Disabilities, Opportunities, Internetworking, and Technology Program. (2016c). *Introduction to Universal Design in Education: Principles and Applications.* Retrieved from http://www.washington.edu/doit/programs/center-universal-design-education/introduction-universal-design-education

Wilson, L. (2015). *Creating Inclusive Environments with DeafSpace Architecture.* Sourceable, Architecture News. Retrieved from https://sourceable.net/creating-inclusive-environments-deafspace-architecture/

World Declaration on Education for All. (1990). *Outcomes on Education: World Conference on Education for All.* Retrieved from http://www.un.org/en/development/devagenda/education.shtml

ADDITIONAL READING

Association on Higher Education and Disability. (2016). *Universal Design Resources.* Retrieved from https://www.ahead.org/resources/universal-design/resources

Davis, L. J. (2016). *Enabling Acts: The Hidden Story of How the Americans With Disabilities Act Gave the Largest US Minority Its Rights.* Boston, MA: Beacon Press.

KEY TERMS AND DEFINITIONS

Abelism: A term coined by Dr. Thomas Hehir, Harvard University, to describe negative attitudes and assumptions towards students with disabilities that specifically favors students who are considered able bodied (AB).

Augmentative/Alternative Communication (AAC): Refers to communication other than speech. AAC devices, sometimes called Speech Generating Devices (SGD's) may include sign language or symbol or picture boards to aid in communication.

Barrier-Free (BF) Concepts: A broad term that incorporates Universal Design (UD) principles so as to provide maximum usability and access for end users by removing physical architectural and access barriers for members of the public and persons with disabilities. Ceiling Lift: A hydraulic lift attached to a track on a ceiling with a sling for the ease of transfer of people with limited mobility from one area to another, such as from a bed to a shower.

Curbcuts or Curbramps: These sidewalk features are designed as solid ramps or cutouts in the sidewalk leading from the top of the sidewalk to the street level. They provide wheelchair access onto the sidewalk.

Disability Discrimination: A term that describes a situation where a person or student with a disability is excluded from participating equally with his or her peers without disabilities due to physical access barriers or other inclusion barriers.

Eye-Gaze Technology: A technology with a camera and computer used for people who may have limited use of their body to write or communicate but have use and movement of their eyes.

Inclusion: The ability of students of all abilities, cultures, races, to be provided access to join together in pursuit of all education and recreation and community activities with a feeling of equity and welcome.

Institutions of Higher Education (IHE): IHE are post-secondary institutions including 2 year or 4 year colleges, vocational schools, trade or professional schools that award academic degrees and certificates.

Universal Design (UD): A design paradigm coined by Ronald Mace in the 1970's with the principles to provide the maximum access and inclusion for the most number of persons in the community, including person with characteristics and abilities that are typical to those on the outer edges of typical.

This research was previously published in Disability and Equity in Higher Education Accessibility edited by Jennie Lavine, Roy Y. Chan, and Henry C. Alphin, Jr.; pages 178-203, copyright year 2017 by Information Science Reference (an imprint of IGI Global).

Chapter 27
Addressing Accessibility of MOOCs for Blind Users
Hearing Aid for Screen Orientation

Teresita de Jesús Álvarez Robles
Universidad Veracruzana, México

Alfredo Mendoza González
Universidad Juárez Autónoma de Tabasco, México

Alma Rosa García Gaona
Universidad Veracruzana, México

Francisco Alvarez Rodríguez
Universidad Autónoma de Aguascalientes, México

ABSTRACT

The concept of universal access to information society stands for the guaranteed access for all people in the world to internet services, online learning including. Blind users have been benefited by accessible tools such as screen readers, auditory interfaces, etc., nevertheless this kind of external software would not be required if the blind user's requirements were taking into account since the design process. This chapter presents a set of guidelines for designing hearing messages that help blind students to navigate in a MOOC's interface.

INTRODUCTION

The advantages of e-learning have been widely documented in literature. Nowadays more and more institutions have extended their programs to distance and online education, changing the tradition way things in education were doing. MOOCs have enhanced e-learning by giving the opportunity to students to have official certificates, high-qualified instructors in renowned institution. Nevertheless, the pedagogic protocols have to be transformed away from the traditional in-classroom perspective.

DOI: 10.4018/978-1-7998-1213-5.ch027

Universal Access to Information Society is a whole philosophy that encourages efforts to assure equal access to digital services such as internet, e-learning, cloud services and mobile technology to all people in the world. Equal access has a wide meaning, including ease of use and delightful user experience, goals that only can be achieved when the technology includes all users' requirements and goals in its design. On this point, blind users' needs of computer based technology has limited satisfied.

Accessibility tools like screen readers generally requires third party software; implying that users, besides learning the way the main software works, also have to learn to use this accessibility tool (and expend additional money to purchase it).

This situation in MOOCs' field makes the student required a double learning effort: learn the academic content (the main objective of the course) and learn how the user interface (menus, tools, and all interactive elements) works with this third party software. Accessibility in MOOCs must include ways to attend blind people's requirements, with tools that do not require additional cognitive load.

This chapter is focused in presenting a interface navigation tool that facilitates the interaction of blind users with all the element of a graphical user interface of an online course, converting the mouse in a cane.

BACKGROUND

E-Learning Introduction

The concept of e-learning is defined to many ways, from the perspective of conception and development as a learning tool; the e-learning systems have a pedagogical and technological duality. The first because in these systems must not be containers of digital information, but it must be transmitted according to models and pedagogical patterns defined to meet the challenges of these new context. Technology, because the whole process of teaching and learning is based on applications software, mainly developed in web environments, this is known as training platforms.

The e-learning, in its broadest sense may comprise any educational activity using electronic means to carry out all or part of the training process.

There are definitions that open the spectrum of e-learning in any process related to education and technology, such as the definition of the American Society of Training and Development: "term that covers a wide range of applications and processes, such as web-based learning, computer-based, virtual classrooms and digital collaboration learning, including delivery of content via Internet, intranet / extranet, audio and video recordings, satellite transmissions, interactive TV, CD-ROM and more." (Alwi & Fan, 2010).

E-learning, as Marc Rosenberg defined in (Rosenberg, 2001), is the use of Internet technologies to deliver a range of solutions that enhance knowledge and performance. The author also pointed three key criteria for e-learning:

1. It is based on networking: making it able to be instantly updated, stored, retrieved, distributed and shared.
2. It is delivered to the end user through the use of computers using Internet technology.
3. It is focused on broadest view of learning: learning that breaks traditional methods and techniques

Paul Henry indicates that a comprehensive e-learning solution involves three key elements: the technology (platforms, virtual campus, etc.), the content (quality and mentions structuring thereof are taken as capital elements for the success of e-training initiative) and the services (actions of teachers, management elements, communication elements, elements of evaluation, etc.). By varying the weight of these three components, are obtained different models of e-learning.

In practice, to carry out a training program based on e-learning, is made use of platforms or software systems that enable communication and interaction between teachers, students and contents.

A recent popular trend in e-learning is MOOCs or Massive Online Open Courses: MOOCs are a continuation of the trend in innovation, experimentation and the use of technology initiated by distance and online learning, to provide learning opportunities for large numbers of learners (Siemens, 2013).

Research work presented in (Burgos et al., 2013) indicates that MOOCs are a means of facilitating the efficient creation, distribution and use of knowledge and information for learning by taking advantage of freely available online resources such as Open Educational Resources (OER), and that they can be used to support social networking and other forms of "connectivity" among the participants.

Any well-designed e-learning platform must apply the next characteristics (Bruzzi, et al., 2012):

1. Personalization (considering a student's knowledge level, objectives, time and pace)
2. Learning by doing (through practical activities, simulations, virtual laboratory, etc.)
3. Active participation and collaboration with other students in the Virtual Learning Environment (sharing resources with other students, teachers, tutors or mentors).
4. The use of different sensory channels, ideal for understanding their effects on learning and delivering educational content.

Education for Blind People

The purpose of providing an additional curriculum for children with Visual Impaired (VI) is to enable the child to develop independence. Fully sighted children learn much through observation and imitation. Children with severe or profound VI require sustained teaching to learn many of the skills that fully sighted children learn with little input

Education for people with VI begins with some areas that are considered important and are closely related to the Orientation and Mobility (O&M), such as (Villalobos, 2012):

- **Physical Education:** In this regard, to develop physical skills necessary for mobility and displacement are necessary.
- **Activities of Daily Living (ADLs):** This area has a close relationship, as in O&M there is a projection of the subject in the social environment and ADLs techniques that allow the subject to deal appropriately with their means they work perform different daily task.
- **Early Stimulation:** In the case of dealing with a congenital blind or blind child at an early age is important for the sensory-perceptual towards this development work, favor the interpretation of the signals from the environment and the need for a sensory integration correct representation of space.
- **Psychology:** In the case of adults, the contact with the therapist is very necessary, because this is the area where the subject begins to work the disability.

Talking about education of blind and visual impaired people, schools limits all their capacities mainly because the lack of accessibility in the design of their furniture, buildings, classrooms, chairs, walking ways, etc. This barely favorable environment makes very difficult the learning process.

The ignorance about abilities, capacities and limitations of blind students only reflects in fail attempts in academic activities. Generally, the blind student represents a source of stress to instructors, since he/she do not know how to communicate with him/her. This fact makes instructor to believe that the student is the one that cannot communicate, the one that cannot complete the activities, and the one that cannot learn. At this point instructor reduces the work load, the activities number, and the cognitive demand; to the blind student education does not really represent a challenge more than a boring activity.

In (Kinash & Paszuk, 2007) there are seven considerations that teachers and instructors must attend when deal with blind students:

1. **Look at the Person First, and the Disability Second:** Blind students, like all others, have feelings, expectations, capacities, abilities, and limitations. Teachers must ensure a great environment to diminish al barriers.
2. **Blind Learners Deserve Expectations:** Just like all other students, blind students need challenges to test their abilities; have desire for success and must know how to get up when falls.
3. **Make Connections:** The learning process for a blind student must involve every person that can contribute: parents, specialists, teachers, etc.
4. **Review the Blind Student's "Eye Report":** Eye report is a medical document that informs about the visual capacity of the patient and includes (Willings, 2015):
    a. Visual acuity with and without glasses.
    b. The prescription being worn.
    c. The etiology (Cause of a disease or abnormal condition.)
    d. The diagnosis.
    e. The prognosis (The prospect of recovery from disease.)

When teachers analyze it, eye report may help to define a strategy to attend the student limitations.

5. **Braille Means Literacy:** For enhance the blind student abilities and opportunities, they must to learn to read and learn Braille as soon as possible, through formal instruction of qualified teachers.
6. **Planned Redundancy of Information:** To make accessible the information in class, teachers must plan how to provide the same information in multiple channels. This way, not only blind students will be benefited.
7. **Organization is Critical:** Multiple accessible class activities and materials represents a lot of work for teachers, so that they must plan and organize everything before class rather than at the time of presentation.

There is not a specific way to design and present a class to blind students, but there are several key elements that teachers must include in their work. Accessible education for blind students must have nine characteristics (Kinash & Paszuk, 2007):

1. Braille literacy.
2. Know and apply the expanded core curriculum.

3. Access to textbooks in advance of course.
4. Convenience of digital formats.
5. Relationships bridging (and fading of adult supports).
6. Teaching responsibility of classroom teacher with supports.
7. Universal design (include disabled persons up-front).
8. Attitude is paramount.

In order to develop additional skills and reinforce the current, (Davis, 2003) propose a set of extra-class activities for visual impaired (VI) students, but some of them fit for blind students:

- To enhance mobility.
  - Asking the child to fetch or return the register.
  - Asking the child to take messages to other teachers in other parts of the building.
  - Making the child a room monitor, e.g. light monitor.
  - Giving time before school for the child to use a walking machine.
- To enhance tactile awareness
  - Providing as many real objects as possible in class for illustrative purposes. These can be touched by the child with VI but can also enliven the lesson for the other children.
- To reinforce life skills:
  - Making sure that at lunchtime the child eats alongside peers, with or without a support assistant.
  - Making sure that the child plays outside at the same time as peers.
  - Establishing a lunchtime Braille club available for all children to join.
  - Organizing visits to civil associations, accessible enterprises, inclusive schools, etc

MAIN FOCUS OF THE CHAPTER

Issues, Controversies, Problems

E-Learning for Blind Students

General rules of accessibility should benefit all users no matter knowledge, health or disability. Coombs and Banks' (2000) proposed 16 tips for teachers when start working in online learning:

1. It's about people and not technology. Teachers must avoid to lean in technology wanting to show off their knowledge and potential, losing the fact that technology is only the way to share information effectively to the learner.
2. Do not replicate the classroom. Teachers must find a way to create a virtual presence in the course. Having control, authority and support. This way students will behave correctly in a controlled environment feeling comfortable and protected.
3. Be interactive. Promote interactivity between students but do not forget to also be the most interactive member of the course.

4. Keep it simple. All information in the course must be transmitted as clear as possible, since when students misunderstand something, they expend valuable time by trying to resolve what the teacher wants to say.
5. Modularize. In order to have more focused students, it will be better to break the content into small units.
6. Beware of techies. Teachers must be aware of trying to convert students into experts of the software or platform where the course stands. They have to focus in the course's content and only acquire the basic technical skills that allow them to take advantage of technology.
7. Remember e-mail. A powerful tool to maintain individual and group communication is the e-mail. Teachers must remember this when try to reinforce instructions, solutions and solving problems.
8. Design for universal access. All materials in the course must meet a wide variety of learning styles including off course the needs of students with disabilities.
9. Understand the problems of students with disabilities.
10. Be a virtual host.
11. Be accessible.
12. Make it a team project.
13. Provide redundant communication modes.
14. Have a system to deal with special problems.
15. Understand adaptive technologies.
16. Set Boundaries.

It is clear that all ideas about enhancing accessibility implemented in the course design will benefit students with disabilities including those with blindness, but is important to satisfy the particular needs of them by defining particular design rules.

A very important part of an online course is its interface. It is a whole world the issue of interface design, full of standards, process, frameworks, etc. Nevertheless, there are easy understandable and basic rules focused in particular characteristics of users or trying to enhance a particular characteristic of the interface. For example, (Kinash & Paszuk, 2007) propose 10 golden rules for programmers to enhance interface's accessibility.

1. Images and animation. Use the alt attribute to describe the function of all visuals.
2. Image maps. Use client-side MAP and text for hotspots.
3. Multimedia. Provide captioning and transcripts of audio, descriptions of video and accessible versions in case inaccessible formats are used.
4. Hypertext links. Use text that makes sense when read out of context. For instance, do not use "click here."
5. Graphs and Charts. Summarize or use the longest attribute.
6. Page organization. Use headings, lists, and consistent structure. Use Cascading Style Sheets (CSS) for layout and style where possible.
7. Frames. Label with the title or name attribute.
8. Scripts, applets, and plug-ins. Provide alternative content in case active features are inaccessible or unsupported.
9. Tables. Make line-by-line reading sensible. Summarize. Avoid using tables for column layout.
10. Validate. Check your work

SOLUTIONS AND RECOMMENDATION

Designing Software for Blind Users

In the design of users' interfaces for the blind, (Bruzzi, et al., 2012) propose three initial elements:

1. Making accessible and usable interfaces for blind students: this feature will also facilitate and simplify the interaction of other users.
2. Increasing the accessibility of awareness information on other collaborators: every user (especially the blind) want to know who is collaborating, what, when and where she/he is doing something, and desire to be updated on her/his and others' status.
3. Providing educational content in different sensorial channels: interaction and integration between blind students and students without disabilities will develop perception of less exploited internal sensorial representations in everyone

As mentioned in (Bruzzi, et al., 2012) interaction based on screen readers may be difficult and frustrating for blind people because:

1. Content serialization produces an overload of vocal information in sequence.
2. A blind user has no overall perception of the whole interface.
3. The screen reader announces information mixing content and structure (related to description of interactive elements).
4. The screen reader can announce information in the wrong order, depending on theHTML code (for instance a table's content is generally organized in columns but it isread by rows).

In (Bruzzi, et al., 2012), authors analyze five disadvantages of screen readers:

1. Many interactive elements cannot be detected by a screen reader nor be accessed via keyboard (since they are not standard (X)HTML elements and their labels are announced by the screen reader as simple text), making some tasks impossible to complete.
2. Blind users have difficulty orienting themselves during interaction, listening to the interface contents sequentially, with no possibility of quickly moving from one part of the interface to another or using main editing functions (such as creating or accessing a document) or the document list.
3. Lack of a summary attribute for table used as layout purposes for the list of documents in the Main page does not quickly provide useful information on its content, and this requires and extra effort for blind users who have to read all cells sequentially to understand the content of the table (see area 5 of Figure 2).
4. The editor is not practically accessible. The main menu (file, edit, view, insert, format, etc.) and the style formatting toolbar (font type or size, etc.) are inaccessible because they cannot be reached via keyboard, while bold, italic or underlined functions can only be used through keyboard shortcuts (CTRL+b, CTRL+i, etc).
5. Some dialogue windows are not accessible at all and messages notifying the presence of other users are not announced by the screen reader, against the awareness principle

In (Perisa, et al., 2011), an approach to usability guidelines for interfaces designed to blind and visually impaired users, proposes that any interface must provide:

- The exact position of the elements in the screen
- Simple design
- The option of changing font size
- The option of changing background color
- Correct description of images
- Adequate language support for letters
- In case of video files, voice and text support must be included
- Web frames with designated names
- Standard web forms
- Text cannot be in image form
- If web page uses visual verification (CAPTCHA), alternative auditory verification must be available

Designing Screen Orientation Trough Hearing Aid

One of the first skills that blind people acquire, commonly by instruction in a formal program, is orientation and mobility. They learn to:

- Sensory development: Obtain information about the environment through sound, smell, touch and perception.
- Spatial concepts: Realize that there are objects around, even if they cannot be touch or heard, and notice the relation between them.
- Search skills: To locate things and places efficiently.
- Independence in movement.
- Self-protection: Skills to maintain face in unknown places

In a previous empirical study, authors made a mobile application that help blind users in the orientation of key elements in an indoor environment. By using markers (QR codes printed in floor) read by the phone's cam, users receive information about their location, clues to a previously defined destination, or characteristics of the object (e. g. stair with 12 steps, 10 inch potted cactus, 20 feet long bridge, etc.). This is a pilot test that is still in progress, but the idea was to provide certain useful information through hearing aid to blind people about the objects in around them

All markers were detected by the phone's camera (which was always enabled), every time a marker was detected a sound was played, then the user choose to hear the information of the marker or to skip it (Figure 1).

Sound Markers were classified in three categories; each of them makes a particular sound in detection.

1. Indicators. Indicator markers help users by informing about directions: corners, long corridors (to keep same direction), crossroads, turns, etc.
2. Descriptors. These markers provide information about relevant objects and places: stairs, elevators, ramps, doors, trees, chairs, etc.

Addressing Accessibility of MOOCs for Blind Users

Figure 1. Blind user interacting wiyh a marker.

3. Helping. This is a special category for those markers designed to provide extra help for the user: emergency phones, alarms, evacuation routes, shelters, etc

This idea was taken by authors and mapped to help in the orientation and mobility through a user interface: specifically through the elements of a MOOC's interface.

Navigation with Sound Markers

Each interactive element (button, menu, icon, etc.) of the interface will have a marker; even elements as borders, rulers, organizers, divisions, etc. This way, markers will be grouped in the next categories:

1. Layout: These markers inform about elements of the interface that conformed the structural design layout.
2. Interactive: These markers provide information about all elements that require direct interaction with the users to trigger some action.
3. Help: These markers provide common user help

Markers will trigger different sounds for each category, and in the learnability process it will be accompanied by vocal feedback about the category (Figure 2). Over time users will relate the sound with the action and this feedback will turn unnecessary. All interfaces must be as configurable as possible, in order to adapt the user knowledge of the interface. This way, users will recognize all categories by sound (Figure 3), and for blind users this process is very quick.

Users will have the option between hear the information of the marker by keeping the pointer in the position where the sound were played, or to skip it by leaving from there (Figure 4).

Markers will play the information if the user does not move the mouse after the initial warning sound, designers must leave a time for tolerance that may be the duration of the sound or the whole area of the element. Also they must define the area of the element where it is possible to trigger the sound; it can be a point at the center (Figure 5a) or a specific area (Figure 5b).

Addressing Accessibility of MOOCs for Blind Users

Figure 2. When mouse stands over an element triggers sound and vocal feedback.

Figure 3. For already-familiarized users, when mouse stands over an element triggers only sound.

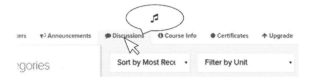

Figure 4. Marker triggers sound about the information of the element

Figure 5. Area of action

Layout Markers

Since there is not a single general layout format for MOOCs' interfaces, these markers orient about the user's position in the screen, indicating things like corners, dividers, windows, etc. For instance, Figure 6 shows a screen layout style where markers a, b, and c, indicate:

1. The divisor between the Menu and the activity area.
2. The division between the menu and tabs.
3. The top left corner of the window

Figure 6. Screen layout with four markers

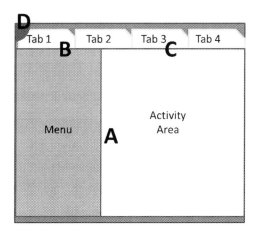

E-Learning Interactive Markers

Interactive markers provide specific information about an interactive element such as hyperlink, menu bar, button, icon, etc. This particular information includes:

- The identifiers of the element (name, tag, class, etc.)
- The action that triggers
- The way to interact with it.

Figure 7 shows the message that markers play (after the identifier sound is played) when users interact with a) button, b) Hyperlink.

Help Markers

Sometimes users lose the track of the spatial organization interface's elements, when it happens, users may use help parkers by activating some specific key (like ESC or F1) or by finding them in a specific area at the screen (like in the upper right corner). Minimize, maximize and close buttons were arranged in this category since they always have the same location (upper right in windows systems and upper left

Figure 7. Examples of two interactive markers

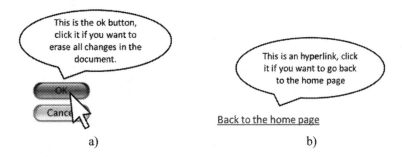

Addressing Accessibility of MOOCs for Blind Users

in IOS systems) and they can be used as escape way. For instance, in Figure 8, the user press ESC key, it triggers a marker that indicates how to close the interface. Help markers, unlike others, have additional information in order to assist, for example by indicating what action did just do, what should be done, what kind of sound should be listened, and what action to expect.

Additional Considerations

General rules of accessibility should benefit all users no matter knowledge, health or disability. Coombs and Banks'
    There are several characteristics that hearing aid must include.
    About general interface design

1. About general interface design
   a. Frequent users must be able to skip additional information.
   b. Interface must be error friendly especially with beginners.
   c. Additional feedback when errors happen.
2. About audible messages
   a. An audible marker is composed of one or more sequential audible messages.
   b. An audible massage provides specific information in the clearest way as possible.
   c. At more messages in a sequence, more specific is the information provided by each one.

FUTURE RESEARCH DIRECTIONS

This chapter presents an initial research of interface orientation guided through audible markers. There are many opportunity research points in this issue: usability of interfaces, user's learning enhances, markers guidelines, markers learnability, markers usability, metrics for markers and audible messages,

Figure 8. Example of a help marker

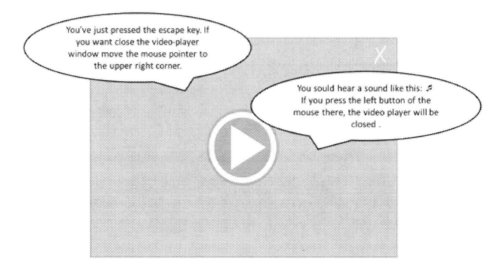

etc. Also, a very interesting line of this research is how an interface can be usable for beginner, intermediate and expert users, since they may process information at different levels and understand audible messages at very different speed.

CONCLUSION

Despite all progress in technology accessibility and inclusivity, designers, developers and researchers still have much work to do. Fortunately, there is not a single restricted way to do it, and therefore, there is not unworthy effort. Authors of this chapter were compromised with blind users by exploring alternative ways to enhance accessibility of online-courses' interfaces. It is very difficult to visual-guided designers (and researchers) to achieve this goal, especially with visual-based interfaces, but it is not compared with the difficulty that blind users have when dealing with regular interfaces.

Audible markers are now a very powerful tool to provide extra information about the environment to blind people; authors introduce this idea to interface design. This way, users move a pointing device (such as mouse) through the interface and markers inform him/her about the elements that are in its way. User chooses the amount of audible information that receives by holding or moving the pointing device. Initially, only a simple sound (such as "ding") is triggered, if user does not move the pointer, additional messages are played, until full information is provided or until user move the pointer.

Markers where divided in three categories according with the information that is provided: layout markers, inform about elements of the interface that conformed the structural design layout, interactive markers, which provide information about all elements that require direct interaction with the users to trigger some action, and finally, help markers, which provide common user help.

Additional markers may be also useful, such as markers that inform about the location in the screen, not in pixels or coordinates, but as spatial orientation like above, center, right, upper right; or like cardinal directions: north, south; and even by using clock orientation (known by blind people that had receive such training) 12 o'clock, 6 o'clock, etc. The advantage with markers is mainly its interaction. Users may hear as many as they need or avoid as many as they want.

REFERENCES

Alwi, N., & Fan, I. (2010). E-learning and information security management. *International Journal of Digital Society*, *1*(2), 148–156.

Arnim, D., Piuzzi, B. S., Nam, C. S., & Chung, D. (2007), Guidelines for the Development and Improvement of Universal Access Systems for Blind Students. *Proceedings of The 4th International Conference on Universal Access in Human-Computer Interaction,* Beijing, China, LNCS (Vol. 4554, pp. 603-612). Springer. 10.1007/978-3-540-73279-2_67

Burgos Aguilar, J. V., Cox, G., Czerniewicz, L., D'Antoni, S., Diallo, B., Downes, S., . . . Lane, A. (Eds.), (2013). Perspectives on Open and Distance Learning: Open Educational Resources: Innovation, Research and Practice, Athabasca, Alberta, Canada. Commonwealth of Learning.

Buzzi, M. C., Buzzi, M., Leporini, B., & Mori, G. (2012). Designing E-Learning Collaborative Tools for Blind People. In E. Pontes, A. Silva, A. Guelfi & S.T. Kofuji (Eds.), E-Learning - Long-Distance and Lifelong Perspectives, Rijeka, Croatia. InTech Open Access.

Davis, P. (2003). *Including Children with Visual Impairment in Mainstream Schools: A Practical Guide.* London, England: David Fulton Publishers.

Kinash, S., & Paszuk, A. (2007). *Accessible Education for Blind Learners: Kindergarten Through Postsecondary.* Charlotte, North Carolina, USA. Information Age Publishing.

Rosenberg, M. (2001). *E-Learning: Strategies for Delivering Knowledge in the Digital Age.* New York, NY, United States: McGraw-Hill.

Siemens, G. (2014). *The Future of MOOCs.* Retrieved from http://www.educause.edu/blogs/gbayne/george-siemens-future-moocs-0

Villalobos, L. (2012). *Orientación y movilidad. Notes from the Course "Orientación y Movilidad".* Universidad Popular de Veracruz.

Willings, C. (2015). *Interpreting the Eye Report,* Retrieved April 01, 2015, from: http://www.teachingvisuallyimpaired.com

ADDITIONAL READING

Bonk, C., Lee, M. M., Reeves, T., & Reynolds, T. (2014). MOOCs and Open Education around the World: Recapping the Past Year, Mapping the Road Ahead. *Proceedings of World Conference on E-Learning in Corporate, Government, Healthcare, and Higher Education 2014* (pp. 238-241). Chesapeake, VA: Association for the Advancement of Computing in Education (AACE)

Kilgore, W., & Lowenthal, P. R. (2015). The Human Element MOOC. In R. Wright (Ed.), *Student-Teacher Interaction in Online Learning Environments* (pp. 373–391). Hershey, PA: Information Science Reference.

LeClair, J., & Ferrer, T. (2014). A case for MOOCs, In *Proceedings of the ASEE Gulf-Southwest Conference* (1 - 8) New Orleans, Louisiana, United States, American Society for Engineering Education.

Thrun, S. (2013). MOOCs: The Future Is Here. [PubMed]. *The Journal of Nursing Education, 52*(1), 3.

Valentin, C. (2015). MOOCs Global Digital Divide: Reality or Myth? In F. Nafukho & B. Irby (Eds.), *Handbook of Research on Innovative Technology Integration in Higher Education* (pp. 376–397). Hershey, PA: Information Science Reference.

KEY TERMS AND DEFINITIONS

Accessibility: Accessibility refers to the design of products, devices, services, or environments for people with disabilities. The concept of accessible design ensures both "direct access" and "indirect access" meaning compatibility with a person's assistive technology (for example, computer screen readers). Accessibility can be viewed as the "ability to access" and benefit from some system or entity.

Blindness: According to the National Institutes of Health (NIH), blindness is a lack of vision. It may also refer to a loss of vision that cannot be corrected with glasses or contact lenses.

Braille: According to the Oxford Dictionary, braille is a form of written language for blind people, in which characters are represented by patterns of raised dots that are felt with the fingertips.

Disability: Is the consequence of an impairment that may be physical, cognitive, mental, sensory, emotional, developmental, or some combination of these. A disability may be present from birth, or occur during a person's lifetime.

Screen Reader: Is a software application that attempts to identify and interpret what is being displayed on the screen. This interpretation is then re-presented to the user with text-to-speech, sound icons, or a Braille output device. Screen readers are a form of assistive technology (AT) potentially useful to people who are blind, visually impaired, illiterate or learning disabled, often in combination with other AT, such as screen magnifiers.

Techies: According to the Oxford Dictionary, is a person who is expert in or enthusiastic about technology, especially computing.

Visual Impaired: Is when a person has sight loss that cannot be fully corrected using glasses or contact lenses.

This research was previously published in User-Centered Design Strategies for Massive Open Online Courses (MOOCs) edited by Ricardo Mendoza-Gonzalez; pages 142-156, copyright year 2016 by Information Science Reference (an imprint of IGI Global).

Chapter 28
The Educational Rights of Students with Chronic Disease

Thomas C. Gibbon
Shippensburg University, USA

Jenifer Cline
Great Falls Public Schools, USA

Christopher L. Schwilk
Shippensburg University, USA

Patricia D. Hosfelt
Frederick County Maryland Public Schools, USA

David F. Bateman
Shippensburg University, USA

ABSTRACT

Effective implementation of services for students with chronic disease in any school district relies on a solid understanding of the rules and regulations governing the educational rights of those with disabilities. This chapter enumerates the history of the educational rights of students with disabilities, describes the key laws as promulgated by the federal government, provides a definition of a disability based on these laws, possible categories of special education services and the qualification process for 504 or special education services. This chapter discusses the consideration for education in the least restrictive environment, and key components in the development of both IEP's and Section 504 plans, issues related to providing a free appropriate public education, and the Family and Educational Rights Privacy Act. It concludes with a discussion of working with related services personnel. The two main ways students with chronic disease receive services is under IDEA in the category of Other Health Impaired or under Section 504 of the Rehabilitation Act.

DOI: 10.4018/978-1-7998-1213-5.ch028

The Educational Rights of Students with Chronic Disease

OVERVIEW

Effective implementation of services for students with chronic disease in any school district in the United States relies on a solid understanding of the rules and regulations governing the educational rights of those with disabilities. This chapter enumerates the history of the educational rights of students with disabilities, describes the key laws as promulgated by the federal government, provides a definition of a disability based on these laws, possible categories of special education services and the qualification process for 504 or special education services. This chapter will discuss the consideration for education in the least restrictive environment, and key components in the development of both IEP's and Section 504 plans, issues related to providing a free appropriate public education, and the Family and Educational Rights Privacy Act. It concludes with a discussion of working with related services personnel.

The two main ways students with chronic disease receive services is under IDEA in the category of Other Health Impaired or under Section 504 of the Rehabilitation Act. Each will be discussed in turn, describing the background on both, along with the United States federal definition of disabilities. Additionally, information will be provided on eligibility for the category of Other Health Impaired, especially clarifying the two-part test, examples of conditions, along with suggestions for programming. Section 504 of the Rehabilitation Act will also be clarified as well as expected programming needs for students with chronic disease. Specific accommodations will be delineated, along with tips for working with students with chronic disease. It is important to note the specific regulations in a state may be slightly different from those promulgated by the federal government. The regulations provided by the federal government serve as the minimum required for implementation.

The most important laws governing the education of students with chronic diseases are the Individuals with Disabilities Education Act (IDEA), and Section 504 of the Rehabilitation Act of 1973. In addition to the laws as passed by Congress, are the codifying regulations that provide the specific "rules" for how special education should be implemented in order to get federal reimbursement. For purposes of this chapter, we will be using two definitions of disability; first the federal definition of disability from the Individuals with Disabilities Education Act and the second definition we will be using is from Section 504 of the Rehabilitation Act of 1973. Each will be addressed in turn. Understanding each will assist in providing appropriate services in your school.

Brief History of Rights of Students with Disabilities

Prior to the mid-1970s students with disabilities were often in programs away from their neighborhood school, if educated at all. Schools had the option to refuse to provide educational services to students whose abilities were different. Students with disabilities were denied access to public education and were in turn segregated and spent their days in settings outside of the educational setting. Section 504 of the Rehabilitation Act of 1973 and PL94-142 grew out of court cases where parents of students with disabilities challenged the public schools to give their children access to public education. *Section 504 of the Rehabilitation Act of 1973* was the first civil rights statute for those with disabilities. However, it did not take effect until 1977. Section 504 gained momentum over the years and paved the way for the Americans with Disabilities Act. Section 504 of the Rehabilitation Act of 1973 is a civil rights law administered by the Office for Civil Rights that does not provide funding but accompanies other sources of federal funding and essentially states that no program receiving federal funds may discriminate against a person based on their disability. Section 504 is an anti-discriminatory act ensuring individuals with disabilities received the same rights as those students without disabilities. Since Section 504 is an anti-discriminatory act and protects any person with a disability, Section 504's definition of disability is broader than the IDEA definition. Section 504 defines an individual with a disability in pertinent part as having (a) a physical or mental impairment that (b) substantially limits (c) a major life activity. This disability definition provides broader coverage than does the IDEA (Yell, 2012).

Individuals with Disabilities Education Act (formerly the Education of All Handicapped Children Act) (P.L. 94-142) is the law providing the basis for the implementation of special education as it is known and practiced today. Following the passing of Section 504 of the Rehabilitation Act of 1973, the advocacy community continued to work to open the doors of public schools to children with disabilities and from work came P.L. 94-142. This law allowed students with disabilities the rights to access public education. As P.L. 94-142 was amended in 1990 it became the Individuals with Disabilities Education Act (IDEA). IDEA is now more than an access to education law; there are expectations and accountability for the achievement of student with disabilities as well. Some have written that, in fact, we have a profession that is defined by this law (Yell, 2011). This is only partially correct. Special education clearly existed before 1975 when this law was enacted, but students with disabilities were legally often denied services. Since 1975, the manner in which it is practiced and the experiences of teachers and students are clearly very different because of this law.

The reauthorization of IDEA in 1997 placed greater emphasis on improving students' inclusion in accountability systems, giving them access to the general education curriculum, and improving their academic performance. The most recent reauthorization of IDEA in 2004 brought further evolution in the law. Although IDEA 2004 continues to ensure all children with disabilities receive a "free appropriate public education" (FAPE), amendments affected state and local policies by stipulating children with disabilities must make progress in the general education curriculum and improve their academic and developmental outcomes. The 2004 reauthorization was aligned more clearly with the guiding federal legislation, the No Child Left Behind Act of 2001 (NCLB). Specifically, states are expected to align their performance goals and indictors for children with disabilities with their definition of adequate yearly progress (AYP). Children with disabilities are expected to participate in state assessment systems and demonstrate continued improvement and progress in their academic outcomes, including those students who take an alternate assessment (Cortiella, 2006).

In 2005, states reported 7,013,238 children ages birth through 21 years had been identified for early intervention and special education services under IDEA, including both children newly identified in the year represented by the count and children identified in earlier years who continued to receive services (National Center for Education Evaluation and Regional Assistance, 2010). The following year marked the first time since the enactment of IDEA in 1975 where special education participation numbers declined. Since then, the number and proportion of students with disabilities has decreased steadily, falling to 13.1 percent of the national student body by 2009-2010, or 6.48 million students. This national trend is driven by shifting populations of particular disability types. The federal government requires all states to report student population numbers across twelve categories of disability, along with an optional thirteenth termed "developmental delay." Those categories are as follows: autism, deaf-blindness, emotional disturbance, hearing impairments, mental retardation (now termed intellectually disabled), multiple disabilities, orthopedic impairments, other health impairments, specific learning disabilities, speech or language impairments, traumatic brain injuries, and visual impairments. While many disabilities identified in these categories declined, there was a sharp increase in the population of students with other health impairments over the last decade. Between 2000-2001 and 2009-2010, the number of other health impaired (OHI) students more than doubled from 303,000 to 689,000; still only constituting 1.4 percent of all special education students in 2009-2010 (Scull & Winkler, 2011). Students with a chronic disease will often qualify for special education services under IDEA as a student with an Other Health Impairment.

A federal funding statute administered by the Office of Special Education Programs (OSEP), the IDEA defines disability as (a) fitting one or more specified categories, "mental retardation, hearing impairments (including deafness), speech and language impairment, visual impairments (including blindness), emotional disturbance, orthopedic impairments, autism, traumatic brain injury, other health impairment, or specific learning disability," and (b) "by reason thereof" needing special education. In turn, the IDEA regulations define each of the categories, with the final criterion for all of them, except the category specific learning disability, being that it "adversely affects educational performance." For specific learning disability, this criterion is presumably implicit (Goelz, 2014).

P.L. 94-142 established all children with disabilities were to receive a free appropriate public education. Additionally, they were to receive this education as a result of a non-discriminatory evaluation completed with parental permission and assistance, resulting in the child receiving an individualized education program (Turnbull, Stowe, & Huerta, 2007). There are several other important characteristics of this law, states (and in turn localities) were to receive financial assistance to meet the demands of providing services and the law was to be revisited every five years to see if any changes were warranted. The federal government made a commitment to provide 40% of the funding for the educational expenses of students with disabilities. States currently receive 15.4% of the excess costs of educating students in special education (NAESP, 2014), a far cry from what was originally promised. However, this law has shaped the educational practices for student with disabilities.

What Is IDEA?

In providing appropriate education for students with chronic disease, administrators must be vigilant regarding key components of the law:

1. All children with disabilities are entitled to receive a free appropriate education;
2. Parents are expected to participate in all decision-making;
3. Identification, placement, and evaluation procedures must be unbiased;
4. Students with disabilities are to be educated in the least restrictive environment;
5. Related services must be provided, if needed;
6. Transition plans are to be developed for when the student leaves school; and
7. Due process procedures need to be followed.

Regulations. When writing a law in the United Stares, it contains parts in which key sections (§§) of the legislation are described, defined, and delimited. This part of the chapter describes the purposes, to define key terms such as, a child with a disability, a free appropriate public education, least restrictive environment, parent involvement, and related services, to delimit basic practices such as identification, evaluation, and placement, due process, and transition that are represented in the most current Individuals with Disabilities Education Act.

§300.1 Purposes. The fundamental purpose of special education law is to ensure *all* children with disabilities have available to them a free appropriate public education, often referred to as FAPE, empha-

sizing special education and related services designed to meet their unique needs and prepare them for employment and independent living. The original title of IDEA was the Education for All Handicapped Children Act (PL 94-142). Congress used that title to emphasize how important it was for all children to be included. The title emphasis is very important to students with chronic disease, or any child with a disability because it makes evident the purpose of the law; that all children in the United States would receive an education.

§300.8 Child with a Disability. The term *child with a disability* means a child who is evaluated as having mental retardation, a hearing impairment including deafness, a speech or language impairment, a visual impairment including blindness, serious emotional disturbance (hereafter referred to as emotional disturbance), an orthopedic impairment, autism, traumatic brain injury, an other health impairment, a specific learning disability, deaf-blindness, or multiple disabilities, and who, by reason thereof, needs special education and related services.

The IDEA definitions are not as broad or as inclusive as the definitions put forward by Section 504 of the Rehabilitation Act of 1973. For example, an individual who has multiple chemical sensitivities could have a disability under Section 504 if they are doing fine in school both academically and socially. Eligible individuals under Section 504 have an impairment, have a record of an impairment, or are regarded as having an impairment--see definition below. The definitions under IDEA are categorical in nature, whereas definitions under Section 504 are functional in nature, meeting one of the three life-defining criteria.

§§300.17 Free Appropriate Public Education. The term free appropriate public education or FAPE means special education and related services that

1. Are provided at public expense, under public supervision and direction, and without charge;
2. Meet the standards of the State Education Agency;
3. Include an appropriate preschool, elementary school, or secondary school education in the State; and,
4. Are provided in conformity with an individualized education program (IEP) that meets the requirements of §§300.320-300.324.

§§300.501-520 Parental Involvement and Procedural Safeguards. Historically, professionals viewed parents as ignorant of their children's educational needs, or we knew what was best for the children (Turnbull, et al. 2004). Parents and guardians have essential information about their children with disabilities. Legislators realized this and outlined provisions in IDEA ensuring parental participation in the special education process (Yell, 2012). Procedures were enumerated for notification, access to records (see the discussion of FERPA below), consultation, and participation in advisory panels.

Shared decision making protects the rights of students by ensuring there is someone involved in the process who has a long-term interest in the child (Turnbull & Turnbull, Turnbull, Erwin, & Soodak, 2006). Additionally, it could be argued that what affects the student with a disability also affects the parents (Bateman, 2001); therefore, most educators regard parents as important stakeholders.

IDEA states parents need to be aware of, and consent to, every step of the process (Yell, 2012). This includes the initial evaluation, the eligibility meeting, the development of the IEP, annual reviews, and the triennial evaluation process. Parents also need access to all the records kept on their child and the assurances about confidentiality (Yell, 2012).

The early childhood amendments to IDEA have added requirements for parent involvement: districts must establish a public awareness campaign, a comprehensive child find program, and a central director of information. School systems also have an obligation to work with families when the child is identified as needing special education services. Early childhood personnel should start working with families as soon as possible after the child is born, providing the child with as much assistance as possible before he or she enters school for the first time. The federal regulation provides funds for services for children from birth to age the age of 21. Some states have established birth to three providers and in other states the school districts have taken on this task.

Similar to the development of the IEP, the Individualized Family Services Plan (IFSP) includes a heavy family component because there is a realization that families play a vital role in the development and nurturing of their child (Epley, Gotto, Summers, Brotherson, Turnbull, & Friend, 2010). One component is working with the family to help them meet the needs of their family member. This can be accomplished either through training of family members to carry out specific duties or in collaborating with them to determine the best methods for working with their family member who has a disability (Turnbull, Turnbull, Erwin, Soodak, & Shogren, 2011). The IFSP is more than just an IEP with a family twist, though; it is a multidisciplinary document designed to enhance children's development and minimize delays by enhancing the family's capacity to meet family members' needs (Yell, 2012). Ideally, multiple agencies must work together to provide combinations of approaches and interventions This important component of the early childhood amendments is the realization that one service provider does not have to be the sole discipline working to address circumstances for the child with a disability and their family members (Bateman & Bateman, 2014). However, prior to the development of and IFSP or an IEP the district has the obligation for pre-referral activities.

Pre-Referral Strategies. Pre-referral strategies consist of professional problem solving (i.e., consultation) and intervention based on screening data as the first steps of special education referral. Multiple strategies need to be tried and found to be unsuccessful for the student in accessing and making progress in the general curriculum. These strategies are documented and reported as a portion of the referral for special education.

Screenings. To ascertain whether or not it is appropriate to refer the student for testing to determine if the student is eligible for and needs special education, school personnel work with families and community agencies to conduct screening activities. Screening activities in the referral process can help in instructional and behavioral decisions to determine appropriate support strategies in general education classes, based on individual students' needs and strengths. Activities can also provide important clues in how to serve students if and when they become eligible and require special education. Accordingly, the first screening activity in the referral process focuses on collecting important data about the nature and extent of the student's problems or concerns. Screening data include, but are not limited to the following:

- *Demographics and Relevant Family Information.* Parents or guardians and other family members can provide a plethora of relevant data regarding the student's early developmental milestones, such as age of crawling, walking, or talking. Home data may include information on the family dynamics, including the family members with whom the student lives, his or her living arrangements, number of siblings, and home roles or responsibilities. Parents or guardians may describe the student's social interactions with family members, neighbors, or community members. Their home data also may provide input into family members' perspectives of the problems exhibited by their children, which may differ greatly from descriptions provided by agency personnel. The family can also provide strategies that they use at home and their effectiveness in that setting.

- *Health and Sensory Information.* Additional home data that help in screening activities include information on the student's health needs and senses. For example, families may provide information on the child or family history of illnesses or diseases. Parents or guardians may describe relevant genetic predispositions common to parents, siblings, or other relatives. They may provide important information on the student's wellness checks and health-care visits, or medications prescribed by physicians. This family data may also offer insights into health care workers' reporting on family-obtained speech and language, vision, hearing, motor, or other sensory testing results.

- *Cumulative School Files.* Screening activities may target data on the student's attendance records, school health records, lunch-program status, grades, achievement scores, permanent record cards, discipline incidents, and progress-reporting notations to parents, including remarks on report cards such as "*approach to learning*" (e.g., follows directions, uses time and materials productively, completes tasks) or "*citizenship*" (e.g., shares material and supplies, accepts responsibility for behavior, is responsible). These prior school records help in the referral process to ascertain trends in grade levels repeated, school achievement, past test results, anecdotal information, attendance patterns, and other important school variables, (e.g., the student's participation in school or general education class activities; success of behavioral or instructional strategies already provided to students).

- *Current Classroom Progress.* Screening activities include the obtainment of progress descriptions in the present educational setting and written records of individual student progress in various general education curricula. Classroom progress data may focus on observation records by educators or other agency personnel. Anecdotal records, informal notations, or formal observations on students' behavior and academic functioning under varied conditions or settings can be useful. Many local education agency (LEA) or school personnel observe and screen students daily either by formal methods (e.g., checklists, rating scales, tests) or by informal methods (e.g., discussions with past teachers, observations, unstructured comments based on informal meetings).

Effective screening activities entail being able to discern students' patterns of normal and deviate behaviors or academic progress as students operate in their current placements. One of the most important activities in the pre-referral process is the interventions and the results of those interventions. The school district is required to try multiple interventions prior to making a referral for special education. The evaluation team will look at the results of the interventions and consider that when determining if the referral is appropriate and developing an evaluation plan. Once the screening and interventions have taken place and the team determines that a referral for special education is appropriate, the team will move forward to the evaluation process.

§§300.300-311 Evaluation Procedures. Historically, there have been problems in the testing and placement of children with disabilities, including things such as not testing in their primary language, not measuring adaptive behavior, or the reliance on a single test for classification and placement. These practices resulted in court cases stipulating expected procedures for the assessment and classification of children with disabilities (Rothstein & Johnson, 2013).

The courts have issued guidelines stating (and the federal regulations have further codified):

1. All children are to be tested in their primary language;

2. IQ tests alone cannot be used for the placement of children into special education programs;
3. Unvalidated tests cannot be used;
4. Parents must be notified before any testing may begin (there are procedures for bypass if parents do not consent to testing);
5. Group tests are not to be used for determining eligibility; and
6. Adaptive behavior must be taken into account when considering eligibility.

There are two other important points:

1. Districts need to seek out and evaluate each child with a suspected disability in their jurisdiction; and
2. Districts need to implement procedures to screen preschool-age children for disabilities.

School districts do not only have the responsibility of evaluating those in their buildings. IDEA outlines the expectations that districts will notify the public and families that they will and have a responsibility to assess any child where a disability is suspected. This includes students attending public or private schools as well as homeschooled students. Procedures for notifying parents of testing can include announcements in the newspaper, as well as notices in grocery stores, gas stations, physician's offices, and churches. These notices would have dates and locations for screening to determine eligibility for services before entering school at age five or six. Regardless of the age of the child, school districts must identify the specific nature of a child's disability and determine the type and extent of special education and related services required.

Additionally, the evaluation of the child must be an individualized assessment of all areas related to the suspected disability. Individualized means that if the child has a suspected math disability, the focus relates to the problems in math. If the suspected problem is a behavior problem, the focus is on the behavior problem and how it manifests itself in school. A team must make the eligibility decision, with at least one member of the team experienced in the suspected disability category. The job of the team is to determine whether a child is eligible for special education and related services. Districts must also notify parents of their right to an independent evaluation at public expense if they disagree with the results or procedures of the school districts evaluation. If the team finds the student eligible, an individualized education program needs to be developed based on the results of the assessments.

The eligibility process is repeated every three years. For students with chronic disabilities, this is not usually an issue. The law, however, mandates at least a three-year or triennial evaluation, to determine that a child still qualifies for special education services.

After the individualized evaluation with a finding of eligibility, the team develops an Individualize Education Program (IEP). The IEP is a legal document developed by a team of individuals describing the special education and related services designed to meet the needs of a child who has a disability. To do this team will write an IEP to define goals and detail the provisions in writing. The IEP goals will be based on the student's present level of educational performance and functioning. In the IEP's *Present Levels of Academic and Functional Performance* section, the statement of how the child's disability affects the child's "involvement and progress in the general education curriculum" must reflect relevant concrete data that had been collected on the child's academic performance and contain objective criteria. The IEP will outline the evaluation procedures as well as a schedule for determining, on a regular basis (at least as regularly as non-disabled students get feedback), progress toward those IEP goals.

In addition to the goals, the IEP describes the following in detail:

1. Who will provide the services;
2. Where the services will be provided;
3. The dates and anticipated duration of services to be provided;
4. The related services necessary to reach those goals and objectives; and
5. The extent to which they are to be provided.

As the IEP team is considering and making decisions on who will be providing the services outlined, they also need to consider where those services will be delivered. The team needs to ensure the services are provided in the least restrict environment.

§§300.114 Least Restrictive Environment. Providing access to general education classrooms for students with disabilities was one of the main forces behind the implementation of P.L. 94-142 (Turnbull, Stowe, & Huerta, 2007). As a result of this new law, there were increases in the number of students receiving special education services being educated in the least restrictive environment. From 1976 to 2011, the percentage of students with disabilities who were placed in regular education for at least some part of the school day had grown from 58% to 73% (U.S Department of Education, 2014).

Congress made it explicit then and now (IDEA, 2004) that students with disabilities, including those with chronic disease, have the ultimate right to be "educated with children who are non-disabled." This is spelled out in the requirement for education of a child with a disability to happen in an environment that is as close as possible to that of nondisabled peers while providing the services in a setting which allows the student to have access to and make progress in the general education curriculum; referred to as the "least restrictive environment' (LRE). Simply, IDEA does not "require" inclusion; rather, the presumption of the law is that:

to the maximum extent appropriate, children with disabilities, including children in public or private institutions or other care facilities, are educated with children who are nondisabled; and that special classes, separate schooling or other removal of children with disabilities from the regular educational environment occurs only if the nature or severity of the disability is such that education in regular classes with the use of supplementary aids and services cannot be achieved satisfactorily. 20 U.S.C. 612(a)(5)(A).

The above statement has been part of the law regarding the education of students with disabilities since 1975, remaining unchanged to this day. What has changed is the interpretation of the legislation and the debate that has ensued regarding where students with disabilities should be educated. Furthermore, the "general education curriculum" is defined by the Department of Education as the "same curriculum as that for nondisabled children (34 C.F.R. 320(a)(1)(i))." In other words, students with disabilities should not merely be in the same room as nondisabled students, but are to be following the same curriculum, accommodated accordingly. The intent of the law is not that every child with a disability has to be included in the general classroom all the time. The presumption of the law is that a continuum of placement be available for every student. So, when developing the IEP, the team must consider placement in a general education classroom as the 'starting point;' however, if the team concurs that the LRE for the individual student is not in general education, it must be explained with adequate evidence why the determined placement on the continuum is least restrictive for that student. The law intends that the degree of inclusion be determined at least annually; that it be based upon the IEP of the child, that it be as close as possible to the child's home, and with the child being educated in the school he or she would attend if nondisabled (34 C.F.R. 300.116). Section 116(b)(3) now reads that the child's placement is to be "as close as possible to the child's home, unless the parent agrees otherwise" and subsection (c) of that section provides, "Unless the IEP of a child with a disability requires some other arrangement, the child in the school that he or she would attend if nondisabled, unless the parent agrees otherwise."

It is not the intent of this chapter to discuss full inclusion, rather to clarify the law. The law states:

Schools must maintain a continuum of alternative placements such as special classes, resource rooms, and itinerant instruction to meet the needs of students with disabilities (Yell, 2012).

The services and location of those services are listed on the individualized education program. Some students appropriately placed solely in the regular classroom with little additional assistance from special education teachers; however, some students require residential settings, totally separated from students without disabilities (Friend & Bursuck, 2009).

Often forgotten is that the law stipulates services are to follow students; that is, services are to be tailored to the unique needs of the individual in the most appropriate setting. It is not acceptable for students to be assigned solely those services designated for a particular disability or those programs that are available or convenient. Just because a student is identified as having a severe disability does not mean the student has to be placed in a self-contained classroom when a partial-day program or a resource room might be more suited for that child. The school district needs to have available a continuum of services including everything between the regular classroom and hospital-type settings (Friend & Bursuck, 2009). The IEP team decides where the child is to receive their education. It is important that this be a team decision, one not based solely on available space in the district special education classrooms. The IEP describes the special education placement to be provided (this should not be decided until the IEP meeting), and the amount and location of the participation with students who do not have disabilities (Bateman & Linden, 1998; Rothstein & Johnson, 2013). If a student is not going to participate with students without disabilities, documentation is necessary stating why this will not occur, and when such placement might occur. In addition to determining where services will be provided, the IEP team will need to determine what services will be provided. Those services can be general education, special education, or related services.

§300.34 Related Services. Related services are other services the child might require to benefit from special education. Related services include many components:

(a) General. Related services means transportation and such developmental, corrective, and other supportive services as are required to assist a child with a disability to benefit from special education, and includes speech-language pathology and audiology services, interpreting services, psychological services, physical and occupational therapy, recreation, including therapeutic recreation, early identification and assessment of disabilities in children, counseling services, including rehabilitation counseling, orientation and mobility services, and medical services for diagnostic or evaluation purposes. Related services also include school health services and school nurse services, social work services in schools, and parent counseling and training.

Several conditions must be met before the child receives related services. First, to be entitled to related services a child must be eligible for special education services. Unfortunately, there are students who might benefit from these related services but because they are not eligible for special education, they cannot receive related services. In the absence of this eligibility, the student does not qualify for related services. Second, only those services necessary to aid a child with a disability to benefit from special education must be provided, regardless of how easily a school nurse or lay person could furnish them. For example, if a particular medication or treatment may appropriately be administered to a child other than during the school day, a school is not required to provide nursing services to administer it. Third, the regulations state medical services must be provided only if they can be performed by a nurse or other qualified person, not if a physician is required (Yell, 2012).

Just as classroom placement is individually determined for the child with a disability, the need for related services should be determined in the same manner and listed on the IEP. Finally, this requires school districts to provide delineated IEP related services.

The IEP is more than a document outlining goals and objectives. It serves as a written commitment by the local education agency to provide the services (Bateman & Linden, 1998; Rothstein & Johnson, 2013). This is an important point for special education administrators. When a representative of the district signs the IEP, it states to the student with a disability and their parents that the program will be in place for their child with the requisite finances. Additionally, the district is stating to the parents that the program as delineated in this IEP will provide a free appropriate public education for the child.

§§300.506-517 Due Process. One main component of the law for children with disabilities is the opportunity for parental decision-making on all the different levels affecting the child's eligibility for special education services. If parents or guardians disapprove of the methods used for determining eligibility and educational programming for children with disabilities or disapprove of the resulting decisions, due process procedures allow interested parties to challenge the school system. This part of the law is provided as a check on the system.

What Is an Appropriate Education for Students with Chronic Disabilities?

The term appropriate has caused confusion both before and after the implementation of the Act. What one parent, supervisor, principal, or teacher finds appropriate, another might deem completely inappropriate. This term has caused a great deal of confusion relating to the education of students with disabilities. The Supreme Court tried to help define the definition on appropriateness in their first case they heard on the implementation of the Education for All Handicapped Children's Act, the Rowley case (1992).

In the Rowley case, Amy Rowley was a child with a hearing impairment who was fully mainstreamed in regular education except for one hour of instruction by a hearing therapist. She also received speech therapy and had the use of an FM amplification system. Her classroom performance was better than average when measured against her peers and she was advancing regularly from grade to grade. It was also clear that if Amy had the benefit of a sign language interpreter at all times, she would have performed even better. It is important to keep in mind that the Court as "one important factor in determining educational benefit" viewed the achievement of passing marks and advancing from grade to grade Amy was not only passing from grade to grade, she was in the upper half of her class. Therefore, the IEP team process was used to determine if the plan provided for "appropriate" public education. The Court stated in Rowley, "we do not hold today that every handicapped child who is advancing from grade to grade in regular public schools is automatically receiving a free appropriate public education." Further, the Court stated, "we do not attempt today to establish any one test for determining the adequacy of educational benefits conferred upon all children covered by the Act." However, the Court adopted the following general principles for determining when a program is appropriate, and these should serve as guidelines for working with students with chronic disabilities:

1. Compliance with procedural requirements of the Act is required in every case.
2. The program must be personalized, individually designed and reasonably calculated to enable the child to receive educational benefit.
3. The school district is not required to maximize the potential of every student with a disability.

Therefore some questions that need to be kept in mind by the IEP team in the determination of an appropriate education and the correct process include:

1. Was the child evaluated in a nondiscriminatory fashion?
2. Is everybody certified for his or her role in the development and implementation of the IEP?
3. Is the IEP individualized?
4. Are the necessary related services listed?
5. Are all the components listed for service on the IEP being implemented?
6. Is there clear documentation on the level of functioning of the child with a disability in comparison to the goals and objectives on the IEP?
7. Is the child receiving educational benefit from the program?
8. Are all the objectives of the IEP behaviorally written?
9. Have the parents or guardians been involved in every step of the development of the IEP?
10. Have the parents or guardians been made aware of their due process rights?
11. Is the student integrated with non-disabled students to the maximum extent possible?
12. If there is no provision for integration, is there a plan for the future integration of the student with students who are non-disabled? (Bateman & Bateman, 2014).

One of the most important component of the process definition is it places the burden on professionals who develop and implement the IEP to show it was based on correct information (testing and observations). Districts also need to show it was properly developed and implemented, and that proper monitoring occurred during its implementation (Yell, 2012).

Definition of Other Health Impairment

According to the federal regulations:

Other health impairment means having limited strength, vitality or alertness, including a heightened alertness to environmental stimuli, that results in limited alertness with respect to the educational environment, that—(i) Is due to chronic or acute health problems such as asthma, attention deficit disorder or attention deficit hyperactivity disorder, diabetes, epilepsy, a heart condition, hemophilia, lead poisoning, leukemia, nephritis, rheumatic fever, and sickle cell anemia; and (ii) Adversely affects a child's educational performance (Grice, 2002).

In order to qualify as OHI eligible under IDEA, a child must meet four conditions. First, he or she must suffer from a chronic or acute health condition. Second, the health condition must cause limited alertness to the educational environment due to limited strength, vitality, or alertness or heightened alertness to the surrounding environment. Third, the child's educational performance must be adversely affected by the disability. A child with limited alertness whose educational performance is not affected does not qualify for placement as OHI. Finally, OHI, like all other qualifying conditions, must create a need for special education services (Grice, 2002).

Health Conditions That May Qualify a Child as OHI

OHI eligibility first considers the child's health condition(s) and the general effects on the child, and then looks separately at the disability's effect on the child's educational performance. While not exhaustive, and not automatically qualifying for eligibility under OHI, the following are medical conditions that may be considered:

- ADHD
- ADD
- AIDS/HIV
- Allergies and chemical sensitivities
- Asthma
- Chronic fatigue syndrome
- Spina bifida
- Epilepsy
- Tourette's syndrome
- Injuries brought on by accidents
- Diabetes
- Heart conditions
- Hemophilia
- Lead poisoning
- Leukemia
- Nephritis
- Rheumatic fever
- Sickle cell anemia

Attention Deficit Disorder and Attention Deficit Disorder/Hyperactivity Disorder (ADD/ADHD) are the most frequent medical conditions under which students qualify for services under OHI. These conditions are characterized by the inability to focus, which usually contributes to a decreased alertness to the educational environment (Grice, 2002). The American Psychiatric Association currently uses the term ADHD rather than ADD for all types of the disorder even the predominantly inattentive type not characterized by hyperactivity. To avoid confusion, the federal regulations implementing IDEA include both terms, ADHD and ADD.

The 2004 Amendments IDEA not only guarantee the right to a FAPE, but if implemented as intended, can provide the level of support children with ADHD need to succeed in school. ADHD is a relatively common child behavioral disorder, affecting 3%–10% of children in the United States (Barkley, 2014; Martin & Zirkel, 2011). Applying the prevalence rates of ADHD to the school setting equates to an estimated one child in every classroom meeting the diagnostic criteria of the disorder (Martin & Zirkel, 2011).

In an educational setting, behaviors characteristic of ADHD can result in a range of school difficulties, which may negatively affect educational performance, such as problems with peer and adult relationships, inability to sustain attention to instruction and tasks, challenges in completing independent seatwork, and difficulty with study and organizational skills (Barkley, 2014; Martin & Zirkel, 2011). ADHD, therefore, puts children at risk for a variety of problems, including school failure, social rejection, antisocial behavior, substance abuse, psychiatric disorders, and involvement with the juvenile justice system (Gregg, 2000).

For a child with ADHD to be classified under OHI depends on the way the condition affects his or her alertness or responsiveness to the educational environment. OSEP has stated a doctor's statement alone does not establish the basis for an ADD/ADHD student's OHI eligibility. Although a school district may choose to require a medical diagnosis to establish IDEA eligibility, a multidisciplinary team must independently determine the student needs special education and related services due to the impairment. For example, in a New York case, a kindergarten child diagnosed with allergies, ADHD, and otitis media but demonstrated "generally satisfactory" work habits, social and emotional development, and readiness skills was found ineligible for special education services (Bd. of Education of the East Syracuse-Minoa Cent. Sch. Dist., 1994). A hearing officer determined the child did not suffer limited strength, vitality, or alertness as a result of any condition (Grice, 2002). If the school system requires a medical diagnosis to help determine eligibility, the diagnosis must be provided at no cost to the parents. If a school district uses alternative assessment measures administered by "qualified personnel" in place of a medical diagnosis by a licensed physician and these measures meet the evaluation procedures, the evaluation will be sufficient to establish OHI eligibility (Grice, 2002).

While ADHD is the most frequent medical condition classifying a student under OHI, a number of specific health conditions qualify as disabling conditions, and some have met the limited-alertness criterion in particular cases. A medical diagnosis alone is insufficient in itself to qualify a child as OHI. For example, in *Jefferson County Board of Education, 1998*, a child in Alabama who had experienced asthma attacks and was diagnosed with asthma but had no issues with attendance nor school performance did not qualify as OHI. The hearing officer determined the child showed no signs of limited alertness, strength or vitality. Conversely, a child with chronic fatigue syndrome in California (Placentia-Yorba Linda Unified School District 1995), who had difficulty getting up in the morning and staying alert though out the day, did qualify under OHI. The hearing officer determined the student missed school because of these symptoms and was described as "low energy" (Grice 2002). The finding of a medical condition causing limited alertness is not enough, as the condition and diminished alertness caused by the condition must also adversely affect the student's educational performance.

In another case, a student being served by a Section 504 plan started having more difficulty in school. The student had multiple sclerosis started to have increasing difficulty with her courses as a result of her medical condition. The school continued to provide her with 504 accommodations but failed to evaluate her to determine if there were adverse effects of educational performance and test to determine if she needed an IEP under the category of Other Health Impaired (Simmons v. Pittsburgh United School District, 2014). School districts should be open to the fact that a student may switch from a 504 plan to an IEP if conditions warrant.

Adverse Effects on Educational Performance

IDEA eligibility initially hinges on the existence of a disability adversely affecting the child's "educational performance," yet IDEA does not define the term. Decision-makers are split as to whether "educational performance" means exclusively academic performance, such as grades and standardized test scores, or whether it also encompasses non-academic performance, such as behavior, emotional development, and interpersonal relationships. Authorities employing a narrow academic-centered definition of "educational performance" deny eligibility to children whose disability affects any area of performance other than academic performance. Decision-makers, utilizing a broad definition, find disabilities which adversely affect attendance, socialization or behavior, are qualifying even though the disability does not effect the child's grades (Garda, 2004). In *Kristopher H.* (1985), the school denied IDEA eligibility to a child who was distractible and had problems staying on task and in social relationships, relying on the fact that he performed at grade level. The hearing officer disagreed, and turning to the dictionary, found that educational performance "includes not only the narrow conception of instruction, to which it was formerly limited, but embraces all forms of human experience" (Garda, 2004).

IDEA does not explain when a disability "adversely affects" educational performance. Two areas of disagreement arise when authorities interpret this provision. They first disagree on whether an adverse effect is determined with or without the non-special education services already provided the child. Many children with disabilities receive non-special education services to address their disabilities, usually under Section 504. If the child performs well with these services then there is a question as to the disability "adversely affecting" the child's educational performance (Garda, 2004). The Office of Special Education Programs has stated the meaning of the terms "educational performance" and "adversely affects" must be established on a case-by-case basis (Grice, 2002). However, there are a number of cases where the court has determined and supported the idea that education performance goes beyond grades earned. For example, in *Yankton School District v. Schramm* (1995), the Eighth Circuit Court found a child's orthopedic impairment adversely affected her educational performance because "but for the specialized instruction and services provided by the school district, her ability to learn and do the required class work would be adversely affected by her cerebral palsy" (Garda, 2004). Another example, in *Lyons v. Smith* (1993), a student diagnosed with ADHD scored in the average to superior range on almost all standardized tests but experienced social problems. The parents challenged the hearing officer's determination the student was not OHI, arguing his difficulties in "social emotional" development had not been taken into account. The court upheld the hearing officer's decision, stating, "the achievement of passing marks is one important factor in determining educational benefit" (Grice, 2002).

Behavior is also a factor in some cases. In *Venus Independent School District v. Daniel S.* (2002), a federal district court determined a student with ADHD qualified for special education as OHI despite well above average grades and test scores. The behavior scales submitted by the child's teachers indicated significant levels of oppositional behavior, hyperactivity, restlessness, impulsivity, anxiety, and problems with social interaction. The court stated "educational need" is not strictly limited to academics, but also includes behavioral progress and the acquisition of appropriate social skills as well as academic achievement" (Grice, 2002).

In defining if a disability "adversely affects the child's educational performance" the courts must decide if the disability, and no other factors, has had any effect, no matter how slight, on any area of instruction mandated in the state curriculum or any area of performance formally tracked by the state's schools (Garda, 2004). Taking into account the type and degree of outside or additional learning support the child receives from a teacher, parent, or tutor will also assist school administrators to assess whether the child is progressing in accordance with his or her age and ability (Grice, 2002).

The IEP

Once it is established a child has a disability and is classified OHI, the issue becomes whether "by reason thereof, the child needs special education and related services" (Garda, 2004). However, remember that in order for a child qualify for special education services they much have 1) met the criteria for the disability category and 2) demonstrate a need for individualized instruction. If the child is deemed in need of special education services through educational and cognitive assessments, then the team must decide on an Individualized Education Plan (IEP) best meeting the student's needs. For every student, an IEP is just that, individualized. For a student classified under OHI, the impact of the disability on the child's educational performance will vary based on the health impairment.

The present level of performance is the starting point of the IEP as it provides the IEP team with the basic information concerning the child's specific levels of educational performance at the time the program is to be developed. In this, a baseline of performance is documented which leads into the necessary goals. The present legislation changes the term "educational performance" to "academic achievement and functional performance." This change is included to clarify and expand the more narrowly defined focus of the individual student's educational program to include academic achievement and functional performance (Gartin & Murdick, 2005). The functional performance inclusion is most important for a student classified under OHI, as this related directly to limited strength, vitality, or alertness.

As with any student who has an IEP, accommodations for students classified under OHI will vary on a case-by-case basis depending on the child's disability and educational need. Some general recommended accommodations, modifications and variations to the curriculum might include:

- Reviewing the student's IEP to determine activities appropriate and desirable for the student considering their specific conditions.
- Reviewing pertinent medical data and become familiar the student's condition.
- Preparing work packets for the student to complete at home should there be a medical necessity preventing the student attending school.
- Allowing for non-competitive participation.
- Watching for any changes in student behavior that may indicate the student is having medical difficulties, discomfort or any evidence of medication side effects.
- Understanding the side effects of the medications the student is taking.
- If in doubt, discussing these issues with the student and/or parent, and their case manager.
- Encouraging socialization and interaction with others.
- Using peer helpers in appropriate ways.
- Understanding any protocols that may be specified in the IEP should there be a medical emergency (i.e. seizure protocol) (Rodrigues, 2007).

The Rehabilitation Act of 1973

The Rehabilitation Act of 1973, commonly referred to as the "Rehab Act," or "Section 504," greatly affects the education of students with disabilities in the public school setting. Section 504 of the Rehabilitation Act (Section 504) makes programs and activities accessible and functional to all individuals with disabilities.

The main component of Section 504 of the Rehab Act states:

No otherwise qualified individual with handicaps shall solely by reason of her or his handicap, be excluded from the participation in, be denied the benefits of, or be subjected to discrimination under any program or activity receiving Federal financial assistance. (29 U.S.C. Sec. 706)

This law authorized federal funds to be paid to institutions after they comply with regulations concerning the education of students with disabilities (and withholding of funds for noncompliance).

Section 504 protects from the discrimination of any person, including students who meets one of three criteria who

"(i) has a physical or mental impairment which substantially limits one or more of such person's major life activities, (ii) has a record of such an impairment, or (iii) is regarded as having such an impairment" (29 U.S.C Sec. 706) is considered as having a disability under this law. For the purposes of Section 504, major life activities include: caring for one's self, performing manual tasks, walking, seeing, hearing, speaking, breathing, learning, and working. The law protects individuals who are discriminated against both intentionally and unintentionally. Under Section 504, individuals who have a disability might need assistance to qualify for the related services necessary for them to benefit from education. In addition, Section 504 has provisions for non-discriminatory employment.

Regulations

General

No qualified individuals with a disability... shall solely by reason of her or his disability, be excluded from participation in, be denied the benefits of, or otherwise be subjected to discrimination under any program or activity which receives or benefits from Federal financial assistance. 29 U.S.C. § 794 (a).

Definitions

A person is considered to be an individual with a disability under section 504 when he or she has a physical or mental impairment which substantially limits one or more of such person's major life activities, has a record of such an impairment, or is regarded as having such an impairment. 29 U.S.C. § 706(8) (B).

Discrimination Prohibited

For purposes of this part, aids, benefits, and services, to be equally effective, are not required to produce the identical result of level of achievement for handicapped and nonhandicapped persons, but must afford handicapped persons equal opportunity to obtain the same result, to gain the same benefit, or to reach the same level of achievement, in the most integrated setting appropriate to the person's needs.

The Educational Rights of Students with Chronic Disease

Definitions

The Rehabilitation Act of 1973, a civil rights act, protects the rights of people with disabilities. It states any recipient of Federal financial assistance cannot discriminate on the basis of disability. The original act focused mostly on employment. Section 504 was expanded in 1993 to include all who receive Federal financial assistance including schools. Compliance with Section 504 however does not grant the programs additional state or federal funding. This statutes' purpose is to prevent discrimination, both intentional and unintentional, against individuals with disabilities, those who are believed to have a disability, or family members of a person with a disability.

The key element of the definition and in determining eligibility is if the individual's disability affects their ability to perform a major life activity, whether permanent or temporary. Disabilities are not always readily evident or obvious are also covered by Section 504.

Disabilities, mental or physical, that are not noticeable to others are known as hidden disabilities. These disabilities include such things as learning disabilities, ADHD, allergies, and some chronic disabilities. Section 504 requires programs to seek out all individuals with disabilities to ensure they are receiving services.

Educational Aspects

Section 504 is enforced by the Office of Civil Rights (OCR) in programs and activities receiving funds from the U.S. Department of Education (ED). Each Federal agency has its own set of Section 504 regulations applying to its programs. Part 104 of the Code of Federal Regulations states the guidelines for implementing Section 504 in educational settings.

Subpart D: Preschool, Elementary, and Secondary Education (34 C.F.R.)

§ 104.32 Location and Notification

A recipient that operates a public elementary or secondary education program shall annually: (a) Undertake to identify and locate every qualified handicapped person residing in the recipient's jurisdiction who is not receiving a public education; and

(b) Take appropriate steps to notify handicapped persons and their parents or guardians of the recipient's duty under this subpart.

§ 104.33 Free Appropriate Public Education

(a) General. A recipient that operates a public elementary or secondary education program shall provide a free appropriate public education to each qualified handicapped person who is in the recipient's jurisdiction, regardless of the nature or severity of the person's handicap.

(b) Appropriate education.

(1) For the purpose of this subpart, the provision of an appropriate education is the provision of regular or special education and related aids and services that (i) are designed to meet individual educational needs of handicapped persons as adequately as the needs of nonhandicapped persons are met (ii) are based upon adherence to procedures that satisfy the requirements of §104.34, §104.35, and §104.36.

§ 104.34 Educational Setting

(a) Academic setting. A recipient to which this subpart applies shall educate, or shall provide for the education of, each qualified handicapped person in its jurisdiction with persons who are not handicapped to the maximum extent appropriate to the needs of the handicapped person.

Determining Need for Section 504

The responsibility of the educational program, under the Section 504 regulation, is to seek out and serve qualified individuals. The recipients of Federal financial assistance must:

- Identify and locate all children with disabilities annually.
- Provide a "free appropriate public education" to students with disabilities.
- Provide education in the "least restrictive environment." This means that students with disabilities will be educated to the maximum extent possible with nondisabled peers.
- Construct evaluation and placement guidelines to ensure appropriate identification of the student.
- Provide parents and/or guardians with procedural safeguards allowing them to participate in the evaluation and placement of their children.
- Give all students with disabilities an equal opportunity to participate in all activities and services.

The greatest challenge to the educational program is the responsibility to identify the students with hidden disabilities, such as those with some who have chronic disabilities. These students represent the part of the student population who are typically not properly diagnosed. Due to this, they appear to be "problem" students who are often described by others as missing school or unmotivated. However, it is important to know that because of a hidden disability these students cannot demonstrate their true potential and academic ability. Due to a disability they are not able to benefit the same as students without disabilities. An appropriate education is one that meets the needs of all students and provides them with the same opportunities.

Appropriate Evaluation and Placement

§ 104.35 Evaluation and Placement

(a) **Preplacement evaluation**. *A recipient that operates a public elementary or secondary education program shall conduct an evaluation in accordance with the requirements of paragraph (b) of this section of any person who, because of handicap, needs or is believed to need special education or related services before taking any action with respect to the initial placement of the person in a regular or special education program and any subsequent significant change in placement.*

(b) **Evaluation procedures**.

(1) *Tests and other evaluation materials have been validated for the specific purpose for which they are used and are administered by trained personnel in conformance with the instruction provided by their producer;*

(2) *Tests and other evaluation materials include those tailored to assess specific areas of educational need and not merely those which are designed to provide a single general intelligence quotient; and*

(3) *Tests are selected and administered so as best to ensure that, when a test is administered to a student with impaired sensory, manual, or speaking skills, the test results accurately reflect the student's aptitude or achievement level or whatever other factor the test purports to measure, rather than reflecting the student's impaired sensory, manual, or speaking skills (except where those skills are the factors that the test purports to measure).*

(c) **Placement procedures**. *In interpreting evaluation data and in making placement decisions, a recipient shall –*

(1) *draw upon information from a variety of sources,*

(2) *establish procedures to ensure that information obtained from all such sources is documented and carefully considered,*

(3) *ensure that the placement decision is made by a group of persons, including person knowledgeable about the child, the meaning of the evaluation data, and the placement options, and*

(4) *ensure that the placement decision is made in conformity with §104.34.*

Evaluation and Re-Evaluation

Each local education agency is responsible to identify and locate all students with disabilities. Every year the school must attempt to find every qualified student in their district, whether receiving a public education or not.

The evaluation process begins with a team of individuals knowledgeable of the student. The focus of this team is to ensure the student's interests are represented and that s/he is not incorrectly labeled or misclassified. Parents must receive a notice informing them of the identification, evaluation, and placement of their child. It does not have to be written consent, however many districts obtain it as documentation. There is no requirement for consent under Section 504. This is different in IDEA where parental consent for testing is required.

An evaluation must be conducted before any placement changes or decisions are made. The evaluation procedures that pertain to Section 504 parallel those under IDEA. The evaluation procedures must make certain:

- Tests and other evaluation materials have been validated;
- Evaluations are administered by trained personnel;
- Evaluations are tailored to assess specific areas of educational need;
- Tests are selected and administered that accurately reflect the factors the test purports to measure.

At the conclusion of the evaluations and observations, data is collected and all the information is used to make a collaborative decision.

There are no timelines for evaluations, however they must be conducted in a reasonable amount of time. After evaluations have been conducted and completed the school must document the information that has been considered. This will ensure that they have taken all the steps necessary for a proper identification.

Re-evaluations are periodically required to determine continued need for services. This can be conducted at parent's request, schools request, or at set interval of time. This re-evaluation is very similar to the IDEA regulations.

504 Accommodation Plans and Responsibilities

It is very important the school and parents of the student with a disability work together to create an accommodation plan. This plan will provide the student with accommodations for them to be successful in the school setting. There are no legal requirements of what the accommodation plans need to contain. The plan should set forth what the student needs in order to help the individual benefit from their educational program. Key elements of a 504 accommodation plan:

- Identification of student. Name, Date, …
- Team Members. Identify individuals on team and their relationship with the student.
- Sources of evaluation information. Section 504 requires a variety of sources and each should be listed on the plan.
- The physical or mental impairment. Name the impairment for which services, accommodations, and modifications are necessary.
- The major life activity that is affected.
- Degree of impact. The severity of the impairment and that it impairs a major life activity.
- Required accommodations, modifications, aids, and services that are necessary for the student to receive an educational opportunity proportionate to his/her peers.
- Parent signature and date stating that s/he received notification of the plan and the procedural rights.

The possible accommodations for students with chronic disabilities vary significantly depending on the individual needs of the child. The following list is not meant to be all-inclusive, only illustrative of possible Section 504 accommodations. With students with chronic disabilities, the individual need is paramount, but remember the needs may be more intense during some periods, while lessened at others. It is also very important to make sure educators working with students with chronic disabilities are aware of this, and work to adjust the flow and demands of the work required.

Organization

- Teach organizational skills,
- Teach study skills,
- Schedule tutoring/homework assistance,
- Reinforce organizational systems (i.e. color-coding),
- Write out homework assignments, check student's recording of assignments,
- Tailor homework assignments toward student strengths,
- Set time expectations for assignments, but be flexible,
- Teach towards an understanding of length of assignments.

Classroom or Work Space

- Utilize study carrels,
- Alter location for classroom supplies for easier access,
- Alter location for classroom supplies for easier access,
- Provide breaks for sensory activities,
- Provide a clear schedule,
- Provide a structured learning environment,
- Provide separate "space" for different types of tasks,
- Possible adapting of non-academic times such as lunch, recess, and physical education,
- Change student seating.

Behavioral Management

- Establish a home/school communication system,
- Post rules for classroom behavior,
- Have daily/weekly progress report/contract,
- Reinforce self-monitoring and self-recording of behaviors,
- Use behavioral management techniques consistently within a classroom and across classes,
- Implement behavioral/academic contracts,
- Utilize positive reinforcements,
- Utilize logical consequences,
- Confer with the student's parents frequently (and student as appropriate).

Instruction

- Utilize peer tutoring.
- Simplify and repeat instructions about in-class and homework assignments.
- Vary instructional pace.
- Reinforce the use of compensatory strategies, i.e., pencil grip, mnemonic devices, "spell check."
- Vary kind of instructional materials used.
- Assess whether student has the necessary prerequisite skills. Determine whether materials are appropriate to the student's current functioning levels.
- Reinforce study skill strategies.
- Introduce definition of new terms/vocabulary and review to check for understanding.
- Pre-teach and/or re-teach important concepts.
- Prepare advanced organizers/study guides for new material.
- Allow students to tape lessons.
- Use computer-aided instruction and other audiovisual equipment.
- Select alternative textbooks, workbooks, or provide books on tape.
- Highlight main ideas and supporting details in the book.
- Provide copied material for extra practice (i.e. outlines, study guides).
- Prioritize drill and practice activities for relevance.
- Ask student to repeat/paraphrase context to check understanding.

Assignments

- Lower reading level of assignments,
- Break assignments into a series of smaller assignments,
- Use highlighted texts,
- Modify the amount of homework,
- Use written directions to supplement oral directions,
- Reduce paper and pencil tasks,
- Allow for assignments to be word processed.

Evaluation

- Limit amount of material presented on a single page,
- Provide a sample or practice test,
- Provide for oral testing,
- Provide tests in segments so student hands in one segment before receiving the next part,
- Provide personal copy of test tools and allow for color-coding/highlighting,
- Adjust time for completion,
- Modify weights of tests when grading.

504 Support Plans

If the child has a disability but does not need special education services, the child may be entitled to protections under Section 504 of the Rehabilitation Act. As noted above, Section 504 is a civil rights statute protecting individuals with disabilities from discrimination for reasons related to their disabilities. Section 504 requires schools to make reasonable accommodations to ensure full access to educational programs. For diverse needs, 504 plans are widely used and typically address accommodations in academic areas, but they can also be applied to nonacademic areas (such as music classes and participation in the lunchroom) and extra-curricular activities, to allow the student to have the whole school experience. The 504 plan can follow the student to college and is also applicable in the workplace. These plans are typically not as involved and therefore do not cover the multitude of details as compared to an IEP. A 504 plan should provide for staff training and specify who will provide that training. The plan should also include review dates and can be requested by the family or school personnel. The parents and a team of school staff develop a 504 plan. The school team usually includes an administrator and a case manager. In many cases where the issues addressed in the 504 are related to the child's medical conditions, the medical team is also included as an active participant (United States Department of Health and Human Services, 2006).

One important fact often forgotten about 504 accommodations is they not only are for students with disabilities, but also for parents who may have disabilities. Schools need to make sure the services for parents, including meetings dissemination of information is provided to parents so as not to discriminate.

Usually, services included in a 504 plan include accommodations in the classroom such as extra time to complete assignments. But the plan may also include the use of assistive technology, such as computer-aided instruction, or access to therapy. Since students with 504 plans do not have IEP's are therefore not eligible for special education, these students receive no assistance from special education teachers or staff. This means they are typically the sole responsibility of general education program-many of the general education staff is not trained in dealing with students with disabilities, much less students with chronic disabilities.

Similar to an IEP, the 504 plan is dependent on the needs of the child. The 504 team will need to create and implement needed accommodations within the educational setting. For example, the following general recommendations for accommodations for a student with a chronic disability such as epilepsy might include (this is by no means a definitive list, but one that could help staff think about the needs of a child who has a seizure disorder):

- Document the characteristics of each seizure.
- Call the parent after each seizure.
- Assess breathing after seizure.
- Document the activities immediately prior to the seizure.
- Train staff for proper dispensing of medication(s).
- Monitor for side effects.
- Train staff about the needs of students with seizure disorders and identifying characteristics.
- Talk with students in the class about what to expect.
- Anticipate recovery process should a seizure occur. Move seating/clear space during seizure.
- Do not insert objects into the student's mouth during seizure.
- Administer no fluids if student is unconscious. Turn the unconscious student on his or her side to avoid aspiration of vomit.
- Provide rest time and return to academic considerations following seizure.
- Arrange a buddy system, especially for field trips.
- Avoid portable chalk boards or furniture that would topple over easily.
- Provide an alternative recess, adapt activities such as climbing and/or swimming.
- Plan for academic make-up work.
- Alter door openings to allow access from the outside (i.e. bathroom stall doors that swing both ways).
- Observe for consistent triggers (e.g. smells, bright light, perfume, hair spray).
- Provide post-secondary or vocational transition planning (Bateman & Bateman, 2014).

Here are some examples of accommodations for students with Leukemia:

- Involve school nurse in assessing current limitations and development of health plan.
- Provide homebound instruction if needed.
- Provide the student with an adjusted school day.
- Make needed accommodations during physical education/recess.
- Provide rest periods.
- Have medical services and medication available at school. Train for proper dispensing of medications; monitor and/or distribute medications; monitor for side effects.
- Support the proper diet as per physical recommendation.
- With parent/student permission, have area nurse to educate teachers/staff/peers.
- Notify parents of existing communicable diseases at school (i.e. chicken pox, flu, strep throat, etc.).

- Consult with medical staff about individual needs and/or concomitant factors (Bateman & Bateman, 2014).

It is important to remember when developing the 504 plans for whatever the disability; the accommodations defined within are those interventions not typically available to all students.

Family Education Rights and Privacy Act

In addition, known as the Buckley Amendment, the Family Educational Rights and Privacy Act of 1974 (FERPA) defines who may and may not see student records. There are several major points that are important to consider as a principal relating to FERPA.

1. FERPA guarantees the parents or guardians of a student to inspect and review their child's records;
2. FERPA establishes policies through which parents can challenge the accuracy of student records;
3. FERPA also establishes a mechanism through which parents can appeal concerning alleged failures to comply with the law;
4. FERPA prohibits the release of information about a student without the parent(s) or guardian(s) consent, except to those who have a legitimate right to know, such as teachers or related services personnel.
5. Districts need to establish a written policy about who will have access to student records.

Special education administrators and 504 coordinators need to realize that all of the information obtained as a part of the assessment process to determine whether a student has a disability is to be placed in the student's file. The only exceptions to this may be the actual test protocols used by the individual administering the psychological and educational assessments. Additionally, the file should include evaluation reports, IEP's, and summaries of attainments toward the IEP goals and objectives.

The important component about FERPA is that all of a student's records are located in the files, parents have access to them, they can challenge them, and the files contain confidential information. Knowing this, one should be very judicious about who has access. In addition, it is necessary to safeguard the files, and ensure the appropriate information remains in the files.

SUMMARY

Many conditions and diseases can significantly affect a child's health and ability to function successfully in school. OHI classification has been called the "catch all" classification in special education. OHI, however, does have specific criteria under IDEA for students to have met before a determination for special education services can be made. To be served under the OHI category, the student's health condition must limit strength, vitality, or alertness to such a degree that the student's educational progress is adversely affected. Unless a student with a chronic disability has another disability, such as a learning disability, intellectual disability, emotional disturbance, the most possible category in which they would receive special education services is the category of Other Health Impairment. OHI as category has grown significantly in the past ten years due to the inclusion of Attention Deficit/Hyperactive Disorder.

Adding AD/HD has caused a significant increase in the size of the category (United States Department of Education, 2007). But, this category is the best possible choice for students with chronic disabilities who are lacking another disability.

One of the main considerations in the education of students with chronic disabilities is the use of the team approach in developing and carrying out the educational program. The team generally includes the parents, teachers, medical professionals, and health-related professionals such as a physical therapist. Parents are critical members of the team and should be involved in all educational decisions. This is vitally important to a child who has a chronic disability that may fall under the category of OHI, as a medical determination alone does not qualify students for special education services.

Accommodations and modifications may be provided through either an IEP or a 504 plan and must provide the necessities for the child to have access to and make progress in the education environment. As with any student with a disability, modifications should be no more restrictive than absolutely necessary so the student's school experiences can be as similar to peers as possible.

REFERENCES

Barkley, R. A. (2014). *Attention-deficit hyperactivity disorder: A handbook for diagnosis and treatment* (4th ed.). New York: Guilford Press.

Bateman, B. D., & Linden, M. A. (1998). Better IEP's: How to develop legally correct and educationally useful programs (3rd. ed.). Denver, CO: Sopris West.

Bateman, D. F. (2001). Families of adult individuals with disabilities. In D. J. O'Shea, L. O'Shea, B. Algozzine, & D. J. Hammitte (Eds.), *Families and teachers: Collaborative orientations, responsive practices* (pp. 205–222). Needham Heights, MA: Allyn and Bacon.

Bateman, D. F., & Bateman, C. F. (2014). *A principal's guide to special education* (3rd ed.). Arlington, VA: Council for Exceptional Children.

Bd. of Educ. of the East Syracuse–Minoa Cent. Sch. Dist., *21 Individuals with Disabilities Education Law Report, 1024* (SEA N.Y. 1994)

Board of Education of Hendrick Hudson School District v. Rowley, 458 U.S. 176 (1982)

Cortiella, C. (2006). *NCLB and IDEA: What parents of students with disabilities need to know and do*. Minneapolis, MN: University of Minnesota, National Center on Educational Outcomes; Retrieved from http://www.cehd.umn.edu/nceo/onlinepubs/parents.pdf

Epley, P., Gotto, G. S., Summers, J. A., Brotherson, M. J., Turnbull, A. P., & Friend, A. (2010). Supporting families of young children with disabilities: Examining the role of administrative structures. *Topics in Early Childhood Special Education*, *30*(1), 20–31. doi:10.1177/0271121410363400

Family Educational Rights and Privacy Act of 1974, 20 U.S.C. § 1232g (2006).

Friend, M., & Bursuck, W. D. (2009). *Including students with special need: A practical guide for classroom teachers* (5th ed.). Upper Saddle River, NJ: Pearson.

Garda, R. (2004). Untangling eligibility requirements under the individuals with Disabilities Education Act. *Missouri Law Review, 69,* 441–512. Retrieved from http://ssrn.com/abstract=1125004

Gartin, C., & Murdick, N. (2005). IDEA 2004: The IEP. *Remedial and Special Education, 26*(6), 327–331. doi:10.1177/07419325050260060301

Goelz, K. (2014). The definition of "adversely affects the child's educational performance" under the IDEA. Retrieved June 16, 2014, from http://www.spigglelaw.com/the-definition-of-adversely-affects-the-childs-educational-perfo.html

Gregg, S. (2000). *At a glance: ADHD and IDEA 1997: A guide for state and local policymakers.* Washington, DC: Office of Educational Research and Improvement.

Grice, K. (2002). Eligibility under IDEA for other health impaired children. *School Law Bulletin,* Summer, 7-12. Retrieved from http://www.pathfinder-nd.org/pdf/EqualityOHIIDEA.pdf

In re: Kristopher H., *1985-86 EHLR Dec 507:183* (Wash. Sept. 4, 1985).

Individuals With Disabilities Education Improvement Act of 2004, 20 U.S.C. §§ 1400 *et seq.* (2004).

Jefferson County Bd. of Education *(1998). 29 Individuals with Disabilities Education Law Report 690,* (SEA Alabama 1998).

Lyons By Alexander v. Smith, 829 F. Supp. 414 (1993).

Martin, S. D., & Zirkel, P. A. (2011). Current issues in eligibility decisions for students with ADHD: What the courts say. *School Psychology Review, 40*(4), 26–27.

National Association of Elementary School Principals. (2014). Federal education funding. Retrieved from http://www.naesp.org/advocacy/education-funding

National Center for Education Evaluation and Regional Assistance. (2010). *Patterns in the identification of and outcomes for children and youth with disabilities. (AHCPR Publication No. ED-04-CO-0040/0007).* Washington, DC: Author.

No Child Left Behind Act of 2001, 20. U.S.C. §§ 6301 et seq. (2006 & Supp. V. 2011).

No Child Left Behind regulations, 34 C.F.R. § 200 (2012).

Placentia-Yorba Linda Unified School District. (1995). *22 Individuals with Disabilities Education Law Report 305.* SEA California.

Rodrigues, J. (2007). *Making modifications, accommodations and variations for student success.* Retrieved from www.jimrodslz.com/sped.html

Rothstein, L. F., & Johnson, S. F. (2013). *Special education law.* Los Angeles, CA: SAGE Publications.

Rutten-McClay, I., & Rousseau, R. (2012). *Special education and behavior modification: An online guide to special education processes and behavior modification principles for educators and parents.* Retrieved from http://www.specialeducationbehaviormodification.com/articles/other_health_impairment.html

Scull, J., & Winkler, A. (2011). *Shifting trends in special education*. Washington, DC: The Thomas B. Fordham Institute. (ERIC Document Reproduction Service No. ED520416).

Section 504 Regulations, 34 C. F. R. § 100 (2012).

Simmons v. Pittsburgh Unified School District (2014). 63 IDELR 158 (N.D. Cal).

Turnbull, A. P., Turnbull, H. R., Erwin, E., & Soodak, L. (2006). *Professionals, families, and exceptionality: Outcomes through partnerships and trust* (5th ed.). Upper Saddle River, NJ: Merrill/Prentice Hall.

Turnbull, A. P., Turnbull, H. R., Erwin, E., Soodak, L., & Shogren, K. (2011). *Professionals, families, and exceptionality: Positive outcomes through partnerships and trust* (6th ed.). Upper Saddle River, NJ: Merrill/Prentice Hall.

Turnbull, A. P., Turnbull, R., Poston, D., Beegle, G., Blue-Banning, M., Diehl, K., et al. (2004). Enhancing quality of life of families of children and youth with disabilities in the United States. In A.P. Turnbull, I., Brown, & H.R. Turnbull (Eds.), Family quality of life: An international perspective (pp. 51-100). Washington, DC: American Association on Mental Retardation.

Turnbull, H. R., Stowe, M. J., & Huerta, N. E. (2007). *Free appropriate public education: The law and children with disabilities*. Denver: Love Publishing.

United Stated Department of Health and Human Services. (2006). *Your rights under section 504 of the rehabilitation act*. Retrieved June 16, 2014 from http://www.hhs.gov/ocr/civilrights/resources/factsheets/504.pdf

United States Department of Education. (2007). *Children with ADD/ADHD: Topic brief*. Retrieved June 16, 2014 from http://www2.ed.gov/policy/speced/leg/idea/brief6.html

U.S. Department of Education, Special Education Programs. (2014). *Thirty-fifth annual report to Congress on the implementation of the Individuals with Disabilities Education Act*. Washington DC: Author.

Venus Independent School District v. Daniel S. (2002). Civil Action No. 3:01-CV-1746-P (N.D. Tex. Apr 11, 2002).

Yankton School Dist. v. Schramm, 900 F. Supp. 1182 (1995).

Yell, M. (2012). *The Law and Special Education* (3rd ed.). Upper Saddle River, NJ: Pearson Publishing.

This research was previously published in Challenges Surrounding the Education of Children with Chronic Diseases edited by Maria Gordon; pages 199-226, copyright year 2016 by Information Science Reference (an imprint of IGI Global).

Chapter 29
Educating Students with Chronic Illness:
How the Old Service Model Fails

Margaret Tseng
Marymount University, USA

Rebecca Magee Pluta
Special Education Advocate, USA

ABSTRACT

Students with chronic illness have historically received an education via home and hospital instruction during their absences. This instruction is significantly inferior in both quality and quantity when compared with the educational experience of students able to attend school. This case study details the experiences of a middle school student in the mid-Atlantic Region of the United States whose chronic illness presented unique and multifaceted challenges that could not be met by her district's inflexible policies and disconnected resources. This case illuminates the need for schools to break away from the traditional administrative special education mold when responding to the challenges of educating frequently absent students with chronic illness. The educational Civil Rights of these students can be preserved, however, by utilizing affordable, available technology to minimize the impact of frequently missed classes, provide continuity of instruction and allow educational access regardless of a student's physical location during their absences from school.

INTRODUCTION

Nearly 31% of school-aged children in the United States suffer from some type of chronic health condition (McCabe & Shaw, 2008). This percentage has risen significantly in the past decade. Chronic illness is defined as a "medical condition of extended duration that creates impairment in adaptive behavior and socially defined roles" (McCabe & Shaw, 2008). Adaptive behavior includes communication, daily living, self-care, academic functioning, and motor behaviors. Socially defined roles include play, social

DOI: 10.4018/978-1-7998-1213-5.ch029

interaction, family roles and schooling. Chronic illness can be as basic as exercise-induced asthma or as complex as an active HIV infection (Gortmaker & Sappenfeld, 1984). While the types of chronic illnesses may vary, they all negatively impact a student's attendance and performance in school. Over 45% of children with chronic illness report struggling with academic progress and nearly 60% regularly miss school (Lynch, Lewis, & Murphy, 1992). Children with chronic illnesses often push themselves to their limits in school and attend school despite feeling quite ill, when their "healthy" peers would have stayed home. This fact can have a negative effect on the academic performance of chronically ill students, as well. In addition, absences necessitated by chronic illness often have adverse consequences on peer relationships (Cook, Schaller, & Krischer, 1985). Further, when chronically-ill students do interact socially, they eventually recognize the differences between themselves and their healthy peers (Isaacs & McElroy, 1980). This can have deleterious consequences on their self-esteem.

To further complicate their existing challenges, many children present with more than one chronic illness, requiring teams of educators to think creatively about ways to meet the needs of these students within the federal legal framework. School districts in the US must comply with a range of prescriptive laws designed to ensure all students receive an appropriate education, including the Individuals with Disabilities Educational Improvement Act, Section 504 of the Rehabilitation Act of 1973, the Americans with Disabilities Act and the partially-repealed No Child Left Behind Act. Prior to 1973, there was no intersection of health and education because they truly existed in separate spheres; and even after four decades of intertwining these arenas, healthcare professionals and educators lack clear, collaborative guidelines governing the provision of an appropriate, inclusive education for children with chronic illness.

All these factors together create an even greater need for educators and administrators to adapt to this changing and evolving group. The needs of this growing population are significant placing a high premium on school districts to meet those needs; and yet, school districts are underfunded and ill-equipped to meet these challenges (Leachman & Mai, 2014). Some districts have gone so far as to reduce individualized education plan goals and remove students altogether from special education programs in an effort to meet the requirements of unfunded mandate within the constraints of their budgets. In order to save money, one district in Connecticut illegally changed students' individualized education plans without parental consent (DeNisco, 2013). A New York district denied students with disabilities the proper educational services in order to meet the budget needs of their district (Petrellese, 2013).

The purpose of this chapter is to present a case study and show how it relates to federal laws and schools. Specifically, the chapter will illustrate and identify universal challenges facing educators and administrators charged with providing an education to children with chronic illness and offer solutions that will prevent them from bankrupting their budgets and breaking the law.

BACKGROUND

During the 2011-2012 academic school-year, one of the largest school districts in the US Mid-Atlantic region was grappling with how to resolve the legal and health issues presented by a newly-enrolled middle school student with multiple chronic illnesses. This case highlights the need to break away from the traditional administrative special education mold in order to tackle the exceptional challenges of preserving the educational Civil Rights of a student with a life-threatening chronic illness. This particular student and her family presented the District with unique and multifaceted challenges that seemed to stack higher and higher, dwarfing the shallow pool of resources designed to meet them.

Up until August 2011, this student, who we will refer to by the alias "Sarah Smith" for the purposes of protecting her privacy, had never been enrolled in public school, or any school for that matter. Sarah and her two siblings had been home-schooled by their mother for their entire educational careers. While school absenteeism is often used to assess functioning level for children with chronic illness we do not have such a measure for Sarah because her condition rendered it impossible to place her in public school with peers. Up until the 1980's, children like Sarah were often educated in hospitals or institutions. The pressure to deinstitutionalize and to drive down healthcare costs has pushed children with chronic illness into the community and public schools (Schwab & Gelfman, 2005). This logistical shift in responsibility was not accompanied by a corresponding shift in human or financial resources. Thus, public school districts that were theoretically and functionally designed to academically educate healthy children now find themselves in the business of coordinating and providing educational environments that can meet the diverse needs of a student population with an enormous range of medical and mental health conditions that naturally interfere with academic instruction and learning. School districts throughout the country will continue to struggle with providing these children with a free an appropriate public education in the least restrictive environment.

Sarah had a very rare and potentially life-threatening genetic metabolic condition. Her condition is estimated to occur in 1 out of every 40,000 to 120,000 children. Her body lacked the correct instructions for how to produce and maintain energy. This condition had devastating consequences on Sarah's health. It required her to remain in a relatively sterile environment away from other children. The pediatric geneticist leading the team of doctors who cared for Sarah said her condition required her to remain outside of the traditional public school classroom "for life". The consequences of her deficiencies could be triggered by exercise, illness or any short periods of time without food (fasting). Even when she was home, in a relatively sterile environment, Sarah's medical condition caused her to be frequently hospitalized and placed in the Intensive Care Unit, sometimes for weeks at a time.

By all measures, Sarah was medically-fragile. She had to follow a very strict diet. Even when following the diet, Sarah required supplemental feeding via a feeding tube. She needed to wash her hands frequently to avoid pathogens on surfaces touched by others and she needed to be in an environment where no airborne pathogens could infect her. The traditional school environment could in no way provide her the needed sterile environment. A recent NSF International study analyzed the grimiest places in public schools. Water fountains, cafeteria trays, students' hands, desks and door knobs all had high levels of bacterial cells. For a typical student these germs might lead to a common cold and a few days of absence from school. For a student like Sarah, exposure to these levels of bacteria on a daily basis could be life threatening.

Her family members were constantly attempting to balance Sarah's need for sterility with their need to live a somewhat normal life. At work, her father came in contact with numerous individuals every day that could unintentionally transmit viruses or bacteria to him that he could unknowingly bring into their home environment. The same situation occurred when Sarah's siblings began attending public schools and carrying the germs inherent in a public school environment home with them. Sarah was fortunate to have a mother who stayed home with her, but this was not enough to protect her from periodically becoming seriously ill.

While Sarah's frequent hospital stays were disruptive, these were not the only source of instability for her family. Her father's job required her family to relocate every two to three years. The frequent upheaval of her social and medical networks had been disruptive and difficult for Sarah and her family. This constant state of flux clearly played a part in her mother's decision to homeschool Sarah for the first six years of her academic career. In addition to the challenges presented by their frequent moves and Sarah's fragile medical condition, Sarah's family endured additional challenges.

Sarah, and at least three of her four immediate family members had been diagnosed with Autism Spectrum Disorders. These disorders caused developmental delays for Sarah and her family members in pragmatic speech and language, fine motor skills, written expression, socialization, self-care, time management, requisite learning skills, organization and behavior. Understandably, Sarah had the lowest functional skills because she had the least amount of life experience and completely lacked appropriate peer models. Children learn a great deal from watching typically-developing peers play and from engaging in pretend play with these peers (Wolfberg, Bottema-Buetel, & DeWitt, 2012). Peer play has been found to be critically important in childhood development and can be especially challenging with children on the autism spectrum. Sarah simply did not have access to peer play or any other common childhood experiences.

Because it is so rare to have a student enroll in a public school with this many unique challenges, the District Sarah's parents eventually enrolled her in was unprepared to ensure Sarah's Civil Rights and could not meet her educational, social, medical, therapeutic, environmental and/or logistical needs.

The rest of the case study in this chapter will highlight the continued challenges Sarah experienced with the district and educators and discuss solutions that can better serve children with chronic illness in this country and around the world. The discussion will include the difficulties with home and hospital teaching; exposure to typical peers, classroom instruction, daily structure and rigorous expectations as functional life skills, and providing a sanitary classroom environment for her that afforded her access to teachers, special educators, therapists, a paraprofessional behavioral aide and a nurse. Many of the solutions presented will elucidate how technology can be used to meet the educational needs of students with chronic illness without placing an undue burden on the resources of educators or the budgets of administrators.

SARAH'S NEEDS VERSUS THE DISTRICT'S STANDARD OPERATING PROCEDURES AND RESOURCES

Sarah's mother and her behavioral therapist initially went to the public school to register Sarah and her two siblings in August of 2011. At the time she was also registering Sarah's siblings, Sarah's mother informed the school that Sarah was unable to physically enter the school building due to her medical condition. She provided the school staff members with medical documentation from her doctors regarding her medical conditions and the resulting restriction from entering the school environment. At this time, Sarah's mother also informed the school that Sarah had Asperger Syndrome and needed to be comprehensively evaluated for an Individualized Education Plan (IEP).

Asperger Syndrome is a complex neurodevelopment disorder that was classified, at that time, under the umbrella of autism spectrum disorders. Children with Asperger Syndrome may exhibit communication and behavioral deficits. In addition, children with Asperger Syndrome may experience delayed motor skill development and challenges with coordination. It is important to note that Asperger Syndrome is not a disease but a syndrome. In Sarah's case, her chronic health issues and Asperger syndrome necessitated an Individualized Education Plan (IEP). Children with delayed skills or other disabilities that adversely affect their educational performance legally have the right to Individualized Education Plan. The IEP is a coordinated plan created by a team of educators, counselors and professionals and includes input from the family. Typically, a child is identified at a young age in the school setting. Students may receive support services if they struggle with anything ranging from learning disabilities to emotional disorders. In Sarah's case, she had never been in the traditional school environment and had been homeschooled for her whole life. Therefore, she never had the opportunity for teachers or administrators to observe her in her learning environment.

IEPs outline goals and services for students and often are carried out in the traditional school environment. However, in Sarah's situation, she clearly needed intense intervention that necessitated a unique learning environment. Unfortunately, the school district insisted that Sarah be evaluated to determine whether she required special education services in the traditional school environment. Sarah's mother requested that this evaluation take place at Sarah's home because Sarah was unable to safely enter the school building due to her medical condition. Upon hearing about her unique condition and these restrictions, the staff members at the school refused to allow Sarah's mother to register her for school. Instead, they gave Sarah's mother several forms for Sarah's doctor to complete and instructed her to come back with this additional medical information and then they would allow her to register for school. Because of her disability, therefore, the school staff members applied a different set of rules to Sarah's enrollment. The resulting effect of these additional rules was that Sarah was not even allowed to enroll in public school until her doctors provided much more detailed information about her medical condition.

In the United States, federal laws protect persons from discrimination in any activity that accepts federal funding. The school staff's refusal to allow Sarah's mother to enroll Sarah in their local public school violated Sarah's federal legal rights under Section 504 of the Rehabilitation Act of 1973 (hereinafter, Section 504). Section 504 provides that:

No otherwise qualified individual with handicaps in the United States . . . shall, solely by reason of her or his handicap, be excluded from the participation in, be denied the benefits of, or be subjected to discrimination under any program or activity receiving Federal financial assistance....

Public schools in the United States cannot legally deny or delay the enrollment of a student who has a chronic illness simply because of their medical condition. It is essential that school districts be prepared in advance with a range of procedures that are sufficiently flexible to meet unique needs presented by students with various chronic illnesses. Failure to plan for these scenarios in advance results in a District's inability to comply with federal laws designed to protect these students' Civil Rights. When violations are found, there are a host of remedies available to correct the violation that resulted in discrimination. If the federal government sees a pattern of violations or a refusal to promptly correct and remedy violations resulting in discrimination, the federal government can withhold the federal funding received by the state or local agency or organization.

Sarah's public school received paperwork signed by Sarah's physician that stated that Sarah could not attend school "for life" due to her need to remain in a sterile environment. Nevertheless, after allowing Sarah's mother to enroll Sarah's siblings, the school required "further medical documentation" before they would allow Sarah to enroll. This delay in enrollment was solely based on Sarah's "handicap" and she was "excluded from participation" and "denied the benefits of" a public school education that a student without her handicaps would have been allowed to receive. While the school undoubtedly needed to know more about Sarah's educational and medical needs, enrolling her would have been the first step in compliance with the law. Following this, the school could have started setting up virtual tutoring with a home and hospital teacher until they had obtained all of the information they needed.

Educating Students with Chronic Illness

Because the school denied enrollment to Sarah, they also violated a second federal law designed to protect students with disabilities. The Individuals with Disabilities Educational Improvement Act, was designed to ensure that students with disabilities receive a Free and Appropriate Public Education (FAPE). This federal law requires a local educational authority (LEA) to conduct a comprehensive psycho-educational evaluation within 60 days of the time a parent provides written consent for this evaluation. Once Sarah was enrolled, the school would have had the ability to start the process of inviting all of the necessary professionals into one room to create a comprehensive psycho-educational evaluation plan for Sarah. The failure to allow Sarah to enroll in public school also caused the school district to violate Sarah's right to have a thorough evaluation in a timely manner. On the same day Sarah's mother attempted to register her, she informed the school in writing that Sarah had a diagnosis of Asperger's Syndrome and requested that she be comprehensively evaluated for the purposes of developing an IEP. This written request and consent created an obligation to convene a multidisciplinary team meeting to begin the IEP process.

When a parent in the United States requests that their child be evaluated for the purposes of determining if they qualify for an IEP as a student with a disability, the LEA should schedule a multidisciplinary team meeting to review the parent's concerns within a reasonable amount of time. Either at this meeting or in a subsequent meeting, the multidisciplinary team puts together a proposed evaluation plan that delineates each area in which the student will be evaluated. In most cases where a student is school-aged, these evaluations occur in the school. In the case of students with chronic illness, sometimes it is not possible to evaluate them in their school building. As previously noted, Sarah's medical condition required her to remain in a sterile environment and her mother presented documentation of this medical necessity at the time she requested her daughter be evaluated by the school. Unfortunately, this school, like most other schools in the United States, had no other procedural guidance from their District besides the standard procedures for evaluating a student in school or at a hospital. The District was unable to adapt their procedures to meet Sarah's evaluation needs within the 60-day timeline required under federal law.

Sadly, Sarah's parents were placed in the position of having to choose between their daughter's health and her education. They did not have the financial means to hire an attorney to advise and assist them in challenging the school's decision. It is quite expensive to hire an advocate or lawyer to deal with due process. Costs can range from anywhere from $1500 to $7500. Due process is the formal hearing where disputes about IEPs take place. Disputes typically center on disagreements between parents and the school district about procedural violations of the law or which services are appropriate to enable the student to obtain some educational benefit from their IEP. Due process can also address the district's failure to provide needed special education or related services in a student's IEP, a denial of special education services, the provision of an independent educational evaluation, or private placement reimbursement (Webster, 2014). Unfortunately, most families cannot afford to engage in due process; and therefore do not attempt to fight the school district, which is exactly the predicament the Sarah's family found themselves in when the school administration insisted Sarah be evaluated in the traditional school environment.

Against her doctor's advice, Sarah's parents took her into the school for her educational evaluations because they felt they had no other choice. Had Sarah become ill from this exposure to pathogens inside the school, the District would have surely found itself in the midst of a very expensive lawsuit. If a more up-to-date set of procedures been developed in advance by a multidisciplinary team within the District, it would have afforded the school staff with the flexibility to evaluate Sarah in a location that was medically-safe for her and would have enabled her school district to remain in compliance with federal laws. Because no alternative procedures had been developed in advance, however, the District was unable to proceed with the flexibility needed to evaluate a student with a serious chronic illness who was not able to safely undergo educational evaluations within the school or hospital settings. Curriculum access must be uninterrupted and instructional quality must be high for any student. The Home and Hospital Teaching provided was woefully inadequate. The curriculum access and educational instruction to Sarah Smith was without any meaningful educational benefit and was in violation of federal law.

In any community around the globe where education, opportunity and productivity are common values, educational systems must ensure that all students, regardless of the quality of their health or the limitations on their mobility, have continuous, uninterrupted access to an appropriately challenging educational curriculum and high-quality instruction. To accomplish this, educational systems must establish a procedural framework that is flexible enough to adapt, adjust and recover somewhat seamlessly when presented with the continuum of environmental and instructional needs that will undoubtedly arise and change without warning within their educational community. Chronic illness and other disabilities are increasing in frequency each year in most developed countries. Students across every race are affected. Communities that embrace this concept and philosophy will inevitably cultivate more educated graduates with greater access to employment and greater opportunities to become productive members of society. This community-wide investment to ensure equal access to a primary and secondary public education, therefore, will inevitably shift these individuals from being the historical consumers of the community tax base to being producers of greater independence and wealth.

The United States Supreme Court, in the landmark set of cases that are collectively referred to as *Brown v. Board of Education*, 347 U.S. 483 (1954), declared that state-sponsored segregation in public schools was unconstitutional. This decision provided the legal scaffolding upon which anyone with certain visible or publically-discoverable reasons for being discriminated against (national origin, race, alienage, gender, illegitimacy, etc.) could hang their legal rights to an inclusive education. Since *Brown*, most political and administrative leaders have, at least publically, embraced the concept that a neither person's looks nor their family's heritage / dynamics can be used as a basis to limit their access to an education. The legal rights to a non-segregated, non-discriminatory education for students with chronic illness, however, are much thinner. While many states have enacted laws granting students with certain illnesses the right to "home and hospital" instruction outside of the school building, this is generally viewed by the district as a temporary service until the student is well again. In the case of students, like Sarah Smith, who have a chronic illness that will never go away, these "alternative" education plans reluctantly offered by the school district significantly fail to meet their long-term educational needs.

The rights conferred via federal and state anti-discrimination and special education laws are only as good as they are enforced. This is because there is no additional, meaningful consequence (other than the expense of litigation) for a local educational authority that decides to disregard a student's legal rights. Across much of the United States, the forum where a parent of a student with a disability who has been denied his civil rights to an education must begin is to request a due process hearing. In the state Sarah Smith lived in, due process entitled her parent to "notice and an opportunity to be heard" by a state-appointed administrative law judge (hereinafter, ALJ). Should the ALJ agree that the student's federal or state rights were violated, the remedy is for the ALJ to order the school to follow the same laws the educators and administrators knew they were supposed to follow in the first place. As you are about to see in the facts of Sarah Smith's case, sometimes school districts display a blatant disregard for the law and the needs of a student. Without meaningful consequences, school districts, like Sarah's, see little reason to take on the financial and logistical expense involved in following the law. School districts across the United States have realized that only a small percentage of parents have the vast financial

Educating Students with Chronic Illness

resources it takes to ensure that they follow the law Consequently, the unwritten policy is to only give the limited grease (curriculum and instructional resources) to the squeakiest of wheels (parents who hire professionals to assist them in persuading the District to follow the law).

According to the state laws that governed the home and hospital instruction in the state Sarah Smith resided in, she was entitled to *a minimum of* six hours of instruction per week and this instruction was legally required to start no later than ten days after the District received a physician's documentation of the inability of a student to attend school and the need for home and hospital teaching. Sarah, unfortunately, did not receive the minimum amount of instruction. During the first 61 days after home and instruction was requested, Sarah received just three hours and one minute of instruction. She should have received a minimum of more than 40 hours of instruction during this time. The three hours and 1 minute of instructional time was broken up into one twenty-minute session, one hour-and-a-half-session and one hour and eleven-minute session.

It took three weeks for the District to arrange for a home and hospital instructor to contact Sarah's family. One would hope that this significant delay was a result of the District's search for an experienced instructor who understood Sarah's disability and her emotional volatility. This was clearly not the case. The state law required home and hospital instructors to have a bachelor's degree in any field. There was no requirement to understand or have any information about the unique learning needs of students, particularly those with specific learning disabilities, special needs, chronic illness, or any other educational or physical disability.

While they waited to be notified of when their daughter's home and hospital instruction would begin, various administrators, special educators and a nurse from the school made comments to Sarah's parents that they did not "believe" she could not come to school. They alleged that the District had received students previously with her same diagnosis and these students and did not consider Sarah's condition to be "severe enough" for her to not come to school, despite what Sarah's doctor said.

The first Home and Hospital Instructor hired on an hourly-wage basis by the District to educate Sarah finally called the house on a Thursday afternoon in mid-October and told Sarah's mom that she would be there the following day to work with Sarah "after 3pm". Sarah sat at the table at 3pm on Friday waiting for the instructor to come for two full hours but she never arrived and never called to say she was not coming. Failing to meet a student's expectations to this degree without any explanation was particularly difficult for a student, like Sarah, with an Autism Spectrum Disorder. Later that weekend, on Sunday evening, the instructor called Sarah's mom again and said she would be coming on Monday at 4:30pm. The instructor did not reference her failure to appear on Friday, but counseled Sarah's mom that she must ensure that Sarah was "ready to work" when she arrived.

The following day, the Home and Hospital Instructor arrived and stayed for just twenty minutes without providing any explanation for why she was leaving after such a short period of time. Prior to her departure, the instructor asked Sarah's mother to sign a document saying she had provided a full hour of direct instruction to Sarah that day. Sarah's mother refused to sign the paper because the woman had only been in their home for 20 minutes. Sarah's mother also explained that she was not comfortable signing the paper because the woman did not have any of the textbooks or materials with her that Sarah needed. The instructor then began arguing with Sarah's mother and alleged that Sarah's mother was required to sign the paper because the instructor had spent time photocopying documents at Sarah's school and that according to the District's policies that preparation time counted toward Sarah's minimum six hours per week of direct instruction. When Sarah's mother questioned her, the instructor informed Sarah's mother that she did not have any of Sarah's assignments or books because the school had not made any of these available to her.

At this point, Sarah's mother noticed two young children who were sitting in the woman's vehicle unaccompanied by any adult. The vehicle was parked in the driveway of the Smith home. The instructor then announced that she needed to get some books from the library and said she would return to work with Sarah the following morning. She again counseled Sarah's mother that Sarah must be at the table and ready to work when she arrives. Once again, however, the instructor failed to show up and failed to call Sarah's mother whatsoever that morning. Later that afternoon, around 4:30, the woman arrived at the Smith home. She still had no textbooks, and only arrived with a few papers in her hand. Sarah's mother noticed that the woman, once again, left her two young children unaccompanied and unattended in her vehicle in the driveway of the Smith home. This time, the woman stayed for 90 minutes, but repeatedly left her instructional sessions with Sarah to go out to her vehicle and speak to her children. In addition, the instructor took several personal cell phone calls, unrelated to her instruction of Sarah, during Sarah's instructional time. Again, the instructor insisted Mrs. Smith sign a document verifying her hours so that she would be compensated for each minute she was on their property despite the fact that a significant portion of the 90 minutes she was at the Smith residence was spent, not providing direct instruction to Sarah, but rather speaking to her children in the driveway or on the front porch talking on her cell phone.

Prior to leaving that day, the instructor told Mrs. Smith that Sarah's instructional schedule would be just six hours per week and the days would be Monday, Tuesday and Thursday from 4:30-6:30pm. Sarah's mom explained that Sarah is much more productive during the day when it was quiet in their home, while her siblings were in school. She also explained that the 4:30 to 6:30 time slot disrupted the family's dinner schedule. The instructor was unwilling to consider any of Sarah's needs and told Mrs. Smith that Sarah would have to work around the schedule of her own children; and therefore, 4:30 to 6:30pm was the only time she was willing to provide home and hospital instruction to Sarah.

The Smith's contacted the Home and Hospital Teaching Office and requested that they send a new home and hospital instructor due to the myriad of issues posed by the first one. They specifically informed the office that they had cats and asked the office to ensure that whomever they sent was not allergic to cats. They also requested that the Home and Hospital Teaching Office coordinate with the Office of Special Education to find an instructor who had some training or experience with the unique challenges that accompany teaching a child with Asperger's Syndrome. The director informed them that they are unable to coordinate with the Office of Special Education and that it was up to that office to find a person to provide Sarah with special education services. Despite the outrageous behavior exhibited by the initial instructor, the director informed Mr. and Mrs. Smith that it would take "quite some time" to find a home and hospital instructor who was not allergic to cats.

Twelve days later, Mrs. Smith received a call from a new instructor who said she would be arriving at the Smith's home the following morning at 9:00am to work with Sarah. She arrived more than 20 minutes late without any curriculum or educational materials. Though home and hospital instruction is designed to cover the entire academic curriculum, (language arts/literature, math, science, and history), the instructor informed Sarah that she was supposed to be doing her math and history classes online on her own. Mrs. Smith said no one informed her of this and said that she had no idea what online programs Sarah was expected to be completing. The instructor told Sarah that she had been told this by the Office of Home and Hospital Teaching in an email but she was unable to locate the email.

That day, the only subject the instructor worked on with Sarah was literature, though she had no lesson plans prepared or materials prepared to work with Sarah. In addition to these surprises, the instructor

Educating Students with Chronic Illness

informed Sarah and her mother that she has a severe cat allergy. She was coughing and sneezing the entire time she was in the Smith home. Just over an hour after she arrived, she said she could no longer work with Sarah due to her cat allergy. She then asked Sarah's mother to sign the timesheet paperwork she had filled out stating that she had arrived at 9:00am. Mrs. Smith corrected the time on the sheet to the actual time the instructor arrived at their home and then signed it. The instructor informed Mrs. Smith that she would not be returning to work with Sarah due to her cat allergy. It was several more weeks before the Home and Hospital Teaching Office decided to send out a different instructor. When the third home and hospital instructor finally arrived, Sarah's family learned that, she too, was allergic to cats.

Sarah Smith's experiences (or lack thereof) in public education are so appalling that they almost seem like a satire that could never have actually happened to a student in the United States. One of the reasons this case study is so important to discuss is that Sarah's bad experiences, when viewed collectively, as she and her parents experienced them, should paint a very clear picture of the need for major changes in our very broken system of providing educational services to students with chronic illness.

Many different professions require post-secondary (college) degrees. There is nothing about that basic qualification that makes the people in those career positions interchangeable. Education is no exception. If a teaching certificate is required for educators who teach students who are healthy enough to attend school inside the school building, the same requirement should exist for educators who teach students who are not healthy enough to attend school inside the school building. Likewise, just as educators inside the traditional school building are not allowed to late arrive to the classrooms (and leave their children inside their parked vehicles while they teach) or just skip days without notifying parents, then obviously educators who instruct students outside traditional school buildings should be held to that same standard of ethics and punctuality. Families of students with chronic illnesses are constantly going to medical and therapeutic appointments and they need to have a professional working with their child who is dependable so that they can maintain their already rigorous schedules.

Moreover, schedules of the instructional sessions must be scheduled based on the needs of that student and should occur, if at all possible, sometime within the window if instructional time inside the school building. This will ease the transitions back into the school building for students whose chronic health status frequently fluctuate.

Unfortunately, there are no federal guidelines for home and hospital instruction. Guidelines vary from state to state and district to district. In most cases, if guidelines are offered by districts, they are broken down into four categories: responsibilities of the instructor, school, parents and student. Typically, the guidelines for the instructor are very vague and include coordinating teaching material with the school, providing instruction and contacting parents to establish a teaching date and time.

Sarah Smith was a student who was eager to experience school for the first time and further her education. Her academic capabilities were superior when compared to her peers. Research has shown that children with chronic illness often perform lower on achievement tests, experience reading problems, and may experience overall academic delays unrelated to cognitive ability. While Sarah's Achievement Test Scores nearly all exceeded her actual grade level, she was achieving at a level that was well below her intelligence level, which was in the very superior range (see Table 1). In comparing her educational achievement to her intelligence, it is clear that Sarah's chronic illness and the district's inflexibility was severely handicapping her education. Sarah, and every student, with a chronic illness who requires instruction outside of the school building deserve to receive instruction from a qualified educator.

SOLUTIONS AND RECOMMENDATIONS

According to Hamlet and Herrick (2011), students who are frequently unable to attend classes fall behind peers who are in school on a regular basis. For students with chronic illnesses frequent absences from school are often unavoidable. Maintaining educational achievement becomes increasingly problematic for children chronic illnesses because the lessons in core subjects like mathematics and reading build upon one another, and that prior knowledge becomes an essential foundation for future learning (Schlieper, 1985). For example, it is almost impossible to learn how to perform multi-digit multiplication if a student has not first learned to perform the foundational skill of completing multi-digit addition. That child will also not be able to move on to learning the skill of long division, without first mastering the skills of adding, subtracting and multiplying.

This same foundational deficit theory applies in language arts education. Spelling and vocabulary, which are heavily emphasized in first through third grades, are the foundational bases for reading comprehension skills that are emphasized throughout the fourth-grade curriculum. A child who has been frequently absent from class and has not acquired these foundational literacy skills will not only struggle to comprehend fourth-grade reading material but also will continue throughout the later grades to self-select texts that are below their grade level, but have pictures or other literary aides that make them easier to comprehend. Failing to fill those foundational literary holes, will cause a student to quickly find themselves stuck in a perpetual cycle of being unable to catch up to their peers because they are continuously unable to comprehend grade-level curriculum and instruction.

Furthermore, Hamlet and Herrick (2011) point out that, in addition to the failure to acquire important foundational skills, students with frequent absences due to chronic illnesses do not have sufficiently consistent opportunities to practice the metacognitive skills of problem solving and critical thinking that are acquired through daily interaction with teachers, peers, and curriculum materials. Frequent absences, therefore, rob a student with chronic illness of the ability to acquire skills that lead to advanced mastery of subject material. This fact places students with chronic illnesses at a distinct disadvantage when compared to their peers who are healthy and rarely absent.

Because many of the absences that are necessary for students with chronic illnesses are unavoidable, school communities must find a way to adequately support students learning outside the classroom to prevent that downward academic spiral caused by a lack of foundational skills. One of the most promising

Table 1. Test scores

Sarah's Achievement Scores Age: 12 Grade Level: 7		
Subject	**Grade Equivalence**	**Percentile**
Reading Vocabulary	9.8	95%
Reading Comprehension	13.5	99%
Math Computation	6.1	52%
Math Concepts/Problems	8.5	91%
Language Mechanics	10.1	92%
Language Usage/Structure	13.1	98%
Spelling	10.0	91%

Educating Students with Chronic Illness

methods of ensuring that students can remain connected to the high-quality instruction occurring inside the classroom is through the use of assistive technology. Assistive technology, like videotelephony, can provide students with chronic illness an academic bridge when they experience long or short absenteeism from school.

ASSISTIVE TECHNOLOGY

While many educators across the country have attempted to modify lesson plans and curriculum to better adapt to different learning styles, the use of technology has certainly increased the number of options available to educators. Technology specifically tailored to students with disabilities is known as assistive technology. Assistive technology was first envisioned as a means to help students with disabilities to engage in activities more easily and independently. Assistive technology is addressed in the 1997 reauthorization of The Individuals with Disabilities Education Act (IDEA), The American with Disabilities Act, and Section 504 of the Rehabilitation Act. The Assistive Technology Act of 1998 and the Technology Related Assistance Act of 1988 define assistive technology as "any item, piece of equipment, or product, whether acquired commercially off the shelf, modified, or customized, that is used to increase, maintain, or improve the functional capabilities of child with a disability" (Martinez and Erickan, 2009). Therefore, assistive technology encompasses a wide range of resources. It includes the purchase or lease of technologies, the fitting and customization of technologies, and the training for the child in the use of the needed technology.

The budgets of school Districts everywhere are squeezed and there simply is not money to hire additional part-time educators of the same caliber, passion and experience as those who are hired to educate our students in the classroom. Therefore, the greater use of assistive technologies may be the way to bridge the needs of children with chronic illness and the districts struggling with budget constraints. The abysmal experiences Sarah Smith had with home and hospital instructors should serve as a call to action for educational administrators everywhere. Today, technology allows people all over the world to communicate their thoughts and share resources and ideas. In the educational arena, Khan Academy is perhaps the best example of how technology has been used to reach out to those who wish to learn but may not be able to attend school. The use of technology inside the classroom is definitely on the rise with the shift toward the Universal Design for Learning in the United States. For students with chronic illness, like Sarah Smith, however, it is not enough to simply use technology to reach students inside the classroom. Technology must be utilized to allow educators to reach students wherever they are, whether inside the classroom, at their homes, in the hospital, inside a hyperbaric oxygen chamber, on vacation or at any other off-site location.

While Sarah Smith presented her school district with a unique set of very permanent medical circumstances, the lessons learned from her situation can be applied universally to students who have a permanent or temporary condition that prevents them from attending school. Whether the absences are sporadic or lengthy, technology is the only way to provide students with chronic illness the chance to experience what they missed in school and to participate at a time and place that is acceptable for them. Technology can be embraced, incorporated and utilized in multiple ways that are meaningful for students both inside and outside of the classroom. Some teachers use technology as a tool to enhance learning in the classroom, and then employ technology as a means of promoting greater student independence and offering two-way communication between the teacher and the students outside of the classroom. Through the use of websites and "Google Drives" the type of information that has traditionally only been available to students with disabilities who have Individualized Education Plans or Section 504 Accommodation Plans can now be made available for all students.

With the proper use of technology, parents never have to wonder what their children are learning in the classroom and have much less to worry about when their children need to miss school. Students who are absent from classes as a result of an appointment, illness or vacation can access all of the information they need to understand the concepts that were covered in class and to complete the assigned homework without even having to inquire about what they missed.

A few teachers who are fully embracing the transparency that technology can provide offer websites that give the syllabus for each course they teach as well as the lesson plans for each week of each course. Often, all of the information posted on the website remains posted from the very first day of the school year in case a student wants to review what they have learned. The week's lesson plans can be shared online at the beginning of each week for administrators, parents and students to see. If a student knows they will be absent for a medical appointment, they will know, in advance, what topics will be covered, what assignments will be due and when to expect tests and quizzes to occur. Online lesson plans can offer incredible detail that is very helpful to students with chronic illnesses who often must plan ahead when they know they will have treatments that will tap their time or energy. Some educators post actual screen shots photos of their lecture notes (including example problems and solutions) that were presented to the class on either the chalkboard, overhead, interactive white board or on a handout paper.

Having electronic access to this information allows students with chronic illness to view not only concepts they missed, but it allows them to learn those concepts in the same way their instructor taught them. This type of access to the instruction that took place inside the classroom is particularly vital for students now that so many states in the United States have adopted the Common Core Curriculum. The Common Core Standards Initiative was initiated by the National Governors Association and the Council of Chief State School Officers. The intent of the initiative was to create common academic standards across states in the areas of language arts and mathematics. Forty-three states have adopted these standards including the state in which Sarah resides. In a recent Gallup poll, parent and teachers alike expressed frustration with these new common standards (Brown, 2014). Teachers expressed frustration with school districts and the lack of support to implement the standards. Parents expressed frustration in their inability to help their children with their homework, which demonstrates an even greater need for assistive technology not only for children in special education, but also in the mainstream classroom (Ludlow, 2014).

Particularly in Mathematics, it is crucial that a student with chronic illness receive instruction on mathematical concepts that mirrors what was presented in the classroom as college graduates who would be qualified to serve as home and hospital instructors have absolutely no knowledge or understanding of the new way mathematics is being taught. Home and hospital instruction that is aligned with the pre-common core era of mathematics education would not only leave gaps in a student's educational foundation, but it would create unnecessary confusion that might set a student even further behind.

The true value of this methodology is in how educators can use resources to promote independence among their students. In the Rochester Community Unit School District in Illinois, where Stephanie Webster teaches mathematics at Rochester Junior High School, all students have the opportunity to participate in a rent-to-own technology program where they can rent a Google Chromebook computer for $75 per year. At the conclusion of three years (and the cumulative payment of $225), the students own their Chromebooks. For students who are unable to afford the annual rental costs, the school has a bank

Educating Students with Chronic Illness

of computers that can be checked out in the morning and back in at the conclusion of school at no cost to the student. When students have questions about their homework or about concepts that were taught in class, Ms. Webster asks her students not to ask their parents to help them with their homework (because their parents were not taught using the Common Core State Standards that are currently being taught). Instead, she asks students to email her if they have questions. If she believes that other students might have the same question, she can email the student back a response, and can also post any question and her answer anonymously on her classroom blog. While this ensures that all students, even those with a chronic illnesses and frequent absences, have the same access to information, it also serves at least six other important functions.

First, it helps her students to learn vital self-advocacy skills. It is essential that students with chronic illnesses and other disabilities develop and hone self-advocacy skills if they are going to have their needs met in high school and college where much more autonomy is required. Second, it requires students to take more responsibility for accessing the wide array of resources available to them. Third, it also allows parents, who frequently lament about not understanding the methodologies being taught under the new Common Core State Standards, to learn what these methods are and exactly how and why their children are using them.

Fourth, this use of technology allows students to essentially bring lectures home with them to study for upcoming quizzes and exams. Vital resources such as these were previously only available to students with documented diagnosed disabilities who had Individualized Education Plans or Section 504 Accommodation Plans, which did not always include students with chronic illnesses. The very best way to truly level the educational playing field is to provide every student with equal access to information (see Table 2). With the broadening definition of assistive technology these tools are being used in mainstream and special education classrooms. Therefore, assistive technology is applicable to any student who might overcome their academic challenges through the use of these tools. The wider use of assistive technology in the classroom allows for an increased use of lesser expensive, but highly useful technologies like Google Docs and Skype.

A fifth function of providing such information to students in an electronic format is that, students can manipulate the presentation of the information to suit their individual needs. For example, students with visual impairments can increase the size of the text to whatever is comfortable for them to read or can use software that will read the information to them over the computer. Students with ADHD or Dyslexia can create the equivalent of electronic colored overlays that function like Irlen lenses. Students with disabilities that affect their writing can type their notes, highlight and electronically copy text for

Table 2. These notes capture what was presented to the math class regarding writing equations. The instructor shared the file virtually with all of her students in real time.

(2-1) Writing Equations (p.42 in IMN)
The perimeter of a square equals four times the length of a side. If the perimeter is 46, what is the side length?
Step 1: Define your variable(s) l= the side of length
Step 2: Write a verbal model. Perimeter= length of a side x # of sides
Step 3: Write an equation 46 =4l
4   4
11.5=l
Step 5: Check and write answer as a sentence v= 46 = 4(11.5)
46=46
The length of a side is 11.5 units

their own note-taking. The possible combination of electronic accommodative supports that students can access independently seems endless.

Technological supports like those discussed here allow students to self-select, experiment with and utilize almost any accommodation that will best suit their learning style. A sixth and likely unintended but welcome benefit of using technology in this manner is that it undoubtedly saves a school district a significant amount of money each year. This money is saved, in part, because these accommodations are now available to all students without the District having to staff Individualized Education Plan and Section 504 Accommodation Plan multidisciplinary team meetings (and hire substitutes to cover the classrooms and special education sessions for the team members who previously spent hours in each of these meetings at least annually and often quarterly) where parents, educators and administrators sit in a room and hypothesize about what might help a student better access the curriculum.

Had Sarah Smith been a student in a classroom that embraced transparency through technology, her home and hospital instructors would not have needed to even go to the school to talk with her teachers about lesson plans, lectures, assignments, quizzes, or review sheets, because each possible piece of information would have already been accessible online. On days when Sarah's home and hospital instructor did not arrive as scheduled, Sarah would have been able to independently acquire the information and email her teacher directly with any questions she had.

In Sarah Smith's case, her parents requested to use technology to bridge the divide between Sarah's needs for both an education and contact with her peers and her inability to enter the school building and be physically present with her peers safely. After experiencing the abysmal quantity and quality of instruction offered to students who required home and hospital teaching, Sarah's parents proposed an alternative solution. They requested that she be allowed to virtually attend her classes via Skype technology from a private portable classroom placed on school grounds outside the school building so that Sarah could still safely participate in the closest possible experience to actually attending school. They explained that being near to the school (and no longer confined to her house) might help Sarah feel more like she was a part of a school community. The Smith's request was denied because the District's portable classrooms had no plumbing and, consequently, no functioning bathrooms or sinks. Sarah would, therefore, have had to enter the school building when she needed to use the restroom. Her doctors explained that it was simply not medically safe for Sarah to come in contact with the pathogens harbored inside the school, particularly those that existed in the school's restrooms.

Sarah's parents also requested that Sarah be allowed to connect virtually via Skype (or a similar videotelephony program) with her classes from the safety of her own home. This would allow her to hear and see the teacher's instruction and to hear and even participate in class discussions with her peers. Their request was denied because the school did not have the required technology in each of their classrooms and would need time to train each of their teachers in the use of this technology. Furthermore, because Sarah required special education, the assistance of a behavioral specialist, a paraprofessional aide and a full-time nurse, the school district decided that it would be cheaper to pay for Sarah to attend a private school that could meet her medical and special education needs. This was their final decision. Sadly, because she could not attend public school, Sarah had zero access to typically-developing peer models. Further, a special education placement in a private school did not afford Sarah any access to the advanced placement courses that she clearly would have been qualified to take in a public school.

CONCLUSION

The details presented in this case study demonstrate the complete ineffectiveness of Sarah Smith's home and hospital instruction beg the future research question of whether, given the lack of required experience and the lack of supervision, home and hospital instruction is a practice that should be continued in educational communities where resources are limited. Future research is also necessary to determine whether there are legal roadblocks that would prevent school districts from utilizing videotelephony technologies like Skype to allow students with chronic illness to access the education their illness so often requires them to miss. Similarly, if this is possible, it would then be necessary to research whether technology could be legally used to videotape classes in the event a student's chronic illness prevents them from being available to participate in real-time as the class is occurring.

In the higher education field, the idea of podcasting lectures and flipping classrooms is increasingly being used. If the wide use of such teaching models can be used in higher education, it stands to be reasoned that they would be useful in the primary grades as well. Further, it would be beneficial to research whether the interactive capabilities of videotelephony technologies can be dually beneficial in also combating the feelings of social isolation that impact so many students with chronic illness as a result of the frequent absences that prevent them from fostering and maintaining typical peer relationships. Finally, Sarah Smith's experiences highlight the need to research more effective ways to ensure the assessment for and provision of special education services can be intertwined as significantly as necessary with whatever alternative form of education is offered to a frequently-absent student with a chronic illness.

REFERENCES

Brown, A. (2014) Teachers Feel Worried, Frustrated About Common Core. *Gallup*. Retrieved from http://www.gallup.com/poll/179048/teachers-feel-worried-frustrated-common-core.aspx

Cook, B. A., Schaller, K., & Krischer, J. P. (1985). School absence among children with chronic illness. *The Journal of School Health*, 55. PMID:3851099

DeNisco, A. (2013). Connecticut school district responds to IDEA violations. *District Administration*. Retrieved from http://www.districtadministration.com/article/connecticut-school-district-responds-idea-violations

Gortmaker, S. L., & Sappenfeld, W. (1984). Chronic childhood disorders: Prevalence and impact. *Pediatric Clinics of North America*, *31*(2), 3–18. PMID:6366717

Hamlet, H. S., & Herrick, M. A. (2011). Who's on first: Professional collaboration and children with chronic illness. Retrieved from http://counselingoutfitters.com/ vistas/vistas11/Article_82.pdf A

Issacs, J., & McElroy, M. R. (1980). Psychosocial aspects of chronic illness in children. *The Journal of School Health*, *50*(2), 318–321. doi:10.1111/j.1746-1561.1980.tb08172.x PMID:6903677

Leachman, M., & Mai, C. (2014). Most states funding schools less than before the recession. *Center on Budget and Policy Priorities*. Retrieved from http://www.cbpp.org/cms/?fa=view&id=4011

Ludlow, B. L. (2014). Blurring the Line Between Assistive and Mainstream Technologies. *Teaching Exceptional Children*, *47*(1), 7. doi:10.1177/0040059914542766

Lynch, E. W., Lewis, R. B., & Murphy, D. S. (1992). Educational services for children with chronic illnesses: Perspectives of educators and families. *Exceptional Children*, *59*(4), 210–220. PMID:8432304

Martinez, Y., & Erickan, K. (2009). Chronic illness in Canadian children: What is the effect of illness on academic achievement, and anxiety and emotional disorders? *Child: Care, Health and Development*, *35*(3), 391–401. doi:10.1111/j.1365-2214.2008.00916.x PMID:19397602

McCabe, S., & Shaw, P. (2008). Hospital to school transition for children with chronic illness: Meeting the new challenges of an evolving health care system. *Psychology in the Schools*, *45*(1), 74–87. doi:10.1002/pits.20280

Petrellese, S. (2013). Parents sue schools for civil rights violations. *The Garden City News Online*. Retrieved from http://www.gcnews.com/news/2013-01-31/Front_Page/Parents_Sue_Schools_For_Civil_Rights_Violations.html

Schlieper, A. (1985). Chronic illness and school achievement. *Developmental Medicine and Child Neurology*, *27*, 67–79. PMID:3884414

Schwab, N. C., & Gefman, M. H. B. (2005). *Legal issues in school health services: A resource for school administrators, school attorneys, school nurses*. Lincoln: Authors Choice Press.

Webster, J. (2014). Due process - - How parents assert their rights: When the IEP process goes wrong. *About.com*. Retrieved from http://specialed.about.com/od/iep/a/Due-Process-How-Parents-Assert-Their-Rights.htm

Wolfberg, P., Bottema-Buetel, K., & DeWitt, M. (2012). Including children with autism in social and imaginary play with typical peers: Integrated play group models. *American Journal of Play*, *5*(1). Retrieved from http://www.journalofplay.org/sites/www.journalofplay.org/files/pdf-articles/5-1-article-including-children-with-autism.pdf

ADDITIONAL READING

Betz, C. L., Redcay, G., Betz, C. L., & Redcay, G. (2005). An exploratory study of future plans and extracurricular activities of transition-age youth and young adults. *Issues in Comprehensive Pediatric Nursing*, *28*(1), 33–61. doi:10.1080/01460860590916753 PMID:15824028

Boyle, C. A., Decoufle, P., & Yeargin-Allsopp, M. (1994). Prevalence and health impact of developmental disabilities in U.S. children. *Pediatrics*, *93*(1), 399–403. PMID:7509480

Brown, R. (1993). An introduction to the special series: Pediatric chronic illness. *Journal of Learning Disabilities*, *26*(2), 4–6. doi:10.1177/002221949302600101 PMID:8463745

Cayce, K. A., Krowchuk, D. P., Feldman, S. R., Camacho, F. T., Balkrishnan, R., & Fleischer, A. B. (2005). Healthcare utilization for acute and chronic diseases of young, school-age children in the rural and non-rural setting. *Clinical Pediatrics*, *44*(6), 491–498. doi:10.1177/000992280504400604 PMID:16015395

Erickson, J. D., Patterson, J. M., Wall, M., & Neumark-Sztainer, D. (2005). Risk Behaviors and Emotional Well-being in Youth with Chronic Health Conditions. *Children's Health Care*, *34*(3), 181–192. doi:10.120715326888chc3403_2

Hoffman, C., Rice, D., & Sung, H. Y. (1996). Persons with chronic conditions: Their prevalence and costs. *Journal of the American Medical Association*, *276*(18), 1473–1479. doi:10.1001/jama.1996.03540180029029 PMID:8903258

Johnson, M. P., Lubker, B. B., & Fowler, M. G. (1988). Teacher needs assessment for the educational management of children with chronic illnesses. *The Journal of School Health*, *58*(6), 232–235. doi:10.1111/j.1746-1561.1988.tb05871.x PMID:3216627

Stein, R. E., Bauman, L. J., Westbrook, L. E., Coupey, S. M., & Ireys, H. T. (1993). Framework for identifying children who have chronic conditions: The case for a new definition. *The Journal of Pediatrics*, *122*(3), 342–347. doi:10.1016/S0022-3476(05)83414-6 PMID:8441085

Stein, R. E. K. (2001). Challenges in long-term health care for children. *Ambulatory Pediatrics*, *1*(5), 280–288. doi:10.1367/1539-4409(2001)001<0280:CILTHC>2.0.CO;2 PMID:11888416

Weller, L., Fredrickson, D. D., Burbach, C., Molgaard, C. A., & Ngong, L. (2004). Chronic disease medication administration rates in a public school system. *The Journal of School Health*, *74*(5), 161–165. doi:10.1111/j.1746-1561.2004.tb08214.x PMID:15283496

KEY TERMS AND DEFINITIONS

Americans with Disabilities Act: "The Americans with Disabilities Act (ADA) was signed into law on July 26, 1990, by President George H.W. Bush. The ADA is one of America's most comprehensive pieces of civil rights legislation that prohibits discrimination and guarantees that people with disabilities have the same opportunities as everyone else to participate in the mainstream of American life -- to enjoy employment opportunities, to purchase goods and services, and to participate in State and local government programs and services. Modeled after the Civil Rights Act of 1964, which prohibits discrimination on the basis of race, color, religion, sex, or national origin – and Section 504 of the Rehabilitation Act of 1973 -- the ADA is an "equal opportunity" law for people with disabilities. To be protected by the ADA, one must have a disability, which is defined by the ADA as a physical or mental impairment that substantially limits one or more major life activities, a person who has a history or record of such impairment, or a person who is perceived by others as having such an impairment. The ADA does not specifically name all of the impairments that are covered" as defined by http://www.ada.gov/ada_intro.htm.

Asperger Syndrome: "Asperger syndrome is an autism spectrum disorder (ASD) considered to be on the "high functioning" end of the spectrum. Affected children and adults have difficulty with social interactions and exhibit a restricted range of interests and/or repetitive behaviors. Motor development may be delayed, leading to clumsiness or uncoordinated motor movements. Compared with those affected by other forms of ASD, however, those with Asperger syndrome do not have significant delays or difficulties in language or cognitive development. Some even demonstrate precocious vocabulary – often in a highly specialized field of interest." as defined by http://www.autismspeaks.org/what-autism/asperger-syndrome.

Free and Appropriate Education (FAPE): "Mandates that school districts provide access to general education and specialized educational services. It also requires that children with disabilities receive support free of charge as is provided to non-disabled students. It also provides access to general education services for children with disabilities by encouraging that support and related services be provided to children in their general education settings as much as possible" as defined by http://www.ncld.org/parents-child-disabilities/ld-rights/what-is-fape-what-can-it-mean-my-child.

Individualized Education Plan (IEP): "Each public school child who receives special education and related services must have an Individualized Education Program (IEP). Each IEP must be designed for one student and must be a truly individualized document. The IEP creates an opportunity for teachers, parents, school administrators, related services personnel and students (when appropriate) to work together to improve educational results for children with disabilities. The IEP is the cornerstone of a quality education for each child with a disability. To create an effective IEP, parents, teachers, other school staff and often the student must come together to look closely at the student's unique needs. These individuals pool knowledge, experience and commitment to design an educational program that will help the student be involved in, and progress in, the general curriculum. The IEP guides the delivery of special education supports and services for the student with a disability" as defined by http://www.ncld.org/students-disabilities/iep-504-plan/what-is-iep.

Individuals with Disabilities Educational Improvement Act: "The Individuals with Disabilities Education Act (IDEA) is a law ensuring services to children with disabilities throughout the nation. IDEA governs how states and public agencies provide early intervention, special education and related services to more than 6.5 million eligible infants, toddlers, children and youth with disabilities. Infants and toddlers with disabilities (birth-2) and their families receive early intervention services under IDEA Part C. Children and youth (ages 3-21) receive special education and related services under IDEA Part B" as defined by http://idea.ed.gov/.

Local Educational Agency: "A public board of education or other public authority legally constituted within a State for either administrative control or direction of, or to perform a service function for, public elementary schools or secondary schools in a city, county, township, school district, or other political subdivision of a State, or for a combination of school districts or counties that is recognized in a State as an administrative agency for its public elementary schools or secondary schools" as defined by http://www.ed.gov/race-top/district-competition/definitions.

No Child Left Behind Act: "The No Child Left Behind Act of 2001 (NCLB) is the most recent iteration of the Elementary and Secondary Education Act of 1965 (ESEA), the major federal law authorizing federal spending on programs to support K-12 schooling. ESEA is the largest source of federal spending on elementary and secondary education. Although NCLB covers numerous federal education programs, the law's requirements for testing, accountability, and school improvement receive the most attention. NCLB requires states to test students in reading and mathematics annually in grades 3-8 and once in grades 10-12. States must test students in science once in grades 3-5, 6-8, and 10-12. Individual schools, school districts and states must publicly report test results in the aggregate and for specific student subgroups, including low-income students, students with disabilities, English language learners, and major racial and ethnic groups. NCLB required states, school districts, and schools to ensure all students are proficient in grade-level math and reading by 2014. States define grade-level performance. Schools must make "adequate yearly progress" toward this goal, whereby proficiency rates increase in the years leading up to 2014. The rate of increase required is chosen by each state. In order for a school to make adequate yearly progress (AYP), it must meet its targets for student reading and math proficiency each year. A state's total student proficiency rate and the rate achieved by student subgroups are all considered in the AYP determination" as defined by http://febp.newamerica.net/background-analysis/no-child-left-behind-overview.

This research was previously published in Challenges Surrounding the Education of Children with Chronic Diseases edited by Maria Gordon; pages 227-246, copyright year 2016 by Information Science Reference (an imprint of IGI Global).

Section 5
Diversity and Culturally Responsive Teaching

Chapter 30
Social Inclusion and Intercultural Values in a School of Education

Olga M. Alegre de la Rosa
University of La Laguna, Spain

Luis M. Villar Angulo
University of Seville, Spain

ABSTRACT

The aim of the study was to analyze the contextual and personal factors associated with student teachers' inclusive and intercultural values to minimize barriers to learning and participation. It also examined the role higher education played as a facilitator of social inclusion. Method. The sample was comprised of 1234 university students. Researchers applied the Guide Index for Inclusion (Booth & Ainscow, 2000) composed of three dimensions: Culture, Politics and Inclusive Practices. Positive elements emphasized the gender variable with highly significant scores on all dimensions. Besides, younger students with no cooperation between teachers and families didn't collaborate between teachers and family to promote inclusive attitudes. Moreover, it was noted that experience increases to more predisposition to the inclusion and recognition of barriers to learning and participation. As a conclusion, it was recognized that the principles of social inclusion may be influenced by variables such as gender, age, cultural experience and experience with people.

INTRODUCTION

Diversity is an inherent quality in human beings; consequently, each person thinks, feels and acts in a specific way in their lives. That mentioned diversity is expressed naturally in educational groups according to students' capacities, needs, interests, maturing rate and socio-cultural situations, among others.

Education authorities must equalise students' opportunities regardless of their personal or social situation in order to allow them to achieve a complete development of their potentials which will let them

DOI: 10.4018/978-1-7998-1213-5.ch030

be thoroughly part of the society. According to Pérez and Sarrate (2013), the university is an institution highly valued by students because it facilitates cultural, social and labour promotion, and since it impulses inclusive education. From this point of view, the university must help in training those pre-service university teachers which make them able to prevent and give answers to students' needs. This approach is related to teacher professionalism, motivation and continuous training, whereas working to promote inclusion in education is arranged as a way to answer to school diversity.

How teachers approach their educational work towards their students responds to the concept *barriers for the inclusion* was first developed by Booth and Aisncow (2000). This concept emphasises a contextual or social perspective on learning difficulties or disability, placing them between students and their context interaction: social and economic situations, educational policy and culture among schools.

The shortage of teachers who are qualified in inclusiveness complicates the quality of the education students receive, regardless of its type: religious or linguistic diversity, lack of culture or related to gender, different abilities, or use of various cognitive types (Alegre, 2006). The limited attention to student attitudes and especially to student diversity is part of the problem of an inclusive and intercultural education (Lalueza & Crespo, 2012).

In this sense, the authors' aim was to know the attitudes towards inclusiveness and interculturality of students of the Degrees in Preschool Education, Primary Education and Pedagogy at the School of Education of La Laguna, since they were going to be teachers and/or career advisers, and they could improve inclusive culture and integrative practice at school (Booth & Ainscow, 2000). Likewise, the fact of having carried out the study about future professionals in education allows authors to investigate the role of personal attitudes in the teacher training process, and to see if these attitudes will be modified during his or her university progress, affecting their school students (Antoniou & Kyriakides, 2013).

The study has taking place with primary and secondary school children (Darretxe, Goikoetxea, & Fernández, 2013; Furuta & Alwis, 2013; Roselló, 2010) and with university student teachers (Chireshe, 2011; Lambe, 2007; Sánchez, 2011). This work has been held on the Canary Islands, in particular on Tenerife, because it is a very important area placed between three different continents (Wedell, 2005, 2008), maximising changes in order to make inclusive attitudes more effective (Avramidis & Norwich, 2002).

BACKGROUND RESEARCH

Future teachers' attitude in any part of the world is seen as an essential concept for a better educational practice and policy, which progress to inclusiveness and respect towards the existing diversity (Delgado, 2003; Rajovic & Jovanovic, 2013). To manage this success will depend on the positive attitudes professionals in education have related to inclusiveness of any special educational needs (Doménech, Esbrí, González, & Miret, 2003).

In order to find a solution to these problems, it is necessary to change not only teacher training programs (Costello & Boyle, 2013), but also to analyse factors that might impact upon teacher approval of the inclusive principle and use of different and appropriate methodologies to make everyone feel included (Avramidis & Norwich, 2002).

The above-mentioned needs are not new, as inclusiveness has been consolidated in the philosophical basis used by Warnock's inform (1978), in the role of incorporating families in the education of children (Esquivel, 1995), and in current approaches of the *Index for Inclusion* (Booth & Ainscow, 2000), as positive mindsets to take.

Through these approaches and thanks to the combination of tools and resources used in the process of inclusiveness development at school, the interest is focused on how professionals in education mature and develop their own attitudes towards students, in order to help those students to build significant meanings, which let everyone's integration. In this way, inclusiveness becomes a valuable device system to make appropriate school programs and practices to cover students' educational needs with their schoolwork, communication or behavior (De Boer, Pijl, Minnaert, & Post, 2014; Sentenac, Ehlinger, Michelsen, Marcelli, Dickinson, & Arnaud, 2013).

According to Idol's idea (2006), this does not mean students with higher educational needs should receive an academic curriculum which is different to the rest of students, as for inclusiveness only happens when students with learning difficulties or disabilities receive the complete academic curriculum from the general education programme. The author emphasized that inclusive attitudes are reinforced by beliefs in a highly attractive whole group.

Current contributions related to inclusive education (Alegre & Villar, 2010; Poon-McBrayer & Wong, 2013; Unianu, 2011; Verdugo, 2009; Vlachou, Didaskalou, & Voudorri, 2009; Wehmeyer, 2009) have shown that inclusiveness demand an analysis of change processes and a follow-up of educational cognitive, physical, emotional and cultural practices, and most important of all suggestions for home-to-school connections and real life classroom settings improvement.

Symeonidou and Phtiaka (2009) have carried out an analysis of inclusive and intercultural education through training courses for teachers related to the change of attitudes via educational practice. In this sense, the aim of inclusive education was to enlarge values that lead to the improvement and development of a secure, educational, integrated and conciliatory community. Those inclusive values must be common among teachers, students and families as a model to enrich the school setting.

It is also necessary to know about how student teachers assume school children inclusiveness and integration, being essential to deal with those two concepts from a wider perspective, which takes into account a culture of school transformation to look after diversity and current student educational needs, such as reading, writing, number work or understanding information expressing themselves or understanding what others are saying.

This culture, in support of engaging students who seem unreachable, and for diversity of learning activities must develop cooperative, plural and respectful attitudes and behaviours, regardless of student origin or their physical, psychological or social condition (Alegre, 2012). Examining future teacher attitudes helps in knowing the process of inclusive-attitude constructions in students, facilitating that production of meanings that let everyone's integration. These concepts on developing intrinsic motivation where analysed by Alegre and Villar (2010). Their work was focusing on how skilled teachers think and concluded that teachers' positive attitudes were key points for developing a right climate for inclusive and intercultural education.

According to Essomba (2008), the search of an inter and multicultural awareness are outlined among ten challenge questions and also ten key ideas presented to teachers concerning people immigration, civil rights, social reality, linguistic projects, intercultural curriculum, identity construction, religious practices, cooperation, school community, and racism.

TENTATIVE HYPOTHESIS

Tentative hypothesis of this study was designed to increase the knowledge on how demographic variables such as gender, age, contact with different people and intercultural factors affect the acceptance of principles of social inclusiveness by university student teachers.

MAIN FOCUS OF THE CHAPTER

Sample Issue

The sample was composed of 1234 individuals of the 1st and the 3rd year of Degree in Pre-school Education (PSED), Degree in Primary Education (PE) and Degree in Pedagogy (P) from the School of Education at the University of La Laguna.

Variables like gender, age, credentials, year of studies and experience in special and intercultural education were taken into account. The students selected for the sample were at their 1st year – because those have been students for a shorter period of time – and 3rd year of university studies – because it was the last set up year on progress. The sample was tried to be intentionally similar among the different degrees.

Women percentage ($n= 927, 75.1\%$) was higher than men percentage ($n=307, 24.9\%$). Regarding degrees, the highest weight was for PE (37.8%), followed by PSED (35%) and P (27.1%). Ages varied between 18-22 years ($n= 790, 64\%$), 23-27 years ($n= 329, 26.7\%$), 28-32 years ($n= 64, 5.2\%$), 33-40 years ($n= 44, 3.6\%$), 41 years or more ($n= 7, 0.6\%$). 55.2% of students was on the first stage and 44.8% was on the second stage. On the one hand, the obtained information indicated that most part of students did not have experience – or have a short period of experience, between 0-3 years ($n= 1177, 95.4\%$) – in the intercultural field. On the other hand, there was a low percentage of students with experience, between 4-8- years ($n= 56, 4.5\%$). Related to experience and/or contact with disable people, 97.3% ($n= 1201$) answered they had had experience for about 0-3 years, while 2.7% ($n= 33$) had had it for about 4-8 years.

Debate: Instrument Selection

The instrument used for this work was a questionnaire adapted from the guide *Index for Inclusion* (Booth & Ainscow, 2000), called *Questionnaire about Attitudes towards Inclusion and Interculturality* (QAII), validated adaptation in previous studies by Alegre and Villar (2012) and initially suggested as a programme by Booth and Ainscow (2000).

Controversies: Validity of Measures

The questionnaire QAII measured attitudes in students and their conceptualization of inclusiveness and interculturality, thanks to 45 items, classified in the three dimensions of *Index for Inclusion* (Booth & Ainscow, 2000) and designed in a Likert scale of four alternatives (1= Not important; 2= Not very important; 3= Important; 4= Very important). The three dimensions of QAII are the following:

- **Creating Inclusive Culture:** 13 items composed this dimension. Its objective is to impulse values to improve and develop a secure community. This dimension is divided into two sections: *Building community* and *Establishing inclusive values*.
- **Producing Inclusive Policies:** 15 items constitute this dimension. Its objective is a demand as a guaranteed success in measures and implication of teachers in order to secure student inclusiveness. This dimension is distributed in two sections: *Developing the school for all* and *Organising support for diversity*.
- **Involving Inclusive Practices:** 17 items comprise this dimension. Its objective is to advance forward in collaboration, cooperation and implication of the educational community. This dimension is split in two sections: *Orchestrating learning* and *Mobilising resources*.

The questionnaire was anonymous and voluntary. It was given to the whole sample of individuals and it was completed during teaching classes' timetable.

The QAII analysis was made through the statistics software package SPSS (v. 19). A descriptive analysis was carried out through ANOVA and *t of Student* for each of the items used on the sample of individuals. Cronbach's alpha coefficient for reliability was obtained for QAII (.919), which guaranteed exploratory research of student attitudes. Likewise, reliability coefficient of each section of the *Index for Inclusion* (see Table 1) was calculated and showed that *Orchestrating learning* was noticeably higher ($\alpha = .811$), followed by *Mobilising resources* ($\alpha = .757$).

Demographic Problem Results: Descriptive and Inference Analysis of Questionnaire QAII Dimensions

Related to students' age, some differences were found among higher punctuations depending on the section used in QAII. *Establishing inclusive values* obtained the highest punctuation on average among 41 years old or more (M= 3.74; TD= .406) and also among 33-44 years old (M= 3.64; TD= .348). On the contrary, the lowest punctuations were seen in *Organising support for diversity* among 18-22 years old (M= 3.32; TD= .456) and among 23-27 years old (M= 3.44; TD= .446) (see figure 1). The highest punctuation is in the section called *Developing the school for all* among people who are 33-40 years old (M=3.63; TD= .397), 41 years old or more (M= 3.59; TD= .251), 23-27 years old (M= 3.57; TD= .391), 28-32 years old (M= 3.47; TD= .476), and 18-22 years old (M= 3.54; TD= .391).

Table 1. Distribution of dimensions, sections and items

Dimensions	Sections	Distribution of items	Reliability	TD
Inclusive culture	Building community	1,2,3,4,5,6,7.	.669	.400
	Establishing inclusive values	8,9,10,11,12,13.	.590	.421
Inclusive policies	Developing the school for all	14,15,16,17,18,19.	.673	.399
	Organizing support for diversity	20,21,22,23,24,25,26,27,28.	.665	.489
Inclusive practices	Orchestrating learning	29,30,31,32,33,34,35,36,37,38,39,40.	.811	.389
	Mobilizing resources	41,42,43,44,45.	.757	.471

Figure 1. Average punctuation of the sample of individuals, according to Age

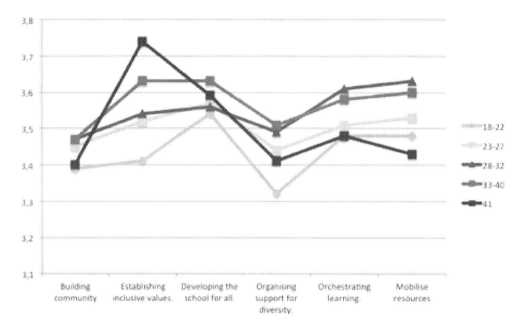

Taking gender into account (Figure 2), the highest values in women were in *Developing the school for all* (M= 3.60; TD= .386). Likewise, there were similar values in men (M= 3.40; TD= .462). In general, punctuation in both, women and men, showed positive attitudes towards inclusiveness and interculturality, being the lowest values on average those from the section *Organising support for diversity*, not only for men (M= 3.41; TD= .477), but also for women (M= 3.24; TD= .441).

Regarding intercultural experience, the sample with 4-6 years of experience had obtained a higher average on all sections, standing out results obtained in the necessity and importance of *mobilising resources* (M= 3.65; TD= .434). The lowest average punctuations were found in *Organising support for diversity*, among students in the sample with 0-3 years of experience (M= 3.30; TD= .456).

Lastly, and related to experience and contact with disable people, the statistic sample obtained was 97.3% of students have had a limited experience, the most relevant average punctuations were found in *Building community* among people with 4-6 years of experience (M= 3.78; TD= .782) and in the necessity and importance of *Mobilising resources* (M= 3.67; TD= .489). The lowest average punctuations were found in *Organising support for diversity* among students with 0-3 years of experience (M= 3.24; TD= .546).

Problem Analysis of Student Perceptions for QAII Questionnaire

T of Student tests (statistics software package SPSS, version 19) were carried out for each social demographic variable from the sample of students in each one of the QAII items (gender, intercultural experience and experience in disability) through the variance analysis (ANOVA) in age and following a statistic signification criterion .05. Significant differences were revealed in the variable gender, and it was even more noticeable in the dimension *Inclusive Culture*, specifically in the section *Building community*, t (471.426/1234)= -5.726, p< .000, and *Establishing inclusive values*, t (1232/1234)= -4.639, p< .000.

Figure 2. Average answers of the sample of students, according to Gender

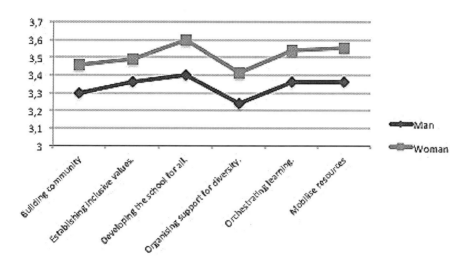

The dimension *Inclusive Policy* showed significant differences related to gender in both sections, *Developing the school for all*, t (472.678/1234)= -7.212, and *Organising support for diversity*, t (490.824/1234)= -5.517. Lastly, the dimension *Inclusive Practice* also showed significant differences in both sections: *Orchestrating learning*, t (462.541/1234)= -6.739, and *Mobilising resources*, t (471.717/1234)= -5.710.

After having taken *Experience in disability* into account, some differences were seen in the section *Building community*, t (1232/1234)= -2.215, p< .027, and related to *Intercultural experience*, there were only significant differences in the section *Organising support for diversity*, t (1232/1234)= -2.394, p< .017 (table 2).

Last, and taking into account the effect of age (table 3), results showed that the higher the range is, the more differences in three of the six sections (*Building community, Developing the school for all* and *Organising support for diversity*). The age ranges with the biggest difference between each other were 18-22 and 23-27 years old.

SOLUTIONS AND RECOMMENDATIONS

This study shows attitudes towards inclusiveness and interculturality among a sample of 1234 students of Degrees in Pre-School Education, Primary Education and Pedagogy at the University of La Laguna.

Once students were classified by their age, more attitudes towards inclusiveness and interculturality were showed in older individuals. This is a relevant aspect because those students were at the last stages of their studies and/or their age let them have some experience in inclusiveness and interculturality. Consequently, it facilitated their future professional labour in inclusive and intercultural curricular competencies (Arteaga & García, 2008).

Differences in *Organising support for diversity* are significant, as younger students do not think collaboration among teachers and/or families is necessary in order to strengthen inclusive attitudes. Related to this, there are numerous authors (O'Rourkey & Houghton, 2008; Villar, 2004, 2008) who claim that type of collaboration is a decisive element to promote inclusive curricular competencies. This situation

Table 2. Significant associations based on t of Student

Measure	Effect (Items)	Levene	t	p<	M	TD
Gender	Building community					
	5	.587	-3.336	.001	V= 2.82 M= 3.05	.923 .879
	Establishing inclusive values					
	8	.067	-3.581	.000	V= 3.00 M= 3.34	.849 .826
	9	.863	-3.027	.003	V= 3.14 M= 3.45	.816 .714
	Developing the school for all					
	17	.000	-4.191	.010	V= 3.58 M= 3.76	.589 .474
	Organising support for diversity					
	21	.001	-5.144	.000	V= 3.20 M= 3.71	.738 .625
	Orchestrating learning					
	35	.000	-4.483	.000	V= 3.34 M= 3.76	.678 .519
	Mobilise resources.					
	45	.000	-5.194	.000	V= 3.40 M= 3.70	.722 .577
	42	.016	-3.514	.001	V= 3.29 M= 3.62	.781 .682
Experience in disability	Building community.					
	5	.056	-2.215	.027	4-8= 3.27 0-3= 2.98	.849 .929
	Organising support for diversity					
	20	.032	-3.007	.003	4-8= 3.73 0-3= 3.38	.555 .616

implies the necessity of a deep analysis of competency development and achievement in the analysed Degrees with the purpose of obtaining a higher use and coordination.

As it has remarked, the importance of an inclusive education consists in involving all the children from a specific community, so they will learn together, regardless of their personal, cultural or social conditions, including those children with any disability (Reyes, 2010). Moreover, student academic training in inclusive competencies has to stand up to the necessity of reinforcing this knowledge and experience of future teachers.

In relation to gender, women are more receptive than men when applying *Inclusive culture, policy and practice*, standing out a higher difference between men and women in items of the section *Building community*, which alludes to the importance of working as a team in an educational community in order to create an inclusive philosophy. Some authors like Firestone (1996), Graham (1996) and Alegre (2006) emphasized that it was necessary to have a teaching commitment regardless of gender or attitude for a good school working.

Table 3. Significant feature associations based on ANOVA by Age

Measure	Effect (Items)		Levene	gl	F	p<	Post hoc Tukey	M	TD
Age	Building community								
	5		.631	4	7.118	.000	18-22 with 23-27 23-27 with 33-40	18-22=2.90 23-27=3.20 33-40=2.70	.936 .874 .991
	Developing the school for all								
	14		.087	4	3.864	.004	18-22 with 23-27	18-22=3.41 23-27=3.60	.709 .671
	Organising support for diversity								
	20		.283	4	3.698	.049	18-22 with 23-27	18-22=3.40 23-27=3.56	.619 .587
	25		.634	4	4.491	.001	18-22 with 23-27	18-22=3.25 23-27=3.48	.691 .662
	27		.578	4	4.666	.001	18-22 with 23-27	18-22=3.21 23-27=3.47	.843 .782

Besides, the necessity of a better collaboration between teachers and families is the second more valued item by women. Connected with this, authors like Gallavan (1998), Mateos, Torrejón, Parra, and Pérez (2008), and Kugelmass (2001) support the importance of communication among members who are part of the school community, especially between mothers and fathers. This contributes to create learning communities where the whole group is involved and it contributes to remove those barriers that damage learning and participation (Ainscow, 1999, 2002, 2004).

Meanwhile, Aguado (2004) described in her work the importance of the family-community dimension in students' and teachers' attitudes, as the means to reach global quality in educational contexts and to develop the intercultural approach. Like this, the author supported the active representation of an educational community on its whole as part of the usual innovation and school change environment.

Concerning intercultural experience among students, most differences were found in the section *Building community*. Results showed that the more teaching experience, the better willingness towards the construction of a secure community. Lambe and Bones (2006), and Cook, Cameron, and Tankersley (2007) pointed out that the more experience in diversity students had, the higher positive effects on social inclusion principles.

In relation to the effect of teaching children with disabilities, there were some significant differences in the importance and/or necessity related to collaboration between teachers and families, organising support for diversity and coordinating all ways of children support. Results of the study revealed longer teaching experience in special education brought more importance to that practice action.

In this way, Minke, Oso, Deemer, and Griffin (1996) showed that special education teachers held the most positive views of inclusion, as regular teachers in the inclusive classrooms. In these studies results highlighted that those teachers who were in contact with disabled children had more positive attitudes towards inclusiveness. In addition, they also had a higher perception of self-efficacy, competency and satisfaction.

It was equally necessary to point out the higher percentage of survey respondents who do not have teaching experience in working with disabled people. Previous studies presented by López, Echeita, and Martin (2009) proved that it was necessary to reformulate teacher training strategies so that reflexion about future situations in the classroom related to disabilities would be strengthened, in particular, those situations which could reinforce this type of students segregation.

FUTURE RESEARCH DIRECTIONS

In short, this study suggested teaching competencies, which make the whole university community be involved in values, related to support for diversity and to the importance of an education that favours inclusive and intercultural teaching-learning processes (UNESCO, 2011).

Authors provided recommendations to develop inclusive practices for School of Education students. They were committed for a program improvement tool at the University of La Laguna to assist university students in creating a safe, inclusive and caring school and classroom environment (Alegre & Villar, 2009).

However, in order to build a more just, inclusive and intercultural school community it is necessary to include and develop an environment by:

- Introducing effective practices that encourage barrier removal, as long as those material or non-material obstacles limit a secure and sustainable inclusive and intercultural education.
- Implementing academic programs for university students to increase their knowledge and understanding of inclusive and intercultural competences.
- Improving pre- and in-service teacher training, mentorship and team-building in order to share emotional attitudes, and inclusion and intercultural experiences, and
- Developing inclusive competencies about shared educational leadership based on cooperation and coordination among all members of the educational community.

CONCLUSION

Index for Inclusion had made it possible to share a sensitive and appropriate point of view of inclusive culture, policies and practices. *Index for Inclusion* dimensions and sections are suitable to be used in order to analyse and interpret the approval of social inclusion principles and values among students of Degrees in Education and Pedagogy at the University of La Laguna.

As a general conclusion, the initial hypotheses – which claimed that social inclusion for future student teachers may be influenced by variables like gender, age, intercultural experience and experience with different people – were accepted.

Particularly, data revealed existing differences between students due to age, regardless of degrees: the older the student teacher is and the longer experience he or she has, the higher predisposition towards inclusiveness and the better recognition of barriers to learning and participation.

REFERENCES

Aguado, T. (2004). Investigación en educación intercultural. *Educatio Siglo XXI, 22*(0), 39–58.

Ainscow, M. (1999). *Understanding the Development of Inclusive Schools*. London: Falmer.

Ainscow, M. (2002). Using research to encourage the development of inclusive practices. In P. Farrell & M. Ainscow (Eds.), *Making Special Education Inclusive: from Research to Practice* (pp. 25–37). London: David Fulton.

Ainscow, M. (2004, December 9-11). Developing inclusive education systems: what are the levers for change? *Paper presented at the Seminario Regional UNESCO "Salamanca 10 años después"*, Santiago, Chile. 10.100710833-005-1298-4

Alegre, O. M. (2006). Evaluación del programa de posgrado Educar en la diversidad por parte de los profesores participantes. *Revista de Educación, 340*, 299–340.

Alegre, O. M. (Dir.) (2012). Investigación sobre Competencias y Tecnología para la Inclusión y la Interculturalidad. Sevilla: Arial.

Alegre, O. M., & Villar, L. M. (2009). Desarrollo de competencias de diversidad en graduados y predicción de la calidad global de un postgrado. *Revista Brasileira de Formaçao de Professores, 1*(2), 69–103.

Alegre, O. M., & Villar, L. M. (2010). *Evaluación del postgrado universitario educar en la diversidad. Estudios y Ensayos*. Tenerife: Servicio de Publicaciones de la Universidad de La Laguna.

Alegre, O. M., & Villar, L. M. (2012). Ögretmenlik Mesleginin Degerlendirilmesi: Kariyer Gelisimine Yönelik Montorlugun Etkileri. In R. Yirci & I. Kocabas (Eds.), *Dünyada Mentorluk Uygulamalari* (pp. 115–132). Ankara: Pagen Aladami.

Antoniou, P., & Kyriakides, L. (2013). A dynamic integrated approach to teacher professional development: Impact and sustainability of the effects on improving teacher behaviour and student outcomes. *Teaching and Teacher Education, 29*(0), 1–12. doi:10.1016/j.tate.2012.08.001

Arteaga, B., & García, M. (2008). La formación de competencias docentes para incorporar estrategias adaptativas en el aula. *Revista Complutense de Educación, 19*(2), 253–274.

Avramidis, E., & Norwich, B. (2002). Teachers' attitudes towards integration / inclusion: A review of the literature. *European Journal of Special Needs Education, 17*(2), 129–147. doi:10.1080/08856250210129056

Booth, T., & Ainscow, M. (2000). *Index for inclusion*. Bristol: Centre for Studies on Inclusive Education.

Chireshe, R. (2011). Special Needs Education In-Service Teacher Trainers Views on Inclusive Education in Zimbabwe. *Journal of Social Sciences, 27*(3), 157–164.

Cook, B. G., Cameron, D. L., & Tankersley, M. (2007). Inclusive teachers' attitudinal ratings of their students with disabilities. *The Journal of Special Education, 40*(2), 230–238. doi:10.1177/00224669070400040401

Costello, S., & Boyle, C. (2013). Pre-service Secondary Teachers' Attitudes Towards Inclusive Education. *Australian Journal of Teacher Education, 38*(4), 129–143. doi:10.14221/ajte.2013v38n4.8

Darretxe, L., Goikoetxea, J., & Fernández, A. (2013). Análisis de prácticas inclusivas y exclusoras en dos centros educativos del País Vasco. *Actualidades Investigativas en Educación*, *13*(2), 105–134.

De Boer, A., Pil, S. J., Minnaert, A., & Post, W. (2014). Evaluating the Effectiveness of an Intervention Program to Influence Attitudes of Students Towards Peers with Disabilities. *Journal of Autism and Developmental Disorders*, *44*(3), 572–583. doi:10.100710803-013-1908-6 PMID:23982486

Delgado, M. (2003). Quién puede ser "inmigrante" en la ciudad? In M. Delgado, W. Actis, D. Martucelli, I. Palacín, & P. Sáez (Eds.), *Exclusión social y diversidad cultural* (pp. 9–24). San Sebastián: Tercera Prensa.

Doménech, V., Esbrí, J. V., González, H. A., & Miret, L. (2003). *Las actitudes del profesorado hacia el alumno con necesidades educativas especiales derivadas de la discapacidad*. Jornadas de Fomento de la Investigación. Universidad de San Jaume.

Esquivel, L. A. (1995). Análisis de la tríada familia-escuela-sociedad: Un estudio comparativo. *Revista Educación y Ciencia*, *12*(4), 51–61.

Essomba, M. A. (2008). *10 ideas clave. La gestión de la diversidad cultural en la escuela*. Barcelona: Grao.

Firestone, W. (1996). Images of teaching and proposals for reform: A comparison of ideas from cognitive and organizational research. *Educational Administration Quarterly*, *32*(2), 209–235. doi:10.1177/0013161X96032002003

Furuta, H., & Alwis, K. A. C. (2013). Differing process of inclusive education in Sri Lanka: Teachers' statements in government schools. *Journal of Policy and Practice in Intellectual Disabilities*, *10*(2), 122–122.

Gallavan, N. P. (1998). Why Aren't Teachers Using Effective Multicultural Education Practices? *Equity & Excellence in Education*, *31*(2), 20–27. doi:10.1080/1066568980310203

Graham, K. (1996). Running Ahead: Enhancing Teacher Commitment. *Journal of Physical Education, Recreation & Dance*, *67*(1), 45–47. doi:10.1080/07303084.1996.10607182

Harris, A. (2008). *Distributed school leadership*. London: Routledge.

Idol, L. (2006). Toward Inclusion of Special Education Students in General Education. A Program Evaluation of Eight Schools. *Remedial and Special Education*, *27*(2), 77–94. doi:10.1177/07419325060270020601

Kugelmass, J. W. (2001). Collaboration and compromise in creating and sustaining an inclusive school. *International Journal of Inclusive Education*, *5*(1), 47–65. doi:10.1080/13603110121498

Lalueza, J. L., & Crespo, I. (2012). Diversidad cultural, investigación psicológica e intervención educativa. *Cultura y Educación*, *24*(2), 131–135. doi:10.1174/113564012804932056

Lambe, J. (2007). Northern Ireland student teacher's changing attitudes towards inclusive education initial teacher training. *International Journal of Special Education*, *22*(1), 59–71.

Lambe, J., & Bones, R. (2006). Student teachers' perceptions about inclusive classroom teaching in Northern Ireland prior to teaching practice experience. *European Journal of Special Needs Education, 21*(2), 167–186. doi:10.1080/08856250600600828

López, M., Echeita, G., & Martín, E. (2009). Concepciones sobre el proceso de inclusión educativa de alumnos con discapacidad intelectual en la educación secundaria obligatoria. *C&E, Cultura y Educación, 21*(4), 485–496. doi:10.1174/113564009790002391

Mateos, G., Torrejón, M., Parra, M., & Pérez, Y. (2008). Necesidades de asesoramiento de acuerdo con padres y maestros de una escuela primaria. *Revista Intercontinental de Psicología y Educación*, enero-junio, *10*(1), 63-74.

Minke, K., Oso, G., Deemer, S., & Griffin, S. (1996). Teachers' Experiences with Inclusive Classrooms: Implications for Special Education Reform. *The Journal of Special Education, 30*(2), 152–186. doi:10.1177/002246699603000203

Morales, P., Urosa, B., & Blanco, A. (2003). *Construcción de escalas de actitud tipo Likert*. Madrid: La Muralla.

O'Rourke, J., & Houghton, S. (2008). Perceptions of Secondary School Students with Mild Disabilities to the Academic and Social Support Mechanisms Implemented in Regular Classrooms. *International Journal of Disability Development and Education, 55*(3), 227–237. doi:10.1080/10349120802268321

Pérez, G., & Sarrate, M.L. (2013). Diversidad y ciudadanía. Hacia una educación superior inclusiva. *Educación XX1, 16*(1), 85-104.

Poon-McBrayer, K. F., & Wong, P. M. (2013). Inclusive education services for children and youth with disabilities: Values, roles and challenges of school leaders. *Children and Youth Services Review, 35*(9), 1520–1525. doi:10.1016/j.childyouth.2013.06.009

Rajovic, V., & Jovanovic, O. (2013). The Barriers to Inclusive Education: Mapping 10 years of Servian Teacher's Attitudes Toward Inclusive Education. *Psychological and Pedagogical Survey, 14*(3-4), 78–97.

Reyes, M. M. (2010). La formación del profesorado. *Revista de Educación Inclusiva, 3*(3), 89–102.

Rosselló, M. R. (2010). El reto de planificar para la diversidad en una escuela inclusiva. *Revista Iberoamericana de Educación, 51*(4), 1–10.

Sánchez, A. (2011). La Universidad de Almería ante la integración educativa y social de los estudiantes con discapacidad: Ideas y actitudes del personal docente e investigador. The University of Almería and the educational and social integration of students with disabilities: ideas and attitudes held by teaching/research staff. *Revista de Educación, 354*, 575–603.

Sentenac, M., Ehlinger, V., Michelsen, S. I., Marcelli, M., Dickinson, H. O., & Arnaud, C. (2013). Determinants of inclusive education of 8–12 year-old children with cerebral palsy in 9 European regions. *Research in Developmental Disabilities, 34*(1), 588–595. doi:10.1016/j.ridd.2012.09.019 PMID:23123872

Symeonidou, S., & Phtiaka, H. (2009). Using teachers' prior knowledge, attitudes and beliefs to develop in-service teacher education courses for inclusion. *Teaching and Teacher Education, 25*(4), 543–550. doi:10.1016/j.tate.2009.02.001

UNESCO. (2011). *Enhancing Effectiveness of EFA Coordination*. Paris: UNESCO.

Unianu, E. M. (2012). Teachers' attitudes towards inclusive education. *Procedia: Social and Behavioral Sciences*, *33*, 900–904. doi:10.1016/j.sbspro.2012.01.252

Verdugo, M. A. (2009). El cambio escolar desde una perspectiva de calidad de vida. *Revista de Educación*, *349*, 23–43.

Villar, L. M. (Ed.). (2004). *Capacidades docentes para una gestión de calidad en Educación Secundaria*. Madrid: McGraw-Hill.

Villar, L. M. (2008). Competencias básicas para uso y dominio de los nuevos medios e instrumentos. In M. L. Sevillano (Coord.). *Nuevas tecnologías en educación social* (pp. 53–84). Madrid: McGraw Hill.

Vlachou, A., Didaskalou, E., & Voudouri, F. (2009). Adaptaciones en la enseñanza de los maestros de educación general. *Revista de Educación*, *349*, 179–201.

Warnock, H. M. (1978). *Special Educational Needs. Report of the Committee of Enquiry into the Education of de Handicapped Children and Young People*. London: HMSO.

Wedell, K. (2005). Dilemmas in the quest for inclusion. *British Journal of Special Education*, *32*(1), 3–11. doi:10.1111/j.0952-3383.2005.00363.x

Wedell, K. (2008). Confusion about inclusion: Patching up or system change? *British Journal of Special Education*, *35*(3), 127–135. doi:10.1111/j.1467-8578.2008.00386.x

Wehmeyer, M. (2009). Autodeterminación y la tercera generación de prácticas educativas de inclusión. *Revista de Educación*, *349*, 45–67.

This research was previously published in the Handbook of Research on Administration, Policy, and Leadership in Higher Education edited by Siran Mukerji and Purnendu Tripathi; pages 518-531, copyright year 2017 by Information Science Reference (an imprint of IGI Global).

Chapter 31
Critical Practices for Teaching and Learning in Global Contexts:
Building Bridges for Action

Ann E. Lopez
University of Toronto, Canada

Elsie L. Olan
University of Central Florida, USA

ABSTRACT

This chapter examines critical practices and agency of teachers as they wrestle with issues of diversity in the teaching and learning process. Using a framework of transcultural education and culturally responsive teaching it draws on research conducted in Southern Ontario, Canada and Central Florida, areas with large and growing diverse populations. We posit that schools are sites of social learning and cultural border crossing, where dominant discourses must be disrupted and the lived experiences of diverse students brought into the center of the teaching and learning process. Through the use of narratives and critical reflection teachers critically examined ways to develop agency and take action to create change. The findings highlighted in this chapter have significance for experienced and novice teachers, teacher educators and faculties of education and school leaders who are seeking to address issues of diversity and equity in critical ways.

INTRODUCTION

In this chapter we examine critical practices and agency of teachers as they wrestle with issues of diversity in the teaching and learning process. Advances in technology, the movement of capital, and the migration of people have created a world where borders are shrinking and social issues are global as well as local. We argue that schools are sites of social learning and cultural border crossing, where

DOI: 10.4018/978-1-7998-1213-5.ch031

dominant discourses must be disrupted and the lived experiences of diverse students brought into the center of the teaching and learning process. Focus on critical practices and actions of teachers can illuminate possibilities and impact agency. Economically advanced countries are becoming more ethnically, culturally, racially, linguistically and religiously diverse. People are living in multiple and overlapping communities and students have become increasingly diverse (Haan, 2012). In Canada, the population is projected to become more diverse over the next two decades. According to Statistics Canada (2016), by 2031 between 25 and 28% of Canada's population could be foreign born, between 20 and 32% could belong to a visible minority group, and visible minorities will make up 63% of the population in Toronto and 59% of the population of Vancouver. In the United States by 2044 more than half of all Americans are projected to belong to a minority group (any group other than non-Hispanic White alone), and by 2060 nearly one in five of the nation's total population is projected to be foreign born (United States Department of Commerce, 2015).

With these kinds of population movements and demographic shifts, it is important that students are prepared to live in a world that extends beyond their own experiences and engage in dialogue to gain deeper understanding of others so that they can participate fully in civic life. The new civic life calls for students to move across and within cultural borders. Critical discourses and actions are needed to broaden our knowledge of others, where transformation takes place through activism and creativity in classrooms and schools. Au (2009) suggests that discourses on transnational identities and multicultural classrooms take place within a context of immigration, globalization and colonization, where students' identities today are multidimensional and transnational. Educators must be brave and respond to difference and diversity within the schooling population, ensuring that curriculum, pedagogy, and texts reflect the diverse knowledge, experiences of students' history, ideas, lived experiences and struggles (Dei & Doyle-Woods, 2009).

We draw on transcultural education and culturally responsive pedagogy as theoretical frames to ground this work. These approaches open up spaces for discussion about diversity and equity in our increasingly globalized world where new epistemologies are formed and critical questions raised. They provide avenues through which existing knowledge can be critiqued, and power dynamics and injustices identified (McLaren, 2003). We came together on this project as scholars and researchers who live and work in areas of Canada and the United States that are very diverse, with common interests to better understand ways that educators can more effectively and critically respond to the growing diversity that are in schools. Teachers are called on to ensure that students are engaged in learning so that they can become global civic learners armed with the skills and knowledge that current realities demand. Robinson (2011) argues that if we are to efficiently teach and employ research to benefit ethnically, culturally and linguistically diverse learners toward what we perceive as being academic success, then major changes are required and education cannot be business as usual. The chapter represents part of larger studies that were conducted in Southern Ontario, Canada and Central Florida in the United States, areas with large and growing diverse populations as represented by the statistics. The United States population increased by 9.7% or 27.3 million people between 2000 and 2010 and net international migration accounted for 3.2% of the 2010 population. In Canada, net international migration for this period was 2.2 million people, representing 6.5% of the 2010 population (Norris, 2012). While Canada appears to be taking in more immigrants than the United States the trend is still up for both.

With countries, cities, and schools becoming increasingly more diverse, the focus on student achievement and engagement has become front and center. To achieve this there is greater need for deeper cultural understanding by teachers. First we explore transcultural education and culturally responsive pedagogy as frameworks that allow for the disruption of taken-for-granted practices and possibilities for the critical action and agency. Next we share the research context and methodology and end with a discussion of findings from our research that offer critical praxis and agency and concluding thoughts. Through participants' narratives and reflections we examine ways that diverse students are brought into the center of the teaching and learning process. We believe that if we are to have a more prosperous society, where all students feel valued and are fully prepared to participate in a global world, as educators we must act in the face of immense change in the social fabric of our societies.

Transcultural Education and Culturally Responsive Pedagogy

Transcultural education interrogates difference and raises critical questions (Cahill, 2013). Aldridge, Kilgo, and Chrisensen (2014) suggest that transcultural education allows for issues of equity and diversity to be examined critically, where culture is seen as fluid, challenging stereotypes and all forms of discrimination. Hou (2013) argues that a transcultural approach builds capacity for individuals and groups to navigate and traverse shifting cultural terrains, connects across social and cultural boundaries and offers educators a way to address the challenges that they face. Drabble, Sen, and Oppenheimer (2012) suggest five interrelated dimensions of transcultural education:

1. Recognizing the importance of culture;
2. Examining the dynamics of power, privilege and oppression;
3. Positionality and self-reflexivity;
4. Respectful partnerships with others; and
5. Culturally responsive practices.

Ladson-Billings (2014) suggests that researchers and practitioners embrace a more dynamic view of culture, that is fluid and encompasses all aspects of emergent global identities, multiplicities of identities, and experiences. This requires critical reflection and self-reflexivity on the part of teachers. Positionality and self-reflexivity looks at how the self is implicated in relation to others influenced by our shifting and multiple identities. Sultana (2007) argues that being reflexive about one's own positionality means reflecting on how one behaves when faced with differing power relations and how this influences methods, interpretations, and knowledge production. As such we must examine the context of institutional, social, and political realities in schools. Through respectful partnerships with others in the teaching and learning process, educators respond to diversity and promote equitable school practices that build connections between schools and communities.

Theorists, such as Gay (2000; Villegas & Lucas, 2002) suggest that culturally responsive pedagogy recognizes that students learn differently and these differences may be connected to background, language, family structure and social or cultural identity. Brown-Jeffy and Cooper (2011) argue that diverse students must be intentionally nurtured in order to create and facilitate effective conditions for learning. Student diversity is seen in terms of student strengths; and opportunities are presented for enhancing learning rather instead of seeing diversity as challenges and/or deficits of the student or particular community (Ontario Equity and Inclusive Strategy, 2014). Culturally responsive pedagogy embodies professional, political, cultural, ethical, and ideological dispositions that supersede mundane teaching acts, but is centered in fundamental beliefs about teaching, learning, students, their families, their communities.

Culturally responsive pedagogy is unyielding commitment to see student success become less rhetoric, and more of a reality (Howard, 2012). Howard further suggests that

Culturally responsive pedagogy is situated in a framework that recognizes the rich and varied cultural wealth, knowledge, and skills that diverse students bring to schools, and seeks to develop dynamic teaching practices, multicultural content, multiple means of assessment, and a philosophical view of teaching that is dedicated to nurturing student's academic, social, emotional, cultural, psychological, and physiological well being" (p. 3).

Culturally responsive pedagogy empowers students intellectually, socially, emotionally, and politically by using cultural referents to impart knowledge, skills, and attitudes (Ladson-Billings, 1995). Like transcultural education, culturally responsive pedagogy is multidimensional and encompasses all aspects of education. These frameworks provide spaces where theory can be brought to action and alternative ways of knowing or counter narratives to dominant ideologies posited. Counter narratives center voices that have been excluded from educational discourse to bear on the teaching and learning process.

By examining teachers' narratives both in Canada and the Unites States, scholars, researchers, and practitioners gain deeper understandings of the possibilities and importance of critical engagement in an increasingly global context. Building understanding across experiences calls for the disruption and interrogation of practices that exclude many marginalized groups from the educative process. Dialogic interactions presented in these narratives are important because it is through dialogic expression that ideas are probed, questioned and reflected upon. Social encounters that characterize the nature of narratives are weaved throughout the teachers' stories. They share a common assumption that there is a connection between life as it is lived and life as told in personal narratives (Milner & Howard, 2013). According to Milner and Howard (2013), "similar to narrative, counter-narrative provides a space for researchers to share teachers' (and others') experiences in ways that have not necessarily been told" (p. 541).

Through the process of reflection, self-discovery, and inquiry, teachers engaged with ways to disrupt the taken-for-granted notions of schooling, connecting students' experiences to the curriculum, across boundaries and the experiences of others. Through this process counter-narratives also emerge. Milner and Howard (2013) argue that "a counter-narrative provides space for researchers to *reinterpret, disrupt* or *to interrupt* pervasive discourses that may paint communities and people, particularly communities and people of color, in grim, dismal ways" (p. 542). Ladson-Billings (1998) argues in favor of counter-narratives as a means to study and define realities that are juxtaposed to prevalent narratives. Counter-narratives open doors to disruptions and re-interpretations of reality as expressed through pervasive, socially accepted stories.

RESEARCH CONTEXT

Research was conducted with teachers all of whom worked schools located in urban settings in South Eastern United States and Southern Ontario, Canada. In the United States, teachers were in-service teachers enrolled in a large publicly funded university serving graduate and undergraduate students. In Canada, research participants all worked in diverse schools in Southern Ontario. This represents part of a larger study parts of which have been published elsewhere see (Lopez, 2011, 2014). Schools and classrooms in Southern Ontario and South Eastern United States are filled with students from all over the world. Classrooms and communities are more diverse than ever before, with many different cultural experiences and languages spoken. This chapter draws on data from eight teacher participants in Canada and the United States, all of whom were engaged in critical culturally responsive practices to enhance the educational experiences of diverse students as well as critical reflection and dialogic inquiry about their work as teachers. In the research process, we were both insider/outsider researchers as we have both been classroom teachers and school administrators. As such, we understand the tensions and possibilities of school life as teachers engage in dialogic inquiry.

Data Collection

Data were collected through semi-structured interviews, journals, and personal narratives. Teachers developed their stories as storied responses to issues that created moments of tension for them on their educational journey. The following questions guided the research:

1. How have the actions that you have taken in your classroom changed the experiences of diverse students in your classrooms?
2. How can the learning needs of diverse students be better reflected in the curriculum?
3. What moments of tension have you experienced on your journey to become more culturally responsive?

Through narrative pedagogy (Goodson & Gill, 2011; Olan, 2012) and narrative inquiry (Connelly & Clandinin, 1990) participants were also asked to critically reflect on the question: What happened in your class today? Narrative pedagogy as an interpretive pedagogy encourages teachers to inquire and challenge preconceptions and assumptions they may hold, and to think through and interpret situations they encounter from multiple and diverse perspectives while envisioning new possibilities for action. When teachers engage in narrative pedagogy students and teachers share and revisit their narratives while engaging in public and communal thinking, and dialogue turns to sharing and interpreting their experiences to discover new understandings (Dahlberg, Ekebergh & Ironside, 2003).

Data Analysis

Using a qualitative narrative study design, data were collected from in-service teachers. Researchers analyzed and interpreted narratives and counter-narratives using Goodson and Gill's (2011) three narrative features:

1. "All narratives encompass a sequence of events",
2. "All the personal significance and meaning[s] are externalized through the telling of lived experiences", and
3. "All narratives are told to an audience and will inevitably be shaped by the relationship between teller and the listener" (p.4).

These three features are salient in teachers' narratives and counter-narratives and evidenced by our own examination of participants' process of self-discovery, inquiry, and growth. According to Bakhtin (1986) "at any moment in the development of the dialogue there are immense, boundless masses of forgotten contextual meanings, but at certain moments of dialogues subsequent development along the way they are recalled and invigorated in renewed form (in a new context)" (p.170).

Through critical dialogues teachers inform their pedagogical and leadership practices and beliefs, recognizing opportunities where students, community members and educators can engage in transformative learning and action. Mezirow (2003) defined transformative learning as a process where "the learner undergoes a conscious recognition of the difference between [the learner's] old viewpoint and new one and makes a decision to appropriate the newer perspective as being of more value" (p. 105). Through critical narratives teachers become aware of their assumptions, suppositions, and expectations of others while making an interpretation of their experiences. Narratives and inquiries about classroom events or practices facilitate reflections about the shifts in pedagogical practices experienced daily, critical reflection, dialogue and appreciation for practitioners' contextual realities. When teachers are afforded opportunities to share their narratives, they revisit their assumptions and make decisions regarding their cultural awareness and pedagogy and pedagogical practices and beliefs. Reissman (2008) suggests that the narrative form gives stories more power than even the resistant subversive acts and "makes the moment live beyond the moment" (p.63). Narratives were transcribed and coded thematically using a qualitative inductive design (Strauss & Corbin, 1990). These narratives were analyzed through narrative analysis where themes were examined based on reflexivity of the participant, transformation, critical action, and disrupting of traditional practices and knowledge. Rex and Juzwik (2011) argue that narrative discourse analysis helps educators to learn about themselves and others and to act more effectively.

Findings

We share the following narratives and stories that emerged from the research as themes of critical actions from which we might draw further insights and possibilities to engage diverse students and bring their experiences to the fore and build critical praxis. Critical praxis connects theory to action in ways that are transformative, creating meaningful change in the lives of students.

Language as a Site of Resistance

Language has become a flashpoint in the diversity discourse. We have seen in current times both in Canada and the Unites States, language has become a source of debate and dialogue (Tannen, 2012). As more immigrants whose first language is not English enter economically advanced countries or who do not speak what Paris and Alim (2014) refer to as Dominant American English (DEA) tensions have emerged. During a class about language, in-service teachers David and Ali[1] engaged in dialogue on what it means to embrace the experiences of students in the learning process. Tension emerges in the dialogue between David and Ali that speaks to the conundrum many teachers face. Both teachers struggle with ways to effectively teach diverse students about their culture that is valuing and empowering.

If we are to accept the idea that there is no correct form of English, as we all use this language differently, then how do teachers assess a student's performance with English in a fair manner? (David)

I don't completely agree with putting so much of the blame on standards. Of course, it makes our jobs very challenging and assessments can be unfair to all, but I think we, as educators, need to find the best option for our students. There is always a way to make it our own, it just requires more effort. Something

I agree with is English language can mean so many things in relation to a school subject, children's background and culture and teachers' understanding of students' learning and their own teaching. I think educators need to think about what and how they are teaching (Ali).

Ali reflects on the meaning of English language for her students and her role as a teacher and teachers' autonomy. Helman (2012) suggests that language is personal and it is a way to strengthen bonds and build relationships. When educators acknowledge and validate their students' language resources, students become more confident and empowered (Lopez, 2011). Despite the implementation of standards, curricula and new initiatives, this dialogue and exchange speak about the overt and covert ways of what, as Wink (2005) comments, is the "grooming" of students for academic success based on dominant values. Nicole reflects on the value of including the experiences and home cultures in the teaching and learning process, what Gonzales, Moll and Amanti (2005) call the 'funds of knowledge'.

From my experiences and theoretical knowledge, I was able to determine that people's experiences with literacy and language heavily influence students' interactions over time. Furthermore, the relationships that those connected to an individual (family, culture, community, etc.) have with literacy can directly influence how students' interacts with language. How then can teachers incorporate these collective temporal experiences when instructing an individual student and teaching a class? When teachers, family members or peers were supportive and provided opportunities and diverse contexts for authentic writing experiences, Dana's use of language and writing developed in positive ways. She invented forms to fit the purposes of her writing.

Nicole questions teachers' ability to foster collective temporal experiences in a changing world where multiple types of literacies are reflected in students' daily lives (learning and schooling). Wink (2005) reiterates that literacies "do not develop in isolation; rather, literate processes grow from families, from schools, from work, from cultures, from knowledges, from technologies, and so on" (p. 47). There is a difference between the language we use to interact on a daily basis, socially, and academic language. "Because learning takes place through academic language, teachers need to guide students to experience not only the content of their subject matter, but also the language with which it is learned" (p.29). Teachers need to be conscientious about students' literacies, cultures, and language learning experiences. Nicole's reflection speaks volumes about her awareness of students' literacies and the importance of teachers taking a united front to foster students' learning and their teaching. Lopez (2014) argues that leaders are teachers and must find agency within their work.

Identifying and Challenging Bias in the Classroom

Wynne (2001) and others suggest that teacher in addition to having expertise in their instruction should become socially conscious and politically involved and be risk-takers who participate in school decisions. The teacher must be a learner in order to teach, and in so doing, the teacher comes to own and produce knowledge rather than being controlled by it. With this liberating process, the teacher becomes a leader as well as develops the knowledge and makes decisions that shape practice (Darling-Hammond, 2006). Ryan and Rottman (2009) suggest that equity-minded educators find ways to make their schools and communities better places to work and live and employ political skills to better understand how those who advocate social justice principles can accomplish their goals. Teacher must take time to raise consciousness and create awareness about race, gender, social class, disability status and other forms of social identity to meet the needs of all students (Sledge & Morehead, 2006). Janet[2] who had been a teacher for five years recognized that she must identify and challenge her biases in order to disrupt the taken-for granted practices that might harm marginalized students.

In O's research course, I have learned how to identify my biases and how to switch my lenses to prevent those biases from affecting my pedagogical practices. Through dialogic interaction with O. and my peers, I feel confident in my ability to use culturally responsive teaching within diverse populations of students. In addition to this empowering confidence, I was also able to develop a revelation about my desire to teach English Language Learners with the help of dialogic practices.

As we develop cross-cultural understanding among students, it is also important for them to examine their own biases and assumptions about people who are different from them. Nicole recognized the importance of engaging students in work that allowed them to examine their beliefs. She noted:

Our discussion about culturally relevant teaching made me realize that the best way for me to choose the proper route of executing it within my classroom will be to really get to know my students. The students will be working on a "This I Believe" essay, in which they will espouse their deepest beliefs. From the feedback from this essay, I will work towards choosing appropriate supplemental instructional material for this unit.

Gravett and Peterson (2002) state that in "dialogic teaching the teacher mediates between students existing ways of thinking and doing and the formal knowledge (new learning content) with its associated way of thinking and doing, which students need to appropriate" (p.282). In an attitude of reciprocity among themselves, teachers reflect on their newfound sense of awareness, biases and pedagogical practices that will be conducive to transformative learning and teaching. This dialogic interaction creates an environment where teachers discuss, disrupt and negotiate with themselves and students while creating a space where cultures, languages and experiences are welcomed and valued. In one account Jill recalls her experience in her classroom with a student that created moments of tension for her and deep reflection:

He walks into my room every day with a brand new pair of shoes (every day of the week), he is Hispanic, he is in my intensive class, and he has a bad attitude. Second week of school it starts- he slides into class barely making it to class on time. Sinks into his chair, unprepared, no pencil, no paper, and no clue. I ask him why he doesn't have his supplies. His reply, "I ain't got any." No problem. I give him what he needs, we go a week completing a close reading lesson. I tell the students to please keep all of their work in their binder and do not lose it. We will need it later. Well that day is here and he again has no supplies and no work, but he has on a brand new pair of shoes that he must not make a scratch on. I get frustrated and he and I get into a little confrontation about being responsible, being prepared, and being successful. I say to him "If you spent as much time worrying about your work as you do about your shoes you wouldn't have as many issues in class." He kind of laughs, yet he still doesn't seem to care about his classwork. The next day he is suspended for ten days with the possibility of expulsion for pulling a knife on the bus. What I have learned from this interaction with this child and what I've learned through the readings is that his values and cultural identity are different from my own and that even trying to connect with him or to understand his background, his values is challenging to me. Perhaps even break down the barriers that stand between this child and his view on education, and authority. When I look more closely at this behavior it could be a product of his own self-efficacy. He is low in reading and writing, and he seems to be saying "Why bother". If only I could relate to him before it's too late. If only I'd have been more open. If only I tried to establish a positive interaction with him... to understand him as a person, he wouldn't be facing expulsion. Maybe I can be better at creating that "kind space" in my classroom. The what-ifs I feel I could be better prepared to create a more trusting environment in my class- not get bogged down with curriculum.

Jill's story is not only reflective, but is one of self-awareness. As she tells this story, she steps back and deconstructs events and subjects. All of these become objects of reflection and reflexive stances. She now is a spectator of this event, perhaps with different lenses. Before she can accept who her students are, she needs to recognize and accept her actions. Gay (2010a) suggests "culturally responsive teachers scaffold instruction and build bridges between the cultural experiences of ethnically diverse students and the curriculum content of academic subjects to facilitate higher levels of thinking" (p. 45). Jill examines the dynamics of power, privilege, and oppression her student might be facing while hoping to cultivate culturally responsive practices in her classroom. As Jill shares her story, she lifts the veil of the authoritarian figure and questions the multiple cultural perspectives that pervade her classroom and acknowledges her disassociation from her students' culture and community.

Disrupting the Scripted Curricula

Culturally responsive teachers that promote transcultural education and engage in culturally responsive teaching attempt to determine the multicultural strengths and weaknesses of curriculum designs and instructional materials and make the changes necessary to improve their overall quality. In her grade nine English class, Joan looked for ways to disrupt the scripted curricula. Teachers' dialogic inquiries are about their need to reflect, their concerns about materials, curricula and policies, and ways to improve and make these more culturally responsive. Joan moved away from the canon that did not connect with her students' experiences.

In her grade nine English comprised of predominantly boys who were struggling readers and disengaged from the prescribed text that had been used for many years, Joan made the conscious decision to embrace alternative forms knowledge, moving away from the traditional canons used in English classes. Dominant forms of knowledge have been 'canonized' and elevated to positions of importance that both teachers and students have difficulties disrupting. They hold positions and value in our education and lives that everyone believes students and teachers should know and revere (Nicol, 2008). It takes courage and leadership in the classroom and in pedagogical choices that are bold, which requires a kind of bottom-up activist teacher leadership that this article articulates. This means breaking with the tradition of the status quo. Taking an alternative approach was not easy or welcomed by some members of the department that she worked in. Joan introduced *Romiette and Julio,* a book about a young Hispanic boy and a young Black girl falling in love that addresses issues such as interracial relationships, gang violence, belonging, identity, bullying and acceptance as the choice of novel study instead of the established 'canon' *Romeo and Juliette*. In her reflections Joan wrote:

I had to find a book that they wanted to read and made sense to them. I am not saying that Shakespeare is not relevant, but I need to find ways to make them want to read...They are not leaving the books behind anymore in the classroom and some of them are eager to see what is coming next. They were struggling readers and I wanted a book that connected to their experiences. Each class one person was responsible to for a section, that way they were accountable. At first they were reluctant but as the story developed they got more into the book...Everything did not change overnight, some students still came late and I still had to stand at the door and look for them, but at least they were now becoming more interested in reading.

Changes in curriculum that meet the needs of diverse learners do not happen by themselves but require bold action on the part of teachers, in many instances going against the traditions in their schools and without the support of the school administration. Ornstein and Hunkins (2004) argue that limited engagement of teachers in meaningful decision-making has been a major flaw in educational reform efforts. Similar to Joan, Jill felt the urge and need as a teacher who believes in culturally responsive approaches to include materials that reflected her students. Jill asked in her class: "How do teachers find the time to research and find materials suited to teach? It is very time consuming and the pressures of standardized testing this can be very challenging."

Practitioners and scholars alike have sounded the alarm on the pressures and impact of the movement towards standardized testing on the learning of students, and particularly those who have been marginalized. According to Helman (2012), the one thing most everyone can agree on is that the accountability systems that are in place for schools, teachers, and students will not be going away soon. He suggests that formative assessment provides valuable information about students' strengths and pinpoints areas for growth. The hidden curriculum is real for many students of colour, diverse students and marginalized students. Wink (2005) defines the hidden curriculum as the "unexpressed perpetuation of dominant culture through institutional processes" (p.46). In a class discussion, Melba posed the following questions:

In the textbooks that we use for our students why aren't there more diverse authors whom are excellent writers being published and read? If we don't keep our students in mind (by doing research of what interests our students and what trends are happening within their generation) when creating the curriculum content how do we expect them to engage in the learning that we are hoping to take place?

Melba recognized, questioned and, challenged previously unexamined norms, trends, and practices that make up the curriculum she is required to use in her classroom. She initiated a discussion around curriculum implementations that perpetuates fragmented and disjointed teaching and learning. Self-reflexivity acknowledges that these disparities defines the educational inequality her students experience. Teachers who are not prepared to teach in ways that disrupt the scripted curricula can feel inadequate as they claim space for critical action. Stacy, a tenth grade teacher, in her reflections expressed feeling inadequate, but highlighted the benefits of co-constructing new knowledge in her graduate seminar. She wrote:

Fellow co-workers of mine boast about their paper/pencil rigor and their intensity to prepare students for every test that is thrown at them- I, however, don't teach to the test. I teach for significance, relevance, engagement, and motivation purposes; I teach to mold, to burgeon, and to ignite passions they didn't even know existed. I've always been this way; I've always tried to create a "third space," but prior to this class I felt (on occasion) that I wasn't as good as the other teachers in my Professional Learning Community, and maybe their test scores would be higher than mine. The research I have conducted in this class has *drowned out my concerns of "not being good enough- or rigorous enough." I am confident in who I am in my "third spaces," My students (just today) completed a group project that was engaging for all. They trust me, and in return, I trust them. I facilitated the classroom, but I didn't need too- I could have left for 20 minutes and everyone would have stayed on task. That is the epitome of a "third space" to me! A space where everyone feels safe, where everyone's engaged, where everyone feels challenged in a positive way, where everyone feels important and validated because w/o them there, class just wouldn't be the same. The greatest reward I have received so far this year came from the father of one of my 4th period boys. His email stated, "Mrs. Stacy, I don't know what you do in English class that makes my son so happy and interested, but yours is the only class he talks about when he gets home. Thank you!"*

Stacy admitted to disrupting the scripted curricula and examined her positionality in her professional learning community and acknowledged that while she is part of this school community she does not follow the system of scripted curricula that focus on deficits and deficiencies identified in students' achievement scores. Stacy in her opposition strives to provide her tenth grade students with learning environments where they work with others collaboratively in ways that not only use existing knowledge, but advances it by taking advantage of the interactions that occur in classrooms where diverse students work together.

From Fear to Care

Culturally responsive teachers avoid practicing superficial "caring" to a deeper caring that delves further into understanding students' backgrounds and cultures. Noddings (2005) asserts that caring and love is at the heart of all good teaching. In recent years, practitioners and scholars have foregrounded other inclusive ways of being in the classroom and caring, while implied this has not been at the front and center of the discourse in teaching. According to Nieto (2015) it is a deep caring that best defines teachers' commitment to students. Nieto argues that caring and love are more than just sentimental or superficial affection, it is about having high expectations and great hopes for all students, believing in their abilities, and respecting their identities. Nicole echoed the importance of care as an effective pedagogical tool, particularly in diverse classrooms. Nicole theorized what caring means after engaging with the text by Wilhelm and Novak (2011), *Teaching Literacy for Love and Wisdom*, in her class.

The chapter focuses on moving away from superficial "caring" to a deeper caring that delves further into understanding students' backgrounds and cultures. How can teachers work to ensure a culturally inclusive mindset through self-analysis, as suggested within the text?

Nicole's critical stance when inquiring about the implementation of culturally responsive pedagogy in their public school settings speaks to her willingness to engage at a deeper level. Gay (2010a) argues that in working with students of color, more teachers need to exhibit culturally responsive caring and to be "tough" and "take no stuff," in the sense of having high performance expectations and diligence in facilitating their achievement. Nicole recognized the importance of caring in the classroom and how it should be integrated into curricula.

Jill also saw the need to care and reflected on her actions in the classroom as she engaged or disengaged with her students that populated a new course and grade level she had not taught before. Jill noted:

That all seemed to change when I started teaching high school. For some reason I had it in my head that I had to be "hard", stern, serious with the high schoolers, because they were older and they had to buckle down and learn. They weren't babies anymore, they were old enough to know better, to act "right", and be responsible. I found myself struggling to connect with my students, as I was unhappy and frustrated. It wasn't until this past year that it dawned on me that these are still kids that still need nurturing, guidance, compassion, flexibility, and those creative fun loving opportunities. What I have learned from this course is that I need to be very responsive just the same as before; maybe even more.

As for Jill's sense of awareness, she to the conclusion that she needed to be responsive and foster an environment where caring permeates during and throughout instruction. Noddings (2005) purports that it is a mistake to restrict teachers to a curriculum that is entirely pre-specified. Good teachers need the flexibility to introduce new material and discard old in accordance with the needs of their students and shifting events. Jill's concern with the rigid curricula illuminates the challenges of implementing culturally responsive practices in the classroom. There is no quick fix for the problems teachers are facing. Teachers that care for their students' learning today will have their students' future present during all instructional activities. Teachers need to establish and maintain environments where caring and culturally responsive pedagogy are conditions for learning and teaching (Noddings, 2005).

CONCLUSION

Population movements and information flows have made the world more accessible and more diverse. In this increasingly globalized world where borders are shrinking and people from all corners of the world share the same space, particularly in schools, culturally responsive and transcultural education have a role to play, and educators must have what we call *global proficiency*. This refers to the knowledge about others that educators need to engage across cultural boundaries and gain deep understanding of the experiences and customs of others who are different from us. Culturally responsive and transcultural teaching that focuses on issues of equity and diversity that challenges the status quo and embraces a notion of culture that is fluid and shifting is useful in preparing educators for an increasingly globalized and shrinking world where different epistemologies and ways of knowing are valued. Culturally responsive pedagogy raises the critical consciousness of students to see beyond their immediate environments and take action to end oppression and discrimination no matter where that may be. New teachers will be entering a world that will be different from the one that they were socialized in and as such must be "globally proficient" to engage with an increasingly diverse student population. According to Gay (2010a), students must use the cultural knowledge, prior experiences, frames of reference, and performance styles of ethnically diverse students to make learning encounters more relevant and effective because students today bring various cultures, languages, and abilities to the classroom. Gay also argues that teachers must learn to communicate effectively in cross-cultural environments that characterize classrooms today. We posit the following tenets of *globally proficient* education building on culturally responsive and transcultural frameworks. Teachers in an increasingly globalized world:

1. Deconstruct/disrupt notions of globalization grounded within capitalist discourses and begin to the think of globalization in more culturally responsive ways that value the knowledge and experiences of groups that have been traditionally oppressed.

2. Create learning environments where achievement and excellence are not based on standardized tests, but on the ability of each student to make sense of their world utilizing critical thinking skills and demonstrating the ability to engage with and include diverse bodies of knowledge.
3. Embrace and include technology not as a panacea and vehicle for oppression, but as means of facilitating communication between communities.
4. Include resources and information that represents the various ways of knowing from different global and local communities.
5. Utilize pedagogies that include Aboriginal and Indigenous ways of teaching and approaches.
6. Posit counter narratives in response to hegemonic and dominant discourses.

This is not an exhaustive list of *global proficiencies*, but a place to begin the conversation and dialogue.

In order for these teachers to be effective, they can't and shouldn't stand alone. Teachers need to find support and productivity by collaborating with colleagues and community members (Lopez, 2005; 2013). Helman (2012) suggests that the most effective teacher (and one that will survive in the profession!) is the person who knows how to include others as team members. Janet, a teacher with five years of service questioned out loud the need for more training and supports for teachers on this journey. She reflected on this conundrum for teachers:

What workshops, seminar or trainings are there to inform educators of these different culturally learning strategies to better assist our students? Although I have learned several ways to accommodate and modify my instruction to benefit ELLS in my ...class, I would like to obtain more information so that I can help each individual ELL that walks through my classroom doors. In addition, I hope to gain more experience with working with these techniques in my internship. My goal is to never again experience "the sinking feeling" I get when it comes to not being able to effectively help an ELL succeed academically. I hope to achieve this by immersing myself into a plethora of research and theory pertaining to ELLs and their educational experience.

As these teachers engage in dialogic interactions, inquiries and reflections, their critical stance is being nurtured. Wink (2005) reminds us that critical pedagogy asks: Whose standard? Whose culture? Whose knowledge? Whose history? Whose language? Whose perspective? Through these questions, teachers disrupt the norm as they answer the call for more socially just and culturally responsive approaches to education are growing louder (Lopez, 2014). It is important to enhance this work and move towards that critical action through which teachers critically examine their acquisition of skills and knowledge, interpretations and assumptions and take action. Throughout these interactions, teachers recognize and share their discontent with curricula and institutional practices and policies. They identify disruptions that lead to their transformations and transformative learning and teaching. Finally, they share and explore new practices they have implemented in their classrooms.

REFERENCES

Aldridge, J., Kilgo, J., & Christensen, L. (2014). Turning culture upside down: The role of transcultural education. *Social Studies Research and Practice, 9*(2), 107-119. Retrieved from http://www.socstrpr.org/wpcontent/uploads/2014/10/MS06572_Aldridge.pdf

Au, W. (2009). Rethinking multicultural education. In W. Au (Ed.), *Rethinking multicultural education: Teaching for racial and cultural justice* (pp. 1–5). Milwaukee, WI: Rethinking Schools.

Bakhtin, M. (1986). *Speech genres and other late essays* (V. McGee, Trans.).

Brown-Jeffy, S., & Cooper, J. E. (2011). Toward a conceptual framework of culturally relevant pedagogy: An overview of the conceptual and theoretical literature. *Teacher Education Quarterly*, *38*(1), 65–84.

Cahill, C. (2013). Transcultural Community Building. *Transcultural Cities: Border Crossing and Placemaking*, 193.

Clark, C., & Medina, C. (2000). How reading and writing literacy narratives affect preservice teachers understandings of literacy, pedagogy, and multiculturalism. *Journal of Teacher Education*, *51*(1), 63–76. doi:10.1177/002248710005100107

Connelly, F. M., & Clandinin, D. J. (1990). Stories of experience and narrative inquiry. *Educational Researcher*, *19*(5), 2–14.

Dahlberg, K., Ekebergh, M., & Ironside, P. M. (2003). Converging conversations from phenomenological pedagogies: Toward a science of health professions education. In N. Diekelmann & P. Ironside (Eds.), *Teaching practitioners of care: New pedagogies for the health professions* (Vol. 2, pp. 22–58). Madison, WI: University of Wisconsin Press.

Darling-Hammond, L. (2006). Constructing 21st-century teacher education. *Journal of Teacher Education*, *57*(3), 300–314.

Dei, G. J. S., & Doyle-wood, S. (2009). Is wo whohaffi ride di stamm: Critical knowledge/multiple knowings – possibilities, challenges, and resistance in curriculum/cultural studies. In Y. Kanu (Ed.), *Curriculum as cultural practice: Postcolonial imaginations* (pp. 151–180). Toronto: University of Toronto Press.

Drabble, L., Sen, S., & Oppenheimer, S. (2012). Integrating a transcultural perspective into the social work curriculum: A descriptive and exploratory study. *Journal of Teaching in Social Work*, *32*(2), 204–221. http://www.tandfonline.com/loi/wtsw20 doi:10.1080/08841233.2012.670087

Garza, R. (2009). Latino and White high school students perceptions of caring behaviors: Are we culturally responsive to our students? *Urban Education*, *44*(3), 297–321. doi:10.1177/0042085908318714

Gay, G. (2000). *Culturally responsive teaching: Theory, research, and practice*. New York, NY: Teachers College Press.

Gay, G. (2010a). Acting on beliefs in teacher education for cultural diversity. *Journal of Teacher Education*, *61*(1–2), 143–152. doi:10.1177/0022487109347320

Gonzales, N., Moll, L., & Amanti, C. (2005). *Funds of knowledge. Theorizing Practices in Households, Communities, and Classrooms*. Mahwah, NJ: Erlbaum.

Goodson, I., & Gill, S. (2011). *Narrative pedagogy: Life history and learning* (Vol. 386). Peter Lang.

Gravett, S., & Petersen, N. (2002). Structuring dialogue with students via learning tasks. *Innovative Higher Education*, *26*(4), 281–291. doi:10.1023/A:1015833114292

Haan, M. (2012). Immigrant learning. In K. S. Gallagher, R. K. Goodyear, D. J. Brewer, & R. Rueda (Eds.), *Urban education: A model for leadership and policy* (pp. 328–341). London: Routledge.

Helman, L. (2012). *Literacy instruction in multilingual classrooms: Engaging English language learners in elementary school.* Teachers College Press.

Hou, J. (2013). *Transcultural cities: Border crossings and placemakers.* New York: NY Routledege.

Howard, T. C. (2012). *Culturally responsive pedagogy.* Change, Series Number: PPBP001-X052-2012, 1-9. Retrieved from https://centerx.gseis.ucla.edu/xchange/culturally-relevant-teaching/...pdf/at.../file

Ladson-Billings, G. (1995). Toward a theory of culturally relevant pedagogy. *American Educational Research Journal, 32*(3), 465–491. doi:10.3102/00028312032003465

Ladson-Billings, G. (1998). Just what is critical race theory and whats it doing in a nice field like education? *International Journal of Qualitative Studies in Education, 11*(1), 7–24. doi:10.1080/095183998236863

Ladson-Billings, G. (2014). Culturally relevant pedagogy 2.0: A.k.a. the remix. *Harvard Educational Review, 84*(1), 74–84. doi:10.17763/haer.84.1.p2rj131485484751

Lopez, A. E. (2005). *Implementing integrative anti-racist education: Negotiating conflicts and tensions utilizing experiential collaborative mentorship.* Unpublished Doctoral Dissertation, University of Toronto.

Lopez, A. E. (2011). Culturally relevant pedagogy and critical Literacy in diverse English Classrooms: Case study of a secondary English teacher's activism and agency. *English Teaching, 10*(4), 75–93.

Lopez, A. E. (2013). Embedding and Sustaining Equitable Practices in Teachers' Everyday Work: A Framework for Critical Action. *Teaching & Learning, 7*(3), 1–15.

Lopez, A. E. (2014). Re-Conceptualizing Teacher Leadership Through Curriculum Inquiry in Pursuit of Social Justice: Case Study From the Canadian Context. In C. Shields & I. Bogotch (Eds.), *International Handbook of Educational Leadership and Social (In) Justice* (pp. 465–484). Springer Publishing.

Lopez, A. E. (2015). Navigating cultural borders in diverse contexts: Building capacity through culturally responsive leadership and critical praxis. *Multicultural Education Review, 7*(3), 171–184.

McLaren, P. (2003). Critical pedagogy: A look at the major concepts. *The critical pedagogy reader*, 1.

Mezirow, J. (2003). Transformative learning as discourse. *Journal of Transformative Education, 1*(1), 58–63. doi:10.1177/1541344603252172

Milner, H. R. IV, & Howard, T. C. (2013). Counter-narrative as method: Race, policy and research for teacher education. *Race, Ethnicity and Education, 16*(4), 536–561.

Nicol, J. C. (2008). Questioning the canon: Issues surrounding the selection of literature for the high school English curriculum. *English Quarterly, 38*(2/3), 22–28.

Nieto, S. (2015). *The light in their eyes: Creating multicultural learning communities.* Teachers College Press.

Noddings, N. (2005). *The challenge to care in schools.* New York: Teachers College Press.

Norris, D. (2012). Cultural Diversity May Be Increasing in Both Canada and the United States, But Important Differences Remain. *Environics Analytics*. Retrieved from http://environicspr.com/wp-content/uploads/2012/08/US_Canadian_Diversity.pdf

Olan, E. L. (2012). *Stories of the past and present: What preservice secondary teachers draw on when learning to teach writing* (Doctoral dissertation, THE PENNSYLVANIA STATE UNIVERSITY).

Ontario Ministry of Education. (2014). *Ontario Equity and Inclusive Strategy. Reach Every Student: Energizing Ontario Education*. Retrieved from http://www.edu.gov.on.ca/eng/policyfunding/inclusiveguide.pdf

Ornstein, A. C., & Hunkins, F. P. (2004). *Curriculum foundations, principles and issues* (3rd ed.). Boston: Allyn and Bacon.

Paris, D., & Alim, H. S. (2014). What are we seeking to sustain through culturally sustaining pedagogy? A loving critique forward. *Harvard Educational Review*, *84*(1), 85–100. doi:10.17763/haer.84.1.982l873k2ht16m77

Reisman, C. K. (1993). Narrative analysis. *Qualitative Research Methods Series, 30*.

Rex, L., & Juzwik, M. M. (2011). *Narrative discourse analysis for teacher educators: Managing cultural differences in classrooms*. Cresskill, NJ: Hampton.

Robinson, K. (2011). *Out of our minds: Learning to be creative*. West Sussex, United Kingdom: Capstone.

Ryan, J., & Rottmann, C. (2009). Struggling for democracy: Administrative communication in a diverse school context. *Educational Management Administration & Leadership*, *37*(4), 473–496. doi:10.1177/1741143209334579

Sledge, J. R., & Morehead, P. M. (2006). Tolerated failure or missed opportunities and potentials for teacher leadership in urban schools? *Current Issues in Education*, *9*(3), 1–10.

Statistics Canada. (2016). *Ethnic Diversity and Immigration*. Retrieved from http://www.statcan.gc.ca/pub/11-402-x/2011000/chap/imm/imm-eng.htm

Strauss, A., & Corbin, J. (1990). *Basics of qualitative research* (Vol. 15). Newbury Park, CA: Sage.

Sultana, F. (2007). Reflexivity, positionality and participatory ethics: Negotiating fieldwork dilemmas in international research. *ACME: An International E-Journal for Critical Geographies*, *6*(3), 374–385.

Tannen, D. (2012). *The argument culture: Moving from debate to dialogue*. Ballantine Books.

United States Department of Commerce. (2015). Retrieved from http://www/census.gov/content/dam/Census/library/publications/2015/demo/p25-1143.pdf?

Villegas, A. M., & Lucas, T. (2002). Preparing culturally responsive teachers: Rethinking the curriculum. *Journal of Teacher Education*, *53*(1), 20–32. doi:10.1177/0022487102053001003

Wilhelm, J. D., & Novak, B. (2011). *Teaching literacy for love and wisdom: Being the book and being the change*. New York: Teachers College Press.

Wink, J. (2005). *Critical pedagogy: Notes from the real world*. Boston: Pearson/Allyn & Bacon.

Wynne, J. (2001). *Urban teacher leaders: Testimonies of transformation*. Unpublished paper presented at the AACTE conference, Dallas, Texas.

KEY TERMS AND DEFINITIONS

Critical Literacy: Critical literacy is an instructional approach, stemming from Marxist critical pedagogy that advocates the adoption of "critical" perspectives toward text. Critical literacy challenges the status quo in an effort to discover alternative paths for self and social development. This kind of literacy connects the political and the personal, the public and the private, the global and the local, the economic and the pedagogical, for rethinking our lives and for promoting justice in place of inequity (Shor, 2009).

Culturally Responsive Pedagogy: Culturally relevant pedagogy encourages teaching and learning that foregrounds learning across cultures. In order to maximize learning opportunities, teachers must gain knowledge of the cultures represented in their classrooms, then translate this knowledge into instructional practice" (Villegas, 1991). According to Ladson-Billings (1992) the primary goal of culturally relevant pedagogy is to empower students to examine critically the society in which they live and to work for social change. Culturally responsive pedagogy encourages learning environments that create space for students to utilize their cultural knowledge in the teaching and learning process in order to enhance their schooling experience and academic success.

Language and Literacy: Language has become a flashpoint in the diversity discourse. Using language to inform and develop students' literacy is imperative for teacher candidates' knowledge and understanding of the diversity of students, their experiences and school literacy learning. In our chapter, we share our views of language and literacy acquisition that is characterized as constructive within a sociocultural and culturally relevant context.

Narrative Pedagogy: The study of narrative pedagogy – as indicative in the research on reflective practice, life history and autoethnography – has its origins in the collection of interpretive 'thick descriptions' as developed by Geertz and other anthropologists (Frazier, 1937). They have also developed a sociocultural approach to pedagogy. Narrative pedagogy aims to explore how individuals, and in this case, teachers develop their intercultural knowledge and its influence in shaping their future role and practice as teachers; it is concerned with teachers' holistic attitude towards knowledge and its relationship to practice (Cochran-Smith & Lytle, 1999).

ENDNOTES

[1] The names of participants are pseudonyms
[2] Pseudonym

This research was previously published in Convergence of Contemporary Art, Visual Culture, and Global Civic Engagement edited by Ryan Shin; pages 46-62, copyright year 2017 by Information Science Reference (an imprint of IGI Global).

Chapter 32
The Role of Multi-Media in Expanding Pre-Service Teachers' Understanding of Culturally and Linguistically Diverse Classrooms and Furthering Their Professional Identities

Latisha Mary
Université de Lorraine, France

Andrea Young
Université de Strasbourg, France

ABSTRACT

This chapter details a qualitative study conducted with pre-service elementary school student teachers enrolled in a Masters course on cultural and linguistic diversity at one university teacher education institute in France. The study aimed to evaluate the impact of the course on the student teachers' understanding of culturally and linguistically diverse classrooms and questioned whether the use of multimedia resources throughout the course could contribute to fostering a greater sense of empathy towards their future culturally and linguistically diverse students. The data analysis reveals that the use of video in particular, in combination with theoretical readings, was highly instrumental in helping the students to understand the concepts linked to second language acquisition and in providing them with strategies for their linguistically and culturally diverse classrooms. The authors question whether the use of multimedia is sufficient to foster a sense of empathy in students and suggest further pedagogical interventions.

DOI: 10.4018/978-1-7998-1213-5.ch032

INTRODUCTION

The power of using multi-media resides in its ability to increase cognitive and emotional interest and attention by creating more coherent and authentic representations of knowledge. (Wankel & Blesinger, 2013, p.6)

According to many researchers and education professionals in Europe and around the world, pre-service teachers are increasingly faced with cultural and linguistic diversity in the classroom for which they are only slightly or not at all prepared. (Cajkler & Hall, 2012; Kuiken, 2014; Murakami, 2008; Schwartz & Mor-Sommerfeld, 2010; Thomauske, 2011). It has thus become necessary to develop intercultural skills and sensitivity to otherness among teachers. In 2005, a bi-national team (France-Scotland) attempted to address this problem within the European project *TESSLA* (Teacher Education for the Support of Second Language Acquisition) by designing, piloting and evaluating a teacher education course. The aim of the course was to sensitize pre-service elementary school teachers to the needs of their culturally and linguistically diverse students and to generate strategies and classroom practices that would support all students in their learning (Hancock et al, 2006).

Since its conception, the course has been adapted and delivered in a variety of contexts (Mary & Young, 2010; Young & Mary, 2010; Young & Mary, 2016). However, the sensitization of student teachers to the needs of their culturally and linguistically diverse pupils through collective reflection, and the development of tools and practices to support their learning, has remained a central concern. One of the objectives in the study described in this chapter was that, through participating in the course, student teachers would not only gain important knowledge but would also acquire the ability to empathize and become agents of change. Previous research has highlighted the fact that many student teachers come to such courses with already established attitudes and ideologies about language (conscious or unconscious) which act as roadblocks to gaining new awareness (Banks, 2001; Commerford, 2005; Garmon, 2004) and that knowledge of content and pedagogy alone are not sufficient in helping teachers to be effective (Horan & Hersi, 2011). In light of this challenge, the didactic model *Problem Based Learning* (Komur & Kogut, 2006) was chosen as the most appropriate approach for the course. It was hoped that this instructional method, based on authentic or real world problems, in conjunction with theoretical reading and the use of multimodal and multimedia resources and tools would provide a rich context in which the students could confront their ideas and engage with their learning within a safe space. This chapter aims to highlight in particular the types of resources used, the reasons underlying the choice of these, the ways in which they were implemented and their role in expanding pre-service teachers' understanding of culturally and linguistically diverse classrooms and in furthering their professional identities.

BACKGROUND

The training of teachers and educators to better take into account the linguistic and cultural diversity present in schools is a challenge teacher educator's face. Teachers and education professionals in general often lack the training necessary (Murakami, 2008; Wiley, 2008; Schwartz et al, 2010; Thomauske, 2011; Cajkler & Hall, 2012; Kuiken, 2014) to assist the increasing number of children for whom the school language is not the language spoken at home. Schools need professionals who have developed the capacity to empathize and an ability to understand others in their differences in order to reduce the gap between students and effectively teach increasingly heterogeneous classes. The barriers schools face are manifold and include future-teachers' limited knowledge of issues related to culture and identity (Santoro & Allard, 2005; Abdellak & Heidenreich, 2004), negative representations with respect to migrant students (Goï & Huver, 2013), and a lack of critical thinking enabling them to analyse school language education policies that can create inequality and marginalization (Gay, 2010; Jokikokko, 2005; 2010).

The European Comenius 2.1 project TESSLA (Teacher Education for the Support of Second Language Acquisition), supported by the Socrates program, was designed to meet these challenges. The specifications of the project included the development of curricula and materials for teachers to understand why and how they need to consider and develop the bilingualism of their students.

The Role of Empathy in Expanding Teachers' Professional Identities

Empathy is thought to contribute to an increased sensitivity to different cultures (Germain, 1998; McAllister & Irvine, 2002; Tiedt & Tiedt, 2010) and is seen as an essential quality to be promoted in teacher education, especially in courses which aim to raise student teachers' awareness of issues concerning diversity and social justice in their classrooms (Dolby, 2012).

The concept of empathy, which has both an affective (feeling what other people feel) and a cognitive (understanding others' situations) component, has also been described as 'taking on another's perspective' as well as being able to respond to another from that perspective (McAllister & Irvine, 2002, p. 433). One educational expert, Dolby (2012) emphasizes the important role that empathy plays for educational communities stating that educators in particular 'need to be able to empathize in order to act in a meaningful way' (p. 69). Dolby highlights the fact that although recent research in the area of neuroscience has shown that most humans possess the biological ability to empathize, other studies point to the fact that individuals are most likely to empathize with others who are most similar or closest to themselves (Bailenson, Iyengar, Yee and Collins, 2008; Ehrlich & Ornstein, 2010). This is in line with Acquah & Commins (2013), who remark that:

several studies have shown that most predominantly white and middle-class pre-service teachers have limited experience outside 'their world'; that is, they have had limited or no experience with persons from different ethnicities or social class prior to enrolling in a diversity course (Larke 1990; Nieto 1998; Ahlquist 1991; Carpenter 2000). This lack of or limited exposure to different ethnicities or social classes tends to reinforce pre-service teachers' stereotypical beliefs. (p. 2).

These findings contribute to our understanding of why this area remains a challenge for teacher educators desirous of raising students' awareness of and sensitivity to the needs of their linguistically and culturally diverse students, who, for the most part, do not share the same background and characteristics of many of their students and their families.

Various attempts have been made by teacher educators in the area of multicultural education to foster empathy in their students. Among the most successful initiatives are those in which students had the opportunity to come into contact with and/or spend time with individuals who were part of a minority group (McAllister & Irvine, 2002, Houser, 2008). Students reported that these experiences allowed them to better understand these individuals in a very personal way which contributed to a more positive vision of them and increased feelings of empathy. However, providing students with such experiences is not always possible, and raises the question of whether teacher educators could draw on alternative strategies/methods, such as the use of multimedia, to increase students' feelings of empathy.

For the purposes of this chapter the concept of using multi-media within the educational context is defined as the use of or combination of more than one means of presenting information with the goal of instruction. Mayer (2003) echoes this definition stating that during multimedia learning 'the student receives an instructional message that is presented in two formats- as words (spoken or printed text) and pictures (animation or illustrations) (p. 126). Brophy (2004) expands on this and describes multimedial narratives as those "in which *educational stories* are told in sound and picture, sometimes connected with text" (p. 133, highlighting by authors). The use of video in instruction in combination with texts and classroom interaction could thus be seen as a possible alternative strategy towards fostering empathy in students as illustrated below.

In one study by Lin and Bradford (2010) which aimed to evaluate the effectiveness of video in raising student empathy towards professors from ethnic minority background, one half of the students in the group watched a video giving general background knowledge of a particular professor (information on his home country and culture), while the other half watched a video giving more personal information on him. After each group watched the videos, the personal information group had more positive personal views of the professor, while the second group, who received general information, showed increased negative stereotypes of this professor. With regards to this study Dolby states that:

while preliminary, their research suggests that personal knowledge and connection – that which decreases the distance between human beings – increases empathy. As students began to know more about the professor as a person, they moved him/her from 'far' to 'near', or from outside of their circle of moral regard, to inside. (Dolby, 2012).

The results of this study also suggest that where personal contact experiences are not possible, the use of videos/multimedia presenting personal information regarding minority language children and their families, can be effective in altering students' perceptions and knowledge of them and can possibly contribute to increased feelings of empathy towards them. Several of the video extracts used in the course described in this chapter allowed the authors to present such personal testimonies. One of these video extracts presented a school project conducted in an elementary school in a multilingual classroom in France (Hélot, Young & Delforge, 2005a; Hélot, Young & Delforge, 2005b; Young, 2008). When showing extracts the authors were able to describe the background and school experiences of two Turkish children and to point out how they suddenly came alive during the project when their home culture and competences in their home language were valued at and by the school. The authors were able to focus attention on the expressions on the children's faces and to "tell their stories," which appeared to have a noticeable impact on the student teachers.

Other videos used during the course presented the web documentary 'Photo de Classe' (http://www.photo-de-classe.org/#/accueil) which featured children from a multilingual school interviewing their parents and/or grandparents about their experiences and feelings as a result of migration to France. The video *In Safe Hands* (Hyder & Rutter, 2001), about refugee children, presented the testimony of a mother who tells the harrowing story of why her family had to leave their country and speaks of the shame she feels at having to rely on the social services of the country to which she has fled. From the same video, a child from Sri Lanka speaks of the anxiety refugee families feel, living in constant fear that they might be forced to leave their new life in the UK, whilst another boy from war-torn Afghanistan explains how he misses his grandparents who had to stay behind. The very personal feelings of sadness and fear expressed by these children and their families seemed to raise the students' awareness of the hardships some of the children in their classroom may have had to face.

Giving Students Real-Life Examples of Good Practice

The use of video in teacher education has also been touted as an effective means of showing student teachers the realities of the classroom. Case studies of classroom practice presented through video provide rich details of classroom life and place the viewer within the action as a result of the distinct visual and aural qualities they provide (Clarke and Hollingsworth, 2000). Brophy (2004) highlights the affordances using videos of classroom practice can provide over the practice of sending students into different schools to observe classroom practices and specifies that viewing video extracts allows teacher educators to focus on one particular practice or aspect of practice and so to ask specific questions about what exactly is being viewed. In addition, video extracts enable teacher educators to choose examples of model practices which may be difficult to observe during random student teacher observations. According to one survey among teacher educators who regularly used video viewing as part of their curriculum (Perry & Talley, 2001), presenting examples of good practice was cited as being the most desired objective for using videos in teacher training classrooms.

The use of multi-media in the classroom has also been advocated as a means of promoting deeper understanding and learning. The rationale supporting this claim as stated in Mayer's (2002) cognitive theory of multimodal learning is, stated simply, that "people learn more from words and pictures than from words alone" (p.31). This element is linked to the nature of information processing and the fact that information processed through multiple channels is processed more deeply. In addition to this, Berk (2009) states that certain forms of multimedia, the use of video in particular, automatically elicit an array of feelings which can have powerful cognitive and emotional impacts on learners. Moreover, various authors have highlighted the ability of multimodal resources and multimedia in enhancing students' "sense-making", increasing their levels of motivation, participation and engagement (Wankel & Blessinger, 2013) and encouraging deeper forms of understanding (Veenema & Gardner, 1996).

Dolby (2012) warns, however, that just "understanding" the material is not enough to motivate people to act, and that teacher educators using multi-media to further students' professional identities need to ensure that the resources used present quality and carefully selected pieces of personal information, and in addition that the methodology chosen engages the learners in reflexion (for example, "social perspective taking", see Rios et al. 2003).

CONTEXT OF THE STUDY: EXPERIENTIAL LEARNING AND THE USE OF MULTI-MEDIA FOR DEEPER UNDERSTANDING AND ENGAGEMENT: THE CASE OF DEVELOPING EMPATHY AND CULTURAL AND LINGUISTIC SENSITIVITY IN THE TESSLA COURSE

Problem Based and Multimodal Learning

In close collaboration with our Scottish colleagues from the University of Edinburgh, the authors developed a training course for students in initial teacher training. The main teaching model chosen by the team, Problem Based Learning (PBL), was supplemented by theoretical lectures, personal narratives and videos of teachers, parents and children interacting in school and family contexts. A wide range of additional resources were used in the course to illustrate the content, to further understanding of the issues and to suit different learning styles. By adopting a multimodal approach including simulation, discussion and group work as recommended by Gellevij et al. (2002); Jewitt et al. (2000, 2001) and Sternberg et al. (1998), it was hoped that the course would have a greater impact on the students' representations and learning than more traditional models.

One of the central goals of the TESSLA course was to provide materials and resources which would enable the students to decentre and to develop a greater capacity for empathy with regard to their linguistically and culturally diverse students. As emphasized above, research supports the idea that in order to adopt another's perspective, students need multiple contact points with different viewpoints and experiences. Therefore, the videos that were integrated into the course were situated within different contexts and presented a variety of perspectives including those of practising teachers, immigrant and refugee children, parents, guest lecturers, and specialists in the area of bilingual education. These particular types of resources have been found to increase empathy in children and adults (Feshbach & Feshbach, 2011).

The course also implemented videos of authentic classroom practice, models of teaching and the effective implementation of these models. This allowed students to see extracts of innovative practices that they would most likely not have been able to see in their local observation assignments as suggested by Brophy (2004). In line with Dolby's (2012) review of research on empathy, Brophy also warns that simply viewing the videos is not sufficient to make a lasting impact on student teachers' future teaching practices. They suggest rather that video extracts need to be embedded in the curriculum and introduced with specific objectives in mind. As the video extracts in this course were selected and implemented in the context of a problem based learning model, they were carefully selected to correspond to the problem situation and to the particular aspect of the problem under discussion in a specific class in order to provide student teachers with complementary visions of the situation and of the possible responses to the problem.

Course Content and Choice of Resources

The resources implemented in the course were chosen in relationship to the course content presented in Table 1.

Among the expected outcomes of the course were: the development of a critical awareness of the nature of linguistic and cultural diversity, knowledge of language development and of the differences between language learning at home and in the school context, knowledge of first language acquisition, bilingual language acquisition, second language acquisition and early foreign language learning, an awareness of the knowledge and skills emergent bilingual children bring to the classroom, and the demands that are placed on these children by the school as well as an examination of how lesson and classroom planning can accommodate these children.

Table 1. TESSLA course content

1. Introductions: participants, tutor, methodology, PBL approach, course contents, evaluation.
2. Linguistic and cultural diversity.
3. L1/2 acquisition and foreign language learning.
4. Bilingualism.
5. Language sensitive teaching.
6. Identity and home school relationship.
7. Linguistic policies, official documentation and terminology, National, European levels portfolios.
8. Student presentations & peer assessment.

As mentioned above, the didactic model chosen for the course was Problem Based Learning (PBL), an instructional method based on the use of *authentic* or *real world* problems (Kumar & Kogut, 2006; Williams, 2001). Within the PBL model, students work together in small groups to reflect on a problem or set of problems in order to generate various solutions in a collective, collaborative way. The role of the teacher is to facilitate the process and to provide various sources of information and support to the groups. PBL has been shown to be a practice that engages students in critical reflection and promotes active learning. The *real life* problem with which student teachers were presented was the following:

Mme Martin teaches a class of 7 year olds which contains a number of children whose home language (their mother tongue) is different from the language of the school. Mme Martin is really concerned that these children don't seem to be making the same progress as the native speakers of the school language. Some of them don't participate in learning activities. The French/francophone children in the class are losing patience with these children's attempts to communicate. Mme Martin would really like to help these pupils more and would like to help the class as a whole to be more welcoming. She is discussing with you what she might do. (Hancock, A., Hermeling, S., Landon, J. & Young, A., 2006)

In the first half of each course the authors presented new content and materials: theoretical readings illustrated by personal testimonies, video recordings and a wide variety of other resources (music, children's literature, website materials including games and classroom ideas). During the second half of the course, students were expected to engage in discussion around the problem situation and to propose new solutions and strategies to be put into practice in light of the new content and material presented in the first half of the course. During the first course on linguistic and cultural diversity, students were asked to complete the answers to a quiz in groups with the help of various documents and a web quest. They were also asked to identify different languages in a multilingual song "Le Pétrin" (La Tordue, 2002) while they listened to it. For themes 2 through 6, in addition to the reading materials provided, videos were selected to raise students' awareness of the concepts covered in order to present materials from personal, first hand perspectives and to show authentic examples of classroom practices (see Table 2 for list of resources). One of the main criterion in selecting the video extracts involved choosing extracts which gave personalized accounts to illustrate the ways in which individuals experienced their pluri-/bilingualism, which has the potential for fostering a sense of empathy in students.

Online Platform and Access to Online Resources and Digital Classroom Resources (Videos, Web-Conferences) as a Means to Foster Understanding and Empathy Among the Student Teachers

The courses implemented in the teacher education institutions made use of an online platform which provided access to the course objectives and course content, academic articles (first and second language acquisition, bi-plurilingualism, questions around language and identity, language policies and ideologies), links to relevant websites and online resources and interactive discussion forums used for posting and responding to weekly student group reports.

Online resources were provided throughout the course with the aim of engaging student teachers in reflection around the questions of second language acquisition and the needs of their linguistically and culturally diverse pupils. The resources not only presented current information on first and second

The Role of Multi-Media in Expanding Pre-Service Teachers' Understanding

language acquisition and linguistic diversity, but also provided access to videos and examples of classroom practice, example lesson plans, pedagogical resources, materials, and resources for welcoming and supporting parents (Table 2).

METHODOLOGY, DATA COLLECTION

The data collected from the various versions of the course over the past 10 years have included identical pre & post course questionnaires, working group minutes, and post course evaluations (for an analysis see Young & Mary, 2010 and Mary & Young, 2010). Concerning the data collected in the spring term of 2015 the course evaluation by students (see appendix) contained additional questions specifically pertaining to their evaluation of the use of resources (multi-media and written) during the course. The data analysed in this chapter pertains to the students' responses to the course evaluation.

Impact of Multi-Media Resources on the Students Learning and Understanding

This data collected in 2015 was drawn from two classes comprising 18 students total enrolled in the TESSLA course in their first year of their two-year Master of Education degree as part of their initial

Table 2. List of resources used during the course

Title of Resource	Content/Themes Addressed
Original research footage from the Didenheim project *La diversité linguistique et culturelle à l'école* (Hélot, Young & Delforge, 2005)	Primary classroom activities about languages and cultures co-constructed by parents and teachers.
Original research footage from a multilingual pre-school in Mulhouse (Horvart, Mary & Young, 2014-15)	Pre-primary classroom activities showing how the teacher includes minority language children and families through translanguaging
Raconte-moi ta langue/Tell me how you talk (Feltin, 2008)	Documentary about the Didenheim project and teacher education for diversity, includes interviews with parents, teachers and researchers
Jim Cummins' conference in Strasbourg 28th January 2015 Bilingual Education: International Perspectives on Research and Policy	Clip during which a minority language girl shares personal memories about learning a second language in school.
Comparons nos langues (CRDP de Languedoc-Roussillon-Montpellier, 2005)	Clips showing classroom footage of how to use multiple languages as resources for learning
Tuning into children (BBC Educational Publishing, 1999)	Video sequence of a young Chinese girl making a cake in a nursery setting.
'Sharing stories' from *'Progress with Purpose: Supporting Continuity in Children's Learning 3-8 Additional Materials* (LTS, 2003)	Emergent bilingual pupils and a bilingual teaching assistant read and talk about a picture book story first in L2 only, then using L1
In safe hands, (Save the Children & the Refugee Council, 2001)	Documentary about life as a refugee child (interviews with parents, school staff & children)
Photo de classe http://enseigner.tv5monde.com/collection/photo-de-classe (TV 5 Monde, 2014)	Web documentary presenting a project and video extracts from one multilingual/multicultural class in which the children interviewed their parents and grandparents on their feelings/experiences concerning their recent migration.

teacher training and took place from January 2015 to April 2015. The course was part of the core curriculum required to earn a Masters in Education preparing them to teach children from age 2 to 11 years old. During their first semester, students also had courses in subject didactics (Math, French, History etc…), child development and psychology, as well as a foreign language course in either English, German, Spanish, or Italian. At the end of their first year in the Masters programme, the students usually take a national competitive teaching exam. Those who succeed on the exam are taken on as student teachers for the second year of their Masters degree and are then granted official full-time teacher status upon successful completion of their course work and teaching internship. Students whose exam scores are not high enough to qualify as student teachers, continue as full-time students into the second year of the Masters programme with the intention of sitting the exam a second time in the Spring. The university teacher education institute in which the study was conducted was situated in a small city in the East of France. The students were between the ages of 20 and 42, and comprised seventeen female and one male student with a general socio-economic status ranging from average to low. Only two of the students enrolled in the course were from ethnic minority groups.

The 18-hour course was divided into nine 2-hour weekly sessions. As mentioned above, one of the central goals of the TESSLA course was to sensitize student teachers to the needs of their linguistically and culturally diverse pupils so they could develop teaching strategies to support these children in the classroom. A pre-course questionnaire was administered with the aim of providing information on their linguistic and cultural background and experience and their attitudes toward and knowledge of second language acquisition and its role and influence in the classroom. Identical questionnaires were completed at the close of the course to evaluate the impact of the course on the students. In addition, the students completed an anonymous course evaluation (Appendix) during the last session which contained a total of 8 questions regarding their perception of the didactic model chosen for the course (PBL), their evaluation of the resources implemented, what they liked about the course, and their suggestions for improvement. The questionnaire and course evaluation were distributed by the instructor on the last day of the course. The students were allowed as much time as necessary to complete the two documents and were informed that the course evaluation was anonymous, and that their answers would remain confidential. The analysis detailed below focuses in particular on their evaluation of the resources implemented throughout the course (online, video, audio and written; in class and outside of class). The qualitative analysis of these data was undertaken using the « constant comparative method » (Ryan, Bernard & Beck, 2000; Wellington, 2004). Emerging themes and concepts were identified and then refined, compared, and contrasted in order to form a coherent picture in relation to the research questions and course objectives.

Concrete Situations: A Means to Providing Deeper Understanding

With regards to Q5, "Did the use of the different resources (written, audio-visual, paper, internet etc.) during the course and outside of the course (for example, the resources consulted on the online course platform) help you to gain a deeper understanding of the concepts/issues surrounding second language learning and culturally and linguistically diverse classrooms? If Yes/No, please explain", 16 out of the 18 students surveyed stated that the videos in particular helped them to understand the course content better. A large majority (14 out of 18) of the students pointed to the benefits of videos stating that these allowed them to see "concrete" or "real-life classroom situations":

The Role of Multi-Media in Expanding Pre-Service Teachers' Understanding

Les vidéos sont très parlantes puisque ce sont des situations réelles qui ont été filmées. Elles permettent de voir concrètement comment cela se passe. Les liens vers les ressources sont également très intéressantes et peuvent être réutilisés plus tard (Student E1).

The videos are very meaningful because they are real situations that were filmed. They allow you to concretely see what really happens. The links to resources are also very interesting and can be reused later.

Oui, car on peut voir différents points de vue qui nous aident à nous faire un avis ou à changer notre propre idée de départ. (Student E3)

Yes, because you can see different perspectives that help you to form an opinion or to change your own initial idea.

Oui, car témoignages (par exemple), vidéos de véritables situations. (Student E14)

Yes, because of the personal accounts (for example), videos of real situations.

Some students (E4, E13), mentioned the ways in which the videos allowed them to reinforce concepts they had read about in the written documents, with one student stating that the videos helped her to see the different dimensions present in certain classroom situations:

La diversité des documents m'a permis d'envisager le problème dans ses différentes dimensions. J'ai particulièrement apprécié les vidéos qui permettent de voir la mise en œuvre et les comportements des enfants (Student E7).

The diversity of materials allowed me to see the problem in its different dimensions. I particularly enjoyed the videos that allowed us to see the implementation [of practices] and the children's behaviour.

Role of Multi-Media Resources in Structuring Thought and Fostering Memorization

Several students (E6, E13) specifically spoke of how the videos supported their understanding specifying that they were able to learn better through visual resources:

Oui, une compréhension via différents supports aide à la mémorisation. (Student E6)

Yes, understanding via various media helps memorization.

Oui, je comprends mieux sur support visuel mais j'ai besoin de lire des textes ensuite pour structurer ma pensée. (Student E13)

Yes, I understand better through visual aids but I need to read texts then to structure my thoughts.

Cela permet de revenir sur des notions qui n'étaient pas forcément comprises en cours. (Student E4)

It allows you to reflect back to notions that you hadn't necessarily understood in class.

Others (7 out of 18) pointed to increased understanding through seeing strategies being put into action, which they felt they could draw on later.

In response to Q6, "Which resources, if any, helped deepen your understanding of the issues related to second language learning/acquisition and culturally and linguistically diverse classrooms?", 12 out of 18 students specified videos as the resource that helped them best understand the concepts and issues related to learning a second language and welcoming linguistic diversity in the classroom. However, 6 students mention gaining a better understanding of these issues through the theoretical readings or a combination of the two resources. This is an interesting finding when contrasted with their responses to Q7 "Which resources did you *like* the most" for which the majority of students indicated the videos. In this same vein, the students who indicated an answer for Q8 (only 5 of them responded to this question) "Are there any resources you didn't like, if so which ones and why?" all five mentioned disliking the use of theoretical texts in the course as they felt these were either "too long" (students E1, E5, E11, E16), "too theoretical/too difficult" (Students E5 & E16) or "too numerous" (E3, E8).

The analysis of the data highlights the use of multi-media resources in the course as a resource, which allows most of the students to gain practical knowledge of teaching strategies to implement in the classroom, and that this was much appreciated by them. However, one particular student specifically stated that for her the only way to gain an accurate idea of the reality of a linguistically and culturally diverse classroom would be direct observation, while another student suggested, as a means to improve the course, being able to "test out" these strategies in a real classroom.

What has emerged through the course evaluation data is that the resources used (audio-visual, online and written) allowed the students to understand different classroom situations with regards to second language learning, acquisition and development and enabled them to gain knowledge of teaching strategies they could draw on in a linguistically and culturally diverse classroom. However, what seems to be absent from many of the students' responses is, in effect, signs of them having gained in empathy towards these students. Banks states that in the 21st century, citizens (and therefore, the teachers responsible for their education) will need to "know, to care and to act" (Banks, 2001, p. 9). The students who followed this course seemed to have learned important concepts and gained effective "tools" to implement in the classroom but in analysing the data the question remains as to whether the course and its resources had a long lasting impact on them on a *personal level*, and whether this would enable them to 'care' about their future linguistically and culturally diverse pupils?

Issues for Reflection

In reflecting on the question of how to not only increase student teachers' *understanding* of the theories and concepts linked to second language acquisition, and awareness of the pedagogical interventions possible in their linguistically culturally diverse classrooms, but also to foster a sense of empathy for their future pupils in these classrooms, several issues have emerged.

The Issue of Time

Over the past ten years, the authors, as teacher-educators, have struggled with shifts in curriculum requirements and procuring the spaces in which students can be provided with knowledge, and also given sufficient time for discussion and reflection. In previous analyses of this course (Young & Mary, 2016), the difficulties of finding spaces in which students can be provided with a sufficient amount of time to discuss the materials and confront their own opinions and points of view in groups is discussed. The results of these analyses indicate that when there is insufficient time for discussion of the problem situation (the basis of PBL) the students are not able to engage with the materials in meaningful ways and therefore demonstrate fewer signs of gaining in empathy. This indicates that the use of multimedia alone in this course is not enough to make a lasting impact on students and cannot replace the benefits of time for discussion. This, however, is a difficult task for teacher educators as they are often faced with an increasingly limited number of hours in the curriculum.

In addition, it appears that in order to have a lasting impact on student teachers, one that would be transformative and allow them to "care" and to "act", sensitization to the questions of intercultural education and equity should not take place in 'isolation' but rather needs to be established through links across the curriculum. Garmon (2004) and Pohan (1996) stress the need to multiply student teachers' experiences throughout their training and academic courses in order to create more opportunities for them to revisit and review their own attitudes and representations. In one case study, Garmon found that it was not a single course that contributed to changes that had occurred in one particular student's attitudes and willingness to change but rather an accumulation of experiences she had encountered, either through course work or direct contact with minority students and individuals with backgrounds different from her own. Burns & Shadoian-Gersing (2010) mirror this point of view:

Improved teaching for diverse student populations is an increasingly important competency for current and future teachers. However, too often these topics are addressed through a sole course, often as an elective. As systems increasingly recognise the need to prepare teachers for a diversifying student population, there must be a systematic effort to integrate this topic and strategies into the curriculum. Moreover, a crucial component of teaching for diversity lies in examining one's own beliefs and how they influence behaviour. Much like any other teacher competency, the requisite skills for teaching and motivating diverse classrooms and attitudinal awareness cannot be simply absorbed through a one-off course during initial education or professional development. Instead, it is important to build on this training throughout teachers' careers, so that they gain transversal exposure to knowledge and perspectives that can have a meaningful impact on how they practice. (p. 290)

Direct Contact with Diversity

Another issue addressed in the literature is the impact that experiences and/or direct contact with diversity has on individuals (Dolby, 2012; Garmon, 2004; McAllister & Irvine, 2002) and the lack of such experiences among student teachers. Acquah & Commins (2013) highlight that:

Several studies have shown that most predominantly white and middle-class pre-service teachers have limited experience outside 'their world'; that is, they have had limited or no experience with persons from different ethnicities or social class prior to enrolling in a diversity course (Larke 1990; Nieto 1998; Ahlquist 1991; Carpenter 2000). This lack of or limited exposure to different ethnicities or social classes tends to reinforce pre-service teachers' stereotypical beliefs. Shultz, Neyhart, and Reck (1996) suggest that pre-service teachers are naive and hold stereotypical beliefs about urban children, for example that they bring attitudes that interfere with their education." (p. 2)

Without a doubt, real immersion experiences in a culture other than the students' own is more effective than vicarious exposure. However, providing students with such experiences remains a challenge for teacher educators.

SOLUTIONS AND RECOMMENDATIONS

One student stated in the course evaluation that in order to understand the issues at stake in diverse classrooms, student teachers need to be immersed in the classroom setting, stating that "nothing replaces direct observation" (Student E10). McAllister & Irvine's study (2002) also showed that many teachers in their programme felt that the "direct contact experience" (e.g. going into communities/families' homes) they had had was vital to nurturing their own feelings of empathy. The authors also point to further studies (Chambers et al., 1998) which show that gaining knowledge alone makes no difference in changing student teachers beliefs. However, when working in contexts where providing quality observations for all student teachers and/or providing them with such direct contact experience with different cultures are not possible, teacher-educators must reflect on ways to simulate these experiences in the classroom or in the surrounding environment, in order to cultivate empathy. As a starting point, it is possible to draw on the success of previous programmes in this area in an attempt to attain this goal. Below are outlined three programmes that have had success in implementing what Dolby (2012) refers to as "exercises in empathy" (p. 98) and which have been shown to have had an impact on students' beliefs and understanding.

Social Perspective Taking

This multi-cultural course implemented at two different universities, with students enrolled in a teacher education degree, was based on the idea that the use of personal narratives in class could have a powerful impact on students. Rios et al. explain that "by engaging narratives of 'others,' we are provided with alternative worldviews that enable us to challenge/trouble our own. Through the use of narratives, readers situate themselves in the other and then determine degrees of connectedness." (Rios, Trent & Castaneda, 2003: p.6).

The social perspective taking activity took place in several stages. At the first stage, students watched two videos of interviews with adult professionals who had been denied their language and culture in school when they were children and who recalled the painful memories they had of these experiences. Students were then asked to take on the role of one of the professionals and to write a letter to the teacher from their perspective. This was followed by a second stage, during which the students were then asked to imagine they were the recipients of these same letters (meaning they then took on the role of the teachers who had denied the children their language and culture) and to write about how they would feel upon receiving the letter and what they would then do. Rios et al. argue that:

By assuming the position of "other," ... students are forced to become consciously aware and awakened to their specific location as they adapt an identity mediated by life experiences different (in many cases) from their own. ... Social perspective-taking may move future and current teachers to consider and challenge their understandings as well as their (explicit or implicit) acceptance of teaching philosophies/notions associated with deficit understandings, disadvantage, advantage, privilege, and oppression. (2003, p. 11)

Reflection Paper

As part of her multicultural education course, Dolby (2012) requires her students to attend an event where they will be in the minority among one of the following categories: race, sexual orientation, religion, or national identity. After the event the students must reflect on the experience and write a paper about their feelings during the event stating what they felt, experienced and learned from the activity. Dolby specifically insists on the fact that they are to attend as the minority participant and not to pretend that they are part of the group itself. The students are also told that that they must not attend the event in which they take on a "helping role" (Dolby, 2012: p. 99) in any way.

Empathy through Global Experience

Suarez describes an increase in empathy on the part of in-service second language teachers after having had the experience of language immersion classes and living with a family in Venezuela and/or Mexico. This first-hand experience helped move the teachers from a position of sympathy towards their pupils to one of empathy with them. The students described experiencing feelings of isolation and frustration with monolingual courses and teaching strategies. Having "walked in their students' shoes" (Suarez, 2013: p. 181), they became acutely aware of the difficulties of learning a second language and how exhausting this could be.

FUTURE RESEARCH DIRECTIONS

The exercises in empathy described above present various means of engaging students in reflection and of helping them to decentre. Two of the strategies mentioned require students to engage in these activities outside the classroom and to reflect on these experiences individually. Both of the authors' teacher education departments strongly encourage students to take part in teaching practices/exchanges in foreign countries and both are working actively to continue to develop partnership programs in order to provide these experiences for student teachers. However, in reality only a small percentage of the student teachers choose to/are able to participate in such programs which means that the majority of newly qualified teachers begin their teaching careers without the benefit of such experiences. In the TESSLA course, one of the goals of Problem Based Learning is to allow students with such experiences to share them with others through the group discussions. It is hoped that through this sharing of experiences, students with limited exposure to diversity will be able to benefit vicariously from these. However, when there is a lack of diversity within the working groups or class itself and thus an insufficient number of experiences with diversity and different viewpoints to share, teacher educators must rely on additional stimulus from outside sources to stimulate reflection. It is in this context that the use of videos and the practice of "social perspective taking" could have a strong impact. The data presented in this chapter has highlighted the impact the video extracts had on the student teachers' understanding of the issues but also underlined the lack of identifiable signs of the students having gained in empathy. Combining social perspective taking exercises with the use of video in the course, however, could be an effective means of enabling the students to "put themselves in another's shoes" and to "experience" a situation from another's perspective and possibly foster a greater sense of empathy.

In addition, with the goal of extending students' opportunities to engage in their reflection on diversity and equity in schools, and in line with Garmon's (2004) and Burns & Shadoian-Gersing's (2012) suggestions our teacher education institutions need to provide training in the area of second language acquisition and linguistically and culturally diverse classrooms not only for their graduate students but for the whole of the teaching staff in order to facilitate the weaving of these questions into the entire fabric of the curriculum and not just into one course on multi-cultural/lingual education. Addressing these issues early on in teacher training programs allows students to be aware of certain questions and to pay attention to them throughout their practice and during their encounters with others. Returning to the same questions through the lenses of different disciplines and within different contexts can help broaden student teachers' visions and beliefs.

CONCLUSION

This chapter aimed to describe and analyse the role of multi-media resources in expanding pre-service teachers' understanding of culturally and linguistically diverse classrooms and furthering their professional identities. The data indicated that knowledge about culture, language and identity and how it was acquired, namely through the teaching framework of Problem Based Learning and the use of multi-media resources, and the selection of pertinent video extracts and access to online resources was instrumental in the evolution of the students' essentially mono-cultural, monolingual frameworks. Students stated that the use of video in particular in the course helped them to gain a greater understanding of the issues related to second language acquisition and linguistic and cultural diversity. In order to foster a greater sense of empathy towards students from culturally and linguistically diverse backgrounds practices in which students vicariously experience diversity or in which they try to imagine an experience from another's point of view are proposed. We also suggested that teacher education institutions develop continuing professional development for members of their teaching staff in order to address questions of diversity and multicultural/multilingual education throughout the curriculum.

REFERENCES

Acquah, E. O., & Commins, N. L. (2013). Pre-service teachers' beliefs and knowledge about multiculturalism. *European Journal of Teacher Education*, *36*(4), 445–463. doi:10.1080/02619768.2013.787593

Bailison Bailenson, J.N., Iyenger, S., Yee, N., Collins, N.A. (2008). Facial similarity between voters and candidates causes influence. *Public Opinion Quarterly*, 72(5) 2008, 935–961

Banks, J. A. (2001). Citizenship Education and Diversity. *Journal of Teacher Education*, *52*(1), 5–16. doi:10.1177/0022487101052001002

Berk, R. A. (2009). Multimedia teaching with video clips: TV, movies, YouTube, and mtvU in the college classroom. *International Journal of Technology in Teaching and Learning*, *5*(1), 1–21.

Brophy, J. (2004). *Using Video in Teacher Education*. Bingley: Emerald Group Publishing Limited.

Brush, T., & Saye, J. (2008). *The effects of multimedia-supported problem-based inquiry on student engagement, empathy, and assumptions about history. Interdisciplinary Journal of Problem-Based Learning, 2(1)*. Available at; doi:10.7771/1541-5015.1052

Burns, T., & Shadoian-Gersing, V. (2010). Supporting effective practice: the pending agenda. In T. Burns & V. Shadoian-Gersing (Eds.), *Educating Teachers for Diversity: Meeting the Challenge*. Paris: OECD. doi:10.1787/9789264079731-16-en

Cajkler, W., & Hall, B. (2012). Languages in primary classrooms: A study of new teacher capability and practice. *Language Awareness, 21*(1-2), 15–32. doi:10.1080/09658416.2011.639889

Clarke, D., & Hollingsworth, H. (2000). Seeing is understanding. *Journal of Staff Development, 21*, 40–43.

Commerford, S. A. (2005). Engaging through Learning-Learning through engaging: An alternative approach to professional learning about human diversity. *Social Work Education, 24*(1), 113–135. doi:10.1080/02615470520003250017

Dolby, N. (2012). *Rethinking Multicultural Education for the Next Generation*. New York: Routledge.

Ehrlich, P. R., & Ornstein, R. (2010). *Humanity on a tightrope: Thoughts on empathy, family and big changes for a viable future*. New York: Rowman and Littlefield.

Fechbach, N. D., & Fechbach, S. (2011). Empathy and Education. In J. Decety & W. Ickes (Eds.), *The Social Neuroscience of Empathy*. Massachusetts: MIT Press.

Garmon, M. A. (2004). Changing Preservice Teachers' Attitudes/Beliefs About Diversity What are the Critical Factors? *Journal of Teacher Education, 55*(3), 201–213. doi:10.1177/0022487104263080

Gay, G. (2010). Classroom practices for teaching diversity: an example from Washington State (United States). In T. Burns & V. Shadoian-Gersing (Eds.), *Educating Teachers for Diversity: Meeting the Challenge*. Paris: OECD. doi:10.1787/9789264079731-15-en

Gellevij, M., Meij, H., & Jong, T. (2002). Multimodal versus unimodal instruction in a complex learning context. *Journal of Experimental Education, 70*(3), 215–239. doi:10.1080/00220970209599507

Hancock, A., Hermerling, S., Landon, J., & Young, A. (2006). *Building on language diversity with young children: Teacher education for the support of second language acquisition*. Münster, Germany: LIT Verlag.

Hélot, C., Young, A. & Delforge, O. (2005) *La diversité linguistique et culturelle à l'école* (original version in French).

Hélot, C. Young, A. & Delforge, O. (2005) *Windows on the World: A language awareness project in a French primary school* (English subtitled version).

Horan, D. A., & Hersi, A. A. (2011). Preparing for diversity: the alternatives to 'linguistic coursework' for student teachers in the USA. In S. Ellis & E. McCartney (Eds.), *Applied Linguistics and Primary School Teaching* (pp. 44–52). Cambridge, England: Cambridge University Press. doi:10.1017/CBO9780511921605.007

Houser, N. O. (2008). Cultural plunge: A critical approach for multicultural development in teacher education. *Race, Ethnicity and Education, 11*(4), 465–482. doi:10.1080/13613320802479034

Hyder, T., & Rutter, J. (2001). *Safe Hands*. London: Save the Children and Refugee Council.

Jewitt, C., Kress, G., Ogborn, J., & Tsatsarelis, C. (2000). Teaching and learning: Beyond language. *Teaching Education, 11*(3), 327–341. doi:10.1080/713698977

Jewitt, C., Kress, G., Ogborn, J., & Tsatsarelis, C. (2001). Exploring learning through visual, actional and linguistic communication: The multimodal environment of a science classroom. *Educational Review, 53*(1), 5–8. doi:10.1080/00131910123753

Komur, M., & Kogut, G. (2006). Students' perceptions of problem-based learning. *Teacher Development, 10*(1), 105–116. doi:10.1080/13664530600587295

Kuiken, F. (2014). Competencies of preschool educators in Amsterdam: A Dutch perspective on language proficiency, language targets and didactic skills. *European Journal of Applied Linguistics, 2*(1), 101–119. doi:10.1515/eujal-2014-0006

La Tordue. (2002). *Champs libre* (Album, music CD).

Lin, X., & Bransford, J. (2010). Personal background knowledge influences cross-cultural understanding. *Teachers College Record, 112*(7), 1729–1757.

Mary, L., & Young, A. (2010). Preparing teachers for the multilingual classroom: Nurturing reflective, critical awareness. In S.H. Ehrhart, C., Hélot & A. Le Nevez, (Eds), Plurilinguisme et formation des enseignants: Une approche critique / Plurilingualism and Teacher Education: a critical approach. Frankfurt: Peter Lang.

Mayer, R. E. (2002). Multimedia learning. *Psychology of Learning and Motivation, 41*, 85–139. doi:10.1016/S0079-7421(02)80005-6

McAllister, G., & Irvine, J. J. (2002). The role of empathy in teaching culturally diverse students: A qualitative study of teachers' beliefs. *Journal of Teacher Education, 53*(5), 433–443. doi:10.1177/002248702237397

Murakami, C. (2008). 'Everybody is just fumbling along': An investigation of views regarding EAL training and support provisions in a rural area. *Language and Education, 22*(4), 265–282. doi:10.1080/09500780802152556

Perry, G., & Talley, S. (2001). Online video case studies and teacher education: A new tool for preservice education. *Journal of Computing in Teacher Education, 17*(4), 26–31.

Rios, F., Trent, A., & Castaneda, L. (2003). Social Perspective taking: Advancing empathy and advocating justice. *Equity & Excellence in Education, 36*(1), 5–14. doi:10.1080/10665680303506

Ryan, G. W., Bernard, H. R., & Beck, C. T. (2000). Data management and analysis methods. In N. K. Denzin & Y. S. Lincoln (Eds.), *Handbook off qualitative research* (2nd ed.). Thousand Oaks: Sage.

Schwartz, M., Mor-Sommerfeld, A., & Leikin, M. (2010). Facing bilingual education: Kindergarten teachers' attitudes, strategies and challenges. *Language Awareness, 19*(3), 187–203. doi:10.1080/09658416.2010.491919

Sternberg, R. J., Torff, B., & Grigorenko, E. L. (1998). Teaching triarchically improves school achievement. *Journal of Educational Psychology, 3*(3), 374–384. doi:10.1037/0022-0663.90.3.374

Suarez, D. (2003). The Development of empathetic dispositions through global experiences. *Educational Horizons, 81*(4), 180–182.

Thomauske, N. (2011). The relevance of multilingualism for teachers and immigrant parents in early childhood education and care in Germany and in France. *Intercultural Education, 22*(4), 327–336. doi:10.1080/14675986.2011.617425

Tiedt, P. l., & Tiedt, I. M. (2010). *Multicultural Teaching: Activities, Information, and Resources*. Boston: Allyn and Bacon/Pearson Education.

Veenema, S., & Gardner, H. (1996). Multi-media and multiple intelligences. *The American Prospect, 29*, 70–75.

Wankel, L. A., & Blessinger, P. (2013). Inventive approaches in Higher Education: An introduction to using multimédia technologies. In L. A. Wankel & P. Blessinger (Eds.), *Increasing Student Engagement and Retention using Multimedia Technologies*. Bingley: Howard House Publishing. doi:10.1108/S2044-9968(2013)000006D003

Wellington, J. (2000). *Educational Research: Contemporary issues and practical approaches*. London: Continuum.

Williams, B. (2001). Developing critical reflection for professional practice through problem-based learning. *Journal of Advanced Nursing, 34*(1), 27–34. doi:10.1046/j.1365-2648.2001.3411737.x PMID:11430603

Young, A. S. (2008). Diversity as an asset: Multiple language integration. In M. Dooly & D. Eastment (Eds.), *How we're going about it. Teachers' voices on innovative approaches to teaching and learning languages* (pp. 51–65). Newcastle upon Tyne: Cambridge Scholars Publishing.

Young, A. S., & Mary, L. (2010). Une formation des professeurs des écoles en phase avec le 21ème siècle. In J.-M. Mangiante (Ed.), *Langue et Intégration* (pp. 349–363). Frankfurt: Peter Lang.

Young, A. S., & Mary, L. (2016). Dix ans d'expérimentation dans la formation de (futurs) acteurs de l'éducation pour une meilleure prise en compte de la diversité linguistique et culturelle des élèves: Enjeux, défis et réussites. *Carnet des Ateliers Sociolinguistiques*.

This research was previously published in the Handbook of Research on Foreign Language Education in the Digital Age edited by Congcong Wang and Lisa Winstead; pages 296-314, copyright year 2016 by Information Science Reference (an imprint of IGI Global).

APPENDIX

Student Questionnaire Compiled by Latisha MARY and Andrea YOUNG: Course Evaluation (April 2015)

1. What have you learned from the course?
2. Has your opinion changed?
3. What suggestions do you have to improve the course?
4. What do you think of Problem Based Learning?
5. Did the use of the different resources (written, audio-visual, paper, internet etc.) during the course and outside of the course (for example, the resources consulted on the online course platform) help you to gain a deeper understanding of the concepts/issues surrounding second language learning and culturally and linguistically diverse classrooms?
    a. If Yes, please explain
    b. If No, please explain:
6. Which resources, if any, helped deepen your understanding of the issues related to second language learning/acquisition and culturally and linguistically diverse classrooms.
7. Which resources did you *like* the most? Why?
8. Were there any resources you didn't like, if so which ones and why?'

Chapter 33
Teacher Preparatory Programs and Culturally Responsive Teaching

Nadira Raghunandan-Jack
Charter School Sector, USA

ABSTRACT

This text focuses on culturally responsive education programs within higher education institutions. The first section traces the historical roots of culturally responsive teaching and explores why it is a pivotal component necessary for pre-service students to comprehend. The next section emphasizes strategies that are currently used within the higher education sector to expose students to culturally competent practices in the classroom. Among the strategies that are discussed are community based immersion experiences, diversity and multi-cultural courses and student teaching experiences. The chapter then closes with a framework for recommendation and improvements for higher education institutions to implement to further refine and strengthen teacher preparatory programs.

BACKGROUND

Common Core Curriculum Standards

The Common Core Curriculum State Standards refers to a high-quality of academic standards in the area of English Language Arts Literacy. The standards collectively outline the learning goals of concepts, knowledge and foundational levels that students should be able to master at the end of each grade level. Through the collaborative efforts of educators, chief school administrators as well as other experts in the field of education, the Common Core provides a framework for educators and heavily emphasizes college and career readiness for students. The standards also focus on the application of content knowledge through the development of higher order thinking skills.

DOI: 10.4018/978-1-7998-1213-5.ch033

Culturally Relevant Resource

A contributing factor to the foundation and development of an individual's culture indicative of shared realities and lived experiences that is central to students lives. A culturally relevant resource reflects the diversity of the student population within a given classroom and is used as a critical tool by which to create equitable learning experiences, introduce concepts and ideas to students while demonstrating appreciation, respect and value of their culture as well as assist in the process of reframing perspectives.

Curriculum

In the context of this study, the term curriculum refers to an in-depth instructional guide incorporating all educational foundations, standards and benchmarks relevant to each grade level within a sequential order, inclusive of all resources and materials necessary for educators to successfully implement lessons. The curriculum is a detailed plan of instruction with categorical elements that define learning experiences and opportunities as well as multiple measures of assessment for students.

MAIN FOCUS OF THE CHAPTER

Each day, students across the nation engage in a daily battle aimed at receiving a high quality education thoroughly designed to quench their thirst for knowledge while simultaneously meeting their distinct needs. They crave a foundation of knowledge that is applicable to their daily lives as they experience and observe a world around them with uncharted wisdom to explore; they yearn for learning modules that can heighten their awareness beyond all that is factual and transform from beings that simply exist towards manifesting their life's purpose. Similarly, educators struggle to provide meaningful learning experiences, as they are coerced to solely rely upon adopted state standards and benchmarks that neglect to integrate meaningful culturally relevant concepts. Overwhelmed by dramatic shifts and transitions in the field of education that link student performance and academic achievement directly to their professional level of efficacy, educators are faced with many limitations and stipulations that bind their instruction in the classroom. Increasing emphasis on accountability measures and standardized assessments related to the Common Core Standards have collectively impacted both educators and students in a negative manner, as both participants are inundated with unrealistic measures of success-none of which truly focus on the innate needs of learners. Thus, it becomes impossible to win the battle both are faced with on a daily basis, and even more difficult for learners to fully grasp content deemed detrimental to their success without relevancy to their personal lives. The end result provides much clarity and insight: We are losing our children to the ills of society and failing to provide them with the adequate tools necessary to develop an intrinsic love for learning and the ability to question the larger world in which they exist. Research suggests that students that reside in high poverty levels are more susceptible to engage in lives of crime, drugs and violence, as it is a part of the community they reside in (Waddell, 2013). Furthermore, unrealistic demands and measures ultimately compromise the quality of instruction that students receive in classrooms throughout the nation on a daily basis, often shattering the spirit of true educators that seek to truly transform the lives of their students.

Such changes present an overwhelming responsibility to the courageous few that choose to enter this rapidly changing field amidst barriers to effectuate the lives of learners in a positive way. While it gener-

Teacher Preparatory Programs and Culturally Responsive Teaching

ally known that the most successful educators are those that are adaptable and flexible, it is imperative for future ones to fully understand and study effective strategies that can be used in the instructional environment to experience success. Success begins when an educator is truly committed and invested in developing positive relationships with students and can demonstrate an appreciation for cultural diversity by utilizing this essential element as a pivotal tool that can enhance the learning process for all. Nonetheless, many teacher education preparatory programs neglect to integrate courses and fieldwork that directly focus on appreciating cultural diversity and using culturally relevant pedagogy as a means to capture student attention and further develop their innate skills and abilities. When we can foster a strong sense of awareness and respect among educators in a culturally responsive manner, we can provide them with the insight necessary to value multiple perspectives and develop a nation of prospective learners that truly respect each other in a dignified manner.

TRACING THE ROOTS OF CULTURALLY RESPONSIVE TEACHING

From a historical standpoint, the concept of education served a singular aristocratic purpose as the nation's founding fathers devised a universal system that would ultimately seek to educate the most elite members of society. This idea, initially proposed by Thomas Jefferson, was to preserve and further the capitalistic ventures of the small few deemed as possessing far superior and noble gifts of talent in comparison to their counterparts. Jefferson believed that individuals possessed a fixed or assigned nature of intelligence (Brick, 2005). This original ideology, fraught with both inequity and injustices, heavily relied upon elements of capitalism as the core basis to further both educational pursuits of knowledge in an effort to exert control and maintain a seemingly structured society. Eventually, as time passed, activist and reformer Horace Mann soon awakened to this devastating reality while serving as the Secretary of Education for the state of Massachusetts. Mann proactively conducted site visits to over 1,000 educational institutions and discovered a system of schooling that was inaccessible and unavailable to children stemming from low socio-economic incomes. Thus, he strongly advocated for the reorganization of the American school system, aiming to transform schoolhouses into institutions focused on furthering human development (Mondale, 2002). Known to have developed the widely adopted common school, Mann developed and implemented a standardized model of education, in which children were taught uniform concepts and ideas relevant to an American, democratic ideal in each state. Mann also sought to embrace diverse populations by propelling the philosophy that education should be free of charge, non-sectarian in nature and emphasized a specific set of core knowledge students were expected to learn. By controlling the content that was taught to students, the nation could control the future outcome of its children, reproducing citizens that rarely deviated from the traditional parameters of society. Students that exhibited leadership characteristics and traits were those that highly functioned in an educational setting, never defying standard rules or protocols or questioning authority figures.

But while many of these "progressive" ideas in education were increasingly readily available to members of certain races, such was not the case for minority students. Interpretations of historical events has erased and denied minorities the accuracy of their inherent truths, minimized their contributions to the worlds as myths and ultimately portrayed their existence as one of inferiority. Historical depictions of minorities within curricular materials and textbooks trace their roots to forced systemic slavery leading to the degradation of an entire civilization. However, prior to being coerced into slavery and intentionally confined, deep historical analysis reveals that minorities were among notable kings and queens that ruled large portions of countries, which flourished and thrived under their guidance and development. In fact, minorities developed an advanced civilization with citizens that valued humanity in general and lived by a devised code of ethics in which all members of society were equal to each other and were held accountable and responsible for their actions (Williams, 1987). Despite such significant success, powerful representations of African Americans in the form of carvings and portraits and images of royalty were destroyed and diminished in an effort to lead humanity to state of confusion and misinterpretation (Williams, 1987).

History is the quintessential starting point necessary to assess cultural strengths and how minorities were robbed of inherent intellectual capabilities (Cress-Welsing, 1992; Williams, 1987). Woodson (1933) presents strong evidence to suggest that although minorities were eventually freed, they still remained economically enslaved. Through the process of standardization, minorities that were able to attend school were taught how to conform to principles and ways of life that did minimal to propel the development of their culture. Thus, continued feelings of degradation perpetuated among minorities, as they were limited to explorations of knowledge regarding the Americanization of European cultures as opposed to significant contributions made by individuals from their inherent cultural background (Gay, 2001). This widely adopted belief and perspective continues to plague minorities, stagnate their development and is immensely prevalent in educational systems today. As victims of unequivocal poverty and continued systemic oppression it becomes almost impossible to provide equitable learning opportunities without demonstrating a sense of appreciation and awareness of cultural diversity.

In fact, education for minority children became solely dependent upon the efforts of the community in which the child resided in. In such communities, learning opportunities were characterized and cultivated in an environment of equitable access, respect and trust among parents and teachers and the acquisition of concepts and knowledge relevant to the inherent culture and ethnic philosophical dispositions. During the early years of schooling, education consisted of general training combined with natural play. As children grew, they then began primary education, which was composed of mental math exercises, storytelling, exposure to cultural dance and songs and an exploration of nature, as children learned to embrace Mother Nature and the gifts she had to offer. Children also learned how to associate with their community and family members, treating each other with both kindness and respect. Life skills were embedded into hands-on learning experiences as children completed household chores, tended to the farm and cared for younger siblings among other activities as well. Male members of the community attended village council meetings and listened intently to the debates of elder male role models including fathers, grandfathers, uncles and brothers. As children entering the next stage of adolescence, they received intense training and accepted responsibilities that were increasingly complex. Sample learning opportunities consisted of exploring one's family history and role in society, exploring the geographical features of the community as well as understanding geographical relations with neighboring states. Developing strong character values and morals were highly emphasized and exhibiting discipline in all forms of life were important concepts students needed to master. In contrast, training for females differed quite extensively from that of the males. Females generally participated in explorations in topic areas such as history, geography, mathematics and poetry. However, they also engaged in training regarding childcare, housekeeping, gardening and social relations as well. Learning opportunities were facilitated by women representatives from the local community. As these children grew and matured into adults, they would then in turn, aide the community and village in performing the tasks and activities incumbent to its survival.

Teacher Preparatory Programs and Culturally Responsive Teaching

This was the birth of culturally responsive teaching in its truest form. Culture refers to patterns of behaviors, shared customs and traditions, and the values that guide people from one generation to another. It affects how an individual interprets, applies information and explore issues on the surface. Deeper explorations into the term culture reveals that it is defined by concepts of attitude, habits, problem-solving strategies, and the notion of tolerance. Drawing reference to the work of Ladson-Billings (2009), educators can capitalize on the cultural backgrounds of students to facilitate instructional connections and link new knowledge to previous experiences and learning. Culturally responsive educators integrate collaborative measures to support diverse cultures in the classroom. Gay (2010), also adopts a similar ideology and defines culturally responsive teaching as one in which educators make a conscious effort to integrate and link students cultural knowledge, daily lived experiences and learning styles to opportunities that solidify what they already know to be true. Others define culturally responsive teaching as a pedagogy that combines both disciplines and cultures while promoting empowerment and integrity among learners (Wlodkowski & Ginsberg, 1995).

Collectively, in this regard, culturally responsive classrooms are cultivated by a high level of communication; hands on teaching modules, inclusion of culturally and linguistically diverse students, collaboration, negotiation and student participation (Ladson-Billings, 1994). In order for students to become contributing and productive members of society, their cultural background needs to be fully embraced and valued as a pivotal starting point from which to build upon existing knowledge, connecting frameworks and models of thinking to the standards relevant to their grade level.

Much of society has changed since the establishment and development of the American education school system and it appears that while some progress has been made, it is of minimal significance in terms of meeting and addressing the innate needs of minority students from diverse cultural and ethnic backgrounds (Emdin, 2013; Morrell, 2004). Such a different lens and frame of mind by which to view educational inequities requires higher education institutions to reflect upon how they may address student awareness and engage pre-service educators in critical teaching practices to foster a culture and climate that nurture student experiences. Conscious insights from students can offer a profound voice in the process of educational reform. Without providing the necessary environment for students and educators to engage in constructive dialogue regarding inequities in education, it becomes impossible to thoroughly ensure that the very needs that impact education and achievement are being addressed.

As such, Gay (2000) reports that teacher preparatory programs serve a critical role, as culturally responsive teachers integrate student experiences as a paradigm that supports instructional models of learning. New educators must be trained on how to organize classrooms into communities that promote cultural excellence and propel social interactions in which diverse opinions and perspectives are perceived as invaluable to all participants (Gay, 2010). In such classrooms, the roles of both educators and students shift dramatically, as the educators transform into facilitators of instruction while the learner assumes higher levels of accountability and responsibility for their own learning. These shifting dynamics in the classroom environment provides opportunities for both sets of participants to collaborate with each other in the learning process. Effective teaching requires a strong foundation and background knowledge of the diverse student populations present within in a specific classroom. As new teachers are faced with countless responsibilities, it becomes critical for them to develop positive relationships with students that thrive in development over time based on facets of mutual respect and trust. Higher education institutions possess the responsibility to efficiently implement education-training programs that will integrate these pertinent principles and ideals.

WHY IS CULTURAL COMPETENCY CRITICAL?

Equity in education consists of various components: equity in treatment, educational opportunities and adequacy (Fisk and Laud, 2004.) In order to be successful in the classroom, students have an inherent right to be exposed to educational opportunities that integrate diversity. The National Center for Education Statistics continues to report that the achievement gap is widening among minority students (NAEP, 2007). There are a disproportionate number of minority students that are struggling below grade level when compared to their counterparts. Schools need to remedy this issue so that learning is maximized to its full potential. The key begins with transforming the mindset of prospective educators even before they enter the educational sector. Higher education institutions possess a great responsibility in preparing educators and assuring they have the adequate training necessary.

When analyzing why there is a need for cultural competency, Milner (2007) reports that many educators have inaccurate perceptions about minority students, which can be detrimental to their success in schools across the nation. Insufficient resources and culturally unresponsive educational school settings promote the idea of hopelessness and underachievement among minority populations of students. A collective body of research has demonstrated that minority students experience low rates of degree completion, are ill-prepared for the rigors of higher education and remain quite disengaged from academic and social activities both inside and outside of the classroom environment (Lynn et al., 2010; Palmer, Davis & Hilton, 2009 and Palmer and Young, 2009). This has fostered a belief among minorities, most notably African-American males, that efforts to nurture and promote their achievements are not dominating perspectives among educators. These perceptions are generally formulated early in the training stages and solidified by adopting the beliefs and opinions of veteran educators. Higher education institutions can ultimately shift pre-service educators thoughts and perspectives by presenting them with opportunities to engage and experience diverse students in different social contexts. As such, Lynn et al., (2010) reports that educators have failed to motivate, inspire students and provide them with stimulating curricula designed to challenge and assist them in the process of confronting social norms that are root causes of epidemics in communities around the world. In fact, proponents of an oppositional identity theory argue that the very label of minority in and of itself has damaged many races and attributed to a history of enslavement, victimization and the overall resistance of culturally dominant spaces (Emdin, 2013; Morrell & Andrade, 2002). Fordham and Ogbu (1986) traced the origins of cultural dispositions towards the disbelief of inequitable education among minorities. Fordham and Ogbu (1986) alluded that the very belief that minorities were incapable of success rooted in American historical dispositions, has impeded their ability to learn in an educational setting and continues to foster racial gaps. This particular mindset, which was initially developed during the early developmental years of the nation, is one that has created an atmosphere of hostility that at present has not been completely acknowledged nor remedied.

Many researchers (Emdin, 2013; Morrell, 2004; and Gecker, 2014) continue to stress the notion that the issue of class within the context of the classroom environment is often hidden within a core belief system of educators and becomes transparent through stigmatized activities that repress cultural knowledge and aim for conformity. Traditional schooling practices promote specific forms of behavior, conduct and etiquette in which students are rewarded for complying with rules and regulations and are submissive to authoritative figures in control. This model assumes that students are deficient in many areas and attempts to deviate from the norm or critique social structures and institutional processes generally result in disciplinary consequences of referral to special education services. Collectively, these attempts coerce minority students to adopt trending models of action and behavior by concealing cultural identities and minimizing their overall complexities as individuals. There is a lack of trust and respect for one another as opportunities for access and equity shrinks (Killion, J. and Hirschi, 1998). Higher education institutions can assist in developing cultural competency among educators by exposing them to diverse methodologies and hands-on experiences that will shift their mindset. Pre-service educators need to engage in interactive opportunities with students from culturally diverse backgrounds that will assist them in attaining the foundational knowledge and core experience needed to effectively teach students from a wide array of cultures.

CURRENT STRATEGIES USED TO DEVELOP CULTURALLY RELEVANT COMPETENCY IN PROSPECTIVE EDUCATORS

Many researchers argue that it is imperative for educators to understand the characteristics conducive to a particular culture, including values, traditions, methods of communication and learning patterns. Goodman (2011) reports that a number of higher education institutions recognize the importance of developing cultural competency among students whom choose career paths in which they must collaborate with diverse populations, particularly those that enter the field of education. The relationships educators build with learners can be enhanced through understanding and applying principles of cultural competency thereby enabling students to become productive citizens. Higher education programs that focus on developing interpersonal skills should align course goals with initiatives needed to serve people from a wide array of racial and ethnic backgrounds as a means to address systemic oppression. Although many higher education programs provide a course in this particular topic area of study, advocates of social justice contend that it is not nearly enough time needed to sufficiently train pre-service educators in diversity.

Researchers call for a more centralized focus to enable educators to maximize upon the diversity present within the classroom. Goodman (2011) develops a framework for cultural competency that integrates the social identities of individuals and the interactions that shape their experiences and lives. There are five essential elements in this particular model, which include self-awareness, understanding and valuing others, possessing knowledge of societal inequities, learning and applying the skills necessary to effectively interact with diverse people in different social contexts (2011) and finally, utilizing critical skills to foster environments of equity and inclusion. Goodman (2011) reports that the first step in the process to becoming culturally competent lies in the art and ability of gaining a sense of self-awareness. She defines this first component as the consciousness of one's social identities, cultural biases and perspectives collectively combined to assist in the understanding of complexities that exist within a person. In comparison, in the second stage, one must learn how to value others in a positive way by appreciating the diverse perspectives of others. In the next stage that follows, Goodman (2011) reports that it is essential to understand societal inequities and injustices that are part of the larger world we dwell in. By understanding how barriers of systemic oppression and social inequities have negatively affected and impacted the lives of various cultural ethnicities, one can engage in reflection as to how oppression has stagnated their growth and progress in society. As individuals strive to transform their way of thinking they confront systemic barriers, which in turn, leads to organized action against oppression. There is a commitment and dedication to challenge societal norms to understand the root causes of underlying issues faced as well as to liberate oneself and society towards a better future. The next step in this proposed model focuses on the skills necessary to collaborate with diverse people in different contexts. Thus, it becomes imperative to embrace and adapt to different cultures and the dynamics unique to each.

Finally, cultural competence requires educators to identify and address inequities and systems of oppression that impact diverse cultures in a negative way. In this category it is important to engage in critical self-reflection to experience personal change that will ultimately transform institutions as change agents. Goodman (2013) argues that cultural competency is a continuous ongoing process that never ceases. Higher education institutions and teacher preparatory programs can integrate cultural competency in a variety of ways. Among her recommendations, Goodman (2013) urges training and preparatory programs to develop and assess learning outcomes aligned to cultural competency goals and ensure that staff and faculty have the necessary cultural competency needed to foster environment of equity and inclusion. Goodman (2013) poignantly points out that it is necessary to prepare students in programs of service to become culturally competent and promote heightened levels of awareness and commitment to equity.

The startling reality is that many educators are not thoroughly prepared or trained to teach students from a wide array of diverse and ethnical background. It then becomes imperative for future educators to understand specific cultural characteristics that are unique to each race. Researcher Gay (2001) outlines a series of pertinent information that educators should possess knowledge on prior to entering the teaching field. First and foremost, she argues that instructors need to understand how family lifestyles coupled with cooperative problem-solving directly impacts educational motivation and task performance among students. She further purports that educators should understand the customs and traditions related to how adults and children interact with each other in an instructional environment. Consistent with this theme, Sleeter (2001), reports that students of color possess rich cultural experiences and perspectives that impact teacher education programs and has pertinent implications that shape the manner in which students learn and how they connect and relate information. A large number of pre-service students remain aware that they will directly work with children from various ethnicities and in urban areas. Nonetheless, a multitude of educators are inadequately prepared with both the knowledge and experience to teach culturally diverse students in an efficient manner. According to Gay (2010) pre-service student teachers adopt stereotypical beliefs about urban children and their ability to achieve significant growth in schools. They attribute their lack of achievement to negative attitudes that incapacitate their ability to succeed in the classroom. Understanding the complex dynamics of racism is peculiarly important as well as systemic inequalities that have been fostered in society play crucial role in the lives of students. These social inequities transcend into the classroom environment as structures of dominion in which educators exhibit a high level of unpreparedness to deal with such major issues. By means of comparison pre-service students of color innately possess the background knowledge, experience and are committed to providing minority students with challenging rigorous curriculum.

Students are more than likely to trust and respect an educator with identical or similar cultural affiliations and characteristics as opposed to someone from a different race that is unable to relate to how racial interactions have impacted student performance. Research illustrates that minority teachers are more than likely to exhibit higher expectations for students, increase their confidence and motivate them in ways that positively promote learning. Although it may be unintended, some educators exhibit racial biases towards minority students and neglect to provide attention and feedback to them (Sleeter, 2001).

DIVERSITY AND MULTI-CULTURAL COURSES

Many higher education institutions typically employ the use of an urban education, diversity or multi-cultural course as a requirement necessary to successfully complete their education training program. This one semester course usually emphasizes general strategies and techniques to serve ethnically diverse students from high poverty levels that are subject to crime, drugs, family issues and violence in their neighborhood on a daily basis. Students in urban areas experiences a lack of self-esteem, which impacts their ability to apply and retain concepts and knowledge learned.

According to the NEA, only one third of the states currently require perspective educators to enroll in a diversity or multi-cultural course and/or participate in student teaching in a culturally diverse setting. Approximately nine states have adopted standards in cultural knowledge and competency, requiring higher education institutions to thoroughly ensure that pre-service educators are familiar with the characteristics, history, values and beliefs of predominate cultures. Aimed to increase student awareness of cultures and diversity, *multi-cultural courses* often require students to engage in critical analyses and reflection regarding the future students they will encounter in the classroom. Waddell (2013) report that higher education institutions have a responsibility to prepare pre-service educators in developing new perspectives, thereby assisting students in the process of gaining personal empowerment and embracing diversity as a valuable tool that can foster learning (Scully, 1986). To remedy this issue, many higher education institutions have integrated multicultural teacher education courses as part of their graduation requirements. A number of college faculty members strongly feel that multicultural education is necessary to transform assumptions and perceptions about teaching minority children while striving towards effective instructional pedagogy that embrace diversity and humanity all around. However, such institutions do not require more than a minimum of one or two courses at best and many argue that this is not sufficient enough to thoroughly prepare prospective educators as they only explore cultural diversity on the surface.

While such programs can have a positive and lasting impact on educators, Sleeter (2001) argues that many of these courses are solely dependent upon the interests of the professors that teach them. Many faculty members experience great levels of difficulty and uncertainty in effectively designing courses to meet student needs. In fact, researchers report that faculty members in higher education institutions are hesitant to engage in deep dialogue and conversations about race and racism in America (Assad et al, 2010). This notion perpetuates an environment of systemic oppression by failing to explicitly address inequities that impact minority students. In a qualitative study conducted by Assad et al (2010), which analyzed teacher perceptions pertaining to multicultural teacher education, researchers reported that teacher educators felt that dialogue and transparency about race or socio-economic status would lead to resistance and manifest into conversations beyond their comfort zone and control. Thus, multicultural education programs tend to embed sheltered activities such as cultural celebrations, traditions and the exploration of ethnic literature in the classroom environment. This notion permeates the belief that schools are institutions in which minorities continue to struggle as the achievement gap widens.

There needs to be a coherent and centralized focus to create and develop sustained programs in multiculturalism in which higher education institutions are held accountable for the implementation of diversity and multi-cultural programs. Cochran-Smith (2003) identifies several elements in a conceptual framework designed to thoroughly educate pre-service teachers on multiculturalism. Those elements consist of mainly on issues relating to diversity, philosophical dispositions, core knowledge, teacher learning and practice, outcomes and teacher candidate selection. This model has been adopted by various researchers in the process of exploring how educators feel about the components of multicultural pre-service education (Capella-Santana, 2003).

When pre-service educators are encouraged to freely discuss and challenge issues that occur in urban school settings, they experience an increase in positive attitudes and beliefs about diversity (Capella-Santana, 2003). Many researchers argue that teacher education preparation programs should enable candidates to reflect on the political and cultural ideologies represented with an education. Issue such as language barriers, cultural identity and patterns in socio-economic status continue to impact teaching and learning.

COMMUNITY BASED IMMERSION PROGRAMS

Cultural misconceptions can potentially lead to sustained disconnections and strained relationships among educators and students within the classroom environment. Researcher Gay (2010) asserts that novice teachers generally hold negative stereotypical perceptions of certain ethnic groups based on the manner in which the media portrays them, as well as beliefs passed down from one generation to the next among members of various races. Coupled with content taught regarding the historical development of the country, it then becomes quite difficult for some to understand how issues of discrimination and inequality impacts culturally diverse students. As such pre-service teachers tend to engage in avoidance tactics to dismiss issues of classism and race that are deeply rooted, prevalent issues that have impacted and stagnated the growth of many cultures. Future educators must understand how to effectively interact with other cultures if they are to experience success in the classroom.

To this end, higher education institutions have developed community immersion programs to specifically immerse teaching candidates in the communities and environments they are more than likely to teach in. *Community-based immersion programs* are defined as experiences in which pre-service students are required to spend time in a culturally diverse community. Community immersion experiences combine experiential learning and exposure to forms of systemic oppression that requires students to step outside of their traditional comfort zone and examine their inherent beliefs and perceptions. These experiences typically are focused on assisting pre-service educators in developing positive attitudes towards the community; creating a sense of awareness in understanding how complex issues impact education; develop the skills necessary to actively engage in collaboration with community members; and transform perceptions. Pre-service educators have a hands-on opportunity to interact with members of a diverse community, as they listen to each individual story and connect with the storyteller(s) in an emotional way that leads to compassion. It is a learner focused investigative experience and increases the candidates' personal sense of responsibility and purpose in the field of education, as they are faced-to-faced with the challenges and barriers that minorities have struggled with. This affords prospective educators the opportunity to learn strategies and techniques to interact with students from a wide array of ethnicities and learn about the priorities and values that are important to students and residents.

Cooper (2007) reports that community immersion activities that are integrated into teacher preparation programs can ultimately enable future educators to develop and maintain positive relationships with learners and create a positive impact upon student achievement. Cultural immersion experiences can benefit students when they proactively participate and engage in opportunities for learning with diverse students. Many researchers argue that such experiences allow novice teachers to critically engage in self-reflection, shifting their mind set and creating higher levels of both cultural and community awareness (Burant & Kirby, 2002; Ladson-Billings, 2001 & Sleeter, 2001).

According to Miller (2010), pre-service educational programs should assist prospective educators in the process of gaining invaluable knowledge and exploring belief systems, inclusive of both cognitive an analytical skills. This journey should integrate opportunities for educators to understand their own cultural identities and create culturally responsive learning opportunities that will benefit students. Research indicates that pre-service teachers have substantially limited background information in regards to the circumstances of low socioeconomic and minority students (Amatea, Cholewam & Mixon, 2012). These students lack both the training and philosophical dispositions needed to thoroughly address students from a wide array of ethnicities. Furthermore this results in negative thinking and reinforcement of stereotypical views that equate academic performance among poor minority students to deficiencies within their community and home environment (Valencia, 1997). As such, Waddell (2013) asserts that education preparatory programs utilize an integrated approach in which components of self-reflection and diversity intersect with the learning experiences of students enrolled in the program. In this process it becomes necessary for prospective educators to examine their inner thoughts and beliefs systems as it relates to culturally responsive teaching.

A growing body of research purports that pre-service teachers are strictly limited to university classrooms in which there are not sufficient opportunities to interact with community members from culturally and linguistically diverse backgrounds (Leland & Murtadha, 2011). Waddell (2013), argues that meaningful real life experiences can enable teaching candidates to gain a sense of awareness and understand the historical and social aspects that the concept of a community has on schools, students and families. Such alternative authentic experiences can assist potential educators in developing a sense of cultural diversity, by applying analytical thinking and the use of critical consciousness. In this regard, they confront various life scenarios, which impact the academic, behavioral, emotional, psychological challenges they are bound to face in the context of the classroom. Furthermore, such emergent experiences help educators to develop a professional teacher identity, helping to shape beliefs about students' capacity to be successful. Additionally, community immersion experiences provide an authentic real world environment for candidates to delve into pertinent issues such as classism, diversity, analyzing power structures of dominance and race. Multiple avenues within the community can ultimately diminish negative stereotypes and provide invaluable information and insight regarding the strengths and weaknesses of the community.

In an effort to provide a structured community immersion program, researcher Cooper (2007), specifically designed and implemented a study focused on a series of requirements that would allow 42 participants enrolled in a south eastern public university to engage in diversity activities. Each structured activity required students to engage in deep analysis and critical self-reflection regarding who they were inside, how they wanted the world to perceive them and they viewed the students they were expected to encounter as future educators. Among those activities, participants were required to compose a written autobiography, conduct a privilege walk to discover how their inner beliefs and perceptions directly affected how they perceived others, conduct visits to site staples within the community, engage in real life experiences that mirrored similar activities that students and families conducted on a daily basis. These range of activities were purposely designed so participants would experience the journey of discovery and gain a strong sense of the communities that their students resided in. Cooper (2007) reports that a series of three themes emerge from this project include emotions of fear and resistance; nervousness and a concern for safety, a sense of revelations and transformation. While initially met with both fear and resistance, the development of these community immersion activities in a structured program allowed pre-service educators to gain a new lens of understanding and preparedness as they begin to transform their mindset.

FIELD EXPERIENCES AND STUDENT TEACHING

Many teacher education preparatory programs culminate in fieldwork opportunities otherwise known as the student teaching experience. Student teachers in programs are typically one semester in length and require teaching candidates to utilize content knowledge attained from previous education courses in formal application and synthesis activities. As a significant part of training and experience, student teaching requires educators to develop instructional materials, design and implement lesson plans, establish classroom management, create and maintain relationships with parental figures and students as well as complete additional tasks incumbent to the position of educator.

Student teaching experiences help to mold expectations of future educators regarding their individual performance and their beliefs about students overall ability to achieve. According to the National Council on Teacher Quality (2011), state regulations differ tremendously in providing guidance regarding student teaching experiences and many have neglected to adopt a universal model. At the present time, no specific state has a comprehensive set of regulations or guidelines to inform student teaching programs and practices. From an international standpoint, in countries such as Finland and Japan, teaching candidates must engage in a full year of clinical experiences under the supervision of highly effective educators and faculty members. Additionally students that complete field experiences are placed in areas that resemble their childhood upbringing. As a direct result, new graduates entering urban school districts are usually in a state of shock and awe and experience great difficulty in the classroom their first year. Having attained these notions in mind, it then becomes imperative to design training programs that focus on thoroughly prepare potential teachers for the daily realities that occur in the classroom. As such the National Council on Teacher Quality has developed five critical standards to allow higher education institutions to implement programs of student teaching in a manner that would ultimately allow candidates to gain the knowledge and experience necessary to function effectively as future educators.

Research suggests that there are many inconsistencies across higher academic institutions regarding the placement of pre-service educators, which ultimately impact their perception of students from diverse backgrounds. This implies and suggests that state regulations should enforce policies that allow teacher candidates to demonstrate competency of content knowledge and multicultural education to provide a high caliber of academic excellence to students.

Additional research suggests that prospective teachers that engage in fieldwork based exercises and experiences are able to successfully use such scenarios to develop meaningful opportunities for students and accommodate instructional modalities to meet the needs of diverse learners, incorporating their cultural background into learning experiences. This enables teachers to create and build positive relationships with students and parental figures from various cultural background. Field based experiences provide critical opportunities for teaching candidates to implement theoretical dispositions into practice and gain a strong sense of awareness of diversity. It provides practical ways and authentic for students to gain hands on experience. In addition field-based learning opportunities provides pre-service educators with the chance to dialogue and interact with veteran educators and work directly with learners.

A FRAMEWORK FOR IMPROVEMENT AND RECOMMENDATIONS

Teacher education preparatory programs should make a conscious effort to recruit as many pre-service teachers that have the knowledge experience and commitment that will enable them to successfully teach students from a wide array of cultural backgrounds. Given the content and scope of research presented the following framework has been developed to assist higher education institutions in the process of assuming accountability and responsibility of future educators.

Table 1. Timeline

Timeframe	Process
	Stage I: Setting the Stage
	• Create and establish a nurturing and positive atmosphere based on principles of exploration and support • Ensure that themes of cultural competency are embedded throughout multiple facets of the curriculum and the overall program design via hands-on exploratory modules
	Stage II: Research and Reflect
	• Provide multiple opportunities for prospective educators to engage in an exploration and deep analysis of individual cultural identity • Invest time in learning about diverse cultures, including dialect, customs, communication/linguistic patterns, traditions and values • Provide mandatory courses in Race and Racism. For many centuries, minority students have been taught that their history begins with the manifestation of physical slavery; this inaccurate portrayal of historical events has impacted cultures in a negative manner. It is essential to explore historical truths to truly understand and value the significant contributions made by others to all off humanity • Exploration in Cultural Competency from its core meaning to the value that it adds in the educational sector including how a core knowledge in diversity can impact student achievement and close the achievement gap • Engage in critical consciousness
	Stage III: Hands-On Exploration
	• Conduct an in-depth community site visits in a suburban and urban area; compare the differences observed from leadership, educators, students, parents to the overall community • Conduct ongoing interviews of educators, students, parents and local citizens and actively engage in conversations regarding the strengths/weaknesses of the community and how education can be utilized as a means to improve targeted areas of weaknesses • Select an issue identified by community members as a potential weakness and develop an Action Research Project to investigate the issue throughout the duration of the next stage.
	Stage IV: Teaching Practicum
	• Student Teaching: Requirement 1 year in desired grade level in an urban area, (preferably a high stakes testing grade); candidates should engage in ALL activities conducive to the job requirements of the hired educator including but not limited to, demonstrating classroom management skills, participating in professional development sessions and staff meetings, meeting with parents, composing and implementing lesson plans etc. • Implement Action Research study by investigating and developing proactive solutions regarding a specific issue relevant to cultural competency and culturally responsive educators as identified in the previous stage
	Stage V: Reflection
	• Engage in self-reflection regarding all Stage IV experiences to assess and evaluate experience and knowledge attained • Present Action Research and proposed solutions • Formulate a formative Philosophy on Education

FUTURE RESEARCH DIRECTIONS

Future research in this particular area should focus on measuring the overall quality and effectiveness of culturally relevant teacher preparatory programs by obtaining feedback from administrative leaders, educators, and student participants.

CONCLUSION

This chapter explored the current mechanisms currently used by higher education institutions in the process of developing culturally relevant practitioners including, student teaching, diversity and multicultural introductory courses and community immersions programs. According to the NEA not only does the concept of culture play a significant role in the overall learning process, but it is essential for educators to attain the knowledge necessary regarding distinctive cultural backgrounds of students in order to facilitate effective instruction. Lesson connections between home, school and the broader community at large have proven to substantially increase student achievement.

As educators, the concept of cultural competency is one that provides an invaluable opportunity for us to look within and delve deep into our own perspectives of humanity and the larger world. As we begin to live our lives through such an awakened lens and a shifting mindset, we learn to demonstrate elements of cultural competency through both our actions and thoughts. Working with children from diverse backgrounds requires educators to engage in consistent and constant self-reflection. In essence, this creates an atmosphere of belonging and respect among our students.

Discussion and Reflection Points

- Do you think that higher education institutions thoroughly prepare pre-service educators for a career in teaching and successful interacting with students from diverse cultures?
- Why are the concepts of "cultural competency" and a "culturally responsive" educator essential to the growth and development of minority students?
- How can higher education institutions and professors embrace change and create an innovative environment for student learning and growth?
- How can the proposed model of design transform the educational sector?
- How can the awareness of self transform the dynamics of education?

REFERENCES

Amatea, E., Cholewa, B., & Mixon, K. (2012). Influencing preservice teachers attitudes about working with low-income and/or ethnic minority families. *Urban Education*, *47*(4), 801–834. doi:10.1177/0042085912436846

Brick, B. (2005). Changing concepts of equal educational opportunity: A comparison of the views of Thomas Jefferson, Horace Mann and John Dewey. *American Educational History Journal*, *32*(2), 166–174.

Burant, T. J., & Kirby, D. (2002). Beyond classroom-based early field experiences: Understanding an educative practicum in an urban school and community. *Teaching and Teacher Education*, *18*(5), 561–575. doi:10.1016/S0742-051X(02)00016-1

Capella-Santana, N. (2003). Voices of Teacher Candidates: Positive Changes in Multicultural Attitudes and Knowledge. *The Journal of Educational Research*, *96*(3), 182–190. doi:10.1080/00220670309598806

Cochran-Smith, M. (2004). The multiple meanings of multicultural teacher education. In F. Schultz (Ed.), Annual editions: Multicultural education 04/05 (pp. 51-53). Guilford, CT: McGraw-Hill.

Cooper, J. E. (2007). Strengthening the case for community-based learning in teacher education. *Journal of Teacher Education*, *58*(3), 245–255. doi:10.1177/0022487107299979

Emdin, C. (2013). The rap cypher, the battle, and reality pedagogy: Developing communication and argumentation in urban science education. In M. L. Hill & E. Petchauer (Eds.), *Schooling hip-hop: Expanding hip-hop based education across the curriculum* (pp. 118–136). New York, NY: Teachers College Press.

Fisk & Laud. (2004). *Elusive Equity: Education Reform in Post-Apartheid South Africa*. Washington, DC: Brookings Institution Press.

Fordham, S., & Ogbu, J. U. (1986). Black students school success: Coping with the burden of acting White. *The Urban Review*, *18*(3), 176–206. doi:10.1007/BF01112192

Gay, G. (2000). *Culturally responsive teaching: Theory, research, practice*. New York: Teacher College Press.

Gay, G. (2001). Preparing for culturally responsive teaching. *Journal of Teacher Education*, *53*(, 2), 106–116.

Gay, G. (2010). *Culturally responsive teaching: Theory, research and practice* (2nd ed.). New York, NY: Teachers College Press.

Gecker, W. (2013). *A pedagogy of openness: Queer theory as a tool for class equity*. The Poverty and Education Reader.

Goodman, D. J. (2011). *Promoting Diversity and Social Justice: Educating People from Privileged Groups*. New York, NY: Routledge.

Goodman, D. J. (2013). *Cultural Competency for Social Justice*. Commission for Social Justice. Retrieved from https://acpacsje.wordpress.com/2013/02/05/cultural-competency-for-social-justice-by-diane-j-goodman-ed-d/

Killion, J., & Hirschi. (1998). A crack in the middle. *Education Week, 17*(27), 44–49.

Ladson-Billings, G. (1994). *The dreamkeepers: Successful teachers of African American children*. San Francisco: Jossey-Bass Publishers.

Lynn, L. M., Bacon, J. N., Totten, T. L., Bridges, T. L., III, & Jennings, M. E. (2010). Examining teachers' beliefs about African-American male students in a low-performing high school in an African American school district. *Teachers College Record, 112*(1), 289–330.

Milner, H. R. (2010). What does teacher education have to do with teaching? Implications for diversity studies. *Journal of Teacher Education, 61*(1-2), 118–131. doi:10.1177/0022487109347670

Mondale, S. (2002). *The story of American public education*. Boston, MA: Beacon Press.

Morrell, E. (2004). *Linking literacy and popular culture: Finding connections for lifelong learning*. Norwood, MA: Christopher-Gordon.

Morrell, E., & Duncan-Andrade, J. (2002). Toward a critical classroom discourse: Promoting academic literacy through engaging Hip-Hop culture with urban youth. *English Journal, 91*(6), 88–92. doi:10.2307/821822

Palmer, R. T., Davis, R. J., & Hilton, A. A. (2009). Exploring challenges that threaten to impede the academic success of academically underprepared African-American male collegians at an HBCU. *Journal of College Student Development, 50*(4), 429–445. doi:10.1353/csd.0.0078

Palmer, R. T., & Young, E. M. (2009). Determined to succeed: Salient factors that foster academic success for academically unprepared Black males at a Black college. *Journal of College Student Retention, 10*(4), 465–482. doi:10.2190/CS.10.4.d

Scully, M. G. (1986). Study finds colleges torn over division, confused over roles. *The Chronicle of Higher Education, 1*, 16.

Sleeter, C. (2001). Preparing teachers for culturally diverse schools: Research and the overwhelming presence of Whiteness. *Journal of Teacher Education, 59*(3), 212–219. doi:10.1177/0022487108317019

Sue, D. W., & Sue, D. (2007). *Counseling the Culturally Diverse: Theory and Practice*. Hoboken, NJ: John Wiley and Sons.

The National Center for Education Statistics. (2007). *NAEP Data Explorer*. Retrieved from http://nces.ed.gov/nationsreportcard/nde/

Valencia, R. R. (1997). Conceptualizing the notion of deficit thinking. In R. R. Valencia (Ed.), *The evolution of deficit thinking*. New York: Taylor and Francis. Retrieved from http://reader.eblib.com.proxy.library.umke.edu/

Waddell, J. (2013). Communities as critical partners in teacher education: The impact of community immersion on teacher candidates' understanding of self and teaching in urban schools. *Current Issues in Education*, 2(16), 1–15.

Welsing, F. C. (1991). *The Isis (Yssis) papers*. Chicago: Third World Press.

Williams, C. (1987). The destruction of Black civilization: Great issues of a race from 4500 B.C. to 2000 A.D. Chicago: Third World Press.

Wlodkowski, R. J., & Ginsberg, M. B. (1995). *Diversity and Motivation: Culturally Responsive Teaching*. San Francisco: Jossey-Bass.

Woodson, C. G. (1933). *The Mis-Education of the Negro*. Trenton, NJ: Africa World Press.

This research was previously published in Cultural Awareness and Competency Development in Higher Education edited by Sherrie Wisdom, Kelly Leavitt, and Lynda Leavitt; pages 207-222, copyright year 2017 by Information Science Reference (an imprint of IGI Global).

Chapter 34
Fusing Culturally Responsive Teaching, Place Conscious Education, and Problem-Based Learning With Mobile Technologies:
Sparking Change

Nykela H. Jackson
University of Central Arkansas, USA

ABSTRACT

Students must be provided meaningful learning opportunities to employ content through active learning opportunities that capitalize their interests (mobile technologies), fuse real life issues (problems that they face in school or local community), and sustain their curiosity (creative learning experiences). Using mobile technologies for culturally responsive, problem based learning is a powerful and unique way to prepare students for the four C's: critical thinking, communication, collaboration, and creativity. This chapter provides theoretical and practical support of the innovative impact of using mobile technologies in student selected, problem focused learning.

INTRODUCTION

Throughout history, nations have experienced contentious and hostile social and/or cultural incidents (e.g., Holocaust, Apartheid, AIDS epidemic, slavery, genocide, Jim Crow law). Even today with all of the advancements in manufacturing, transportation, security, medicine, and technology, these social justice events continue to occur in the United States and around the world (e.g., racial intolerance; large populations without access to clean water, food, and medical care to cure preventable diseases; ISIS; poverty; deplorable living and working conditions).

DOI: 10.4018/978-1-7998-1213-5.ch034

Fusing Culturally Responsive Teaching

News reports affirm that communities continually face "wicked problems," formerly described by Rittel and Webber (1973) as the social or cultural problems that are challenging to solve due to inconsistent, conflicting, and changing factors. Challenges such as water cleanliness, air quality, climate control, agricultural issues, population migration, unemployment, poverty, violence, industries moving overseas, health concerns (e.g., Zika virus, obesity, cancer, new illnesses), and economic crisis are just a few issues that have impacted students' communities in some way. Murgatroyd (2010) stressed that it is crucial for students to realize that change is not other people's responsibility but an obligation for everyone. To experience this notion of accountability, students need chances to respond to both culturally relevant and place-based problems using technology resources for innovation and design to solve real problems in their local contexts.

The power of technology has made information about social justice incidents accessible and readily available. Through social media and news, society has firsthand access to dig deeper, to critically analyze issues, and to create platforms for people to voice their opinions and/or raise awareness. There are numerous apps and social media options that support communication, advocacy, means for financial assistance, and activism. This technology has assisted with transforming our roles in society from one of bystander to one where we can take a more visible presence in recognizing and supporting talk around issues. Technology has made a huge impact providing learners with immediate access to information and sharing of ideas. The next step is to find more ways to use technology to solve problems and make a social impact.

Integrating technology to affect social change in students' communities and local society structures is the perfect venue to show students how to directly address social and cultural issues on a small-scale level and that can be used as a platform to tackle bigger issues. Cultivating students' dispositions from a young age with the gift of empathy, the power of understanding, and the promotion of social action has the potential to empower positive change on a large scale.

Teachers are accountable to nurture and prepare the next generation to have the necessary skills to live and work successfully in a multicultural society (Roehrig, Moore, Wang, & Park, 2012). Although academic content is extremely important, many problems that students will encounter once they graduate high school center on injustices some groups may face and will not be related to a specific content area (Duch, Groh, & Allen, 2001) or tied to scores on standardized tests. Instead, the problem-solving strategies and cross-disciplinary knowledge that students apply to real life contexts can serve as a baseline for creating innovative solutions to issues and problems.

This is the work teachers now must engage in. Memorizing and regurgitating facts out of a textbook removed from the world as it exists outside of school is not an effective method of deep learning (Towler, 2014). Teachers' goals should not be simply to encourage learners to access and understand content, but to apply what they learned by building authentic experiences encouraging them to share information with peers and community stakeholders, to investigate multiple perspectives, and to execute social action (Sharples, Kloos, Dimitriadis, Garlatti, & Specht, 2015).

Students must be provided meaningful learning opportunities to use their content knowledge and to develop higher order thinking skills through active learning opportunities that capitalize on their interests -- issues around them and in their local communities. Active engagement occurs when students work on issues that they personally care about and that are relevant to what is going in their lives. In these learning situations, mobile technologies can be used as a tool for exploration and communication and as a method to approach these problems through creative learning experiences. These hands-on experiences provide students with the opportunity to be actively engaged to create and to create change. Potential solutions to issues come from a collective group of engaged activists and/or a fervent individual.

Mobile Technologies and Social Action

Teachers who use mobile technologies to blend culturally responsive teaching with place-conscious education and problem-based learning are creating a perfect storm for their classrooms. They are using technology to spark change and to show students how to take social action in the world.

Using mobile technologies to help achieve this academic goal allows teachers and students the freedom and flexibility for deeper learning as well as moving learning into the context of students' lives outside the classroom. Technology access can assist with the research of the issue at hand to discern facts from opinions, communicate with a group to generate point of view, and analyze the presented information to develop perspective. Teachers are expected to implement inventive practices and lessons that require engagement, exploration, explanation, extension, and evaluation (Bybee, Taylor, Gardner et al., 2006). Mobile technologies employed within a specific, local context help with achieving these goals.

Intentional integration of mobile technologies used for authentic learning (used for brainstorming, collaboration, communication, inquiry, constructive feedback, access to learning resources, research, data collection, record of evidence, assessment) instead of addition (used only for research, presentations, and educational games that meet the teacher's needs) provides students the chance to investigate issues in their local communities and develop relevant questions to solve or issues to explore. By allowing the element of choice in selecting problems to analyze and examining areas of interest, students have more autonomy and motivation to be creative and innovative (Strimmel, 2014). Through this process students construct knowledge and innovation, which are essential skills for 21st century college and career readiness (Tambouris, Panopoulou, Tarabanis et al., 2012).

The skills promoted by problem-based, placed-based, and culturally responsive approaches supported by mobile technology integration allows schools to equip students for careers/jobs that do not even exist, demand proficiencies that are not fully outlined, and utilize technologies that have yet to be created (Murgatroyd, 2010). To prepare current and future mobile literacy (Pacansky-Brock, 2013), students need practice in and with 21st century learning goals. Mobile technologies enable the implementation of authentic learning that may otherwise seem problematic to implement due to classroom constraints, cost, and time (Lombardi, 2007). The purpose of this chapter is to provide theoretical and practical supports that demonstrate the importance of using mobile technologies to integrate culturally relevant teaching, place-conscious education, and problem-based learning.

THEORETICAL FOUNDATION

Students learn best through active engagement, discovery, and application of concepts in real life contexts (Dewey, 1915; Vygotsky, 1978). These are the same ideas embedded in culturally responsive teaching, place-conscious education, and problem-based learning approaches to learning. Using mobile technologies for problem based learning, rooted in student generated interests or problems that are relevant to students' environments and responsive to students' cultures, allows for creativity and unique learning opportunities (McFalls, 2013).

Culturally Responsive Teaching

The goal of culturally relevant teaching is for students to develop sociocultural consciousness, have opportunities to construct their own knowledge to shape their personal views, and connect learning with relevant experiences (Kea, Campbell-Whatley, & Richards, 2006). The focus is changed from the conception of information to the creation of knowledge and collective ownership.

Culturally responsive teaching is a thoughtful and methodical process of attentiveness to cultural significances, concerns, and problems (Gay, 2010). In an effort to combat misconceptions, interpret and recognize different viewpoints, and inspire students to think, students are challenged to take risks to not only embrace their own beliefs but understand the value of others' perceptions (Gay, 2002; Gay, 2010). students are encouraged to become an integral part of the learning community and decision making process through this learner-centered approach as they engage in active participation, critical thinking, and deep discussions. (Rychly & Graves, 2012).

There is a misconception that culturally responsive teaching is simply adding multicultural resources (e.g., books that include underrepresented populations, posters/images that showcase the accomplishments of minorities, highlights of notable minority people (Banks, 2002). But culturally responsive teaching is so much more than simply adding a few resources into a standing curriculum. Gay (2002, 2010) emphasized that students must witness people they identify within the curriculum, see other cultural groups reflected in the curriculum, and engage with people who are different from them. Ladson-Billings (1994) outlined the following foundations:

- Communication of high expectations.
- Active teaching methods (student engagement and active participation in planning what is being studied in the curriculum).
- Teacher as facilitator (learner centered environment).
- Inclusion of culturally and linguistically diverse students and their families (addressing meaningful issues to these communities and/or including individuals and cultural issues in the classroom curriculum and experiences).
- Cultural sensitivity.
- Reshaping the curriculum (e.g., experiences to engage in social situations for learning, valuing student's cultural knowledge, opportunities to practice cultural competence).
- Student controlled classroom discourse (e.g., chances for student led discussions, interest based problem solving, student choice in the direction of curriculum).
- Small group instruction and collaboration (Ladson-Billings, 1994).

Implementation of the fundamentals that comprise culturally responsive teaching allows students to participate in learning experiences that fit well in the context of problem-based learning. Additionally, culturally responsive teaching also dovetails nicely with the literature base describing place-conscious education.

Place-Conscious Education

Culturally responsive teaching can be complemented when paired with the tenants of place-conscious education to focus instruction on experiences encountered in students' neighborhoods, community, city, or state and/or challenges of particular groups/individuals (Gruenewald, 2008; Greenwood, 2011; Murgatroyd, 2010). Using place-conscious education, students will not only see the relevance in what they are learning, but they will become more aware of cultural issues while learning to analyze and view issues from different perspectives (Gay, 2010).

Place conscious education connects learning with the life of the community and with students' lived experiences. Using this theoretical lens in the classroom to stage instruction, students get firsthand experience with recognizing local and community issues and have opportunities to impact the community through problem based learning. Students are able to use a crucial lens to link learning with the community and culture outside the school walls (Greenwood, 2011; Gruenewald, 2008). Local and community problems (e.g., social, cultural, ecological, political, economic, history, community) are investigated, empowering social action at the local level which could serve as a springboard for an even bigger impact.

Fusing culturally responsive teaching and place conscious education allows students to connect real life experiences with what is happening in society. Additionally, using culturally responsive teaching practices with emphasis on social justice issues, can help students identify potential issues in their own communities and raise awareness. Students can then address issues and apply what they learned on a local, more tangible level.

Problem Based Learning

Problem based learning provides students with the ideal opportunity to build critical and creative thinking skills, explore issues to identify problems, develop research questions, gather and analyze data, develop possible solutions, and disseminate this information to others (Lambros, 2002). A fusion between culturally responsive teaching and place-conscious education into problem-based approaches not only enhances the learning experience, but surpasses the last step of problem-based learning of disseminating information, to social action. This approach is transformational, taking an abstract idea and responding to it with concrete action.

Problem based learning is an instructional approach that enhances learning by presenting students with authentic problems to analyze and solve (Duch, Groh, & Allen, 2001; Hung, Hwang, Lee, Wu, Vogel, Milrad, & Johansson, 2014; Lambros, 2002; Tambouris, Panopoulou, Tarabanis et al., 2012; Torp & Sage, 2002; Wattinger, Nguyen, Fornaro et al., 2006). Students work in small collaborative groups to identify "complex, real world problems" and use current knowledge and newly learned information to determine feasible solutions through investigation (Duch, Groh, & Allen, 2001; Torp & Sage, 2002; Wattinger et. al 2006). Problems are embedded in the curriculum (addressing state and national standards), connecting school content to real life experiences. Teachers serve as facilitators to coach learning through inquiry, questioning, and active participation. Through these authentic experiences students develop problem solving and self-directed learning skills (Torp & Sage, 2002).

As shareholders and agents of change, students not only formulate answers but suggest resolutions for social action. Students' move through the following criteria for problem based learning:

- Acknowledge a relevant, open-ended problem (can be teacher selected but to be more culturally-responsive should be student driven issues and/or learner centered action research, focused on the population and community students identify and/or community, local, and/or state issues).
- Investigate concerns (research and define important components).

Fusing Culturally Responsive Teaching

- Recognize multiple perspectives (e.g., discuss situations, value teammates' viewpoints, empathize with different beliefs that challenge own feelings, accept everyone's contributions).
- Empower student voice in learning (collaborative group problem statement, action steps).
- Launch student investigation and research (e.g., resources, collaboration, communication, speculations, active examination).
- Devise quality solutions (authorize multiple outcomes, supporting evidence, recommendations based on data analysis and interpretation of research, present and defend conclusions).
- Allocate for reflection (implement or propose social action, apply learning in a situation or personal life) (Lombardi, 2007; Northern Illinois University, n. d.).

Mobile Technologies to Spark Change

The use of mobile technologies as tools to target culturally responsive, place based problems is a fusion for change. Similar to how fusion is the source of energy to power the sun, stars, and universe, integration of mobile technologies is the fuel and spark students need to immerse in this type of learning. To effectively infuse this combination, teachers will have to embrace a learner centered pedagogy that stimulates students through creative and purposeful use of technology (Montrieux, Vanderlinde, Schellens, & De Marez, 2015).

Mobile technologies (e.g., wearable devices, tablet computers, smartphones) provide portability, immediate access, and availability from anywhere (Davidson & Lazaros, 2015; Watson, 2001). Students have more flexibility to participate in learning experiences at their convenience. These perks permit students to engage in contextual learning both at school and in their community. The broad array of online resources (e.g., internet resources, databases journals, books) to retrieve information and diverse tools for communication and collaboration endorse more efficient problem-based work (Watson, 2001). Beyond research, students can use mobile technologies to discuss, deliberate, distribute, and debrief ideas/evidence with peers and the teacher instantly and from anywhere (Hung, Hwang, Lee, Wu, Vogel, Milrad, & Johansson, 2014).

Mobile technologies allow teachers to combine the ideals of culturally responsive teaching, place-based consciousness, and problem based learning to tackle local/community problems and to offer students the opportunity to examine and work within real life contexts. Mobile technologies make this assimilation easier, since students have readily available support and resources to facilitate learning. Through processes encouraged by these models and through allowing student choice in selecting problems to examine, teachers can use students' passion as an anchor to connect content and inspire students to take ownership.

Investigating practical questions to make a difference in the school and/or families/community embraces these ideals and focuses students on exploring their world in an authentic way and then seeking positive change (Hung, Hwang, Lee et al., 2014). For example, history students could interview immigrants who have gone through the process to become a citizen to find out positives and shortcomings they endured. After analysis of local and national issues with immigration, students could then publish their findings and recommendations through an online documentary to improve the current process. This information could be shared with congressmen who are currently battling immigration reform at the national level. The technology tools could assist students with gathering interview/video data, research information, collaborative means, and publishing.

Integrating social justice projects that students are passionate about can also serve as a springboard for students to develop apps or cloud service technology to address problems. Mobile technologies can be used to immerse students in culturally relevant, authentic problem focused learning that impacts them, the needs of the community, and/or people in need (Blackburn, 2015). For example, the "Love Clean Streets" app was created and is used in some countries to report environmental issues (e.g., potholes. Graffiti, litter accumulation). Once the app is opened, the location is automatically detected. Then the user takes a photo of the problem, enters a few details, and the report is sent to the correct authority to address the issue and will keep the user updated on the progress. This app was developed in response to a problem.

Parallel to the Universal Design for Learning principles (CAST, 2015) where mobile technologies are seen as a method to promote change, to engage students in their learning, and to promote social agency, this chapter promotes change from the classic approach of what students should learn (using technology for content delivery) to the focal point on why students should engage in solving the problem and how the students will apply what they learned (intentional use of technology to assist in reaching these goals) is essential:

The challenges faced by communities are so substantial and the demands for the solution so demanding that we cannot assume that doing what we always do (but slightly better) will produce different results. It is time for bold, imaginative change which embraces a new view of learning as a process founded upon a different understanding of the focus of the curriculum and the nature of knowledge processes. (Murgatroyd, 2010, p. 276)

The integration of mobile technology is a feasible method to assist student participation in real life contexts and a means to supporting them to recognize problems, actively collect data, and work to find solutions. Mobile technologies allow an extension outside of the classroom for more meaningful learning experiences and allow students to apply content into practice. Mobile technologies are invaluable tools and resources for inquiry, collaboration, communication, and assessment (Torp & Sage, 2002). The unique features (mobility, connectivity, flexibility, social interactivity, individuality, and immediacy) make learning goals achievable (Lan, Sung, Tan et al., 2010). Nielson and Webb (2011) highlight the advantages of using mobile technologies and how they serve as vehicles for reciprocal learning:

- Organizational tools (e.g., calendar, calculator, stopwatch, note taking, voice recording, reminder lists).
- Response systems (e.g., communication, collaboration, audience response and feedback through social networking).
- Research (e.g., social networking, hashtags, information resources, news, primary and secondary sources, YouTube, search engines).
- Hands on activities (e.g., exploration, inquiry, assessment, reflection, presentations).
- Recording evidence (e.g., pictures, video, audio, words).
- Assistance (e.g., support, assistive technology).

A Fusion for Change

A search through peer reviewed works in the field of education and/or internet for the confluence of these terms produces limited results: problem-based learning, place conscious education, culturally responsive teaching, and mobile technologies. However, individual search results for each component highlight many documented benefits and many common themes. Additionally, the combination of any two of the search terms often yields some small subset of articles. Common terms emerge throughout these searches, such as learner centered, intrinsic motivation, collaboration, cooperative learning, active engagement, inquiry based learning, critical thinking, multiple perspectives, etc. Discussions about how all these instructional approaches foster deep learning, increase motivation, make learning relevant, and promote higher-order thinking are omnipresent. With these obvious benefits, why do all teachers and schools not approach learning this way?

Transitioning to or just implementing small components of these student-centric learning approaches may require major changes in the ways schools function and deliver curriculum. Change always provokes controversy and concern. This apprehension is based on 3 C's: coverage, control, and complications. How can teachers cover state mandated objectives? What if students do not have enough background or content knowledge to venture into a culturally responsive and/or community based problem? How can teachers ensure that students have met the required objectives through problem based learning? How can teachers have time to coordinate these efforts?

Coverage

Additionally, many teachers ask with state mandated standards and prescribed scope and sequence plans, how can teachers cover all of the standards and have time to implement culturally responsive teaching, place-conscious education, and problem-based learning? Teachers may feel that standardized tests are not designed to evaluate the type of learning goals of these constructivist approaches. Anxiety is increased over whether students will possess the knowledge they need to pass the end of year tests (Torp & Sage, 2002). While passing a test may seem important in the moment, the skills promoted by student-centric approaches described in this chapter might prove more meaningful in the long run. For example, workforce demands innovation, creativity, critical thinking, and cultural competence, which are better taught and enforced through a problem based curriculum. (Murgatroyd, 2010).

Society has not aligned what they deem as "proficient" in school (measured by standardized tests) to the real-life benefits of problem based learning: critical thinking, problem solving, and integrative knowledge. To address this concern over coverage, it is essential for teachers to create problem focused lessons based on specific standards (Torp & Sage, 2002). A few examples might help illustrate how this confluence could work.

For example, history class students could investigate population decline (e.g., crime, white flight, urban decay, rural flight, unemployment) in their local community/city and the reasons why people decide to leave or stay. Students can compare and contrast their local situation with population decline in other parts of the nation and/or world (e.g., Chicago, Flint). In this scenario, history, geography, technology, and reading/writing standards would be used to meet the educational objectives (Wieseman & Cadwell, 2005). The examination of this problem would spill over to migration of communities (e.g., California Gold Rush, railroad, mining, white flight, Native Americans, tourism, industry).

Another example that would meet specific math, science, and technology standards would be the scenario to design, fund, and create a "tiny house" village for homeless people. Where would be the best place to build this village to ensure people would have access to public transportation to travel to a job? How would the city work this rental model to pay for costs of utilities? What amenities would be offered (e.g., financial education, health care)? What are potential issues with this plan?

Control

The issue of control relates to teachers feeling uncomfortable allowing student choice in the problems and learning experiences they pursue. If curriculum is student driven, how does the teacher ensure that students seek the right direction that integrates pre-set standards and intended learning outcomes? Although the teacher's role is to facilitate this process, he/she is already overcommitted and may be challenged for time. Acknowledging student choice and interests in the problems that students explore is one of the key components. Depending on the situation, teachers may have to accept the role of a director-oriented facilitator. To assure that teams address the prescribed learning standards, the teacher may assist in planning directional goals while at the same time, guide students to find their own path to solving the problem (Lambros, 2002).

Complications

Some projects may require students to do research in the community, which could stimulate logistical concerns such as safety and coordination. In addition, some teachers may be nervous about taking the risk of implementation in their classrooms; since it is not the norm and may be viewed negatively by administration or parents (Torp & Sage, 2002). Coordination of problem-based learning requires recruitment and support from administrators, parents, extended family (e.g., retired grandparents), and community stakeholders. The amount of planning and expertise required to mentor and assist students with devising solutions for problems should be a joint effort, but does add layers of complication to the instructional design process.

One solution teachers might consider is building Partnerships with nonprofit organizations, parent affiliate groups, city offices (e.g., police, medical facilities, fire department, Chamber of Commerce), and community resources (e.g., restaurants, national/state parks, local industries). These partnerships could not only offer educational backing but possibly financial support as well. But again, the teacher would have to facilitate these connections and build these partnerships.

Practical Applications

In order to combat questions of coverage, control, and complications, teachers should look to resources and examples that already exist in instructional contexts. Teachers do not need to re-invent the wheel. In addition to the examples already layered into this chapter, I offer here additional examples and resources for teachers to consider. These examples illustrate four methods teachers might consider in designing student-centric learning experiences:

1. Instructional connections.
2. Community integration.

Fusing Culturally Responsive Teaching

3. Community participation.
4. Citizen action.

Instructional connections are one way to connect content to local issues and situations (Glossary of Education Reform, 2014). For example, a math teacher could use socioeconomic data in students' city/community to teach numerous concepts. Analysis of poverty rates, cost of living, minimum wage, and governmental assistance could be investigated. Students retrieve the public information and participate in an inquiry, web-based activity to answer specific questions about their data (e.g., average household earnings versus cost of living average, educational impact, economic impact, statistics, probability). Through the research process students gather, analyze, visualize, and explain the significance of data. To add the action piece, collaborative groups could present a proposal to the city council including congressman/representative with the analytics and possible recommendations. This communication component can be created using a number of apps or technology resources (e.g., infograph, report, video, virtual gallery walks).

An extension of the previous example is a focus on financial education. Education on credit cards, managing debt, saving money, budgeting money, credit score, and high cost loans can benefit all individuals. In lower socioeconomic areas, check cashing and rent to own businesses are prevalent. Why do people cash checks at one of these businesses when they could get this same service at their bank for free? Why do people rent electronics, paying higher interest rates, when they could buy it outright? Through research and analysis, students can partner with financial experts to offer face-to-face (e.g., library, nonprofit organization, community events) and/or virtual community forums to the public. Even information on buying a vehicle (e.g., credit score affecting interest rate, invoice price, base price, sticker price, Kelly Blue Book value, rebate, financing options) could be included. Numerous types of technology can be used to help in researching and publicizing financial education.

Community integration is a second way for teachers to invite local experts to serve as guest speakers and develop mentoring partnerships with students for independent research projects (Glossary of Education Reform, 2014). For example, for a history lesson on the Civil Rights movement teams could interview local community members who experienced oppression and those who did not as a result of segregated law. As part of this process, students investigate how their lives were impacted negatively and positively after integration. With guidance from the teacher, students could interview someone internationally via visual communication (e.g., Facetime, Hangout, Skype) about similar experiences in their native country (e.g., Apartheid in South Africa) to compare and contrast events. Students can analyze how what they learned relates to the social and cultural unrest happening in society/local community to suggest recommendations for change.

Another social studies example is to use mobile technologies to participate in a historical journey through examination of primary resources (e.g., landmarks, cemeteries, Library of Congress, local museums) in the community. Students conduct research to determine how their community was impacted by societal events (e.g., immigration, illnesses, financial crisis, racism). Findings from these primary resources in combination with historical texts, graphs, etc. illustrate what makes the community unique. This evidence can be shared via a face-to-face or remote presentation at a community event or meeting, website, video reenactment, or handouts/brochures at the local library.

Community participation is the third method to integrate culturally responsive and place-based problems. This process includes collaboration and active participation with community groups such as local organizations, nonprofit organizations, and advocacy groups (Glossary of Education Reform,

2014). For example, in science students can collaborate with local experts to determine the carbon dioxide, carbon monoxide, and other pollutant levels that derive from the school, local nursing home, and/or community home. Students could explore how to reduce the levels (Murgatroyd, 2010). They can also apply this research to their homes to analyze their home safety. Another science example might be investigating local environmental issues (e.g., sinkholes, flooding, water cleanliness, environmental concerns) and working with professionals in the field of environmental science to present suggestions to the City Council or another appropriate action group.

Citizen action is the last and most authentic learning alternative for students. Students participate in social action, using what they learned to make a difference in the community in a meaningful way (Glossary of Education Reform, 2014). Although the previous three approaches challenge students to create products that are appreciated by others, social action empowers students to serve as agents of change. Murgatroyd (2010) provided an example of examining social isolation and loneliness of elderly. Students explore the services of their local assisted living/nursing home facility and outreach assistance. As a result, students increase social cohesion by recommending ways the community can utilize elderly individuals' knowledge and skill. Evaluating data, argument, understanding social history, etc. are all utilized in this problem focus.

Another example would be to decrease homelessness in a nearby community. With established partnerships with local psychologists, sociologists, nonprofit organizations, unemployment offices, and technical training schools, students can assist in determining viable solutions to help this population. An example is to offer technical and skills based training to individuals. Students could also design and offer financial data for a green "tiny home" community park (using SketchUp or a 3D app) that could offer a support system for former homeless people. This information could be used as supporting evidence in a grant sought by the city or nonprofit organization.

There are ongoing problems that arise in local communities. Examination of School Board minutes, City Council department minutes, and local newspapers/news reports reveal the problems that teachers can use to facilitate culturally relevant, problem based learning. Analysis of what issues the community faces illustrates the "why" learning related content is important. Then the teacher has to assist in figuring out the "how" and "what" students will learn based on the problem's focus. In addition, a web search of problem based learning examples and/or lessons reveals numerous websites that provide activities that can be adapted. Mobile technology has made collaboration (e.g., sharing information via Google Drive, social networking, online interactive books, videos), communication (e.g., chat, discussions, interviews, backchannels, visual communication, narrative recordings), and investigation/exploration (e.g., hashtag research, online polls, blogs, customizable circles, bookmarking) more attainable than ever. The teacher has to start small and intentionally integrate culturally-relevant, problem-based activities in the curriculum.

CONCLUSION

The same approach to education that was used in the past is not enough to prepare students for current and future society and workforce (Duch, Groh & Allen, 2001). Students need a fluid mentality and mindset to handle the issues and complicated problems they will face, and they need tools to manage the complex decisions they will be forced to make. Using mobile technologies for culturally responsive, place-conscious, problem-based learning is a powerful and unique technique that will expose students to these these critical 21st century skills and equip them to use these skills to better their worlds.

Research confirms that problem-based learning is effective without question (Duch, Groh, & Allen, 2001; Hung, Hwang, Lee et al., 2014; Lambros, 2002; Tambouris, Panopoulou, Tarabanis et al., 2012; Torp & Sage, 2002; Wattinger, Nguyen, Fornaro et al., 2006). Students are actively involved, develop a deeper understanding of the content, learn problem solving skills, engage in techniques that teach them how to be resourceful and how to apply what they learned instead of regurgitating factual answers that can be found through a simple web search (Torp & Sage, 2002). Integrating culturally-responsiveness and place-conscious education in a problem based approach to the classroom changes the focus from contrived problems found on the internet to practical and meaningful learning experiences to which students can identify and relate.

Mobile technologies support learning and enable students in all of these student-centric context to meet these goals by offering unique options to be more innovative, reflective, transparent, and creative. The abundance of mobile technology resources to help achieve project objectives may seem overwhelming and spark hesitation. However, the focus should be on why students should engage in this instructional approach and how to support them in doing this work. Technology is constantly changing, and students have a wealth of information at their fingertips. With mobile technologies, students have access to information instantly. It is up to educators to prepare students to use this massive amount of information effectively, to communicate and collaborate efficiently, and to think and problem solve in order to function successfully in current and future situations.

REFERENCES

Banks, J.A. (2002). *An introduction to multicultural education*. Boston, MA: Allyn & Bacon.

Blackburn, G. (2015). Innovative eLearning: Technology shaping contemporary problem based learning: A cross-case analysis. *Journal of University Teaching & Learning Practice*, *12*(2), 1–17.

Bybee, R. W., Taylor, J. A., Gardner, A., Van Scotter, P., Powell, J. C., Westbrook, A., & Landes, N. (2006). *The BSCS 5E instructional model: Origins and effectiveness*. Colorado Springs, CO: BSCS.

CAST. (2015). *About universal design for learning*. Retrieved from http://www.cast.org/our-work/about-udl.html#.VyJNNPkrLIU

Davison, C. B., & Lazaros, E. J. (2015). Adopting mobile technology in the higher education classroom. *The Journal of Technology Studies*, *41*(1), 30–38.

Dewey, J. (1915). *School and society*. Chicago: The University of Chicago Press.

Duch, B. J., Groh, S. E., & Allen, D. E. (2001). Why problem-based learning? A case study of institutional change in undergraduate education. In B. J. Duch, S. E. Groh, & D. E. Allen (Eds.), *The power of problem-based learning* (pp. 3–12). Sterling, VA: Stylus Publishing.

Gay, G. (2002). Preparing for culturally responsive teaching. *Journal of Teacher Education*, *53*(2), 106–116. doi:10.1177/0022487102053002003

Gay, G. (2010). *Culturally responsive teaching: Theory, research, & practice* (2nd ed.). New York: Teachers College Press.

Glossary of Education Reform. (2014). *Community based learning*. Retrieved from http://edglossary.org/community-based-learning/

Greenwood, D. (2011). Why place matters. Environment, culture, and education. In S. Tozer, B. P. Gallegos, A. Henry, M. Greiner, & P. Groves-Price (Eds.), *Handbook of research in social foundations of education* (pp. 632–640). New York: Routledge.

Gruenewald, D. (2008). Place-based education: Grounding culturally responsive teaching in geographical diversity. In D. Gruenewald & G. Smith (Eds.), *Place-based education in the global age: Local diversity* (pp. 137–153). Mahwah, NJ: Lawrence Erlbaum Associates.

Hung, P., Hwang, G., Lee, Y., Wu, T., Vogel, B., Milrad, M., & Johansson, E. (2014). A problem-based ubiquitous learning approach to improving the questioning abilities of elementary school students. *Journal of Educational Technology & Society*, *17*(4), 316–334.

Kea, C., Campbell-Whatley, G. D., & Richards, H. V. (2006). *Becoming culturally responsive educators: Rethinking education pedagogy (NCCREST Practitioner Brief H326E020003)*. Tempe, AZ: U.S. Department of Education Office of Special Education Programs.

Ladson-Billings, G. (1994). *The dreamkeepers: Successful teachers of African-American Children*. San Francisco: Jossey-Bass.

Lambros, A. (2002). *Problem-based learning in K-8 classrooms: A teacher's guide to implementation*. Thousand Oaks, CA: Corwin Press.

Lan, Y., Sung, Y., Tan, N., Lin, C., & Change, K. (2010). Mobile device supported problem based computational estimation instruction for elementary students. *Journal of Educational Technology & Society*, *11*(3), 55–69.

Lombardi, M. (2007, May). *Authentic learning for the 21st century: An overview*. Retrieved from http://net.educause.edu/ir/library/pdf/ELI3009.pdf

McFalls, M. (2013). Integration of problem-based learning and innovative technology into a self-care course. *American Journal of Pharmaceutical Education*, *77*(6), 1–5. doi:10.5688/ajpe776127 PMID:23966730

Montrieux, H., Vanderlinde, R., Schellens, T., & De Marez, L. (2015). Teaching and learning with mobile technology: A qualitative explorative study about the introduction of tablet devices in secondary education. *PLoS ONE*, *10*(12), 1–17. doi:10.1371/journal.pone.0144008 PMID:26641454

Murgatroyd, S. (2010). Wicked problems and the work of the school. *European Journal of Education*, *45*(2), 259–279. doi:10.1111/j.1465-3435.2010.01428.x

Nielson, L., & Webb, W. (2011). *Teaching generation text: Using cell phones to enhance learning*. San Francisco: Jossey-Bass.

Northern Illinois University, Faculty Development and Instructional Design Center. (n.d.). *Problem-based learning*. Retrieved from http://www.niu.edu/facdev/resources/guide/strategies/problem_based_learning.pdf

Pacansky-Brock, M. (2013). *Best practices for teaching with emerging technologies*. New York: Routledge.

Rittell, H. W., & Webber, M. M. (1973). Dilemmas in a general theory of planning. *Policy Sciences*, *4*(2), 155–169. doi:10.1007/BF01405730

Roehrig, G. H., Moore, T. J., Wang, H., & Park, M. S. (2012). Is adding the E enough? Investigating the impact of k-12 engineering standards on the implementation of STEM integration. *School Science and Mathematics*, *112*(1), 31–44. doi:10.1111/j.1949-8594.2011.00112.x

Rychly, L., & Graves, E. (2012). Teacher characteristics for culturally responsive pedagogy. *Multicultural Perspectives*, *14*(1), 44–49. doi:10.1080/15210960.2012.646853

Sharples, M., Kloos, C. D., Dimitriadis, Y., Garlatti, S., & Specht, M. (2015). Mobile and accessible learning for MOOCs. *Journal of Interactive Media in Education*, *4*, 1–8. doi:10.5334/jime.ai

Strimmel, G. (2014, April). Authentic education by providing a situation for student-selected problem based learning. *Technology and Engineering Teacher*, 8-18.

Tambouris, E., Panopoulou, E., Konstantinos, T., Ryber, T., Buus, L., Peristeras, V., ... Porwol, L. (2012). Enabling problem based learning through web 2.0 technologies: PBL 2.0. *Journal of Educational Technology & Society*, *15*(4), 238–251.

Torp, L., & Sage, S. (2002). *Problems as possibilities: Problem based learning for K-16 education* (2nd ed.). Alexandria, VA: Association for Supervision and Curriculum Development.

Towler, L. (2014, November). *Deeper learning: Moving students beyond memorization*. Retrieved from http://neatoday.org/2014/11/25/deeper-learning-moving-students-beyond-memorization-2/

USC. (n.d.). *Using active learning in the classroom*. Retrieved from http://cet.usc.edu/resources/teaching_learning/docs/Active_Learning_Florida.pdf

Vygotsky, L. S. (1978). *Mind in society*. Cambridge, MA: Harvard University Press.

Watson, G. H. (2001). Problem based learning and the three c's of technology. In B. J. Duch, S. E. Groh, & D. E. Allen (Eds.), *The power of problem-based learning* (pp. 109–120). Sterling, VA: Stylus Publishing.

Wattinger, C., Nguyen, D. P., Fornaro, P., Guggisberg, M., Gyalog, T., & Burkhat, H. (2006). Problem-based learning using mobile devices. *Proceedings of the Sixth International Conference on Advanced Learning Technologies* (pp. 835-839). IEEE. 10.1109/ICALT.2006.1652571

Wieseman, K. C., & Cadwell, D. (2005). Local history and problem-based learning. *Social Studies and the Young Learner*, *18*(1), 11–14.

This research was previously published in Empowering Learners With Mobile Open-Access Learning Initiatives edited by Michael Mills and Donna Wake; pages 288-306, copyright year 2017 by Information Science Reference (an imprint of IGI Global).

Chapter 35
A Forensic Psychological Perspective on Racism in Schools of Educational Leadership:
Impact on Organizational Culture

Ronn Johnson
Creighton University Medical School, USA & VA Nebraska-Western Iowa Health Care System, USA

JoJo Yanki Lee
University of San Diego, USA

Ji Youn Cindy Kim
University of Iowa, USA

ABSTRACT

Schools theoretically operate under a shared value of fairness in the workplace. The fairness includes a notable sense of egalitarian beliefs, values, and people who hold themselves out to be unprejudiced. When defensible and culturally responsive justice measures are applied in schools of education, leadership in Schools of Education must consistently demonstrate clear and convincing evidence of fairness. The chapter is an analysis of aversive or unconscious racism and in the ways that it might manifest itself through individuals in leadership positions. Evaluating the impact of the institutional racism. In the analysis of forensic psychological perspective, ways of using a forensic psychological approach to assess the stakeholders in the School of Education as it pertains to the experience of racism will be discussed. A forensic psychological portrait of racism in schools of education is examined. Finally, implications for practice, training, and research are discussed.

DOI: 10.4018/978-1-7998-1213-5.ch035

A Forensic Psychological Perspective on Racism in Schools of Educational Leadership

INTRODUCTION

The roots of what is currently known as colleges or schools of education can be traced back to the "Normal School," whose creation was fueled by the westward expansion in America. The intent of these schools across the country was to enhance the standards for teaching. The 19th century marked a period where these normal schools were in almost each part of the country. The normal schools also provided an opportunity for women to attend college to become teachers. Historically, schools of education were plagued by an undeniable reality of inadequate standards, low wages, and a reputation for being a less prestigious occupation. The confluence of the aforementioned realities may also explain why so many schools of education remain locked in a seemingly inescapable historical and cultural quagmire related to standards that is now mixed with race-based tensions. That is, some of the same ethnoracial injustices perceived in the broader American society can also be observed in schools of education. Some might assess these inequities as a byproduct of historic positional advantage for some individuals that has resulted in oppression, race-based privilege, acts of racial supremacy and self-serving ignorance of the imbalance in the organizational power structure. Some might even argue that schools of education have become extensions of a larger culture that includes the 21st century version of racially coded lynchings (i.e., academically underperforming schools, criminalization of Black males, and disproportionate unemployment rates. These circumstances coincide with race based reflexive tendency to blame the victim for their plight. Examples of this trend include an accusatory finger pointing to a decline in the Black family (i.e., single-headed households and teen pregnancy rates). In this case, Blacks are seemingly universally blamed as a major part of the community demise reflected in these unwanted circumstances (e.g., people faced with extreme hardships are blamed for the hardships) (Capezza & Arriaga, 2008).

Racism can have forensic psychological (i.e., psycho-legal) implications. For example, racism was alleged in three high profile shooting incidents involving Black males. In two of the cases, timely medical attention was not provided and in a third, the corpse was allowed to remain on the street for hours after the incident. In the case of the 12-year-old 6th grader, he was shot dead by police within two seconds of them arriving on the scene for waiving a fake gun. American history is littered by lynchings that took place and often followed by a time when the bodies were displayed, souvenirs were collected, or victims were tortured in a way in order to terrorize (i.e., racial domination) Blacks (Bonilla-Silva, 2009, 2012). This type of terrorism (i.e., group inducing fear) functions as a form of collective punishment for Blacks. In this case, these acts of lynching were highly publicized at the time but now with the access to camera phones it means the size of the crowds that view them exponentially dwarf those hangings that occurred following reconstruction. The handling of the bodies was designed to communicate possible ethnoracial message that resonates today. Like lynchings, the killings of Black males were ruled as legitimate actions, both by the officers themselves and by legal authorities charged with subsequently reviewing them.

In fact, these events were assessed as legitimate criminal punishments. These high profile police shootings of Black males serve as a culturally responsive platform for initiating conversations regarding racism in schools of education and leadership. Racism refers to discriminatory behavior attached with prejudicial beliefs towards an entire race that places that group in a subordinate position in society (Anderson, 1996; Beamon, 2014; Feagin & Feagin, 2012; Singer, 2005). Organizationally, there are at least two types of racism. Structural racism refers to a tapestry of institutional barriers that result in inequalities (e.g., disparities in pay or other financial rewards for academic productivity) between diverse faculty and their colleagues.

A Forensic Psychological Perspective on Racism in Schools of Educational Leadership

The other type of racism is observed in what may be experiences as private acts of interpersonal vengeance that may be assessed as microaggressions (Sue, 2010) or personal racism. For example, the only Black male graduate student is mocked for his petition to switch into programs where he can get more exposure to the only tenured Black professor in the department. This seeming indifference to the request or taking vicarious pleasure in deriding the Black student's request is revealing. This type of cloaked scorn is a form of personal racism whereby faculty or students of color frequently assess themselves as being harassed, stereotyped, and ridiculed (e.g., Banks 1984; Johnsrud & DesJarlais 1994; Johnsrud & Sadao 1998; Stanley, 2006). As a potential crisis management scandal, the full dimensions of the perceptions of racism can have a ripple effect on any organization (e.g., police department or School of Education) that can ostensibly result in psycho-legal consequences (e.g., litigation where forensic psychological testimony may be used). For example, the aforementioned recent spate of killings of Black males by police has once again raised questions about the role that race-based motives could be operating within police departments and by extension schools of education.

The denial, discounting or dismissal of race base motives may actually overshadow bad cops whose poor judgment under stressful circumstances may have unwittingly contributed to the deaths of these males. It is certainly plausible that a combination of a bad cop that also holds racist views may be operating as well. Or, an otherwise good cop could have made a mistake under the fog of carrying out their duties (i.e., split second life and death decisions). Finally no less relevant, carrying out police duties during the scene management situation for various public safety circumstances can legally warrant lethal force to be executed in a lawful way. These killings beg a legitimate forensic psychological question for organizations. Were the White officers involved in these incidents negligently hired or retained (Johnson, 2010, 2013) Because the officers involved in these incidents were all White and the untried Black males were killed, the historical concern about racism is reignited. Why, maybe because of a denial or self-serving amnesia of racism that is deeply ingrained in American history.

On a less violent level, a well-recognized organizational entity like Colleges or Schools of Education are not immune from the same race based brush when it comes to leadership. To be clear, racism does not include every faculty member or is predominantly represented by any one group of faculty (Schuman, Steeh, Bobo, & Krysan, 1997). Yet, disentangling racism is complex but is socially constructed in a way that is experienced through attitudes, actions, policies, or perceptions. Racism can be intentional or unintentional (e.g., unconscious) and can be found in a variety of life experiences with individuals. The power structure of schools of education is over-represented by the collective strength of one racial group that operates in ways to maintain the cultural security of their status in that organization. In schools of education and organizations like police departments, it is declared to be important that a general perception of security of the structure of the organization must be maintained even sometimes at the expense of the unpalatable truth that racism is a widespread element within the culture of the institution (Kääriäinen, Sirén, 2011; Flexon, Lurigio, & Greenleaf 2009; Cochran, & Warren 2012). Instead, a failure to properly assess and address issues stemming from racism may actually result in restrictive oversight (e.g., expansion of civilian oversight committees for police misconduct).

A historical review of racism reveals the problem that is larded within the organizational and institutional structures and practices (Byrd & Clayton, 2000, 2001). In this case, racism can maintain a rather cozy existence in the absence of what historically has been known as racial prejudice or stereotypes. Some institutions are hesitant to assess if race-based issues are in fact caused by various organizational processes (Bell & Nkomo 2001; Karlsen & Nazroo 2004; Kivel 1996). Yet, there is persistent evidence that at least the perceptions of racism still exist within the society as a whole and within various orga-

A Forensic Psychological Perspective on Racism in Schools of Educational Leadership

nizations like schools of education. For example, the dynamics of the organizational atmosphere within which diverse faculty and students have to function may serve as quite an eye opener. A culturally relevant snapshot might show the attitudes, expectations, and perceptions when ethnoracial factors are examined (Hurtado et al. 1998). Collectively, the overall racial repression that is reserved for these diverse faculty and students can result in a critical loss in the inspired motivation or sense of satisfaction that can result in drop off in engagement and decline in academic productivity (Jayakumar et al., 2009; Turner & Myers 2000). Perhaps the aforementioned consequence is the actual intended goal, which may to a calculated way to maintain racial domination. Broadly speaking, the perceptions of racism can further threaten an already endangered diversity element in a School of Education. It also seems blatantly hypocritical for an organization to trumpet that racial diversity is desired and even engages in then engages in celebratory ceremonial activities around Martin Luther King or Cesar Chavez but note there is scant evidence of it in practice based on the experience of faculty or students of color. Ethnoracial factors matter to people of color because of a well-documented history of racism (i.e., historic racial trauma) that has been ubiquitously experienced as a form of aggression by every minority group in this country.

In this chapter, the racism within the context of organizational culture will be examined, specifically in the level of higher education. That is, how does racism function as a barrier to organizational justice in a higher education setting? Ideally, universities promote and educate about diversity to promote a future generation can have a chance for a cross-culturally safe environment. However, the paucity of culturally responsive competence within those in roles of leadership may result in a detrimental impact on faculty and students of color. The first section of the chapter discusses the history and development of organizational racism. Then, the chapter transits into analyzing how aversive or unconscious racism may manifest it through individuals in leadership positions. The chapter also explores the potential impact of institutional racism across various populations of racial minorities. The final section examines the forensic psychological perspective of racism within schools of education. A forensic psychological perspective is used to expose realistic race-based situations and experiences that can result in litigation as a means to securing some sense of justice. The chapter proposes implications for practice, training, and research to promote antiracist practices in schools of education.

BACKGROUND

Brown v. Board of Education of Topeka (1954)

The organizational functioning of Schools of Education is more or less shaped by several landmark court decisions. The Supreme Court decision for *Brown v. Board of Education of Topeka* (347 U.S. 483, 495) probably represents the most clear, progressive, and compelling legal ruling on racial educational policy in the twentieth century. In this case, there was a challenge to educational policy implementation about whether and how to best achieve its ethical ends in race relations, school facilities, transportation, parent choices, and funding (Henderson, 2004). *Brown* consolidated through five cases, all of which challenged the constitutionality of racial segregation in public schools, ascending from the United States court of appeals in Delaware, the District of Columbia, Virginia, South Carolina, and Kansas. From a forensic psychological perspective, the work of Dr. Kenneth Clark (Doll Experiment) was instrumental in making the counterargument that separate but equal was untrue. Through his research, he was able to show that when given a preference, Black children would prefer White dolls over Black. The lawsuit in Kansas emerged when the National Association for the Advancement of Colored People (NAACP) began the suit through its Legal Defense Fund on behalf of plaintiff Oliver Brown (Henderson, 2004; Roberts & Sttraton, 1995). With Charles Summer School, an all-White school, in her immediate neighborhood, Oliver Brown's daughter, Linda, had been forced by the local public schools in Topeka, Kansas, to walk across railroad tracks miles away from her home to attend a segregated school. The NAACP brought suits in the other four cases on similar grounds and challenged the "separate but equal" doctrine that had been firmly established in the 1896 *Plessy v. Ferguson* (163 U.S. 537) Supreme Court case, in which Justice John Harlan presaged the precepts of *Brown* by rejecting the separate-but-equal principle as a contradiction of the intent of the Fourteenth Amendment (Henderson, 2004; Leonard, 1980). Successfully, Thurgood Marshall, then head of the NAACP Legal Defense Fund, and his colleagues ended school segregation with the death of Chief Justice Vinson in September 1953 and the appointment of California governor Earl Warren as chief justice (Henderson 2004; Roberts & Stratton, 1995).

Breaking grounds in changing federal policy, the NAACP was also effective in ending segregation in several colleges and universities during the early 1950s with *Sweatt v. Painter* (339 U.S. 629 [1950]) and *McLaurin v. Oklahoma State Regents for Higher Ed.* (339 U.S. 637 [1950]; Henderson, 2004). The Supreme Court directed two universities to end discrimination against Blacks seeking admission and, once admitted, to provide them full access to instruction, library, and other student rights and privileges (Henderson, 2004; Roberts & Sttraton, 1995). *Brown* continues to raise controversial and volatile issues related to policy implementation and ethics of race relations.

With strong opposing sides, it was clear that the implementation of the new policy would be a challenge. Many school districts followed the new policy, but many publicly announced they would not desegregate; therefore, the Supreme Court issued a sequel to its previous ruling in 1955 (*Brown v. Board of Education* 349 U.S. 294, 301; Henderson, 2004). This ruling affirmed the Supreme Court's 1954 opinion and indicated that desegregation in public schools should advance "with all deliberate speed." This second ruling concurred with the development of the modern civil rights movement and protests (e.g., 1955 Montgomery bus boycott, Resistance of Governor Faubus of Arkansas, Resistance of Governor Wallace of Alabama to the admission of Black students at Central High School in Little Rock and the University of Alabama; Henderson, 2004). Governor Wallace's 1963 inaugural statement of "Segregation now, segregation tomorrow, segregation forever" still resonates in education. The resistance to racial desegregation and the civil rights movement amplified local battles within national and international media, and fifty years late, the *Brown v. Board of Education of Topeka* decision continues to contribute to current issues with ethics of race relations in the United States of America (Beamon, 2014; Henderson, 2004). While no school district overtly segregates students on the basis of race as official policy, clear racial and ethnic concentrations of students exist in many metropolitan areas (Clark & Clark, 1939; Duncan, 2002; Henderson, 2004; Sleeter, 2001), including schools of education (Taylor & Clark, 2009).

ORGANIZATIONAL AND INSTITUTIONAL RACISM

Emotional Segregation

Emotional segregation is an organization process, whereby racially oppressed groups are denied sharing the same human emotions and experiences (Beeman, 2007). To be emotionally equal, it is helpful to distinguish sympathy and empathy. Sympathy is found to be more passive compared to empathy and

A Forensic Psychological Perspective on Racism in Schools of Educational Leadership

requires less emotional energy; however, empathy is a more active feeling or feeling with another person (Beeman, 2007). The psychological construct known as emotional segregation refers to the lack of empathy that has been noted in the relationships between African Americans and 'whites.' Organizationally, emotional segregation is supported by structures of educational institutions and it coincides with a well-documented history of systemic racism in the United States of America (Beeman, 2007; Rush, 2006). When examining emotional responses of children to the teachings of "Huckleberry Finn" in public schools, emotional segregation is thought to have developed within a legal context (Rush, 2006) that is best noted by segregating 'white' and 'black' children through eliciting different emotional responses (Beeman, 2007). Schools of education then become an academic platform whereby 'whites' and 'blacks' have reflect the structural barriers noted throughout history that prevents the full sharing of empathetic bonds. Unfortunately, it is a race-based circumstance that continues to be at least tacitly supported in schools of educations (Beeman, 2007; Rush, 2006). The unique system of emotional segregation has been operating at a dysfunctional level throughout the history of miscegenation in the United States of America (Beeman, 2007). Some of the most pointed examples of this is reflected in the relationships of 'black'/'white' that are located historically within laws related to interracial marriage. Following the end of slavery, miscegenation was criminalized (Williams, 2001), marking the beginnings of emotional segregation in what might be assessed as an organizational form (Beeman, 2007). The statutes of anti-miscegenation were primarily concerned with the maintaining what was rationalized as the purity of the 'white' race, as 'whites' could only marry other 'whites' but non-'whites' could marry other non-'whites' (Applebaum, 1964; Beeman, 2007). This glaring racial double standard allowed for the maintenance of whiteness as a space of 'privilege and purity' (Romano, 2003) offering additional insight into why interracial intimacies remain offensive and taboo (Beeman, 2007). With disputes beginning as early as the 1800s, laws against interracial marriage were repealed in the late 1960s (Beeman, 2007). Despite the repeals, United States citizens in Mississippi, Alabama, and South Carolina have struggled to maintain symbolic bans on interracial marriage (Romano, 2003). Research on sexuality demonstrates how interracial sexual relationships elicit strong negative emotions from 'whites' (Beeman, 2007). By introducing the concept of sexual racism, Stember connected emotions related to racism (1976). African American men have been stigmatized by being labelled as inhuman in a race-based scheme to prevent interracial intimacies (Stember, 1976). The labelling has resulted in an unwanted form of stigmatization that has even circulated into organizational policies as various forms of racism (Beeman, 2007).

Organizational Policies

The recognition of systemic racism within an organization is challenging and often dismissed (Blitz & Kohl, 2012). Organizational racism relies upon public authority to ration resources and power in order to exclude people designated as belonging to allege racially inferior categories (Dominelli, 1988, 1998; Bozalek, 2010). Whites and people of color may work together as colleagues, but deeper equity work requires using diverse workforce as a resource to identify and rectify hidden and unconscious forms of bias that may go unrecognized by managers and administrators. 'Race' and racism are socially constructed and how these constructions may function in organizations can perpetuate into certain kinds of unwanted social relations (Ahmed, 2008; Ahmed, Nicolson, & Spencer, 2000). Most universities have 'Equality and Diversity' and/or 'race equality' policies that promote anti-racism in an effort to combat oppressive practices such as racism in the way university settings operate while establishing an environment that acknowledges and celebrates the diversity within its own population (Ahmed, 2008). The policies articulate complaints procedures for instances of individual discrimination and oblige the university population to promote 'Equality and Diversity' (e.g., faculty are asked to ensure providing in their teaching examples of research that reflect many cultures varying from western views; Ahmed, 2008). The following quote is an example of those found in many Equality and Diversity or 'race' equality policies:

Students will have opportunities to discuss equal opportunities issues as part of their learning where the context permits, for example anti-racism or how different groups may be stereotyped and represented. Where appropriate, the learning outcomes of the particular program modules will include an appreciation of the changing needs of a modern culturally diverse society.

When policy statements are too vague or over-general in the strategies they recommend, such vagueness can support multiple interpretations as to what can reasonably be done, ranging from radical ideas to simple solutions (Ahmed, 2008; Sonn, 2004). This vagueness also does not necessarily demand a substantial commitment to actively engaging with issues within one's teaching and leadership, but also in interactions between staff and students to truly develop anti-racist practice (Sonn, 2004).

Curriculum Content: The Topic of Racism

Within schools of education, there is increasing concern of rather issues of equality and diversity (e.g., race, sexuality, disability, gender, etc.) should be more clearly embedded in teaching content (Ahmed, 2008; Henwood & Phoenix, 1996). This debate also raises the question about who should do such teaching. Some lecturers imply that as White lecturers they would feel uncomfortable talking about 'race' issues because they are not a person of color; other lecturers claim they do not have the time, is irrelevant to the content, or do not have the resources to include 'race' issues within their curriculum (Ahmed, 2008). This commonly debated scenario often leads to the 'ethnic minority' staff members to be overburdened with the role of teaching issues of equality and diversity (Jacobs & Hai, 2002). The common ideology that 'race' is relevant to only 'non-white' people arises with White staff lecturers giving privilege to 'whiteness' by feeling they cannot or should not try to tackle 'race' issues (Ahmed, 2008; Ahmed, 2008; Howarth & Hook, 2005).

There has been much discussion on the issues related to teaching 'race'-related issues in the social sciences (i.e., psychology; Jacobs & Hai, 2002). To move towards understanding the psychology of racism, there has been over a century of psychological research relating to 'race' (Ahmed, 2008). With this research, there also has been much criticism charging that it is either unintentionally or overtly racist (Ahmed, 2008; Henwood, 1994; Howitt & Owusu-Bempah, 1994; Richards, 1997). It has been suggested that some psychologists have a racist agenda (Henwood & Phoenix, 1996), or that for theoretical, epistemological, and methodological reasons (Ahmed, 2008), psychologists fail to consider the possible consequences following the research (Ahmed, 2008; Wetherell & Potter, 1992). Critical psychology research examines how categories such as 'race' are socially constructed, and how particular constructions function in maintaining oppressive power relations (Ahmed, 208; Wetherell & Potter, 1992). The topic of 'race' issues in educational curriculums in higher education developed into a political debate; Engagement with the discussion of the issues necessitate understanding the privilege enclosed with 'Whiteness' and also the consequences of criticism (Ahmed, 2008).

Social scientists have argued that despite a decline in racist attitudes, much opposition to interracial intimacy remains (Beeman, 2007; Knox, 2000; Romano 2003). To enhance culturally responsive education, faculty, and staff members (i.e., those in the position of leadership within the institution) from marginalized or socially oppressed groups need to know they are valued by the organization (Blitz & Kohl, 2012). Significance and value can be established through practices that allow all members of the entire school of education to compete on a playing field that addresses factors of organizational culture that privilege certain groups over others (Beeman, 2007; Blitz & Kohl, 2012). Overlooking the social and historical impact of race privilege and racism risks propagating injustice through race-based practices that highlight the achievements and strengths of privileged members without recognizing the full cultural context that supports their success (Blitz & Kohl, 2012).

Organizational Trickle-Down Model

The dominant paradigm in organizational justice involves the assessment of members' justice perceptions and linking these perceptions to a variety of attitudinal and behavioral outcomes (Ambrose, Schminke, & Mayer, 2013). Organizational justice perceptions are positively related to satisfaction with the organization, organizational commitment, evaluations of authority, trust, organizational citizenship behavior (OCB), and performance (Ambrose, Schminke, & Mayer, 2013; Cohen-Charash & Spector, 2001; Colquitt, Conlon, Wesson, Porter, & Ng, 2001). The "trickle-down" model is an emerging perspective explaining the experience of one individual in an organization and how it can affect his or her perceptions of the organization as well as his or her behavior toward other individuals (Ambrose, Schminke, & Mayer, 2013). For example, individuals who feel fairly treated by their organization are more likely to engage in positive behavior, including fair behavior directed at others; thus the experiences one individual has with the organization and its representatives "trickles down" from the leadership of the organization to affect other individuals (Ambrose, Schminke, & Mayer, 2013; Masterson, 2001; Masterson, Lewis, Goldman, & Taylor, 2000).

Masterson (2001) first examined the effects of the model with employee perceptions of procedural and distinctive and distributive fairness and the relations with customer reactions through their influence on employee commitment and customers' perceptions of fairness. Other research on the model focuses on the effect of supervisors' experiences on their subordinates (Shanock & Eisenberger, 2006; Tepper & Taylor, 2003). Supervisors' perceptions of procedural justice have been found to affect their subordinates' perceptions of procedural justice and organizational citizenship behavior (Tepper & Taylor, 2003), and supervisors' perceived organizational support was related to subordinates' perceived supervisor support (Shanock & Eisenberger, 2006). The trickle down effect affects behavioral integrity (Simons, Friedman, Liu, & McLean Parks, 2007) across different constructs as well. Supervisors' perceptions of procedural justice were associated with subordinates' perceptions of abusive supervision (Ambrose, Schminke, & Mayer, 2013; Tepper et al., 2006). The quality of leader-member exchange influences subordinates' job satisfaction and performance (Ambrose, Schminke, & Mayer, 2013; Erdogan & Enders, 2007).

Recent research on the model has moved beyond the study of parallel supervisor and subordinate constructs; however, all research related to the trickle down effect to date shares the common focus on individual level perceptions, attitudes, or behavior (Ambrose, Schminke, & Mayer, 2013). When supervisors model the behavior of their managers, that behavior has an impact beyond subordinates' individual experiences; it also influences work group climate. This model illustrates the effect racism has within leadership of educational institutions on its students.

Organizational Racial Culture

The multidimensional elements of racism as part of the organizational climate in Schools of Education must start with a discussion of racism as a leadership issue. Racism in the 21st Century usually does not take place in a direct way, but rather in an indirect way (Solorzano et al., 2000). Indirect racism typically takes place in a manner that is often referred to as racial microaggressions (Sue, 2010; Sue, Capodilupo, et al., 2007). The racial perpetrators are not wearing white pointy-headed sheets, burning crosses, or shouting racial slurs. Instead, the racism in Schools of Education has a restrained, but nonetheless sends delivers an unmistakable ethnoracial message that may be assessed as aversive racism (AR).

According to the AR perspective, many individuals who believe they support egalitarian and non-judgmental also unconsciously maintain negative feelings and stereotype toward Blacks and other historically disadvantaged groups (Dovidio & Gaertner, 2000). Dovidio & Gaertner (1998, 2000, 2005) proposes the theory of aversive racism (AR). They suggested that AR is subtle, indirect expressions of prejudice by White Americans. Aversive Racists are hypothesized to have internalized the genuine egalitarian attitudes (e.g., fairness equality), and promote non-prejudiced self-image. However, Dovidio & Gaertner argues that such individuals still hold non-conscious negative, race-based feelings toward others.

AR is noted by at least four ethnoracial factors (Dovidio & Gaertner, 2000). First, AR can be assessed claim to hold egalitarian values and beliefs. Second, they perceive themselves as not motivated by ethnoracial biases. Third, they are unconsciously racially biased as observed by negative beliefs about Blacks and other out-groups. Finally, they covertly discriminate in ways that are more passive, but nonetheless racially selective with an entrenched self-delusional cognitive schema in which they reflexively use rationalization for their actions.

Therefore, AR is an unconscious emotional conflict for individuals who explicitly support egalitarian principles and believe themselves to be non-prejudiced also experience involuntary, negative, race-based feelings at the same time (Nail, Harton, Barnes, 2008). The negative consequences of AR are not easy to recognize (by oneself, and by others) as racial bias. "Aversive racists recognize prejudice is bad, but they do not recognize that they are prejudiced… Like a virus that had mutated, racism has also evolved into different forms that are more difficult not to recognize but also to combat" (Dovidio & Gaertner, 1998, p. 25).

Dovidio & Gaertner (2005) designs to extend their research on AR by exploring changes in expressed racial attitudes and patterns of discrimination in hiring recommendations for a Black or White candidate for a position of peer counselor, in a 10 year period. Participates (34 White males and 48 White female undergraduates) are asked to utilize the interview excerpts to evaluate candidates for a new program for peer counseling in their university. Three profiles are developed, including one strong qualification, one clearly weak qualification, and one marginally acceptable but ambiguous qualification. Participants are asked to evaluate and identify a single candidate who is Black or White based on the candidate's profile.

The study's result supports their hypothesis that subtle and covert forms of discrimination are persisting even when expressed prejudice is expected to decline. Dovidio and Gaertner (2005) emphasize that racial stereotypes are most influential in ambiguous situations. When a Black candidate has clearly strong qualification, or when his/her credential is clearly not qualified, there is no discrimination against him/her. In the evaluation process, the bias against Blacks is primarily manifested when a candidate's qualifications for the position are ambiguous. The authors suggest that the effects of AR may be rooted from the intergroup biases based on social categorization processes (Gaertner et al., 1997). In other words, the biases reflect on "in-group favoritism" and "out-group derogation." For example, one school

A Forensic Psychological Perspective on Racism in Schools of Educational Leadership

of education faculty member was serving on a search committee for the director of public safety. Two of the finalists were Black. Both had advanced terminal degrees and had extensive prior experience directing large public safety departments. The third candidate was a White female who did not have an advanced degree and had never held any administrative position. When it was abundantly clear that the White female was going to be recommended, the school of education faculty member objected. He cited the fact that the female candidate had no advanced degree or prior administrative experience. Disappointedly, he was told by the chair, "Yes, it is true that she has no advance degree or administrative experience but sometimes you have to just go with your instincts." The school of education member resigned from the selection committee. When the behaviors are performed by the out-group members, people tend to judge potentially negative behavior more aversive and intentional, and more likely to attribute those behaviors to the person's personality (Hewstone, 1990). Given that explanation and applied to the ambiguous-qualification condition, participants in this study may perceive White candidates as "the benefit of the doubt." Yet, this benefit is not extended to the Black candidates. Consequently, the moderate qualification with ambiguous profile is viewed as strong qualification when the candidate is White, but weak qualification when the candidate is Black. The authors propose that this kind of subtle, rationalizable in-group favoritism can pose unique challenges to the legal system.

Unconscious Racism in Organizational Culture

From childhood experiences, individuals receive images from the media and experience personal observations that convey racial inequality in the American society (Quillian, 2008). These images often include stereotypical distortions. For examples, African Americans and Latinos are often in trouble with the law (i.e., criminalized), and have lower social class than Whites. Contradictory to these images, individuals are told that race should not be matter. Individuals are not supposed to judge others based on their skin color, but evaluate them based on what Martin Luther King exhorted as the content of their character A logical questions is, what are the effects of these contradictory images and messages on people's actions during cross-racial interactions?

The public rejection of racism in the United States begins with the previously discussed Supreme Court's denouncement of "separate but equal" in Brown v. Board of Education of Topeka. This court case leads some Whites to evaluate their stereotypical beliefs about African descendants. Yet, Aiyetoro (2009) argues that the case also brings what is identified as intentional or "in-your-face" discrimination underground. The term transforms to become unconscious racism (i.e., more invisible or carefully coded). This unconscious racism does not lessen the harm observed across age groups for African Americans or other ethnoracial groups, including Whites.

As previously mentioned, there is an example that demonstrates the unconscious racism impact on children. Drs. Kenneth and Mamie Clark performed "The Doll Test" (Clark & Clark, 1939). The test measures children's racial awareness and preferences. In a collection of studies, children are given a White doll and a Black doll. Eight different requests were asked including "give me the doll that: (a) like to play with or the doll you like best, (b) is the nice doll, (c) looks bad, (d) is a nice color, (e) looks like a White child, (f) looks like a Negro child, (h) looks like you." The results reveal that 67% of the Black children prefer White dolls to play with, 59% express the White doll as the nice doll, and 60% believe the White doll had a nice color. In contrast, 59% choose the brown doll as "looks bad." The study also demonstrates that the child's racial awareness begins around age 3. Also, children are aware of the advantages and negative connotations assign to the White and Black racial groups.

Thirty years later, Powell-Hopson & Hopson (1988) replicated the Clark doll test techniques, and adds the treatment intervention component to the study. One hundred and five Black preschoolers and fifty White preschoolers are presented with dolls that are identical except for skin color and hair texture. Similar to the Clark & Clark's (1939) study, the majorities of the children in the pretest are favored in the White doll and picture the Black doll as "bad". In the second phase of the study, the intervention involves children who choose a Black doll as their preferences are reinforced (verbal praise) and allowed to sit closer to the researchers. The children who choose the White dolls have to sit in the back. The researchers also choose the Black doll as their preferences and model pro-Black response to the preference questions. Story about the positive images of Black children is read in front of the group. Also, researchers ask children to hold up the Black dolls and repeats positive adjectives such as "pretty, nice, and smart" and "we like these dolls the best." No doll is referred as Black or White in the intervention phase.

After the intervention phase, 69% - 71% of Black children respond the Black roll as their preferences compare to 22% - 40% in the pre-test. For the White children, preference responses rages from 62%-66% choosing the Black doll after the intervention phase versus 18% - 38% in the pre-test phase. This study does not indicate that the children wish they were White. However, it suggests their awareness of society's preferences. Furthermore, the study results show the importance and positive impact on the children's attitudes and choices of having a role model (Powell-Hopson & Hopson, 1988). With the same idea, it is essential to have culturally responsive educators and leaders among the school of leadership in order to provide high-quality educations to the future generations.

Colorblindness

In today's society, many work groups consist of people from different cultural backgrounds. Because of these cross-cultural dynamics, the culturally responsive management skills are important for group performance. Multiculturalism recognizes and celebrates the differences between members from diverse cultural backgrounds. It enhances the feeling of accepted among minority members. On the contrary, leader's colorblindness is associated with group distancing and relationship conflict among minority members (Meeuseen, Otten, & Phalet, 2014). Applying the same idea into higher education, it underlines that multiculturalist and colorblind climates play a crucial role in students' psychological well-being.

Gordon (2005) evaluates and explores the colorblindness among teacher education. Based on the National Center for Education Statistics (2002), approximately 84% of public school teachers are White while almost 40% of their students are children of color. Cross (2003) states that this is "an enormous gap between who prepare teachers, who the teachers themselves are, and who they will likely teach… that results in a significant detachment of White teacher educators and White teacher education students from children of color" (204). Ignorance about cultural differences can lead to frustration and perpetuate a cycle of failure (Gordon, 2005). The result, could lead to unwanted consequences for the students of color.

Colorblindness proposes that all individuals are equal and that cultural differences are irrelevant (Meeuseen et al., 2014). Bonilla-Silva's (2009) book, Racism without Racists: Colorblind Racism and the Persistence of Racial Inequality in the United States, illustrates that some individuals make regarding to their racial "color-blindness." He argues that Whites use color-blind racism to explain racial differences in ways that exculpate them of any responsibility (Harper, 2012). For example, the higher rates of college attrition among Black male students are usually explained by factors that have little to deal with racist stereotypes or the maintenance of White supremacy in the campus environments (Harper, 2009).

Colorblindness is not blindness: it is not an inability to see color. In fact, it is a refusal. Jervis (1996) refers as "White resistance to seeing" (533). This resistance is learned and nurtured to preserve the status quo, which protect White privilege in individual and systemic levels. On the individual level, a person will claim, "I don't see color. We are all just people" to deny themselves of racism (Bell, 2003). On the systemic level, it denies "the system of rules, procedures, and tacit beliefs that result in Whites collectively maintaining control over the wealth and power of the nation and the world" (Sleeter, 1994, p. 6).

Harper (2012) completes a meta-analysis of the 255 peer-reviewed articles in regards to higher education institutional racism. Studies have shown that the individuals of color perceived and experienced campus racial climates are different than their White counterparts. Harper (2012) claims that many studies minimize the racial differences as byproducts of institutionalized racism. It requires systemic organizational change by investing and responding to the realities of race on campus. For example, institutional researchers states that Asian Americans are more likely to complete their education, but also experience higher rate of dissatisfactions on campus life. The study suggests assessment administrators to develop interventions that address Asian student's dissatisfaction and mental health concerns. Harper argues that the study not only emphasize on helping students, but also focus on the environmental factors that lead to dissatisfaction and psychological distress for particular minorities on campus.

Microaggression

The number of racial and ethnic minority students in college is high, yet many campuses still struggle to maintain an open and welcoming climate for diversity (Boysen, 2012). Microaggressions on university campus have recently caught the attention of popular media and literature (Vega, 2014). Microaggression is described as, "brief and commonplace daily verbal, behavioral, or environmental indignities, whether intentional or unintentional, that communication hostile, derogatory, or negative slights and insults toward people of color" (Sue et al., 2007, p. 271). Microaggression has also broadened to include other identity markers such as gender, disability, and sexual orientation (Alleyne, 2004; Sue, 2010).

On college campuses, cases of racially charged occurrences continue to occur. For example, "blackface" party incidents and "noose" hangings occur at numerous universities all over the country (Beamon, 2014). Mostly in urban areas of the Northern United States, Blackface minstrelsy began in the nineteenth century as a form of American musical theater performed for White working-class male audiences (Bucholtz & Lopez, 2011). In minstrel shows, White performers portrayed comic southern Black characters in skits and songs with their faces 'blacked' with the use of burnt cork as make-up (Bucholtz & Lopez, 2011; Strausbaugh, 2006). The shows originated with the 'white' man's characterizations of plantation slaves and free Blacks during the era of the 1800s, and the negative stereotypes developed from this process exist on schools of education amongst the students. As a form of entertainment, "blackface" parties exist causing difficult challenges beyond the academic scope of tests papers, and projects (Bucholtz & Lopez, 2011; Strausbaugh, 2006). This is especially true at predominantly White institutions (PWIs) where coping with racism has been identified as a risk factor and an impediment of achievement for African American students (Feagin, Heman, & Imani, 1996; Feagin & Feagin, 2012). Many of which can be explained by past and present perceived and actual discrimination, African Americans face a wealth of difficulties in the United States (Anderson, 1996; Beamon, 2014). Campuses where African American students, faculty, and administrators are underrepresented, they face overt acts of discrimination and institutional racism (Beamon, 2014).

Microaggressions have been extensively researched in everyday life to identify a comprehensive typology of microaggressions (Sue et al., 2007). There are three types of microaggression: microinsult, microinvalidation, and microassault. Microinsults are behaviors, actions, or verbal remarks that perceives as rude, insensitive, humiliate toward a person's group or social identity or heritage (Sue et al., 2007). An example would be a student asks his peer of color how he/she got his/her scholarship, implying he/she may have landed it through an affirmation action or minority quota system. Micro-invalidations are communications or actions that subtly exclude, negate, or nullify the psychological thoughts, feelings or experiential reality of a person of color (Sue et al., 2007). For instances, denying the continued existence of racism and sexism, treating minorities like foreigners, and claims of color blindness. Microassaults are consciously and intentionally put down meant to hurt the victim (e.g., using racial epithets, displaying White supremacist symbols). Although there are only limited studies have examined college students' perceptions of microaggressions, the results are consistent, in that students experience microaggression in college classroom (Solorzano et al., 2000; Sue et al., 2007).

Some teachers might be tempted to believe that any incident of bias in the classroom should be ignored to avoid attention to the behavior; however, students have been found to favor instructors who address microaggression within the classroom. For example, Boysen and colleagues (2009) asked students to recall incident of subtle bias in the classroom and rate of effectiveness of the teachers' method of responding to the incident. The study shows that ignoring subtle bias is ineffective overall, and it is significantly less effective than other response methods. Moreover, some teachers may not perceive microaggression as incidents of bias. The results show that older, male teachers are less likely to perceive and report noticing bias in the classroom than younger, female teachers (Boysen & Vogel, 2009).

Boysen (2012) addresses the importance of teachers' responses to the microaggressions. By providing vignettes describing classroom microaggressions, teachers of courses with diversity perceive microaggression negatively compared to teachers from nondiverse courses. Also, diversity teachers are more likely to recognize microaggression as necessitating a response and discuss microaggression in the classroom than nondiversity teachers.

Microaggression require a response, and it should be handled with moderate directness and intensity. Both teachers' and students' data indicate that responding rather than ignoring as the preferred course of action. Since teachers of diversity courses tend to have more knowledge about the topic, they are more likely to address and manage microaggression in the classroom due to the nature of their courses.

In the contrary, college employees, similar to students, they also experience varying degrees of power and privilege on college campuses, including privileges related to their professional roles. Young, Anderson, and Stewart (2014) explores the types of microaggressions experience by university employees on a college campus. The authors introduce the term "hierarchical microaggression" to represent "everyday slights found in higher education that communicate systemic valuing (or devaluing) of a person because of institutional role held by that person" (Young et al., 2014, p.2). The study explores the hierarchical microaggression through examining qualitative data from multiple cultural competence trainings.

The study highlights the importance of examining the role of hierarchical microaggression in higher education. The four main types of hierarchical microaggressions are: valuing/devaluing based on role/credential, changing accepted behavior based on role, actions (e.g., ignoring, excluding, surprise, interrupting) related to role, and terminology related to work position. The findings indicate that hierarchical microaggression are more than just insensitive comments. It significantly impact people because people take on an identity associated with their status at the university (Young et al., 2014). The individuals who receive privilege with a doctoral degree reinforce the microaggressions in this setting. The lack of privilege associates with those with lesser or no degrees (e.g., students, staffs). Sue (2010) also argues that these microaggressions are made more problematic because the perpetrators may not acknowledge their comments or actions and view it as "innocent and harmless slight(s)." This absence of recognition creates a challenge for the receivers of these microaggressions to report (Ashburn-Nardo, Morris, & Goodwin, 2008).

At a professional level, workplace racism has been found in experiences of college faculty of color (Young, et al., 2014). Orelus (2013) states that it is a considerable challenge for many professors of color to teach in a predominately White institution. Professors of color constantly need to fight against institutional racism and White hegemony (Delgado, 2011). Professors of color may only become visible to meet the universities' diversity propaganda purposes. Orelus (2013) lists an example from Professor Uvanney Maylor, a Black British female professor and researcher: Maylor states that there have been many times where her identity as a Black academic researcher has been misrecognized. There was one incident that when she was introduced to a White European visiting professor, Maylor was asked if she was "one of the helpers." Maylor was automatically viewed as less intelligent and placed in a lower status due to her "Blackness" perceived by the European professor. Unfortunately, what had happened to Professor Maylor has happened to countless other professors of color.

It is clear to conclude that microaggressions in higher education have a significant impact on college students, faculty, and staff. In order to improve positive campus climates and broaden the goals of inclusive excellence, campus can use an "Inclusive Excellence Toolkit" (Treviño, Walker, & Leyba, 2009; Young et al., 2014). The Inclusive Excellence Toolkit focuses on infusing the practices and philosophies that promote diversity in every aspects of an organization (e.g., increasing a supportive environments for all students, faculty, and staff; increasing the numbers of historically underrepresented students, faculty, and staffs). In addition, Sue (2010) indicates that the ability to properly address microaggression requires an individual to raise awareness of what microaggressions are, awareness of personal cultural values, and awareness of personal bias. By doing so, it encourages everyone to develop knowledge about, and interactions with, diverse groups (Williams, Berger, & McClendon, 2005).

RACISM ACROSS DIFFERENT MINORITIES IN HIGHER EDUCATION

The climate of a university often is the prominent factor that influences the depth and level of learning among students (Vaccaro, 2010). Hurtado, Milem, Clayton-Pedersen, and Allen (1998) defines campus climate as a combination of psychological climate, behavioral climate, structural diversity, and institutional history. Tierney (1990) suggests that the campus climate is intricately related to students' complex attitudes and perceptions of their environments. Studies have supported that a negative and hostile environments may lead to detrimental impact on the success and retention rate of students of colors (Chang, 2000; Feagin, Vera, & Imani, 1996; Hurtado, 2002; Nora & Cabrera, 1996; Watson, 2002).

Organizations and the Model Minority Myth

Discrimination based on racial and ethnic group has been identified as a lifelong struggle for many minorities in the United States (Lee, 2003). In many Americans' views, Asian Americans do not encounter racial discrimination, or that they experience minimal discrimination compared to other ethnic and racial minority group. These beliefs largely stem from the community misconception of Asian Americans as the "model minority" (Lee, 2003). For more than two decades, Asian Americans have been portrayed by the press and media as a successful minority. Asian Pacific Americans (APAs) often misidentify as being overrepresented at 4-years colleges/universities (Hartlep, Ecker, Miller, & Whitmore, 2013). APAs are stereotyped as being "model minorities" (Brydolf, 2009; Pang, Han, & Pang, 2011). This label portrays that APAs are educationally and socially successful, high-achieving individuals, diligent and docile worker, problem-free in mental health and crime (Hartlep et al., 2013; Huynh, Devos, Goldberg, 2014).

Holding a minority status does not only link to negative social consequences, but more importantly, it also correlates with increased risk for psychopathology (i.e., abnormal behaviors) among Asian Americans (Alegria et al., 2004). Psychologically compared to Whites, Asian American college students are more likely to seek medical leave, more likely to go on academic probation, and are less likely to graduate in four years (Cornell University, 2004). At Cornell University, 13 of the 21 student suicide victims between 1996 and 2006 were Asian or Asian American. This number is even more alarming when accounting for the fact that Asians make up of only 14 percent of the total Cornell student body. Ly (2008) stated that Asian American students were more likely to report difficulties with stress, sleep and feelings of hopelessness compare to White students, yet they are less likely to seek counseling (Ly, 2008).

Asian Indians are also a part of this growing Asian population, but "Calling Asian Indians the new 'model minority' isn't a compliment. It's an attempt to fit them into a convenient box for political purposes" (Srivastava, 2009, p. 1). Srivastava argues that the phase of 'Model Minority' (MM) is potentially creating interracial tension by labeling one community as the "model". Indeed, the analysis of census data seems to back up this contention (U.S. Census Bureau, 2011). Of those, over the age of 25, half of Asian/Pacific Islanders have bachelor's degrees or higher degree of education, compared with 28.5% of all Americans. With all these data published in the company as a whole, it is not hard to anticipate that this stereotypical view can become more entrenched and supported within the company.

Due to this label, APAs oftentimes are not considered as "underrepresented." Thus, they are ineligible for affirmation action protection (Wu & Wang, 1996). The purpose of the affirmation action is to promote social equality, to address minority underrepresentation, to increase diversity, and to provide equal opportunity (Dong, 1995; Ball, 2000). However, the model minority stereotype has masked APAs from the underrepresented subgroup.

According to the Commission on Asian American and Pacific Islander Research in Education (CARE; 2011), Pacific Islanders have a very high rate of attrition during college. Among the Pacific Islanders, 47% of Guamanians, 50% of Native Hawaiians, 54% of Tongans, and 58.1% of Samoans have failed to earn a degree when they entered college.

Moreover, there are a large proportion of Southeast Asian and Pacific Islanders college attendees earned associate's degrees as their highest level of education. On the other hand, East Asian and South Asians were more likely to earn bachelor's degree or advanced degree. This report has demonstrated the large disparity among APAs groups. The within-group differences make it more complicate concludes any generalized summary of the APAs populations.

The Sexual Orientation: "Dual Minority Stress"

Ideally, university campus should able to allow and encourage students from diverse social groups to interact across differences (Holley, Larson, Adelman, Trevino, 2007). Unfortunately, studies show that students who are lesbian, gay, bisexual, or transgender (LGBT) and/color often report hostile campus climates (Ancis, Sedlacek, & Mohr, 2000; Rankin, 2003; Brown, Clarke, Gortmaker, & Robinson-Kelig,

2004). As LGBT students become more visible on college campus, it is important for higher education educators and administrators to assist the students in becoming more safe and comfortable in their identities. This section will focus on exploring the institutional racism among individuals who are racial and sexual minorities, the dual minority status.

Scholars have been explored the issues about that LGBT students face in higher education (Goode-Cross & Tager, 2011). Howard & Stevens (2000) argues that the barrier to higher education and individual development for LGBT students include the fear of being out, isolation, verbal harassment, and physical violence. In a survey that consists that 1669 LGBT-identified students, faculty, and staff/administrators at 14 universities, 20 percent of the respondents report fear for their physical safety due to their sexual orientation or gender identity. Moreover, one out of two respondents prefer to conceal their sexual orientation or gender identity to avoid intimidation (Evans, 2002; Rankin, 2003).

Not surprisingly, LGBT students and student of color perceive a more hostile campus environment than do their heterosexual and White peers. Holley et al. (2007) states that students report significantly higher levels of negative attitude toward LGBT individuals than any of the specific ethnic/racial groups. Gender, religion, sexual orientation, and ethnicity can influences students' attitudes toward some social groups. Studies show that African American sexual gay and bisexual men often suffer from a varying degrees of psychosocial challenges at the universities, especially predominantly White institutions. Being racism and sexual minorities, these students often experiencing feelings of isolation and marginalization, and struggle in finding a safe and comfortable environment (Goode-Cross & Good, 2008; Mobley, 2000; Schueler, Hoffman, & Peterson, 2009). In Goode-Cross & Tager's study, the African American gay and bisexual men choose minimize their sexual identity in order to gain affiliation and acceptance from peers in other races.

Gay and bisexual African American male students often struggle from low self-esteem and identity confusion from their experience at predominantly White institution (Washington & Wall, 2006). Herek, Gillis, & Cogan's (2009) study states that LGBT African Americans are more likely to experience higher internalized homophobia than other races and ethnicities. The internalized homophobia is associated with greater relationship issues, lower self-esteem, and higher psychological distress among LGBT African Americans (Frost & Meyer, 2009; Szymanski & Gupta, 2009). In particular studies, internalized homophobia is associated with a variety of psychological distress: demoralization (depression, anxiety, hopelessness, helplessness, psychosomatic symptoms, and confused thinking), sense of guilt, sexual problems, suicidal ideation, and AIDS-related psychological distress (Meyer, 2003; Rosser, Bockting, Ross, Miner, & Coleman, 2008). Because of that, these students report difficulty in finding supportive community at the predominantly White institution.

Asian American gay men have also been found in facing unique challenge in managing stressors associated with dual minority status that is coming from their ethnicity and sexual orientation (Wilson & Yoshikawa, 2004). Homophobia, racism, anti-immigrant expression, and discrimination based on stereotype of passivity and submission place these individuals at high risk for stress and poor psychological wellbeing (Cochran, Mays, Alegria, Ortega, & Takeuchi, 2007; Wilson & Yoshikawa, 2004). Due to the unique cultural experience of Asian Americans, study shows that Asian American gay men who experiences higher levels of stress relate to their Asian ethnicity also tend to report higher levels of stress associate to their sexual orientation (Chen & Tryon, 2012). It emphasizes the significant impact of racial/ethnic identity toward the perception of their sexual orientations.

Effect on Education

Colleges of education are part of a larger education system, which are elaborate and have a ubiquitous demonstrations presence in modern society (O'Brien, 2009). It composes with many players who have different levels of power and variety of influences. Among all the players, teachers usually are the central forces. The perspectives and actions of teachers shape the way society deals with racism. In result, it directly influences the worldviews and behaviors of all students.

Much of what the teacher do in the classroom are associated to their own prior educational experiences and the beliefs they have constructed from their exposure to schools of education (Gordon, 2005). The majority of teacher education students are heterosexual women from European culture backgrounds. Their experiences will in turn influences the lives and experiences of their students (Martin & Van Gunten, 2002). Many teachers have limited contact with the racial groups that are different from their own. Not surprisingly, many White, middle-class, monolingual teachers hold negative perceptions of minority students (Milner, 2003; Terrill & Mark, 2000). Gay (2002) argues that minority students are places in double jeopardy by expecting them to perform academic excellence and functioning under the cultural conditions unnatural to them. These students are expected by their teachers to accept and learn the European American cultural norms while disregarding their cultures. A significant cross-cultural burden can lead to psychological distress among students.

In the UK, Black academics claim that they are viewed as "outsiders" at universities by a mentality of racism (Grove, 2014). William Ackah, a lecturer at University of London states that the "outdated Victorian views on the 'wild and untamed' nature of 'the Negro' still persisted at some level in UK universities." Shirley Anne Tate, an associate professor at the University of Leeds, note that the university still view Black academics as "out of place" in an academic setting; therefore, Because of that, she claims that Black academics struggled to find mentors.

Compared to the teachers who serve predominantly White student populations, teachers who serve African American students are tend to be less well trained, less well paid, and less experienced (Kalogrides & Loeb, 2013). On the other hand, schools that serve a large population of African American students are usually underfunded and in greater disrepair (Knaus, 2014). Knaus (2014) argues that such disparities reiterate that inequalities are built into the curriculum, school funding, teaching method, and the ways knowledge is constructed.

Orelus (2013) argues that it is a terrific challenge for many professor of color to teach in a predominantly White institution. On top of fulfilling the professional obligation such as publishing, teaching, advising, professor's of color need to constantly fight against institutional racism (Delgado, 2011). In Orelus's study (2013), he described his personal experience as being a Black professor in a predominantly White institute. Orelus states that being a professor of color is exhausted. He often serves the purpose of having "diversity" on campus, and expects to participate in many activities that are related to his race. He feels that he is obligated to fight for the respect for his credentials and professionalism. Unfortunately, the racially constructed reality leads many non-White individuals to feel that they are expected to fight against all forms of racial aggression at work and beyond (Orelus, 2013).

In order to minimize the institutional racism toward students and faculties, education programs need to examine the racism oppression at both the individual and systemic levels. The first step is to acknowledge the failure of colorblindness and recognize the racial oppression within the educational system. Professors and educational students need to see beyond their worldviews in order to provide academic excellence and cultural competence education to the future generations.

FUTURE RESEARCH DIRECTIONS

From the perspective of the chapter's focus, future movements within research can provide antiracist practices in schools of education leadership. In an effort to provide successful institutional environment, universities across the nation has developed groups (e.g., racial affinity groups) to cultivate a culturally responsive competence amongst the university population. In view of a legal stance, it is necessary for institutions to consider legal consequences following social injustice. With further research in the forthcoming areas, schools of education can deliver interculturalism with race-based forensic psychological perspectives.

Culturally Responsive Competence

Institutions of higher education can provide environments for students to develop new capacities for learning across differences (Musil et al., 1999; Vaccaro, 2010); however, negative, hostile, and unwelcoming campus climates have a detrimental impact on the success and retention of students of color (Chang, 2000; Feagin, Vera, & Imani, 1996; Hurtado, 2002; Vaccaro, 2010; Watson, 2002). Institutions with diversity programs (i.e., programs that foster intergroup communication) can have a profound impact on their students' development of identity, respect for cultural differences, and self-growth through self-awareness (Vaccaro, 2010). Cross group interaction can influence both motivation to reduce an individual's own prejudice and executing actions to promote inclusion for social justice (Vaccaro, 2010; Zúñiga, Williams, & Berger, 2005). Cultural receptiveness within an organization can be seen as a developmental development with stages of growth and conflict emerging as that organization becomes increasingly inclusive (Blitz & Kohl, 2012; Constantine & Sue, 2005)

Racial Affinity Groups

Racial affinity groups, or race-based caucuses, are processes where people of the same racial group meet on a regular basis to discusd institutional racism, oppression, and privilege within their organization (Blitz & Kohl, 2012). Race-based caucusing is utilized to address cultural responsiveness and can function to promote antiracist practice, effective organizational change, and support individual growth (i.e., professional, personal; Blitz & Kohl, 2012). Recognition and validation of institutional racism within an organization can foster accountability further support the members of the organization (Blitz & Kohl, 2012; Zúñiga, Williams, & Berger, 2005). Diversity initiatives of an institution can minimize psychological, sociological, identity, cognitive, structural, and cultural factors that undergird individual resistance to diversity (Goodman, 2001).

Forensic Psychological Perspective

Forensic psychology involves the application of professionally trained skills in assessment of culturally responsive approaches, investigation quantitative methods, the law, and research within schools of education. Individual racism is powerfully augmented by the power of institutions (e.g., schools of education) to apply racism across social groups (Cross, 2005; Henkel, Dovidio, & Gaertner, 2006; Vaught, 2012). All levels of an institution need the understanding of the history and how it has shaped society (Cross, 2005; Leonardo, 2012).

It is essential for teacher education programs to examine interculturalism and to have the opportunities to reflect on their own personal bias (Haran & Tormey, 2002). "In order to get beyond racism, we must first take account of race. There is no other way" (Harper & Hurtado, 2011, p.viii).

Critical Race Theory

Giving educational scholars an arsenal of concepts (i.e., knowledge apartheid, microaggressions, critical race pedagogy), Critical Race Theory (CRT) legitimizes the intellectual practice and study of race and education (Delgado Bernal, 1998; Leonardo, 2012; Solorzano, 1998). Critical Race Theory is a paradigm to produce a better comprehension of the racial dilemma, revealing how racial stratification is enduring than is initially evident (Beamon, 2014; Delgado & Stefancic, 2000, 2001). The theoretical perspective began during the era of civil rights litigation: a time legal scholars began to recognize how racial oppression within American society and the law works to perpetuate racial stratification instead of fostering the deconstruction of oppressive conditions (Beamon, 2014). For the first time, Critical race theorists examined the contemporary legal thought and doctrine with the viewpoint of the law's role in the construction and maintenance of social subordination (Beamon, 2014; Crenshaw et al., 1995). Critical race theorists argue that race and racism permeate the entire educational enterprise, from aspirations, to spatial configurations, and teacher education within education (Leonardo, 2012; Yosso, 2002). Today, Critical Race Theory is utilized by scholars in sociology, psychology, political science, critical race feminism, Native American studies, sport psychology, and education to examine how racial stratification operates in various levels to affect 'blacks' and 'whites' (Beamon, 2014; Brown, 2003). With thorough examination of schooling as a racial state apparatus, CRT demonstrates, in essence, how education is a racial project and race consist of an educational project (Fasching-Varner, 2009; Leonardo, 2012).

Antiracist Multicultural Organization

Race-based perspectives emphasize the need to examine policies, practices, and organizational culture to understand how the agency and/or institution may privilege 'white' people and/or subordinate people of color (Blitz & Kohl, 2012; Carter, 2000; Crossroads Ministry, 2008). With this identification, a plan can be developed to move through the process of becoming antiracist (Blitz & Kohl, 2012). Since 'white' people are often in key decision-making roles within organizations, they must take several actions: do something daily to earn the title of ally; identify and name racism directly; take responsibility for self-education without relying on people of color; confront racism; and interrupt racist statements and behaviors, regardless of whether a person of color is present (Blitz & Kohl, 2012; Safehouse Progressive Alliance for Nonviolence, 2007).

An institution's motivation for responding to structural racism is based on a desire to provide the best possible education to students (Blitz & Kohl, 2012). The organization would be taking a philosophical stance, grounded in research on multicultural clinical competency, that institutional factors that tend to be inhibited by staff (Blitz & Kohl, 2012). The implementation of training program managers who oversee the dissemination of antiracism information allows antiracist practices (Blitz & Kohl, 2012; Safehouse Progressive Alliance for Nonviolence, 2007).

CONCLUSION

The globalization of higher education cannot occur if it is a culture that contains perceptions of racism. Despite improvements in the diversity of students and campus climate, there are still many reasons for racial minorities to feel unwelcome in schools of education. The findings add a new layer of interpretation to organizational racism by introducing comprehensive history of racism with examples of court cases. *Brown v. Board of Education* rings the bell to the society. Throughout history, the rulings of the *Brown* case allowed individuals to reflect on their own biases. Unfortunately, emotional segregation continues to function as a barrier to antiracist practices and is tacitly supported in schools of education (Beeman, 2007; Rush, 2006).

Organizational policies are another barrier to promote antiracism. Even though most campuses have "Equality and Diversity" policies, the policy statements are too vague or over-general to provide practical strategies (Ahmed, 2008; Sonn, 2004). In addition, the curriculum content within the schools of education has developed into a political debate. The topic of who and what should be required within the curriculum to promote antiracist practices remain unsolved. Although there is a decline in racist attitudes, the opposition to interracial intimacy remains (Beeman, 2007; Knox, Zusman, Buffington, & Hemphill, 2000; Romano, 2003). Addressing the factors of racial privilege and racial oppression enhance culturally responsive education (Beeman, 2007; Blitz & Kohl, 2012). Moreover, the "trickle-down" model provides a different viewpoint to explain the impact of supervisors' experience on their subordinates. It emphasizes the hierarchical model of how one's experience in an organization can affect his or her perceptions of the organization, as well as his or her behaviors towards others (Ambrose et al., 2013). Similarly, this model also illustrates the similar effect of institutional racism has within leadership of educational institutions on its students and subordinates.

As mentioned earlier in the chapter, racism does not present itself in a direct way nowadays (i.e, old versus new racism). Instead, it usually manifests in an indirect and subtle way. Aversive racism and unconscious racism are examples of indirect racism. Being colorblind and acting with microaggression toward other racial minorities can manifest these types of racism. These acts are subtle and not easy to recognize by the perpetrators. These behaviors often serve as the status quo, which protect the privilege in certain racial group in individual and systemic level (Bell, 2003; Sleeter, 1994). The impact of institutional racism in colleges of education does not only affect the students, but also expand to the faculty and staff. Minority students often report higher level of psychological distress, lower self-esteem, lower level of satisfaction of college experience compare to the White students (Chang, 2000; Feagin et al., 1996, Alegria et al., 2004; Ancis et al., 2000). Moreover, professors of color are also constantly experiencing racial microaggression, especially at predominantly White institutions (Orelus, 2013). Effective management of racism within the classroom should not only improve campus climates for diverse students, but also train all those aspiring to be leaders about mindfulness and responsibility to a larger multicultural society. It is with hope that this chapter raised the awareness of institutional and organizational racism for individuals on campus, and for campuses in general, to reduce tension and dissatisfaction in the college climate.

REFERENCES

Ahmed, B. (2008). Teaching critical psychology of race issues: Problems in promoting anti-racist practice. *Journal of Community & Applied Social Psychology, 18*(1), 54–67. doi:10.1002/casp.912

Ahmed, B., Nicolson, P., & Spencer, C. (2000). The social construction of racism: The case of second generation Bangladeshis. *Journal of Community & Applied Social Psychology, 10*(1), 33–47. doi:10.1002/(SICI)1099-1298(200001/02)10:1<33::AID-CASP529>3.0.CO;2-B

Aiyetoro, A. A. (2009). Can we talk: How triggers for unconscious racism strengthen the importance of dialogue. *National Black Law Journal, 22*, 1–60.

Alegria, M., Takeuchi, D., Canino, G., Duan, N., Shrout, P., Meng, X. L., ... Vera, M. (2004). Considering context, place and culture: The National Latino and Asian American Study. *International Journal of Methods in Psychiatric Research, 13*(4), 208–220. doi:10.1002/mpr.178 PMID:15719529

Alleyne, A. (2004). Black identity and workplace oppression. *Counselling & Psychotherapy Research, 4*(1), 4–8. doi:10.1080/14733140412331384008

Ambrose, M. L., Schminke, M., & Mayer, D. M. (2013). Trickle-down effects of supervisor perceptions of interactional justice: A moderated mediation approach. *The Journal of Applied Psychology, 98*(4), 678–689. doi:10.1037/a0032080 PMID:23477377

Ancis, J. R., Sedlacek, W. E., & Mohr, J. J. (2000). Student perceptions of campus cultural climate by race. *Journal of Counseling and Development: JCD, 78*(2), 180–185. doi:10.1002/j.1556-6676.2000.tb02576.x

Anderson, P. M. (1996). Racism in sports: A question of ethics. *Marq. Sports L. J., 6*, 357–408.

Applebaum, H. M. (1964). Miscegenation statutes: A constitutional and social problem. *The Georgetown Law Journal, 53*(1), 49–91.

Ashburn-Nardo, L., Morris, K. A., & Goodwin, S. A. (2008). The confronting prejudiced responses (CPR) model: Applying CPR in organizations. *Academy of Management Learning & Education, 7*(3), 332–342. doi:10.5465/AMLE.2008.34251671

Ball, H. (2000). *The Bakke Case: Race, Education, & Affirmative Action*. Lawrence, KS: University Press of Kansas.

Banks, W. M. (1984, January/February). Afro-American scholars in the university: Roles and conflicts. *The American Behavioral Scientist, 27*(3), 325–338. doi:10.1177/000276484027003005

Beamon, K. (2014). Racism and stereotyping on campus: Experiences of African American male student-athletes. *The Journal of Negro Education, 83*(2), 121–134. doi:10.7709/jnegroeducation.83.2.0121

Beeman, A. K. (2007). Emotional segregation: A content analysis of institutional racism in US films, 19802001. *Ethnic and Racial Studies, 30*(5), 687–712. doi:10.1080/01419870701491648

Bell, E. L. J., & Nkomo, S. M. (2001). *Our Separate Ways: Black and White Women and the Struggle for Professional Identity*. Boston: Harvard University Press.

Bell, L. A. (2003). Telling tales: What stories can teach us about racism. *Race, Ethnicity and Education, 6*(1), 3–28. doi:10.1080/1361332032000044567

Blitz, L. V., & Kohl, B. J. Jr. (2012). Addressing racism in the organization: The role of White racial affinity groups in creating change. *Administration in Social Work, 36*(5), 479–498. doi:10.1080/03643107.2011.624261

Bonilla-Silva, E. (2009). *Racism Without Racists: Colorblind Racism and the Persistence of Racial Inequality in the United States* (3rd ed.). Lanham, MD: Rowman & Littlefield.

Bonilla-Silva, E. (2012). The invisible weight of whiteness: The racial grammar of everyday life in contemporary America. *Ethnic and Racial Studies, 35*(2), 173–194.

Boysen, G. A. (2012). Teacher and student perceptions of microaggressions in college classrooms. *College Teaching, 60*(3), 122–129. doi:10.1080/87567555.2012.654831

Boysen, G. A., & Vogel, D. L. (2009). Bias in the classroom: Types, frequencies, and responses. *Teaching of Psychology, 36*(1), 12–17. doi:10.1080/00986280802529038

Boysen, G. A., Vogel, D. L., Cope, M. A., & Hubbard, A. (2009). Incidents of bias in the classrooms: Instructor and student perceptions. *Journal of Diversity in Higher Education, 4*(4), 219–231. doi:10.1037/a0017538

Bozalek, V. (2010). The effect of institutional racism on student family circumstances: A human capabilities perspective. *South African Journal of Psychology. Suid-Afrikaanse Tydskrif vir Sielkunde, 40*(4), 487–494. doi:10.1177/008124631004000409

Brown, R. D., Clarke, B., Gortmaker, V., & Robinson-Keilig, R. (2004). Assessing the campus climate for gay, lesbian, bisexual, and transgender (GLBT) students using a multiple perspectives approach. *Journal of College Student Development, 45*(1), 8–26. doi:10.1353/csd.2004.0003

Brown, T. N. (2003). Critical race theory speaks to the sociology of mental health: Mental health problems produced by racial stratification. *Journal of Health and Social Behavior, 44*(3), 292–301. doi:10.2307/1519780 PMID:14582309

Brown v. Board of Education of Topeka, 347 U.S. 483 (1954).

Brydolf, C. (2009). Getting real about the "Model Minority": Asian Americans and pacific islanders fight their stereotype. *Education Digest: Essential Readings Condensed for Quick Review, 74*(5), 37–44.

Bucholtz, M., & Lopez, Q. (2011). Performing blackness, forming whiteness: Linguistic minstrelsy in Hollywood film. *Journal of Sociolinguistics, 15*(5), 680–706. doi:10.1111/j.1467-9841.2011.00513.x

Byrd, W. M., & Clayton, L. A. (2000). *An American Health Dilemma*. New York: Routledge.

Byrd, W. M., & Clayton, L. A. (2001). Race, medicine, and healthcare in the United States: A historical survey. *Journal of the National Medical Association, 93*(3), 11S–34S. PMID:12653395

Capezza, N. M., & Arriaga, X. B. (2008). Why do people blame victims of abuse? The role of stereotypes of women on perceptions of blame. *Sex Roles, 59*(11-12), 839–850. doi:10.100711199-008-9488-1

Carter, R. T. (Ed.). (2000). *Addressing Cultural Issues in Organizations: Beyond the Corporate Context*. Thousand Oaks, CA: Sage Publications.

Chang, M. J. (2000). Improving campus racial dynamics: A balancing act among competing interests. *The Review of Higher Education, 23*(2), 153–175. doi:10.1353/rhe.2000.0003

Chen, Y. C., & Tryon, G. S. (2012). Dual minority stress and Asian American gay mens psychological distress. *Journal of Community Psychology, 40*(5), 539–554. doi:10.1002/jcop.21481

Clark, K. B., & Clark, M. P. (1939). The development of consciousness of self and the emergence of racial identification in Negro preschool children. *The Journal of Social Psychology, 10*(4), 591–599. doi:10.1080/00224545.1939.9713394

Cochran, J. C., & Warren, P. Y. (2012). Racial, ethnic, and gender differences in perceptions of the police: The salience of officer race within the context of racial profiling. *Journal of Contemporary Criminal Justice, 28*(2), 206–227. doi:10.1177/1043986211425726

Cochran, S. D., Mays, V. M., Alegria, M., Ortega, A. N., & Takeuchi, D. (2007). Mental health and substance abuse disorders among Latino and Asian American lesbian, gay, and bisexual adults. [PubMed]. *Journal of Consulting and Clinical Psychology, 75*(5), 785–794. doi:10.1037/0022-006X.75.5.785 PMID:17907860

Cohen-Charash, Y., & Spector, P. E. (2001). The role of justice in organizations: A meta-analysis. *Organizational Behavior and Human Decision Processes, 86*(2), 278–321. doi:10.1006/obhd.2001.2958

Colquitt, J. A., Conlon, D. E., Wesson, M. J., Porter, C. O., & Ng, K. Y. (2001). Justice at the millennium: A meta-analytic review of 25 years of organizational justice research. *The Journal of Applied Psychology, 86*(3), 425–445. doi:10.1037/0021-9010.86.3.425 PMID:11419803

Commission on Asian American and Pacific Islander Research in Education. (2011). *The Relevance of Asian Americans & Pacific Islanders in the College Completion Agenda*. Retrieved on November 24, 2014 from http://apiasf.org/research/2011_CARE_Report.pdf

Constantine, M. G., & Sue, D. W. (2005). Effective multicultural consultation and organizational development. In M. G. Constantine & D. W. Sue (Eds.), *Strategies for building multicultural competence in mental health and educational settings* (pp. 212–226). Hoboken, NJ: John Wiley & Sons.

Cornell University. (2004). *Asian and Asian American campus climate task force report*. Retrieved from http://www.gannett.cornell.edu/downloads/campusIniatives/mentalhealth/AAATFreport2004.pdf

Crenshaw, K., Gotanda, N., Peller, G., & Thomas, K. (Eds.). (1995). *Critical race theory: The key writings that formed the movement*. New York: The New Press.

Cross, B. E. (2003). Learning or unlearning racism: Transferring teacher education curriculum to classroom practices. *Theory into Practice, 42*(3), 203–209. doi:10.120715430421tip4203_6

Cross, B. E. (2005). New racism, reformed teacher education, and the same ole' oppression. *Educational Studies: A Journal of the American Educational Studies Association, 38*(3), 263–274. doi:10.120715326993es3803_6

Crossroads Ministry. (2008). *Racial identity caucusing: A strategy for building antiracist collectives.* Retrieved from http://www.crossroadsantiracism.org/wp-content/themes/crossroads/PDFs/Racial%20 Identiy%20Caucusing%20Strategy.pdf

Delgado, R. (2011). Unveiling Majoritarian Myths and Tales about Race and Racism: A conversation with Richard Delgado. *Rethinking race, class, language, and gender: A dialogue with Noam Chomsky and other leading scholars*, 7-15.

Delgado, R., & Stefancic, J. (Eds.). (2000). *Critical race theory: The cutting edge* (2nd ed.). Philadelphia, PA: Temple University Press.

Delgado, R., & Stefancic, J. (2001). *Critical race theory: An introduction*. New York: New York University Press.

Delgado Bernal, D. (1998). Using a chicana feminist epistemology in education research. *Harvard Educational Review*, *68*(4), 555–583. doi:10.17763/haer.68.4.5wv1034973g22q48

Dominelli, L. (1988). *Anti-racist Social Work*. Basingstoke, UK: MacMillan.

Dominelli, L. (1989). An uncaring profession? An examination of racism in social work. *Journal of Ethnic and Migration Studies*, *15*(3), 391–403. doi:10.1080/1369183X.1989.9976127

Dong, S. (1995). Too many Asians: The challenge of fighting discrimination against Asian-Americans and preserving affirmative action. *Stanford Law Review*, *47*(5), 1027–1057. doi:10.2307/1229181

Dovidio, J. F., & Gaertner, S. L. (1998). On the nature of contemporary prejudice: The causes, consequences, and challenges of aversive racism. In J. L. Eberhardt & S. T. Fiske (Eds.), *Confronting Racism: The Problem and the Response* (pp. 3–32). Thousand Oaks, CA: Sage.

Dovidio, J. F., & Gaertner, S. L. (2000). Aversive racism and selection decisions: 1989 and 1999. *Psychological Science*, *11*(4), 315–319. doi:10.1111/1467-9280.00262 PMID:11273391

Dovidio, J. F., & Gaertner, S. L. (2005). Understanding and Addressing Contemporary Racism: From Aversive Racism to the Common Ingroup Identity Model. *The Journal of Social Issues*, *61*(3), 615–639. doi:10.1111/j.1540-4560.2005.00424.x

Duncan, G. (2002). Beyond love: A critical race ethnography of the schooling of black males. *Equity & Excellence in Education*, *35*(2), 131–143. doi:10.1080/713845286

Erdogan, B., & Enders, J. (2007). Support from the top: Supervisors perceived organizational support as a moderator of leader–member exchange to satisfaction and performance relationships. *The Journal of Applied Psychology*, *92*(2), 321–330. doi:10.1037/0021-9010.92.2.321 PMID:17371081

Evans, N. (2002). The impact of an LGBT safe zone project on campus climate. *Journal of College Student Development*, *43*(4), 522–539.

Fasching-Varner, K. J. (2009). No! The team ain't alright! The institutional and individual problematics of race. *Social Identities: Journal for the Study of Race Nature and Culture*, *15*(6), 811–829.

Feagin, J., & Feagin, C. (2012). *Racial and Ethnic Relations* (9th ed.). Upper Saddle River, NJ: Pearson.

Feagin, J., Heman, V., & Imani, N. (1996). *The agony of education: Black students at White colleges and universities*. New York: Routledge.

Feagin, J. R., Vera, H., & Imani, N. (1996). *The Agony of Education: Black Students at White Colleges and Universities*. New York: Routledge.

Flexon, J. L., Lurigio, A. J., & Greenleaf, R. G. (2009). Exploring the dimensions of Trust in the police among Chicago juveniles. *Journal of Criminal Justice*, *37*(2), 180–189. doi:10.1016/j.jcrimjus.2009.02.006

Frost, D. M., & Meyer, I. H. (2009). Internalized homophobia and relationship quality among lesbians, gay men, and bisexuals. *Journal of Counseling Psychology*, *56*(1), 97–109. doi:10.1037/a0012844 PMID:20047016

Gaertner, S. L., Dovidio, J. F., Banker, B., Rust, M., Nier, J., Mottola, G., & Ward, C. (1997). Does racism necessarily mean anti-blackness? Aversive racism and pro-whiteness. In M. Fine, L. Powell, & L. Weis (Eds.), *Off White* (pp. 167–178). London: Routledge.

Gay, G. (2002). Preparing for culturally responsive teaching. *Journal of Teacher Education*, *53*(2), 106–116. doi:10.1177/0022487102053002003

Goode-Cross, D. T., & Good, G. E. (2008). African-American men who have sex with men: Creating safe spaces through relationships. *Psychology of Men & Masculinity*, *9*(4), 221–234. doi:10.1037/a0013428

Goode-Cross, D. T., & Tager, D. (2011). Negotiating multiple identities: How African-American gay and bisexual men persist at a predominantly White institution. *Journal of Homosexuality*, *58*(9), 1235–1254. doi:10.1080/00918369.2011.605736 PMID:21957857

Goodman, D. J. (2001). *Promoting Diversity and Social Justice: Educating People from Privileged Groups*. Thousand Oaks, CA: Sage.

Gordon, J. (2005). Inadvertent complicity: Colorblindness in teacher education. *Educational Studies: A Journal of the American Educational Studies Association*, *38*(2), 135–153. doi:10.120715326993es3802_5

Grove, J. (2014). Black Scholars Still Experience Racism on Campus. *Times Higher Education*. Retrieved from http:// www.timeshighereducation.co.uk/news/black-scholars-still-experience-racism-on-campus/2012154.article.

Haran, N., & Tormey, R. (2002). *Celebrating Difference, Promoting Equality; Towards a framework for intercultural education in Irish classrooms*. Academic Press.

Harper, S. R. (2009). Niggers no more: A critical race counternarrative on Black male student achievement at predominantly White colleges and universities. *International Journal of Qualitative Studies in Education*, *22*(6), 697–712. doi:10.1080/09518390903333889

Harper, S. R. (2012). Race without racism: How higher education researchers minimize racist institutional norms. *The review of higher education*, *36*(1S), 9–29. doi:10.1353/rhe.2012.0047

Harper, S. R., & Hurtado, S. (Eds.). (2011). *Racial and ethnic diversity in higher education. Pearson Learning Solutions*. Limerick: CEDR and TED.

Hartlep, N. D., Ecker, M. M., Miller, D. D., & Whitmore, K. E. (2013). Asian Pacific American college freshman: Attitudes toward the abolishment of affirmative action in college admissions. *Critical Questions in Education*, 4(1), 1–20.

Henderson, L. J. (2004). Brown v. Board of Education at 50: The Multiple Legacies for Policy and Administration. *Public Administration Review*, 64(3), 270–274. doi:10.1111/j.1540-6210.2004.00371.x

Henkel, K. E., Dovidio, J. F., & Gaertner, S. L. (2006). Institutional discrimination, individual racism, and Hurricane Katrina. *Analyses of Social Issues and Public Policy (ASAP)*, 6(1), 99–124. doi:10.1111/j.1530-2415.2006.00106.x

Henwood, K. L. (1994). Resisting racism and sexism in academic psychology: A personal/political view. *Feminism & Psychology*, 4(1), 41–62. doi:10.1177/0959353594041003

Henwood, K. L., & Phoenix, A. (1996). Race in psychology: Teaching the subject. *Ethnic and Racial Studies*, 19(4), 841–863. doi:10.1080/01419870.1996.9993938

Herek, G. M., Gillis, J. R., & Cogan, J. C. (2009). Internalized stigma among sexual minority adults: Insights from a social psychological perspective. *Journal of Counseling Psychology*, 56(1), 32–43. doi:10.1037/a0014672

Hewstone, M. (1990). The ultimate attribution error? A review of the literature on intergroup attributions. *European Journal of Social Psychology*, 20(4), 311–335. doi:10.1002/ejsp.2420200404

Holley, L. C., Larson, N. C., Adelman, M., & Trevino, J. (2007). Attitudes among university undergraduates toward LGB and five ethnic/racial groups. *Journal of LGBT Youth*, 5(1), 79–101.

Howard, K., & Stevens, A. (2000). *Out & about campus: Personal accounts by Lesbian, Gay, Bisexual & Transgendered college students* (1st ed.). Los Angeles, CA: Alyson Books.

Howarth, C., & Hook, D. (Eds.). (2005). Towards a critical psychology of racism. *Journal of Community & Applied Social Psychology*, 15(6), 425–431. doi:10.1002/casp.840

Howitt, D., & Owusu-Bempah, J. (1994). *The Racism of Psychology*. New York: Harvester-Wheatsheaf.

Hurtado, S. (2002). Creating a climate of inclusion: Understanding Latina/o college students. In W. A. Smith, P. G., Altbach, & K. Lomotey (Eds.), The Racial Crisis in American Higher Education: Continuing Challenges for the Twenty-First Century (pp.121–135). Albany, NY: State University of New York Press.

Hurtado, S., Carter, D. F., & Kardia, D. (1998). The climate for diversity: Key issues for institutional self study. *New Directions for Institutional Research*, 1998(98), 53–63. doi:10.1002/ir.9804

Hurtado, S., Clayton-Pedersen, A. R., Allen, W. R., & Milem, J. F. (1998). Enhancing campus climates for racial/ethnic diversity: Educational policy and practice. *The Review of Higher Education*, 21(3), 279–302. doi:10.1353/rhe.1998.0003

Huynh, Q., Devos, T., & Goldberg, R. (2014). The role of ethnic and national identifications in perceived discrimination for Asian Americans: Toward a better understanding of the buffering effect of group identifications on psychological distress. *Asian American Journal of Psychology*, 5(3), 161–171. doi:10.1037/a0031601 PMID:25258674

Jacobs, S., & Hai, N. (2002). Issues and dilemmas: 'Race' in higher education teaching practices. In F. Anthias & C. Lloyd (Eds.), *Rethinking Anti-Racisms: From Theory to Practice*. London: Routledge.

Jayakumar, U. M., Howard, T. C., Allen, W. R., & Han, J. C. (2009). Racial privilege in the professoriate: An exploration of campus climate, retention, and satisfaction. *The Journal of Higher Education, 80*(5), 538–563. doi:10.1353/jhe.0.0063

Jervis, K. (1996). How Come There Are No Brothers on That List? Hearing the Hard Questions Children Ask. *Harvard Educational Review, 66*(3), 546–577. doi:10.17763/haer.66.3.mv0034808237266r

Johnson, R. (2010). Forensic assessment and clinical intervention for juvenile firesetters: The San Diego model. *Matchbook: A Journal on the Prevention & Treatment of Juvenile Firesetting, 1*(2), 14–16.

Johnson, R. (2013). Forensic Psychological Evaluations for Behavioral Disorders in Police Officers: Reducing Negligent Hire and Retention Risks. In J. B. Helfgott (Ed.), *Criminal Psychology* (Vol. 3). Praeger.

Johnsrud, L. K., & Des Jarlais, C. D. (1994). Barriers to tenure for women and minorities. *Review of Higher Education, 17*(4), 335–353. doi:10.1353/rhe.1994.0007

Johnsrud, L. K., & Sadao, K. C. (1998). The common experience of otherness: Ethnic and racial minority faculty. *Review of Higher Education, 21*(4), 315–342. doi:10.1353/rhe.1998.0010

Kääriäinen, J., & Sirén, R. (2011). Trust in the police, generalized trust and reporting crime. *European Journal of Criminology, 8*(1), 65–81. doi:10.1177/1477370810376562

Kalogrides, D., & Loeb, S. (2013). Different teachers, different peers the magnitude of student sorting within schools. *Educational Researcher, 42*(6), 304–316. doi:10.3102/0013189X13495087

Karlsen, S., & Nazroo, J. Y. (2004). Fear of racism and health. *Journal of Epidemiology and Community Health, 58*(12), 1017–1018. doi:10.1136/jech.2004.020479 PMID:15547063

Kivel, P. (1996). *Uprooting Racism: How White People Can Work for Racial Justice*. Gabriola Island, Canada: New Society Publishers.

Knaus, C. B. (2014). Seeing what they want to see: Racism and leadership development in urban schools. *The Urban Review, 46*(3), 420–444. doi:10.100711256-014-0299-0

Knox, D., Zusman, M. E., Buffington, C., & Hemphill, G. (2000). Interracial dating attitudes among college students. *College Student Journal, 34*(1), 69–69.

Knox. (2000). Interracial dating attitudes among college students. *College Student Journal, 34*(1), 69–71.

Lee, R. M. (2003). Do ethnic identity and other-group orientation project against discrimination for Asian Americans? *Journal of Counseling Psychology, 50*(2), 133–141. doi:10.1037/0022-0167.50.2.133

Leonard, W. (1980). Brown v. Board of Education: An Historical Background and Development. *Howard Law Journal, 23*(1), 43–50.

Leonardo, Z. (2012). The race for class: Reflections on a critical race class theory of education. *Educational Studies: Journal of the American Educational Studies Association, 48*(5), 427–449. doi:10.1080/00131946.2012.715831

Ly, P. (2008). Caught between two cultures. *Diverse Issues in Higher Education*. Retrieved from http://diverseeducation.com/article/11578/

Martin, R. J., & Van Gunten, D. M. (2002). Reflected identities: Applying positionality and multicultural social reconstructionism in teacher education. *Journal of Teacher Education*, *53*(1), 44–54. doi:10.1177/0022487102053001005

Masterson, S. S. (2001). A trickle-down model of organizational justice: Relating employees and customers perceptions of and reactions to fairness. *The Journal of Applied Psychology*, *86*(4), 594–604. doi:10.1037/0021-9010.86.4.594 PMID:11519644

Masterson, S. S., Lewis, K., Goldman, B. M., & Taylor, M. S. (2000). Integrating justice and social exchange: The differing effects of fair procedures and treatment on work relationships. *Academy of Management Journal*, *43*(4), 738–748. doi:10.2307/1556364

Meeussen, L., Otten, S., & Phalet, K. (2014). Managing diversity: How leaders multiculturalism and colorblindness affect work group functioning. *Group Processes & Intergroup Relations*, *17*(5), 629–644. doi:10.1177/1368430214525809

Meyer, I. H. (2003). Prejudice, social stress, and mental health in lesbian, gay, and bisexual populations: Conceptual issues and research evidence. *Psychological Bulletin*, *129*(5), 674–697. doi:10.1037/0033-2909.129.5.674 PMID:12956539

Milner, H. R. (2003). Teacher Reflection and Race in cultural Contexts: History, Meanings, and Methods in teaching. *Theory into Practice*, *42*(3), 173–180. doi:10.120715430421tip4203_2

Mobley, M. (2000). Cultural guardians: A model for supporting gay-African American boys/men in higher education. In M. C. Brown & J. E. Davis (Eds.), *Black Sons to Mothers: Compliments, Critiques, and Challenges for Cultural Workers in Education* (pp. 173–192). New York, NY: Peter Lang.

Musil, C. M., García, M., Hudgins, C. A., Nettles, M. T., Sedlacek, W. E., & Smith, D. G. (1999). *To Form a More Perfect Union: Campus Diversity Initiatives*. Washington, DC: American Association of Colleges and Universities.

Nail, P. R., Harton, H. C., & Barnes, A. A. (2008). Test of Dovidio and Gaertner's integrated model of racism. *North American Journal of Psychology*, *10*(1), 197–220.

National Center for Education Statistics. (2002). *NCES Digest of Education Statistics*. Available online at http://nces.ed.gov/programs/digest/d02/dt068.asp

Nora, A., & Cabrera, A. F. (1996). The role of perceptions of prejudice and discrimination on the adjustment of minority students to college. *The Journal of Higher Education*, *67*(2), 119–148. doi:10.2307/2943977

OBrien, J. (2009). Institutional racism and anti-racism in tech education: Perspectives of teacher educators. *Irish Educational Studies*, *28*(2), 193–207. doi:10.1080/03323310902884326

Orelus, P. W. (2013). The institutional cost of being a professor of color: Unveiling micro-aggression, racial [in]visibility, and racial profiling through the lens of critical racial theory. *Current Issues in Education*, *16*(2), 1–10.

Pang, V. O., Han, P. P., & Pang, J. M. (2011). Asian American and Pacific Islander Students: Equity and the achievement gap. *Educational Researcher, 40*(8), 378–389. doi:10.3102/0013189X11424222

Powell-Hopson, D., & Hopson, D. S. (1988). Implications of doll color preferences among black preschool children and white preschool children. *The Journal of Black Psychology, 14*(2), 57–63. doi:10.1177/00957984880142004

Quillian, L. (2008). Does unconscious racism exist? *Social Psychology Quarterly, 71*(1), 6–11. doi:10.1177/019027250807100103

Rankin, S. (2003). *Campus Climate for Gay, Lesbian, Bisexual and Transgendered People: A National Perspective*. Washington, DC: National Gay and Lesbian Task Force.

Richards, G. (1997). *'Race' Racism and Psychology: Towards a Reflexive History*. London: Routledge.

Roberts, P. C., & Stratton, L. M. (1995). *The New Color Line: How Quotas and Privileges Destroy Democracy*. Washington, DC: Regnery Publishing Co.

Romano, R. C. (2003). *Race-Mixing: Black-White Marriage in Post-War America*. Boston, MA: Harvard University Press.

Rosser, B. R. S., Bockting, W. O., Ross, M. W., Miner, M. H., & Coleman, E. (2008). The relationship between homosexuality, internalized homo-negativity, and mental health in men who have sex with men. *Journal of Homosexuality, 55*(2), 185–203. doi:10.1080/00918360802129394 PMID:18982569

Rush, S. (2006). *Huck Finns Hidden Lessons: Teaching and Learning Across the Color Line*. Rowman & Littlefield.

Safehouse Progressive Alliance for Nonviolence (SPAN). (2007). *Tools for Liberation packet 2007 for building a multi-ethnic, inclusive, and antiracist organization*. Retrieved from http://www.safeplaceolympia.org/wp-content/uploads/2011/08/Tools_for_Liberation_Packet_2007-SPAN-Abridged_Version.pdf

Schueler, L. A., Hoffman, J. A., & Peterson, E. (2009). Fostering safe, engaging campuses for lesbian, gay, bisexual, transgender, and questioning students. In S. R. Harper & S. J. Quaye (Eds.), *Student Engagement in Higher Education* (pp. 61–79). New York, NY: Routledge.

Schuman, H., Steeh, C., Bobo, L., & Krysan, M. (1997). *Racial Attitudes in America: Trends and Interpretations* (Rev. ed.). Cambridge, MA: Harvard University Press.

Shanock, L. R., & Eisenberger, R. (2006). When supervisors feel supported: Relationships with subordinates perceived supervisor support, perceived organizational support, and performance. *The Journal of Applied Psychology, 91*(3), 689–695. doi:10.1037/0021-9010.91.3.689 PMID:16737364

Simons, T., Friedman, R., Liu, L. A., & McLean Parks, J. M. (2007). Racial differences in sensitivity to behavioral integrity: Attitudinal consequences, in-group effects, and trickle down among Black and non-Black employees. *The Journal of Applied Psychology, 92*(3), 650–665. doi:10.1037/0021-9010.92.3.650 PMID:17484548

Singer, J. N. (2005). Understanding racism through the eyes of African American male student-athletes. *Race, Ethnicity and Education, 8*(4), 365–386. doi:10.1080/13613320500323963

Sleeter, C. E. (1994). White Racism. *Multicultural Education, 1*(4), 5–8.

Sleeter, C. E. (2001). Preparing teachers for culturally diverse schools: Research and the overwhelming presence of Whiteness. *Journal of Teacher Education, 52*(2), 94–106. doi:10.1177/0022487101052002002

Solorzano, D. (1998). Critical race theory, racial and gender microaggressions, and the experiences of chicana and chicano scholars. *International Journal of Qualitative Studies in Education, 11*(1), 121–136. doi:10.1080/095183998236926

Solorzano, D., Ceja, M., & Yosso, T. (2000). Critical race theory, racial microaggressions, and campus racial climate: The experiences of African American college students. *The Journal of Negro Education, 69*, 60–73.

Sonn, C. C. (2004). Reflecting on practice: Negotiating challenges to ways of working. *Journal of Community & Applied Social Psychology, 14*(4), 305–313. doi:10.1002/casp.779

Srivastava, S. (2009). *Nobody's model minority*. Retrieved from http://www.theroot.com/articles/politics/2009/03/nobodys_model_minority.html

Stanley, C. A. (2006). Coloring the academic landscape: Faculty of color breaking the silence in predominantly White colleges and universities. *American Educational Research Journal, 43*(4), 701–736. doi:10.3102/00028312043004701

Stember, C. (1976). *Sexual Racism: The Emotional Barrier to an Integrated Society*. Elsevier.

Strausbaugh, J. (2006). *Black like you: Blackface, Whiteface, insult and imitation in American popular culture*. New York: Tarcher.

Sue, D. W. (2010). *Microaggressions in Everyday Life: Race, Gender, and Sexual Orientation*. Hoboken, NJ: John Wiley & Sons.

Sue, D. W., Capodilupo, C. M., Torino, G. C., Bucceri, J. M., Holder, A. M. B., Nadal, K. L., & Esquilin, M. (2007). Racial microaggressions in everyday life: Implications for clinical practice. *The American Psychologist, 62*(4), 271–286. doi:10.1037/0003-066X.62.4.271 PMID:17516773

Szymanski, D. M., & Gupta, A. (2009). Examining the relationship between multiple internalized oppressions and African American lesbian, gay, bisexual, and questioning persons self-esteem and psychological distress. *Journal of Counseling Psychology, 56*(1), 110–118. doi:10.1037/a0013317

Taylor, D. L., & Clark, M. P. (2009). Set up to fail: Institutional racism and the sabotage of school improvement. *Equity & Excellence in Education, 42*(2), 114–129. doi:10.1080/10665680902744220

Tepper, B. J., Duffy, M. K., Henle, C. A., & Lambert, L. S. (2006). Procedural injustice, victim precipitation, and abusive supervision. *Personnel Psychology, 59*(1), 101–123. doi:10.1111/j.1744-6570.2006.00725.x

Tepper, B. J., & Taylor, E. C. (2003). Relationships among supervisors and subordinates procedural justice perceptions and organizational citizenship behaviors. *Academy of Management Journal, 46*(1), 97–105. doi:10.2307/30040679

Terrill, M. M., & Mark, D. L. (2000). Preservice teachers expectations for schools with children of color and second-language learners. *Journal of Teacher Education, 51*(2), 149–149. doi:10.1177/002248710005100209

Tierney, W. G. (Ed.). (1990). *Assessing academic climates and cultures (No. 68).* Jossey-Bass Inc Pub.

Treviño, J., Walker, T., & Leyba, J. (2009). *Inclusive Excellence Toolkit.* Retrieved December 14, 2014, http://www.du.edu/gsg/media/documents/InclusiveExcellenceToolkit-DUCME3-09.pdf

Turner, C. S. V., & Myers, S. (2000). *Faculty of Color in Academe: Bittersweet Success.* Needham Heights, MA: Allyn & Bacon.

U. S. Census Bureau. (2011). *Asian/Pacific American Heritage Month: May 2011.* Retrieved from https://www.census.gov/newsroom/releases/archives/facts_for_features_special_editions/cb11-ff06.html

Vaccaro, A. (2010). What lies beneath seemingly positive campus climate results: Institutional sexism, racism, and male hostility toward equity initiatives and liberal bias. *Equity & Excellence in Education, 43*(2), 202–215. doi:10.1080/10665680903520231

Vaught, S. E. (2012). Institutional racist melancholia: A structural understanding of grief and power in schooling. *Harvard Educational Review, 82*(1), 52–77. doi:10.17763/haer.82.1.e3p454q1070131g4

Vega, T. (2014). Students see many slights as racial 'microaggressions'. *New York Times.* Retrieved from http://www.nytimes.com/2014/03/22/us/as-diversity-increases-slights-get-subtler-but-still-sting.html?_r=0

Wang, T. H., & Wu, F. H. (1996, Winter). Beyond the Model Minority Myth: Why Asian Americans Support Affirmative Action. *Guild Practitioner, 53,* 35–47.

Washington, J., & Wall, V. A. (2006). African American gay men: Another challenge for the academy. In M. J. Cuyjet (Ed.), *African American men in college* (pp. 174–188). San Francisco, CA: Jossey-Bass.

Watson, L. W. (2002). *How minority students experience college: Implications for planning and policy.* Stylus Publishing, LLC.

Wetherell, M., & Potter, J. (1992). *Mapping the Language of Racism: Discourse and the Legitimation of Exploitation.* London: Harvester Wheatsheaf.

Williams, D. A., Berger, J. B., & McClendon, S. A. (2005). *Toward a model of inclusive excellence and change in postsecondary institutions.* Washington, DC: Association of American Colleges and Universities.

Williams, L. (2001). *Playing the Race Card Melodramas of Black and White from Uncle Tom to O.J. Simpson.* Princeton, NJ: Princeton University Press.

Wilson, P. A., & Yoshikawa, H. (2004). Experiences of and responses to social discrimination among Asian and pacific Islander gay men: Their relationship to HIV risk. *AIDS Education and Prevention, 16*(1), 68–83. doi:10.1521/aeap.16.1.68.27724 PMID:15058712

Yosso, T. (2002). Toward a critical race curriculum. *Equity & Excellence in Education, 35*(2), 93–107. doi:10.1080/713845283

Young, K., Anderson, M., & Stewart, S. (2014). Hierarchical microaggressions in higher education. *Journal of Diversity in Higher Education*, 8(1), 61–71. doi:10.1037/a0038464

Zúñiga, X., Williams, E. A., & Berger, J. B. (2005). Action-oriented democratic outcomes: The impact of student involvement with campus diversity. *Journal of College Student Development*, 46(6), 660–678. doi:10.1353/csd.2005.0069

KEY TERMS AND DEFINITIONS

Aversive Racism: A form of contemporary racism that individuals believe they are egalitarian and non-judgmental, yet unconsciously maintain negative and stereotypical thoughts toward other historically disadvantaged groups; It often manifests at an unconscious level, in subtle and indirect ways.

Institutional Racism: Any system of unequal treatment based on race or skin color, and that an individual or group based on one's race or skin color. It can occur in institutions, such as universities, business corporations, and public government bodies.

Leadership: A process in which a group and/or person support and aid others with social influence in the accomplishment of a common goal and/or task.

Microaggression: An intentional or unintentional daily verbal, behavioral, or environmental slights that convey hostile, derogatory, or negative message toward the marginalized group.

Organizational Culture: The values and behaviors within an organization and the meanings individuals attach to those values and behaviors. It includes the organization's expectations, experiences, and philosophy, which can potentially affect its productivity and performance.

Pedagogy: An instructional method with a goal to promote the best practices of teaching.

Racism: Any acts of prejudice and discrimination, intentional or unintentional, that are against certain racial groups based on the belief that one's own race is superior.

Stereotype: Without accurate reflection of reality, a thought or belief that can be adopted about specific types of individuals, groups, or certain ways of doing things.

This research was previously published in the Handbook of Research on Organizational Justice and Culture in Higher Education Institutions edited by Nwachukwu Prince Ololube; pages 225-256, copyright year 2016 by Information Science Reference (an imprint of IGI Global).

Chapter 36
Channeling Race:
Media Representations and International Student Perceptions

Kenneth Robert Roth
California State University, USA

Zachary S. Ritter
University of Redlands, USA

ABSTRACT

The late Stuart Hall argued depictions of race in media most appropriately should be examined as ideology, since a main sphere of media operation is the production and transformation of ideologies. These ideologies are not isolated concepts but articulations of a variety of cultural signifiers into a chain of meanings that are often presented as statements of nature. Such meanings can produce troubling outcomes on U.S. college campuses when arriving international students' first and often only exposure to race in America is the nation's continued struggle with equality as portrayed in exported film and news spectacles portraying blackness as a social threat. This chapter examines how media representations can flavor cross-cultural interactions, and the implications these interactions may have for campus climate, diversity initiatives, and the increasingly multicultural and globalized work place.

INTRODUCTION

"Why don't you have your license on you?" asked Cincinnati, Ohio Police Officer Tensing, while standing outside of the car window of Ray Dubose. Mr. Dubose responded: "I just don't – I'm sorry, sir. I'm just gonna go [in] the house." Then Officer Tensing asked Mr. Dubose to get out of the car. Several quick moves later by both parties and Mr. Dubose is fatally shot in the head, his car propelled forward by the weight of a dying man heavy on the accelerator (Williams, 2015). There is almost no need to mention the race of either man, since we see this scenario in America with increasing frequency: An allegedly fearful white police officer looming over a clearly fearful black driver. The whole tragic moment is captured on the officer's body cam and the video circumnavigates the globe via social media. These

DOI: 10.4018/978-1-7998-1213-5.ch036

Channeling Race

tragedies play out almost daily in the U.S., as an unarmed black man is routinely killed by a U.S. police or other security officer approximately every 28 hours (Hudson, 2013).

This apparent form of Constitutional racism has haunted non-white U.S. citizens since America's inception, but has only recently sprung onto our high definition nightly news screens and mobile devices in alarmingly skyrocketing frequency. One scholar calls it Negrophobia – the irrational fear of black people –, resulting in the regular harming or homicide of blacks by whites based almost exclusively on stereotypes of monolithic proportion (Armour, 1997). Given America's dominance in global media markets, distributing a full one-third of all filmed entertainment alone (PwC, 2015; Roth, 2015b), these representations likely have implications for perceptions of African Americans by global citizens in general and specifically for international students arriving for their first extended stay in the United States.

Meanwhile, American politicians struggle to address a public groundswell proclaiming "Black Lives Matter", and depictions of people of color in other nation's media also are becoming increasingly troubling. As the 2008 U.S. Presidential campaign heated up, an eMobile cell phone advertisement in rotation on Japanese television featured a chimpanzee dressed in a suit, giving a speech to a cheering crowd holding signs calling for "Change!" The thinly veiled reference to then-candidate Barack Obama was not lost on either Japanese or American audiences who called for the commercial to be taken off the air because of its racist overtones (The Guardian, 2008).

Hall (2011) argued media representations of race and racism are problems of ideology, since a main sphere of media operation is the production and transformation of ideologies. His definition of ideology encompassed images, concepts and premises "which provide frameworks through which we represent, interpret, understand and *make sense* of some aspect of social existence" (Hall, 2011, p. 81). These ideologies are not separate or isolated concepts but are an articulation of meanings producing different forms of social consciousness, and tend to disappear into a taken-for-granted world of common sense (Hall, 2011). While ideologies are worked on in a variety of social settings, media are important sites for their production, reproduction and transformation, since media represent the social world and provide frames for understanding how the world is and why it works in the ways it does. While media assist us to grasp the meanings of success, unemployment, freedom and democracy, the media also construct for us representations of what race is, what meanings racial imagery carry, and what the *problem* of race is understood to be (Hall, 2011).

Media depictions of people of African descent exported from America to the rest of the world are often problematic and fraught with stereotypes (Dikotter, 1997; Fujioka, 2000; Johnson, 2007; Russell, 1991; Talbot, 1999). As international students, particularly Chinese, become a larger portion of the U.S. higher education landscape, it is unclear how relations between these students and domestic African American students will unfold. However, it is apparent media representations of race likely will have implications for cross-cultural interactions.

Previous perception studies of visual media suggest media does more than simply provide information about events, and individuals take in and interpret information selectively (Blackman, 1977; Gilliam, 2000). Further, Tobolowsky (2001, 2006) argued U.S. prime time television has implications for minority women's perceptions of what to expect from college campus life, and both Postman (1979) and Horn (2003) concluded media possess the elements of curriculum and, arguably, should be viewed as such, given their ability and purpose to train, inform, inspire, enlighten, entertain or otherwise engage the mind of an individual (Roth, 2015c). These findings are consistent with Kretch and Crutchfield (1973) who argued individuals perceive and interpret information in terms of their "own needs, own emotions, own personality, own previously formed cognitive patterns" (p. 251).

Stack (2006) identified the pervasiveness of media in our daily lives and its potential as an informal pedagogy to surpass the effects of formal pedagogies, placing citizenship at risk of reduction to mere consumerism. In these ways, media possess a profound and not completely understood form of cultural pedagogy, teaching us about gender, discussing race, and contributing on almost every level to what we think, feel, believe, fear and desire (Kellner, 2011).

U.S. media representations of race, and particularly those of black men, most likely scaffold tensions between international students and domestic black students on U.S. college campuses. These interactions can complicate campus diversity initiatives and campus climate (Cuyjet, 2006; Hanassab, 2006; Lee, 2007a, 2007b; Rankin, 2005), and may have implications for how black students view themselves (Roth, 2011; Roth, 2015c). Together, these perceptions and outcomes create the likelihood misunderstandings will persist and be reproduced in the globalizing workplace.

Girded by two recent independent qualitative studies conducted principally at the University of California, Los Angeles (UCLA) (Ritter, 2013; Roth, 2015c), this chapter examines how media representations can flavor cross-cultural interactions, and their implications for campus climate, and the rates of college going among African American men. The latter has been stagnate at 4.3% of America's college going student body since 1976 (Harper, 2008). Examples of recent initiatives at U.S. colleges and universities to address cross-cultural issues show the deconstruction of media representations and stereotypes are often the linchpin to these efforts (Althen, 2009; Chow, 2013; Gordon, 2010; Zuniga, 2002), suggesting educators need to seek more ways to integrate the interrogation of media representations across the curriculum, given the ever-increasing role media consumption plays in our lives (Horn, 2003; Stack, 2006).

PROBLEM STATEMENT

The United States is home to some of the best known and well-regarded universities in the world, with 14 American institutions ranking in the top 20 of a recent and annual report on institutional prestige (Gurney-Read, 2015). Students arrive from everywhere on the planet to study in America. Often, these international students have had limited exposure to American culture outside of their perceptions drawn from U.S. news, film, and pop culture, including television, music, dance, dress, and demeanor (Fujioka, 2000; Kim, 2008). As a result, they often hold negative racial stereotypes, particularly in relation to African Americans and specifically males (Ritter, 2013). Due to these perceptions, many international students tend to fear and avoid contact with African American males on college campuses and elsewhere (Talbot, 1999).

Attending these same colleges and universities are black males who are all too aware of their often-marginalized representation in media and in other social domains (Harper, 2009, 2010; Roth, 2011; Roth, 2015c). They also are aware of the real world consequences they may encounter as a result of these representations: in classrooms (Carter, 2006), in lunchrooms (Tatum, 1997), in courtrooms (Alexander, 2010; Harris, 2003), on elevators (Solórzano, 2000), in interactions with police (Clarke, 2014; Egelko, 2013; Fantz, 2015; Hensley, 2015; Medical Examiner Rules Eric Garner's Death a Homicide, Says He Was Killed by Chokehold, 2014) and in a multiplicity of other settings. One 22-year-old UCLA student described an encounter with police while walking with friends in the community surrounding the university, an upscale multicultural enclave in West Los Angeles. He attributed this encounter to the near-constant flow of negative media representations of black men, particularly in television news: "When I walk down the street or with a group of my friends, they don't see UCLA. I could have my *Bruin* (ID)

Channeling Race

Card on my head, and they don't see a UCLA student. They see a black guy in Westwood" (Roth, 2011). Westwood is just south of the UCLA campus. At its north and east boundary, UCLA is bordered by two other upscale and predominantly white communities, Bel Air and Beverly Hills.

Similarly, when an undergraduate Korean international student was asked whether she might date an black male, she said: "They will hurt me because they are so big and I don't like their curly hair and big lips…it's not my style." (Ritter, 2013). Even today, black men on East Asian screens are portrayed as large and oversexed and ready to physically dominate Asian women (Russell, 2012). Further, the delimited and stereotypical representation of black men as entertainers, athletes, and criminals also is promulgated on Asian screens (Russell, 2012). These stereotypes and prejudices not only hamper international students' ability to interact positively with racial *out groups* – a racial/ethnic group outside of one's own race (Talbot, 1999) –, they also can mar black student college going experiences (Cha, 1992; Cuyjet, 2006; Dixon, 2003; Fujioka, 2000; Smith, 2007a; Talbot, 1999).

At the institutional level, international students are portrayed as not having a clear understanding of American racial dynamics (Gordon, 2010). Yet, year in and year out, American colleges and universities find themselves the subject of news stories showing fraternities, sororities, and institutional others engaging in activities that result in backlash due to racist overtones, from nooses hanging in campus trees to racially-themed Greek parties and chants (Clifton, 2015; Grenoble, 2015; Jonsson, 2015; Mashhood, 2011; Parkinson-Morgan, 2011; Rocha, 2015). At the same time, campus and other police routinely stop, question, and in some cases assault black males on or near campus and images of takedowns or news articles of holding students at gunpoint circulate the globe (Fantz, 2015; Faulders, 2015; Williams, 2015), likely contributing to the rise of racial fear. Meanwhile, American colleges and universities insist they are seeking ways to admit more African-American and Latino students, in an effort to live up to America's promised meritocracy (Hoxby, 2012). This seemingly contradictory stew of intents and outcomes has implications well beyond the college campus.

For young black men, negative depictions in media tend to serve as the stereotypical representation of *all* African American men (Bjornstrom, 2010; Entman, 2008; Jackson, 2005; Kitwana, 2002). So, when a single black man does act out and approximates these stereotypes, there is never any discussion about psychological wounding (hooks, 2004). But when young white males, especially those of privilege, act violently, media discussions invariably turn to exploring psychological issues as a partial explanation for their crimes, representing them not as inherently evil but as disturbed (Colorado Shooting Suspect Was Brilliant Science Student, 2012; hooks, 2004). Black males, however, are typically portrayed as inherently defective – "always the killer in the making," (hooks, 2004, p. 92).

These portrayals in television news, blockbuster films, on the Internet, in music videos, and newspaper crime reports paint black men as a social threat (Bjornstrom, 2010; Boswell, 2014; Chiricos, 1997, 2001). Perceived as such, black men have experienced differential treatment in general (Harper, 2009), and in campus interactions specifically, especially when interacting with international students (Kobayashi, 2010).

What this means for campus climate as increasing numbers of international students find themselves rooming with domestic black students and taking classes together, without either possessing a firm grasp of the other's communication styles and cultural backgrounds, is at the very least a question seeking an answer.

BACKGROUND

While the day has not come where a media text can alter itself in response to verbal or other cues by viewers, let's consider mass media as one participant in a dialogue. In an attempt to attract broad appeal, mass media must be polysemic and capable of carrying and transmitting multiple meanings simultaneously (Condit, 1989; Fiske, 1986). The importance of these various meanings is dependent on where we, as the viewer or listener, are situated (Harding, 2004) in relation to the content of the media text, both in terms of its representation of the world and the affinity to us of the world it represents (Bourdieu, 1984; Condit, 1989; Fiske, 1986; McDonough, 1997; Scahill, 1993). So, ultimately, the meaning of an object, person, or thing, is not necessarily held intrinsically by the person or thing, or even by the word describing the person or thing, but rather in our meaning making that, after awhile, suggests the way we view things is natural, obvious, and inevitable (Hall, 2003a). For instance, take traffic signals. There is nothing intrinsic to the color red signifying stop, or green signifying go. Yet, throughout the world, we recognize and respond to these signals as if their very existence is a well-known canon of the natural world. In this way, a shared language system and codes that govern relationships of translation allow members of a culture to share ideas and concepts that all members agree upon (Hall, 2003a). Further, these ideologies tend to disappear, as their underpinnings become seeming idioms of common sense. Since race, like gender, stems from nature, racism is one of the most naturalized of all ideologies (Hall, 2011).

Some researchers have argued contemporary U.S. media representations of race were shaped by a nascent television industry in the mid-20th Century (Gray, 2005). However, others acknowledge even Thomas Edison's peepshow nickelodeons enacted stereotypical and negative representations of African Americans as early as the 1890s (Vera, 2003). The formative years of television (1948–1960) most certainly helped to maintain and disperse these representations due to their necessity for the ongoing legitimization of a social order built on racism and white supremacy (Cabrera, 2009; Gray, 2005b; Harris, 1993; Olson, 2008; Vera, 2003).

However, as a more constructivist view emerged (Patton, 2002), representation took on a role of linking people, events and experiences that was negotiable and even contestable (Hall, 2003b; Kellner, 1995, 2010). These contested views can be mediated by socioeconomic status (SES), gender, politick or race (Morley, 1980, 1992, 1993). Further, Bourdieu (1977) examined the addition of power relations, arguing media messages often correspond with the interests of dominant groups and classes. This argument raises interesting questions about the ongoing and seemingly rising racial conflict in the U.S., as well as the often media-driven assessments or declarations of a post-racial America.

Shared meanings through media representations, then, help to define who we think we are, and where we think we belong – as well as where we think *others* belong –, and are constantly being produced and shared in all personal and social interaction (Hall, 2003b; Kellner, 1982, 1995, 2011). But these actions and reactions, as already mentioned, are often constrained by social forces in advance of individuals enacting their own interpretations. Individuals often express ideological positions but those ideologies are not necessarily the product of individual consciousness (Hall, 2003a). Instead, such positions or intentions are formulated within already-established ideologies that pre-date individuals and are formed from conditions into which the individual was born and lives (Bourdieu, 1977; Hall, 2003a). In effect, individuals speak through the ideologies present in society, which provide citizens a way of making sense of social relations, and the individual's position within them (Hall, 2003a). The rise of hip-hop as a cultural representation is an example. Boyd (1997) has claimed hip-hop and "gangsta" culture, as popularized in mass media, may contribute to a greater apathy and alienation among African-American males in a misdirected attempt at reaffirming culture and identity. In its formative years, hip-hop sought emancipation by drawing attention to social injustice while promoting cultural uplift. However, once recognized as a potent and viable market from which to sell inner-city angst, the representations took on a style of dress and language and messaging that changed social uplift into an increasingly dangerous social unrest. A 21-year-old black male studying at another Southern California university characterizes these media representations this way:

I think the media is – from my observation – the media projects a certain amount of images of people who look like me, black men. And they're really narrow.

They're either, you know, that we're committing a crime or dressed a certain way or speaking a certain way…Like, I mean, I've seen positive things on the media as well but, you know, it's just…it's distorted (Roth, 2015c).

These perceptions increasingly associate young black men with violence and crime (Gilliam, 2000; Gray, 2005b; Hunt, 1994, 1997). Characterizations of successful African-American males outside of entertainment or sports are limited, and in many media representations, which some researchers have asserted are "coextensive with life itself" (Houston, 1994), African-American males simply aren't there at all. What is not held within the media frame tends to lose its "liveness" and ceases to exist in the public eye (Couldry, 2000).

Culture is primarily concerned with the production and exchange of such representations between society members in order to make meaning. This concept of culture, then, depends on participants to interpret what is happening around them by making sense of the world in broadly similar ways. With regard to black males, their representation as a social threat has risen with the ascent in popularity of hip-hop and associated black cultural representations, often to monolithic proportion (Chiricos, Eschholz, & Gertz, 1997; Gilliam, 2000; Harper, 2009, 2008; Hunt, 1994, 2005; Jackson & Moore, 2008).

As a result, African Americans are overrepresented in portrayals of crime and civil decay, and these portrayals, at least in part, may be responsible for a concurrent overrepresentation of black males in the U.S. prison system, since law enforcement uses race and ethnicity in crime profiles to determine suspects for further investigation (Davis, 1997). In addition, due to competition for viewership, U.S. news organizations have focused on an action format, which centralizes attention on crime, accounting for as much as 75% of all news coverage in some U.S. cities (Bjornstrom, 2010; Gilliam, 2000; Henkin, 2008). These local images are often broadcast worldwide due to global fascination with their sensationalized content (Bjornstrom, 2010; Chiricos, 1997; Dixon, 2003). Given the visuality of these media, and the importance of a suspect in the standard crime news "script", reportage or filmic depictions of crime stories are often imbued with racial imagery. Since African Americans comprise the largest percentage of minority suspects depicted in news media, despite not having committed the majority of violent crime (Alexander, 2010) may indicate the standard crime news script serves other ends than to merely report news.

Further, despite a lower crime rate than the international norm, U.S. incarceration rates are 6 to 10 times greater than those of other industrialized nations (Alexander, 2010). This explosive growth in penal population has been fueled by the errant War on Drugs, which is the single most significant factor in soaring incarceration rates (Alexander, 2010). Approximately one-quarter of the 2 million prisoners under federal and state authority are serving time for non-violent drug offenses, and approximately 80-90%

of all drug offenders *sent to prison* are African American (Alexander, 2010), despite studies indicating African Americans consume illicit drugs at or below levels of use by white Americans (Kitwana, 2002).

So, while there are some positive examples of men of color in blockbuster American films – the like of Will Smith and his son, Jaden Smith, Denzel Washington, Morgan Freeman, Danny Glover, Cuba Gooding, Jr., Sidney Poitier, Laurence Fishburne, and Samuel L. Jackson, among others – and even as a twice-elected U.S. president, there are a greater number of representations of black men as gangsters, thugs, drug dealers, pimps and murderers. In fact, many of the actors cited for playing positive roles can be and often still are cast in films as good people caught up in serious wrongdoing. Morgan Freeman as the character, "Red", a convicted murderer serving a life sentence behind bars in *The Shawshank Redemption* (King, 1994), is just one such example. Wesley Snipes as a fugitive from alleged corrupt government in *U.S. Marshalls* (Baird, 1998) is another. *Enemy of the State* (Scott, 1998), starring Will Smith as an attorney targeted by a corrupt federal bureaucrat, is yet another. These three examples also demonstrate another trend: portraying black males as if they are on the other side, altogether different, and in opposition to the *rest of us*, and our established way of life, even when that way of life may be shown to be perverse and corrupt (Roth, 2015c).

A result of these portrayals may be a heightened vigilance in the monitoring of African American men, and this heightened vigilance has resulted in more than 1 million black males incarcerated in U.S. prisons (Alexander, 2010). Further, approximately one-third of all African American males, ages 20-29, are under some form of correctional supervision (Kitwana, 2002). In other words, 1 in 3 black men can expect to go to prison at some point in their life, compared to 1 in 17 white males (Knafo, 2013). No other racial group in America faces as many obstacles to the benefits of full citizenship, positive representation in media, or the specter of eventual imprisonment.

Clearly, there can be little doubt media representations present particular codings in the public space, and in many cases these codings have deleterious outcomes for African Americans. Still, not all media representations of blackness are negative. Kellner (2010) has argued Hollywood may have facilitated the ascendancy of U.S. President Barack Obama by and through its positive and presaging depictions of a not-completely dissimilar looking Will Smith. But, even if there are an equal number of positive and negative media representations of blackness, positive representations of White America significantly outnumber negative representations, and negative representations are generally constrained by class and criminality (Callinicos, 1993). Cultivation theory posits after an individual sees an image repeatedly, such as televisual accounts of robberies or unsolved homicides where black perpetrators are inferred or represented as *persons of interest*, these representations can lead viewers to see *all* black men as criminals due to their disproportionate representation as oversexed law breakers of physicality (Potter, 2014).

Still, Hall (2003a) cautions there is neither a conspiratorial racist media or ruling class and such simple and reductive views lack credibility and weaken the case they are making when the theories and critiques assume such a limited view. But this is not to say there isn't room for rigorous interrogation of media representations and the often taken for granted assumptions they signify. For our purposes here, it is important to remain mindful of the ways representation may influence perception and as educators how we engage students, both international and domestic, in ways to demystify how they perceive one another through consumed media representations in advance of personal contact.

CAMPUS CONTEXTS

The American university is thought to be the site where democratic values and principles are enacted and instilled in future generations (Gutmann, 1999). In addition, research has shown campus diversity and an acceptance of difference are tantamount to a positive campus climate (Chang, 2013; Chang, 2010; Cuyjet, 2006; Hurtado, 1992, 2000, 1998). International students likely choose to study at U.S. campuses for these very reasons. Still, if American university and college campuses do not vigorously attempt to mediate negative racial perceptions, and promote racial equality, then American campuses likely become little more than sites of reproduction of racial tensions (Lieber, 2002; Locke, 1987; Morey, 2004; Torres, 2006; Torres, 2002; Van Heertum, 2009), that ignore the increasing diversity of college student bodies (Bowman, 2010; Locks, Hurtado, Bowman, & Oseguera, 2008; McMurtie, 2012), and the identified cognitive and educational benefits diverse racial interactions provide (Bowman, 2012; Chang, 1996, 1999; Denson, 2009; Lee, 2004). But we believe these concerns are but a few of the potentially adverse effects associated with antagonistic cross-cultural encounters on college campuses. With some 274,439 Chinese international students studying in the U.S. and international students as a group contributing some $27 billion to the U.S. economy in 2014, begs for an associated increase in cultural sensitivity across this growing multicultural community and work force (Dillard, 2001; Kellner, 2011; Leonardo, 2005; Morgan, 2014; Nemetz, 1996).

Two of the stronger arguments associated with minimizing ongoing racial antagonisms are many future jobs and professions have yet to be conceived; and given the growing number of social, environmental, economic and political problems that transcend national boundaries, the need for increased cooperation across continents, culture, and color has never been greater. The future leaders and potential solutions to address these changes and challenges most likely will either germinate or mature within the portals of higher education.

Yet, the number and variety of potential racial conflicts on college campuses impairing relationships between international students and domestic students of color grow by the day. Justin Simien's film, *Dear White People* (2014), explored racially complex issues on college campuses, but it also shed light on the troubling ritual of blackface parties at fraternities. Similar to scenes from the film, the Tau Kappa Epsilon fraternity at Arizona State University held a Martin Luther King Jr. *Black Party*, where partygoers were encouraged to wear sagging jeans, basketball jerseys, and drink from watermelon cups, portraying less-than-attractive black stereotypes (Clifton, 2015). The campus chapter of the fraternity was eventually expelled for this racist behavior.

In a similar incident, University of Florida's Beta Theta Pi had a *Rock Stars and Rappers Party* where students dressed in black face, donning gold chains and baseball caps, outraging many members of the student body and the National Association for the Advancement of Colored People (NAACP) (Photo of University of Florida Frat Members Wearing Blackface Sparks Controversy, 2012). Another and direct example of racist perceptions by international students was evidenced at Columbia University during the 2008 presentation of a Chinese Scholars and Students Association play entitled, *Finding Li Wei*. One actor proclaimed America is a nice place, but "we need to get rid of those black people in Harlem. I'm terrified by black people!" (The Blaaag: Official Tumblr of Columbia University's Asian American Alliance, 2012; Cheng, 2011). This punch line received enthusiastic laughter, causing some black organizations and bloggers to question the racial equity and sensitivity in China (Cheng, 2011). This dialogue referenced an incident at Columbia in which Ming-Hui Yu, a graduate student in Statistics, was fatally struck by a car after fleeing a fourteen-year-old African-American assailant near the campus (Amzallag, 2008).

Examples of racist portrayals of international students also exist, as evidenced by a video rant by a white female UCLA student who deplored how the university admitted "hordes" of Asian students who she felt didn't exhibit "American manners." In a YouTube video that went viral, she mocked the Chinese language by mimicking the way she perceived it sounded: "ching, chong, ling, long, ting, tong" (Gordon, 2011; Parkinson-Morgan, 2011). More recently, Duke University's Kappa Sigma chapter held an Asian themed-party where partygoers were encouraged to wear Sumo outfits, conical Vietnamese hats, pose giving the peace sign in photos, and speak in Asian accents. The Facebook invite page included phrases such as "Herro nice Duke peopre" and "Chank you" (Clifton, 2015). Again, we believe these incidents have far-reaching implications beyond the college campus.

The campus climate literature has explored racial tensions between various groups on campuses (Hurtado, 1992; Locks, Hurtado, Bowman, & Oseguera, 2008), but little research has been done on how international students perceive and interact with racial diversity on American campuses. This is certainly an area seeking further study.

DIVERSITY MATTERS

The college years are critical ones in which cognitive, social, and academic growth take place (Pascarella, 2005). Educational benefits accrue from college campus diversity and cross-racial interaction. Greater degrees of cross-racial interaction have been attributed to increased cognitive development (Astin, 1993; Hurtado, 1992), more positive academic and social self-concept (Chang, 1999), positive intergroup attitudes (Chang, 2002), greater cultural awareness (Antonio, 2001), the promotion of racial tolerance, and increased college satisfaction (Astin, 1993). Interactions with diverse peers can be a formidable catalyst for growth (Astin, 1993), and with an increased presence of diversity on campus, students are more likely to have interaction with racial out groups (Hurtado, 1994). Whether explicit or no, this body of literature speaks to the inevitability of greater diversity on U.S. college campuses and in every other walk of life. As a result, American institutions of higher education would be remiss if they did not attempt to prepare students for the greater diversity that lies ahead. In addition, college students become graduates and as graduates become leaders in the work force, and other areas of society. Their opinions, perceptions, sense of justice, equity and tolerance are key factors for shaping the world that lies ahead. For these reasons, educational institutions cannot simply pay lip service to diversity initiatives, but must enact diversity and its ethos in every vein of operation. Diversity is no longer a concept, like space travel once was. Diversity is.

However, for individuals and institutions to benefit from diversity, concerted efforts must be made. The University of California in general, and UCLA in particular, has made significant efforts to bolster structural diversity by and through the increase of international student populations. Still, despite these efforts, racial tensions exist on California's flagship university campuses. At UCLA, international students represent 15% of the student population of 43,239, including graduate students (Quick Facts – UCLA Undergraduate Admissions, 2015). But rapid increase in structural diversity, which refers primarily to the ethnic and racial makeup of a student body, without accounting for implications to other dimensions of campus climate, can be fraught with unforeseen problems (Hurtado, 1999; Milem, 2001). An increase in minority group populations increases the likelihood of conflict with majority group members (Blalock, 1967; Olzak, 2011). There also is the potential for conflict with and between minority populations.

As a result, campus climate is not only a structural issue, but it can also have a psychological and behavioral impact on campuses (Chang, 2010; Tanaka, 2007). How these dimensions affect faculty, staff, and students tends to depend on how each group individually views campus racial climate, which is based largely on their varied level of power within the institution, and their sense of belonging within specific communities (Hurtado, 1998). Studies show white students (68%) often think their universities are supportive of minority students, while minority students (28%) consider their campuses to be supportive (Loo, 1986; Rankin, 2005). This disparity may be attributed to most white students growing up in predominantly white communities and consequently having limited exposure to racial others prior to college (Radloff, 2003). Minority students, on the other hand, more than likely have had previous experience with racism in advance of college. Just as racism in the broader society can have deleterious effects, a discriminatory campus climate can negatively impact minority student grades and lead to feelings of alienation and ultimately affect persistence (Ancis, 2000; Cabrera, 1994; Roth, 2015c).

When black males are investigated at gun point for attempting to enter buildings at elite private schools on weekends (Fantz, 2015), or ordered to stop playing sandlot football and disperse from campus fields where white students regularly play the same games without incident (Smith, 2007b), what is driving this differential treatment? Is it simply bald racism, to which we must admit a pervasive, ongoing, and virulent white supremacy and toxic racism in the U.S., or are these incidents the result of an almost unconscious response to near-constant representations in media and elsewhere that promote racial animus and racial fear, either directly or indirectly, in the ways they signify blackness and difference?

These perceptions of discrimination affect all students, some more indirectly than others. Isn't it incumbent on us as educators and citizens within a democracy to call upon our institutions to make special efforts to create a campus climate that is fair, tolerant, and peaceful (Hurtado, 1998)? All too often, universities do not have policies and programs in place to generate positive cross-racial interactions, so these interactions, if and when they do occur, do so by happenstance (Hurtado, 1998; Pascarella, 2005). This is an important area where U.S. campuses must focus efforts to engage both international and domestic students in dialogue around perceptions of one another, and where they believe or can identify those perceptions came from.

For the most part, most of us do not want to admit how media influences the way we see ourselves and others (Stack, 2006). As Kellner (1982, 2010) and others have argued (Condit, 1989), we all have the ability to critically assess what we see and think and hear, both by and through media and other institutions. Still, media is a linchpin through which society is maintained, recreated and in rarer cases contested (Bourdieu, 1977; Gramsci, 1971; Hall, 2011, 2003b; Kellner, 2010). So, if American colleges and universities are to truly live up to their recently devised diversity initiatives, they cannot leave racial media representations uninterrogated, especially those that rely on the reification of stereotypes. Educators must offer a robust critique of media representations, not only in media literacy courses, but across the curriculum (Stack, 2006). Concurrently, diversity requirements in the form of living situations and intergroup dialogue may need to be considered essential requirements for matriculation. When the U.S. Supreme Court decided the outcome of *Grutter v. Bollinger* (Grutter v. Bollinger (02-241) 539 U.S. 306, 2003), a case challenging affirmative action practices at the University of Michigan Law School, Jurist Sandra Day O'Connor cited a "compelling interest" in creating and maintaining diversity since many future leaders emerge from law schools. A similar case was set for argument before the U.S. Supreme Court challenging similar admission policies at The University of Texas at Austin, with arguments scheduled after this chapter was submitted for publication. Given the increasing diversity of the college-seeking population, there seems to be no better time than the present to engage how best to reproduce our national diversity on our college and university campuses.

DISCRIMINATION ON CAMPUS

American college campuses have seemingly become racial tinderboxes. At no time in recent memory have race relations in campus contexts been so openly divisive and pervasive. The Fall of 2015 seemed to be a tipping point, resulting in the resignations of college presidents, sports teams refusing to compete in protest of campus climate, and an uptick in student activism seeking change or in solidarity with students at other campuses seeking to right racial wrongs. At the University of Missouri, students frustrated with the campus racial climate after swastikas were painted in human feces on walls, and racial epithets routinely hurled at the student body president, who was black, students organized a tent city in protest, a hunger strike was started, and the university's football team refused to finish its season unless President Tim Wolfe stepped down (Criss, 2015; Eligon, 2015). When estimates surfaced the boycott by the football team would cause $1 million in losses to the university, Wolfe resigned. Head football coach, Gary Pinkel, a white man, supported his players' protest. This act alone is unprecedented, as was the boycott by a major university football team in support of racial concerns (Eligon, 2015). It also seemed to put college administrators nationwide on notice that campus officials may need to respond more quickly to a wide array of student concerns, of which racial intolerance and the need for increased diversity among students, faculty and staff seemingly rank at the top of the list.

The spirit of student activism at University of Missouri spread to campuses across the nation. At Ithaca College in upstate New York, students demanded the resignation of their college president for what they described as poor response to complaints of racism on campus (Hartocollis, 2015). At Claremont McKenna College, one of seven colleges comprising the Claremont Colleges, the junior class president resigned after a Facebook photograph was found of her posing with sombreros and mustaches for Halloween (Hartocollis, 2015). A few days later the dean of students resigned after responding to a student opinion piece in the school newspaper, indicating she would work to serve students "who don't fit our CMC mold" (Watanabe, 2015). Two students on this campus also started a hunger strike after the dean's response and in the wake of some 30 students of color writing President Hiram E. Chodosh in April, expressing they felt excluded, isolated and intimidated among the 1,300-member student body (Watanabe, 2015).

At Yale University, 1,000 students participated in a "March of Resilience" due to an "emotionally draining" and "traumatic" environment for students of color. In addition, Yale's Sigma Alpha Epsilon fraternity allegedly held a "white girls only" party, prompting protests from women of color refused entry (Grenoble, 2015; Shire, 2015). At a University of Kansas Town Hall meeting on diversity, a student group called Rock Chalk Invisible Hawk interrupted the chancellor with a list of 15 demands. This was in response to events at University of Missouri, but also because the Black Student Union President was attacked by men at a party who addressed him with racial slurs (Donovan, 2015). Also at the University of Kansas, four students were expelled from the Zeta Beta Tau fraternity after posting an Islamophobic video of students dressed in what appeared to be faux Middle Eastern garb, chanting "Allah Akbar" (Clark, 2015). These incidents were just a few examples of an apparently increasingly hostile climate on many U.S. campuses. There are more. Some of them, like the activism at University of Missouri, were

Channeling Race

spurred by a growing "Black Lives Matter" movement started in the aftermath of the shooting death of unarmed 18-year-old Michael Brown in nearby Ferguson, MO by a white police officer (Clarke, 2014; Kearney, 2014). Making matters worse, Brown's inert body was left uncovered in the middle of the street in his neighborhood for more than four hours in the hot summer sun and these images were circulated widely in all media forms (Clarke, 2014).

However, some have viewed this growing indignation on college campuses as students of color being too sensitive or overly dramatic. We disagree. Black males are the most vulnerable U.S. racial-gender group for nearly every health condition medical researchers monitor (Smith, 2011). Our social, educational, and professional institutions, in addition to society-at-large, must come to realize the enormous physical, emotional and psychological costs of gendered racism. These experiences shape identities, motivations, dreams, activities and the psychological and physiological well-being of men and women of color (Roth, 2015c; Smith, 2011).

In addition, several scholars have found the increase of international students on U.S. campuses has led to an increase in discrimination on campuses. International students themselves are stereotyped and mistreated based on their cultural background (Hanassab, 2006). Often, these stereotypes are thrust upon unsuspecting international students, causing them to internalize and adopt American racial categories (Lee, 2007b). These racial dynamics encourage international students to seek and understand their place in the context of the U.S. racial hierarchy, and potentially adopt what they perceive is widespread animus toward African Americans (Lee, 2007b). Asian students, in particular, are keenly aware European international students face less discrimination, and assimilate more easily, which likely can be explained by the historical dominance of whiteness in America, a legacy of colonialism, and the privilege associated with white skin (McIntosh, 2008). These experiences coupled with imported perceptions of threat driven by mass media representations have the potential to create volatile cross-cultural interactions, leading to another dimension of substantive disruptions to positive campus climate.

While the higher education literature explores domestic students' stereotypes and prejudiced behavior toward international students, it is significantly more muted when it comes to international students' racial attitudes and prejudices toward domestic students. However, one study reported Asian international students view African-Americans as *violent hoodlums* and *second-class citizens* (Talbot, 1999). These findings are troubling.

Given international students are not only members of U.S. college communities, but also likely future leaders and policy makers (Locke, 1987), and micro aggressions (Solórzano, 2000) by international students against black students can be powerful deterrents in particular to black male college success (Harper, 2008), educators must seek ways to cross-culturally dismantle the American black-white dichotomy. Otherwise, international students, and particularly Asian students, may leave the U.S. with continued negative perceptions of African Americans, almost assuring they will not develop the cross-racial communication toolkit necessary for success in our increasingly globalized workplaces.

RECOMMENDATIONS

To address these long-established and structural stereotypes reproduced by mass media representations and then exported to the rest of the world, some universities have turned to innovative ways to broaden cross-racial/ethnic interactions between African American and Asian international students. We have discussed many of these initiatives in other publications, including another chapter in this book (Ritter,

2014; Roth, 2015a; Roth, 2016). A key area of focus, as we have suggested, is the examination, critique, and deconstruction of media representations across disciplines and to interrogate the ideologies scaffolding them. Stack (2006) has argued the under emphasis by educators on media deconstruction is an area of needed improvement across the curriculum. Like Kellner (2010, 2011), Stack (2006) sees opportunities for students to resist damaging and dominant representations with efforts to invent new ones, emancipating spaces within the media sphere to democratize representations and to effect change in the actual production of media. Education, in the past, has attempted to inoculate students against media consumption, but given the pervasiveness of the medium, this is no longer a practical effort. That so many representations have been naturalized and are often taken-for-granted axioms, such as race, the processes and assumptions that lead to these conclusions must be interrogated (Hall, 2011).

One approach is the formation of intergroup dialogue programs, where students study structural racism in society, dissect media images, and examine the dynamics of privilege and oppression through collaborative team building exercises (Roth, 2015a; Zuniga, 2012). This social justice curriculum promotes interaction and dialogue across identities, and provides for an examination of race and ethnicity through both an international and domestic lens. Student facilitators typically lead peer discussions, interactive games, listening activities, and the sharing of personal narratives with the intended outcome of a greater understanding among participants of societal oppression and privilege across race and culture.

While such dialogue is a good place to start, there may also need to be a diversity curriculum for all incoming students to an institution. To effectively combat racial stereotypes imposed by media and other cultural representations, both international and domestic students need a deeper understanding of racial diversity throughout the world. Technology and transportation have brought every corner of the world within access to nearly every global citizen. No doubt these citizens will encounter cultures and social nuances they may be unfamiliar or uncomfortable with. However, our efforts as educators should not necessarily be to prepare students to master the world they encounter but to assist them to engage that world with tolerance and openness to difference. Given the rapidity with which human experience is globalizing, the ability to acknowledge, tolerate, and accept difference across culture may be the most important skills to prepare citizens to participate in the inevitably multicultural workplaces and public spaces of the future. But these important skills and sensibilities cannot be taught or learned in institutions that don't reflect them. For these reasons, another critical aspect to creating tolerance and openness to difference among students is to have a tolerant and openly diverse faculty and staff.

Research shows having diverse faculty has proven to aid in student success, especially among black male students (Dogan, 2010; Williams, 2012). Faculties of Color serve as mentors and advisers to students of color (Smith, 2009). But, all too often, faculty outside the majority identity group find themselves pigeon-holed pedagogically, teaching courses associated with their race, or their gender (Epps, 2002), or other generalizable personal characteristic. These types of outcomes scaffold a culture of tokenism and insensitivity (Smith, 2009), and the call for greater diversity among faculty and administrators has been a cornerstone of increasing student activism nationwide (Criss, 2015; Donovan, 2015; Eligon, 2015; Patton, 2013; Stanley-Becker, 2015).

Hiring diverse faculty also cultivates diverse future leadership within the promotion pipeline (Smith, 2009). Since tenure is a significant way for faculty to move into administration, where they create policy and programs, it is vital each and every college department strives to develop a diverse faculty that in turn enables a potentially rich and varied pool of future administrators (Patton, 2013).

While these few suggestions may seem obvious, we have found examples where institutional leaders are performing a form of racial quietism in constructing curricula and campus climate. At the University of Southern Alabama, Director Brenda Hinson explains, "Here in the South we spend so much time trying to overcome our past images that we wait until [foreign students] arrive and answer questions they might have about race at that time" (Althen, 2009, p. 90). This is likely not a national norm and ignoring potential racial misunderstandings is problematic, given the history of slavery in America and only a cursory understanding of that history among most international students (Ritter, 2013). However, throughout the nation, programming tying America's racial past to current practices and polices is sporadic at best, and even sparser for graduate students. Tuft University's International Center director Jane Etish-Andrews explains graduate students "do not have the issue of race on their radar screen... they are only interested in doing well academically and do not want to address issues outside of their academic performance" (Althen, 2009, p. 92). Again, this is not a productive posture, especially in light of widespread student activism and unrest on U.S. college campuses nationwide. Neither do we agree this is an accurate assessment. Race is on all students' radar, and it may be time to fully acknowledge the U.S. has not achieved a *post-racial* climate and may never get there unless concerted efforts are made throughout society, and as we have previously said some of the most potent germinating ground is the American college and university.

CONCLUSION

Media representations and their underlying ideologies assist individuals to make meaning of social experiences. Given the ubiquity and frequency of certain ideologies carried by media representations, it is not much of a leap to imagine how individual ideas and opinions may be shaped in the process. In fact, Cultivation Theory asserts individuals accept certain beliefs and opinions if they are heard or seen repeatedly in the course of social interaction. For this reason, Hall (2011) has argued for an interrogation of the ideologies behind representations over the representations themselves, since it is the ideologies or agreed-upon social constructs that scaffold representations, giving them meaning. Of course, individuals are not hostage to media representations and can interpret, accept, and reject representations and ideologies as they see fit (Kellner, 1982, 1995, 2011). Still, this may require an additional level of work individuals may choose not to engage if they are unaware of the right or need to do so. In this way, monolithic representations of black males as a social threat, or inauspicious academically, likely have implications for college campus climate.

Further, college campuses remain both bastions for social change and stalwarts for the status quo, and for these reasons they are important sites for addressing the implications of globalization in raced relations and acceptance of difference as represented in media and other cultural contexts. The surge in racial incidents on some of the nation's most venerable campuses, as well as many others, may signify cultural and media representations of race, particularly with regard to black males, have reached a tipping point of intolerance, and this intolerance is being played out and reproduced in campus interactions nationwide. These are not incidental or geographical issues due in part to the vast reach of media representations.

Clearly, at least in America, students of many races on many college campuses throughout the country are reacting to perceived local or global issues of racism and social injustice. The college years have typically been characterized as a time when young people test their vision and views of the world en route to adulthood. Yet, we believe the issues briefly highlighted here may have serious implications well beyond the assertion of coming of age among current college cohorts. Racial issues and racism have plagued the U.S. for centuries, with few moments of intermittent remedy and redress. Similarly, these same injustices have surfaced elsewhere in the world and typically have not been addressed due to those nations' lack of the same egalitarian credo we teach our students from their first days in school. It may be time to either reinvigorate that commitment to social justice, or clearly pull back the curtain on an illusory system of higher education that allegedly rewards meritocracy regardless of the color with which it arrives.

REFERENCES

Alexander, M. (2010). *The New Jim Crow: Mass Incarceration in the Age of Colorblindness*. New York: The New Press.

Althen, G. (2009). Education International Students About 'Race'. *International Educator, 18*(3).

Amzallag, D., Peacocke, A., & Pianin, A. (2008, April 5). Grad Student Fled Assault before Killed by Car; Suspect Arrested for Manslaughter. *The Columbia Spectator*. Retrieved from http://www.columbi-aspectator.com/2008/04/05/grad-student-fled-assault-killed-car-suspect-arrested-manslaughter

Ancis, J. R., Sedlacek, W. E., & Mohr, J. J. (2000). Student Perceptions of Campus Cultural Climate by Race. *Journal of Counseling and Development, 78*(2), 180–185. doi:10.1002/j.1556-6676.2000.tb02576.x

Antonio, A. L. (2001). The Role of Interracial Interaction in the Development of Leadership Skills and Cultural Knowledge and Understanding. *Research in Higher Education*, *42*(5), 593–617. doi:10.1023/A:1011054427581

Astin, A. W. (1993). Diversity and Multiculturalism on the Campus: How Are Students Affected? *Change*, *23*(2), 44–49. doi:10.1080/00091383.1993.9940617

Baird, S. (1998). U.S. Marshals [Film]. K. Barrish, & A. Koppelson (Producer). Hollywood, CA.

Bjornstrom, E. E. S., Kaufman, R. L., Peterson, R. D., & Slater, M. D. (2010). Race and Ethnic Representations of Lawbreakers and Victims in Crime News: A National Study of Television Coverage. *Social Problems*, *57*(2), 269–293. doi:10.1525p.2010.57.2.269 PMID:20640244

Blalock, H. M. (1967). *Toward a Theory of Minority-Group Relations*. New York: Wiley.

Boswell, F. (2014). In Darren Wilson's Testimony, Familiar Themes About Black Men. *Code Switch: Frontiers of Race, Culture and Ethnicity*. Retrieved from npr.org website: http://www.npr.org/sections/codeswitch/2014/11/26/366788918/in-darren-wilsons-testimony-familiar-themes-about-black-men

Bourdieu, P., & Passeron, J. C. (1977). *Reproduction in Education, Society and Culture*. Beverly Hills, CA: Sage Publications.

Bowman, N. A. (2010). Disequilibrium and Resolution: The Nonlinear Effects of Diversity Courses on Well-Being and Orientations toward Diversity. *The Review of Higher Education*, *33*(4), 543–568. doi:10.1353/rhe.0.0172

Bowman, N. A., & Denson, N. (2012). What's Past Is Prologue: How Precollege Exposure to Diversity Shapes the Impact of College Diversity Experiences. *Research in Higher Education, 53*, 406–425. doi:10.100711162-011-9235-2

Cabrera, A. F., & Nora, A. (1994). College Student Perceptions of Prejudice and Discrimination and Their Feelings of Alienation: A Construct Validation Approach. *Review of Education, Pedagogy & Cultural Studies, 16*(3-4), 387–409. doi:10.1080/1071441940160310

Callinicos, A. (1993). *Race and Class*. Chicago: Bookmarks Publications, Ltd.

Carter, P. L. (2006). Straddling Boundaries: Identity, Culture, and School. *Sociology of Education, 79*(4), 304–328. doi:10.1177/003804070607900402

Cha, J., & Choi, I. (1992). College Students' Attitude toward Foreigners. *Psychological Science, 1*(1), 1–23.

Chang, M. J. (1996). *Racial Diversity in Higher Education: Does a Racially Mixed Student Population Affect Educational Outcomes?* (Dissertation). University of California, Los Angeles, CA.

Chang, M. J. (1999). Does Racial Diversity Matter? The Education Impact of a Racially Diverse Undergraduate Populations. *Journal of College Student Development, 40*(4), 377–395.

Chang, M. J. (2002). Preservation or Transformation: Where's the Real Educational Discourse on Diversity. *Review of Higher Education, 25*(2), 125–140. doi:10.1353/rhe.2002.0003

Chang, M. J. (2013). Post-Fisher: The Unfinished Research Agenda on Student Diversity in Higher Education. *Educational Researcher, 42*(3), 172–173. doi:10.3102/0013189X13486764

Chang, M. J., Milem, J. F., & Antonio, A. L. (2010). Campus Climate and Diversity. In J. H. Schuh, S. R. Jones, S. R. Harper, & ... (Eds.), *Student Services: A Handbook for the Profession*. San Francisco: Jossey-Bass.

Cheng, Y. (2011). From Campus Raciscm to Cyber Racism: Discourse of Race and Chinese Nationalism. *The China Quarterly, 207*, 561–579. doi:10.1017/S0305741011000658

Chiricos, T., Eschholz, S., & Gertz, M. (1997). Crime, News and Fear of Crime: Toward an Identification of Audience Effects. *Social Problems, 44*(3), 342–357. doi:10.2307/3097181

Chiricos, T., McEntire, R., & Gertz, M. (2001). Perceived Racial and Ethnic Composition of Neighborhood and Perceived Risk of Crime. *Social Problems, 48*(3), 322–340. doi:10.1525p.2001.48.3.322

Clark, M. (2015, April 27). Zeta Beta Tau Fraternity Expels Four Members Following Anti-Muslim Yeti Post. *The University Daily Kansan*. Retrieved from http://www.kansan.com/news/zeta-beta-tau-fraternity-expels-four-members-following-anti-muslim/article_343d281e-ed60-11e4-8222-a79781d7894c.html

Clifton, D. (2015). Leaked Video of Disturbingly Racist Frat Song Exposes an Ugly Truth About the Greek System. *Identities.Mic*. Retrieved from mic.com website: http://mic.com/articles/112240/12-incidents-that-prove-fraternity-and-sorority-racism-isn-t-just-an-oklahoma-problem

Colorado Shooting Suspect Was Brilliant Science Student. (2012). *Victoria Advocate*. Retrieved from victoriaadvocate.com website: https://www.victoriaadvocate.com/news/2012/jul/20/colorado_suspect_072012_182974/

Condit, C. M. (1989). The Rhetorical Limits of Polysemy. *Critical Studies in Mass Communication*, 6(2), 103–122. doi:10.1080/15295038909366739

Criss, D. (2015). University of Missouri Campus Protests: This Is Just the Beginning. *CNN Breaking News*. Retrieved from cnn.com website: http://www.cnn.com/2015/11/10/us/missouri-football-players-protest-presidents-resigns/

Cuyjet, M. J. (2006). *African American Men in College* (1st ed.). San Francisco: Jossey-Bass.

Davis, A. J. (1997). Race, Cops and Traffic Stops. *University of Miami Law Review*, 51(425).

Denson, N., & Chang, M. J. (2009). Racial Diversity Matters: The Impact of Diversity-Related Student Engagement and Institutional Context. *American Educational Research Journal*, 46(2), 322–353. doi:10.3102/0002831208323278

Dikotter, F. (1997). *The Construction of Racial Identities in China and Japan: Historical and Contemporary Perspectives*. Honolulu, HI: University of Hawaii Press.

Dillard, A. D. (2001). *Guess Who's Coming to Dinner Now? Multicultural Conservatism in America*. New York: New York University Press.

Dixon, T. L., Asocar, C. L., & Casas, M. (2003). The Portrayal of Race and Crime on Television Network News. *Journal of Broadcasting & Electronic Media*, 47(4), 498–524. doi:10.120715506878jobem4704_2

Dogan, R. (2010). *Schools Need Black Male Teachers*. Retrieved from http://www.menteach.org/news/schools_need_black_male_teachers

Donovan, E. (2015, Nov. 12). Black Students Interrupt University of Kansas Town Hall in Wake of Missouri Protest. *USA Today*. Retrieved from http://college.usatoday.com/2015/11/12/black-students-interrupt-univeristy-of-kansas-town-hall/

Egelko, B. (2013). Blame in Oscar Grant BART Death May Shift. *SFGate*. Retrieved from Blame in Oscar Grant BART Death May Shift - SFGate website: http://www.sfgate.com/bayarea/article/Blame-in-Oscar-Grant-BART-death-may-shift-4713100.php

Eligon, J., & Pérez-Peña, R. (2015). University of Missouri Protests Spur a Day of Change. *The New York Times*. Retrieved from http://www.nytimes.com/2015/11/10/us/university-of-missouri-system-president-resigns.html?_r=2

Entman, R. M., & Gross. (2008). Race to Judgment: Stereotyping Media and Criminal Defendants. *Law and Contemporary Problems*, 71(4), 93–133.

Epps, A. W., Suh, S., & Stassen, M. (2002). Outsiders Within: Race, Gender and Faculty Status in U.S. Higher Education. In W. A. Smith, P. G. Altbach, & K. Lomotey (Eds.), *The Racial Crisis in American Higher Education: Continuing Challenges for the Twenty-First Century* (pp. 189–220). Albany, NY: State University of New York Press.

Fantz, A. (2015). New York Times Columnist: Yale Police Detained My Son at Gunpoint. *CNN Breaking News*. Retrieved from CNN Breaking News website: http://www.cnn.com/2015/01/26/us/yale-blow-son-detained/

Faulders, K. (2015). Brutality Eyed in Arrest of UVA Student by Alcohol Agents. *ABC News*. Retrieved from http://abcnews.go.com/Entertainment/leah-remini-break-church-scientology-wanted/story?id=34854744

Fujioka, Y. (2000). Television Portrayals and African American Stereotypes: Examination of Television Effects When Direct Content Is Lacking. *Communication Abstracts*, *23*(1), 3–149.

Gilliam, F. D., & Iyengar, S. (2000). Prime Suspects: The Influence of Local Television News on the Viewing Public. *American Journal of Political Science*, *44*(3), 560–573. doi:10.2307/2669264

Gordon, L. (2010, January 12). UC Freshman to Include Record Number of out-of-State and International Students. *Los Angeles Times*. Retrieved from http://www.latimes.com/news/local/la-me-uc-enroll-20100715,0,2160250.story

Gordon, L., & Rojas, R. (2011). UCLA Won't Discipline Creator of Controversial Video, Who Later Withdraws from University. *Los Angeles Times*. Retrieved from http://articles.latimes.com/keyword/education

Gramsci, A., Nowell-Smith, G., & Hoare, Q. (1971). Selections from the Prison Notebooks of Antonio Gramsci: Ed. And Transl. By Quintin Hoare and Geoffrey Nowell Smith. International Publishers.

Gray, H. (2005). The Politics of Representation in Network Television. In D. M. Hunt (Ed.), *Channeling Blackness: Studies on Television and Race in America* (p. ix). New York: Oxford University Press.

Grenoble, R. (2015). Yale Investigates Claims of 'White Girls Only' Fraternity Party. *Huffingtonpost.com*. Retrieved from Huffingtonpost.com website: http://www.huffingtonpost.com/entry/yale-fraternity-white-girls-only-party-sae_5637c091e4b0631799134506

Grutter v. Bollinger (02-241) 539 U.S. 306 (U.S. Supreme Court 2003).

Gurney-Read, J. (2015). Top 100 World Universities 2015/16 – the Rankings. *The Telegraph*. Retrieved from The Telegraph website: http://www.telegraph.co.uk/education/universityeducation/11896268/Top-100-world-universities-201516-THE-rankings.html

Gutmann, A. (1999). *Democratic Education with a New Preface and Epilogue*. Princeton, NJ: Princeton University Press.

Hall, S. (2003a). What Is This "Black" in Black Culture? In V. Smith (Ed.), *Representing Blackness: Issues in Film and Video* (p. 240). New Brunswick, NJ: Rutgers University Press.

Hall, S. (Ed.). (2003b). *Representation: Cultural Representation and Signifying Practices*. London: Sage Publications.

Hall, S. (2011). The Whites of Their Eyes: Racist Ideologies and the Media. In G. Dines & J. M. Humez (Ed.), Gender, Race, and Class in Media (pp. 81-84). Los Angeles, CA: Sage Publications.

Hanassab, S. (2006). Diversity, International Students, and Perceived Discrimination: Implications for Educators and Counselors. *Journal of Studies in International Education*, *10*(2), 157–172. doi:10.1177/1028315305283051

Harper, S. R. (2009). Niggers No More: A Critical Counternarrative on Black Male Student Achievement at Predominantly White Colleges and University. *International Journal of Qualitative Studies in Education, 22*(6), 697–712. doi:10.1080/09518390903333889

Harper, S. R. (Ed.). (2010). *An Anti-Deficit Achievement Framework for Research on Students of Color in Stem*. San Francisco: Jossey-Bass.

Harper, S. R., & Nichols, A. H. (2008). Are They Not All the Same? Racial Heterogeneity among Black Male Undergraduates. *Journal of College Student Development, 49*(3), 199-214. doi: 10l1353/csd.0.0003

Harris, A., & Allen, W. (2003). Lest We Forget Thee …: The under- and over-Representation of Black and Latino Youth in California Higher Education and Juvenile Justice Institutions. *Race and Society, 6*(2), 99–123. doi:10.1016/j.racsoc.2004.11.008

Hartocollis, A., & Bidgood, J. (2015, Nov. 11). Racial Discrimination Protests Ignite at Colleges across the U.S. *The New York Times*. Retrieved from http://www.nytimes.com/2015/11/12/us/racial-discrimination-protests-ignite-at-colleges-across-the-us.html?_r=0

Henkin, D. M. (2008). On Forms and Media. *Representations (Berkeley, Calif.), 104*(1), 34–36. doi:10.1525/rep.2008.104.1.34

Hensley, N. (2015). Man Dies in Baltimore Police Custody with Spinal Injuries One Week after Arrest. *Daily News*. Retrieved from nydailynews.com website: http://www.nydailynews.com/news/crime/man-spinal-injuries-dies-baltimore-police-custody-article-1.2190933

hooks, b. (2004). *We Real Cool: Black Men and Masculinity*. New York: Routledge.

Horn, R. A. Jr. (2003). Developing a Critical Awareness of the Hidden Curriculum through Media Literacy. *The Clearing House: A Journal of Educational Strategies, Issues and Ideas, 76*(6), 298–300. doi:10.1080/00098650309602024

Hoxby, C. M., & Avery, C. (2012). *The Missing 'One-Offs': The Hidden Supply of High-Achieving, Low Income Students*. National Bureau of Economic Research. Retrieved from http://www.nber.org/papers/w18586

Hudson, A. (2013). 1 Black Man Is Killed Every 28 Hours by Police or Vigilantes: America Is Perpetually at War with Its Own People. *Alternet*. Retrieved from ALTERNET.ORG website: http://www.alternet.org/news-amp-politics/1-black-man-killed-every-28-hours-police-or-vigilantes-america-perpetually-war-its

Hurtado, S. (1992). The Campus Racial Climate: Contexts of Conflict. *The Journal of Higher Education, 63*(5), 539–569. doi:10.2307/1982093

Hurtado, S. (2000). The Campus Racial Climate: Contexts of Conflict. In M. C. Brown (Ed.), *Organizational Governance in Higher Eduation* (pp. 182–202). Boston, MA: Pearson.

Hurtado, S., Clayton-Pedersen, A. R., Allen, W. R., & Milem, J. F. (1998). Enhancing Campus Climates for Racial/Ethnic Diversity: Educational Policy and Practice. *The Review of Higher Education, 21*(3), 279–302. doi:10.1353/rhe.1998.0003

Hurtado, S., Dey, E. L., & Trevino, J. G. (1994). *Exclusion or Segregation? Interaction across Racial/Ethnic Groups on College Campuses*. Paper presented at the American Educational Research Association, New Orleans, LA.

Hurtado, S., Milem, J., Clayton-Pederson, A., & Allen, W. (1999). *Enacting Diverse Learning Environments: Improving the Campus Climate for Racial/Ethnic Diversity. ASHE/ERIC Higher Education Reports Series 26, No. 8*. Washington, DC: George Washington University/ERIC Clearinghouse on Higher Education.

Jackson, D. Z. (2005). Stereotyping Black Men. *The Boston Globe*. Retrieved from http://www.boston.com/news/globe/editorial_opinion/oped/articles/2005/05/27/stereotyping_black_men/

Johnson, D. (2007). *Race and Racism in China: Chinese Racial Attitudes toward Africans and African Americans*. Bloomington, IN: AuthorHouse.

Jonsson, P. (2015). Noose on Duke Campus: Do Colleges Have a Growing Racism Problem? *The Christian Science Monitor*. Retrieved from http://www.csmonitor.com/USA/Education/2015/0402/Noose-on-Duke-campus-Do-colleges-have-a-growing-racism-problem-video

Kearney, L., & Stein, L. (2014). *Ferguson Officer Testified He Feared for His Life in Confrontation with Teen*. Retrieved from http://www.reuters.com/article/2014/11/26/us-usa-missouri-shooting-wilson-idUSKCN0J92DE20141126

Kellner, D. (1982). TV, Ideology, and Emancipatory Popular Culture. In H. Newcomb (Ed.), *Television: The Critical View* (3rd ed.; pp. 386–421). New York: Oxford University Press.

Kellner, D. (1995). *Media Culture*. New York: Routledge. doi:10.4324/9780203205808

Kellner, D. (2010). *Cinema Wars: Hollywood Film and Politics in the Bush-Cheney Era*. Malden, MA: Wiley-Blackwell.

Kellner, D. (2011). Cultural Studies, Multiculturalism, and Media Culture. In G. Dines, & J. M. Humez (Ed.), Gender, Race and Class in Media (3rd ed.; pp. 7-18). Thousand Oaks, CA: Sage Publications, Inc.

Kim, N. (2008). *Imperial Citizens: Koreans and Race from Seoul to L.A.* Palo Alto, CA: Stanford University Press.

King, S., & Darabont, F. (1994). *The Shawshank Redemption* [Film]. L. Glotzer, D. Lester, & Niki Martin (Producer). Hollywood, CA.

Kitwana, B. (2002). The Hip Hop Generation: Young Blacks and the Crisis in African American Culture. New York: Basic Civitas Books.

Knafo, S. (2013). 1 in 3 Black Males Will Go to Prison in Their Lifetime, Report Warns. *The HuffingtonPost.com*. Retrieved from Huffingtonpost.com website: http://www.huffingtonpost.com/2013/10/04/racial-disparities-criminal-justice_n_4045144.html

Kobayashi, Y. (2010). Discriminatory Attitudes toward Intercultural Communication in Domestic and Overseas Contexts. *Higher Education, 59*(3), 323–333. doi:10.100710734-009-9250-9

Lee, J., & Bean, F. D. (2004). America's Changing Color Lines: Immigration, Race/Ethnicity, and Multiracial Identification. *Annual Review of Sociology, 30*(1), 221–242. doi:10.1146/annurev.soc.30.012703.110519

Lee, J. J. (2007a). Bottomline: Neo-Racism toward International Students. *About Campus: Enriching the Student Learning Experience, 11*(6), 28–30. doi:10.1002/abc.194

Lee, J. J., & Rice, C. (2007b). Welcome to America? International Student Perceptions of Discrimination and Neo-Racism. *Higher Education, 53*(3), 381–409. doi:10.100710734-005-4508-3

Leonardo, Z. (2005). Through the Multicultural Glass: Althusser, Ideology and Race Relations in Post-Civil Rights America. *Policy Futures in Education, 3*(4), 400–412. doi:10.2304/pfie.2005.3.4.400

Lieber, R. J., & Weisberg, R. E. (2002). Globalization, Culture, and Identities in Crisis. *International Journal of Politics Culture and Society, 16*(2), 273–296. doi:10.1023/A:1020581114701

Locke, D. C., & Valesco, J. (1987). Hospitality Begins with the Invitation: Counseling Foreign Students. *Journal of Multicultural Counseling and Development, 15*(3), 115–119. doi:10.1002/j.2161-1912.1987.tb00386.x

Locks, A. M., Hurtado, S., Bowman, N. A., & Oseguera, L. (2008). Extending Notions of Campus Climate and Diversity to Students' Transition to College. *The Review of Higher Education, 31*(3), 257–285. doi:10.1353/rhe.2008.0011

Loo, C. M., & Rolison, G. (1986). Alienation of Ethnic Minority Students at a Predominantly White University. *The Journal of Higher Education, 57*.

Mashhood, F., & Parkinson-Morgan, K. (2011). Viral YouTube Video Called "Repugnant" by UCLA Administration. *Daily Bruin*. Retrieved from http://www.dailybruin.com/index.php/blog/off_the_press/2011/03/viral_youtube_video_called_repugnant_by_ucla_administration

McIntosh, P. (2008). White Privilege: Unpacking the Invisible Knapsack. In P. S. Rothenberg (Ed.), *White Privilege: Essential Readings on the Other Side of Racism*. New York: Worth Publishers.

McMurtie, B. (2012). China Continues to Drive Foreign-Student Growth in the United States. *The Chronicle of Higher Education*.

Medical Examiner Rules Eric Garner's Death a Homicide, Says He Was Killed by Chokehold. (2014). Retrieved 12/7/2014, 2014, from http://www.nbcnewyork.com/news/local/Eric-Garner-Chokehold-Police-Custody-Cause-of-Death-Staten-Island-Medical-Examiner-269396151.html

Milem, J. (2001). Increasing Diversity Benefits: How Campus Climate and Teaching Methods Affect Student Outcomes. In Diversity Challenged: Evidence on the Impact of Affirmative Action. Cambridge, MA: Harvard Education Publishing Group.

Morey, A. I. (2004). Globalization and the Emergence of for-Profit Higher Education. *Higher Education, 48*(1), 131–150. doi:10.1023/B:HIGH.0000033768.76084.a0

Morgan, R., & O'Connel, K. (2014). *International Students Contribute $26.8 Billion to the U.S. Economy New state and congressional level economic data and U.S. study abroad demographic data with accompanying policy recommendations now available from NAFSA*. New York: NAFSA.

Nemetz, P. L., & Christensen, Sandra L. (1996). The Challenge of Cultural Diversity: Harnessing a Diversity of Views to Understand Multiculturalism. *Academy of Management Review, 21*(2), 434–462.

Olzak, S. (2011). Does Globalization Breed Ethnic Discontent? *The Journal of Conflict Resolution, 55*(1), 3–32. doi:10.1177/0022002710383666

Parkinson-Morgan, K. (2011). *Updated*: UCLA Student's YouTube Video 'Asian in the Library' Prompts Death Threats: Violent Responses Criticized as Equally Damaging. *The Daily Bruin*. Retrieved from http://dailybruin.com/2011/03/14ucla_student039s_youtube_video_039asians_in_the_library039_prompts_death_threats_violent_re-sponses_c/

Pascarella, E. T., & Terenzini, P. T. (2005). *How College Affects Students: A Third Decade of Research* (Vol. 2). San Francisco: Jossey-Bass.

Patton, S. (2013). *At the Ivies, It's Still White at the Top*. Retrieved from http://chronicle.com/article/At-the-Ivies-Its-Still-White/139643/

Photo of University of Florida Frat Members Wearing Blackface Sparks Controversy. (2012). *Huffingtonpost.com*. Retrieved from huffingtonpost.com website: http://www.huffingtonpost.com/2012/10/29/university-of-florida-blackface-beta-theta-pi_n_2038326.html

Potter, W. J. (2014). A Critical Analysis of Cultivation Theory. *Journal of Communication, 64*(6), 1015–1036. doi:10.1111/jcom.12128

PwC. (2015). *Filmed Entertainment Revenue Worldwide from 2012 to 2017, by Region (in Billions U.S. Dollars)*. New York: Statista, Inc.

Quick Facts – UCLA Undergraduate Admissions. (2015). *Campus Profile*, from http://www.admissions.ucla.edu/campusprofile.htm

Race, Racism and International Students in the United States. (2013). *NACADA Academic Advising Today: Voices from the Global Community*. Retrieved from http://www.nacada.ksu.edu/Resources/Academic-Advising-Today/View-Articles/Race--Racism--and-International-Students-in-the-United-States.aspx#sthash.Tgew30Vv.dpuf

Radloff, T. D., & Evans, N. J. (2003). The Social Construction of Prejudice among Black and White College Students. *NASPA Journal, 40*(2), 1–16. doi:10.2202/0027-6014.1222

Rankin, S. R., & Reason, R. D. (2005). Differing Perceptions: How Students of Color and White Students Perceive Campus Climate for Underrepresented Groups. *Journal of College Student Development, 46*(1), 43–61. doi:10.1353/csd.2005.0008

Ritter, Z. (2013). *Making and Breaking Stereotypes: East Asian International Students' Experience with Cross-Racial Interactions*. (Ph.D. Dissertation). UCLA, Los Angeles, CA.

Ritter, Z., & Roth, K. (2014). Realizing Race: Media Representations and the Uneasy Adjustment of Asian International Students and African American Males on U.S. College Campuses. In N. D. Erbe (Ed.), *Approaches to Managing Organizational Diversity and Innovation* (p. 387). Hershey, PA: IGI Global. doi:10.4018/978-1-4666-6006-9.ch006

Rocha, V. (2015, Oct 9). Kanye West-Themed Frat Party at UCLA Sparks Protests, Claims of Racism. *Los Angeles Times*. Retrieved from http://www.latimes.com/local/lanow/la-me-ln-ucla-blackface-kanye-party-20151008-story.html

Roth, K. (2011). *The Other Curriculum: How Mass Media Can Shape Perceptions of College Going for African American Males*. Paper presented at the Association for the Study of Higher Education (ASHE), Charlotte, NC.

Roth, K., & Ritter, Z. (2015a). Diversity and the Need for Cross-Cultural Leadership and Collaboration. In Cross-Cultural Collaboration and Leadership in Modern Organizations. Hershey, PA: IGI Global, Inc. doi:10.4018/978-1-4666-8376-1.ch012

Roth, K., & Ritter, Z. (2015b). *Racial Spectacle and Campus Climate: The Intersection of U.S. Media Representations and Racial Stereotype Formation among Asian International Students, and Cross-Racial Interaction on College Campuses*. Paper presented at the Schools of Education Biennial Conference, Bridgetown, Barbados.

Roth, K. R. (2015c). *The Other Curriculum: Media Representations and the College Going Perceptions of African American Males. (Ph.D. Dissertation)*. UCLA. Retrieved from http://escholarship.org/uc/item/1rw2n0t8

Roth, K. R., & Ritter, Z. S. (2016). Racial Spectacle and Campus Climate: Media Representations and Asian International Student Perceptions at U.S. Colleges. In J. Prescott (Ed.), *Handbook of Research on Race, Gender, and the Fight for Equality*. Hershey, PA: IGI Global, Inc.

Russell, J. (1991). Race & Reflexivity: The Black Other in Contemporary Japanese Mass Culture. *Cultural Anthropology*, *6*(1), 3–25. doi:10.1525/can.1991.6.1.02a00010

Russell, J. G. (2012). Playing with Race/Authenticating Alterity: Authenticity, Mimesis, and Racial Performance in the Transcultural Diaspora. *CR (East Lansing, Mich.)*, *12*(1), 41–92. doi:10.1353/ncr.2012.0022

Scott, T. (1998). *Enemy of the State* [Film]. J. Bruckheimer (Producer). Hollywood.

Shire, E. (2015). Inside Yale's 'Whites-Only' Panic. *thedailybeast.com*. Retrieved from thedailybeast.com website: http://www.thedailybeast.com/articles/2015/11/11/inside-yale-s-whites-only-panic.html

Simien, J. (2014). *Dear White People [Film]. E. Brown, Le, A., Lebedev, J. Lopez, A., Simien, J., Waithe, L. (Producer)*. Minneapolis, MN: Lionsgate.

Smith, D. G. (2009). *Diversity's Promise for Higher Education: Making It Work*. Baltimore, MD: The Johns Hopkins University Press.

Smith, T. B., Bowman, R., & Hsu, S. (2007a). Racial Attitudes among Asian and European American College Students: A Cross-Cultural Examination. *College Student Journal*, *41*(2), 436–443.

Smith, W. A., Allen, W. A., & Danley, L. L. (2007b). Assume the Position...You Fit the Description. *The American Behavioral Scientist*, *51*(4), 551–578. doi:10.1177/0002764207307742

Smith, W. A., Hung, M., & Franklin, J. D. (2011). Racial Battle Fatigue and the Miseducation of Black Men: Racial Microagressions, Societal Problems, and Environmental Stress. *The Journal of Negro Education, 80*(1), 63–82.

Solórzano, D., Ceja, Miguel, & Yosso, Tara. (2000). Critical Race Theory, Racial Microaggressions, and Campus Racial Climate: The Experiences of African American College Students. *The Journal of Negro Education, 69*(1/2), 60–73.

Stack, M., & Kelly, D. M. (2006). Popular Media, Education, and Resistance. *Canadian Journal of Education, 29*(1), 5–26. doi:10.2307/20054144

Stanley-Becker, I. (2015). Minority Students at Yale Give List of Demands to University President. *The Washington Post.* Retrieved from https://www.washingtonpost.com/news/grade-point/wp/2015/11/13/minority-students-at-yale-give-list-of-demands-to-university-president/

Talbot, D., Geelhoed, R., & Ninggal, M. T. (1999). A Qualitative Study of Asian International Students' Attitudes toward African-Americans. *NASPA Journal, 36*(3). doi:10.2202/0027-6014.1081

Tanaka, G. (2007). *The Intercultural Campus: Transcending Culture & Power in American Higher Education.* New York: Peter Lang Publishing, Inc.

Tatum, B. D. (1997). *Why Are All the Black Kids Sitting Together in the Cafeteria? And Other Conversations About Race.* New York: Basic Books.

The Blaaag: Official Tumblr of Columbia University's Asian American Alliance. (2012). Retrieved from http://theblaaag.tumblr.com/post/4415598604/cucssas-finding-li-wei

Torres, C. A., & Rhoads, R. A. (2006). Introduction: Globalization and Higher Education in the Americas. In C. A. Torres & R. A. Rhoads (Eds.), *The University, State, and Market: The Political Economy of Globalization in the Americas.* Stanford, CA: Stanford University Press.

Torres, C. A., & Schugurensky, D. (2002). The Political Economy of Higher Education in the Era of Neoliberal Globalization: Latin America in Comparative Perspective. *Higher Education, 43*(4), 429–455. doi:10.1023/A:1015292413037

Van Heertum, R., & Torres, C. (2009). Globalization and Neoliberalism: The Challenges and Possibilities of Radical Pedagogy. In M. Simons (Ed.), *Re-Reading Education Policies: Studying the Policy Agenda of the 21st Century.* Netherlands: Sense Publishers.

Watanabe, T., & Rivera, C. (2015). Amid Racial Bias Protests, Claremont Mckenna Dean Resigns. *Los Angeles Times.* Retrieved from http://www.latimes.com/local/lanow/la-me-ln-claremont-marches-20151112-story.html

What Happened When Michael Brown Met Officer Darren Wilson. (2014). Retrieved 12/02/2014, 2014, from http://www.cnn.com/interactive/2014/08/us/ferguson-brown-timeline/

Williams, K. (2012). *A Phenomenological Study: African-American Males in the Educational Profession.* (Ph.D. Dissertation), Liberty University Lynchburg, VA.

Williams, K., Lowery, W., & Berman, M. (2015). University of Cincinnati Police Officer Who Shot Man During Traffic Stop Charged with Murder. *The Washington Post*. Retrieved from https://www.washingtonpost.com/news/post-nation/wp/2015/07/29/prosecutors-to-announce-conclusion-of-probe-into-cincinnati-campus-police-shooting/

Zuniga, X., Lopez, G. E., & Ford, K. A. (2012). Intergroup Dialogue: Critical Conversations About Difference, Social Identities, and Social Justice: Guest Editors' Introduction. *Equity & Excellence in Education*, 45(1), 1–13. doi:10.1080/10665684.2012.646903

Zuniga, X., Nagda, B. A., & Sevig, T. D. (2002). Intergroup Dialogues: An Educational Model for Cultivating Engagement across Differences. *Equity & Excellence in Education*, 35(1), 7–17. doi:10.1080/713845248

ADDITIONAL READING

Barger, S. S. (2004). *The Impact of International Students on Domestic Students in U.S. Institutions of Higher Education*. (Doctoral dissertation) University of Wisconsin, Madison.

Berryman-Fink, C. (2006, September 01). Reducing Prejudice on Campus: The Role of Intergroup Contact in Diversity Education. *College Student Journal*, 40(3), 511–516.

Bogle, D. (2001). *Toms, Coons, Mulattoes, Mammies, & Bucks: An Interpretive History of Blacks in American Films* (4th ed.). New York: The Continuum International Publishing Group, Inc.

Brown, L., & Peacock, N. (2007, September). *Crisis of Cross-cultural Communication on Our Campuses*. Paper presented at the conference on Education for Sustainable Development: Graduates as Global Citizens, Bournemouth, UK.

Deardorff, D. K. (2009). Connecting International and Domestic Students. In M. S. Andrade & N. W. Evans (Eds.), *International Students: Strengthening a Critical Resource* (pp. 211–215). Lanham, MD: Rowman & Littlefield.

Gilliam, F. D., Valentino, N. A., & Beckmann, M. N. (2002, January 01). Where You Live and What You Watch: The Impact of Racial Proximity and Local Television News on Attitudes about Race and Crime. *Political Research Quarterly*, 55(4), 755–780. doi:10.1177/106591290205500402

Gould, S. J. (1996). *The Mismeasure of Man*. New York: W. W. Norton & Company.

Grant, R. A., & Lee, I. (2009). The Ideal English Speaker. In *Kubota, R., & Lin, A. M. Y. (2009). Race, Culture, and Identities in Second Language Education: Exploring Critically Engaged Practice*. New York: Routledge.

Guerrero, E. (1993). *Framing Blackness: The African American Image in Film*. Philadelphia: Temple University Press.

Levin, S., Van Laar, C., & Sidanius, J. (2003). The Effects of In-group and Out-group Friendships on Ethnic Attitudes in College: A Longitudinal Study. *Group Processes & Intergroup Relations*, 6(1), 76–92. doi:10.1177/1368430203006001013

Masterman, L. (2001). A Rationale for Media Education. In R. W. Kubey (Ed.), *Media Literacy in the Information Age: Current Perspectives*. New Brunswick, NJ: Transaction Publishers.

Shook, N. J., & Fazio, R. H. (January 01, 2008). Interracial Roommate Relationships: An Experimental Field Test of the Contact Hypothesis. *Psychological Science: a Journal of the American Psychological Society / Aps, 19,* 7, 717-23.

Smith, V. (Ed.). (2003). Representing Blackness: Issues in Film and Video (2nd Paperback printing ed.). New Brunswick, NJ: Rutgers University Press.

Tan, A., Zhang, Y., Dalisay, F., & Zhang, L. (2009, July 01). Stereotypes of African Americans and Media use among Chinese High School Students. *The Howard Journal of Communications, 20*(3), 260–275. doi:10.1080/10646170903065803

Woo, H.-J., & Dominick, J. R. (2001, January 01). Daytime Television Talk Shows and the Cultivation Effect Among U.S. and International Students. *Journal of Broadcasting & Electronic Media, 45*(4), 598–614. doi:10.120715506878jobem4504_4

Xuexin, L. (2005). The Hip Hop Impact on Japanese Youth Culture. *Southeast Review of* Asian Studies.

This research was previously published in the Handbook of Research on Race, Gender, and the Fight for Equality edited by Julie Prescott; pages 172-197, copyright year 2016 by Information Science Reference (an imprint of IGI Global).

Chapter 37
Using Narrative and Team-Teaching to Address Teaching About Racial Dynamics

Stephen Brookfield
St. Thomas University, USA

ABSTRACT

Diversity training and multicultural competency workshops typically work from a top down logic in which educators or trainers skilled in working in multi-racial settings inform less enlightened colleagues about what they need to do to communicate across difference. This 'expert to novice' dynamic can easily create resentment as participants feel blamed for their lack of racial awareness. A missing component of this work is the use of narrative disclosure by expert instructors of how they struggle with their own learned racism as they seek to navigate racial complexities. This chapter outlines a pedagogy of narrative disclosure in which an instructor's personal experience is placed front and center as a teaching tool. It emphasizes the importance of team teaching as a way of modeling respectful disagreement and an openness to multiple perspectives for students.

INTRODUCTION

Programs designed to help people create and negotiate workforce diversity are typically framed around the construct of difference. Difference is seen as positive, as part of the infinite variety of the world. A workplace characterized by differences in culture, race, gender, age, religion, ability, and sexual orientation is held to be one with a competitive edge (Cox, 2001). This is because the kaleidoscope of diversity is assumed to create a kind of creative synergy, a spontaneous combustion of multiple perspectives and experiences. If we can create a workplace where differences are respected and valued, so the argument goes, this will be the catalyst for an unending exploration of new possibilities.

What this harmoniously appealing scenario often omits, however, is the presence of various 'isms'; racism, sexism, ableism, ageism and so on. From a humanistic viewpoint, difference is a gift, a manifestation of the multitude of individual talents in the world. From the standpoint of critical theory (Brookfield,

DOI: 10.4018/978-1-7998-1213-5.ch037

2004) however, difference is often structured in ways that reflect wider inequities. So, in the case of racial and cultural difference, the broader material inequities that exist in the world are linked to racial and cultural identity. When Black, Brown and Red Americans are disproportionately poorer, less educated, and more frequently incarcerated than White Americans, critical theory inquires into the ways that structural barriers constantly marginalize those racial groups.

In this chapter I explore how instructors can use personal narratives – particularly when they work in teams – to teach about the ways that structural and systemic racism is internalized and then enacted. This kind of racism is not an individual choice, but a set of ideas and practices transmitted and learned from birth, and embedded in the way organizations and communities function day to day. I want particularly to look at the pedagogy of anti-racism involving White educators and trainers working with mostly White groups. How can White educators help other Whites, become aware of the ways they unwittingly and unknowingly reinforce structural racism and enact racist ideology on a daily basis? I propose the use of personal narrative as a relatively unexplored approach.

MAIN FOCUS OF THE CHAPTER

The Theoretical Background to Understanding Racism

In this chapter racism is viewed not as an expression of individual prejudice or as a matter of personal choice, but as a learned ideology; that is, as a interlinked set of beliefs and practices that are embedded in social systems and structures. This understanding is grounded in the analytical framework of critical theory, so a brief explanation of this body of work is in order.

Critical theory is a term associated with thinkers from the Frankfurt School of critical social theory, such as Horkheimer and Adorno (1972), Marcuse (1964), and Habermas (1987). The theory describes the process by which people learn to accept as obvious and common sense the dominant ideologies (such as White supremacy, capitalism, patriarchy and representative democracy) that are embedded in everyday situations and practices. These ideologies shape behaviour and keep an unequal system intact by making it appear normal.

As a body of work, critical theory is grounded in three core assumptions regarding the way the world is organized: (1) that apparently open, Western democracies are actually highly unequal societies in which economic inequity, racism, and class discrimination are empirical realities; (2) that the way this state of affairs is reproduced as seeming to be normal, natural, and inevitable, thereby heading off potential challenges to the system, is through the dissemination of dominant ideology (n the case of the perpetuation of racism this ideology would be White supremacy), and (3) that critical theory attempts to understand this state of affairs as a prelude to changing it.

Dominant ideology comprises the set of broadly accepted beliefs and practices that frame how people make sense of their experiences and live their lives. When it works effectively it ensures that an economically unequal, racist, homophobic, and sexist society is able to reproduce itself with minimal opposition. Its chief function is to convince people that the world is organized the way it is for the best of all reasons and that society works in the best interests of all. So if Whites are overwhelmingly in possession of power and advantage, dominant ideology makes that fact seem unremarkable, not worth commenting on. Critical theory regards dominant ideology as inherently manipulative and duplicitous.

From the perspective of critical theory, a critical person is one who can identify this manipulation and discern how the ethic of capitalism, and the logic of bureaucratic rationality, push people into ways of living that perpetuate economic, racial, and gender oppression. Teaching critical thinking, therefore, involves teaching people to see behind the apparently normal façade of daily life to realize how ideological manipulation works to keep people quiet and in line. In terms of anti-racist work, this would entail helping people see how ideological manipulation ensures that the majority accept these ideologies unquestioningly. Those working within the critical theory paradigm are often regarded as troublemakers who see power, race, class, sexism, ableism, and homophobia everywhere, even when the majority is convinced these do not exist.

Critical theory defines racism as a system of beliefs and practices (i.e. an ideology) that legitimizes the power of one racial group and justifies it viewing all others as inherently inferior. Racism is simultaneously overt (in law, the economy, political participation and education) and covert (in the media, social mores, fashion). When structural and systemic racism is threatened it responds sometimes with overt force (torture, police brutality, political imprisonment, murder) and sometimes with covert manipulation (symbolic festivals, media, prominent 'success' stories). Structural racism is expert at reconfiguring itself by appearing to have ceded important territory while in reality maintaining its power.

Racist ideology – often referred to as White supremacy – is embedded in the institutions and conventions of everyday lives. This ideology places 'Whiteness' as the preferred norm, 'White people' as the 'natural' authorities that ought to be entrusted with decision-making power and White knowledge (and White forms of knowledge production) as the most valid produced by humankind. This ideology is often implicit and its perpetrators such as myself frequently denied that they are disseminating it, even when doing so.

As I mentioned earlier, racist ideology is often so embedded in the daily business of life that the White majority finds it impossible to see other than in dramatic events such as hate crimes, racial chants or beatings. As overt racism has become punishable by law, and as politically correct language gains wider acceptance, racist ideology moves underground. The knapsack of taken-for-granted privileges Whites enjoy is rarely acknowledged. There are no more signs declaring "Whites Only" and people are not told that they are not being hired because of the color of their skin. Although news media report dramatic instances of overt racism, endemic racism today is far more likely to be carried in everyday instances of racial micro-aggression.

Popularized by Wing Sue (2010) micro-aggressions are the small acts of exclusion and marginalization committed by a dominant group towards a minority. They are the kinds of seemingly natural, instinctive and unthinking behaviors that keep dominant ideology intact. Moreover, they never overt or explicit, nothing as obvious as using a racist epithet or telling a person of color to shut up. The two constituent defining elements of a micro-aggression underscore this subtlety. First, receivers of micro-aggressions are usually left wondering 'did that really happen?' and asking 'should we be offended by that?' or 'did he/she mean to be insulting?' Second, when enacters of micro-aggressions are confronted with their actions they typically, and in a sense quite honestly, deny that there was any aggressive intent. They explain, with full sincerity, that no exclusion or diminution was planned, and that the receiver is indeed imagining things. They will explain their action away by saying that they had a temporary moment of forgetfulness, or that they got their words mixed up.

The key point about micro-aggressions is that they are never consciously intended to diminish a person of color. Instead, they are so ingrained in the repertoire of daily behaviors Whites employ to manage interpersonal interactions – the tone of voice we use, the gestures we make, where we direct eye contact, the analogies that unconsciously suggest themselves to us, the jokes we use, the shorthand terms we employ – that we never experience them as deliberately focused on insulting someone. In this sense they are truly ideological, so fully assimilated as to be unnoticeable until someone brings them to our attention. Helping people uncover and address these micro-aggressive expressions of dominant ideology is one of the tasks to be examined in this chapter.

Repressive Tolerance: A Key Critical Theory Idea in Analyzing Racism

An important idea drawn from critical theory that helps illuminate how racism persists is Marcuse's (1965) concept of repressive tolerance. Marcuse was interested in how institutions managed to deflect any serious challenge to their power and presumed legitimacy by appearing to cede territory and embrace change while staying the same. Token gestures such as changing the language and images representing the institution would be one example. I know of many higher education institutions that have changed their brochures and publicity materials to make it look as though their student body is a multi-ethnic, multi-racial rainbow coalition, all the while retaining an overwhelmingly White student body. Similarly, the creation of a 'Diversity' unit on campus is often assumed to have addressed effectively the problem of racism, hate speech, bigotry and so on. The institution can point to the new office or unit as evidence of substantive change. Meanwhile institutional procedures and culture can remain exactly the same.

The contemporary discourse of diversity, of opening up the field of higher education to diverse voices, perspectives and traditions, can be analyzed quite effectively using the idea of repressive tolerance. An honorable and emancipatory position to take is that higher education research, theorizing and practice needs to include alongside the grand narrative of Eurocentric rationality work that draws on other cultural traditions and represents different racial perspectives. Providing an array of alternative perspectives and sensibilities seems to be a major step in moving away from a situation in which White, male, European voices dominate. Yet Marcuse alerts us to the possibility that this apparent broadening of voices can actually reinforce the ideology of White supremacy that it purports to undercut.

By widening curricula to include a variety of traditions we appear to be celebrating all positions. But the history of White supremacy, and the way that language and structures of feeling frame Whiteness as the natural, inevitable conceptual center, means that the newly included voices, sensibilities and traditions are always positioned as the exotic other. Higher educators can soothe their consciences by believing progress is being made towards racial inclusivity and cultural equity, and can feel they have played their small but important part in the struggle. But as long as these subjugated traditions are considered alongside the dominant ideology, repressive tolerance ensures they will always be subtly marginalized as exotic, quaint, other than the natural center. The logic of liberating or discriminating tolerance would require an immersion only in a racial or cultural tradition that diverged radically from mainstream ideology; for example, a higher education graduate program that allowed only the consideration of Africentric ideas and perspectives. The logic of repressive tolerance holds that as long as Africentrism is considered as one of many possible perspectives, including Eurocentrism, it will always be positioned as the marginal alternative to the White supremacist center.

Pedagogically, the logic of Marcuse's argument is that we need to ensure students' extended immersion in a radically different set of ideas and perspectives that challenge the dominant ideology. An example of this would be an instructor establishing a ground rule that when students of color express their being on the receiving end of racism, that White students do not try to talk them out of it by saying that it wasn't systemic racism they were experiencing, just an act of individual foolishness, naiveté or forgetfulness. For example, the New Orleans based *People's Institute for Survival and Beyond* does not allow any debate of whether or not widespread endemic racism exists in the USA. Participants in workshops sponsored by the institute are told to accept this as fact. This kind of strong declaration has its roots in Marcuse's notion that sometimes educators just need to insist that learners ignore mainstream ideas and focus only on a radically different perspective.

Moving from Analysis to Action: Organizing Education for Diversity

For the rest of this chapter I want to move beyond a preliminary analysis of how systemic and structural racism is learned to focus on how personal narratives – particularly shared amongst a multiracial teaching team – can help people understand and challenge the persistence of structural and systemic racism. As a participant in diversity and anti-racist professional development workshops over the years I have often noticed a particular dynamic at play. Essentially the workshop is set up to help participants learn about cultural and racial difference and to help them be more alert to the ways they fall into reproducing racist behaviors by perpetuating cultural stereotypes and holding inaccurate assumptions about different racial groups. The underlying assumption is that through education and self-reflection people can learn to work in ways free of racist undertones. Anti-racist and diversity education is something done to you by those who have cracked the code of cultural misunderstandings and who have come out the other side of struggling with racism to a point where they can now teach others how to think and work in non-racist ways. In these workshops racism is framed as a personal choice, not a systemic phenomenon that soaks itself into your micro actions.

This paradigm has been challenged by the work of the *European-American Collaborative Challenging Whiteness* (ECCW) in San Francisco. The Collaborative has met monthly for the last 16 years to examine how Whites can educate each other, and themselves, about White supremacy. Its members note how the desire to be seen as 'good White people' "who act as effective allies to people of color by challenging the injustices of white hegemony and privilege" (ECCW, 2010 p. 146) permeates so much of anti-racist education. Paradoxically, as the ECCW notes, "this desire to be and be seen as a good white person often leads each of us to behaviors that have the opposite effect of what we intend" (p. 147).

From examining their own personal experiences, the ECCW members note two very common mistakes committed when Whites try to teach each other about race and racism. The first is that of proselytizing, of "exhorting in an officious and tiresome way" to other Whites the need for anti-racism. The effect of this is that those on the receiving end become defensive or shut down entirely. In the zeal to educate people about racism, proselytizers end up bringing anti-racist endeavors into disrepute. The second error noted by the ECCW is that of disdaining less racially 'enlightened' colleagues as objects of scorn to be pitied or condemned. Disdaining is rarely overt in my experience, but rather the sending of a subtle message that you are one of the many who ' just don't get it' in contrast to the racially cognizant elite few who have cracked the code of how to be non-racist.

As soon as I read the ECCW's analyses of these errors I recognized my own commission of these exact same behaviors. And I realized that what was missing from my own practice was a full disclosure of how the ideology of White supremacy was alive and well within me. Instead of educating people from a supposed position of racial cognizance what I really needed to do was to talk openly about my own struggle with my own racism. Slowly I came to understand that education about racism was often best done through narrative disclosure, rather than sharing tips and techniques of what did, or did not, work.

Pedagogically I now think of anti-racist education as being as much about teaching our own racism as it is about scrutinizing curricula, institutional policies, and organizational practices for evidence of structural disenfranchisement. If racism is understood as a learned ideology, something that pervades everyday speech, media images, peer group learning and family dynamics, then it is surely reasonable to expect that even adult educators committed to dismantling racism have internalized aspects of this ideology.

In this chapter I argue that even the most experienced White anti-racist educators are likely to have elements of the learned ideology of racism living within them. Instead of trying to purge themselves of these, conceal them, or damp them down, an alternative educational approach is to make these racist inclinations public and to engage learners in a consideration of how to recognize and challenge these. This approach uses educators' own attempts to model a critical analysis of their own learned racism. It asks questions such as; (a) How have we learned racism from dominant ideology? (b) How do our racist impulses continue to manifest themselves in our actions? (c) What are ways we can identify these? (d) How are our racist leanings interrupted by disruptive experience? (e) How do we challenge and push back against them?

Learning Racism: A Personal Example

In this section I want to provide an illustration of how racism is learned using myself as an example. As with all Whites in Britain, I grew up in a world in which Whiteness, and all things White, was taken as the 'natural' order of things. I have had 6 decades of ideological conditioning into White Supremacy and, as a result I do not expect it ever to leave me. Attitudes and beliefs I picked up in my childhood, adolescence and young adulthood were that Blacks were alternatively lazy, happy, or violent, Pakistanis and Indians were sexually irresponsible having large families, and Gypsies were thieves out to mark your house as an easy target. White supremacy was not without complications, though. For example, the White Irish were portrayed as lazy, drunken brawlers, with a markedly inferior IQ.

These stereotypes were earned through jokes with peers, family conversations, and media images. They flourished in the vacuum of no contact with anyone other than Whites like myself. I don't think I had a conversation with a Black person until I was 18 years old. This ideology of White supremacy rarely named itself as such. Overt declarations of White racial superiority were rare and, even as racist attitudes were being learned, I was engaged in apparently anti-racist acts. For example, as an undergraduate I participated in demonstrations against the South African Rugby team that represented the then South African apartheid regime. But external behavior often masks learned instincts, and so it was with me.

External events sometimes challenged the power of this ideology. One pivotal event in adolescence helped disrupt the way White Supremacy moved in me. This happened at the age of 17 when I was being beaten up by a gang of White youths (they were 'rockers' I was a 'mod') in Banbury High Street one Friday night. A Black American GI serviceman from Upper Heyford Air Force base crossed the street and broke up the fight telling us "everybody's got to be cool now". That man saved me from potentially severe injury. In my memory I was on the verge of falling to the floor as the GI intervened. Being born in Bootle (Liverpool) I knew that once you were on the floor things got a lot worse because then people could kick you in the kidneys and head. That event formed what Critical Race Theory (CRT) calls a counter-story that disrupted the White Supremacist script forming in my head that said that Black people are violent and start fights and White people are peacemakers who sometimes have to use force to reign in Black instigators of violence. Here was a stunning role reversal that made a big impression on me.

But despite disruptive moments and events such as these White Supremacy moves in me as it does in most Whites. First, my skin color means that for my whole career I am used to seeing as gatekeepers in adult education people who look like me. Now I suppose I am one of those gatekeepers, continuing the unproblematized White Supremacy norm. I never have to question my right to publish something and White epistemology is something bred into my neural synapses. Racism – the ugly operationalization of the ideology of White supremacy – moves in me in ways that constantly catch me by surprise. I see a Black pilot enter the cockpit of the plane on which I'm traveling and catch myself thinking "will this flight be safe?" Interestingly, Nelson Mandela writes about having the same reaction in his autobiography (Mandela, 1994).

In classes I catch myself holding back from challenging students of color and realize my so called 'empathy' or desire to be an ally masks an embedded racist consciousness which says that 'they' can't take a 'strong' challenge from a White person. The ECCW notes how Whites often withhold their contributions in multi-racial dialogues so as not to be seen as enacting White supremacy. They point out that this implies that the White voice is so powerful it will eclipse all others, and that by withholding colleagues of color are left wondering what Whites are thinking.

Clearly, racism moves in me in small, micro-aggressive ways. I find myself quickly granting paper extensions to Black students and can only assume it springs from a White Supremacist judgment that because Black students are not as intelligent as White students, of course they will need more time to complete their work. I keep silent in a presentation given by a scholar of color because (so my internal calculus goes) my voice is so powerful it will diminish the voice of the presenter. It is deeply sobering to realize how strong and enduring is the successful ideological conditioning of White Supremacy.

Outlining the Pedagogy of Narrative Disclosure

For the rest of this chapter I will explore in some detail the ways in which personal narrative disclosure, properly timed, can be an effective instructional tool. I grew up suspicious of the use of narrative, of storytelling, as I would have described it. Storytelling was something that was entertaining but essentially fictional. It was most certainly not academic, chiefly because it was clearly subjective and a-theoretical. It has taken me a long time to realize that narrative is one of the most compelling pedagogic approaches I can use. Nothing draws people more quickly into considering information and perspectives that are challenging than a personal story, and dissertations that are scholarly personal narratives (Nash, 2004; Nash & Bradley, 2011; Nash & Viray, 2013) are often far more likely to influence practice than third person research reports.

The appeal of narrative is powerful yet simple. Narrative draws the reader or listener in. The disclosure of personal experience, particularly when told in the form of a story, has far greater effect than the presentation of research data. People remember examples, metaphors and analogies they hear in a personal story far more than they do a theoretical explanation or a study's empirical findings. So whenever I have a pedagogic aim of teaching about the pervasive nature of racism I always work from the position that before I can ask anyone else to explore how it lives within them I need to engage in a prolonged period of self-disclosure of how it lives within me. I usually begin by defining some constituent elements of the ideology of White supremacy and then proceed to show how each of them flourishes within me. Let me describe three of these.

Using Narrative and Team-Teaching to Address Teaching About Racial Dynamics

Whites are Natural Gatekeepers

This first idea seeps its way insidiously into our consciousness. It does not assert itself as an overt injunction, as in 'you must be white to be editor of this journal, winner of this award, compiler of this handbook'. It's more that the power of the White gatekeeper role is revealed when we come across a gatekeeper who is not White. The instinctive surprise we experience at such moment is the chief indicator of the power of this ideology.

When uncovering this ideology I will usually start by talking about those who, in a four-decade career, have been my boss. There has not been one person of color who has been in a position of direct authority over me. Every dean, department head, principal, president and book editor I have worked with has been White like myself. So I have no model of a person of color who has exercised gatekeeper power or influence over me.

I then talk about my own gatekeeper role. An Endowed Chair is the top of the professorial hierarchy and I now find myself in the role of mentor to junior faculty at the outset of their careers who are trying to get published. Several of these are colleagues of color. So now I'm in the position of the White power broker trying to work as an ally whilst working in an overwhelmingly White field and still being in thrall to learned racist ideology. I talk about how I try to deal with this contradiction. I say that I try not to set any agenda with my mentee but that I always begin any mentoring conversations asking mentees what their agendas and goals are, and how they feel I could be of help. I never agree to a mentoring role unless asked to do so by the mentee, even though superiors have sometimes wanted to foist me on colleagues they see as under performing.

At the outset I try to acknowledge my own identity as a White, Euro-American, and how the rules of the game have been set up to help me. If a junior colleague wishes to play this game of publish or perish I am more then willing to help them do that. I don't try to pretend that I can in any way draw on my own struggles to get to my position as a way of understanding theirs. I don't insist they call me 'Stephen', which is what I'm most comfortable with and would much prefer. The 'Dr. Brookfield' or 'Professor Brookfield' that I am usually called, is always a reminder of the power differential between us.

Colleagues of Color Need Special Help and Assistance: They Can't Make it Without a 'White' Ally

One of the dynamics that the ECCW talks about is the need for 'good' Whites to be seen as an ally. I have to admit, whenever I hear White colleagues declare themselves allies I cringe. This is because the designation of ally is not ever ours to make. Yes, I would like to be considered an ally but I understand that the naming of me in that way is not in my hands. But when working with White students or colleagues I try to keep the cringe internal. Displaying it openly is a clear act of disdaining in the way the ECCW identifies this. Instead I often begin any discussion of being an ally by declaring my core assumptions of this work; that any person of color will never trust me and that this should have no bearing on my readiness to work in ways that seem anti-racist. I also own up to my belief that I should never expect to be acknowledged or thanked for this kind of work.

One of the things I try to talk a lot about is my own practice of interacting with colleagues and students of color. I talk about my own withholding behaviors, of not speaking for fear of seeming authoritarian or racist. I remember the first time I worked with a group in which African American students were present. Whenever one woman spoke I would remain studiously silent, congratulating myself on my empathic support. One day this student pulled me aside and asked me why I never responded to her comments in classroom discussion. She was visibly upset with what she saw as my disinterest in her views. So the supposed act of an 'ally' actually increased her perception of the power I held over her.

I also describe my experiences working in multi-racial teaching teams. I am known as something of a soft touch for any tale of woe, but particular for tales told by students of color. So for years I would unhesitatingly grant extensions, and push back deadlines, for any such student who asked for those. My own rationale was that White institutions needed to bend over backward to make allowances for those students who have not had the privilege of a rigorous academic training. Although I always tried to grade in what I then called a 'color-blind' way, I would feel much more pressure to round up a score for a student of color compared to a White student.

But when working in multi-racial teams it quickly became apparent to me that my teammates of color behaved very differently. They would be much less ready to grant extensions and would frequently ask me why I had graded a student of color so generously. I began to realize that the behaviors that I had imagined were in some way contributing to anti-racist pedagogy could actually indicate a deeply ingrained racism. In essence I was assuming without stopping to question this that students of color were not capable of handling the same full-blown critique I would make of White students' work. Furthermore, I was assuming that students of color could not reach the same standards of excellence as White students, and so I should 'go easy' on them and bump up their mark whenever I was in doubt about the merits of a piece of work. In essence I was giving marks for showing up and for the sheer fact of handing something in, irrespective of the quality of the work, in a way I would never do for White students.

"You're Being Way Too Sensitive": Uncovering Racial Micro-Aggressions

I see racial and gender micro-aggressions everywhere and always try to use my own commission of these as the starting point for examining this concept. So I will typically begin a class or workshop examining these by sharing my most recent micro-aggressions. Let me give two examples here. One is in an academic class on leadership where I asked all the students in a discussion to give their preliminary 'take' on an issue the course was examining. After hearing from each student I summarized what I felt were the main themes and differences revealed in the discussion. Upon finishing my summary a student raised her hand and said I'd missed out one member of the group, a young Asian American woman. I was momentarily flustered, apologized, and invited the overlooked student to speak.

During the coffee break I thought the incident over and realized it was a classic example of a micro-aggression. I certainly had no plans to exclude this student. I had not come to class thinking 'I must make certain student A doesn't have the chance to speak". And, had I been confronted with my behavior in the moment I would have denied any exclusionary intent. So when I returned to class after coffee I began the session by apologizing again and saying that what the students had just witnessed was a classic example of a racial micro-aggression. A representative of the dominant culture had unknowingly and unwittingly marginalized someone from a community of color.

One of the White students told me not to be so hard on myself and said I was reading far too much into a momentary lapse of forgetfulness. I explained that micro-aggressions are never intended. Instead, they are ingrained, seemingly instinctive behaviors that represent years of unconscious assimilation and socialization. They are ideological in the sense that they become part of our daily repertoire, behavioral minutiae that actually represent a socially ordered system of structural inequality. At this point the student I had overlooked spoke up and said that the same thing had happened to her in every class she had taken at the university. Her experience had been that of being repeatedly ignored.

The second example occurred in a professional development workshop I was running. The participants were all leaders within their own organization and we had convened for a day to examine, amongst other things, ways in which the organization could provide services that were more inclusive. At one point in the day we were talking about the influence of machismo in sport and how this connected to homophobic attitudes and I volunteered the comment that there was only one openly Gay athlete in U.S. professional sports, Robbie Rogers of the LA Galaxy soccer team.

A woman at the training immediately spoke up saying, "you mean the first gay *male* athlete" and pointed out the presence of openly gay female basketball players, including the lucrative Nike sponsorship deal just signed by Brittney Griner, the top pick in the 2013 basketball draft. We then mentioned top tennis players of the past such as Billie Jean King and Martina Navratilova. This was a wonderful example of a micro-aggression, this time one reflecting gender and patriarchy. Here was I, the paid outside 'expert' leading a workshop on inclusivity, supposedly aware of a whole range of race, class and gender inequities, and I had never thought about women as I was discussing professional sports. In effect I had dismissed a whole half of the human race without ever thinking about it!

Writing as a Tool of Narrative Pedagogy: The Use of Scholarly Personal Narratives

In the last decade or so the written narrative has been advocated and enacted by Robert Nash (2004) and a series of collaborators (Nash & Bradley, 2011; Nash and Viray, 2013, 2014) as an effective tool of education for diversity. A brief narrative of a racist incident that is put down on paper has a powerful permanence that can evoke hidden feelings far more than a conversation about the same incident. Nash and his collaborators call such writing an example of a scholarly personal narrative (SPN).

This kind of writing is a sustained exploration of one's own narrative experience of a particular question, problem or dynamic that has broader social significance. It is not telling a story of an interesting episode in your life. Whatever aspects of your narrative included in an SPN must illuminate the central question that is being explored. In a dissertation I supervised Sandra Unger (2014) wrote a narrative of her move from the white suburbs to the east side of St. Paul to found a program for Black teens called the Lift. She moved into the community and tried to build relationships with working class African Americans. That was the 'data' she drew on to write her narrative. The central problem she explored was how people of different racial identities learn to build reciprocal relationships across racial and class boundaries.

As stated, an SPN is not just a personal narrative of one's own experience, one's life history or story. The 'S' in the SPN means that this narrative moves beyond simply recounting personal experience. It insists that three 'scholarly' components be threaded throughout the study. Narratives of personal experiences in the study are included *only* if they illuminate the problem or question that has been identified. So you don't just tell your story of whatever you find interesting in your life. Writers *only* include events and experiences that speak directly to the central topic. This is why clarifying the question being explored is so crucial in the early stages, since that question drives what is included from narrative experience and what theory is consulted.

The question that explored in an SPN must be one that has wider social implications. It should refer to some important dynamic in education, leadership, or the world at large that people are trying to figure out. Nash likes to say it should focus on change or transformation of some kind. References to relevant theory that sheds light on the narrative are woven throughout the study. There is not a separate section called 'Theory', 'Research' or 'Literature Review'. Instead, the study moves back and forth between explication of the narrative and then theoretical commentary on it. This means that someone writing an SPN needs to know the different theoretical areas that might pertain to her topic very well.

It's important to emphasize that the theory that is woven throughout the narrative should ***not*** always support the narrative as it is framed. The literature should also challenge the narrative thread, give markedly different perspectives on what happened, give multiple and contrasting readings of experience, and be critical of times when the narrative is becoming too neatly contrived. In this regard the supervisor of the SPN plays a crucial role in identifying 'inconvenient' theory or research that challenges a writer's presentation of their narrative, and insisting that they respond to it.

This constant integration of theory means that the writer's narrative is always deepening and changing. As the writer considers different research and theory that illuminates and questions the way the narrative is being told, he or she continually builds that new awareness of complexity into how the narrative unfolds. Symbiotically, as new aspects of the experiences recounted are revealed, so the writer often branches into theoretical areas not identified in the initial proposal.

Up to this point this chapter has focused on the speaking and writing of personal narratives by individual instructors. Now I wish to switch my focus a little to examine how personal narratives can have even greater pedagogic effect when they used by the members of a teaching team.

The Use of Personal Narrative within Team Teaching

I have a recurring dream that goes like this. One day the President of the United States calls me. "Stephen" she says, "the country has just discovered a new energy source that ensures the national debt is wiped out and we are awash in resources. I'd like you to be the new Tsar of higher education. You can make any change you want with no budgetary restrictions. What's the first change you want to make?" I have no hesitation in replying "Madam President, I'd like to propose that – unless there's a good reason for this not being the case – every college course from now on be team taught". "Done" replies the President.

As you might guess, team teaching, properly done, is something I am passionate about. The 'properly done' caveat is crucial however. Team teaching is not two or three people agreeing to carve up a course into sections so that each person does thirty or fifty per cent of the sessions. Properly conducted, team teaching involves all members of the team planning the course, writing the syllabus, specifying learning objectives, conducting the class, and evaluating student work. This takes far more time than teaching solo. You need to coordinate, discuss and decide multiple matters as a group, something that adds considerably to your faculty load (Pharo, Davison, Warr, Nursey-Bray, Beswick, Wapstra & Jones, 2012).

Obviously within that structure leadership roles vary so that different members of the team have responsibility for teaching certain content, drafting particular assessment rubrics or running specific exercises. But every team member is in class all the time so that she or he can complement and support whatever the lead teacher is doing. This model of teaching parallels the work reality most students will face. In the information age, working in project teams is the norm, so it makes perfect sense for our pedagogy to mirror that reality.

I am such a proponent of this method because of my own experiences working in teams at multiple institutions over the past four decades. Where confronting racial dynamics in the classroom is concerned, a multiracial teaching team is best placed to illustrate how the micro-dynamics of racism play themselves out. I have also made it a point to observe teaching teams in action outside of my own discipline. As chroniclers of team teaching (Eisen & Tisdell, 2000; Ramsey, 2008; Plank, 2011) often point out, this approach has benefits for both students and teachers.

One of the problems trying to work in anti-racist ways is the lack of examples of what an honest conversation across racial differences looks like. Exhortations to conduct dialog across difference are frequent, but actual instances of this are rare. In my own work I rarely get the chance to talk publicly with colleagues from different racial and cultural backgrounds about how our racial identities enter into our exchanges and work practices. However, for several years I was an adjunct faculty member in the adult education doctoral program at National Louis University (NLU) in Chicago, where I regularly team-taught courses with Scipio A.J. Colin Jr. III, the Africentric theorist, and the late Elizabeth Peterson, both African American faculty members.

In our team teaching we would often talk about how our own racial identities framed the ways we negotiated decisions, employed different teaching approaches, and influenced how we responded to students' requests. Dr. C (as Scipio was called) would use a call and response model of communication, regularly asking the group "are you with me now?" and "are you running with me?" Elizabeth would work from a critical race theory perspective, providing the White students with illustrations of how that differed from an Africentric perspective. This was a striking counterbalance to the idea that there was a unified Black or African American perspective on adult education.

Elizabeth and I then delivered a paper at an Adult Education Research Conference (AERC) titled "Race and Racism: A Critical Dialogue" (Peterson and Brookfield, 2007). Our idea was to model a candid exchange about race in which we wove into our conversation some very specific examples of how race played itself out in our own interpersonal relations. We chose as one example an incident involving the *Harvard Educational Review* (HER). In 2002 I was a Visiting Professor at Harvard University and was asked to contribute an article to the *HER*. I suggested to the editorial board that I invite Dr. C, Elizabeth Peterson, Ian Baptiste, Juanita Johnson-Bailey and Vanessa Sheared to contribute articles along with me on the theme of racializing the discourse of adult education, and that the journal issue take the form of a symposium on that topic.

The *HER* editorial board agreed to this suggestion and we all began to write our separate pieces. A few months later the editorial board changed its membership. The new board told us that now the symposium would take the form of a main article written by me, with commentaries on my piece submitted by my colleagues. So now we were faced with Stephen Brookfield's piece being the central academic sun around which the contributions from the scholars of color would revolve. Not surprisingly my colleagues all dropped out from the project. As Elizabeth said in the dialog we had "I can remember feeling like I'd been slapped in the face when it was suggested that your article would be featured and we, as African American scholars, would be invited to respond to it" (Peterson & Brookfield, 2007, p. 5). I went ahead and published my own article reasoning that at a minimum it would be good to have a piece on racializing the discourse of adult education in the *HER*. I still don't know if that was the right thing to do.

Team Teaching Reaches a Wider Variety of Learners

Solo teachers teach out of their preferred learning style and their individual experience. Although we can all expand our repertoire of teaching practices, there is a limit to how much we can change who we are. Moreover, no matter how many books on White racism we read, or how many conversations we have with people of color, we can never claim to be inside that experience. My own positionality as an English male, and more specifically my own racial membership as White, is an important element to acknowledge in this chapter. In their analysis of Black intellectual life Cornel West and bell hooks discuss the ways in which, according to hooks, "White theorists draw upon our work and our ideas, and get forms of recognition that are denied Black thinkers" (hooks and West, 1991, p. 36). She speaks of how "there is a feeling now that a White academic might take your idea, write about it, and you'll never be cited" (West 1991.).

In the same conversation West observes "White scholars are bringing certain baggage with them when they look at Black culture, no matter how subtle and sophisticated the formulations" (West 1991.). I have learned that the baggage of my racial membership and identity means I cannot be an Africentric theorist whose being, identity and practice spring from African values, sensibilities and traditions. I can appreciate the accuracy and explanatory power of something like Du Bois' concept of double consciousness. In so doing I can reflect on how being both African and American means that one is "always looking at oneself through the eyes of others, of measuring one's soul by the tape of the world that looks on in amused contempt and pity" (Du Bois, 1969, p. 45). But though this may illuminate what some of my learners and colleagues are experiencing I can have no real understanding of what this means.

As a White Englishman I have no experiential, visceral access to the philosophy born of struggle that comprises the central dimension of African American thought. My skin pigmentation, White privilege and collusion in racism places me irrevocably and irretrievably outside the Africentric paradigm. I can learn from, and honor, this scholarship. I can be grateful for the way it questions and reformulates aspects of critical theory, or the way it shatters (in a helpful way) my own understandings and practices. But I can never claim to work as an Africentric adult educator. No matter how much I wish to honor this tradition, my racial membership precludes me making such a claim. In the words of a provocative volume, it is problematic to be *Teaching What You're Not* (Mayberry, 1996).

But what I *can* do with some credibility is talk about how I have learned the ideology of White supremacy very efficiently. After all, I have been immersed in it for over six decades, had it rammed down my throat at times, and experienced how it is subtly communicated at others. I can't turn myself into a person of color and I can't use whatever slights I've suffered as an analog of racism. Neither can I become a methodological exemplar of different culturally grounded ways of teaching. I like words so I tend to teach with words. I like order so I tend to teach with lists and itemized classroom agendas. I'm not a visual teacher ready to incorporate body movement into my teaching and I'm not a Whizz at social media. I can try to broaden my skills to incorporate elements of these things but I'm always working from within the framework of who I am as a person.

But add another one or two teachers to the classroom and the experiential background of instruction broadens, as does the range of personalities involved. As an introvert I work well with extraverted colleagues. I can call for pauses and silence in class in a way that extraverts don't. My extraverted colleague can give necessary presentations with greater punch and energy than I'm capable of. As a White I can talk with some authority about how Whites learn racist attitudes, how we don't notice our racial microaggressions, and how we think of diversity and racism as something that 'they' – people of color – are affected by, not us.

When a person of color teaches this material with me, or when we lead a discussion or workshop together, the whole dynamic changes. If we know something of each other's history and experience, and if each member of the team knows each other's methodological preferences, habits and styles, we can keep in mind the need to provide a breadth of instructional approaches. I like to teach through narrative disclosure but have often taught with someone who is a strong theorist. He kept me from overdoing a self-indulgent use of autobiography, and I was able to punctuate his wholly theoretical explanations with narrative examples. Because we knew each of us had these tendencies this alternation worked. We were able to let students know that we brought different things to the pedagogic table.

Team Teaching Models Respectful Disagreement

One of the meta-agendas of higher education is teaching students how to disagree in ways that don't shut down further communication. Models of student development (Evans, Forney, Guido, Patton & Renn, 2010; Jones & Abes, 2013) stress the movement students make from dualistic, right/wrong thinking, through multiplistic relativity, to arrive at a stage of informed commitment. This movement involves learning to live with contradiction and disagreement, something Basseches (2005) explores in his work on the development of dialectical thinking in young adults. He reports how difficult it is for students to hold two contradictory ideas in tension without needing to decide that one is definitively correct and one clearly wrong.

A teaching team can model how to explore a dialectical tension by providing a variety of narratives on a common racial dynamic, stating the different understandings embedded in these narratives, and then demonstrating how each member strives to comprehend the other's viewpoint. Members can summarize each other's arguments, check that they've understood these correctly, and ask questions designed to elicit why these views are held. They can then critique these positions and end by summarizing how the discussion has confirmed and challenged their perspective.

As I have already emphasized this dynamic is crucial when it comes to teaching about racism. We can't expect students to explore raw and contentious issues unless we have shown them we're doing this too. But an added benefit of team teaching is that it allows you to demonstrate and enforce conversational protocols that stand a chance of keeping discussion going. For example, one of the most fundamental ways to demonstrate respect is to communicate to someone that you are actually listening to their narrative. The behavior that lies at the root of such respect is asking good questions; questions that are grounded in someone' earlier comments in the narrative, that seek to understand a key turning point in the narrative, and that express a genuine curiosity regarding how the narrative will unfold.

One of the quickest ways to shut down racial discussion is to move to declarative statements. These are statements that assert one's position, that try to convert people to agreeing with your views, and that, in the face of contrary evidence, are maintained with even greater ferocity. So a useful exercise is to require people only to ask questions that seek to understand another's view by only asking for more information. Typical questions are; 'What leads you to believe that?' What's the strongest piece of evidence you have for that view? Can you tell me more about how you came to that position? How would you respond to 'A's counter argument? These questions are particularly suited to narrative analysis.

Good narrative questions also grow out statements and descriptions already conveyed in the narrative. When a questioner circles back to something someone has said and asks them to develop a sub-point, or when someone asks how two of the events you've described in the narrative connect to each other, it's clear to the storyteller that their arguments are heard. A teaching team can model asking these kinds of questions about each other's narratives in front of students.

A useful way to illustrate the complexity of racially based narratives is to post two or three stations around the room, each of which represents a distinctive position, theory or analytical framework that can be taken when analyzing a narrative. After one of the team has disclosed a particular narrative of an experience of racism the other team members can stand at these geographically separate stations and analyze that narrative – explaining its meaning and identifying its salient points - only in the voice of someone who holds the view represented by that station. So, for example, one instructor can stand under a sign saying 'Critical Race Theory', one under 'Post Racial Society' and one under 'Color Blind'. They then hold a conversation about the narrative as if each of them was bringing only the viewpoint represented by their sign to their discussion of its significance.

Bringing different perspectives to bear on the same piece of content (in this case to the same narrative) is probably the most frequently cited reason for team teaching (Eisen & Tisdell, 2000; Plank, 2011). When a solo teacher tries to convey the different viewpoints or theoretical frameworks that exist he or she is always working within the confines of being a singular voice. Nothing beats team teaching for conveying complexity properly. Team teaching allows your partner to pose a question or contribute an insight that opens you up to a genuinely new way of thinking about something. After all, it's not just students who are learning about the subject in a team taught classroom.

Team Teaching Creates a Learning Environment of Risk and Uncertainty

Discussing how racist ideas and behaviors are learned, and how they remain embedded in everyday actions and wider social structures, is often unsettling to students. But since college is a "dynamic, complex and often unsettling place" (Plank, 2011, p. 3) this dissonance can be productive. In team teaching there is no one clear source of authority and knowledge in the classroom. This can create an environment of discovery and inquiry. For example, Ouellett and Fraser (2011) in their analysis of interracial team teaching describe how one of them would have an unplanned idea in the middle of the class and ask the other in front of the students if she or he would be willing to try something new, on the spot. As they report "we were committed to modeling the intellectual and social learning and risk taking we were asking of students" (p. 76).

Risk-taking involves uncertainty and pause. When a colleague asks me a question about my narrative description in front of the students and I don't have a good answer on the tip of my tongue, I say that I need a moment's pause to think about this before replying. I always try to take plenty of time to think about my response as a way of socializing students to be more comfortable with periods of silence in class. Sometimes I will then say "you know I don't have a good response for that question, I need to think more about it – can we come back to it later?" Alternatively, I will state my answer hesitatingly, maybe saying something like "I'm not really sure how to answer that, but as a first pass what I'm thinking might be the case is A." Students need models of pause and hesitation just as much as they need confident declarations of your disciplinary authority. Team teaching allows students to see how we stumble, pause, and double back as we try on new perspectives or understandings. And understanding racism involves many unexpected turns, dead ends and short cuts.

Sometimes team teachers can disclose how learned racism has framed their interactions. When I teach with colleagues of color I like to discuss in front of the class the way our identities and racial formations have caused problems in our communication. Publicly revealing my own specific micro-aggressions enacted in a teaching team, and asking colleagues and students to critique my actions, entails a level of extreme discomfort on my part. I still have a hard time hearing my actions described as racist, even though cognitively I am in full agreement with that judgment. Laying bare one's own racism as a narrative teaching tool carries the risk of people shutting their ears to any future comments you might make. There is the risk of one's racist behaviors being reported to superiors. Also, you never know how your colleagues will negotiate a conversation in which your, and their, racially based perceptions and judgments are publicly dissected.

When it comes to exploring racial dynamics people are so afraid of saying the wrong thing and being thought of as racist that conversation is inevitably stilted, full of pauses and hesitations. These should not be thought of as instances where the discussion goes awry, but as the natural rhythm when dealing with something as contentious as race. You need to slow the pace down and take plenty of time to think before you speak. The model of effective discussions that seems to hold sway in higher education is one of seamless and animated conversation, with people speaking over the top of each other as they jump in to make their point. Conversations about race will sometimes be likes this. But just as easily they can be disjointed and full of silences. A team talking about race can show they are comfortable with silence and that sometimes they need time to sit with a comment or question before responding to it.

When a team tries to conduct a public conversation regarding their own racial dynamics, and the way that racial factors and racist attitudes influence the ways they make decisions, there is a strong element of unpredictability. Not only are you uncertain how colleagues are going to respond as the discussion deepens, but it is impossible to predict how students will react. Classrooms will often close down as students are unsure how to respond or contribute and as the level of uncertainty rises. I have had White students tell me that they daren't speak because everything they say will be seen as racist, and students of color ask me to stop talking about race due to the deepened racism those conversations produce.

CONCLUSION

In this chapter I have argued that racism is learned through family, media, school and friendships as the ideology of White supremacy seeps into our consciousness. Even Whites like myself who like to think of themselves as anti-racist frequently commit micro-aggressions that remain unacknowledged until a colleague brings them to our attention. Disruptive classroom events can heighten our awareness of these and they can be challenged through narrative disclosure, particularly in team teaching.

Illuminating how racism works on a systemic level is enormously complex and involves drawing upon highly theoretical literature such as critical theory, post-structuralism and post-colonialism. Personal narrative disclosure is an effective teaching approach to break through this theoretical fog and illustrate the relevance of particular concepts. Repressive tolerance, micro-aggressions, the way White supremacy is manifested – all these 'big ideas can be encapsulated in a description of a singular critical incident. So in all kinds of training, teaching and professional development situations the use of spoken, or written (such as SPN's) narratives can bring an intimidating topic to life. When leaders and instructors tell stories about their own experiences of enacting or confronting racism this brings complex concepts down to earth. It also sets a tone for similar disclosure by participants and learners.

Add the dimension of team teaching to this method and you have an effective way to bring a group much more quickly to a point where they are ready to examine racism. An instructional team can use their own narratives of identity formation and racial experiences to illustrate central concepts of racism, identity and White supremacy. And they can model a discussion of how they negotiate different racially and culturally formed viewpoints on racial dynamics.

REFERENCES

Basseches, M. (2005). The development of dialectical thinking as an approach to integration. *Integral Review, 1*, 47–63.

Brookfield, S. D. (2004). *The power of critical theory: Liberating adult learning and teaching.* San Francisco: Jossey-Bass.

Cox, T. Jr. (2001). *Creating the multicultural organization: A strategy for capturing the power of diversity.* San Francisco: Jossey-Bass.

Du Bois, W. E. B. (1995). *The souls of Black folk.* New York: New American Library. (Original work published 1903)

Duchovic, R. J. (2011). Lessons learned from an interdisciplinary course in undergraduate science. In K. M. Plank (Ed.), *Team teaching: Across the disciplines, across the academy* (pp. 97–118). Sterling, VA: Stylus Publishing.

Eisen, M., & Tisdell, E. J. (Eds.). (2000). *Team teaching and learning in adult education. New Directions for Adult and Continuing Education, 87.* San Francisco: Jossey-Bass.

European American Collaborative Challenging Whiteness. (2010). White on white: Developing capacity to communicate about race with critical humility. In V. Sheared, J. Johnson-Bailey, S. A. J. Colin III, E. Peterson, & S. Brookfield (Eds.), *The handbook of race and adult education: A resource for dialogue on racism.* San Francisco: Jossey-Bass.

Evans, N. J., Forney, D. S., Guido, F. M., Patton, L. D., & Renn, K. A. (2010). *Student development in college: Theory, research and practice.* San Francisco: Jossey-Bass.

Habermas, J. (1987). *The theory of communicative action: Volume two, lifeworld and system – A critique of functionalist reason.* Boston: Beacon Press.

hooks, b. & West, C. 1991. *Breaking bread: Insurgent Black intellectual life.* Boston: South End Press.

Horkheimer, M., & Adorno, T. (1972). *Dialectic of enlightenment.* New York: Seabury Press.

Jessen-Marshall, A., & Lescinsky, H. L. (2011). Team teaching in the sciences. In K. M. Plank (Ed.), *Team teaching: Across the disciplines, across the academy* (pp. 13–35). Sterling, VA: Stylus Publishing.

Jones, S. R., & Abes, E. S. (2013). *Identity development of college students: Advancing frameworks for multiple dimensions of identity.* San Francisco: Jossey-Bass.

Mandela, N. (1994). *Long walk to freedom: The autobiography of Nelson Mandela.* Boston: Little Brown.

Marcuse, H. (1964). *One dimensional man.* Boston: Beacon.

Mayberry, K. J. (Ed.). (1996). *Teaching what you're not: Identity politics in higher education.* New York: New York University Press.

Nash, R. J. (2004). *Liberating scholarly Writing: The power of personal narrative.* New York: Teachers College Press.

Nash, R. J., & Bradley, D. L. (2011). *Me-search and re-search: A guide for writing scholarly personal narratives*. Charlotte, NC: Information Age Publishing.

Nash, R. J., & Viray, S. (2013). *Our stories matter: Liberating the voices of marginalized students through scholarly personal writing*. New York: Peter Lang.

Nash, R. J., & Viray, S. (2014). *How stories heal: Writing our way to meaning and wholeness in the academy*. New York: Peter Lang.

Ouellett, M. L., & Fraser, E. (2011). Interracial team teaching in social work. In K. M. Plank (Ed.), *Team teaching: Across the disciplines, across the academy* (pp. 73–90). Sterling, VA: Stylus Publishing.

Peterson, E., & Brookfield, S. (2007). Race and racism: A critical dialog. *Proceedings of the 45th Adult education research conference*. Halifax, Nova Scotia: Department of Adult Education, Mount Saint Vincent University.

Pharo, E. J., Davison, A., Warr, K., Nursey-Bray, M., Beswick, K., Wapstra, E., & Jones, C. (2012). Can teacher collaboration overcome barriers to interdiscplinary learning in a disciplinary university? A case study using climate change. *Teaching in Higher Education, 17*(5), 497–507. doi:10.1080/1356 2517.2012.658560

Plank, K. M. (Ed.). (2011). *Team teaching: Across the disciplines, across the academy*. Sterling, VA: Stylus Publishing.

Ramsey, J. (2008). But can we trust the Lord? Using team-teaching to model trust within and beyond the classroom. In M. J. Hess & S. D. Brookfield (Eds.), *Teaching reflectively in theological contexts: Promises and contradictions*. Malabar, Florida: Krieger Publishers.

Sue, D. R. (2010). *Microaggressions in everyday life: Race, gender and sexual orientation*. San Francisco: Jossey-Bass.

Unger, S. 2014. *We Shouldn't Even Know Each Other: A Scholarly Personal Narrative of the Development of Deeply Reciprocal Relationships Across Differences of Race and Class* [Unpublished Dissertation]. Minneapolis-St. Paul, MN: Department of Educational Leadership, University of Saint Thomas.

ADDITIONAL READING

Nash, R. J., & Viray, S. (2014). *How stories heal: Writing our way to meaning and wholeness in the academy*. New York: Peter Lang.

Plank, K. M. (Ed.), (2011). *Team teaching: Across the disciplines, across the academy*. Sterling, VA: Stylus Publishing.

Sheared, V., Johnson-Bailey, J., Colin, S. A. J. III, Peterson, E., & Brookfield, S. (Eds.). (2010). *The handbook of race and adult education: A resource for dialogue on racism*. San Francisco: Jossey-Bass.

Sue, D. W. (2015). *Race talk: Uncovering the conspiracy of silence*. San Francisco: Jossey-Bass.

KEY TERMS AND DEFINITIONS

Critical Theory: A body of ideas developed by the Frankfurt School that illustrates how an iniquitous social system is rendered normal through the dissemination of dominant ideology.

Micro-Aggressions: Small, subtle daily acts of exclusion that often leave receivers asking 'did that really happen?' or 'am I imagining that?' When identified as aggressions these acts are strongly denied by the perpetrator who insists there is no malicious intent and the receiver is being overly sensitive.

Racism: The systemic exclusion and diminishment of a group of people solely by phenotype. Although expressed in individual action, racism is embedded in institutional policy and functioning.

Repressive Tolerance: The mechanism by which a system appears to change in response to challenges from below whilst concealing the fact that the status quo remains intact.

Scholarly Personal Narrative: A mode of writing that explores personal experience, and research informing that experience, to examine a social change dynamic.

Team-Teaching: Teaching in which two or more instructors collaboratively design curricula, develop teaching plans, conduct class sessions and evaluate students' work. Although individual teachers may take the lead in class their colleagues are always present.

White Supremacy: The ideology that Whites, due to their superior powers of reasoning, evolved morality and innate intelligence, deserve to be the 'natural' leaders and power holders in a system.

This research was previously published in Developing Workforce Diversity Programs, Curriculum, and Degrees in Higher Education edited by Chaunda L. Scott and Jeanetta D. Sims; pages 98-116, copyright year 2016 by Information Science Reference (an imprint of IGI Global).

Chapter 38
Preparing Urban Educators to Address Diversity and Equity through Field-Based Teacher Education:
Implications for Program Design and Implementation

Adam S. Kennedy
Loyola University, USA

Amy J. Heineke
Loyola University, USA

ABSTRACT

This chapter presents a case for field-based teacher preparation through mutually beneficial community partnerships in diverse urban contexts. Such models are a response to calls for change in teacher education, as well as to current policies and research on the central role of field experiences. Extant research is shared on partnerships as a key context for developing programs with depth, effectiveness, and sustainability. Next, information is presented about the development and implementation of one field-based teacher education program designed around mutually beneficial partnerships to prepare effective urban educators. Key themes and practices are demonstrated through data-based vignettes of collaborative field experiences with urban educators. These cases involve unique preparation experiences, stakeholders, and roles, but also serve as illustrations of the ways in which partnerships aimed at achieving mutual benefit must undergo continuous evaluation and redesign. Recommendations for iterative design and implementation of field-based models are offered.

DOI: 10.4018/978-1-7998-1213-5.ch038

INTRODUCTION

Intensified, carefully designed and continuously supervised field-based experiences have long been a cornerstone of teacher preparation. Not only do they provide opportunities for teacher candidates to develop essential knowledge and skills, but they are also aligned with current teacher preparation policy and viewed as both authentic and beneficial to schools and other types of community partners. Field-based teacher education presents one solution to the problem of preparing effective teachers in light of the culturally and linguistically diverse contexts of schools in the United States (U.S.). However, little is known about the necessary supports, design processes, or features of teacher education models which rely entirely on rich clinical experiences to prepare teachers. The objectives of this chapter are to:

- Describe the ways in which shifting policies and emerging research have informed the development and implementation of one field-based teacher education program, Teaching, Learning, and Leading with Schools and Communities (TLLSC), designed around mutually beneficial partnerships to prepare effective urban educators (Ryan et al., 2014).
- Illustrate key practices, themes, and outcomes through data-based vignettes of collaborative, field experiences with urban educators, particularly focused on those serving culturally and linguistically diverse children and children with special needs.
- Share recommendations to inform continuous evaluation and redesign of field-based community partnership models.

BACKGROUND

The field of teacher education in the U.S. faces complex and dynamic changes in both micro-level student demographics and macro-level policies, as well in our understanding of the links between theory, preparation, and practice. Over the past decades, the demographics of the U.S. population have changed dramatically. In 2012, enrollment in public elementary and secondary schools consisted of 51% White, 24% Hispanic, 16% Black, and 5% Asian/Pacific Islanders and smaller percentages of American Indian and multiracial students. The percentage of White students has continued to decline; by 2024, the number and percentage of White students enrolled in public schools is projected to reach 46%, with Hispanic students increasing to 29% and Asian/Pacific Islander students increasing to 6% (National Center for Education Statistics; NCES, 2015). These cultural shifts have been accompanied by increased linguistic diversity (Gándara & Hopkins, 2010). English Learners (ELs) comprise more than 10% of the Pre-Kindergarten-through-grade-12 (P-12) student population, with proportions varying significantly by state and region but continuing to rise. The states with highest EL enrollment serve from 5% to as many as 25% ELs; representation at the school district level is as high as 50% (Ruiz Soto, Hooker, & Batalova, 2015). Teacher diversity has not maintained the same trend. The majority of P-12 teachers remain White, middle-class women, and this majority continues to grow younger and less experienced as veteran teachers leave the field (National Center for Education Information, 2011).

These changes in student demographics have occurred during challenging political times, as the accountability movement in education has expanded its lens to include not only P-12 education, but teacher education as well. In P-12 schools, the accountability movement is characterized by standards and standardized testing, such as the Common Core Standards (CCS) and Partnership of Assessment for Readiness for College and Careers (PARCC). Additionally, school and district administrators use the Danielson framework (2011) to evaluate teachers' practice, including the use of student achievement data on standardized tests. Despite ample critiques of these value-added measures (e.g., Floden, 2012), recently proposed regulations from the U.S. Department of Education would extend federal accountability to teacher education. These proposed regulations emphasize the use of state-determined indicators of quality to assess the performance of teacher education programs, tying program quality ratings to federal funding. Particularly, using the value-added model, teacher education programs would be rated and federally funded based on graduates' ability to procure gains in P-12 student learning as measured by standardized test scores (AACTE, 2015).

Within these shifts in U.S. education, both the diversifying student population and the increasingly political scrutiny, teacher educators must critically consider their preparation practices with teacher candidates. No universally effective common curriculum exists for the initial preparation of teachers at any level of P-12 education; furthermore, a lack of agreement exists as to the specific competencies all new teachers must possess to enter the field. In an era of redesign and realignment with new teacher education standards, the persistent question of how to prepare effective and resilient teachers remains challenging to answer when key questions regarding outcomes and effectiveness remain underexplored (Cochran-Smith & Zeichner, 2010; Whitebook et al., 2012). Additionally, teacher educators must prepare candidates for culturally and linguistically diverse populations, tapping into the rich and unique funds of knowledge of students and families within their communities (AACTE, 2004, 2010; Farell, 2005; Heineke, Kennedy, & Lees, 2013; Moll & Gonzalez, 1997). Teacher education is increasingly a field of many different pathways and degrees, thus compounding the challenges of intentional redesign and substantive systemic change (Whitebook et al., 2012); in other words, the student population continues to change at a more rapid pace than any effort to standardize teacher preparation can keep up with. Still, scholars and policymakers send consistent, universal messages that teacher education must emphasize collaborative problem-solving and redesign of programs to involve school and community stakeholders (AACTE, 2004; Rust, 2010; Zeichner, 2010).

Building intensified, purposeful field-based experiences has been identified repeatedly as a key strategy for preparing candidates to enter the field with the necessary knowledge and skills to serve diverse children, families, and communities (Lim & Able-Boone, 2005; McDonald et al., 2011; Rust, 2010). Nevertheless, teacher educators utilize the term field experiences in a variety of ways within their preparation programs, often in the more traditional sense of teacher candidates spending a set number of hours spent in the field. Going beyond this time-based approach to fieldwork as an add-on to university-based coursework, field-based teacher education programs are built around objectives-based opportunities for candidates to work alongside practicing teachers throughout their preparation, with opportunities to build teaching skills under the dual supervision of classroom teachers and university faculty (Kennedy & Heineke, 2014). When such models are grounded in close partnerships between community schools and teacher education programs, they are much more likely to provide the types of intensive and closely supervised field experiences that characterize high-quality preparation (AACTE, 2012). Alternative certification programs such as Teach for America do not meet this standard.

Field-based teacher education builds upon research linking the quality of field experiences to enhanced readiness to teach upon entering the profession (e.g., McDonald et al. 2011; Zeichner 2010). Authentic field experiences have been extensively linked to positive outcomes in P-12, including teacher retention and satisfaction, teacher-student relationships, classroom climate, and student learning (AACTE, 2010; Adams & Wolf, 2008; LaParo, Thomason, Maynard, & Scott-

Little, 2012; McDonald et al., 2011; Rust, 2010). Field-based models expand and deepen the role of teaching in teacher preparation, exposing teacher candidates to diverse schools and communities throughout their preparation, with opportunities to link research and theory to practice under the guidance of both practicing teachers and university faculty (Zeichner, 2010). Pre-service teachers and faculty work within the shared spaces of schools and community agencies, emphasizing direct experiences over coursework and thus requiring new roles for all stakeholders, including practicing teachers (Heineke, Kennedy, & Lees, 2013; Kennedy & Heineke, 2014), including teachers and administrators have traditionally been viewed as "hosts" for students (Chang, Early, & Winton 2005). Such models involve a deeply shared commitment across stakeholders to support preservice teachers in the field.

While field-based models show promise, evidence of their effectiveness, and an indication of the work involved in developing and sustaining them, are still scarce (Zeichner 2010). The sections to follow present processes, challenges, barriers, and solutions associated with the development, implementation, and systematic study of field-based teacher education, using one model: Teaching, Learning, and Leading with Schools and Communities, offered through the School of Education at Loyola University Chicago and situated in the communities, agencies, and schools of Chicago, Illinois.

TEACHING, LEARNING AND LEADING WITH SCHOOLS AND COMMUNITIES (TLLSC)

Introduction

TLLSC (Ryan et al., 2014) is an innovative approach to teacher education at Loyola University Chicago, a private, urban, Jesuit university in Chicago, Illinois. With 58 community and school partners, 24 full time faculty members, and about 270 undergraduate candidates, TLLSC is an example of teacher education anchored in collaboration between university, schools, and community organizations (Kennedy & Heineke, 2014). Based upon a shared recognition of the need to rethink and rebuild a formerly traditional foundations-methods-clinicals model of teacher education (NCATE, 2010), TLLSC was developed to prepare teachers to support the development, learning, and needs of diverse children within the complex, changing realities of urban schools and communities (Kennedy & Heineke, 2014; Ryan et al., 2014). In this way, rather than delivering coursework on campus for the bulk of teacher candidates' preparation program with disjointed clinical experiences prior to student teaching (Cochran-Smith & Zeichner, 2005; Wilson, Floden, & Ferrini-Mundy, 2001), TLLSC faculty endeavored to situate teacher education in the field where four full years of P-12 teaching, learning, and leading occur in daily practice. This effort required awareness of and access to the rich urban context and all of its challenges in order to engage teacher candidates with students and families from diverse cultural, linguistic, ability, socioeconomic, and religious backgrounds (Heineke, Kennedy, & Lees, 2013). Table 1 presents some of the differences between TLLSC and traditional teacher education programs. Universal dimensions of teacher preparation are presented in the center column, with each row representing a continuum with traditional university-based preparation on the left and the aims of TLLSC on the right.

Table 1. Comparison of TLLSC and traditional university-based teacher education programs

Traditional Approaches	Dimension	TLLSC
Course-based with clinical experiences	Format	Universal four-year continuum of field-based sequences with supporting courses
Foundational coursework with later methods courses and clinical experiences	Model	Field experiences address multiple interrelated themes and competencies in authentic settings; field-based learning begins first semester of freshman year
Instructors work largely independently, with assignments and field experiences linked to individual courses	Integration of knowledge and skills	University and field-based instructors collaborate regularly and share linked activities and assignments with students via a single shared calendar each semester
Faculty teach university courses	Faculty supervision	Faculty travel with candidates to each site every day, and directly supervise field-based sequences
Teachers host pre-service teachers, who complete observation and practicum hours	Role of teacher mentors	Teachers meet with faculty throughout and model, support, and provide feedback on a daily basis
School and center administrators approve and place pre-service teachers	Role of school-based administrators	Administrators collaborate throughout design and redesign processes to ensure mutual benefit

(Kennedy & Heineke, 2014; Ryan et al., 2015)

Theoretical Framework

Grounded in sociocultural theory (Vygotsky, 1978), TLLSC utilizes a *field-based apprenticeship* framework (Kennedy & Heineke, 2014; Rogoff, 1994), which emphasizes the developmental process of teacher learning as situated in and influenced by the unique social and cultural context of P-12 urban schools. Within a framework of cognitive and *field-based apprenticeship* (Brown, Collins, & Duguid, 1989; Rogoff, 1994), TLLSC candidates engage in increasingly sophisticated and authentic practices that make up the dynamic work of teaching (Ball & Forzani, 2009) in partnerships with schools and communities with a goal of mutual benefit (Kruger et al., 2009). Through engagement in a professional preparation continuum (Feiman-Nemser, 2012) of modules and sequences planned with a backward design process (Wiggins & McTighe, 2005) around enduring understandings and related knowledge, skill, and disposition indicators, as well as participation in professional learning communities (PLCs), candidates evolve as adaptive and responsive professionals that effectively meet the needs of all students (García et al., 2010). Within this broader framework (which will be described in greater detail in partner vignettes), TLLSC utilizes four conceptual cornerstones to guide the collaborative preparation of teacher candidates. Depicted in Figure 1, these cornerstones reflect the collective knowledge base regarding the role of field experiences in the preparation of knowledgeable and skilled teachers.

The first conceptual cornerstone, reciprocal mutually beneficial partnerships with schools and communities, recognizes that teacher preparation requires an *all hands on deck* approach, where university, school, and community partners share responsibility to prepare effective educators (Kruger et al., 2009; Zeichner, 2006). The second cornerstone, stakeholders engaged in communities of practice, recognizes that teacher learning occurs through authentic practice with professional apprenticeship within practicing communities (Rogoff, 1994). The third cornerstone, teacher preparation for diverse classrooms, demonstrates our shared belief that *all* teachers must be prepared to serve *all* learners from diverse social, emotional, behavioral, cognitive, cultural, and linguistic backgrounds (Heineke, Kennedy, & Lees, 2013). Guided by these principles, TLLSC embeds teacher preparation in diverse, urban schools and communi-

Figure 1. Cornerstones of field-based teacher education

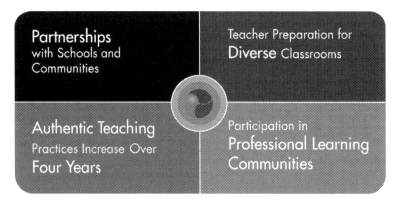

ties to provide candidates with extensive opportunities to work alongside educators, students, and parents in high-need, high-performing educational settings. Apprenticed by multiple experts in the field, we prepare teachers with adaptive expertise and flexible teaching repertoires to meet the multifaceted and unique needs of students. The fourth cornerstone reflects a recognition of the developmental trajectory of teacher preparation, and a shared understanding that expertise is not an endpoint, but a continual growth cycle as teachers' progress and respond to the dynamic nature of the profession (Ball & Forzani, 2009).

Figure 2 depicts the conceptual model of teacher development for diversity and equity in TLLSC. The teacher candidate is represented inside a large sphere of potential influence; each semester applies layers of experience in teaching, learning, and leadership, deepening candidates' knowledge and skills within education settings and communities. Over four undergraduate years, candidates expand their influence within the same community contexts that nurture their development as teachers, and in the same ways that practicing educators influence their own communities. The previously described components of the TLLSC theoretical framework are the engines that drive that process of growing effectiveness and influence.

The emphasis on practices for diverse learners and responsiveness of faculty to the needs of each partnership allow for issues of diversity and equity to be addressed continuously and in real time. The development of these partnerships must involve explicit outlining of the essential underlying universal beliefs and considerations (labeled Enduring Understandings in Figure 2) of effective teaching for all learners. Within community partnerships, teacher educators (including faculty and practicing teachers) then may collaborate to facilitate candidates' development of knowledge and skills over time in both universal major-specific modules. As knowledge and skills grow, so does the influence of the candidate and of the field-based model.

The Four-Year Continuum of TLLSC

In TLLSC, the development of candidates' professionalism is fostered through adaptive teaching, reflective learning, and responsive leading (Feiman-Nemser, 2012). Expertise develops most effectively through interaction; therefore, the program promotes intrapersonal development through reflection, as well as interaction with candidates and professionals in schools and communities (García et al., 2010). In the initial exploration phase, which spans three semesters, candidates learn theory and practice for diverse

Preparing Urban Educators to Address Diversity and Equity through Field-Based Teacher Education

Figure 2. Conceptual model of teacher development for diversity and equity

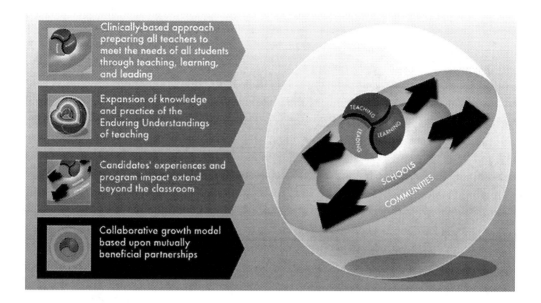

students spanning the birth to grade 12 spectrum, taking part in a variety of school and community field experiences. In the concentration phase, which spans three semesters, candidates become experts in their selected program of study by honing in on knowledge and skills specific to early childhood, elementary, secondary, special education, or bilingual education. Candidates then enter the specialization phase in the final year and participate in one-year internships in diverse urban classrooms. The final phase integrates the multiple facets of student diversity into daily teaching and learning.

Figure 3 displays the universal four-year TLLSC continuum for early childhood special education, one of the five program areas in which undergraduate teacher candidates may specialize (the others consist of elementary, secondary, special education, and bilingual/bicultural education). This Figure will be referenced throughout the remaining sections of this chapter, as it illustrates an example of the three universal TLLSC phases of preparation (depicted in the top row of the Figure 1), as well as the universal semester-long sequences (semesters, displayed as nested spherical layers of field-experiences), along with examples of program-specific adjustments and additions made to address the licensing requirements of a particular major area.

As it emerged from a process of bottom-up redesign, TLLSC uses unique components and nomenclature; these are presented and defined in Figure 4. TLLSC consists of:

- Eight semester-long *sequences*, consisting of twelve weeks of field-based learning followed by three weeks of Professional Learning Communities, in which candidates collaborate with each other and with program area faculty to engage in inquiry, professional development, mentoring activities, group presentations, and other experiences (which vary by program area and from year to year);
- *Modules* (time-limited field-based learning experiences) of varying length, of which each sequence is comprised;

Figure 3. The TLLSC continuum
(Heineke, Kennedy, & Lees, 2014)

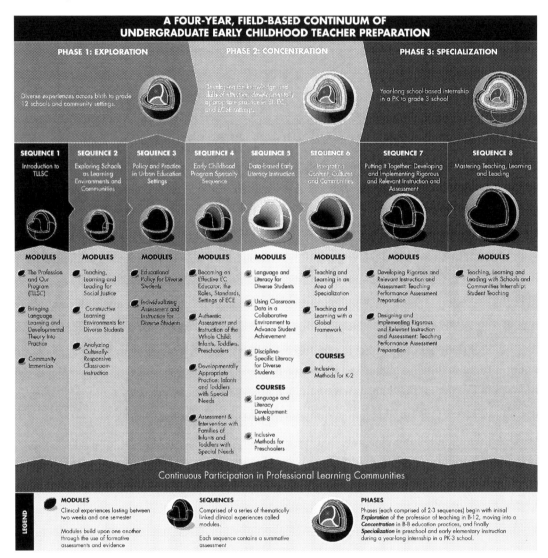

- A handful of *courses*, which address program-specific requirements for licensure or, in some cases, support a specific program sequence;
- Eleven collaboratively developed *Enduring Understandings (or EUs)* of teaching, to which each sequence and its modules are mapped. Each EU (and the knowledge and skills associated with it) is also mapped across the program continuum. For example, EU2 (which emphasizes professional collaboration to ensure optimal development, academic success, and emotional well-being of learners) is addressed (and assessed) at the *exploration, concentration*, and *specialization* phases.

TLLSC was created over a period of two years, requiring ample time and, effort, collaboration, and coordination to initiate, design, and implement. In a bottom-up, collaborative effort between university faculty and administrators, as well as school and community leaders, university faculty engaged in an

Figure 4. Components of the TLLSC model

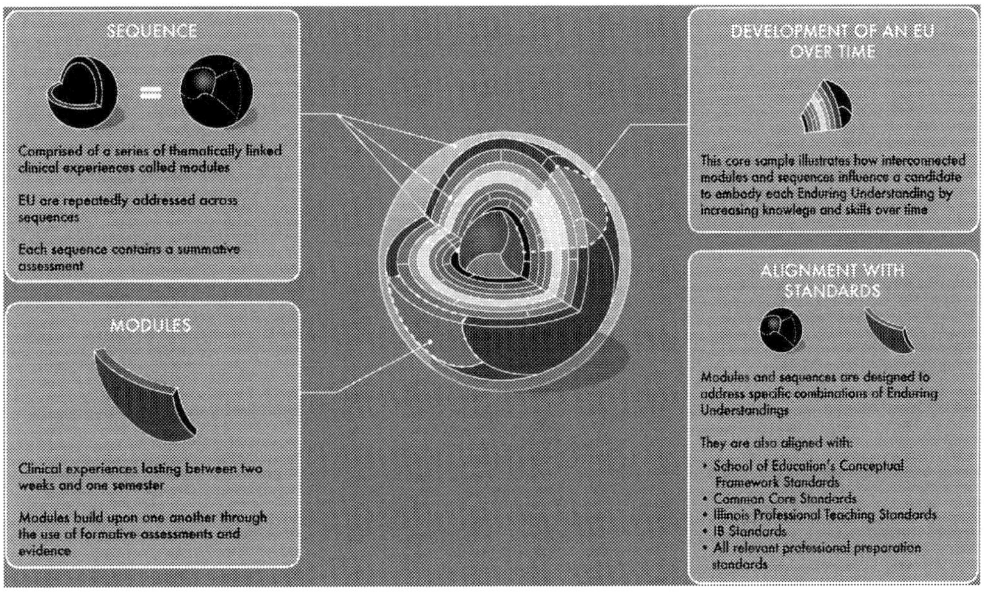

extensive program design process across three years. In the sections to follow, program design and implementation are discussed, focusing first on the micro-level shifts and steps needed to effectively transform a teacher education program at the macro-level.

Collaborative Program Design of Field-Based Teacher Education

Throughout the collaborative program design, faculty engaged in systemic self-study research (Hamilton, Pinnegar, Russell, Loughran, & LaBoskey, 1998; Lunenberg, Zwart, & Korthagen, 2010). In this way, they collected data to capture the individual, interpersonal, and institutional shifts throughout the process, such as individual written reflections, audio-recorded collaborative planning sessions, and institutional documentation and communication. Drawing from these data, the following sub-sections highlight six design steps that proved integral to successful to the TLLSC program: (a) considering institutional supports and structures, (b) designing teacher education curriculum, (c) refining the program with external resources, (d) developing professional knowledge and skills, and (e) strengthening and building partnerships.

Considering Institutional Supports and Structures

Programmatic change began with motivated university stakeholders, rather than from the top-down in response to federal and state mandates (Heineke, Kennedy, & Lees, 2013; Ryan et al., 2014). Aiming to professionalize teaching by strengthening teacher preparation, faculty took up the charge from school leadership to transform its program and think beyond the traditional teacher education structures of courses on educational foundations, followed by courses on instructional methods, and culminating with clinical experiences in schools (Mehta, 2013; Ryan et al., 2013).

Multi-layered institutional support from faculty and leadership is central to helping negotiate various challenges posed by traditional university structures and teacher education discourses. Faculty also had to deconstruct their own use of structures, terminology, and other discourse to move beyond the traditional framework of teacher education programming. Teacher education faculty found the need to explicitly replace certain terminology in the regular discourse of collaborative program design, such as the use of "module" in place of "course" and "sequence" in place of "semester," since those traditional terms reinforced traditional ways of thinking about preparing future teachers. By shifting the discourse, self-study data demonstrated faculty surpassing these challenges related to traditional mindsets and programs.

Designing Teacher Education Curriculum

Following the curricular design process that the program consistently uses with teacher candidates, TLLSC was backward designed using the *Understanding by Design* framework (Wiggins & McTighe, 2005). In this approach to curriculum and instruction, planning begins with the end in mind – setting goals for learning, designing aligned assessments to measure mastery of set goals, and then planning instruction to successfully support students in reaching goals and demonstrating mastery.

Stage One of the process, the most time-consuming and messy of the three stages, included the drafting of enduring understandings, dispositions, knowledge, and skills that would then guide the backward planning of the four-year, field-based program. Following the drafting of 11 enduring understandings, 16 dispositions, and 241 knowledge and skill indicators, Stage Two considered learning goals across the developmental phases across the four-year program and designed assessments to measure candidates' learning. Stage Three then focused on fleshing out the curriculum of sequences and modules, tapping into faculty experts to draft modules within their areas of focus (e.g., literacy, culturally responsive practice).

Across the three stages of backward design, faculty engaged in collaborative efforts with the full faculty, approximately 25 individuals across elementary, secondary, early childhood, special education, and bilingual education. Nonetheless, because of the large number of faculty with varying levels of commitment to the program re-design, leadership convened a *re-design steering committee* with volunteers who wished to engage in behind-the-scenes work to coordinate the whole-group planning and work and engage in the more detailed planning of specific sequence assessments and module curriculum. While it proved challenging to find the correct balance between whole- and small-group engagement, the decision to create and utilize the steering committee was central to move forward the complex and time-consuming work. Self-study data, particularly audio recordings of collaborative planning sessions, revealed the complexity of this process, with multiple faculty perspectives, theoretical frameworks, and areas of priority across program areas and demonstrated the need for a collaborative, respectful faculty willing to engage in dialog around educational issues (Ryan et al., 2013).

Refining the Program with External and Internal Resources

Following the backward design of the four-year TLLSC program, the *iterative* process of reviewing and refining the curriculum began (Erickson, 1987). Key tools in this feedback cycles included teacher preparation standards, professional literature, and targeted faculty expertise, as well as feedback from school and community partners. Faculty set the goal to *target* and *integrate* knowledge and skills for teaching all students, rather than silo expertise to particular teachers (Heineke, Kennedy, & Lees, 2013). In modules where specific proficiencies were *targeted*, faculty ensured explicit focus and learning related to those enduring understandings, knowledge, and skills, such as the EL-focused modules meeting state requirements for EL assessment and EL methods. Other modules then *integrated* these knowledge and skills to support candidates, so as to not silo learning separate from authentic classroom practice; for example, after targeted learning of EL methods in Sequence 5, those knowledge and skills were then integrated in Sequence 6 when candidates engaged in instructional planning and implementation. Because of the initial decision to engage in the program re-design as a full teacher preparation faculty, rather than as separate programs such as elementary and secondary, faculty negotiated various challenges during this process, particularly letting go of their particular areas of responsibility and expertise for the integrated portions of the content.

Developing Professional Knowledge and Skills

With specific sub-sets of knowledge and skills targeted and integrated throughout the programs, faculty now needed to ensure that they themselves had the needed knowledge and skills. At most universities, teacher preparation faculty have been hired for expertise in particular areas, with specialists in areas such as reading, special education, bilingual education, and science education. With faculty experts teaching the targeted portions of the program, such as bilingual and EL faculty experts teaching those targeted modules, the TLLSC program necessitated faculty who were prepared for the integrated component of the program. In other words, to effectively prepare candidates through the integration of content related to ELs, special education, and IB, faculty needed the appropriate knowledge and skills themselves in addition to their own areas of expertise.

Central to the self-study, TLLSC faculty and community partners engaged in self-assessment to reflect upon and set goals for personal and collaborative learning as teacher educators. The re-design steering committee then utilized both sets of reflective data to plan professional development opportunities for both faculty and partners to learn side-by-side as co-teacher-educators in the TLLSC program. While self-study data (Chang et al., in press) indicated the value of this collaborative learning, it is important to note that TLLSC used external funding to support this work (Ryan et al., 2013; Kennedy & Heineke, 2014).

Strengthening and Building Partnerships

NCATE (now *CAEP;* 2010) identifies deep, strategic, and equal partnerships as the critical foundation for the field-based teacher education models emphasized in current policy. For teacher education programs to reflect authentic practice, they must align themselves with the aims and practices of community partners and participate in substantive dialogue about shared priorities (Kruger et al., 2009). During program development, TLLSC faculty worked alongside partners to operationalize principles of effective university-school partnerships (Kruger et al., 2009). Partners played active roles that evolved and deepened during implementation of the resulting program. In the resulting TLLSC sequences, university faculty and school/community organization administrators meet regularly with community partners to develop plans for facilitating modules that work will within the context and community of each field site. These meetings were designed to develop and capitalize on a commitment and trust in shared expertise (Kruger et al., 2009). Faculty, administrators, teachers, and community partners determined roles and responsibilities of stakeholders to address the needs of children, families, and candidates with the goal of reciprocity in partnership roles (Kruger et al., 2009). They identified resources available at field sites during module sessions such as meeting space, curriculum materials, and internet access. Partners engaged in conversations with faculty and candidates about ways that module assignments might align with their classroom needs, as well as identifying local professional development needs. In this way, for example, teachers play a continued role in the adjustment of assignments and module objectives to align with their classroom goals, curriculum, assets, and demographics.

Examples of Field-Based Teacher Education Partners and Sequences

Each partner collaborates with TLLSC faculty and teacher candidates in a unique way, the result of collaboratively designed field-based learning experiences that suit the structure, needs, and assets of each partner. To demonstrate the features and impact of TLLSC in schools and communities, five cases are presented in the sections to follow. Extended vignettes are used to discuss the development of each partnership, its role in TLLSC, practices that support field-based preparation experiences, the perceptions of teachers and administrators from each site, and impact on candidates. These cases were selected based upon two criteria. First, partners who collaborate to deliver TLLSC sequences in the exploration (Indigo Center and St. Bruno's School) and concentration (Early Head Start, Newville School and Nagle High School) phases are included, as these phases involve the most extensive collaboration between university and community partners. Second, partners were selected to represent the developmental continuum from birth-through-grade-12 and a variety of specialty areas in TLLSC.

The Indigo Center: Partnering with Communities to Prepare Teachers

The Indigo Center is an urban Indigenous community organization (ICO) serving the distinct needs of a tribally diverse community residing off reservation lands. Indigo Center partners with TLLSC to offer Sequence 1, which all candidates take in their first undergraduate semester prior to selection of areas of teaching specialty. The modules of Sequence 1 expose teacher candidates to specific knowledge and skills necessary for educators to embody the dispositions of the profession. Modules progress from examining the roles of responsibilities of educators within diverse schools to connecting those responsibilities directly to the learning and development of P-12 students. One unique advantage afforded to teacher candidates during this sequence is preparation focused on the role communities play in educating students.

Indigo was a community partner prior to the TLLSC redesign and thus had an established relationship with faculty, hosting field-experiences before the development and implementation of the field-based model. As an established community partner, Indigo leadership was involved throughout the redesign process, sharing how increased collaboration may support candidate and community needs. Prior to the Community Immersion module held at their center, Indigo leadership and TLLSC faculty met to adapt the module content to match the Indigo context. During these meetings, Indigo leadership and TLLSC faculty shared their respective needs and goals of the partnership, and developed experiences for the candidates that would address the objectives of both parties—thus advancing the goal of mutual benefit. Faculty gained access to a culturally diverse community organization for supporting candidates' understandings of school-community collaboration, while the Indigo community gained information about the resources identified through candidates' asset maps and a voice in preparing teachers for the distinct needs of urban Indigenous children.

The experiences of Indigo partners served as examples of the ways in which mutual benefit is not always a static or predetermined goal for such partnerships. First, simply ensuring that partner sites benefit in some way is insufficient (Lees et al., in press). That benefit must be meaningful in view of community partners' understandings of effective teaching and priorities for future teachers' experiences, knowledge, and skills. In a broader sense, benefit is also perceived through the shared experiences of the partnership, which must in turn adapt in response to those experiences through collaborative and further redesign.

Candidate Experiences and Outcomes in Sequence 1

During Sequence 1, candidates complete a community asset map as part of a community immersion module at the Indigo Center; this serves as a culminating experience of candidates' first semester in the Exploration phase of TLLSC. Under the guidance of faculty and direction of community partners, candidates explore the neighborhood surrounding the agency while learning about and identifying community assets and needs of an urban American Indian community. They present findings to the community, sharing community resources to serve needs of families away from their tribes and lands. As a result of participating in this module, candidates have developed a greater understanding of the community in which a part their professional preparation takes place, as well as networking opportunities with a variety of community agencies which they seek out and visit as part of their asset mapping. Candidates also develop an initial understanding and awareness of community resources that support teaching, which they report that this helps them to expand their thinking of influences and potential beyond their classroom walls in an effort to plan more authentic learning experiences for their students.

St. Bruno's School: A Laboratory for Examination of Education Policy

As a Jesuit Catholic institution, TLLSC partners with Catholic schools in addition to community organizations and public schools, which provides candidates with experiences in multiple educational contexts. A unique P-12 school with early childhood, elementary, and secondary students, St. Bruno's Preparatory School regularly hosts Sequence 3, which includes modules that investigate educational policies in practice (four-week module), as well as individualized assessment and instruction for diverse students (eight-week module). Situated in the final of three semesters in the *exploration* phase of candidate development, the overarching goal of Sequence 3 is to emphasize the role of the teacher as advocate in the complex and dynamic interconnection of macro- and micro-level educational policy in practice (Heineke, Ryan, & Tocci, 2014).

Candidate Experiences and Outcomes in Sequence 3

In the 2013-2014 school year, the first year of TLLSC implementation, Sequence 3 candidates at St. Bruno's considered both macro-level educational policies and micro-level classroom practices at the school. Specifically a focus of this module, sequence, and broader program, they investigated the language diversity in the school, including the specific policies and programs targeting the high number of students who spoke another language other than English. With less federal and state mandates than public schools, candidates discovered in the first policy-focused module that this Catholic school had no formalized procedure to identify ELs, or students who were still learning the English language. As they moved into the second module focused on the individualized assessments of diverse students, their one-on-one work with students led to important realizations about the significant language needs at the school, which remained largely unmet and unaccounted for due to the lack of formalized structures for EL identification and instruction.

At the end of the semester and with the collaborative support of both the university faculty member and school principal, candidates presented these findings to school faculty and administration. St. Bruno's faculty benefited from learning more individualized linguistic needs about specific students in their classrooms, whereas administration realized the need to prioritize EL procedures and program across the school. Emergent from this collaborative work, the school principal made the integral decision to hire an EL coordinator to identify, support, and evaluate the language development of students across the P-12 school. TLLSC continues to support this diverse school's innovative efforts to meet the needs of ELs in a Catholic school system without the structures or resources to otherwise do so.

Case study research and thematic analysis of candidates' Sequence 3 work products have revealed that sequence experiences lead to deepened understandings of both the broad constructs of educational policy and the ways in which it impacts daily teaching practice (Heineke, Ryan, & Tocci, 2014). This includes awareness of the range of actors who influence educational policy, the interaction of a variety of policies in practice, and the appropriation of policy to address individual students' needs.

Early Head Start: Preparing Teachers for Diverse Young Learners

The next featured community partner is an Early Head Start (EHS) center serving culturally and linguistically diverse families on the south side of Chicago. As a response to the call for increased focus on high-quality infant-toddler preparation (Horm, Hyson, & Winton, 2013), redesign of the TLLSC early childhood education program included significant expansion of field-based infant-toddler experiences. An existing partnership with EHS was revisited and discussions focused on providing candidates with increased exposure to a community-based agency, which provides child and family supports within an inclusive and family-centered program philosophy.

As an existing partner, the EHS program manager was involved in each phase of TLLSC's design and implementation, and continues to provide feedback regarding the successes and challenges of the field-based program. During the second semester of EC candidates' sophomore year, Sequence 4 includes a full semester of field-based infant-toddler preparation, part of which takes place in an EHS program serving primarily African-American, Chinese-American, and Latino children from families considered low income. Collaboration within this partnership involves semi-annual team meetings with faculty, teachers, and support staff, at which teachers discuss everyone's roles and responsibilities for supporting the development of teacher candidates.

Candidate Experiences and Outcomes in Sequence 4

In this modules taking place in EHS classrooms, Early Childhood Special Education candidates in Sequence 4 of the Concentration phase learn and practice developmentally appropriate adult-child interaction, activity planning, and daily routines, under the direct supervision of EHS teachers and two faculty. Candidates and faculty travel to the site together three mornings a week for six weeks, where they are provided with an initial orientation to the EHS center before transitioning into their placement classrooms. Typical days include a brief meeting to cover essential content and plan for the day, after which candidates proceed to their classrooms, where teachers provide mentorship, modeling of effective teaching, support in planning activities, and in-class coaching. Faculty rotate among the classrooms, providing individualized feedback and a system of tiered supports, the intensity of which are adjusted to match each candidate's strengths and areas of need (Kennedy & Lees, 2014).

Each day concludes with a seminar session, and weekly meetings are conducted to review candidates' progress. As a result of participation in this module, candidates have demonstrated significant growth on measures of teacher sensitivity, support for positive behavior, and the facilitation of learning and development (Kennedy & Lees, 2015a, Kennedy & Lees, 2015b). Interviews with candidates have revealed benefits such as increased understanding and practice of intentional teaching, recognition of individual strengths and weaknesses, and direct application of feedback to teaching. The candidates also develop close relationships with classroom teachers, who (in subsequent focus groups) have reported that their work with candidates increased their recognition of their importance (as teachers) to the field of teacher education (Kennedy & Lees, 2015b).

Newville School: Supporting the Literacy Development of English Learners

Newville Elementary School, a neighborhood Chicago Public School, serves 1,033 children with 91% qualifying for free and reduced lunch. With 36% of the student body labeled as ELs and 13 languages spoken by students, including Spanish, Arabic, Thai, Farsi, and Tagalog, the university-school partnership prioritized the support of language development for linguistically diverse students. In addition to the TLLSC partnership, a locally funded grant entitled Language Matters provided human and material resources to build capacity at the school for supporting students' language development, thus emphasizing the mutually beneficial nature of the partnership where the school benefited from expertise and funding for professional development for ELs and the university benefited from situating the TLLSC program in Newville classrooms and schools. As a whole, the partnership built capacity of candidates, teachers, leaders, and faculty focused on the curricular content of Sequence 5, specifically language and literacy development.

Candidate Experiences and Outcomes in Sequence 5

Situated in second of three semesters in the *concentration* phase, TLLSC candidates engaged in Sequence 5 modules focused on language development and literacy instruction (four-week module), data-based decision making (four-week module), and discipline-specific language development and instruction (four-week module). Aiming to emphasize the importance of data-based decision making to drive instruction, candidates created a portfolio of authentic assessments of language and content based on teacher identification of students needing individual supports. Within the target on ELs and language development within both literacy and content area instruction, candidates then collaborated and supported teachers' weekly planning through differentiated instruction of interdisciplinary lessons. Apprenticed by expert teachers in bilingual, EL, and mainstream settings, candidates learned to use the New Standards to support language and content learning with students from diverse linguistic backgrounds and abilities.

Candidates were continuously engaged in Newville classrooms three mornings per week for twelve weeks in Sequence 5. During this time they received continuous support and feedback from classroom teachers and TLLSC faculty. Outcomes of Sequence 5 candidates include significant increases in scores on measures of teacher sensitivity, language support, behavior management, and the facilitation of language and literacy development.

Simultaneous to the field-based teacher preparation program, TLLSC faculty collaborated with Newville leadership to develop school-wide foundations, programs, and structures to build capacity and appropriately support students' language and learning needs. With the support of the Language Matters grant project, Newville and TLLSC collaborated to provide professional development and facilitate professional learning communities focused on instructional planning for language development. Additionally, using both grant funds and vouchers for hosting the TLLSC program, three teacher leaders completed a six-course ESL endorsement to lead the capacity building efforts at Newville. With this mutually beneficial partnership impacting classroom- and school-level practice, districts leaders have recognized Newville as a leader in EL teaching and learning, using their multi-faceted efforts as the exemplar for surrounding schools.

Nagle High School: Fostering Holistic Change across Classrooms, School, and Community

A central partner for the university and TLLSC program, Nagle High School is a neighborhood high school serving students from 45 countries of origins and 35 language backgrounds, with 88% of students qualifying for free or reduced lunch. The school implements the International Baccalaureate (IB) program for all students as a way to increase curricular richness and rigor. Because of the wall-to-wall IB program at Nagle, an unprecedented approach to this global curriculum that provides access to all students at the school, TLLSC faculty consistently rely on this site for the IB-focused modules and sequences (Ryan, Heineke, & Steindam, 2014).During the first two years of TLLSC implementation from 2013-2015, Nagle hosted sections of four different sequences, with a total of 135 candidates working in classrooms in capacities ranging from leading whole-class instruction to co-planning with teachers to conducting functional behavior assessments to creating community asset maps and more.

Candidate Experiences and Outcomes in Sequence 6

In Sequence 6, the final of three semesters in the *concentration* phase of the field-based program, candidates engage in deep teaching and learning about the IB program and approach to curriculum and instruction. Focused first on discipline-specific instruction (e.g., mathematics, history; four-week module) and then on the IB-specific, inter-disciplinary teaching and learning (eight-week module), Nagle teachers and TLLSC candidates collaborate to plan and implement a rigorous instructional unit that supports content learning, language development, and international mindedness. Using backward instructional design and IB curricular principles (Ryan, Heineke, & Steindam, 2014; Wiggins & McTighe, 2005), candidates build expertise in planning and facilitating student learning within and across their chosen disciplines.

In addition to supporting candidates' professional learning and development through the TLLSC program, Nagle and TLLSC have partnered to build capacity across the school and community, specifically focused on the wall-to-wall IB program for all students. Both situated in the same geographical region, the university-school partnership runs deep with a shared commitment to one another. TLLSC has committed human and material resources to the Nagle partnership, including a full-time clinical faculty member with the sole focus of coordinating and teaching at Nagle. Through this role, TLLSC has been able to support Nagle and the IB program by tapping into the resources of the School of Education, School of Communications, and Institute for Environmental Studies. Since the partnership began in 2012, Nagle has re-emerged as a strong and viable neighborhood high school with increased enrollment, achievement, and college matriculation - particularly with a large number of Nagle graduates coming to Loyola University Chicago.

An Examination of Partner Experiences and Perceptions of TLLSC

Implementation of TLLSC has unfolded over two subsequent years with a combination of existing community partners and new ones joining the program at every stage. As described above, continuing research focuses on self-study of program planning and design. Implementation research has focused on both candidate outcomes and partner experiences. Interview and focus group research was conducted with a broad spectrum of community partners throughout implementation, with data collected from representatives of a variety of partners participating at each phase of TLLSC. The selection of interviews vs. focus groups was made based upon the context and preference of each partner agency. This section focuses on three broad practices (emerging from these partner interviews and focus groups) supporting the success of field-based teacher education: (a) extending engagement in field sites, (b) valuing partner perspectives and knowledge, and (c) revising curriculum in response to partner need. Each of these three practices represent the views of both community partners *and* faculty on the key essential practices for achieving not only supporting program implementation, but the goal of mutual benefit.

Extending Engagement in Field Sites

Faculty and co-teacher-educators share in the belief that without extended engagement, candidates cannot develop relationships that are critical both for their development and for the benefit of partner sites. The length of each field-based module varies based upon its content (including objectives for candidate knowledge and skills) and its placement in the four-year continuum (generally, the later the four year program, the longer the modules); however, length is also directly related to perceived benefit, as partners have described more effectively sharing knowledge and skills with candidates only when the length of the module provided them with sufficient opportunities to do so. In some cases, partners expressed during focus groups that their time spent with candidates was not prolonged enough to have a meaningful impact on their learning. They believed that for candidates to gain an authentic understanding of the communities they serve (including families and children's educational needs), they required extended cyclical engagements with those communities. As one community agency hosting candidates in the *exploration* phase stated, "*I think the time needs to be spread out. It's too much for them... We expect them to take everything they think and know... and change that.*" Responses such as this fueled the iterative design process, and both the content and duration of TLLSC modules in the exploration phase. In contrast, an interview with another community agency administrator (who hosted modules in the *concentration* phase) depicted the prolonged experiences of candidates in her center as beneficial to their development and readiness when entering the profession. She shared,

I think for the students definitely having a lot of experiences, starting early in their teacher preparation with different populations of students, I think is really valuable so that they're able to really start getting comfortable with children of different ages, abilities with and without special needs, different cultural backgrounds because I think then by the time they're actually entering the profession, they will feel some greater sense of competence and confidence going into it.

She illustrated her impression of the partnership as impactful for participating teachers who serve as mentors. They develop professionally as, over time, they explain their practices in detail to novice candidates and discuss their instructional decision-making. They also benefit from learning current best and evidence-based practices from faculty and, in some cases, alongside candidates. Finally, these experiences gradually build and strengthen relationships among candidates, teachers, and the children and families served by the partner site. Perceptions such as these reinforce the notion that field-based learning experiences must be of sufficient length and depth for candidates and partners to benefit from them.

Valuing Partner Perspectives and Knowledges

The need for field-based teacher educators to value practitioners' knowledge and skills represents another critical element of partners' experiences of mutual benefit. In some cases, field-based modules failed to achieve this aim and were adjusted; in others, teachers developed new awareness of their professional skills through their experiences with candidates, thus reaping the benefit of those skills having recognized value in the partnership. In other cases, teachers who had never before participated in teacher education in this way began to develop a new awareness of their professionalism through their experiences with candidates; in this sense, the fact that their skills had recognized value in the partnership led to its own benefits. In interviews and focus groups, teachers and administrators repeatedly shared observations such as this one: "For our teachers here…I think they really like passing on some of their knowledge and their experience to new teachers." While teachers' level of comfort with active facilitation of candidate learning varied significantly across settings, administrators viewed this as a form of professional development and of needs assessment.

Revising Curriculum in Response to Partner Needs

Despite the need to maintain alignment to teacher education and accreditation standards, field-based models must continually adapt to the changing contexts in which children and families are served. While this often occurs in response to the needs and values of partners, it also stems from a host of logistical considerations, such as number of candidates, days and hours of each site's programming, changes in school staff and structure, and weather-related and transportation issues. Overall, while partners shared positive experiences as co-teacher-educators, ongoing challenges were inevitable. Extended engagement, for instance, requires that faculty and administration align sequences with school and community partner priorities; this required a willingness to continually re-examine and revise the teacher education curricula whenever and wherever possible.

A commitment to addressing the themes outlined above meant that a safe space had to be created for all stakeholders to address systemic and practice challenges throughout the implementation process. For example, partners inevitably must provide support for candidates that extend beyond their typical workload, and consistent collaboration with university faculty requires an investment of time and resources. Partnerships flourished when partners recognized that they possess knowledge, skills, and resources that are to share with candidates, when they were able to access support from administrators and faculty to serve as co-teacher educators while still meeting the needs of their classrooms and communities, and when their investment of time and effort in the shared delivery of TLLSC modules led to benefits of value to them.

Issues, Controversies, Problems

As the landscape of U.S. education continues to change, including the growing diversity among student demographics and increasing accountability in P-12 and teacher education, scholars, policy makers, and other stakeholders have called for substantial changes to traditional teacher education (AACTE, 2010, 2015; Gándara & Hopkins, 2010). With university-based teacher education programs facing scrutiny from state and federal policy makers, as well as from external organizations prioritizing alternative routes to teacher certification such as Teach for America and the National Council on Teacher Quality, teacher educators must critically consider how they prepare candidates for today's classrooms. Traditional teacher preparation programs have been criticized for the divide between theory and practice, as well as the static nature of the foundations-methods-clinicals approach to preparing teachers in the ivory tower of the university far from the realities of schools and communities (NCATE, 2010).

Field-based models such as TLLSC address many of the challenges and limitations of traditional, university-based teacher preparation models. However, they present significant and unique challenges of their own. Mirroring Table 1 from the beginning of this chapter, Table 2 presents examples of the ways in which field-based and traditional approaches must address different practical issues relating to each of teacher education dimension. An additional row highlights implications of teacher education research in these disparate settings.

RECOMMENDATIONS FOR ADDRESSING THESE CHALLENGES

The following recommendations integrate teacher education research, policies, and outcomes from two years of TLLSC design and two years of implementation/outcomes studies. These practices embody tenets of effective university-community partnerships (Lees & Kennedy, in press; Kennedy & Heineke, 2014; Kruger et al., 2009) and stem from a variety of sources of data, including student assignments, partner interviews and focus groups, and measures of candidate growth and effectiveness.

Community Partners Must Be Meaningfully Included in Redesign Efforts

To ensure that partners have a voice in aligning teacher education programs with policies, standards, and assessments, they must engage with university faculty throughout each step of any redesign process. Partners must attend planning sessions, align and adapt field-based experiences, collaborate to address local logistical issues and constraints, and advance local professional development needs. But perhaps most importantly, teacher educators must both learn and demonstrate respect for partners' perspective and knowledges. This extends to field-based research; partners (including teachers) must play a role in identifying the focus of program research in addition to serving as participants.

Consider Goals and Implications of Practitioners as Co-Teacher Educators

To forge co-teaching relationships, adequate preparation and planning time for these new roles is essential; in reality these interactions between educators and candidates are often assumed rather than directly facilitated. Faculty and community partners must explore the particular knowledge and skills they feel prepared to offer candidates, identify practitioners and activities to support candidates, and

Table 2. Issues and challenges associated with traditional vs. field-based approaches to teacher education

Traditional Approaches	Dimension	Field-Based Community Partnership Models
Bridging the gap between course-based learning and clinical experiences presents a challenge when individual students are placed based upon site availability	Format	Integrating the content knowledge and practices associated with effective teaching in the field requires new and context-specific models of collaboration and program delivery
Foundational coursework, methods courses, and clinical experiences may be planned and delivered by different faculty and/or departments, leading to misalignment and discontinuity in candidate development	Model	For field experiences to address interrelated competencies in authentic settings, separations between areas of knowledge and skill must be addressed
Instructors must isolate areas of competency and develop meaningful yet manageable individual courses	Integration of knowledge and skills	Shared assignments and preparation activities require faculty to collaborate to bridge gaps in expertise in a way that responds to diverse community contexts
Faculty work in isolated silos where preparation and practice do not always support one another	Faculty supervision	Direct faculty involvement in community schools and agencies requires a shift in identity and unique skill set
Practicing teachers have little voice in the design of teacher preparation programming and limited communication with university faculty	Role of teacher mentors	Teachers and faculty must serve as teacher educators in an equal partnership with the goal of supporting candidates and the responsibility to impact P-12 students
School and center administrators have little to no contact with individual faculty members outside of approving candidate placements, resulting in limited interaction between candidates and the systems/communities in which they are placed.	Role of school-based administrators	A mutual benefit model requires seats at the teacher preparation table for administrators and community agency leaders.
Teachers (and often school administrators) do not serve as the focus or audience for university research, reinforcing the gap between research and practice	Research	Practice-based research requires the trust and involvement of school and community partners as both participants and researchers, requiring even more from participating educators.

set in place a system of regular collaboration among faculty and teachers. As shifts in faculty identity are examined through self-study research, the changes and challenges experienced by teachers should be brought to light.

Impact on Practitioners Must Transcend "Additional Help"

Partners provide extensive supports to candidates. These roles require a significant investment on the part of teachers, and the advantage of having additional help in the classroom is at times disproportionately small in comparison to the responsibilities of supporting candidates. Strategies for field-based teacher education should uphold mutuality within the partnership and respect teachers, children, and communities as valuable stakeholders in teacher education. One way of working to achieve this involves combining teacher education and teacher professional development by sharing innovative strategies with teachers while supporting teacher candidates as they implement these as novice teachers.

Align Practices with a Goal of Positive Impact on Children and Families

Feld-based teacher education models must enhance, rather than interfere with, schools' and community agencies' efforts to address the needs of students, families, and the community. University faculty must consider contextually meaningful ways to provide benefits such as improved student to staff ratio, exposure to varied and innovative teaching practices (Petti, 2013), English language supports, intervention plans, individual assessment and instructional plans, and asset mapping. With faculty present to support the implementation and delivery of these strategies and approaches as teacher candidates learn about them, partners are more likely to view them as having direct benefit for children and families.

CONCLUSION

This chapter argues for field-based teacher education, calling for teacher educators and school and community partners to proactively and collaboratively respond to the calls for change (and unique challenges) in a way that prioritizes the needs of school and communities and prepares future teachers as professionals who effectively support the learning of all students (Kennedy & Heineke, 2013; Kruger et al., 2009; Ryan et al., 2013). As P-12 teaching is increasingly acknowledged as an academically taught, clinical practice profession (AACTE, 2015), the role of extended and intensive field-based teacher preparation experiences is increasingly critical. In order to form deep, long-lasting, and mutually beneficial partnerships with schools and communities, teacher education programs must discard notions such as "host sites" for teacher candidates and isolated practica or student teaching experiences. In their place, living partnerships must grow and adapt in response to each partner's needs. This adaptation rests upon the willingness and ability of teacher education program faculty to consider both the goals and implications of working alongside community partners as co-teacher educators, going beyond traditional notions of candidates providing additional help in the classroom and considering each partner's needs and priorities. These partnerships must also reject candidate placement and graduation as the central goal of teacher education; rather, the collaborative work of alignment of teaching and preparation practices must address the shared goal of positively impacting students and families. This allows for the integration of preparation, professional development, and practice as shared priorities for collaborative research with the potential to positively benefit teacher educators and their partner schools and communities.

REFERENCES

Adams, S. K., & Wolf, K. (2008). Strengthening the preparation of early childhood teacher candidates through performance-based assessments. *Journal of Early Childhood Teacher Education*, *29*(1), 6–29. doi:10.1080/10901020701878644

American Association of Colleges for Teacher Education. (2012). *The clinical preparation of teachers: A policy brief*. Washington, DC: AACTE. Retrieved from https://aacte.org

American Association of Colleges of Teacher Education. (2004). The early childhood challenge: Preparing high-quality teachers for a changing society (White paper). American Association of Colleges for Teacher Education Focus Council on Early Childhood Education. Retrieved from https://secure.aacte.org/apps/rl/resource.php

American Association of Colleges of Teacher Education. (2010). *21st century knowledge and skills in educator preparation*. Retrieved from http://www.aacte.org

Ball, D. L., & Forzani, F. M. (2009). The work of teaching and the challenge for teacher education. *Journal of Teacher Education, 60*(5), 497–511. doi:10.1177/0022487109348479

Brown, J. S., Collins, A., & Duguid, P. (1989). Situated cognition and the culture of learning. *Educational Researcher, 18*(1), 32–42. doi:10.3102/0013189X018001032

Chang, A., Neugebauer, S., Ellis, A., Ensminger, D., Ryan, A., & Kennedy, A. S. (in press). Teacher educators' experiences around teacher education redesign: A collaborative self-study. *Studying Teacher Education*.

Chang, F., Early, D. M., & Winton, P. J. (2005). Early childhood teacher preparation in special education at 2-and 4-year institutions of higher education. *Journal of Early Intervention, 27*(2), 110–124. doi:10.1177/105381510502700206

Cochran-Smith, M., & Zeichner, K. (2010). *Studying teacher education: The report of the AERA Panel on Research and Teacher Education*. Washington, D.C.: American Educational Research Association.

Erickson, F. (1987). Transformation and school success: The politics and culture of educational achievement. *Anthropology & Education Quarterly, 18*(4), 335–356. doi:10.1525/aeq.1987.18.4.04x0023w

Farell, A. (2005). Globalising early childhood teacher education: A study of student life histories and course experience in teacher education. *International Journal of Early Childhood, 37*(1), 9–17. doi:10.1007/BF03165828

Feiman-Nemser, S. (2012). Beyond SOLO Teaching. *Educational Leadership, 69*(8), 10–16.

Floden, R. E. (2012). Teacher value added as a measure of program quality: Interpret with caution. *Journal of Teacher Education, 63*(5), 356–360. doi:10.1177/0022487112454175

Gándara, P., & Hopkins, M. (2010). The changing linguistic landscape of the United States. In P. Gándara & M. Hopkins (Eds.), *Forbidden language: English learners and restrictive language policies* (pp. 7–19). New York: Teachers College Press.

García, E., Arias, M. B., Harris, M. N. J., & Serna, C. (2010). Developing responsive teachers: A challenge for a demographic reality. *Journal of Teacher Education, 61*(1-2), 132–142. doi:10.1177/0022487109347878

Hamilton, M. L., Pinnegar, S., Russell, T., Loughran, J., & LaBoskey, V. K. (Eds.). (1998). *Reconceptualizing teaching practice: Self-study in teacher education*. London: Falmer Press.

Heineke, A., Kennedy, A., & Lees, A. (2013). Preparing early childhood educators for the culturally and linguistically diverse classrooms and communities of Illinois. *Early Childhood Research & Practice, 15*(2). Retrieved from http://ecrp.illinois.edu/v15n2/heineke.html

Heineke, A. J., Ryan, A. M., & Tocci, T. (2015). Teaching, learning, and leading: Preparing teachers as educational policy actors. *Journal of Teacher Education, 66*(4), 382–394. doi:10.1177/0022487115592031

Horm, D., Hyson, M., & Winton, P. (2013). Research on early childhood teacher education: Evidence from three domains and recommendations for moving forward. *Journal of Early Childhood Teacher Education, 34*(1), 95–112. doi:10.1080/10901027.2013.758541

Kennedy, A., & Lees, A. (2015a). Outcomes of a community-based birth-to-three preparation sequence for undergraduate early childhood teacher candidates. *American Journal of Educational Research, 2*(6), 770–782.

Kennedy, A., & Lees, A. (2015b, June). Preparing undergraduate pre-service teachers through direct and video-based performance feedback and tiered supports in Early Head Start. *Early Childhood Education Journal, 2015,* 1–11. doi:10.100710643-015-0725-2

Kennedy, A. S., & Heineke, A. (2014). Re-envisioning the role of universities in early childhood teacher education: Community partnerships for 21st century learning. *Journal of Early Childhood Teacher Education, 35*(1), 226–243. doi:10.1080/10901027.2014.936072

Kennedy, A. S., & Lees, A. (2014). Merging professional preparation and development through blended practices and a tiered approach in Early Head Start. In K. Pretti-Frontczak, J. Grisham-Brown, & L. Sullivan (Eds.), *Young Exceptional Children Monograph 16 - Blending Practices to Strengthen Quality Early Learning Programs for ALL Children*. Los Angeles: Division for Early Childhood of the Council for Exceptional Children.

Kruger, T., Davies, A., Eckersley, B., Newell, F., & Cherednichenko, B. (2009). *Effective and sustainable university-school partnerships: Beyond determined efforts by inspired individuals*. Canberra, Australia: Teaching Australia - Australian Institute for Teaching and School Leadership Limited.

LaParo, K., Thomason, A., Maynard, C., & Scott-Little, C. (2012b). Developing teachers' classroom interactions: A description of a video review process for early childhood education students. *Journal of Early Childhood Teacher Education, 33*(3), 224–238. doi:10.1080/10901027.2012.705809

Lees, A., & Kennedy, A. S. (in press). Community-based collaboration for early childhood teacher education: Community partner experiences and perspectives as co-teacher educators. *Journal of Early Childhood Teacher Education*.

Lim, C.-I., & Able-Boone, H. (2005). Diversity competencies within early childhood teacher preparation: Innovative practices and future directions. *Journal of Early Childhood Teacher Education, 26*(3), 225–238. doi:10.1080/10901020500369803

Lunenberg, M., Zwart, R., & Korthagen, F. (2010). Critical issues in supporting self-study. *Teaching and Teacher Education: An International Journal of Research and Studies, 26*(6), 1280–1289. doi:10.1016/j.tate.2009.11.007

McDonald, M., Tyson, K., Brayko, K., Bowman, M., Delport, J., & Shimomura, F. (2011). Innovation and impact in teacher education: Community-based organizations as field placements for preservice teachers. *Teachers College Record, 113*(8), 1668–1700.

Mehta, J. (2013). Why American education fails. *Foreign Affairs*, *92*(3), 105–116.

Moll, L. C., & Gonzalez, N. (1997). Teachers as social scientists: Learning about culture from household research. In P. Hall (Ed.), *Race, ethnicity, and multiculturalism: Policy and practice*. New York: Routledge.

National Center for Education Information. (2011). *Profile of teachers in the U.S.* Retrieved from http://www.ncei.com/

Rogoff, B. (1994). Developing understanding of the idea of communities of learners. *Mind, Culture, and Activity*, *1*, 209–229.

Ruiz Soto, A. G., Hooker, S., & Batalova, J. (2015). *States and districts with the highest number and share of English language learners*. Washington, DC: Migration Policy Institute.

Rust, F. (2010). Shaping new models for teacher education. *Teacher Education Quarterly*, *37*(2), 5–18.

Ryan, A., Ensminger, D., Heineke, A., Kennedy, A. S., Prasse, D., & Smetana, L. (2014). Teaching, Learning, and Leading with Schools and Communities (TLLSC): One urban university re-envisions teacher preparation for the next generation. *Issues in Teacher Education*, *22*(2), 139–153.

Ryan, A. M., Heineke, A. J., & Steindam, C. (2014). Preparing globally minded teachers: One teacher education program's incorporation of the international baccalaureate. *Journal of Education*, *194*(3), 39–51.

Vygotsky, L. S. (1978). *Mind in society: The development of higher psychological processes*. Cambridge, MA: Harvard University Press.

Whitebook, M., Austin, L. J., Ryan, S., Kipnis, F., Almaraz, M., & Sakai, L. (2012). *By default or by design? Variations in higher education programs for early care and education teachers and their implications for research methodology, policy, and practice*. Berkeley, CA: Center for the Study of Child Care Employment, University of California at Berkeley.

Wiggins, G., & McTighe, J. (2005). *Understanding by design* (2nd ed.). Washington, DC: Association for Supervision and Curriculum Development.

Wilson, S. M., Floden, R. E., & Ferrini-Mundy, J. (2001). Teacher preparation research: Current knowledge, gaps, and recommendations. Retrieved from https//www.ctp.org

Zeichner, K. (2006). Studying teacher education programs. In R. Serlin & C. Conrad (Eds.), *Handbook for research in education* (pp. 80–94). Thousand Oaks, CA: Sage.

KEY TERMS AND DEFINITIONS

Backward Design: An approach to curriculum design and instructional planning that begins with the end in mind, or the end goals for learning.

Co-Teacher-Educators: Cooperating teachers, school administrators, and community leaders who partner with university-based teacher educators to prepare future teachers.

English Learner: Student who is still in the process of learning the English language, as measured by standardized proficiency tests of listening, speaking, reading, and writing.

Field-Based Teacher Education: Teacher preparation program that is situated primarily in the field at schools and community organizations, rather than at the university.

International Baccalaureate: An international organization that provides P-12 interdisciplinary curriculum focused on supporting individual learners and building international mindedness.

Module: The equivalent of a course, but varying in length from four to twelve weeks and situated in the field at schools and community organizations.

Mutually Beneficial Partnership: Partnership between the university and a school or community organization that supports the goals and growth of both partners.

Sequence: The equivalent of a semester, or the combination of multiple instructional modules situated in the field at schools and community organizations.

Teacher Candidate: A pre-service teacher enrolled in a teacher preparation program.

This research was previously published in the Handbook of Research on Professional Development for Quality Teaching and Learning edited by Teresa Petty, Amy Good, and S. Michael Putman; pages 437-461, copyright year 2016 by Information Science Reference (an imprint of IGI Global).

Chapter 39
#UrbanLivesMatter:
Empowering Learners through Transformative Teaching

Nicole Webster
Pennsylvania State University, USA

Heather Coffey
University of North Carolina at Charlotte, USA

Anthony Ash
University of North Carolina Charlotte, USA

ABSTRACT

In an era marked by major political and social change, teachers of urban students must be prepared to engage and appreciate an ever-changing demographic of learners who come from backgrounds different from their own. In this chapter, we discuss the need for professional development embedded in culturally responsive teaching, multicultural education, and critical literacy, all of which have the power to incite social action. We posit that social action has the potential to empower and engage urban learners in meaningful ways. We believe this work fills the gap that exists in the literature regarding urban education and social and political movements

INTRODUCTION

What can be done to secure a brighter future for today's urban youth? That seems to be the burning question of parents, youth-serving organizations and the greater society at large. Given the past few years were ones of profound injustice and extraordinary resilience in a number of American cities, it still left many youth feeling a sense of hopelessness. Homicides, attacks, and senseless bullying peppered news outlets across the globe, and many times became interwoven into the fabric of the urban classroom. The deep psychological wounds of racism, classism and structural oppression are elements of several movements, like #BlackLivesMatter and #OccupyWallStreet that started within urban contexts and communities.

DOI: 10.4018/978-1-7998-1213-5.ch039

#UrbanLivesMatter

Despite the massive political and ideological synergies created around these movements, we believe a gap exists between the two—urban education and transformative teaching.

Our premise is that there are tenets that tie together intentionality of social movements and core competencies of quality teaching and learning for teachers who choose to work in urban schools. We believe that a deep exploration of these movements will reveal teaching tools, discussions, and techniques that can be used to strengthen quality teaching in urban schools, thus making them vehicles for change that can redefine and deepen democracy and equality (Clemons & Clemons, 2013). What's more, despite significant advances in enhancing educational practices, there is a worry that an intense focus on core subjects such as English, Mathematics and Science are failing students later in life. More specifically, K-12 learners are not being sufficiently equipped with the life skills to make personal and social decisions outside of the classroom which could most affect their future. Our conversation is based on the following:

1. *Schools (and communities) are often sites of reproduction or creation of such discourses.* Power can also repress knowledge (Freire, 1970; Giroux, 1987). Educators who are not critically conscious of the systemic power differentials between students and teachers will likely serve to recreate these oppressive systems. If power is not checked, knowledge can be repressed. As an institution built on the relationship between students, teachers, and knowledge, schools are inherently linked to power.
2. *Power contextualizes almost all aspects of school.* Students interact with people in formal positions of power—principals, teachers, deans—and create their own codes of power. Educators teach curricula authored by people often in institutional powers, which trickles down into school spaces. Students and teachers potentially resist and reinvent the institutional rules promoted by these curricula. As a result, students and educators interact within codes of power, (i.e. implicit and explicit rules of power) (Delpit, 1988) and construct narratives of power (i.e. stories about how power is and should be enacted) as interpreters of these codes. *Power also implicates pedagogy.* Schools are sites of explicit and implicit pedagogies. Extending Gage's (1978) definition of pedagogy as "scientific basis of the art of teaching," pedagogy also implicates the governing system of values, sets of assumptions, discourses *and* the instructional decisions and interactions that come within this system.
3. *School is an active, civic space.* School is the only *compulsory* civic space for most youth. They live within a set of governed rules that promote a closed set of values (Raby, 2008; Warren, 2013). They negotiate action to fulfill their individual needs in relation to the needs of the collective group. In other words, schools are spaces where students are citizens of a broader community. Despite the massive amounts of time students spend in this politically charged space, little is known about how teachers understand, experience, and act upon/with/without power in the context of school (Briggs & Mchenry, 2013; Burke & Greene, 2015; Lenzi, Vieno, Sharkey, Mayworm, Scacchi, Pastore, & Santinello, 2014; Martens & Gainous, 2013).

Engaging Pre-Service and Practicing Teachers in Intentional Experiences in Urban Settings

We shed light on thoughtful, deliberate pathways of action teachers may use to demonstrate for students and the ways in which injustice exists both inside the classroom (through curriculum) and outside of the classroom (social and political situations). We also provide strategies for helping teachers gain background knowledge of the workings of power, governance, and democracy in classrooms and how they might examine their own biases about these concepts. And finally, we challenge teachers to develop a wider understanding of social movements and their potential impact on teacher pedagogy in urban classrooms. We hope to create a powerful discourse that will begin candid conversations around this topic.

More specifically, we provide examples of engaged pedagogy that challenges both pre-service and practicing teachers to develop a clearer understanding of how urban schools are often sites of oppression and how, through careful dialog, they might work to dismantle these inequitable power structures and to empower their future students. Since public school education is one of the only compulsory parts of American citizenry (Beal & Crockett, 2010; Siegesmund, 2013), schools are ripe spaces to have discussions of cultural discrimination and to appreciate that which is "different" from the social norm. We make the case that all teachers need to learn to both check their own biases, stereotypes, and thoughts regarding race, ethnicity, gender, sexual orientation, ability, etc. and then work that dispositional knowledge into conversations in their own classrooms in order to dismantle of power and promote a more socially just society. We support the idea that teachers can be agents of change and provide recommendations for how they can both advocate for the needs of their urban students around issues of social justice and demonstrate for these students how to advocate for themselves.

We explore the ways in which teacher preparation can include education about the specific needs of urban students and should equip teachers in urban classrooms to challenge their own judgments about children in order to create spaces where these children raise their own consciousness and act to create equitable communities both inside and outside the classroom. Historically, K-12 students have advanced social change through engaging in advocacy around issues of oppression. For example, the "Children's Crusade" of 1963 was meant to attract more attention to the American Civil Rights Movement and more importantly, create a platform for youth to contribute to the educational injustices in Birmingham (McWhorter, 2001; Wilson, 2000). During this event, more than 1000 youths marched in downtown Birmingham to bring attention to segregation in American public schools and all public spaces in the south.

Similarly, in movements such as *El Movimiento*, an extension of the 1960s Mexican American Civil Rights Movement in Los Angeles, CA, Chicano students voiced the educational rights of Latino students. While actions, such as walkouts and sit-ins were not activities supported by the administration at large, no one could dispute the unintended outcome of the protests. Chicano student organizations were formed at a number of college campuses and universities to address policy changes and social injustices that impacted their communities (Gómez-Quiñones & Vásquez, 2014), and helped shape current student leaders into modern day change agents in educational spaces. Thus, a raised consciousness gave Chicano students the motivation and empowerment to stand up for equal educational rights.

Taines (2012) argues that the debate over how to improve the education offered at urban schools can be informed by the students who attend them, and that through social activism, urban school reform can be brokered by the voices of students and teachers who are the most valuable stakeholders in this battle for equity. Educational researchers focused on the importance of understanding how student-led activism can improve experiences for urban schools (i.e. Anyon, 2005, 2009 & Taines, 2012), contend that, "The immediate school environment mediates students' experience of wider social inequity" (Taines, 2012, p. 265).

#UrbanLivesMatter

Review of the Literature

As schools and society grow more diverse, educators in the United States are charged with developing a critically-thinking and democratically-minded workforce equipped to promote and sustain the nation's global economic competitiveness (National Research Council [NRC], 2007a, 2007b, 2010; Riegle-Crumb & King, 2010). Chief among concerns of U.S. economic stability in a global society is the ability to effectively educate an increasingly diverse group of students and develop highly-skilled, scientifically-literate workers. With an exceedingly complex geopolitical landscape, the nation's ability to make sound, ethical decisions regarding the course of schools and society will indeed rely on a diverse citizenry proficient in disciplines such as science, mathematics and English. Further, these efforts must be backed by a strong cohort of teacher educators capable of developing teachers for a 21st century knowledge-based economy. A common rejoinder to this political economy of education has been increased pressure on teacher education programs (TEPs) to produce educators who can engage students in diverse classrooms in ways that prepare them to address such needs (Cochran-Smith, 2010; Cochran-Smith & Zeichner, 2009; Darling-Hammond, 2005, 2010; Osborne, Simon, & Collins, 2003). This response, however, often elides more serious discussions regarding the ability of teachers who span a variety of years of experience to reach students from cultural backgrounds disparate from their own.

Approximately 83 percent of the nation's 3.85 million school teachers are white, and 76 percent of whom are female, whereas the growing majority of students they teach are from various ethnic and racial backgrounds (National Center for Education Statistics [NCES], 2013; Swartz, 2003). These demographic differences between student and teacher populations and subsequent effects of cultural mismatches in the classroom tend to have a negative impact on student achievement, particularly in underserved urban schools (Cochran-Smith & Zeichner, 2009; Delpit, 2006; Delpit & Dowdy, 2002; Howard, 2006; King, 1991; Ladson-Billings, 1995a). Such understandings have driven considerable research (both in initial licensure programs and through professional development) on preparing teachers to educate diverse student populations using critical, culturally responsive and multicultural approaches (Barnes, 2006; Bennett, 2013; Castro, 2010; Gay, 2002; Ladson-Billings, 2000; Milner, 2006; Sleeter, 2001). And yet, there remains a dearth of critical self-reflection among many of these teachers which impedes the development of positive and inclusive practices for reaching students from diverse backgrounds (Benton-Borghi & Chang, 2012; Gay, 2003; King, 1991). This lack of self-examination often stems from traditional Eurocentric power structures in society, which now more tacitly reinforce the nearly-imperceptible, internalized sense of privilege espoused by many white teachers (King, 1991; McIntosh, 1989). As a result, many teachers still hold negative views regarding the ability of students from diverse racial and ethnic backgrounds that continue to go unexamined in their respective TEPs (Cochran-Smith & Zeichner, 2009; Howard, 2006).

Overview

With respect to the rapid diversification of society as well as issues of equity and social justice, this review discusses key areas of research involving student diversity and teacher preparation and professional development. These interrelated topics are commonly discussed in the context of critical, culturally responsive and multicultural perspectives of schools and society, and rightly focus on conceptualizing methods for practice that increase students' and teachers' critical awareness of diversity issues of race, class, gender, language, ability, and cultural epistemologies in the classroom, as well as in local and global societies (Abrams, Taylor, & Guo, 2013; Apple, 2010, 2011a, 2011b; Castro, 2010; Freire, 2005; Giroux, 1988; Shizha, 2010; Swartz, 2003).

Concurrent with the diversification of society, social movements and educational reform efforts aimed at mitigating the effects of racial discrimination in schools and society continually emerge. As a broad rubric for teacher education and student diversity, this research generally underscores three major themes in the literature, including critical pedagogy, culturally responsive pedagogy, and multicultural education. In what follows, these topics are discussed and synthesized to help develop a framework of conceptual best practices for teaching in diverse urban settings.

Critical, Culturally Responsive and Multicultural Education

Critical perspectives in educational research are rooted in critical pedagogy, from which culturally responsive pedagogy and multicultural education were largely derived (Cochran-Smith & Zeichner, 2009; Lee & Buxton, 2008). Much of this research is decidedly political and tends to centralize concepts such as critical consciousness, emancipation, agency, social justice and community (Atwater, 1996a, 1996b; Atwater & Riley, 1993; Barton & Yang, 2000; Buxton, 2010; Cochran-Smith, 2010; Hickling-Hudson, 2004; Kanpol & McLaren, 1995; Ladson-Billings, 1995b; May, 1999; Tsurusaki, Barton, Tan, Koch, & Contento, 2013). Along with culturally responsive pedagogy and multicultural education, the critical lens espoused by many educational researchers has increasingly included feminist, postcolonial, and postmodern critiques that open the field to new conceptualizations of learning and teaching diversity (Capobianco, 2007; Carter, 2004, 2006; Haraway, 1988; Hickling-Hudson, 2003; Sharpe, 2005). And while these methods differ in scope and application, their shared commitment to social justice and the empowerment of racially and ethnically marginalized groups through critical and engaging teacher education offer significant insights for teaching effectively in diverse settings.

A common thread in this research is the notion that critical, pluralistic, and human-responsive forms of education have important implications in diverse classrooms. In particular, the literature suggests that effective teaching in diverse settings involves developing critical educators who, because they are attentive to both student and community contexts of race, ethnicity, culture, etc., as well as wider political implications of 'mainstream' education and social norms, continually seek to enhance curriculum and instruction in ways that are more responsive and inclusive (Barton & McLaren, 2001; Basu & Barton, 2010; Hodson, 1999).

Critical Pedagogy

Literature on critical pedagogy focuses on underserved populations and antiracist approaches to teaching and learning and includes authentic and democratic approaches to constructivist education in which students investigate and construct knowledge in real-world contexts alongside their teachers (Atwater, 2010, p. 20; Dewey, 1916; Freire, 1970, 2005; Gill & Levidow, 1987; Hodson & Dennick, 1994; Popkewitz, 1998; Ültanir, 2012). This research demonstrates the political possibilities of education when applied toward personal transformation, and developing the ability to locate and confront social injustice in ways that empower students and teachers as change agents in schools and society (Bandura, 1989; Freire, 1970; Giroux, 1988, 2005; Kanpol, 1992; Kanpol & McLaren, 1995; McLaren, 1999). To this end, such inquiry and investigations are useful for disrupting oppressive discourses in schools and society (Atwater, 1996b; Barton & McLaren, 2001; Basu & Barton, 2010).

Culturally Responsive Pedagogy

Culturally responsive pedagogy (CRP) is an extension of critical pedagogy centered in social justice and inclusion that attends to students' ethno-racial, cultural, and linguistic differences in the learning process. Not unlike its critical and multicultural counterparts, CRP demonstrates the importance of connecting subject area content to "the cultural characteristics, experiences, and perspectives of ethnically diverse students as conduits for teaching them more effectively" (Gay, 2002, p. 106). Likewise, with the goal of empowerment, CRP views students as agents rather than victims and seeks to assist them in developing a critical consciousness with which to confront social disparities in their local communities (Barton, 2003; Barton & Berchini, 2013; Ladson-Billings, 1995b, 1998; Lee, 2001). This research suggests that regardless of subject matter or a student's cultural background, relevant and responsive teaching supports high academic achievement and social mobility (Gay, 2002; Ladson-Billings, 2009; Lee, 2001; Lee & Buxton, 2008; Lee & Fradd, 1998).

As with critical pedagogy, literature on CRP emphasizes the need for greater accessibility to learning for students from diverse backgrounds and in ways that empower them as subjects in the world (Aikenhead, 1996, 1997; Atwater, 1996b, 2010; Gay, 2002; Hickling-Hudson, 2003; Jegede & Aikenhead, 1999; Nieto & Bode, 2012). This aspect of research on critical and culturally responsive pedagogy also points to the need for greater awareness of dominant cultural values and hegemonic discourse embedded in education, including "the selective inclusion and exclusion of material" (Kumashiro, 2001, p. 4) in the curriculum, high-stakes accountability measures that disproportionately affect urban schools attended by racial and ethnic minorities, as well as the increased presence of corporate privatization of education (Asante, 1991; Barton & McLaren, 2001; Hickling-Hudson, 2003; Kumashiro, 2001; Lipman, 2000, 2002, 2004; McLaren & Farahmandpur, 2001). In helping students restore and maintain their humanity, critical and culturally responsive pedagogies provide meaningful entry points for equitable learning opportunities for all students (Irvine, 1992; Ladson-Billings, 1995a; Nola & Irzık, 2005).

Multicultural Education

Following the *Brown Decision* in 1954 and Civil Rights Movement of the 1960s, multiculturalism and cultural pluralism became more prevalent in public and educational discourse and provided a curricular basis for multicultural education (Banks, 1993a, 1993b; Banks & Banks, 2010; May, 1999; Sharpe, 2005).

In doing so, multicultural education (MEd) combines the principles of multicultural education with critical and culturally relevant/responsive perspectives in systematic fashion. Banks and Banks offer MEd as a rejoinder to increased cultural intersections and subsequent need for "gender, ethnic, race, and cultural diversity of a pluralistic society [to be] reflected in all of the institutionalized structures of educational institutions" (2010, p. 447) through intensive efforts to incorporate the "content, concepts, principles, theories, and paradigms from history, the social and behavioral sciences, and particularly from ethnic studies and women's studies" (2004, p. xii).

The initial goal of MEd was to provide equal access and opportunity to all students, and over the course of its development, came to include more critical and culturally relevant approaches. However, as MEd is positioned as a systemic treatment for redressing educational inequalities that most often affect racial and ethnic minorities, it often includes the adaptation of curriculum designed to reflect the achievements and language of nonwhites in order to appeal to more diverse audiences (Banks, 1993a, 1993b; Banks & Banks, 2010; May, 1999; Sharpe, 2005). In striving to make education more accessible and reflective of all students, MEd continues to make valuable contributions for mitigating disparities in academic achievement (Atwater, 2011; May, 1999).

The underlying hope for this new field was to provide a viable means of facilitating increased cultural intersections in society, as well as address issues of achievement disparities among minority students (Atwater, 2011; May, 1999). However, MEd critics argued that the structural effects of racism were understated, and the curriculum, overemphasized (May, 1999). Antiracist criticisms, for example, suggested that multicultural curricula were naïvely touted as a panacea for increasing academic achievement and social mobility among minority students (Gill & Levidow, 1987; May, 1999; Swartz, 2005). Among such debates was the view that MEd was a superficial treatment privileged at the expense of deeper analyses of power differentials affecting race relations in society, and moreover, that it lacked the necessary depth and scope to effectively confront issues of racial discrimination pervading schools and society (May, 1999).

Additionally, some critics were skeptical as to whether the dominant class would even allow MEd to develop as it was proposed. Afrocentric scholars such as Molefi Asante, familiar with the history of suppressed knowledge and cultures of non-dominant groups, were rightly concerned with a hidden agenda of some white multicultural proponents (Asante, 1991; Asante & Ravitch, 1991; Bernal, 1987; Diop, 1974; Swartz, 2005). From this perspective, MEd would amount to little more than a near-passive addition to the already inequitable process of schooling, whose covert purpose would be to reinforce Eurocentric values rather than critically intervene in political debates and educational discourse (May, 1999).

Given the vast influence of critical (and even postmodern) educational approaches on an expanding array of multicultural and culturally responsive modes of teaching and learning in a knowledge-based economy, the above elicits new paths to critical and responsive education.

Adopting Critical Multicultural Education for Social Justice

Along with culturally responsive approaches, the political focus on equity and social justice embodied by critical pedagogy allow for more substantive applications of MEd. This not only helps situate MEd within the context of the political economy of education, but by incorporating the responsive nature of CRP and the emancipatory project of critical pedagogy assists in the development of a more transformative agenda for students and educators (McLaren & Torres, 1999). For instance, critical multicultural and culturally responsive perspectives offer the ability to politicize issues of class, gender, and socioeconomics, and to challenge revisionist histories that distort or omit the contributions of non-white cultures (Swartz, 2005). Embodied within these approaches is a deep respect for the localized, cultural streams of knowledge students bring into the classroom, including contextualized understandings of personal identity and subject area content (Brown, 2006; Emdin, 2008; Gay, 2002; Ladson-Billings, 1995a).

Developing and Supporting Educational Spaces for Transformative Teachers

As we demonstrate, research in the area of preparing culturally responsive teachers suggests a plethora of models that have been successful with encouraging urban students to excel academically. The first necessary step in urban teacher preparation and professional development would be to challenge teachers to check their biases and understandings of the lived experiences of their students by engaging in reflective activities. Teachers at all stages in their careers need to have the tools to be able to explore their own thinking and how their own implicit biases influence their work. In this section, we provide three examples of ways in which teachers can discover the funds of knowledge their students bring to school and how to utilize this new understanding to support the diversity within urban classrooms.

Community Mapping

In order to develop a deeper understanding of students' backgrounds, we argue that all teachers would benefit from participating in a community walking tour or mapping exercise, which would challenge them to learn more about the neighborhoods where students live and the community resources to which they have access. According to Ordonez-Jasis & Myck-Wayne (2012), "Community mapping is an inquiry-based method that situates learning in the context of students' lived realities" (p. 31). In many urban areas, due to the systemic lack of resources, and more importantly, access to them, a community based approach is quite common in supporting youth and their families (Ordonez-Jasis & Jasis, 2011). Community mapping has been used across a variety of fields (i.e. psychology, urban planning, cultural anthropology) to develop a better understanding of a community's assets, needs, resources, and culture (Tindle, Leconte, Buchanan, & Taymans, 2005). In the area of urban education, teachers can first use Google maps to take a digital walking tour of the community in which they are teaching. In this virtual tour, teachers might note all resources available within these communities—for example, major buildings and landmarks (i.e. grocery stores, schools, houses, doctor's offices, etc.), religious institutions, parks and recreational spaces, and community centers. By using street view, teachers can actually see the residential parts of neighborhoods and develop a clearer understanding of the places where their students live.

After this mapping exercise, teachers would benefit from going out into the community, taking pictures of the resources within the service areas of the community organizations, and talking to the residents within the neighborhoods. Using data collected on the physical walking tour (i.e. pictures, fliers, interviews), teachers might create a comprehensive picture of the community and determine how their classroom might be a space where these needs are met.

Teachers and administrators would further benefit from a sort of debriefing or reflective activity where they discuss what resources are available or missing from the residential areas within the school boundaries. Discussions of how these children are positioned by their access to goods (e.g. fresh produce) and services (e.g. access to parks and recreational spaces) might challenge teachers to think more deeply about issues, like childhood obesity, that plague urban communities. This community walking tour might also provide an opportunity to meet stakeholders who can provide resources and insight into meeting the needs of students. When engaging in post-walking tour/community mapping exercises, teachers might respond to the following questions that examine these experiences:

- How has touring the neighborhood in which your students we live informed your understanding of their lived experience?
- How has this experience informed your understanding of your students' behavior and response to curriculum and pedagogy in your classroom?
- What are the ways in which you might include community assets in your own classroom to meet the very specific needs of your students?

Ordonez-Jasis and Myck-Wayne (2012) suggest that pre-service teachers engaged in a community mapping project enabled participants to discover the resources surrounding the schools in which they were conducting clinical observations, raised awareness of the students' social and cultural contexts, and contributed to the development of "critical cultural competencies and positive dispositions" (p. 42) related to working with diverse populations.

Similarly, Fox (2013) suggests that community mapping from the vantage point of the students, has the potential to challenge teachers to walk in their students' shoes, thus a better understanding of their funds of knowledge (Banks, 1990a) and access to resources that support literacy. If teachers learn to view the community as an asset, thus shaking up the view of students from a deficit paradigm, they might find value in these community resources and add them to the curriculum (Moll, Gonzalez, Greenberg, & Velez, 2011). Fox (2013) found that teachers who participated in a community mapping exercise were more likely to understand the students' lives outside of school and were more likely to be engaged in activities and initiatives to make the school, especially libraries, more accessible to parents, families, and community members.

Service-Learning and Outreach

Another strategy that has been shown to be transformative for urban students is engagement in service-learning curriculum and projects (Webster & Coffey, 2011; Comer, 2004). Masucci and Renner (2001) suggest, "when activated for the purpose of the intellectual and practical apprehension of social injustice [service-learning] can become the foundation for a progressive (and transformative) educational experience" (p. 2). Service-learning not only provides the opportunity for teachers to become more familiar with their students, developing deeper connections, but also creates occasions for students to connect learning to their lives and communities.

Service-learning has been well documented in the literature in teacher education (Anderson & Erickson, 2003). In the context of teacher education, service-learning can be used to prepare pre-service teachers to teach in diverse settings (Erickson & Anderson, 1997), develop a sense of social justice (Anderson, Swyck, & Yiff, 2001), and support teacher candidates in the development of cultural competency (Coffey, 2010; Boyle-Baise, 2002; Tilley-Lubbs, 2011; Tinkler, Tinkler, Gerstl-Pepin, & Mugisha, 2014). Wade (2000) suggests that participation in service-learning in the communities in which one teaches has the potential to assist in the development of understanding of diversity in these areas.

Learning about Urban Communities through Service-Learning

One author teaches a service-learning course, Citizenship and Education, at a large public university in an urban area in the southeastern United States. Pre-service teachers (PSTs) enrolled in this course spend at least 25 hours per semester working with middle grades students in a sort of mentor/tutoring program at one of the largest urban middle schools in the state. Each semester, these PSTs collaborate with middle grades students (MGS) on developing a service project based on their interests. One spring, MGS identified bullying as the issue that most concerned them in their homes, school, and community. As a result, PSTs worked with middle grades students to plan and implement a week of activities designed to raise awareness about bullying and to involve the entire school and surrounding community, culminating in a large anti-bullying event. Throughout the week, activities included providing statistics and stories about bullying on the morning announcements; engagement in team building activities; and challenging the entire student body to take a leadership role in being more supportive of their peers. These MGS, in collaboration with the PSTs, also planned a student assembly for the entire seventh grade team, where they invited student and adult speakers and local musicians to entertain while sharing their anti-bullying message. MGS also learned a dance to a popular song with an empowering message and taught the dance to their peers during the assembly.

At the "Anti-bullying Blues Night", dinner was provided for MGS, their families, and community stakeholders. A local business donated T-shirts promoting the MGS-created anti-bullying slogan, "Think before you speak. Don't make others weak!" Local musicians and students performed songs and spoken word related to the theme of empowerment. MGS had the opportunity to make crafts and play games with PSTs outside of school time, thus solidifying the understanding these PSTs were invested in their lives. Furthermore, PSTs contacted local community businesses to attend the event to raise awareness about the concerns of MGS so that these stakeholders would have a deeper understanding of the students who attend George Washington Middle School.

The overall goal of the partnership was to promote engagement among SLPs in support of achieving a more meaningful and purposeful learning experience and to encourage an understanding of the concept of social justice, while providing requested tutoring and mentoring for students and aid for teachers. An examination of the outcomes for the PSTs indicate that they developed a deeper understanding of the issues that cause inequitable schooling experiences, increased awareness of concerns related to adolescence and poverty, and began to understand the potential of becoming culturally competent, especially as future teachers.

The middle grades teachers explained that this opportunity also enabled them to see their students in a different light and to experience a non-academic project with these learners. They felt as if they developed a sense of respect and a deeper understanding of these students and their backgrounds from this experience. One teacher said, "The kids always looked forward to it; they knew Fridays were coming they were able to build relationships, and then I also had the opportunity to see the kids in a different context instead of Monday through Friday…" During these moments, teachers were not primarily concerned with test scores and meeting annual growth, but were able to actually see the students' funds of knowledge.

As a result of this partnership and activity, MGS were able to identify as agents of change; not only did adults finally hear their voices, but they were able to affect change with their peers as well. This service-learning opportunity empowered MGS to identify an area of need, seek a solution for that concern, and voice their opinions about how to make change, thus moving them toward social action that would impact both their school and home communities. This example of how service-learning can demonstrate for PSTs the importance of understanding the background of urban students has implications for the potential of service-learning for practicing teachers who hope to engage and empower their urban students.

Exploring 'Texts' and Developing Critical Literacy

One valuable aspect of a culturally responsive approach to teaching that encourages agency and social action is critical literacy, which is the ability to read texts in an active, reflective manner in order to better understand power, inequality, and injustice in human relationships. According to Robinson and Robinson (2003), text is defined as a "vehicle through which individuals communicate with one another using the codes and conventions of society" (p. 3). Thus, songs, novels, conversations, pictures, movies, etc. are all considered texts.

The development of critical literacy enables one to interpret messages in the modern world through a critical lens, and to challenge the power relations embedded within them. Teachers who facilitate the development of critical literacy encourage students to interrogate societal issues and institutions like family, poverty, education, equity, and equality in order to critique the structures that serve as norms

(Comber, 2001). By selecting texts that represent the culture and lived experiences of urban students, teachers can validate their perspectives and realities. Furthermore, by teaching students how to interpret messages of power and to critique how their voices might be left out of the texts, teachers of urban students create spaces whereby learners can counter mainstream messages and act as agents of change (Behrman, 2006). Through mediums such as blogs and websites, teachers can provide ideal platforms for helping students as young as Kindergarten (Vasquez, 2014) foster acts of change. One of the most powerful mediums being used by urban teachers and within pre-service teacher environments is urban music—ranging from hip hop, to jazz, to classic rhythm and blues (Hill, 2007; Morrell, 2002; Morrell & Duncan-Andrade; Stovall, 2007).

An example of how a teacher might engender a critical literacy approach to analyzing text might be using hip hop music to empower urban students to voice their own critique of inequality in society. Clemons and Clemons (2013) found that if taught how to explore the messages of power in popular music, students often find a vehicle for expression of their own oppression. In particular, Clemons and Clemons posit that Hip Hop music can be used as a transformative educational tool because, oftentimes, urban students identify with the themes contained within the lyrics in these songs, which validate their own experience in words that are familiar to them.

Furthermore, as Ernest Morrell, former president of the National Council for Teachers of English suggests, teachers facilitating critical literacy have the responsibility to make texts written by and representative of their students the focus of the class as opposed to the supplementary or non-existent texts (2008). In order for students to see themselves as potential contributors to the world beyond school, they must provide them with examples of people who look like them and who have made significant contributions to the world. Classroom curriculum is often dominated by texts written by and representative of people who do not exemplify the minority perspective; thus, teachers must seek out those texts and make them central to their curriculum.

Additionally, teaching students how to read and write from a resistant perspective can become a tool for social change (Morrell, 2008), as this type of engagement enables them to interpret text from a viewpoint of the world and not just the common Euro-centric ideology often found in standard texts. By considering how people from different backgrounds (i.e., racial, cultural, gender, religious, socio-economic status, sexual orientation) would read the same text, students gain a better understanding of how the representative group would be affected by a reading of a text (Foss, 2002). Learning how to read from a resistant perspective challenges students to consider how their own world view is not the same as others, using this new understanding, students writing from a resistant perspective might publish works, like blogs, that would encourage social justice.

The production of counter-texts aligns with the practice of resistant reading. Essentially, this practice engages students in generating narratives or other texts, including multi-media creations, from a non-mainstream perspective, thus changing the meaning of the original text. "Producing counter-texts can serve to validate the thoughts, observations, and feelings of students and other underrepresented groups" (Behrman, 2006). This approach to curriculum offers students occasions to speak from the point of view of those voices that are often silenced or marginalized, thereby empowering them instead.

Developing critical digital literacy also enables students to act upon the world. Incorporating media and technology is another popular strategy for including critical literacy in the classroom. With the ever-increasing pervasive nature of digital media and social networks, teachers now, more than ever before, are tasked with showing students how to read and interpret messages they encounter via the Internet. Text messaging, blogging, creating identity profiles on social networking websites, and countless other activities are altering the way ideas are represented and communicated in society; thus, classroom instruction must include lessons in how to navigate and interrogate the impact media and technology has on their lives. Not only do students need to be shown how to interpret the messages, but also how to create their own messages of power in meaningful ways. Engaging students in this type of pedagogy, challenges the traditional teacher/student learning paradigm, creating a classroom where teachers are learners and learners are teachers. In this manner, traditional hierarchical relationships between the students and teacher are diminished.

Implications for Practice

Our main goal in this chapter has been to contribute to the discourse on systemic and coordinated approaches to helping urban teachers become more culturally responsive. We focus on the need for protecting the integrity of the place and space of urban students, and more notably, bringing there lived and real experiences within the classroom. We also acknowledge that in order for teachers to become more comfortable and successful in their urban environments, they must take an active role in establishing classrooms that accept and embrace their students' realities. Notably, those teachers who are truly concerned in the holistic learning of their students must come to the realization that the equation for success is not just academic building blocks. Teachers have the ability to positively influence and possibly change how their students see themselves and the world in which they live.

In the wake of a number of national events that have impacted urban communities, we cannot be ignorant to the fact that the aftermath of these activities have trickled into urban classroom environments. Restructured conversations about race and new realities about urban youth have altered families and communities, and more importantly, how youth see themselves and their futures both in and out of schools. These changing dynamics in the landscape of urban communities creates new challenges for pre-service teachers in urban settings. This sets up a pathway for deliberate and purposeful actions for pre-service teachers to bridge the gap of knowledge of injustice inside and outside of classrooms; to develop wider understandings of transformative teaching in urban classrooms and to deepen the understanding of the urban context through social mediums relevant to students.

1. Bridge the Gap of Knowledge of Injustice Inside and Outside of Classrooms

As we noted earlier, culturally responsive approaches and the political focus on equity and social justice embodied by critical pedagogy allows for more substantive applications of MEd. When teachers have the ability learn and understand the issues that their students might be facing on a daily basis, they are better positioned to be more responsive to their academic and social needs. For example, when pre-service and practicing teachers understand the complexities of many urban communities, they may be less likely to minimize their students' issues to being poor and destitute. They are in a place to better understand and incorporate the lived experiences of their students in their classroom teachings. Building on these revelations of greater understanding and empathy could also include the following within the classroom:

- Deeper appreciation of the classroom and learning environment of students due to the interactions between students and their teachers.
- Inclusion of community leaders and sites in the classroom to better illustrate topics and allow for teachers to help students make better connections of classroom content.

- Assistance in the development of activities for and by students to address social injustices.
- Development of a culturally realistic lens of students in order to be in better positions to advise and facilitate social justice rather than thwarting efforts and seeing the needs of urban students as an unimportant issue.
- Focus on developing civic-minded behaviors and attitudes in students, which can be used in classroom settings and beyond.

2. To Develop a Wider Understanding of how Social Movements can Affect Urban Classroom Teacher Pedagogy

Teachers who have made a choice to work in urban schools have done so for a number of reasons—some for the love of teaching, some for the love of changing lives, and others for the love of the money. Whatever the case, one cannot ignore the fact that teachers in urban settings must be cognizant of the role of power and politics in the school and to the greater extent their classrooms. They cannot distance themselves from these issues, and until they realize and accept these issues are real, they will be unable to truly be effective teachers. When this point is realized, these teachers then have the ability to:

- Evoke awareness among students of their ability to change and challenge the status quo.
- Assisting students in realizing that they can make a difference through classroom activities and discussions can change how teachers structure classroom learning.
- Establish a culture of change agents in school settings and to a greater extent the communities in which they work.
- Assist students in understanding the history and "story" of social ills, injustices and justices in their communities in an academic setting provides opportunities for teachers to form more socially competent and aware citizens—hopefully, leading to organized and relevant civic action to address issues in life.
- Develop a culture of democratic action and civility in classrooms.
- Facilitate more meaningful and deeper conversations and connection in their classes about the role and impact of positive democratic actions and how these have been used both locally and globally to empower and change societies and people.

3. To Deepen the Understanding of the Urban Context Through Mediums and Context Relevant to Students and Their Communities

When groups like Public Enemy came on the rap scene in the late 1980's, their message was meant to illuminate the social and political ills rampant in urban communities, but in a way that would soften the "blow" for those who were not living these realities. Through songs such as "Rebel without a Pause" or "Fight the Power" they began to stream the realities of urban youth and their communities on public radio. Gone are the days of many of these socially conscious rappers such as the 5 Percenters and the Poor Righteous Teachers, who had a vivid way of painting the obstacles of urban life. A wave of social media outlets meant to inform, incite and teach has been ushered onto the scene. With a click and a couple of keystrokes, an individual can immerse themselves in the culture and history of a community unlike their own. Mediums such as Facebook and Instagram have created platforms for not only exposing the realities of urban life, but also the histories, stories, and success that exude from these communities. Pre-service and practicing teachers have no excuse not to be able to understand the world of their students. Yes, we admit that there is a plethora of information streaming the social media airways; however, there are also avenues to find quality sources that will enrich the learning and teaching experiences of teachers.

We challenge teachers at all levels of experience to seize opportunities for classroom growth through these social media pathways and to hopefully use these resources to further develop the minds and attitudes of their students. Incorporating socially relevant sites and media in their classrooms cannot only enhance learning, but create an environment that acknowledges the impact and role of urban culture and history among pre-service teachers and their students. As Anyon (2005) observed, "Middle and high school teachers, in particular, can make a powerful contribution to movement-building by engaging students in civic activism. Both the Civil Rights Movement and successful youth efforts to reduce the voting age from 21 to 18 (legalized in 1971) demonstrate that activism by young people can make a huge impact on American society" (p. 188). Examples of international youth movements include:

- The Youth Justice Coalition, based in Los Angeles, California continuously focuses on empowerment for youth through monthly events that promote educational seminars on legal rights, immigration and deportation, and gang violence. In the wake of the murder of Michael Brown in Ferguson, Missouri, the group has increased activism related to mistreatment of minority groups by law enforcement.
- In the winter of 2011, the youth-led Arab Spring spread throughout the Northern African nations as well as the Middle East. Their fury fueled by repressive political regimes, lack of access to jobs, and economic sluggishness, compelled this powerful group of youth to mobilize through the Internet utilizing social media (Facebook, YouTube, and Twitter) to recruit forces to protest for rights such as political dialogue, job security through unionization, and the highest demand—democracy. Although the movement did not accomplish all of the desired goals, it brought attention to human rights issues in the Arab countries (Slackman, 2011).
- "Si, se puede!" In 2006, responding to legislation that would charge residents in the United States illegally with felony and make it a crime to help illegal immigrants, students throughout Virginia staged a walk-out in protest of national legislation. These youth marched in solidarity for the sake of their loved ones and others who were threatened with deportation despite working hard and contributing to society. This movement was publicized in *The Washington Post* (Bahrampour & Glod, 2006).

Unquestionably, we are poised to make change, to transform the face of American public school education. However, teachers have to understand the specific needs of their students and be willing to empower those students to challenge the status quo in order for this change to occur.

CONCLUSION

The original idea of this paper came from the involvement of the three authors in various aspects of urban communities and teacher education. Each author has a vested interest in the development of future teachers and the impact they have in the classroom, and more importantly the impact of these young lives in society. We hope this chapter will spark conversations about the role of culturally responsive teachers and their place in urban communities. More importantly, the aim is to challenge pre-service and practicing teachers to better recognize how the context in which their students grow up affects their perspective and understanding of the world.

The thoughts and ideas suggested are meant to provide both pre-service and practicing teachers with avenues to becoming stronger teachers and help them to make deeper connections with their students, and even more germane to the conversation, with the communities of their students. It is not enough for teachers to just gain content to *deal with* their students in the classroom; effective teaching in an urban setting also means understanding the culture, context, and realities of students and knowing how to use these complexities in their teaching. We challenge teachers and those who are preparing them to move expand their boundaries of self-learning. We want moments of self-reflection and critique by teachers in order to improve the learning and development of urban youth. If teachers are able to create opportunities for deeper connections with students by better understanding their world, we believe they will be able to affect greater learning within the classroom. Teachers who have the ability to evoke desire and change within students, who often do not see this as an option, should not lack the resources to do so. These educators should be given the space and resources to create classrooms that continuously build the learning environments of urban youth and the communities in which they live. Although these youths are faced with daunting realities that can thwart growth and development, they should not be denied the chance to be a force of change within their own classrooms and communities.

REFERENCES

Abrams, E., Taylor, P., & Guo, C. (2013). Contextualizing culturally relevant science and mathematics teaching for indigenous learning. *International Journal of Science and Mathematics Education*, *11*(1), 1–21. doi:10.100710763-012-9388-2

Aikenhead, G. (1996). Science education: Border crossing into the subculture of science. *Studies in Science Education*, *27*(1), 1–52. doi:10.1080/03057269608560077

Aikenhead, G. (1997). Student views on the influence of culture on science. *International Journal of Science Education*, *19*(4), 419–428. doi:10.1080/0950069970190405

Anderson, J. (1998). *Service learning and teacher education.* ERIC Document ID: ED 421481.

Anderson, J., & Erickson, J. (2003). Service-learning in preservice teacher education. *Academic Exchange Quarterly*, *7*(2), 111–115.

Anderson, J., Swick, K. & Yff, J. (2001). *Service-learning in teacher education: Enhancing the growth of new teachers, their students, and communities.*

Anyon, J. (2005). *Radical possibilities: public policy, urban education, and a new social movement. The critical social thought series.* New York: Routledge.

Anyon, J. (2009). Progressive social movements and educational equity. *Educational Policy*, *23*(1), 194–215. doi:10.1177/0895904808328523

Apple, M. (2010). Theory, research, and the critical scholar/activist. *Educational Researcher*, *39*(2), 152–155. doi:10.3102/0013189X10362591

Apple, M. (2011a). The tasks of the critical scholar/activist in education: The contribution of José Gimeno Sacristán. *Revista de Educación, 356,* 235–250.

Apple, M. (2011b). Global crises, social justice, and teacher education. *Journal of Teacher Education, 62*(2), 222–234. doi:10.1177/0022487110385428

Asante, M. (1991). The Afrocentric idea in education. *The Journal of Negro Education, 60*(2), 170–180. doi:10.2307/2295608

Asante, M., & Ravitch, D. (1991). Multiculturalism: An exchange. *The American Scholar, 60*(2), 267–276.

Atwater, M. (1989). Including multicultural education in science education: Definitions, competencies, and activities. *Journal of Science Teacher Education, 1*(1), 17–20. doi:10.1007/BF03032129

Atwater, M. (1996a). Teacher education and multicultural education: Implications for science education research. *Journal of Science Teacher Education, 7*(1), 1–21. doi:10.1007/BF00118343

Atwater, M. (1996b). Social constructivism: Infusion into the multicultural science education research agenda. *Journal of Research in Science Teaching, 33*(8), 821–837. doi:10.1002/(SICI)1098-2736(199610)33:8<821::AID-TEA1>3.0.CO;2-Y

Atwater, M. (2010). Multicultural science education and curriculum materials. *Science Activities: Classroom Projects and Curriculum Ideas, 47*(4), 103–108. doi:10.1080/00368121003631652

Atwater, M. (2011). Significant science education research on multicultural science education, equity, and social justice. *Journal of Research in Science Teaching, 49*(1), O1–O5. doi:10.1002/tea.20453

Atwater, M., & Riley, J. (1993). Multicultural science education: Perspectives, definitions, and research agenda. *Science Education, 77*(6), 661–668. doi:10.1002ce.3730770609

Bahrampour, T., & Glod, M. (2006, March 26). Students walk out in 2nd day of immigration rights protest. *Washington Post.* Retrieved from http://www.washingtonpost.com/wp-dyn/content/article/2006/03/28/AR2006032800982.html

Bandura, A. (1989). Human agency in social cognitive theory. *The American Psychologist, 44*(9), 1175–1184. doi:10.1037/0003-066X.44.9.1175 PMID:2782727

Banks, J. (1993a). Multicultural education: Historical development, dimensions, and practice. *Review of Research in Education, 19,* 3–49. doi:10.2307/1167339

Banks, J. (1993b). The canon debate, knowledge construction, and multicultural education. *Educational Researcher, 22*(5), 4–14. doi:10.3102/0013189X022005004

Banks, J., & Banks, C. (2010). *Multicultural education: Issues and perspectives* (7th ed.). Hoboken, NJ: Wiley.

Barnes, C. (2006). Preparing preservice teachers to teach in a culturally responsive way. *Negro Educational Review, 57*(1/2), 85–100.

Barton, A. (2003). *Teaching science for social justice.* New York: Teachers College Press.

Barton, A., & Berchini, C. (2013). Becoming an insider: Teaching science in urban settings. *Theory into Practice*, *52*(1), 21–27. doi:10.1080/07351690.2013.743765

Barton, A., & McLaren, P. (2001). Capitalism, critical pedagogy, and urban science education: An interview with Peter McLaren. *Journal of Research in Science Teaching*, *38*(8), 847–859. doi:10.1002/tea.1035

Barton, A., & Yang, K. (2000). The culture of power and science education: Learning from Miguel. *Journal of Research in Science Teaching*, *37*(8), 871–889. doi:10.1002/1098-2736(200010)37:8<871::AID-TEA7>3.0.CO;2-9

Basu, S., & Barton, A. (2010). A researcher-student-teacher model for democratic science pedagogy: Connections to community, shared authority, and critical science agency. *Equity & Excellence in Education*, *43*(1), 72–87. doi:10.1080/10665680903489379

Beal, S., & Crockett, L. (2010). Adolescents' occupational and educational aspirations and expectations: Links to high school activities and adult educational attainment. *Developmental Psychology*, *46*(1), 258–287. doi:10.1037/a0017416 PMID:20053022

Behrman, E (2006). Teaching about language, power, and text: A review of classroom practices that support critical literacy. *Journal of Adolescent and Adult Literacy*, 49(6), 490-498. doi:10.1598/JAAL.49

Bennett, S. (2013). Effective facets of a field experience that contributed to eight preservice teachers' developing understandings about culturally responsive teaching. *Urban Education*, *48*(3), 380–419. doi:10.1177/0042085912452155

Benton-Borghi, B., & Chang, Y. (2012). Critical examination of candidates' diversity competence: Rigorous and systematic assessment of candidates' efficacy to teach diverse student populations. *Teacher Educator*, *47*(1), 29–44. doi:10.1080/08878730.2011.632472

Bernal, M. (1987). *Black Athena: The Afroasiatic roots of classical civilization*. New Brunswick, NJ: Rutgers University Press.

Boyle-Baise, M. (2002). *Multicultural service learning: Educating teachers in diverse communities*. New York, NY: Teachers College Press.

Briggs, J., & McHenry, K. (2013). Community arts and teacher candidates: A study in civic engagement. *Studies in Art Education*, *54*(4), 364–375.

Brown, B. (2006). "It isn't no slang that can be said about this stuff": Language, identity, and appropriating science discourse. *Journal of Research in Science Teaching*, *43*(1), 96–126. doi:10.1002/tea.20096

Burke, K., & Greene, S. (2015). Participatory action research, youth voices, and civic engagement. *Language Arts*, *92*(6), 387–400.

Buxton, C. (2010). Social problem solving through science: An approach to critical, place-based, science teaching and learning. *Equity & Excellence in Education*, *43*(1), 120–135. doi:10.1080/10665680903408932

Capobianco, B. (2007). Science teachers' attempts at integrating feminist pedagogy through collaborative action research. *Journal of Research in Science Teaching*, *44*(1), 1–32. doi:10.1002/tea.20120

Carter, L. (2004). Thinking differently about cultural diversity: Using postcolonial theory to (re)read science education. *Science Education, 88*(6), 819–836. doi:10.1002ce.20000

Carter, L. (2006). Postcolonial interventions within science education: Using postcolonial ideas to reconsider cultural diversity scholarship. *Educational Philosophy and Theory, 38*(5), 677–691. doi:10.1111/j.1469-5812.2006.00219.x

Castro, A. (2010). Themes in the research on preservice teachers' views of cultural diversity implications for researching millennial preservice teachers. *Educational Researcher, 39*(3), 198–210. doi:10.3102/0013189X10363819

Clemons, K., & Clemons, K. (2013). What the music said: Hip Hop as a transformative educational tool. In M. Hanley, G. Noblit, T. Barone, & G. Sheppard (Eds.), *Culturally Relevant Arts Education for Social Justice*. New York: Routledge.

Cochran-Smith, M. (2010). Toward a theory of teacher education for social justice. In A. Hargreaves, A. Lieberman, M. Fullan, & D. Hopkins (Eds.), *Second International Handbook of Educational Change, Springer International Handbooks of Education* (pp. 445–467). London: Springer. doi:10.1007/978-90-481-2660-6_27

Cochran-Smith, M., & Zeichner, K. M. (Eds.). (2009). *Studying teacher education: the report of the AERA Panel on research and teacher education*. Mahwah, NJ: Lawrence Erlbaum Associates.

Coffey, H. (2010). '*They* taught *me*': The benefits of early community-based field experiences in teacher education. *Teaching and Teacher Education, 26*(2), 335–342. doi:10.1016/j.tate.2009.09.014

Comber, B. (2001). Negotiating critical literacies. *School Talk, 6*(3), 1–2.

Comer, J. (2004). *Leaving no child behind: Preparing today's youth for tomorrow's world*. New Haven: Yale University Press.

Darling-Hammond, L. (2005). New standards and old inequalities: School reform and the education of African American students. In J. E. King (Ed.), *Black education: A transformative research and action agenda for the new century* (pp. 197–223). Mahwah, NJ: Lawrence Erlbaum Associates.

Darling-Hammond, L. (2010). *The flat world and education: How America's commitment to equity will determine our future*. Columbia, NY: Teachers College Press.

Delpit, L. (1988). The silenced dialogue: Power and pedagogy in educating other people's children. *Harvard Educational Review, 58*(3), 280–299. doi:10.17763/haer.58.3.c43481778r528qw4

Delpit, L. (2006). *Other people's children: Cultural conflict in the classroom*. New York: New Press.

Delpit, L., & Dowdy, J. (2002). *The skin that we speak: Thoughts on language and culture in the classroom*. New York: New Press.

Dewey, J. (1916). *Democracy and education: An introduction to the philosophy of education*. Macmillan. Retrieved from http://www.gutenberg.org/ebooks/852

Diop, C. A. (1974). *The African origin of civilization: Myth or reality*. New York: Laurence Hill.

Emdin, C. (2008). Urban science classrooms and new possibilities: On intersubjectivity and grammar in the third space. *Cultural Studies of Science Education, 4*(1), 239–254. doi:10.100711422-008-9162-5

Foss, A. (2002). Peeling the onion: Teaching critical literacy with students of privilege. *Language Arts, 79*, 393–403.

Fox, K. (2013). Exploring literacy in our own backyard: Increasing teachers' understanding of literacy access through community mapping. *Journal of Praxis in Multicultural Education, 8*(2), 1–33. doi:10.9741/2161-2978.1071

Freire, P. (1970). *Pedagogy of the oppressed*. New York: Herder & Herder.

Freire, P. (2005). *Teachers as cultural workers: Letters to those who dare teach*. Boulder, CO: Westview Press.

Gage, N. (1978). *The scientific basis of the art of teaching. The Julius and Rosa Sachs memorial lectures*. New York: Teachers College Press.

Gay, G. (2002). Preparing for culturally responsive teaching. *Journal of Teacher Education, 53*(2), 106–116. doi:10.1177/0022487102053002003

Gay, G., & Kirkland, K. (2003). Developing cultural critical consciousness and self-reflection in preservice teacher education. *Theory into Practice, 42*(3), 181–187. doi:10.120715430421tip4203_3

Gill, D., & Levidow, L. (Eds.), (1987). *Anti-racist science teaching*. London: Free Association Books.

Giroux, H. (1987). Educational reform and the politics of teacher empowerment. *New Education, 9*(1/2), 3–13.

Giroux, H. (1988). *Teachers as intellectuals: Toward a critical pedagogy of learning*. Granby, MA: Bergin & Garvey.

Giroux, H. (2005). *Border crossings: Cultural workers and the politics of education* (2nd ed.). New York: Routledge.

Gómez-Quiñones, J., & Vásquez, I. (2014). *Making Aztlán: Ideology and culture of the Chicana and Chicano movement, 1966-1977*. Albuquerque: University of New Mexico Press.

Haraway, D. (1988). Situated knowledges: The science question in feminism and the privilege of partial perspective. *Feminist Studies, 14*(3), 575–599. doi:10.2307/3178066

Hickling-Hudson, A. (2003). Multicultural education and the postcolonial turn. *Policy Futures in Education, 1*(2), 381–401. doi:10.2304/pfie.2003.1.2.13

Hickling-Hudson, A. (2004). Educating teachers for cultural diversity and social justice. In G. Hernes (Ed.), Planning for diversity: Education in multi-ethnic and multicultural societies (pp. 270–307). Paris: International Institute for Education Planning (UNESCO).

Hill, M. (2009). *Beats, rhymes, and classroom life: hip-hop pedagogy and the politics of identity*. New York: Teachers College Press.

Hodson, D. (1999). Critical multiculturalism in science and technology education. In S. May (Ed.), *Critical multiculturalism: Rethinking multicultural and antiracist education* (pp. 236–266). Philadelphia, PA: Falmer Press.

Hodson, D., & Dennick, R. (1994). Antiracist education: A special role for the history of science and technology. *School Science and Mathematics, 94*(5), 255–262. doi:10.1111/j.1949-8594.1994.tb15666.x

Howard, G. (2006). *We can't teach what we don't know: White teachers, multiracial schools. Multicultural education series* (2nd ed.). New York: Teachers College Press.

Irvine, J. J. (1992). Making teacher education culturally responsive. In M. E. Dilworth (Ed.), *Diversity in teacher education: New expectations* (pp. 79–82). San Francisco: Jossey-Bass.

Jegede, O., & Aikenhead, G. (1999). Transcending cultural borders: Implications for science teaching. *Research in Science & Technological Education, 17*(1), 45–66. doi:10.1080/0263514990170104

Kanpol, B. (1992). *Towards a theory and practice of teacher cultural politics: Continuing the postmodern debate*. Norwood, NJ: Ablex.

Kanpol, B., & McLaren, P. (Eds.), (1995). *Critical multiculturalism: Uncommon voices in a common struggle*. Westport, CT: Bergin & Garvey.

King, J. (1991). Dysconscious racism: Ideology, identity, and the miseducation of teachers. *The Journal of Negro Education, 60*(2), 133. doi:10.2307/2295605

Kumashiro, K. (2001). "Posts" perspectives on anti-oppressive education in social studies, English, mathematics, and science classrooms. *Educational Researcher, 30*(3), 3–12. doi:10.3102/0013189X030003003

Ladson-Billings, G. (1995a). Toward a theory of culturally relevant pedagogy. *American Educational Research Journal, 32*(3), 465–491. doi:10.3102/00028312032003465

Ladson-Billings, G. (1995b). But that's just good teaching! The case for culturally relevant pedagogy. *Theory into Practice, 34*(3), 159–165. doi:10.1080/00405849509543675

Ladson-Billings, G. (1998). Just what is critical race theory and what's it doing in a nice field like education? *International Journal of Qualitative Studies in Education, 11*(1), 7–24. doi:10.1080/095183998236863

Ladson-Billings, G. (2000). Fighting for our lives: Preparing teachers to teach African American students. *Journal of Teacher Education, 51*(3), 206–214. doi:10.1177/0022487100051003008

Ladson-Billings, G. (2009). *The dreamkeepers: Successful teachers of African American children*. San Francisco, CA: Jossey-Bass Publishers.

Lee, O. (2001). Culture and language in science education: What do we know and what do we need to know? *Journal of Research in Science Teaching, 38*(5), 499–501. doi:10.1002/tea.1015

Lee, O., & Buxton, C. (2008). Science curriculum and student diversity: A framework for equitable learning opportunities. *The Elementary School Journal, 109*(2), 123–137. doi:10.1086/590522

Lee, O., & Fradd, S. (1998). Science for all, including students from non-English-language backgrounds. *Educational Researcher, 27*(4), 12–21. doi:10.3102/0013189X027004012

Lenzi, M., Vieno, A., Sharkey, J., Mayworm, A., Scacchi, L., Pastore, M., & Santinello, M. (2014). How school can teach civic engagement besides civic education: The role of democratic school climate. *American Journal of Community Psychology, 54*(3-4), 251–261. doi:10.100710464-014-9669-8 PMID:25172202

Lipman, P. (2000). Bush's education plan, globalization, and the politics of race. *Cultural Logic, 4*(1). Retrieved from http://clogic.eserver.org/4-1/lipman.html

Lipman, P. (2002). Making the global city, making inequality: The political economy and cultural politics of Chicago school policy. *American Educational Research Journal, 39*(2), 379–419. doi:10.3102/00028312039002379

Lipman, P. (2004). *High stakes education: Inequality, globalization, and urban school reform*. New York: RoutledgeFalmer. doi:10.4324/9780203465509

Martens, A., & Gainous, J. (2013). Civic education and democratic capacity: How do teachers teach and what works? *Social Science Quarterly, 94*(4), 956–976. doi:10.1111/j.1540-6237.2012.00864.x

Masucci, M. & Renner, A. (2001). The evolution of critical service-learning for education: Four problematics. *Resources in Education: ERIC Clearinghouse*. ED 456962.

May, S. (Ed.), (1999). *Critical multiculturalism: Rethinking multicultural and antiracist education*. Philadelphia, PA: Falmer Press.

McIntosh, P. (1989). *White privilege: Unpacking the invisible knapsack*. Peace and Freedom.

McLaren, P. (1999). *Schooling as a ritual performance: Toward a political economy of educational symbols and gestures* (3rd ed.). Lanham, MD: Rowman & Littlefield.

McLaren, P., & Farahmandpur, R. (2001). Teaching against globalization and the new imperialism: Toward a revolutionary pedagogy. *Journal of Teacher Education, 52*(2), 136–150. doi:10.1177/0022487101052002005

McLaren, P., & Torres, R. (1999). Racism and multicultural education: Rethinking "race" and "whiteness" in late capitalism. In S. May (Ed.), *Critical multiculturalism: Rethinking multicultural and antiracist education* (pp. 42–76). Philadelphia, PA: Falmer Press.

McWhorter, D. (2001). *Carry me home: Birmingham, Alabama, the climactic battle of the Civil Rights Revolution*. New York, NY: Simon and Schuster.

Milner, H. (2006). Preservice teachers' learning about cultural and racial diversity: Implications for urban education. *Urban Education, 41*(4), 343–375. doi:10.1177/0042085906289709

Moll, L., Gonzalez, N., Greenberg, J., & Velez, C. (n. d.). Funds of Knowledge. *USC.edu*. Retrieved from www.usc.edu/dept/education/CMMR/FullText/LuisMollHiddenFamilyResources.pdf

Morrell, E. (2002). Toward a critical pedagogy of popular culture: Literacy development among urban youth. *Journal of Adolescent & Adult Literacy, 46*(1), 72–77.

Morrell, E. (2008). *Critical Literacy and Urban Youth: Pedagogies of Access, Dissent, and Liberation*. New York: Routledge.

Morrell, E., & Duncan-Andrade, J. (2002). Promoting academic literacy with urban youth through engaging hip-hop culture. *English Journal*, *91*(6), 88. doi:10.2307/821822

National Center for Education Statistics. (2013). *Schools and Staffing Survey (SASS): Table 1. Total number of public school teachers and percentage distribution of school teachers, by race/ethnicity and state: 2011–12*. Washington, DC: U.S. DOE. Retrieved from http://nces.ed.gov/surveys/sass/tables/sass1112_2013314_t12n_001.asp

National Research Council. (2007a). *Rising above the gathering storm: Energizing and employing America for a brighter economic future*. Washington, DC: National Academies Press.

National Research Council. (2007b). *Beyond bias and barriers: Fulfilling the potential of women in academic science and engineering*. Washington, DC: National Academies Press.

National Research Council. (2010). *Rising above the gathering storm, revisited: Rapidly approaching category 5*. Washington, DC: National Academies Press.

Nieto, S., & Bode, P. (2012). *Affirming diversity: The sociopolitical context of multicultural education* (6th ed.). Boston, MA: Prentice Hall.

Nola, R., & Irzık, G. (2005). *Philosophy, science, education and culture. Science & technology education library*. Dordrecht, The Netherlands: Springer.

Ordoñez-Jasis, R., & Jasis, P. (2011). Mapping literacy, mapping lives: Teachers exploring the sociopolitical context of literacy and learning. *Multicultural Perspectives*, *13*(4), 189–196. doi:10.1080/15210960.2011.616824

Ordonez-Jasis, R., & Myck-Wayne, J. (2012). Community mapping in action: Uncovering resources and assets for young children and their families. *Young Exceptional Children*, *15*(3), 31–45. doi:10.1177/1096250612451756

Osborne, J., Simon, S., & Collins, S. (2003). Attitudes towards science: A review of the literature and its implications. *International Journal of Science Education*, *25*(9), 1049–1079. doi:10.1080/0950069032000032199

Ozoliņš, J. (2015). Creating the civil society east and west: Relationality, responsibility and the education of the humane person. *Educational Philosophy and Theory*. doi:10.1080/00131857.2015.1048666

Popkewitz, T. (1998). Dewey, Vygotsky, and the social administration of the individual: Constructivist pedagogy as systems of ideas in historical spaces. *American Educational Research Journal*, *35*(4), 535–570. doi:10.3102/00028312035004535

Raby, R. (2008). Frustrated, resigned, outspoken: Students' engagement with school rules and some implications for participatory citizenship. *International Journal of Children's Rights*, *16*(1), 77–98. doi:10.1163/092755608X267148

Riegle-Crumb, C., & King, B. (2010). Questioning a white male advantage in STEM: Examining disparities in college major by gender and race/ethnicity. *Educational Researcher*, *39*(9), 656–664. doi:10.3102/0013189X10391657

Robinson, E., & Robinson, S. (2003). *What does it mean? Discourse, text, culture - an introduction*. Sydney: McGraw-Hill.

Sharpe, J. (2005). Postcolonial studies in the house of US multiculturalism. In H. Schwartz & S. Ray (Eds.), *A companion to postcolonial studies* (pp. 112–125). Malden, MA: Blackwell Publishing. doi:10.1002/9780470997024.ch6

Shizha, E. (2010). The interface of neoliberal globalization, science education and indigenous African knowledges in Africa. *Journal of Alternative Perspectives in the Social Sciences*, 2(1), 27–58.

Siegesmund, R. (2013). Art education and a democratic citizenry. *International Journal of Art & Design Education*, 32(3), 300–308. doi:10.1111/j.1476-8070.2013.12023.x

Slackman, M. (2011, March 17). Bullets stall youthful push for Arab Spring. *The New York Times*. Retrieved from http://www.nytimes.com/2011/03/18/world/middleeast/18youth.html?_r=0

Sleeter, C. (2001). Preparing teachers for culturally diverse schools: Research and the overwhelming presence of Whiteness. *Journal of Teacher Education*, 52(2), 94–123. doi:10.1177/0022487101052002002

Stovall, D. (2006). We can relate: Hip-hop culture, critical pedagogy, and the secondary classroom. *Urban Education*, 41(6), 585–602. doi:10.1177/0042085906292513

Swartz, E. (2003). Teaching white preservice teachers: Pedagogy for change. *Urban Education*, 38(3), 255–278. doi:10.1177/0042085903038003001

Swartz, E. (2005). Multicultural education: From a compensatory to a scholarly foundation. In C. A. Grant (Ed.), *Research and multicultural education: From the margins to the mainstream* (pp. 31–42). London: Falmer Press.

Taines, C. (2012). Educational or social reform? Students inform the debate over improving urban schools. *Education and Urban Society*, 44(3), 247–273. doi:10.1177/0013124510392566

Tilley-Lubbs, G. A. (2011). Preparing teachers for teaching immigrant students through service-learning in immigrant communities. *World Journal of Education*, 1(2), 104–114. doi:10.5430/wje.v1n2p104

Tindle, K., Leconte, P., Buchanan, L., & Taymans, J. (2005). Transition planning: Community mapping as a tool for teachers and students. *Research to Practice Brief*, 4(1).

Tinkler, A., Tinkler, B., Gerstl-Pepin, C., & Mugisha, V. (2014). The promise of a community-based, participatory approach to service-learning in teacher education. *Journal of Higher Education Outreach & Engagement*, 8(3), 209–232.

Tsurusaki, B., Barton, A., Tan, E., Koch, P., & Contento, I. (2013). Using transformative boundary objects to create critical engagement in science: A case study. *Science Education*, 97(1), 1–31. doi:10.1002ce.21037

Ültanir, E. (2012). An epistemological glance at the constructivist approach: Constructivist learning in Dewey, Piaget, and Montessori. *International Journal of Instruction*, 5(2), 195–212.

Vasquez, V. (2014). *Negotiating critical literacies with young people: 10th Anniversary edition*. New York: Routledge.

Wade, R. C. (2000). From a distance: Service-learning and social justice. In C. R. O'Grady (Ed.), *Integrating service learning and multicultural education in colleges and universities* (pp. 93–111). Mahwah, NJ: Lawrence Erlbaum Associates.

Warren, C. (2013). Towards a pedagogy for the application of empathy in culturally diverse classrooms. *The Urban Review*, 46(3), 395–419. doi:10.100711256-013-0262-5

Webster, N., & Coffey, H. (2011). A critical connection between service learning and urban communities: Using critical pedagogy to frame the context. In T. Stewart & N. Webster (Eds.), *Problematizing service learning: Critical reflections for development and action* (pp. 245–262). Charlotte: Information Age Publishing.

Wilson, B. (2000). *Race and place in Birmingham: The civil rights and neighborhood movements*. Lanham, MD: Rowman & Littlefield.

This research was previously published in the Handbook of Research on Professional Development for Quality Teaching and Learning edited by Teresa Petty, Amy Good, and S. Michael Putman; pages 462-485, copyright year 2016 by Information Science Reference (an imprint of IGI Global).

Chapter 40
Multiculturalism in Special Education:
Perspectives of Minority Children in Urban Schools

Zandile P. Nkabinde
New Jersey City University, USA

ABSTRACT

The goal of this chapter is to explore multicultural education in the context of special education. Multicultural education as an effective intervention in urban schools is discussed. Obiakor (2007) describes this era as that of accountability where schools are challenged to leave no child behind, which makes schools more responsive to students' needs including those with special needs who are linguistically and culturally diverse. In addition, Gay (2002) defines culturally responsive teaching as using the cultural knowledge, prior experiences, and performance styles of diverse students to make learning more appropriate and effective for them; it teaches to and through the strengths of these students.

INTRODUCTION

This chapter was conceived with a purpose to contribute on the debate about multiculturalism and special education. The discussion explores how these overlapping spheres of influence affect minority children in urban schools. Many educators acknowledge that teachers need to be able to work well with minority students who have special needs and their families in urban settings in order to ensure that their cultural background is used to support, rather than impede their progress in education (Tepper, Tepper, 2004). The concept of multicultural education and special education when combined with terms like minority children and urban schooling usually carries negative connotations. This brings to mind academic underachievement, helplessness related to race, culture, class, and urban decay. Minority students with special needs in urban schools have triple-layered problems: that of being culturally different, linguistically different and having special needs. Diaz (2001) argued that disability itself, when framed through

DOI: 10.4018/978-1-7998-1213-5.ch040

the lens of special education, tends to be equated with deficiency. Having these odds stacked against them presents challenges for teachers and demands creative ways to help minimize these negative forces.

Multicultural Education Defined

Haberman and Post (1998) define multicultural education as follows:

Multicultural education is a process built on respect and appreciation of cultural diversity. Central to this process is gaining understanding of the cultures of the world and incorporating these insights into all areas of the curriculum and school life with a particular emphasis on those cultures represented in our school community. Growing from these insights is a respect for all cultures and commitment to creating equitable relationships between men and women, among people of different ethnic backgrounds, and for all categories of people. Viewed in this manner multicultural education builds respect, self-esteem, and appreciation of others and provides students with the tool for building a just and equitable society (p. 98).

Banks (1994) defines multicultural education as an education for freedom that is essential in today's ethnically polarized and troubled world. Education according to Banks (1994) should not alienate students from their home and community cultures. However, it should also not confine them by their cultural boundaries.

Special Education Defined

Smith and Tyler (2010) defined special education as a specially designed instruction to meet the individuals' unique needs. It is characterized by individualized services for students with disabilities. The key component to the services provided to students with disabilities and their families is free appropriate education provided in the least restrictive environment.

Multiculturalism and Minority Students in Special Education Classes

Research studies in special education state that minority students in urban schools are more likely to fail grades, drop out of school, and get assigned to special education classes more than their white counterparts (Chu, 2011). The U.S. Department of Education as cited by Obiakor (2007) reported that though Anglo Americans represent about 67% of general public school enrollments, they represent about 43% of special education placements. On the other hand, while African Americans represent about 17% of general public school enrollments, they represent about 20% of special education placements. The report further stated that from 2000 through 2001, there was a national student population of 67% Anglo American, 17% African American, 16% Hispanic, 4% Asian/Pacific Islander, and 1% American Indian/Alaska Native. However, special education placement of these groups was disproportionate in terms of the racial/ethnic composition of students; 43% Anglo American, 20% African American, 14% Hispanic, 2% Asian/Pacific Islander, and 1% American Indian/Alaska Native (U.S. Department of Education, 2001).

While classification of students with disabilities is necessary for the provision of special services, it has also been used to exclude minority groups from receiving education in a meaningful manner. Such exclusion has destroyed the academic and social aspirations of many urban students (Grant, 1980). For instance, black students are more than twice as likely as students of other ethnicities to be labeled as

EMR (Harry, Klingner, Crammer, Sturges, Moore, 2007). According to these authors the state of Black disproportionality is still problematic. Budd (2007) concurs that there is concern regarding the number of students of color receiving special education services. Further, special education legislation has created a vehicle for segregating students of color from mainstream educational opportunities. Mthethwa-Sommers (2014) pointed out that multicultural education for exceptional and culturally different is concerned with assisting students who do not possess the cultural capital of the dominant culture prevalent in schools. Therefore, the overarching objective of multicultural education as described by Mthethwa-Sommers (2014) is to remediate deficiencies or build bridges between the student and the school.

CULTURE AND MINORITY STUDENTS IN URBAN SCHOOLS

Schools have long recognized the importance of engaging minority students in their education. However, educators mainly work with middle and upper social class European Americans and interact less with other races, cultures and ethnic groups. This does not come as a surprise since the majority of the teaching force in institutions of learning is European Americans even in urban schools where there is a large concentration of students from ethnically diverse backgrounds (Obiakor & Mukuria, 2006).

The decreased involvement of both minority students and their families is connected to issues of power, privilege, discourse, and bias practices that silence these families. Culture, socioeconomic status, family and language all play critical roles and interact in complex ways to create unique learners with individual strengths and needs. Cultural identities of students may also be in sharp contrast with their European American teachers. Cultural identity is defined by Hernandez (2001) as an intertwined system of values, attitudes, beliefs, and norms that give meaning and significance to both individual and collective identity.

According to Hernandez (2001) an individual's cultural identity is based upon a number of traits and values related to national or ethnic origin, family, religion, gender, age, occupation, socioeconomic level, language, geographic region, residence (e.g., rural, suburban, or urban), and exceptionality. Garcia and Ortiz (2006) argued that when educators understand that culture provides a context for the teaching and learning of all students, they recognize that differences between home and school cultures can pose challenges for both teachers and students.

Therefore, teachers need to be sensitive to cultural issues when working with students who are culturally and linguistically diverse in special education settings. In addition, teachers need to know how culture affects learning. These students have unique characteristics and learning preferences that distinguish them from other students of their age. These differences may be viewed negatively by their peers and teachers. Stambaugh and Ford (2015) noted that when any individual differs significantly from the general population, whether in beliefs, ability, cultural differences, race/ethnicity, or social status, they may be more susceptible to misunderstanding, a lack of fit and even abuse.

Grant (1980) described schools as normative where dominant cultural practices form the basis of social, academic, and linguistic practices and are used as the basis for varied school experiences. According to Garcia and Ortiz (2006) in cases where dominant cultural practices shape school culture, many culturally and linguistically diverse students and their families find it challenging to function and participate in school. This is also called cultural mismatch. Budd (2007) argued that this cultural mismatch can result in a detachment from the learning environment by the students. In addition, culture clashes can lead to low expectations from the teachers due to preconceived notions about diverse cultures. Teachers can eliminate the negative effects of culture through the implementation of culturally responsive teaching. This can be accomplished by teaching within the cultural context and experiences of the students and their communities. Diaz (2001) stated that when students are given the opportunity to negotiate their cultural backgrounds, interests, and cognitive skills, they are more likely to experience academic success.

According to Gollnick and Chinn (2002), teachers need to engage in the following practices to reflect culture in the academic subjects they teach:

- Know how school knowledge is perceived in learners' cultures. Resistance to school authority and knowledge among low-income, working class, and minority youngsters limit their engagement with academics, especially when they do not see the relevance to their own lives.
- Know what kind of knowledge, skills, and commitments are valued in students' cultures. Such knowledge is critical to developing representations of subject matter that either bridge or confront the knowledge and understandings that students bring with them.
- Know about students' prior knowledge of, and experience with, the subject matter. The frameworks of understanding, based on prior experience that students use to make sense out of new ideas and information are also critical if teachers are to make their subject matter meaningful to students.
- Understand how a given subject matter is taught and learned determines, in part, the kinds of opportunities that teachers create for students to understand.
- Have a repertoire of different representations for a given idea, concept, or procedure. Teachers' abilities to generate or adapt representations, and their capacity to judge the appropriateness of representations for different students depends probably equally, on their understanding of their subject matter and their knowledge about their students.
- Understand the relationship of their subject matter to the world to help students understand these connections. Such connections are critical to the students' need to see the relationship between what they are studying in school and the world in which they live. Such connections are critical if teachers are to help oppressed students increase their control over and within their environment.
- Understand the role that teachers and schools play in limiting access to vital subject matter knowledge by addressing what they define as individual differences through organizational arrangements such as individualization, tracking, and ability grouping.
- Know that, for students, they are representatives of their subject matter. If teachers represent mathematics as repetitious drill and practice and if they express negative attitudes toward mathematics, their students are likely to develop similar beliefs and attitudes.
- Consider their role in the classroom and how that role shapes the roles that students assume. If students are to explore problems and ideas with classmates, teachers need to consider how their behavior facilitates or inhibits such collaboration (pp. 327-328).

TEACHING CULTURALLY AND LINGUISTICALLY DIVERSE CHILDREN WITH SPECIAL NEEDS

There are three educational components that need to be considered when dealing with special needs minority students in urban schools. These are teachers, instructional materials and testing materials

(Grant, 1980). Haberman and Post (1998) identified the following knowledge base for teachers who can offer multicultural programs:

- **Self-Knowledge**: A thorough understanding of one's own cultural roots and group affiliations.
- **Self-Acceptance**: A high level of self-esteem derived from knowing one's roots.
- **Relationship Skills**: The ability to work with diverse children and adults who are different from oneself in ways that these others perceive as respectful and caring.
- **Community Knowledge**: A knowledge of the cultural heritages of the children and their families.
- **Empathy**: A deep and abiding sensitivity and appreciation of the ways in which children and their families perceive, understand, and explain their world. The teacher truly understands what parents in particular cultural groups may want for their children without lowering standards and expectations.
- **Cultural Human Development**: An understanding of how the local community influences development. The teacher knows more than what is supposedly universal for all 7 year olds or all 13 year olds.
- **Cultural Conflicts**: An understanding of the discrepancies between the values of the local community groups and the traditional American values espoused in schools.
- **Relevant Curriculum**: A knowledge of connections that can be made between general societal values and those of the culture groups in the community, and the skills needed to implement this knowledge. The teacher connects specific content goals to specific uses in the students' lives.
- **Generating Sustained Effort**: A knowledge and set of implementation skills that will engage youngsters from this community to persist with schoolwork. The teacher's daily instruction is organized around and rewards effort rather than perceived ability.
- **Coping with Violence**: Skills for preventing and de-escalating violence and the potential for violence. The teacher demonstrates forms of conflict resolution based on criteria other than power.
- **Self-Analysis**: A capacity for reflection and change. Teachers engage in systematic self-reflection. They develop and implement plans for professional development that impact on their classrooms.
- **Functioning in Chaos**: An ability to understand and the skills to cope with a disorganized environment (pp. 98-99).

Instructional Materials

Instructional materials used for diverse learners with special needs in urban environments must accommodate their favored modalities. Tileston (2004) described students from the inner city as more hands-on, kinesthetic learners. On the other hand students from Eastern cultures are said to be auditory learners. Tileston (2004) identified the following instructional strategies to meet auditory learners:

- Direct instruction, in which the teacher guides the learning through the application of declarative (what students need to know) and procedural (what students can do with the learning) objectives;
- Peer tutoring, in which students help each other practice learning;
- Activities that incorporate music;
- Group discussions, brainstorming, and Socratic seminars;
- Specific oral directions;
- Verbalizing while learning, including the use of self-talk by the teacher and the learner;

Multiculturalism in Special Education

- Cooperative learning activities that provide for student interaction. Because cooperative learning also includes movement, more students benefit from its use (p. 17).

Visual learners are described as those students who need to see the information in order to understand how it is applied. Tileston named the following ideas to be used for visual learners:

- Using visuals when possible;
- Using models, puzzles, and DVD tapes;
- Demonstrating the learning, when appropriate;
- Including activities in a mind-game format;
- Showing patterns in the learning (p. 19).

Another preferred modality for students with disabilities who are also culturally and linguistically diverse is kinesthetic. These learners need movement and touching and they may be hyperactive. Ideas identified by Tileston (2004) which may be beneficial for these students are:

- Using hands-on approach to learning;
- Providing opportunities to move;
- Using simulations, when appropriate;
- Bringing in music, art, and manipulatives to expand the learning;
- Breaking up lecture so that verbal communication by the teacher is in manageable chunks;
- Providing opportunities for learning through discovery when appropriate;
- Using such techniques as discussion groups or cooperative learning so that these students have an opportunity to move about and to talk with their peers (pp. 20-21).

Testing Materials

Testing used to identify students with disabilities including those who are culturally and linguistically diverse has been described as overwhelmingly biased against ethnic minorities other than those who are white. Problems with testing are described by Chamberlain (2005) as being twofold:

1. General education teachers lack the ability to discern between underachievement due to a disability (e.g., information processing deficits seen with learning disabilities (LD) and underachievement due to other reasons (e.g., learning English as a second language, culture clashes that lead to low expectations by teachers).
2. Educational diagnosticians are unable to make the same distinction within the context of comprehensive assessment (p. 197).

IDEA requires that all students considered for special education services be tested in their primary language conducted by a multidisciplinary team. These safeguards are aimed at eliminating discrimination in all aspects of assessment. Culturally biased assessment and referral procedures are a major contributing factor in the misidentification of culturally and linguistically diverse students. This may be due partly to administrator's bias, content bias, linguistic bias and cultural bias. Test bias in standardized norm-referenced assessments is described by Chamberlain (2005) as follows:

- **Content Bias:** A test has content bias if it includes items with which a particular cultural group is not familiar or reflects a value system that is different from the value system of that group.
- **Construct Bias:** Tests should measure the constructs they purport to measure. If these constructs are not well defined, the tests are not valid indicators of a student's ability related to those constructs.
- **Lack of Tests in Different Languages:** Other than assessments in Spanish, there are no non-English norm-referenced assessments used in determining LD eligibility in the United States, which is problematic when special education eligibility criteria stipulate the use of such tests.
- **Lack of Opportunity to Learn Content or Lack of Exposure to the Testing Situation:** When CLD students have not had an adequate opportunity to learn the content being assessed, tests are not valid as an indicator of disability.
- **Norm-Referenced Tests Rely on the Melting – Pot Theory of the Typical U.S. Student:** Norms represents an aggregate of a representative sample of people. For norms to be culturally appropriate, they should reflect the cultural and linguistic backgrounds of specific and linguistic groups (p. 198).

These conceptual and procedural flaws and problems according to Artiles and Trent (1994) call for a reform of the current referral and assessment systems in special education. Reschly (1996) suggested the following as causes for disproportionate minority representation in special education: poverty, discrimination or cultural bias in referral and assessment, and unique factors related directly to race or ethnicity (p. 47). The Individuals with Disabilities Education Act (IDEA) 2004's statute noted that:

1. Greater efforts are needed to prevent the intensification of problems connected with mislabeling minority children with disabilities;
2. African-American children are identified as having mental retardation and emotional disturbance at rates greater than their white counterparts;
3. More minority children continue to be served in special education than would be expected from the percentage of minority students in the general school population;
4. In the 1998-1999 school year, African-American children represented 14.8% of the population aged 6 through 21, yet comprised 20.2% of all children with disabilities served in our schools; and
5. Studies have found that schools with predominately white students and teachers have placed disproportionately high numbers of their minority students into special education (U.S. Department of Education, 2009, p.1).

MULTICULTURAL LEARNERS AND THE ASSESSMENT PROCESS

Minority groups in urban schools including children of different racial, cultural, social, ethnic, and linguistic backgrounds have historically been disproportionately represented in special education. Chu (2011) contended that the incompatibilities of culturally and linguistically diverse students with school standards makes teachers view them as deviant and puts them in a disadvantaged position. It is further stated that a disproportionate representation of CLD students in special education is due to inappropriate diagnosis. Garcia and Ortiz (2006) contended that it is critical that the prereferral intervention process is culturally and linguistically responsive; that is, educators must ensure that students' sociocultural, linguistic, racial/ethnic, and other relevant background characteristics are addressed at all stages, including reviewing student performance, considering reasons for student difficulty or failure, designing alternative interventions, and interpreting assessment results (p. 64).

Part of the problem in the placement of students from culturally and linguistically diverse backgrounds into special education classes may be the result of confusing disability with diversity. This is also known as the deficit theory. Several research studies concur that teachers have a greater tendency for racial biases toward culturally and linguistically diverse students, which take the form of lower expectations and negative perceptions (Arnold & Lassmann, 2003; Chu, 2011; Grant, 1980; Obiakor, 2007). Chu (2011) further revealed that the negative perceptions held against minority students are generally not based on cognitive capabilities, but on characteristics unrelated to the learning process. This notion is supported by Artiles, and Trent (1994) who reported that factors such as gender, appearance, and socioeconomic status can all be the basis for eligibility decisions.

Teachers who believe they can make a difference in the learning of students who are at risk are less likely to refer at-risk students for special services. It is revealed that a teacher's sense of efficacy has a significant impact on his/her perceptions of appropriateness of general education for students with learning and/or behavior problems. It is essential for educators to take into consideration the student's culture when administering tests that may not reflect their true abilities due to the testing materials' biased content. Obiakor (2007) cited the following important placement principles for general and special education professionals:

- Race and culture matter in the placement of students.
- Placements must be based on students' need not on racial and cultural identities.
- Language difference should never be misconstrued as a lack of intelligence.
- Empathy is an important ingredient of "good" placement.
- Good placements are usually least restrictive environments.
- Differences are not deficits.
- Students are best served when their due-process rights are respected.
- Appropriate inclusion reduces biased exclusion of students in classroom activities.
- Prejudicial placements have devastating effects on students.
- The unique differences brought by students into classrooms must be valued (p. 150).

As the school population becomes more diverse in terms of its racial and language make-up, teachers need much more cultural sensitivity in order to assess and work fairly with children who are culturally and linguistically diverse (Diaz, 2001).

PARENTAL INVOLVEMENT

Numerous studies have confirmed that parental involvement in children's schooling has significant benefits associated with children's school success, including better achievement and behavior, lower absenteeism, lower dropout rates, and more positive attitudes toward schools (Overstreet, Devine, Bevans, Efreom, 2005; Park, Holloway, 2013). However, educators struggle with the dilemma of how, where, when, and to what extent parents should be involved. The issue of how to empower parents and community has become significant since most teachers struggle to determine the actual role parents should play. Some educators perceive parental involvement in educational matters as an invasion of their "niche or domain." Teachers perceive that they have been thoroughly trained in the craft of their trade and therefore do not see the value of parents' contributions. At the same time, many parents are daunted by the prospect of confronting bureaucratic and often non-responsive school systems. Many parents from culturally diverse backgrounds work more than one job and cannot help their children with school work. Their children in turn fall behind academically and will never be able to catch up with their counterparts whose first language is in English.

According to Palawat and May (2015) if professionals do not understand the goals valued by families of children with disabilities from different cultural backgrounds this may cause conflict when the goal of education has been set. For example, intellectual productivity/strength is a measurement of human worth in Western cultures, people who do not measure up in this area may be considered as non-productive and are also likely to be undervalued. In the context of children with disabilities the ultimate goal may be that of independent living in adulthood. Many parents of children with disabilities struggle as they attempt to reconcile cultural values that are different from theirs.

PARENTS FROM DIVERSE CULTURAL AND ETHNIC BACKGROUNDS

Many parents in urban schools are working class from culturally, ethnically, and linguistically diverse backgrounds whose first language may not be English. Sometimes immigrant parents have the assumption that teachers are in charge of all that goes on at school. According to Vang (2006) many bilingual parents come from cultures in which teachers receive the same respect as civic leaders and clergyman. These parents trust that teachers have great expertise, enabling them to educate their children to become productive citizens (Vang, 2006). The cultural and socioeconomic backgrounds of these parents relegate them to a low-status position within the education context.

Consequently, urban parents who advocate for their children and demand extensive educational reform encounter the challenge of seeking knowledge and power in a system that is inclined to frustrate and resist their efforts. Ideally, the prevailing adversarial relationship between parents and education should be replaced by enhanced collaboration for the benefit of the children. Parental empowerment can be a powerful tool in achieving that goal. Language and cultural differences can cause children to struggle in school and thus be suspected of having a disability.

Parents of minority children with disabilities are perhaps the most valuable resources for both policy makers and teachers whose expertise can be drawn upon to design innovative training programs (Nkabinde, 1995).

Special Education Legal Mandate

In 1974 case of Lau v. Nichols as cited in Vang (2006) established the premise that public schools should give non-native English speaking students extra help to assist them to excel in school. However, according to Vang (2006), the court did not specify what public schools should do to help these learners excel academically. The implementation of PL 99-157 and PL 101-476 signaled a change in the status of parent/school relationships. These enactments stressed the idea that families, but not parents alone, should be the focal point of professional attention. The salient reasons for this shift were the evolving recognition that partnerships should not be limited exclusively to parents but should also include immediate family and the community at large (Turnbull & Turnbull, 2001).

Professionals must now operate under the assumption that the family serves as a primary decision-maker in matters pertaining to setting goals and establishing priorities for the students. The fundamental beliefs underlying focus on family and community are based on the premises that families are interrelated social systems with unique characteristics and needs. The family operates as an interrelated and an independent unit. Whatever affects one family member has ripple effects on other family members and community. Consequently, teachers and other service providers should consider the family constellation as the appropriate focal point of their professional attention. Turnbull & Turnbull (2001) posit that the study of family must take into account family dynamics and include family characteristics, family interactions, family functions and family cycles.

Need for Parental Involvement

Research studies indicate that cultural and/or linguistic differences are often the cause of poor collaboration between minority families and special education providers (Palawat & May, 2015). Berger (2006) reported that parental involvement has become a buzzword in education, a recommended cure for high dropout rates, poor test scores, student attitudes and almost everything else that ails schoolchildren. The author noted that for immigrant parents, helping their children absorb lessons in an inscrutable language in a strange country has always been a distinctive challenge. For over three decades educators have decried disproportional representation of minority groups in special education programs and their underrepresentation in programs for the gifted (Coutinho & Oswald, 2000). A myriad of reasons has been given as an explanation of over-and under representations of children from culturally and linguistically diverse backgrounds in certain programs in special education. No one explanation fully accounts for this situation; the various reasons are complex and frequently intertwined. Patton (1998) and Artiles and Trent, (1994) describe the problems as rooted in socioeconomic, sociocultural and sociopolitical forces. Nzinga-Johnson, Baker and Aupperlee (2009) identified the following as barriers to minority parental involvement, teacher and school practices that are inequitable and reinforce power and privilege, previous experiences of ethnic minority and the poor, and the quality of the relationship between school staff, parents, and students (p. 82).

Parental involvement is one of the major elements of the Individuals With Disabilities Education Improvement Act of 2004 (IDEA). According to Harry (2008) implementation of this mandate is important to all families of children with disabilities. Harry (2008) noted that there are three main areas of concern regarding the participation of culturally and linguistically diverse (CLD) families. These concerns are, first, children of African American, Latino, and Native American groups represent a disproportionately large percentage of certain disability categories and a disproportionately small percentage of gifted programs. Second, our nation's history of exclusion and marginalization of CLD groups continues to present the education system with the challenge of historically embedded prejudices that are reinforced when children from such groups have further characteristics of disability. Third, because the concept of disability is defined differently across cultures, the potential for cross-cultural miscommunication is extremely high when the service provider's cultural framework differs from those of the families they serve (p. 372).

Minority children are at a greater risk to drop out of school when their families are excluded from the educational process. Tepper and Tepper (2004) argued that if a good connection is made with families of children who are culturally and linguistically diverse, a strong bond and a positive working relationship can be developed. According to these authors, when educators view how a particular family operates within the culture they can better serve the child.

Immigrant parents who are also racial and ethnic minorities are more likely to encounter barriers to school involvement as they navigate through the school system and interact with teachers (Turney and Kao, 2009). The disengagement of culturally and linguistically diverse parents in their children's education is due to several factors, including: language barrier, cultural challenges, lack of resources, and lack of knowledge about what is expected of them. Parental involvement is also linked to socioeconomic status. According to Turney and Kao (2009), parents with higher income and greater educational attainment are more involved than parents of lower socioeconomic status.

Turney and Kao (2009) outlined the following as the benefits of parental involvement:

First, parental involvement socializes children; parents who are involved send a message to their children that education is important, and these children are more likely to value education themselves. Second, parental involvement provides parents with a means of social control; involved parents get to know other parents, teachers, and administrators who may then discuss their children's performance with them. Last, involved parents are privy to information about their children; if teachers tell parents their children are struggling, parents are in a better position to intervene (p. 258).

Parents can demonstrate involvement in their children's education in a variety of ways, such as attending parent-teacher conferences, participating in parent-teacher organizations (PTOs), participating in school events, and volunteering at school (Turney and Kao, 2009). Nzinga-Johnson, Baker and Aupperlee (2009) identified a six component typology of behaviors that comprise home/school/community partnerships including parenting, communicating between the home and school, volunteering at school, fostering learning at home, sharing responsibility for decision making in the school, and collaborating with the community (p. 82). Parental involvement is viewed as a crucial element in planning and providing effective services for children with disabilities. Students whose parents are involved in their education tend to do better academically and socially. Olivos et al. (2010) identified the following approaches to foster authentic collaboration with families of culturally and linguistically diverse students:

- Provide CLD families full access to the school and to the people serving their children's needs. Too often CLD families are turned away from the school during times that are convenient because of school professional's lack of sensitivity to the reality of families' schedules.
- Examine collaboration efforts and ensure that all parties share power equally. Parents should be fully informed of where and how they can express a concern with the options presented for assessment and services.
- Inform parents of all options available for their children and support family involvement in authentic decision making. Information is central to assisting CLD families in their quest to serve the needs of their child with disabilities.
- Establish general education teachers as the point person in the school-family collaboration. Their child's teacher is often the person in the school that CLD parents trust most. Teachers play an intimate role in empowering students and parents (pp. 36-37).

As Nzinga-Johnson et al. (2009) highlighted, that when minority and low-SES parents are involved, there are positive outcomes for their children. Research studies have suggested that the role of the community is important in promoting the learning culture. Students must see the connection between the school and their communities (Nkabinde, 1997). This relationship provides continuity, as well as the practical implications of education.

Barriers to Overcome

Many service providers are baffled as to why parents and community often resist being involved in the educational process. Several possible explanations may exist. In addition, many of these parents have had negative or discriminatory school experiences, which have created mistrust. Family members are unwilling to disclose personal or family matters that might reflect negatively on themselves and the family. Further, some groups view school achievement, failure and behavior as direct attacks to their parenting skills. To make the matter worse, school personnel and school structure intimidate some parents from diverse cultural and linguistic backgrounds.

Some parents do not participate in the education of their children due to language barriers, conflicting work schedules, and sometimes lack of transportation. Language is an important modality for fostering meaningful relationships and therefore, language differences impose communication barriers for some. The professional jargon teachers use during teacher-parent conferences is intimidating to many parents. Also the difference between the school and home language can contribute to parents' resistance to participating in school matters. It is pathetic that many service providers have a view of "deficient" which increases the level of discomfort and disrespect among parents. It is erroneous, misleading and unacceptable to view language differences as a deficiency. A viable explanation provided by Lindeman (2001) is that some parents, especially those from immigrant families, do not understand the U.S. school system and its expectations, nor do they have a cultural history of being active, collaborative parents who visit schools regularly.

Other authorities suggest that families may perceive the meaning of disability and the acceptance of certain behaviors differently and that parents from different cultural backgrounds may have different perceptions about schooling (Craig, Hall, Hagart, Perez-Sellers, 2002). Consequently, when working with families from culturally and linguistically diverse backgrounds, it is critical for school personnel to anticipate that there may be a conflict between the home and school culture and be willing to determine the nature of these differences and how to minimize them.

RECOMMENDATIONS

Culturally responsive teaching is an effective intervention for teaching students who are culturally and linguistically diverse. This pedagogy as described by Gollnick and Chinn (2002) affirms the cultures of students, views the cultures and experiences of students as strengths, and reflects the students' cultures in the teaching process. Gollnick and Chinn (2002) identified the following six practices that define culturally responsive teaching:

- Students whose educational, economic, social, political, and cultural futures are most tenuous are helped to become intellectual leaders in the classroom.

- Students are apprenticed in a learning community rather than taught in an isolated and unrelated way.
- Students' real-life experiences are legitimized as they become part of the "official" curriculum.
- Teachers and students participate in a broad conception of literacy that incorporates both literature and oratory.
- Teachers and students engage in a collective struggle against the status quo.
- Teachers are cognizant of themselves as political beings (p. 325).

The underachievement of student of color has been the focus of numerous studies. Gonzalez, Velez, Garrett (2004) identified five school-related factors that influence their underachievement: a lack of exposure to appropriate and challenging curricular experiences at the elementary school level; an absence of opportunities to develop or improve schoolwork discipline; negative interactions with teachers; an unrewarding curriculum; and questionable experiences with guidance counselors (p. 16). If school-related factors have direct impact on underachievement of ethnically diverse learners, then school reform aimed at removing these barriers is a necessity.

CONCLUSION

The success of students who are culturally and linguistically diverse does not depend solely on their academic achievement. However, these students are less likely to succeed when their economic, cultural, socioemotional, affective, and developmental needs are ignored, trivialized, or poorly addressed (Stambaugh and Ford, 2015). It must also be pointed out that multicultural education is not only appropriate for ethnic minorities and linguistically diverse students but it is also appropriate for White mainstream students. According to Banks (1994), many of the reforms designed to increase the academic achievement of ethnic and linguistic minority students, such as pedagogy that is sensitive to student learning styles and cooperative learning techniques, will also help White mainstream students to increase their academic achievement and to develop more positive intergroup attitudes and values (p. 18). Therefore, multicultural education has to do with effective teaching for all learners.

Having more educators from racial and ethnic minorities who share the same experiences and background with students might help reduce the problem of misidentification. Unfortunately, the scarcity of educators of color leaves many students from ethnic/racial minorities without role models.

REFERENCES

Arnold, M., & Lassman, M. E. (2003). Overrepresentation of minority student in special education. *Education, 124*(2), 230–236.

Artiles, A. J., & Trent, S. C. (1994). Overrepresentation of minority students in special education: A continuing debate. *The Journal of Special Education, 27*(4), 410–437. doi:10.1177/002246699402700404

Banks, J. A. (1994). *An introduction to multicultural education.* Boston, MA: Allyn and Bacon.

Berger, J. (2002, November 1). For Hispanic parents, lessons on helping with the homework. *New York Times.*

Budd, E. (2007). Multicultural insights: The importance of culturally responsive curriculum and teaching for culturally diverse student who have special needs. *Black History Bulletin, 70*(1), 31–33.

Chamberlain, S. P. (2005). Recognizing and responding to cultural differences in the education of culturally and linguistically diverse learners. *Intervention in School and Clinic, 40*(4), 195–211. doi:10.1177/10534512050400040101

Chu, S. (2011). Teacher perceptions of their efficacy for special education referral of students from culturally and linguistically diverse backgrounds. *Education, 132*(1), 3–14.

Coutinho, M., & Oswald, D. (2000). Disproportionate representation in special education: A synthesis and recommendations. *Journal of Child and Family Studies, 9*(2), 135–156. doi:10.1023/A:1009462820157

Craig, S., Hall, K., Hagart, A. S. G., & Perez-Sellers, M. (2002). Promoting cultural competence through teacher assistance teams. *Teaching Exceptional Children, 32*(3), 6–12. doi:10.1177/004005990003200302

Diaz, C. F. (2001). *21st century.* New York, NY: Addison Wesley Longman.

Garcia, S. B., & Ortiz, A. A. (2006). Preventing disproportionate representation: Culturally and linguistically responsive prereferral interventions. *Teaching Exceptional Children, 38*(4), 64–68. doi:10.1177/004005990603800410

Gay, G. (2002). Culturally responsive teaching in special education for ethnically diverse students: Setting the stage. *International Journal of Qualitative Studies in Education, 15*(6), 613–629. doi:10.1080/09518390220000014349

Gollnick, D. M., & Chinn, P. C. (2002). Multicultural education in a pluralistic society (6th ed.). Upper Saddle River, NJ: Merrill Prentice Hall.

Gonzalez, R. A., Velez, W., & Garrett, T. (2004). Challenging the academic (mis)categorization of urban youth: Building a case for Puerto Rican high achievers. *Multiple Voices for Ethnically Diverse Exceptional Learners, 7*(1), 16–32.

Grant, C. A. (1980). Education that is multicultural and Urban Schools: Rationale and Recommendations. *British Journal of In-Service Education, 6*(2), 69–78. doi:10.1080/0305763800060202

Haberman, M., & Post, L. (1998, Spring). Teachers for Multicultural Schools: The Power of Selection. *Theory into Practice, 37*(2), 96–104. doi:10.1080/00405849809543792

Harry, B. (2008). Collaboration with culturally and linguistically diverse families: Ideal versus reality. *Exceptional Children, 74*(3), 372–388.

Harry, B., Klingner, J., Cramer, E., Sturges, K. M., & Moore, R. F. (2007). *Case Studies of Minority Student Placement in Special Education.* New York, NY: Teachers College Press.

Hernandez, H. (2001). *Multicultural Education: A teacher's guide to linking context, process, and content* (2nd ed.). Upper Saddle River, NJ: Merrill Prentice Hall.

Lindeman, B. (2001). Reaching out to immigrant parents. *Educational Leadership, 58*(6), 62–66.

Mthethwa-Sommers, S. (2014). *Narratives of social justice educators standing firm*. New York: Springer Cham Heidelberg.

Nkabinde, Z. P. (1997). *An analysis of educational challenges in the new South Africa*. Lanham, Maryland: University Press of America.

Nkabinde, Z. P., & Ngwenya, T. P. (1995). Interviews with African parents of children with disabilities. *Negro Educational Review*, *46*(3-4), 95–102.

Nzinga-Johnson, S., Baker, J. A., & Aupperlee, J. (2009). Teacher-parent relationships and school involvement among racially and educationally diverse parents of Kindergartners. *The Elementary School Journal*, *110*(1), 81–91. doi:10.1086/598844

Obiakor, F. E. (2007, January). Multicultural Special Education: Effective Intervention for Today's Schools. *Intervention in School and Clinic*, *42*(3), 148–155. doi:10.1177/10534512070420030301

Obiakor, F. E., & Mukuria, G. (2006). Special education leadership in urban schools. In F. E. Obiakor, F.A. Rotatori, & S. Burkhurdt. *Advances in Special Education*, *17*, 57–71.

Olivos, E. M., Gallagher, R. J., & Aguilar, J. (2010). Fostering collaboration with culturally and linguistically diverse families of children with moderate to severe disabilities. *Journal of Educational & Psychological Consultation*, *20*(1), 28–40. doi:10.1080/10474410903535372

Overstreet, S., Devine, J., Bevans, K., & Efreom, Y. (2005). Predicting parental involvement in children's schooling within an economically disadvantaged African American sample. *Psychology in the Schools*, *42*(1), 101-111.

Palawat, M., & May, M. E. (2015). The impact of cultural diversity on special education provision in the United States. *Journal of the International Association of Special Education*, *13*(1), 56–61.

Park, S., & Holloway, S. D. (2013). No parent left behind: Predicting parental involvement in adolescents' education within a sociodemographically diverse population. *The Journal of Educational Research*, *106*(2), 105–119. doi:10.1080/00220671.2012.667012

Patton, J. (1998). The disproportionate representation of African Americans in special education: Looking at behind the curtain of understanding and solutions. *The Journal of Special Education*, *32*(1), 25–31. doi:10.1177/002246699803200104

Reschly, D. J. (1996). Identification and assessment of students with disabilities. *The Future of Children*, *6*(1), 40–53. doi:10.2307/1602493 PMID:8689261

Smith, D. D., & Tyler, N. C. (2010). *Introduction to special education: Making a difference*. Upper Saddle River, NJ: Merrill.

Stambaugh, T., & Ford, D. Y. (2015). Microaggressions, multiculturalism, and gifted individuals who are Black, Hispanic, or low income. *Journal of Counseling and Development*, *93*(2), 192–201. doi:10.1002/j.1556-6676.2015.00195.x

Tepper, N., & Tepper, B. A. (2004). Linking Special Education with Multicultural Education for Native American Children with Special Needs. *Rural Special Education Quarterly*, *23*(4), 30–33.

Tileston, D. W. (2004). *What Every Teacher Should Know About Diverse Learners.* Thousand Oaks, CA: Corwin Press.

Turnbull, A. P., & Turnbull, H. R. (2000). *Families, professionals, and exceptionalities: Collaboration for empowerment* (4th ed.). Columbus, OH: Prentice Hall.

Turney, K., & Kao, G. (2009). Barriers to school involvement: Are immigrant parents disadvantaged? *The Journal of Educational Research, 102*(4), 257–271. doi:10.3200/JOER.102.4.257-271

United States Department of Education (2009). *Office of Special Education and Rehabilitative Services* (OSEP 07-09). Author.

Vang, C. T. (2006). Minority parents should know more about school culture and its impact on their children's education. *Multicultural Education, 14*(1), 20–26.

KEY TERMS AND DEFINITIONS

Cross-Cultural Dissonance: A mismatch of home and school cultures.

Culturally Competent: Knowing and understanding the cultural standards of diverse communities.

Culturally Diverse: Being from a cultural group that is not Eurocentric or mainstream America.

Cultural Mismatch: When there are incompatibilities between the home culture and the school culture. For example, in the African tradition one is expected to put his/her head down and not look at the teacher while she/he talks to him/her. In the Western culture eye contact is the norm when being addressed.

Disproportionate Representation: Unequal proportion of group membership; over or underrepresentation.

Language Disorder: Difficulty or inability to master the various systems or rules in language, which interferes with communication.

Linguistically Diverse: Having a native language other than English.

Multicultural Education: Incorporates the cultures of all students into instruction.

Overrepresentation: Too many students from a diverse group participating in a special education category, beyond the level expected from their proportion in the population.

The Individuals with Disabilities Education Act (IDEA): The special education law originally passed in 1975 to guarantee a free appropriate public education for all students with disabilities.

Underrepresentation: Insufficient presence of students from a diverse group in a special education category; a smaller number than would be predicted by their proportion in the population.

This research was previously published in the Handbook of Research on Promoting Cross-Cultural Competence and Social Justice in Teacher Education edited by Jared Keengwe; pages 382-397, copyright year 2017 by Information Science Reference (an imprint of IGI Global).

Chapter 41
Exploring Intercultural Awareness:
International Student Mobility in China and the UK through a Non-Essentialist Lens

Monika Foster
Edinburgh Napier University, UK

ABSTRACT

In the research literature regarding international students' learning experiences, a frequently studied theme is the 'Chinese culture of learning' as contrasted by the 'Western/United Kingdom (UK) culture of learning'. This essentialist approach tends to reduce culture of learning to a static, nationally-bound object that exists a priori. A cross-faculty study examined the complexities underpinning culture of learning in the context of student mobility, using a non-essentialist lens. Using individual experiences, unique perspectives on own and host cultures of learning by students from China studying 'business' in the UK and students from the UK studying 'design' in China are captured in seven distinct themes, including good teaching, good learning, peers and assessment. The results inform the design of student mobility programs with aspects of intercultural empathy, as well as preparation for and benefits from study abroad as a feature of the internationalised of Higher Education (HE).

INTRODUCTION

This chapter is focused on the increased internationalisation of teaching and learning in Higher Education (HE) worldwide (Knight 2006; Caruana & Spurling, 2007) and specifically the ambition to internationalise the student experience (Hyland et al., 2008). The specific interest is 'internationalisation' from the students' perspective as it focuses on 'academic learning that blends the concepts of self, strange, foreign and otherness' (Teekens, 2006, p. 17). This view of internationalisation is also congruent with the perspectives of Appadurai (2001), Haigh (2009) and Sanderson (2011) who foreground the value of personal awareness in intercultural encounters in HE. The interest for the study stemmed from a desire

DOI: 10.4018/978-1-7998-1213-5.ch041

to examine the complexities underpinning the concept of 'a culture of learning' in student mobility through a non-essentialist lens. Exploring the rich and individual student perspectives, the objectives of this study included: (a) to explore how students can benefit from cultural diversity through mobility; and (b) to raise awareness of their own and other cultures of learning, with both points contributing to the development of one's 'intercultural capacity' i.e., a Graduate Attribute.

BACKGROUND

A Culture of Learning

The idea of a culture of learning is not recent to researchers and practitioners engaged in intercultural education. As denoted by the element of 'learning', a culture of learning addresses aspects of a number of learner-oriented concepts, such as *approach to learning*, *learning style* and *learning habit* (Zulu 2012; Pask & Joy 2007). A culture of learning, however, broadens understandings of what happens in the learning context by going further to encompass dimensions of teaching, assessment and the wider social environment in which the learning context is shaped. This has invited a variety of nuanced conceptualisations of this term. For example, Chisholm and Vally (1996) defined culture of learning as 'bringing about of the conditions and disciplines of compulsory schooling to bear on teachers and students, regular attendance, punctuality and acceptance of authority'. 'Culture' is a contested word, but may be summed up as 'the way we do things round here' (Pask & Joy 2007, p. 169). Culture reflects the values in use that have emerged over time; values that can be quite different from the espoused or official values of the organisation (2007, p. 169).

The conceptualisation most relevant to this study concerning HE in an internationalising context is the one proposed by Cortazzi and Jin (1996) based on issues of overseas students' learning around intercultural communication, and especially 'the hidden assumptions about culture, which impact communication and learning' (p. 76). It is a complex whole that consists of key elements including socially transmitted expectations, beliefs and values about *what* good learning is, *what* constitutes a good teacher and a good student, *what* their roles and relationships should be. It further relates to teaching and learning styles, approaches and methods, classroom interaction and activities, and use of resources.

The 'Chinese culture of learning' has been a popular theme in the literature on international students' experiences. For example, in the classroom, they are often observed to be 'quiet learners' (Turner, 2003) and prefer a reflector learning style by taking a less active role (Wong, Pine & Tsang, 2000). Central to their perception of teaching is the authoritative status they assign to their teachers who embody a source of hegemonic norms (Chee & West, 2007). The work students produce for assessment is believed by many researchers to indicate a preference for rote-learning and a view of knowledge as a reproduction of what is being taught (Carson & Nelson, 1994). This impression is usually associated with the understanding that 'Chinese students' tend to 'lack in critical or independent thinking' (Ballard & Clanchy, 1991). The majority of the above perceptions are based on studies and data collected in the host ('Western/UK') culture of learning, which plays an important role in how learners interact in the classroom.

The 'Western/UK culture of learning' has also been well documented in the international education literature (Livingston & Lynch, 2000; Vita, 2001; Hand, 2006). For example, students from this cultural or national background are found to prefer direct and low-context communication and address questions and puzzles in the classroom by interacting with the teacher (Holmes, 2005). 'Western/UK culture of learning' displays a low power distance characteristics (Hofstede, 1994) where students are treated as equals. It is said to promote individual orientation, self-reliance, asking for help, expressing disagreement and striving for reflection (Cortazzi & Jin, 1996).

LITERATURE REVIEW

Interestingly, in the literature, a number of representations appear to contradict with the majority of voices regarding the 'Chinese culture of learning', whilst 'Western/UK culture of learning' has not been so hotly discussed, possibly due to the attention being on overseas' students culture of learning in the context of increased Internationalisation of Western/UK HE. For example, Turner (2003) found that Chinese students can be highly competitive with other students and strive to be the best in the cohort. This seems to cohere with an individualistic orientation rather than a preference for collectivist thinking as noted by Carson and Nelson (1994). According to Huang (2005), Chinese students may find that 'Western' teachers do not logically organise their lectures and do not tend to give clear definitions of terms and concepts in class.

To a certain extent, the depictions cited above about 'Chinese students' and 'Western/UK students' are well resonant with a respective teaching context. However, it is strikingly inconsistent with own teaching experience that in existing research, the 'Chinese culture of learning' or the 'Western/UK culture of learning' is often presented in a singular form, with minimal comment on whether and how this culture of learning may change (or not change) over time.

Another difficulty with the existing research concerning the 'Chinese culture of learning' and the 'Western/UK culture of learning' is the trend that these 'two' cultures of learning are often discussed in juxtaposition. The dichotomised images presented earlier are an illustration of this. Some of these representations do cohere with our impressions of individual students from these two countries. Nevertheless, in the present HE agenda, where the promotion of diversity and inclusivity is becoming a key concern, universities are starting to commit themselves to purposefully providing an equitable international experience for all students (Brooks & Waters 2011; Killick 2011; Sweeney 2012), rather than fostering exclusive experiences through inadvertent segregation by nationality, along with other social groupings.

In the context of increased student mobility and student exchange, students are encouraged to experience different cultures in order to reflect on their own and to develop a sound understanding of other cultures of learning (Killick, 2011). However, the differences between/among students' home and host cultures of learning, can be problematic for students studying abroad, as well as for the HE faculty and staff associated with both HE Institutions (HEIs). This study attempted to address the mismatches in the expectations or perspectives of students and inform program directors involved in student mobility programs. Furthermore, it is the dynamic changes in our students' learning experiences, rather than cultural traits frozen in time, that inspired this research.

A Culture of Learning through a Non-Essentialist Lens

The confirmed impressions, surprises and puzzles in the literature concerning the 'Chinese and Western/UK cultures of learning' began to make more sense when examined through the conceptual lens of non-essentialism. The existing research on culture of learning seems to be largely imbued with an essentialist discourse, whereby students are grouped into broad categories (usually in terms of their nationality).

The complexities of students' experiences that do not appear to relate to their nationalities immediately are often explained away or even deliberately eliminated as not-so-relevant idiosyncrasies or distracting contextual factors. The context for this exploration is student mobility, currently promoted in HE as one of the key areas that enables students to engage with an internationalised education (Prazeres, 2013) and to develop an intercultural awareness of themselves and other cultures; a key attribute of global citizenship (Brooks & Waters, 2011; Waters, Brooks & Pimlott-Wilson, 2011). Although there is a growing body of knowledge on the internationalisation of HE, there is still a lack of research on the students' perspective (Brooks & Waters, 2011).

This study, therefore, sets out its agenda from a unique and more dynamic perspective, based on a non-essentialist belief (Holliday, 1999; Grimshaw, 2007) to offer insights into the present cultures of learning associated with China and the UK by acknowledging, valuing and closely examining their complexities, dynamics and fluidity.

THE RESEARCH STUDY

This chapter explores the results of a study that involved students from China studying Business in the UK and students from UK studying Design in China, both for a period of six months. The study's focus, research aims, method and findings are presented below.

Geertz (1973) argued that culture cannot be defined by a law, rather we can only seek to interpret its meaning. 'The activities of most cultures are unfathomable, unless they are viewed from within the culture, for membership of a culture provides a set of cultural eyeglasses that are the key to understanding and carrying out its activities' (Brown et al., 1989, p. 6). The qualitative study explores the evolving views of a sample of 18 exchange students, not in an attempt to provide categorical 'truths', but to raise questions about how students learn in different cultures of learning through a detailed analysis in non-essentialist approach. Non-essentialist approach is seen as dynamic, complex, subjectively constructed, fluid, and importantly can be associated with non-national entities (Holliday, 1999; Grimshaw, 2007).

This study is dynamic by gathering data at multiple time points. It is complex and fluid by examining the individual trajectories of students' perspectives about their cultures of learning over time, it looks at trends that transcend nationality classifications. It offers an approach that is more sympathetic to the complexities of increasingly international universities, especially the multi-faceted context of student mobility. The combination of four research academics with cultural and subject differences has provided the opportunity for exploring the culture of learning within both Design and Business-related courses.

Research Aims

The study reported here goes beyond existing understandings of 'cultures of learning' linked to China and the UK by opening perspectives on individual experiences to form insights that move from an essentialist view. The intention is to identify areas of support that universities can provide for students participating in such internationalised education. With aspects of intercultural empathy and an inclusive, flexible learning ethos, it could also inform initiatives for increased student mobility at university and beyond.

Using individual experiences rather than a large quantitative sample, the complexities and richness of 'culture of learning' are unpacked and explored with a specific focus on students' evolving perceptions of own and host learning cultures. Specifically, the researchers were interested in the students' perspectives of the foreign culture of learning, how the students' perspectives about the foreign culture of learning are different from their home culture of learning and how the students' perspectives of the foreign culture of learning change over time.

These questions are addressed first through a non-essentialist and dynamic content analysis of interview results and students' learning journals. The themes arrived at from the analysis are then explored in relation to the multi-faceted perspectives on student mobility, especially the cultural aspects of student mobility and how they can be explored and supported to ensure students fully benefit from the experience of study in a new teaching and learning context.

RESEARCH METHOD

Participants

Two different groups of exchange students were identified as research subjects: nine Chinese students coming to study in the UK from China, and nine UK students leaving the UK to study in China. The students involved in this study came from a diverse range of ethnic, cultural and economic backgrounds. The UK students included Anglo-Chinese, Kurdish, Russian, and Scottish backgrounds. Similarly, Chinese students who took part in the study came from different cities in China, representing a spread of backgrounds. As mentioned above, none of the groups of students were given specific pre-departure training about the foreign culture of learning.

The sample size reflects the small number of students on the exchange programs in the Design Department and Business Schools of the universities in which this study is based. On both sets of programs, the students are prepared for study abroad in terms of visas, fees, accommodation etc., but there is little existing preparation regarding students' perspectives of foreign culture of learning and even their understanding of their own culture of learning. During study abroad, the Design students in China, are well-supervised and are given opportunities to experience the host culture, both the academic and local culture. The Business School students tend to be well looked after at the start of the study abroad, but during the experience are left largely to their own devices without any structured introduction to both the academic and the local culture.

Data Collection Instruments

The methodology was not dependent on participants being designers or business people. Following university ethical procedures students were asked in advance to give their informed consent to participate in the study. Qualitative data was generated through in-depth interviews at the start and at the end of their study abroad experience, informed by students' reflective journals, which were undertaken longitudinally in parallel with the students' study in the host countries for four months. The questions for the interviews at the start and the end of the study abroad can be found in the Appendix. Reflective journals are widely used to reflect on the 'encounters' or 'moments' or 'experiences', by briefly recording learning events and then reflect on the meaning of the experience for their own development and learning (Loo & Thorpe, 2002; Wagner, 2006). They provide up to date reflections on events as they happen rather than retrospectively such as in interviews or questionnaires and give strength to other evidence (quantitative or qualitative).

Data Collection Procedure

In-depth, semi-structured interviews taking between 30-40 minutes, were conducted with the students before their departure from the UK and at the end of the exchange in China. The Chinese students were interviewed at the start and end of their exchange in the UK. The students kept reflective learning journals. The participants were asked to use the journals whenever they felt inspired to, there were no fixed writing periods agreed to ensure the participant-led approach. There were no specific prompts provided what to record although the participants were encouraged to reflect on the 'encounters' or 'moments' or 'experiences' i.e., briefly record them and then reflect on the meaning of the experience for their own development/journey/learning. At the end of keeping their journals, students are asked to review themselves what they have gathered in their journals, and write a 'final journal reflection', summarising main points and highlights. Researchers viewed all entries, but through this activity students used their own 'filter' to select the key points/moments so student perspective in selecting key points is maintained. The extracts from the journal used for the thematic analysis and quoted here all come from the 'final journal reflection'.

Data Analysis

Content analysis followed by thematic sampling was conducted on the data from the interviews and reflective journals (Ortlipp, 2008). This triangulation of data collection ensured that rich data was obtained and the varied sources of data provided an opportunity to look at the experience from varied angles, both researcher led and student led (Flick, 2014). This study's non-essentialist approach and focus on individual, dynamic and evolving perceptions, sees it reporting responses from relatively small amount of responses. Nine Chinese participants are coded 1A-I and nine UK participants are coded 2A-I. This offers an opportunity for an in-depth exploration of experiences as seen through students' eyes, shining a new light on the complexities involved in student mobility regardless of essentialist national boundaries.

RESULTS

The results were grouped into *seven* distinct themes that stemmed from the process of thematic analysis of the interview transcripts and analysis of related journals:

Theme 1: Expectations of Good Teaching;
Theme 2: Expectations about the Learning Process;
Theme 3: Expectations about how to Interact with Lecturers;
Theme 4: Perceptions of Good Learning;
Theme 5: Role of Peers in the Learning Process;
Theme 6: Assessment and Learning; and
Theme 7: Preferred Form of Assessment.

The themes correspond to the key features of the culture of learning conceptualisation proposed by Cortazzi and Jin (1996) and the results grouped according to the seven themes are discussed below. The presentation of the results strives to navigate the reader through the trends arrived from the data, emphasising the most common characteristics for the theme and how the students' perceptions changed over time. However, references to 'UK participants' and 'Chinese participants' are made for clarity and to explore the distinctions between home and host culture for these two groups of students.

Theme 1: Expectations of Good Teaching

Cortazzi and Jin (2009) analysed the metaphors of the role of teacher. The outcome was a cultural model to detail the core characteristics of teachers in the mind of Chinese students: *knowledge, cultivation* and *morality*. The nurture role of lecturer resonates with the cultivation characteristic of a 'good teacher' in the eyes of Chinese students. Under the 'Chinese culture of learning', a 'good' lecturer seemed to be 'caring and helpful' and to nurture students' personal learning experience and growth.

This study, however, found that the 'caring and helpful' attribute was mentioned by most UK and some Chinese participants as one of the characteristics of 'good teachers/lecturers', which means that this perception can be noted in both contexts of 'culture of learning'. Chinese participants' perceptions reinforced the nurturing role of lecturers and their interest in the pedagogic aspect of teaching rather than the 'gurus' role or authoritative status of lecturers. Most UK participants identified 'caring and helpful', but their perceptions were rather diverse and personal. These statements from students in both rounds of interviews illustrate their perceptions of 'good teacher':

[S]omeone who did not hesitate to answer anybody's enquiries and just someone, yeah, someone who makes sure and knows what we are doing... (Participant 2I first-round interview)

[T]he teacher here is very friendly and if I have anything problems, I can ask them for help and they all help me very much... (Participant 1G journal)

I think to be a good lecturer, he or she maybe motivate us and engaged in the speech and focus on the speak and we can activity join in the speech I think. (Participant 1D journal)

Looking at evolving perceptions of 'good teaching', before the study abroad, only two UK participants commented that a good lecturer was expected to have an 'amicable personal attribute'. While, after the new learning experience, many participants (both Chinese and the UK) believed that 'amicable personal attribute' was a component for a good lecturer. However, the 'amicable personal attribute' was also mentioned as a characteristic under the 'UK culture of learning'.

I think the teacher should be very friendly and they should smile all the time in class, so that you will not feel the class is boring. (Participant 1G second-round interview)

[T]hey are very approachable, actually you can go up to them and ask some questions if you need to, they are very good for that here and that's a good lecturer... (Participant 2C journal)

The above findings seem to show that the students' perceptions of these values seem to be similar, regardless the nationality and that for all students they have evolved over time and experience of study abroad, regardless of their home culture of learning.

Theme 2: Expectations about the Learning Process

This broad theme revealed further dichotomy between the standard, essentialist perceptions of both cultures of learning and the individual perceptions displayed by the participants in the study, regardless of their home culture of learning.

Most Chinese participants considered that the learning process was 'lecturer-focused' in China. However, nearly all the UK participants commented that their learning process in China was 'self-study-focused' and some UK participants referred to the lecturer guidance within the learning process. UK participant comments in the reflective journal on learning process being '…98% self-directed, 1% tutor input 1% student input…'

It appeared that the UK participants' perceptions of the learning process to be 'self-study-focused' in China, may have been influenced by less access to familiar social media (i.e., Facebook, YouTube). Thus, they had to be more resourceful in research techniques, using other alternatives, doing self-reflecting and peer-discussion. The concept of 'self-study' could be understood differently in two different contexts of 'culture of learning' (Cortazzi & Jin, 2013). It seems to be normal for Chinese students to read books verbally and recite the content, who, even in the UK seem to be treating learning as 'self-study' for practising.

[M]aybe 12 hours and for the class and maybe 24 hours for myself, self-reading I think… (Participant 1D second-round interview)

However, UK students said that they tried to learn from others, through activity, reflection and conversation (Biggs, 1996).

Under the 'UK culture of learning', Chinese participants thought that the pace was fast and that the project and timetable were well-structured. In contrast to their opinions, the UK participants commented that the timetable and program in structure was more erratic, more unpredictable in the 'Chinese culture of learning'. The results may also be complicated by the differences between the pedagogies of Design and Business. There does not seem to be a universal pattern of 'Chinese culture of learning' as its perceptions to students were impacted by their disciplinary background (from one Chinese participant) and unique nature of the subject/program (from some UK participants):

I want to be independent to do my work, but sometimes I just found that I get some difficulties in it. So then I began relying on my teachers and then I found that the teachers always tell me what is right and what is wrong and what is suitable for the exam and how can I get the better marks… (Participant 1A journal)

From the above, it would seem that for the participants in the study what constitutes the main features of 'UK culture of learning' and 'Chinese culture of learning' is far more blurred than what seems to be suggested by the literature. The time spent on study abroad and the perceptions being individual and cannot be generalised, it is intriguing that the participants did not display the standard perceptions and that their opinions reflect individual or subject preferences rather than static, essentialist views of the respective cultures of learning.

Theme 3: Expectations about how to Interact with Lecturers

Theme 3 revealed similar preferences amongst the participants, regardless of their home or host culture of learning. Researchers found that both Chinese and UK participants preferred face-to-face communication. Due to the language issue, for the UK participants, face-to-face communication was dependent on the help of translators. Chinese lecturers had no inhibitions about using mobile text messaging to communicate in English with the UK participants. Mobile communication was not mentioned by Chinese participants.

I just find the teacher when she had a break and she will glad to tell me about the problem or how to solve it and what shall we, just which way should I to do... (Participant 1H first-round interview)

If we have to talk to them, we had translator and they will text us saying you have to be in stuff... (Participant 2B second-round interview)

While email or online communication is the most frequent student digital interaction with lecturers, mobile communication is perceived to be more personal and immediate.

Obviously face-to-face a good start. Yeah email was quite good... (Participant 2A first-round interview)

I think, I often send emails to teachers because I don't want to bother them, yeah, email is the main way I connect to the teacher... (Participant 1C journal)

It seems that the primary preference amongst the participants, regardless of their nationality or subject, is a face-to-face contact with the lecturers, which provides the most support.

Theme 4: Perceptions of Good Learning

In this theme, even though there is clearly an evolving perception of good learning, home culture of learning seemed to impact on preferences for and perceptions of good learning.

Both Chinese and the UK participants' perceptions of 'good' learner in the 'Chinese culture of learning' were rather diverse and difficult to identify the shared perceptions. Only two attributes, namely 'independent study' and 'attentive listening' were mentioned by some Chinese participants and a few UK participants. In addition, some UK participants commented that a good learner had to be 'well-motivated to study' in China. However, researchers noted that Chinese participants and the UK participants seemed to place different emphasis on the perception of a 'good learner'. Relationship with information or knowledge and effort-driven were exclusively mentioned by Chinese participants while individual responsibility and transferred skills were discussed by the UK participants.

I think for a student, the information or the knowledge is not given by the teachers, just need to learn by yourself and you must understand what you have learnt. (Participant 1D second-round interview)

[A]nd I think it's good to be able to do self-study a lot and definitely that the skill we need over here... (Participant 2B second-round interview)

I think you have to have like really strong self-motivation that is one of the most important thing because you are doing it for yourself and you have to be like really keen on learning new things. (Participant 2D journal)

In the home 'culture of learning' there were differences in how the learning process was directed by the lecturer: in China their learning process was 'lecturer-focused', while UK participants had a 'lecturer-guided' learning process. After they came to the host 'culture of learning', most of the participants (both Chinese and the UK) highlighted the 'self-study' in their learning process.

I think I use the time to study in class and we need to study very hard and listen to the teacher what they said very carefully... (Participant 1G journal)

The lecturers should teach you some kind of the foundations... Yeah, the foundation should be settled by the lecturers then you can go on yourself sometimes. (Participant 2A first-round interview)

To summarise, in the 'Chinese culture of learning' a good learner as seen by Chinese participants is indicated by familiarity with a surface approach to learning (Marton et al., 1997) and an emphasis on relationship and is effort-driven; for UK participants there is an emphasis on individual responsibility and transferrable skills beyond academic studies. In the 'UK culture of learning' a good learner is seen by both a few Chinese and UK participants to have an emphasis on transferrable skills beyond academic studies.

Theme 5: Expectations about Role of Peers

Theme 5 discusses a significant aspect of the experience, evolving over time and displayed across the participants' groups, regardless of nationality or the host culture. Only some UK participants mentioned their fellow students as 'a role of helper' in their home 'culture of learning' while the majority of participants—both Chinese and the UK—saw their fellow students as 'a role of helper' in the host places. Uniquely, some individual Chinese participants mentioned peer-influencing and emotional support from peers.

When we get miss something uncomfortable or we may have some failure, we can talk to others. It's very good to release and adjust something... (Participant 1A journal)

Some students are very good at learning, so they just... give me some ideas about how to learn and how to be a good learner. I can learn a lot from them, they just give many ideas to how to organise my studies... (Participant 1C first-round interview)

They play a huge part in my particular subject (Design), I came up with an idea and ask them do you think this is good, this is bad and they will say 'yes'... (Participant 2B journal)

The role of peers is also explored in the UK participants' reflective journals as they commented 'Thank god, the Chinese students helped us, we would've had no hope... They have made me aware more of how to treat foreign students when they come over'. Recent studies (Newstead & Humphreys,

2013) support this comment and UK universities are increasingly aware of the importance of supporting international students through 'buddies'.

The role of peers seems to be more significant that may be suggested by the literature, with the majority of the participants in the study strongly relying on peers or buddies in their experience of mobility. This poses a challenge as well as an opportunity for the universities aiming to develop student mobility; a challenge to ensure students know how to tap into this important support mechanism and use it well i.e., not as an alternative to the support offered by the host institution; and an opportunity for the universities to develop students' peer engagement skills to utilise and offer such support to fully benefit from the study abroad experience.

Theme 6: Assessment and Learning

Assessment is an area evoking strong emotions and it seems from the data that students' home culture of learning exerts a significant influence on how they perceive it in the host culture of learning. Assessment for learning can be understood as any assessment for which the first priority in its design and practice is to serve the purpose of promoting pupils' learning. It thus differs from assessment designed primarily to serve the purposes of accountability, or of ranking, or of certifying competence (Black et al, 2003, p. 9). Assessment of learning focuses on using assessment to provide judgment of student learning and utilising the assessment information for administrative and reporting purposes (Wiliam, 2001).

Some Chinese participants thought that the relationship between assessment and learning is 'assessment over learning' while some UK participants commented that it was 'assessment of learning' in their respective 'home culture of learning'. After the experience in the host 'culture of learning', most of the Chinese and two UK participants said that it was 'assessment of learning'.

The assessment is, I think it's an important part, but it's not the most important for me... (Participant 2D first-round interview)

I think, it's very, the cause relationship with them because, the essence of the assessment I think is to check whether we know the knowledge and learning, so it's very, the relationship is very close. (Participant 1B second-round interview)

Some Chinese and UK participants mentioned that assessment was a tool to measure the outcomes of learning, but participants held different opinions with regard to how useful or valid this tool was. Some Chinese participants tended to view assessment as the priority for their study. A few Chinese and UK participants saw assessment to help them enhance their learning.

[I]n China you don't need to work hard every day, you just need to work hard before exam because teacher will give you everything before the exam and they will appeared completely the same in the exam but after the exam you will forget everything. (Participant 1B journal)

[T]hey probably assess a lot more than what they tell us [right] I think and as if there is something bad, they won't tell us that's bad, I don't know if they just want to be polite or I am wrong, but they maybe say maybe do it this way instead but yeah, it is quite difficult, I think they analysed us a lot more than

Exploring Intercultural Awareness

what they can say and do [ok] from that, it is hard to get what kind of outcomes indeed. (Participant 2H second-round interview)

It seems that assessment is an area that can be explored with students preparing for mobility experience as to the value it offers to capture their learning and how it can be used by the students to demonstrate their evolving perceptions of their own and host culture of learning.

Theme 7: Preferred Form of Assessment

In this theme we explore that what students are used to in their home culture of learning, has a fairly significant influence on their evolving perceptions of preferred form of assessment during their study abroad.

Only three UK participants commented on oral presentation as the experienced or expected form of assessment in their home 'culture of learning' while many (both Chinese and the UK) participants (despite obvious differences in language) mentioned oral presentation as the assessment they experienced or preferred in the host 'culture of learning'.

Well, for projects that we are doing, I actually would like to do several types of presentations, like pen-ups or PowerPoint presentations, or even one chance to do presentations from my choice... (Participant 2E first-round interview)

I think I prefer to do the presentation because if I did the presentation, the marks always very high... (Participant 1E journal)

I prefer the practice...can I say Chinese use this word called 实际操作 means just practice... (Participant 1E first-round interview)

Under the 'Chinese culture of learning', some forms of assessments i.e., essay, practical assessment, and exams, as well as oral forms of assessment, especially oral presentations were preferred by students. Under the 'UK culture of learning', oral forms of assessment and some other forms of assessment i.e., report, essay, group work were preferred/experienced by students.

DISCUSSION

The study reported in this chapter has offered a unique insight into students' evolving perceptions of own and host culture of learning. It seems that students' perceptions of a 'culture of learning' may be fluid rather than fixed, nationally bound objects. Their perceptions also seem to evolve in response to the change of the learning context, which seems to be a stimuli for students to explore their own culture of learning and their host culture of learning. Furthermore, the boundary between what is traditionally perceived as the 'Chinese culture of learning' and the 'UK culture of learning' seems more blurred than being clear-cut. Both student groups seem to develop similar perceptions to a certain extent through shared experiences of cultures of learning. Additionally, it seems that some of the characteristics proposed by the literature do not apply to a specific culture of learning and rather to a Confucian cultural heritage. According to Hadley and Hadley (1996), from the Japanese students' view, 'kind', 'friendly', 'impartial', 'understandable' and 'cheerful' are the five most salient characteristics of a good 'teacher' mentioned under the 'Japanese culture of learning'. To some extent, the 'amicable personal attribute' noted in the data seem to resonate with Hadley and Hadley's (1996) findings. Due to the influence of Confucian cultural heritage on Asian countries in the educational context, this would seem unsurprising.

Therefore, the diversity emerging in 'student experience' seems more striking than the difference between 'Chinese students' and 'UK students' as two nationally distinct groups. To sum up, the non-essentialist perspective has allowed to identify the complexity and fluidity of students' perceptions of a culture of learning, which arises from and is enhanced by the experience of study abroad or student mobility, rather than simply associated with the traditional notions of a 'Chinese culture of learning' and a 'UK culture of learning'. Moreover, the experience of study abroad raises students' awareness of their own culture of learning and new perceptions of the host culture of learning. This aspect of student mobility seems to be a central element of students' reflections on their experience of mobility, but one rarely forming part of the preparations for or record of student mobility.

As educational institutions develop internationalisation strategies, there is a pressing challenge to understand the cultures of learning between and across UK and Chinese students. This study has used a non-essentialist lens to go beyond existing understandings of 'cultures of learning' linked to China and the UK. Identified in the study, was a difference in students' original ideas about their own culture of learning and their perceptions after the study abroad experience, raising the important issue of intercultural awareness of own culture of learning before the mobility experience, which could then serve as a vehicle to better embrace the host culture of learning and therefore benefit more fully from student mobility. The perceived differences between a 'Western/UK culture of learning' and a 'Chinese culture of learning' are revealed here as being much more granular and can be attributed to individual variations in student preferences rather than true distinctions in how things are done in the respective cultures. Likewise, a lot of what is attributed in the data on studies on 'Chinese culture of learning' can be in fact more of a reflection of the styles of teaching and learning that the students are used to.

Additionally, the seven themes arising from the study in relation to how students perceive culture of learning, both host and their own, provide some unique insights into students' evolving concepts of teaching and learning trigged by the experience of study abroad. Despite individual differences and a rather fluid interpretation of 'Chinese culture of learning' and 'UK culture of learning' amongst the participants, what seems to be emerging are some common traits displayed in students' perceptions of key aspects of a teaching and learning culture including an amicable and friendly teacher who can be accessed face-to-face; learning process viewed as a personal and subject specific experience rather than a large and static 'state of things'; a strong role of peers in the learning process, especially in study abroad.

Specific to this study, different perceptions amongst participants about what constitutes a 'Chinese culture of learning' and a 'UK culture of learning' are strongly influenced by a home culture of learning as well as the specific and individual experience abroad, a range of perspectives on the relationship between assessments and learning, as well as a range of preferred assessment types. While it seems that the large essentialist notions of a 'Chinese culture of learning' and a 'UK culture of learning' do not apply, unique insights into students' preferences in teaching and learning in general seem to point that students involved in mobility could benefit from being prepared for it, including their understanding of their own culture of learning, and their preferences, before engaging with the host culture of learning. Additionally, educators involved in designed student mobility programs are informed as to what students value in the process such as face-to-face contact with the teacher and strong peer support.

In addition, of interest here is how the experience of study abroad is captured by the Design and Business students. Apart from the semi-structured interviews, the students kept the reflective journals, which offer a comprehensive and unique insight into their cultural experience and the affect it has on their view of the world. Art and Design students are familiar with documenting reflective analysis of their work and learning process. Business students were unfamiliar with this approach to learning, but they have quickly picked up the necessary skills through the help of their tutors. This asks for a debate whether additional training should be given to student participants for fear it may influence and restrict more spontaneous, personal and authentic self-reflection.

Student mobility experience is often captured through academic assessments and rarely through other means such as reflective tools, which allow for the personal perspective to be prominent and for the intercultural skills development to be recognised. With careful preparation before student mobility, including the development of sound reflective skills, there is a potential additional benefit from the mobility experience in students engaging in ongoing reflection on their experience, which helps them to make sense of their own culture of learning, as well as of the host. Such reflective capture would become an important lens adding depth to our understanding of the richness of experience of students engaged in mobility. It may also serve as an important record of the evolving students' perceptions of own and host teaching and learning contexts that can be used as a promotional material(s) to encourage students to take part in the mobility.

RECOMMENDATIONS

This chapter sought to open and inform the debate to equip HE educators in a rapidly changing globalised society, especially the developments in encouraging global student mobility, and how educators can prepare for this new and growing area of international education. The emerging results point to the importance of study abroad as a key shaping experience for the students' evolving awareness of their own culture of learning and the hosts', hence developing an intercultural dimension to the overall study experience. This essential understanding of own and other cultures is one of the key features of a global citizen (Hyland et al., 2008).

For education providers wishing to increase student mobility, it seems necessary to ensure an effective preparation for students involved, including raising students' awareness of their own culture of learning and preparing students for the intercultural encounters prior to engaging in student mobility. This can be achieved by asking the returning exchange students to present a short video/slideshow describing their experiences studying and living on exchange to prospective exchange students. Another way institutions can prepare students would be through a buddy up scheme with returning exchange students. Finally, students should be equipped with sound independent study skills (Hyland et al., 2008).

Additionally, as motivating students to take part in increased mobility often relates to how they perceive long term benefits from mobility (Brooks & Waters 2011), it is recommended to maximise capturing learning from study abroad experience through a number of mechanisms including getting students to record the experience of developing intercultural awareness and using it to enhance assessments from study abroad and their curriculum vitae. Further, they may share the experience online with other students and visiting exchange students when they are abroad. Student assessment and moderation of marks on their return is an area that needs attention, and so is celebrating diversity in group work by breaking up clusters of students from the same university and integrating them into a broader international student cohort.

Another area worth taking into account, and one that emerges from the reported study, is not a static, essentialist perception of cultures of learning attached to China and the UK, but a more fluid and individual way students interpret and perceive cultures of learning irrespective of the own and host nationalities. Educators involved in developing student mobility between China and the UK, or any other countries, are encouraged to explore with the students their own home culture of learning first, as well as point to the rather misleading way students could approach other cultures of learning they encounter in study abroad. The program of preparation for student mobility should include sessions on exploring the complexities of culture of teaching and learning versus the essentialist, national stereotypes. This would help students to approach mobility with a (more) open-mind, prepared to explore their own and host cultures of learning, with a less static and generalist lens and through their own experience. This contributes to the development of students' intercultural awareness and helps position student mobility as a journey in students' intercultural skills development.

FUTURE RESEARCH DIRECTIONS

This chapter takes a 'small-culture' approach and seeks to take advantage of a study based on a small sample to reach deeper meaning from an analysis of richer and more complex data. It is a study of only two subject disciplines, but within them there are a variety of specialisms and interests, as well as ages and ethnicity. The period of study was restricted to an academic semester and a single cohort, yet the researchers have a longer perspective from several years of international teaching.

Additional exploration via longitudinal studies could further enhance and/or advance the seven themes identified in this study and students' evolving perceptions of the key aspects of teaching and learning as they move from one HEI to another. A longitudinal study involving larger samples of students from a variety of subjects and levels of study is needed to extend the findings and provide more informed recommendations.

Furthermore, the study fits within an emerging understanding of the complexities of student experience involved in student mobility. It would be helpful to find out what study abroad program directors are currently doing to address differences in the cultures of learning in study abroad programs and how they are helping students to identify differences, and make the transition to a new culture of learning, and work through any differences that exist. Furthermore, as this area of HE grows and becomes a well-developed part of an internationalised education, it would be appropriate to explore the interventions that may help prepare students for study abroad, as suggested in the recommendations, and their impact on the benefits of student mobility and overall intercultural skills development. Intercultural awareness in student mobility is a growing area that will hopefully be further developed as an integral part of student mobility.

CONCLUSION

This chapter set to explore the complex notion of culture of learning in the context of internationalisation of HE, specifically a growing ambition to develop student mobility as its key feature. The rich and evolving student perceptions of their own and host culture of learning have been explored with UK students involved in a period of study in China and Chinese students studying in the UK, key destinations of student mobility in HE at present. Student perceptions of their own and host culture of learning seem to be more fluid and complex than those represented in the literature. Instead of the static and essentialist 'Chinese culture of learning' and 'UK culture of learning', this study proposes a more informed approach to viewing students' perceptions as captured in the seven areas representing the breadth of students' experience of mobility.

The findings trigger recommendations for educators and student mobility co-ordinators to consider early development of students' understanding of own culture of learning, and anticipation of host culture of learning. An early and structured development of intercultural awareness can ensure students fully benefit from the mobility experience. It is suggested that it is captured through reflective journals or assessments that are able to (better) embrace the benefits of student mobility. Further, longitudinal study with a wider selection of participants could explore the seven themes of culture of learning and further develop our understanding of the complexities of student experience in mobility identified in this chapter.

ACKNOWLEDGMENT

This chapter is based on the study conducted Edinburgh Napier University with contributions from colleagues Iain Macdonald, Vivien Zhou and Richard Firth to whom I am greatly indebted.

REFERENCES

Appadurai, A. (2001). *Globalization*. Durham, NC: Duke University Press. doi:10.1215/9780822383215

Ballard, B., & Clanchy, J., & International Development Program of Australian Universities and Colleges (IDP). (1991). *Teaching students from overseas: A brief guide for lecturers and supervisors*. Melbourne: Longman Cheshire.

Biggs, J. B. (1996). Western misperceptions of the Confucian-heritage learning culture. In D. A. Watkins & J. B. Biggs (Eds.), *The Chinese learner: Cultural, psychological, and contextual influences* (pp. 45–67). Hong Kong: CERC and ACER.

Black, P., Harrison, C., Lee, C., Marshall, B., & Wiliam, D. (2003). The nature of value of formative assessment for learning. *Improving Schools*, *6*, 7–22. doi:10.1177/136548020300600304

Brooks, R., & Waters, J. (2011). *Student mobilities, migration and the internationalization of higher education*. Basingstoke, UK: Palgrave Macmillan. doi:10.1057/9780230305588

Brown, J. S., Collins, A., & Duguid, P. (1989). Situated cognition and the culture of learning. *Educational Researcher*, *18*(1), 32–42. doi:10.3102/0013189X018001032

Carson, J. G., & Nelson, G. L. (1994). Writing groups: Cross-cultural issues. *Journal of Second Language Writing*, *3*(1), 17–30. doi:10.1016/1060-3743(94)90003-5

Caruana, V., & Spurling, N. (2007). *The internationalisation of UK higher education: A review of selected material*. Project Report. Retrieved from https://www.sussex.ac.uk/webteam/gateway/file.php?name=lit-review-internationalisation-of-uk-he-v2&site=44

Chee, H., & West, C. (2007). *Myths about doing business in China*. Basingstoke, UK: Palgrave Macmillan. doi:10.1057/9780230286771

Chisholm, L., & Vally, S. (1996). *The culture of teaching and learning in Gauteng schools: Report of the committee on the culture of teaching and learning. Education Policy Unit*. University of the Witwatersrand.

Cortazzi, M., & Jin, L. (1996). Cultures of learning: Language classrooms in China. In H. Coleman (Ed.), *Society and the language classroom* (pp. 169–206). Cambridge, UK: Cambridge University Press.

Cortazzi, M., & Jin, L. (2013). *Researching cultures of learning: International perspectives on language learning and education*. New York, NY: Palgrave MacMillian. doi:10.1057/9781137296344

Flick, U. (2014). *An introduction to qualitative research*. London: Sage.

Geertz, C. (1973). *The interpretation of cultures: Selected essays*. New York, NY: Basic Books.

Grimshaw, T. (2007). Problematizing the construct of 'the Chinese learner': Insights from ethnographic research. *Educational Studies*, *33*(3), 299–311. doi:10.1080/03055690701425643

Hadley, G., & Hadley, H. (1996). The culture of learning and the good teacher in Japan: An analysis of student views. *Language Teaching*, *20*(9), 53–55.

Haigh, M. (2009). Fostering cross-cultural empathy with non-Western curricular structures. *Journal of Studies in International Education*, *13*(2), 271–284. doi:10.1177/1028315308329791

Hand, V. M. (2006). Exploring sociocultural perspectives on race, culture, and learning. *Review of Educational Research*, *76*(4), 449–475. doi:10.3102/00346543076004449

Hofstede, G. (1994). The business of international business is culture. *International Business Review*, *3*(1), 1–14. doi:10.1016/0969-5931(94)90011-6

Holliday, A. (1999). Small cultures. *Applied Linguistics*, *20*(2), 237–264. doi:10.1093/applin/20.2.237

Holmes, P. (2005). Ethnic Chinese students' communication with cultural others in a New Zealand university. *Communication Education*, *54*(4), 289–311. doi:10.1080/03634520500442160

Huang, R. (2005). Chinese international students' perceptions of the problem-based learning experience. *Journal of Hospitality, Leisure, Sport and Tourism Education*, *4*(2), 36–43. doi:10.3794/johlste.42.108

Hyland, F., Trahar, S., Anderson, J., & Dickens, A. (2008). *A changing world: The internationalisation experiences of staff and students (home and international) in UK higher education*. Higher Education Academy. Retrieved from http://escalate.ac.uk/downloads/5248.pdf

Killick, D. (2011). Seeing ourselves-in-the-world: Developing global citizenship through international mobility and campus community. *Journal of Studies in International Education*. doi:10.1177/1028315311431893

Knight, J. (2006). *Internationalization of higher education: New directions, new challenges (IAU 2nd Global Survey Report)*. Paris: IAU.

Livingston, D., & Lynch, K. (2000). Group project work and student-centred learning: Two different experiences. *Studies in Higher Education, 25*(3), 325-345. doi:10.1080/713696161

Loo, R., & Thorpe, K. (2002). 'Using reflective learning journals to improve individual and team performance'. *Team Performance Management, 8*(5), 134–139. doi:10.1108/13527590210442258

Marton, F., Hounsell, D., & Entwistle, N. (Eds.). (1997). *The Experience of Learning* (2nd ed.). Edinburgh, UK: Scottish Academic Press.

Newstead, C., & Humphrey, D. (2013). *Internationally engaged campus cultures and UK student mobility*. Retrieved from http://www.heacademy.ac.uk/assets/documents/seminars/Themes_20122013/GEN379/GEN379_Humprey_Engaged_Campus_Culture.pdf

Ortlipp, M. (2008). Keeping and using reflective journals in the qualitative research process. *Qualitative Report, 13*(4), 695–705.

Pask, R., & Joy, B. (2007). *Mentoring-coaching: A guide for education professionals*. Berkshire, England: Open University Press.

Prazeres, L. (2013). International and intra-national student mobility: Trends, motivations and identity. *Geography Compass, 7*(11), 804–820. doi:10.1111/gec3.12080

Sanderson, G. (2011). Internationalisation and teaching in higher education. *Higher Education Research & Development, 30*(5), 661–676. doi:10.1080/07294360.2011.598455

Sweeney, S. (2012). *Going mobile: Internationalisation, mobility and the European higher education area*. Retrieved from http://www.heacademy.ac.uk/resources/detail/internationalisation/Going_Mobile

Teekens, H. (2006). *Internationalisation at home: A global perspective*. The Hague: NUFFIC.

Turner, Y. (2003). *Chinese students in a UK business school: Hearing the student voice in reflective teaching and learning practice*. Paper presented at the Improving Students' Learning Symposium: Diversity and Inclusivity. Birmingham, UK.

Vita, G. D. (2001). Learning styles, culture and inclusive instruction in the multicultural classroom: A business and management perspective. *Innovations in Education and Teaching International, 38*(2), 165–174. doi:10.1080/14703290110035437

Wagner, Z. M. (2006). 'Using student journals for course evaluation'. *Assessment & Evaluation in Higher Education, 24*(3), 261–272. doi:10.1080/02602939902403011

Waters, J., Brooks, R., & Pimlott-Wilson, H. (2011). Youthful escapes? British students, overseas education and the pursuit of happiness. *Social & Cultural Geography, 12*(5), 455–469. doi:10.1080/14649365.2011.588802

Wiliam, D. (2001). An overview of the relationship between assessment and the curriculum. In D. Scott (Ed.), *Curriculum and assessment* (pp. 165–181). Westport, CT: Ablex Publishing.

Wong, K. K., Pine, R. J., & Tsang, N. (2000). Learning style preferences and implications for training programs in the hospitality and tourism industry. *Journal of Hospitality & Tourism Education, 12*(2), 32–40. doi:10.1080/10963758.2000.10685277

Zulu, L. C. (2012). Neoliberalization, decentralization and community-based natural resources management in Malawi: The first sixteen years and looking ahead. *Progress in Development Studies, 12*(2-3), 193–212. doi:10.1177/146499341101200307

KEY TERMS AND DEFINITIONS

Culture: Values in use that have emerged over time that can be quite different from the espoused or official values of the organisation.

Culture of Learning: Aspects of a number of learner-oriented concepts, such as approach to learning, learning style and learning habits.

Essentialist: A static approach, linear or single lens, whereby students are grouped into broad categories usually in terms of their nationality.

Internationalisation: The process of integrating an international/intercultural dimension into the teaching, research and service functions of the institution including a global movement of students and staff in education, promoting cultural diversity and fostering intercultural understanding, respect, and tolerance.

Non-Essentialist: A dynamic, complex, subjectively constructed, fluid, and importantly can be associated with non-national entities, sympathetic to the complexities of increasingly international universities.

Student Mobility: Any opportunity for students to work or study abroad whilst undertaking their degree program; can be both incoming and outgoing.

This research was previously published in the Handbook of Research on Study Abroad Programs and Outbound Mobility edited by Donna M. Velliaris and Deb Coleman-George; pages 349-369, copyright year 2016 by Information Science Reference (an imprint of IGI Global).

APPENDIX

Part 1: Interview Questions before Study Abroad (Table 1)

- *Why have you chosen to go on exchange to a new academic environment?*
- *What information did you have to make this decision?*

[Ending questions]

- *What do you hope to achieve while on exchange in terms of your academic study and in terms of your personal development?*
- *What effect do you anticipate the exchange will have on how you approach learning once you are back home?*

Part 2: Interview Questions after Study Abroad (Table 2)

- *On a scale from -5 to +5, how would you rate your overall learning experience here? Why (give examples)?*
- *What information would you like to have had before the study in the UK?*

Table 1. Questions addressing 'culture of learning'

Suggested Questions	Rationale
What are your expectations of 'good' lecturers?	These questions point to the 'teaching' dimension of 'culture of learning' as perceived by the participants regarding their experience in the home culture of learning.
How do you expect your learning process to be structured e.g., how much input should be provided by the lecturers in the form of conventional 'classes', how much weight should be put on self-directed learning/ practice?	
How do you expect to interact/communicate with your lecturers in your learning process?	
What do you think constitutes 'good' learning? Can you think of any specific learning methods that a 'good' student typically adopts?	These questions point to the 'learning' dimension of 'culture of learning' as perceived by the participants regarding their experience in the home culture of learning.
How do you see the role(s) that your fellow students play in your learning?	
How do you see the relationship between assessment and learning?	These questions point to the 'assessment' dimension of 'culture of learning' as perceived by the participants regarding their experience in the home culture of learning.
How do you expect to be assessed in order to properly demonstrate the outcomes of your learning?	
How do you imagine your learning experience in the new academic environment would be like (give examples)?	These questions invite participants to construct the culture of learning in the host culture of learning.
How are you preparing for studying in the new academic environment?	

Table 2. Questions addressing 'culture of learning'

Suggested Questions	Rationale
Following your experience in (host culture of learning), what are your expectations now of 'good' lecturers?	These questions point to the 'teaching' dimension of 'culture of learning' as perceived by the participants regarding their experience in the host culture of learning.
How was your learning process structured e.g., how much input was provided by the lecturers in the form of conventional 'classes', how much weight was on self-directed learning/practice?	
How did you interact/communicate with your lecturers in your learning process?	
What do you think now constitutes 'good' learning? Can you think of any specific learning methods that a 'good' student typically adopts?	These questions point to the 'learning' dimension of 'culture of learning' as perceived by the participants regarding their experience in host culture of learning.
What role(s) did your fellow students play in your learning?	
What kinds of assessment did you undertake during your studies here?	These questions point to the 'assessment' dimension of 'culture of learning' as perceived by the participants regarding their experience in the host culture of learning.
How do you see the relationship between assessment and learning now?	
How would you like to be assessed now in order to show that you have learnt something useful?	
How did learning experience in the new academic environment differ from what you imagined (give examples)?	These questions invite participants to construct the culture of learning in home culture of learning.

[Ending questions]

- *What did you achieve while studying in the UK in terms of your academic study and in terms of your personal development?*
- *What effect will the study in the UK have on how you approach learning once you return home?*
- *Any other comments?*

Chapter 42
Data System–Embedded Analysis Support's Implications for Latino Students and Diverse Classrooms

Jenny Grant Rankin
University of Cambridge, UK

ABSTRACT

Urban school populations are particularly diverse, requiring teachers to see to a broad spectrum of student needs. Latinos are the largest and fastest growing racial/ethnic minority group of students in the U.S., and the majority of Latino students live in urban areas. Data can be a powerful tool when used by teachers to target specific student needs, especially those of subgroups with a history of academic struggle. Latino students are commonly featured in not just one, but three large subgroups that typically struggle academically when compared to peers outside these subgroups: the Hispanic, Socio-economically Disadvantaged, and English Learner subgroups. It is vital teachers use data to better understand and meet these students' needs. However, such data use can only benefit students if teachers understand its meaning and implications. This chapter highlights study findings that can significantly improve teachers' ability to use data to help Latinos and other students in diverse classrooms.

INTRODUCTION

Urban school populations are particularly diverse, requiring teachers to see to a broad spectrum of student needs. Latinos are the largest and fastest growing racial/ethnic minority group of students in the U.S., comprising 24% of the U.S. children population, which will grow to over 33% by 2050 (Murphey, Guzman, & Torres, 2014). Conversely, according to a report from the U.S. Department of Education, National Center for Education Statistics other racial/ethnic groups have remained relatively stagnant (as with African American students) or are not growing as rapidly (Aud, Fox, & KewalRamani, 2010). Latinos are more likely to live in urban areas. For example, most Latinos (45%) live in urban areas, with

DOI: 10.4018/978-1-7998-1213-5.ch042

31% in suburban areas, 8% in towns, and 14% in rural areas (Aud et al., 2010). Latino students in the U.S. live predominantly in neighborhoods of concentrated poverty, where they are further faced with crime and poor housing, and facing threats to their well-being (Murphey et al., 2014).

Data can be a powerful, pivotal tool when used by educators to target specific student needs, especially those of subgroups with a history of academic struggle (Faria et al., 2012). For example, in a two-year study involving 53 schools, well-implemented data-informed decision-making was found to have a significantly positive impact on students, equivalent to one additional month of schooling; gains were especially significant for socioeconomically disadvantaged students (van Geel, Keuning, Visscher, & Fox, 2016). Latino students in the U.S. comprise particularly relevant subgroups in this respect, as can be seen in 2013 National Assessment of Educational Progress (NAEP) results involving the testing of fourth and eighth grade students throughout the country (see Figure 1). The 2013 NAEP revealed an average of 21% of Hispanic students (the subgroup to which Latino students are assigned) were proficient in *Reading*, as opposed to 46% proficiency averaged by whites, and 23.5% of Hispanic students were proficient in *Mathematics*, as opposed to 49.5% proficiency averaged by whites (National Center for Education Statistics [NCES], 2013). When compared to students in the *White* and *Black* subgroups, Hispanic students are the least likely to be academically ready for kindergarten (ASCD. 2015). Hispanic students are also least likely to have a mother with a bachelor's degree (11%) when compared to students who are Asian (51%), white (36%), black (17%), American Indian/Alaska Native (16%), or of two or more races (31%) (Aud et al., 2010). However, data can only benefit students if teachers understand its

Figure 1.

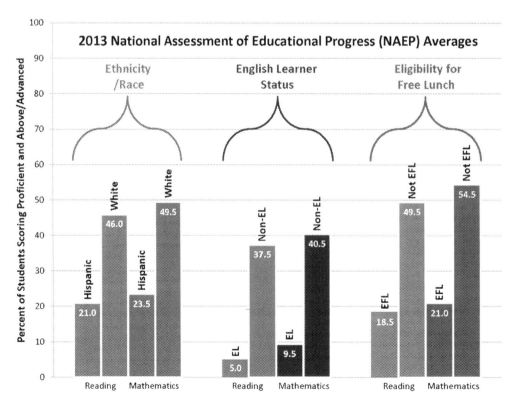

meaning and implications. This chapter will highlight current problems with teacher data use, as well as a cost-free, research based solution to misguided data use that can significantly improve teachers' ability to use data to help Latinos and other students.

BACKGROUND

Multiple Subgroup Significance

All students, regardless of demographics, deserve a quality education on par with that of their peers. Given the high diversity in urban classrooms, teachers in these environments need to be especially proactive in ensuring each student's varied needs are met. This chapter focuses on data-related improvements as they relate to Latino students, specifically, given (a) the high and growing population of Latinos in the U.S., combined with (b) Latino students' strong presence in multiple student subgroups. Those three main subgroups are the race/ethnicity subgroup of *Hispanic*, the status of *Socio-economically Disadvantaged*, and the status of *English Learner*. These federally-established subgroups are targeted by teachers with data, given federal accountability mandates to do so. Since these subgroups have historically struggled academically, and since these are larger than less populated subgroups (such as *American Indians/Alaska Natives* and *Students with Disabilities*) they are particularly targeted by teachers seeking to help students within the groups.

Since 80% of ELs are Hispanic (National Education Association, 2013), EL results are also pertinent to the Latino community. Hispanic students (69%) are more likely than any other subgroup's students to speak a language other than English at home (Aud et al., 2010). Many Hispanic children start school inadequately prepared to meet that institution's expectations, with language issues – that contribute to possible disconnect between families and schools – hindering academic achievement (Murphey et al., 2014). 2013 NAEP results revealed an average of 5% of EL students were proficient in *Reading*, as opposed to 37.5% proficiency averaged by non-ELs, and 9.5% of EL students were proficient in *Mathematics*, as opposed to 40.5% proficiency averaged by non-ELs.

Socio-economic subgroup performance is also pertinent to the Latino community. Nearly 33% of Latino students are classified as impoverished, and another 33% are barely above that classification, simply meeting basic needs (Murphey et al., 2014). 72-76% of Hispanic students are eligible for free lunch (EFL) through the National School Lunch Program (NSLP), one of the main criteria used to determine which students are socio-economically disadvantaged, while only 24-29% of white students are EFL (NCES, 2011). Thus EFL results are also pertinent to the Latino community. An average of 18.5% of EFL students were proficient in *Reading*, as opposed to 49.5% proficiency averaged by ineligible students, and 21% of EFL students were proficient in *Mathematics*, as opposed to 54.5% proficiency averaged by ineligible students (NCES, 2013).

Current Teacher Misunderstandings Using Data

Data disaggregated by criteria such as subgroup and student allow educators to carefully monitor Latino students' progress, identify individual needs, and deliver the best programs and instruction to target those needs, foster success, and thus close achievement gaps (Lachat & Smith, 2005; Mitchell, 2007). However, if educators misunderstand this data, the impact on Latino students can be detrimental. For example, the process of targeting subgroups, such as those with Limited English Proficient (LEP) students, with education data is currently fraught with errors that are unfair to the students in those subgroups (Schwartzbeck, 2003).

Data interpretation has become increasingly vital to school reform (Minnici & Hill, 2007), yet misunderstandings about how to use data and a data system can debilitate data use in a school district (Wayman, Cho, & Shaw, 2009). For example, if (a) educators identify *Literary Analysis* as a Latino subgroup weakness at a particular school district and then reorganize programs, resources, and instruction accordingly when (b) language-related *Word Analysis* is really the weakness that needs to be targeted, then (c) Latino students in that district will likely lose time and support vital to their academic progress as a result of educators' data-*mis*informed decisions. For example, it would seem the students were struggling with analyzing the literature, when in fact the students' vocabulary limitations and struggles with decoding words (i.e., word analysis) would cause them to not be able to comprehend the literature. In other words, they would not be able to analyze the literature if they could not first understand it, but without getting to the root of the problem (the world analysis) the students would not be able to properly analyze the literature.

Consider how this misunderstanding of Latino students' needs could hurt the very students each type of educator is seeking to help. Based on this misunderstanding:

- Teachers and teacher leaders (who came to this conclusion using student- and class-level data reports, among others) might use time with struggling Latino students to work more on literary analysis and less on other areas like word analysis.
- School administrators (who came to this conclusion using class-, grade-, and school-level data reports, among others) might arrange for a "pull out" in which struggling Latino students leave the class during other instruction to attend an intensive workshop on literary analysis.
- School district administrators and curriculum specialists (who came to this conclusion using school-level data reports, among others), might purchase more expanded literary analysis curriculum.

Since in all these example cases the students were actually struggling with world analysis, not literary analysis, the allocated learning time and resources would likely be poorly spent and detract from more appropriate efforts.

Unfortunately, there is strong evidence many users of data system reports have trouble understanding the data (Hattie, 2010; Wayman, Snodgrass Rangel, Jimerson, & Cho, 2010; Zwick et al., 2008). For example, in two national studies of districts known for *strong* data use, teachers' accuracy when interpreting data was only 48% correct and it is unlikely other school districts would perform any better (U.S. Department of Education Office of Planning, Evaluation and Policy Development, [USDEOPEPD], 2009, 2011). When data is particularly convoluted, as that generated for Common Core State Standards (CCSS) is likely to be due to the assessments' computer adaptive testing (CAT) nature, educators' data analysis accuracy within typical data system/reporting environments can be as low as 11% correct (Rankin, 2013).

For example, when educators of all levels were asked to view a data report to identify which students scored *proficient* on the state English language proficiency assessment, only 11% of educators could correctly identify the students or identify the assessment areas that caused a student to not score proficient (Rankin, 2013). Identifying proficiency on this assessment played a primary role in teacher's recommendation of EL students for redesignation. Given that 80% of ELs are Hispanic (National Education Association, 2013), failure to read this data accurately has likely affected Latino students' effective language classification, and thus their receipt of appropriate services.

If data system users do not understand how to properly analyze data, the data will be used incorrectly if it is used at all (National Forum on Education Statistics [NFES], 2011). There are many ethical concerns, some of which can be classified as human rights abuses, currently tainting the use of data systems when targeting vulnerable population subgroups such as the Latino population (Seltzer & Anderson, 2008). For example, school districts have been charged with the federally mandated task of continually examining the performance and progress of student subgroup populations – including the Hispanic/Latino ethnicity subgroup – to identify cases where these populations are struggling and to then make changes to address these problems. Essentially, it is a federal requirement that school districts monitor and see to Latino students' needs. The use of data is necessary to objectively determine if students' needs are being met and to monitor the success of interventions to determine if school districts are remedying any problems. If educators are not understanding data during these steps, as evidence cited in this paper indicates they are not, then educators are not properly seeing to these ethical mandates. Likewise, at the state level, professional standards for educators typically reiterate the requirement that educators analyze data at the subgroup level and use this data to inform appropriate responses. As one state's example, the California Professional Standards for Educational Leaders (CAPSELs) refer to different aspects of this requirement in five separate standards.

Current Teacher Education for Using Data

Training programs for teachers have generally not addressed data skills and data-informed decision-making (USDEOPEPD, 2011). Many teachers and administrators do not know fundamental analysis concepts, and 70% have never taken a college or post graduate course in educational measurement (Zwick et al., 2008). Even for those who do take such courses, it is not guaranteed the courses covered Latino-pertinent topics like the importance of disaggregating and analyzing data by subgroup, and implications for students spanning multiple subgroups like a student can in the areas of ethnicity, EL, special education, and socio-economically disadvantaged status. Given that 80% of ELs are Hispanic (NEA, 2013) and 72-76% of Latino students are socio-economically disadvantaged (NCES, 2011), such issues are of particular relevance to Latino students and the teachers who teach them. Yet few teacher preparation programs cover topics like state data literacy (Halpin & Cauthen, 2011). In fact, most people responsible for analyzing data have received no training to do so (Few, 2008).

Professional development (PD) can improve educators' data use (Lukin, Bandalos, Eckhout, & Mickelson, 2004; Sanchez, Kline, & Laird, 2009; Zwick et al., 2008). Staff resources such as site leaders, data teams, data experts, and/or instructional coaches can also improve educators' data use (Bennett & Gitomer, 2009; McLaughlin & Talbert, 2006). However, PD is not without limitations (Lock, 2006; Kidron, 2012; O'Hanlon, 2013; USDEOPEPD, 2011), nor are staff supports without imperfections (McDonald, Andal, Brown, & Schneider, 2007; Underwood et al., 2008; Wayman et al., 2010). For example, in a study involving teachers who had taken at least one course in measurement, *all* teachers struggled afterwards with statistical terms and measurement concepts and 60% of teachers had difficulty explaining a term used in a score report (Zapata-Rivera & VanWinkle, 2010). Since even districts utilizing PD and staff supports continue to struggle with data use, more avenues for teacher education are needed if their data use is to help rather than hurt Latino students and others targeted with data.

Lack of Data System-Embedded Teacher Education

In order to improve data use, practitioners and researchers need to gather empirical evidence to support different ways in which data is reported (Lyrén, 2009). Most educators have access to data systems to generate and analyze data reports (Aarons, 2009; Herbert, 2011), but there is clear evidence many users of data system reports have trouble understanding the data (Wayman, Snodgrass Rangel, Jimerson, & Cho, 2010; Zwick et al., 2008).

Despite this, labeling and tools within data systems to assist analysis are uncommon (USDEOPEPD, 2009). There are multiple ways in which teacher education, in respect to data use, can be embedded within a data system. For example, a data system can include: (a) labels for data displays, such as footers and/or other annotations, that guide viewers in understanding the data and in avoiding common misunderstandings concerning the displays and/or content; (b) a report-specific, one-page reference sheet for each data report, accessible through a link within the data report, that helps viewers understand a data report's purpose, components, and data; (c) a report-specific, multiple-page reference guide for each data report, accessible through a link within the data report, that covers the content of the reference sheet but goes further by walking viewers through the use of the report, such as in using the data report to answer specific questions; (d) an online, searchable, illustrated, step-by-step help system within the data system that is accessed through an ever-present "help" button and offers technical lessons related to using the data system and also data analysis lessons related to using the system's data; (e) pop-up messages that help with data interpretation every time a user hovers over a particular "hot spot", clicks a question mark icon, or follows a "more information" link, with the message being specific to the given area of the report where it was triggered.

QUANTITATIVE STUDY OF A SOLUTION

The study profiled in this paper (see Rankin, 2013) was used to investigate data system-embedded teacher education designed to improve the accuracy with which educators analyze data, which would then be used to inform decisions that impact students, particularly often-targeted students such as Latinos. This study was conducted to investigate solutions to the problem detailed in this chapter's Problem section, below, which involves the inaccuracy with which educators analyze student data, resulting in misinformed data-driven decisions that impact students. This quantitative study, along with its review here, concerns data analysis issues that affect all students as opposed to just Latino populations. However, due to reasons outlined in this chapter's Background section, the need for effective data analysis is particularly pertinent to Latino students. Thus the study's results will be shared with Latino students specifically in mind.

The study was built on a theoretical framework inspired by over-the-counter medication, where providing a product/treatment without embedded education in its use would be considered negligent. For example, the Food and Drug Administration requires over-the-counter medication to be accompanied by textual guidance proven to improve its use, deeming it negligent to do otherwise (DeWalt, 2010), and inadequate medication labeling has resulted in many errors and tragedy, as it leaves people with no way to know how to use the contents wisely (Brown-Brumfield & DeLeon, 2010). Fortunately, labeling conventions can translate to improved understanding on non-medication products, as well (Hampton, 2007; Qin et al., 2011).

Consider if you were to buy medicine to help your child recover from a cold. The package would give you a general sense of each medicine's function, such as if it were for a child (maybe a photo of a child is on the box with cartoon-like letters) versus an adult. The label would tell you the product's purpose, how to use the product (such as how many teaspoons to give your child and when), and dangers (such as possible side effects). If important information did not fit within the label, an inserted sheet or packet would provide added information. Supports such as these would help you use the product appropriately. Imagine if data systems contained similar supports to ensure their data contents were used appropriately.

In the same way over-the-counter medicine's proper use is communicated by an adequate label and added documentation, a data system used to analyze and address student performance can include components to help users better comprehend the data it contains. Yet computer data systems display data for educators without sufficient support to use report contents – data – wisely (Coburn, Honig, & Stein, 2009; Data Quality Campaign [QQC], 2009, 2011; Goodman & Hambleton, 2004; NFES, 2011). For educators, whose primary purpose for using data is to help students, using data without embedded support is akin to using medicine from an unmarked or marginally marked container. This study considered the impact on educators' data analyses if data systems provided data in an over-the-counter format, meaning teacher education in the form of data usage guidance was embedded within the reporting environment.

Problem

Educators make data analysis errors impacting students, yet data systems do not include data analysis help. Previous researchers had not determined whether adding specific supports to data systems could directly reduce the number of analysis errors. Data-informed decisions can lead to improved learning (Sabbah, 2011; Underwood, Zapata-Rivera, & VanWinkle 2010; Wohlstetter, Datnow, & Park 2008). Yet data use that impacts students serves as a negative factor when educators misunderstand data while using data systems (Wayman, Cho, & Shaw 2009). For example, only 11% of educators could correctly identify which students scored *proficient* on the state English language proficiency assessment or identify the assessment areas that caused a student to not score proficient (Rankin, 2013).

Computer data systems are the standard component schools use to collet, analyze, use, and communicate student data about students (Cho & Wayman, 2013). Yet labeling and tools within data systems to assist analysis are uncommon, even though most educators analyze data alone (USDEOPEPD, 2009). There is a clear need for research identifying how reports can better facilitate correct interpretations by its users (Goodman & Hambleton, 2004; Hattie, 2010).

Purpose and Methods

The purpose of this experimental, quantitative study was to facilitate causal inferences concerning the degree to which including different forms of data usage guidance within a data system reporting environment can improve educators' understanding of the data contents, much like including different forms of usage guidance with over-the-counter medication is needed to improve use of contents. The study's primary independent variables included the following types of data analysis guidance, each of which was framed in two different formats and was used with two reports per study participant to answer four data analysis-based questions of varied complexity:

- **Footer:** A report footer is a brief set of text at the bottom of a report that communicates information an educator would need to know to correctly understand and analyze that particular report's data. The study's footers ranged from 34-58 words, 156-269 characters without spaces, and 224-324 characters with spaces. Footers were either monochromatic or contained minimal color used purposefully; for example, "Warning" was featured in red and "What to Do" was featured in green.

Example: On a report displaying data from a California English Language Development Test (CELDT) teachers would use to inform their reclassification of EL students as Redesignated Fluent English Proficient (RFEP), the footer was featured in these two formats (with the second format following the color guidelines described above):

1. The student's "Overall" score is not the only score that determines CELDT proficiency. A student is Proficient on the CELDT only if earning both of these:
    - Performance level 4 or above overall, and
    - Performance level 3 or above in every domain.
2. Warning: "Overall" is not the only score that determines CELDT proficiency. What to Do: Consider a student CELDT Proficient only with both:
    - 4 or above overall, and
    - 3 or above in every domain.

- **Reference Sheet:** A report-specific reference sheets, also called a reference sheet, is a single page that accompanies a report to help the educator more easily understand the report and analyze its data. The study's reference sheets contained the report's title, description, image, focus (content reported), and warning (vital, cautionary information an educator would need to avoid the most common analysis errors made when analyzing the particular data being displayed). Half of the study's sheets also communicated the report's purpose (key questions the report will help answer) and additional focus information (intended audience, and format in which data is reported).

Example: "Focus" area on a reference sheet accompanying data from a California Standards Test (CST), which was used by teachers to better understand student performance overall and by student subgroup such as *Hispanic*, by which results were disaggregated for the public and local educational agencies (LEAs), was featured in these two formats:

1. **What Data is Reported?** Students' average % correct when answering questions aligned to each CST content cluster is displayed for:
    - A school site.
    - The State Minimally Proficient (meaning all students in California who scored the minimum scale score needed – 350 – to be considered Proficient on this CST).
2. **Who is the Intended Audience?** Teachers and administrators.
3. **What Data is Reported?** Students' average % correct when answering questions aligned to each CST content cluster is displayed for:
    - A school site.
    - The State Minimally Proficient (meaning all students in California who scored the minimum scale score needed – 350 – to be considered Proficient on this CST).

4. **How is the Data Reported?** The school site is graphed in blue, and the State Minimally Proficient is graphed in orange.

- **Reference Guide:** A reference guide, also called an interpretation guide, is a 2- or 3-page reference guide that accompanies a report to help the educator more easily use the report and analyze its data. The study's guides adhered to either of two formats: (a) the report's reference sheet (as described above) functioned as the guide's 1st page, and pages followed containing the report's instructions (how to read the report), essential questions (showing the user where to look on this report – and what to look for – to answer each question listed in the purpose area of the guide's 1st page), and a "more info" section (offering where to get additional information on related topics); or (b) the guide contained the report's title, description, warning, essential questions, and a "more info" section (details for these sections was provided earlier in article).

Example: On a guide accompanying CELDT data teachers would use to inform their reclassification of EL students as RFEP, each guide illustrated exactly how to determine which students were proficient in English, what their scores were, and more. Essentially, one guide went into more detail than the other.

Variables

The dependent variable was accuracy of data analysis-based responses, measured by a survey containing data analysis questions. 211 elementary and secondary educators at nine schools within six school districts answered these questions while viewing one of seven report sets of student data. The primary independent variables included brief, cautionary verbiage in (a) report footers, (b) report-specific reference sheets, and (c) report-specific reference guides, as well as the framing of these supports.

Each of these three (a-c) variables was framed in two different ways. Thus the seven report sets aligned with the variables as follows:

- Report set one included no embedded data analysis guidance (control group).
- Report sets two and three featured footers (variable a) on the data reports framed in two different ways.
- Report sets four and five accompanied the data reports with reference sheets (variable b), framed in two different ways.
- Report sets four and five accompanied the data reports with reference guides (variable c), framed in two different ways.

Secondary variables were investigated to add insight to the primary research questions; these included (a) school site demographics (school level type, school level, academic performance, EL population, Socioeconomically Disadvantaged population, and Students with Disabilities population) and (b) educator demographics (veteran status, current professional role, perception of his or her own data analysis proficiency, data analysis PD time, and number of graduate-level educational measurement courses).

Research Questions

The main research question from the study was:

Q1: What impact does data use guidance in the form of a report footer, reference sheet, or reference guide have on how frequently educators draw accurate inferences from student data reports?

Additional research questions were variations of Q1 and were used to investigate the specific impact of each *individual* form of guidance (such as a research question on the impact of the footer, specifically). Additional research questions were used to question the impact of the variations in how each of these forms of guidance were framed (such as the success of a longer footer versus a more concise footer). Secondary research questions were also used to determine the impact of school site demographics – listed above as (a) – and educator demographics – listed above as (b). All research questions were modeled after Q1, such as being focused on determining the impact on how frequently educators draw accurate inferences from student data reports?

Sample

A priori two-tailed t-test (effect size d = 0.5, α error of probability = 0.05, power = 0.95), rendered a recommended sample size of at least 210 participants. A priori F-test linear multiple regression analysis (effect size f^2 = 0.15, α error of probability = 0.05, power = 0.95, predictors based on independent variables = 7) rendered a recommended sample size of at least 153 participants. The study employed a random, cross-sectional sampling procedure when incorporating responses from 211 educators of all school levels spanning transitional kindergarten (TK) through twelfth grade, at all veteran levels, working in varied roles, and at schools with a range of demographics. These educators were employed at nine schools in six school districts, six cities, and three counties in California. The sample accurately reflected the study's population, which is comprised of public educators of all primary and secondary school levels in the U.S.

Materials/Instruments

Survey

The researcher was present while participant responses were collected through an anonymous, web-based survey crafted and administered in Google Docs, employing the Google Form feature. The survey included 10 multiple choice questions involving respondent background and the analysis of data contained in report handouts. The survey was crafted with attention to validity and reliability considerations, as well as opportunities for within-method methodological triangulation. All *analysis* survey questions concerned data from state assessments with which the study participants were most likely to be familiar with analyzing.

Handouts

All participants received the same data as one another, which was communicated through two different reports. Both reports concerned data from state assessments with which the Californian study participants were most likely to be familiar with analyzing. One report contained school-level data from the CST, which constituted the largest component of California's Standardized Testing and Reporting (STAR) Program on which state and federal accountability was most largely based as the time of the study. This accountability involves subgroup-specific accountability including the *Hispanic/Latino* subgroup and non-ethnicity subgroups of which some Latino students are also included: *EL*, *Special Education*, and *Socio-Economically Disadvantaged*. The other report contained student-level data from the CELDT, which California teachers must use when determining reclassification recommendations for any EL student.

The control group received plain reports with no analysis supports, whereas all other participants also received either footers, reference sheets, or reference guides. Data analysis supports used in the study adhered to research-based best practices inspired by literature such as Odendahl (2011) and Sabbah (2011). However, given controversies concerning framing such as behavioral economics phenomena summarized by Kahneman (2011) and by Thaler and Sunstein (2008), each support was formatted in two slightly different ways. These framing distinctions involved minor differences in length, density, and color usage. In order to mimic real-world conditions, the reference sheets and reference guides addressed all major questions the reports were designed to answer, as opposed to being geared exclusively toward the questions asked in this study's survey.

Likewise, all handouts mimicked real world environments by being distributed in hard copy format. While some teachers (44%) use their data system directly, most (56%) have access but do not use their data system directly and instead only read printed versions (such as in cases where educator leaders use the data system to generate reports for teachers or others) (Underwood et al., 2008). This design was also needed to better isolate the impact of study variables, as viewing a report on the computer can negatively impact how it is interpreted. For example, someone who correctly interprets a printed report can make mistakes when scrolling is involved, users are more likely to scan a report on a computer that they would read carefully when printed, and users' inability to mark on the screen can reduce the credibility users attribute to reports (Hattie, 2010; Leeson, 2006).

Coding and Analysis

The Google Docs Form tool automatically assigned an anonymous ID to each respondent's data, which was used in complete absence of participant names or employee numbers. The data was automatically, securely stored and password-protected online as soon as it was entered, and was exported into Microsoft Excel® shortly afterwards in order to be coded in accordance with a code book (columns A-JH for each respondent) and analyzed with the Microsoft 2010 Data Analysis feature and Predictive Analytics Software (PASW) Version 18 with the Statistical Package for the Social Sciences (SPSS) Data Access Pack. Results were analyzed to (a) answer research questions with related hypothesis strands, and (b) identify themes, patterns, relationships, and implications. Independent samples T-Tests and crosstabulations with Chi-square were used to investigate all variables noted earlier: dependent variable, primary independent variables, and secondary independent variables.

FINDINGS

The study profiled in this paper (see Rankin, 2013) rendered findings that educators' data analysis accuracy significantly increases with the presence of data system-embedded teacher education data analysis support in the forms of footers, reference sheets, and reference guides. Findings are presented using the following terms:

- **Support:** Meaning any or one of the following supports: footer, reference sheet, or reference guide.
- **Support Use:** Meaning instances in which respondents indicated they used the available support.
- **Data Analysis Accuracy:** Meaning the mean value of participants' percent correct scores earned when answering survey questions measuring common, varied types of data analysis accuracy.

All supports used in the study – footers, reference sheets, and reference guides – had a significant, positive impact on the participating educators' data analysis accuracy. Specifically, educators' data analyses were:

1. 264% more accurate (with an 18 percentage point difference) when any one of the three supports was present and 355% more accurate (with a 28 percentage point difference) when respondents specifically indicated having used the support,
2. 307% more accurate (with a 23 percentage point difference) when a footer was present and 336% more accurate (with a 26 percentage point difference) when respondents specifically indicated having used the footer,
3. 205% more accurate (with a 12 percentage point difference) when a reference sheet was present and 300% more accurate (with a 22 percentage point difference) when respondents specifically indicated having used the reference sheet, and
4. 273% more accurate (with a 19 percentage point difference) when an reference guide was present and 436% more accurate (with a 37 percentage point difference) when respondents specifically indicated having used the guide.

Overall, the 211 study participants indicated they used supports 62% of the time. 87% of participants who receive no supports indicated they would have used footers, reference sheets, or reference guides if the supports had been available. Given the discrepancy between 62% and 87%, and given that each participant who had the option of using a support only had access to a single support, it is likely some participants who did not use the offered support would have used the support if they had been offered one of the other two support types. Not only did the supports prove to have a significant, positive impact on data analysis accuracy, but the substantial rate at which they were utilized rendered their value significant for *all* educators as a whole, even when respondents' use of the supports was not considered. Nonetheless, respondents' data analyses were even higher when they indicated having used the available support.

When no supports were used, data analysis accuracy was 11%. All 211 participants, regardless of support use, averaged a data analysis accuracy of 26%. In cases where respondents indicated they used an available support, data analysis accuracy was 39%. See Figure 2 for a visual representation of support impact.

Data System-Embedded Analysis Support's Implications

Figure 2.

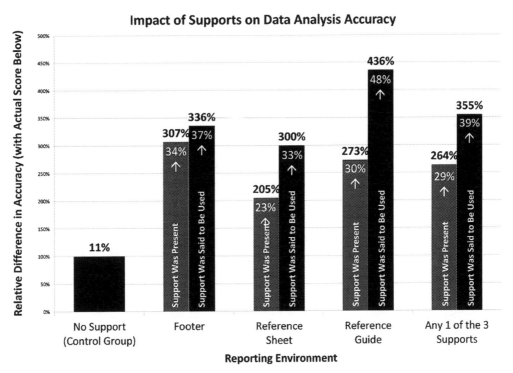

The minor modifications in support format, mainly in terms of length and color usage, had no significant impact on participating educators' data analysis accuracy. It is important to note all support format variations used in the study subscribed to leading best practices in design. Thus the variations were minor and designed to garner more specificity in these best practices. It was thus concluded such minor variations are also minor in their impact on educators' data analyses.

Additional, secondary research questions were used to add insight to the primary research questions. Findings in relation to these questions determined that educators' school site demographics had no significant impact on their data analysis accuracy that might impact the primary research questions. In other words, an educator's school level type, school level, academic performance, EL population, Socioeconomically Disadvantaged population, or

Students with Disabilities population had no significant impact on data analysis accuracy. Likewise, findings in relation to the secondary questions determined that educators' demographics had no significant impact on their data analysis accuracy that might impact the primary research questions. In other words, an educator's veteran status, current professional role, perception of his or her own data analysis proficiency, data analysis PD time, and number of graduate-level educational measurement courses had no significant impact on data analysis accuracy. This resulted in acceptance of the alternative hypotheses for secondary research questions. In addition, there were insignificant differences in data analysis accuracy, support use, and support success when participants viewed differing report types, such as tabular versus graphed or site-level versus student-level; when participants answered different types of analysis questions, such as single-step versus multiple-step or single-answer versus multiple-answer; and when participants viewed data from differing assessments, such as state assessment data versus language proficiency data.

Findings from the study and its accompanying literature review were summarized as a set of education data reporting standards referred to as Over-the-Counter Data (OTCD) Standards (see www.overthecounterdata.com/s/OTCDStandards.pdf). These standards summarize over 300 studies and other expert texts informing best practices for communicating data to educators so the data can be easily and accurately used.

CONCLUSION

Findings rendered implications there are direct benefits to educators' data use when a data system and its reports embed at least one of the three data analysis supports investigated in this study. Findings rendered implications that adherence to key OTCD Standards significantly improves educators' accuracy when analyzing school and student data. Findings also supported experts' assertions that educators desire more data analysis support from their data systems and its reports, and that the majority of educators use such supports when they are available. In addition, secondary research questions concerning educators' personal and school site demographics were answered with the finding that such demographics have no significant bearing on the supports' success, and thus the supports can be implemented with expected success at varied locations and for varied users.

SIGNIFICANCE

The study's findings filled a gap in field literature by containing evidence that can be used to identify whether, how, and to what extent data systems can help increase data analysis accuracy. The study also rendered OTCD Standards for effective education data reporting, examples, and templates for real-world implementation.

Teachers in highly diverse, urban classrooms need to ensure each student's varied needs are met. Latino students, specifically, represent (a) a high and growing population in the U.S. and (b) a strong presence in multiple student subgroups (such as the race/ethnicity subgroup of *Hispanic*, the status of *Socio-economically Disadvantaged*, and the status of *English Learner*). Driven partly by federal mandates, these subgroups are each targeted by teachers with data. Since each of these subgroups has historically struggled academically, and since these are larger than less populated subgroups (such as *American Indians/Alaska Natives* and *Students with Disabilities*) they are particularly targeted by teachers seeking to help students within the groups. Thus findings that can be applied to improve educators' data analysis accuracy are particularly meaningful and powerful for Latino students.

Improvements computer data system and report providers make in light of this study, and/or improvements educators make to reports stemming from data systems, have potential to improve the accuracy with which educators analyze data stemming from these sources. These improvements will likely benefit students affected by educators' data-informed decision-making. Students most directly targeted with data use, such as those experiencing gaps in academic achievement, will likely benefit the most. Given their strong role in multiple subgroups most impacted by data use, Latino students are the stakeholders most impacted by this study's findings.

IMPLICATIONS FOR EDUCATORS, LATINO STUDENTS, AND DIVERSE CLASSROOMS

Most Latinos (45%) live in urban areas (Aud et al., 2010), and they comprise the largest and fastest growing racial/ethnic minority group of students in the U.S. (Murphey, Guzman, & Torres, 2014). Teachers can use data to target specific student needs, especially those of subgroups with a history of academic struggle (Faria et al., 2012). Latino students in the U.S. comprise particularly relevant subgroups in this respect, as they have a history of academic struggle largely due to their presence in two additional subgroups that have historically struggled: namely, the *Socio-economically Disadvantaged* and *EL* subgroups.

Teachers need support in using data to help all students. However, given Hispanic students' common presence in three large, high-need subgroups, teachers especially need help in using data disaggregated to examine the *Hispanic* subgroup.

To offer over-the-counter medication without evidence-based textual guidance would be negligent (DeWalt, 2010). Nonetheless, data systems display data for educators without sufficient support to use their contents – data – wisely (Coburn, Honig, & Stein, 2009; DQC, 2009, 2011; NFES, 2011). Labeling and tools within data systems to assist analysis remain uncommon (USDEOPEPD, 2009). Thus educators' primary option for data use is not typically presented in an "over-the-counter" format, and educators using unmarked or marginally marked data to "help" students can be imagined as akin to ingesting medicine from an unmarked or marginally marked container. This analogy is appropriate considering many – and some studies indicate most – educators are making flawed data analyses when using data to impact students.

These flaws hold particularly significant implications for Latino students, who are overwhelmingly represented in three subgroups most commonly targeted when teachers, administrators, and other educators use data with the goal of closing achievement gaps: 80% of *ELs* are Hispanic (NEA, 2013), 72-76% of Latino students are *Socio-Economically Disadvantaged* (NCES, 2011), and all Latinos are represented in the *Hispanic* subgroup.

Educators can use this study's findings to advocate for improved data use conditions, such as when they are using data to learn more about the needs of particular student subgroups. For example, educators can:

1. Contact their school district administrators who oversee data use (e.g., Director of Accountability, Program Specialist for Assessment, etc.), school district administrators who oversee the data system (e.g., Edtech Coordinator, Information Technology Director, etc.), and key leaders (e.g., principal, superintendent, etc.), and policy makers or state officials influencing how school report cards and other data is displayed (e.g., state Departments of Education).
2. Request (of the above-mentioned stakeholders) that the data system being used within the LEA adhere to OTCD Standards (see see www.overthecounterdata.com/s/OTCDStandards.pdf), which are also featured (with citations) on the author's non-commercial research website at www.overthecounterdata.com/s/OTCDStandards.pdf
3. Include (in the above-mentioned request) mention of with which data reports teachers and other stakeholders need the most help; e.g.:
    a. Specific reports in which subgroups are analyzed, which should indicate areas of overlap where students are in multiple subgroups, and should allow teachers to view gaps in performance between the subgroup and students not in that subgroup.

b. Specific reports used to analyze specific students' needs, which should indicate language proficiency and specific language scores and sub-scores over time; subgroup statuses, academic proficiency, scores, and sub-scores over time; behavioral records and needs; attendance records and needs; etc.
4. Suggest (in the above-mentioned request) the data system provider use the free reference sheet and reference guide templates, based on the formats proven effective in this study, can be downloaded from the author's non-commercial research website at www.overthecounterdata.com/templates.
5. In the meantime, educators should not assume any data is as simple as a data report might make it look. Educators can contact support staff (e.g., a data coach) and agencies that publish and oversee measurement instruments (e.g., assessments) to better understand each data type's analysis guidelines. Educators should be particularly aware of multiple subgroup representation and the multiple needs Latino students might have. For example, 80% of special education referrals are based on teachers' concerns about students' reading, which has historically led to ELs being overrepresented in the *Students with Disabilities* subgroup; though this problem is improving, it still warrants care (NEA, 2013).

Educators do so much to help Latino students and their peers, and using data to target diverse needs becomes especially complex in urban areas. It is not enough to train teachers and other stakeholders to use complex data, as the data itself remains difficult to use when training is the only support offered to users. The data systems educators are using to better understand the needs of subgroups and the students within those subgroups need to better adhere to best practices that make the data, itself, easier to understand and use. Only then are Latino students likely to get the most benefits data use has to offer them and their peers.

REFERENCES

Aarons, D. (2009). Report finds states on course to build pupil-data systems. *Education Week*, 29(13), 6. Retrieved from http://search.proquest.com/docview/202710770?accountid=28180

ASCD. (2015, March). Research alert: The good news. *Educational Leadership*, 72(6), 8.

Aud, S., Fox, M., & KewalRamani, A. (2010). *Status and Trends in the Education of Racial and Ethnic Groups* (NCES 2010-015). U.S. Department of Education, National Center for Education Statistics. Washington, DC: U.S. Government Printing Office.

Bennett, R. E., & Gitomer, D. H. (2009). Transforming K-12 assessment: Integrating accountability testing, formative assessment and professional support. In C. Wyatt-Smith & J. J. Cumming (Eds.), Educational assessment in the 21st century, (pp. 43-61). New York, NY: Springer.

Brown-Brumfield, D., & DeLeon, A. (2010). Adherence to a medication safety protocol: Current practice for labeling medications and solutions on the sterile field. AORN Journal, 91(5), 610-7. doi:10.1016/j.aorn.2010.03.002

Cho, V., & Wayman, J. C. (2013). District leadership for computer data systems: Technical, social, and organizational challenges in implementation. *UCEA Convention*. Retrieved from http://www.vincentcho.com/uploads/9/6/5/2/9652180/ucea_2013_co_data_systems_final.pdf

Coburn, C. E., Honig, M. I., & Stein, M. K. (2009). What's the evidence on districts' use of evidence? In J. Bransford, D. J. Stipek, N. J. Vye, L. Gomez, & D. Lam (Eds.), The role of research in educational improvement, (pp. 67-88). Cambridge, MA: Harvard Education Press.

Data Quality Campaign. (2009). *The next step: Using longitudinal data systems to improve student success*. Retrieved from http://www.dataqualitycampaign.org/find-resources/the-next-step/

Data Quality Campaign. (2011). *Leveraging the power of state longitudinal data systems: Building capacity to turn data into useful information*. Retrieved from http://www.dataqualitycampaign.org/files/DQC-Research%20capacity%20May17.pdf

DeWalt, D. A. (2010). Ensuring safe and effective use of medication and health care: Perfecting the dismount. *Journal of the American Medical Association, 304*(23), 2641–2642. doi:10.1001/jama.2010.1844 PMID:21119075

Faria, A., Heppen, J., Li, Y., Stachel, S., Jones, W., Sawyer, K., ... Palacios, M. (2012, Summer). *Charting success: Data use and student achievement in urban schools*. Council of the Great City Schools and the American Institutes for Research. Retrieved from http://www.cgcs.org/cms/lib/DC00001581/Centricity/Domain/87/Charting_Success.pdf

Few, S. (2008, November 14). Telling compelling stories with numbers: Data visualization for enlightening communication. *Statewide Longitudinal Data Systems (SLDS) Grant Program Third Annual Fall Grantee Meeting*. Retrieved from http://nces.ed.gov/programs/slds/pdf/08_F_06.pdf

Goodman, D. P., & Hambleton, R. K. (2004). Student test score reports and interpretive guides: Review of current practices and suggestions for future research. *Applied Measurement in Education, 17*(2), 145–220. doi:10.120715324818ame1702_3

Halpin, J., & Cauthen, L. (2011, July 31). The education dashboard. *Center for Digital Education's Converge Special Report, 2*(3), 2–36.

Hampton, T. (2007). Groups urge warning label for medical devices containing toxic chemical. *Journal of the American Medical Association, 298*(11), 1267. doi:10.1001/jama.298.11.1267 PMID:17878415

Hattie, J. (2010). Visibly learning from reports: The validity of score reports. *Online Educational Research Journal*. Retrieved from http://www.oerj.org/View?action=viewPaper&paper=6

Herbert, M. (2011). States on track to have top-notch data systems. *District Administration, 47*(4), 12.

Kahneman, D. (2011). *Thinking, fast and slow*. New York, NY: Farrar, Straus and Giroux.

Knapp, M. S., Swinnerton, J. A., Copland, M. A., & Monpas-Hubar, J. (2006). *Data-informed leadership in education*. Seattle, WA: Center for the Study of Teaching and Policy.

Lachat, M. A., & Smith, S. (2005, July). Practices that support data use in urban high schools. *Journal of Education for Students Placed at Risk, 10*(3), 333–349. doi:10.120715327671espr1003_7

Leeson, H. V. (2006). The mode effect: A literature review of human and technological issues in computerized testing. *International Journal of Testing, 6*(1), 1–24. doi:10.120715327574ijt0601_1

Lukin, L. E., Bandalos, D. L., Eckhout, T. J., & Mickelson, K. (2004). Facilitating the development of assessment literacy. *Educational Measurement: Issues and Practice, 23*(2), 26–32. doi:10.1111/j.1745-3992.2004.tb00156.x

Lyrén, P. (2009). Reporting subscores from college admission tests. *Practical Assessment, Research & Evaluation, 14*(4), 3–12. Retrieved from http://pareonline.net/pdf/v14n4.pdf

McLaughlin, M., & Talbert, J. E. (2006). *Building school-based teacher learning communities: Professional strategies to improve student achievement.* New York, NY: Teachers College Press.

Minnici, A., & Hill, D. D. (2007). *Educational architects: Do state education agencies have the tools necessary to implement NCLB?* Washington, DC: Center on Education Policy.

Mitchell, C. (2007, April 9). Disaggregating the data clarifies picture of student achievement. *NSTA News: NSTA Reports.* Retrieved from http://www.nsta.org/publications/news/story.aspx?id=53730

Murphey, D., Guzman, L., & Torres, A. (2014, September). *America's Hispanic children: Gaining ground, looking forward.* Retrieved from http://www.childtrends.org/?publications=americas-hispanic-children-gaining-ground-looking-forward

National Center for Education Statistics. (2011). *Achievement gaps: How Hispanic and whites students in public schools perform in Mathematics and Reading on the National Assessment of Educational Progress.* Washington, DC: National Center for Education Statistics, Institute of Education Sciences, U.S. Department of Education. Retrieved from http://nces.ed.gov/nationsreportcard/pdf/studies/2011485.pdf

National Center for Education Statistics. (2013). *The Nation's Report Card: What proportions of student groups are reaching Proficient?* Washington, DC: National Center for Education Statistics, Institute of Education Sciences, U.S. Department of Education. Retrieved from http://nationsreportcard.gov/reading_math_2013/#/student-groups

National Education Association. (2013). *Hispanics: Education issues.* Retrieved from http://www.nea.org/home/HispanicsEducation%20Issues.htm

National Forum on Education Statistics. (2011). *Traveling through time: The forum guide to longitudinal data systems. Book Four of Four: Advanced LDS Usage* (NFES 2011–802). Washington, DC: National Center for Education Statistics, Institute of Education Sciences, U.S. Department of Education.

Odendahl, N. V. (2011). *Testwise: Understanding educational assessment* (Vol. 1). Lanham, MD: Rowman & Littlefield Education.

Qin, Y., Wu, M., Pan, X., Xiang, Q., Huang, J., Gu, Z., ... Zhou, M. (2011, February 25). Reactions of Chinese adults to warning labels on cigarette packages: A survey in Jiangsu Province. *BMC Public Health, 11*(133). doi:10.1186/1471-2458-11-133 PMID:21349205

Rodriguez, M. (2008, May 1). Learning how to incorporate technology in classrooms. *Inland Valley Daily Bulletin.*

Sabbah, F. M. (2011). Designing more effective accountability report cards. *ProQuest Dissertations and Theses, AAT 3469488.* Retrieved from http://search.proquest.com/docview/893068662?accountid=28180

Sanchez, E., Kline, D., & Laird, E. (April, 2009). Data-driven districts: Building the culture and capacity to improve student achievement. *Data Quality Campaign: Using data to improve student achievement.* Retrieved from http://www.dataqualitycampaign.org/files/DQCbrief_FINAL-lowres_2_.pdf

Schwartzbeck, T. D. (2003, December). Targeting subgroups: How students with disabilities and limited English are unfairly measured under NCLB. In *The School Administrator*. Alexandria, VA: AASA, the School Superintendents Association.

Seltzer, W., & Anderson, M. (2008). Using population data systems to target vulnerable population subgroups and individuals: issues and incidents. *Statistical Methods for Human Rights*, 273-328.

Thaler, R. H., & Sunstein, C. R. (2008). *Nudge: Improving decisions about health, wealth, and happiness*. New Haven, CT: Yale University Press.

Underwood, J. S., Zapata-Rivera, D., & VanWinkle, W. (2008) *Growing Pains: Teachers Using and Learning to Use IDMS®*. ETS Research Memorandum. RM-08-07. Princeton, NJ: ETS.

Underwood, J. S., Zapata-Rivera, D., & VanWinkle, W. (2010). *An evidence-centered approach to using assessment data for policymakers (ETS Research Rep. No. RR-10-03)*. Princeton, NJ: ETS.

U.S. Department of Education Office of Planning, Evaluation and Policy Development. (2009). Implementing data-informed decision making in schools: Teacher access, supports and use. United States Department of Education. (ERIC Document Reproduction Service No. ED504191)

U.S. Department of Education Office of Planning, Evaluation and Policy Development. (2011). Teachers' ability to use data to inform instruction: Challenges and supports. United States Department of Education. (ERIC Document Reproduction Service No. ED516494)

van Geel, M., Keuning, T., Visscher, A. J., & Fox, J. (2016, April). Assessing the effects of a school-wide data-based decision-making intervention on student achievement growth in primary schools. *American Educational Research Journal*, 53(2), 360–394. doi:10.3102/0002831216637346

Wayman, J. C., Cho, V., & Shaw, S. M. (2009, December). *First-year results from an efficacy study of the Acuity data system*. Paper presented at the Twenty-fourth Annual Texas Assessment Conference, Austin, TX.

Wayman, J. C., Snodgrass Rangel, V. W., Jimerson, J. B., & Cho, V. (2010). *Improving data use in NISD: Becoming a data-informed district*. Austin, TX: The University of Texas at Austin.

Wohlstetter, P., Datnow, A., & Park, V. (2008). Creating a system for data-driven decision-making: Applying the principal-agent framework. *School Effectiveness and School Improvement*, 19(3), 239–259. doi:10.1080/09243450802246376

Zapata-Rivera, D., & VanWinkle, W. (2010). *A research-based approach to designing and evaluating score reports for teachers* (ETS Research Memorandum No. RM-10-01). Princeton, NJ: ETS.

Zwick, R., Sklar, J., Wakefield, G., Hamilton, C., Norman, A., & Folsom, D. (2008, Summer). Instructional tools in educational measurement and statistics (ITEMS) for school personnel: Evaluation of three web-based training modules. *Educational Measurement: Issues and Practice*, 27(2), 14–27. doi:10.1111/j.1745-3992.2008.00119.x

KEY TERMS AND DEFINITIONS

Data System (Within the Context of Education): A computerized system that houses and displays student, educator, and school information and allows users to retrieve, manage, and analyze the data. Examples of data systems include an assessment system, data and assessment management system, data mart, data warehouse, decision support system (DSS), information system, instructional management system (IMS), learning management system (LMS), special education system (SES), student information system (SIS), and other educational technology product types that contains a significant feedback component.

Data-Informed Decision-Making: The process of using data to guide decisions. When educators use this process, their decisions ultimately impact students and often impact other stakeholders, such as teachers and administrators. Data-*driven* decision-making is a more common term, but data-*informed* decision-making is a preferable term since decisions should not be based solely on quantitative data (Knapp, Swinnerton, Copland, & Monpas-Hubar, 2006; USDEOPEPD, 2009).

Footer: A type of data report label with data usage guidance, involving brief (such as one to three lines of) text at the bottom of a data report.

Help System: A computerized, online collection of task-based lessons that walk data system users through sequential steps to accomplish tasks within the data system, as well as topic-based lessons that help users understand and use the data housed in the data system.

Over-the-Counter Data: Education data that is accompanied by usage guidance, embedded within the use environment, just as over-the-counter products are accompanied by embedded usage guidance. Data systems and reports can provide over-the-counter data by adhering to Over-the-Counter Data Standards (www.overthecounterdata.com/s/OTCDStandards.pdf) when reporting data to educators and other education stakeholders in order to improve their understanding and use of the data. These standards involve implementation of effective labels, supplemental documentation, a help system, package/display, and content.

Professional Development (PD): Continual process of learning recommended for educators. This process can involve a range of improvement strategies such as online networks, embedded videos, on-the-job training, traditional workshops, weekly collaboration sessions, and more.

Reference Guide: Supplements each report to help users understand and use that specific report's data. The reference guide is sometimes called a data guide, interpretation guide, or interpretive guide. The report's reference sheet (which is described below) functions as the guide's first page, and subsequent pages contain the report's instructions (how to read the report), essential questions (showing the user where to look on this report – and what to look for – to answer each question listed in the purpose area of the guide's 1st page), and a "more info" section (offering where to get additional information on related topics).

Reference Sheet: Supplements each report to help users understand that specific report's data. The reference guide is sometimes called an abstract or summary. This single page features the report's title, description, image, focus (content reported), and warning (vital, cautionary information an educator would need to avoid the most common analysis errors made when analyzing the particular data being displayed). The sheet can also communicate the report's purpose (key questions the report will help answer) and additional focus information (intended audience, and format in which data is reported).

Report: An arrangement of data usually selected for a particular topic and purpose in order to communicate the data to a particular audience through graphs/graphics, tables, text, and/or other means. These data reports can take online forms such as data dashboards or can appear as traditional printed pages.

User: Any person using a data system, such as within the field of Education, where this is likely an educator (including classified staff). However, in some cases the user can be a student, parent, or other stakeholder.

This research was previously published in the Handbook of Research on Classroom Diversity and Inclusive Education Practice edited by Christina M. Curran and Amy J. Petersen; pages 444-464, copyright year 2017 by Information Science Reference (an imprint of IGI Global).

Section 6
Inclusive Classrooms and Campuses

Chapter 43
Creating Inclusive Classroom:
Innovative Practices by Chinese Banzhurens

Jiacheng Li
East China Normal University, China

Yan Li
East China Normal University, China

Ying Huang
Changzhen Elementary School of Guangming District, China

Liujuan Huang
Guangming Experimental School, China

Binyao Zheng
Kennesaw State University, USA

ABSTRACT

From the 1980s, there are three steps to understand and adopt the inclusive education belief and theory in China. In today's Chinese schools, the typical inclusive education is implemented at the classroom level, but with unique context and content compared with the practices in the Western world. Banzhuren, a very special role in Chinese school, has witnessed the development of each child and plays a very important role in student development. Banzhuren creates the inclusive atmosphere for all students, engages every student in the classroom-based activities, and works with other teachers and parents to develop the classroom community. Authors surveyed students in two classes on their experience, values, understanding and expectation on inclusive education in the classroom. Based on the data, the authors found that the banzhurens involved have fulfilled their potentials to achieve the inclusive classroom by multiple ways. The authors discussed the practical application, the limitations of the research, and future research directions about the inclusive classroom in China as well.

DOI: 10.4018/978-1-7998-1213-5.ch043

INTRODUCTION

Inclusive education is an international focus in education reform and social development (Booth & Ainscow, 1998; UNESCO, 1994). With the largest amount of population, Chinese educators' practice and understanding can be an important part in the international society. From PISA 2009 and 2012, Chinese educational reform aroused more attention in the world (OECD, 2010; Tan, 2012; Tucker, 2011). As innovative practice and perspectives about inclusive education, the experience from China can be valuable to the international community. Especially with the development of urbanization in China, the disadvantaged children's education is getting more attention from policy-makers, researchers and other relevant stakeholders. This phenomenon is also the embodiment of inclusive education.

In Chinese education context, inclusive applies to the special education as well as regular schooling or general education. At the compulsory education level, almost all classrooms are divers in terms of gender, ethnicity, SES, and potentials. This chapter will focus on the inclusive classroom in regular schools to illustrate the innovative practice of Chinese teachers.

Inclusive education is adopted by Chinese government for enrolling children with disabilities. After years of efforts, the policy has implemented and developed, and China can now provide good services to children with disabilities in regular classroom settings (Xiao, 2005). However, new problems arise in China in the constructure of the supporting and security system for disabled children's learning in regular classes (Yu & Zhu, 2012). Besides, challenges facing the in-depth development of China's inclusive education arise from the conceptual backwardness in China's special education laws and regulations, including the imperfect mechanism of inclusive education, the imperfect system of special education fund allocation, the poor mechanism of teacher cultivation and training, and the excessively large regular classes (Peng, 2011). Comparing to Western schools, there are always more students in a regular classroom in Chinese schools. In 2013, the average class size at elementary level is 37 students per classroom, 49 students at junior high school level, 55 students at senior high school level, and 13.3% of the elementary schools have over 56 students per class (MOE, 2015a).

Diverse students with different SES, personalities and interests, values and habits, and expectations on education stay together from morning till afternoon in regular Chinese classrooms. A group of teachers teaching the same group of students in the same classroom through the grades in elementary schools, as well as in junior or senior high schools. Among the teachers, there is one teacher who plays the role as the team leader, with key responsibility in student management, collaboration among teachers, and communication with parents (Gu, Chen & Li, 2015). This is Chinese *banzhuren* (Li, 2014; Li & Ni, 2015), literally, the director of a class. Readers can imagine that the Chinese school principal would work with all students, teachers, and parents, as well as the *banzhuren* at the classroom level. It is related to the Chinese culture, school organization, instructional leadership, teacher professional development, school-family partnership, and the living mode of students in school. Unfortunately, Western researchers can hardly find this role in the West, though *banzhuren*'s responsibility is very similar to the homeroom teacher, school counselor, administrative assistant, and classroom teacher in USA (Morgan, 2016).

Banzhuren plays a very important role in Chinese education system, and there are lots of creative moments in children's classroom life created by *banzhuren* along with students. Besides the instruction, this new kind of education is referred to as *classrooming* and mainly conducted by banzhuren (Li & Chen, 2013). The *classrooming* consists of the classroom ceremonies, peer relationships, class meetings, student organizations in the class, and so on. At the classroom level, difference and the intersection of race, gender, ability, social and economic status are taken care of not only in the instruction time

Creating Inclusive Classroom

with various content areas, but also in the *classrooming* time which is the fundamental base of Chinese schooling and regarded as an education area as well as instruction (Bu & Li, 2013; Li & Chen, 2013).

Such context put inclusive education with some new meaning in China. The most important role in the school is that of a *banzhuren*, who cares for the whole group of the students, creates the inclusive learning environment for all students, and works with other teachers and parents to develop the classroom community. *Banzhuren* is one of the important positions in primary and middle schools (MOE, 2009). In a way, *banzhuren* is the key educator responsible for conducting inclusive education in regular schools.

This chapter will introduce the development of inclusive education in China first, and then focus on the classroom based education in regular schools where diverse students live and learn together. After the discussion of the methodology, the chapter will continue discuss the findings about how Chinese *banzhuren* develop the students in spite of the diversity of personalities, interests, abilities and learning needs. The chapter then will discuss the practical application in the Chinese context, the limitations of the study, and future research on inclusive classroom in China.

BACKGROUND

Inclusive education has been gradually recognized across the world (Chen & Wang, 2016; Li, 2013). Chinese scholars and educators learned from the international community, and put new understanding and beliefs into the daily educational practice. From the 1980s, there are three steps to understand and adopt the inclusive education belief and theory in Chinese education: inclusive education as special education, inclusive education as education reform for diversity, and inclusive education as education process for equality and quality.

Inclusive Education as Special Education

The first step is with the reform of special education, people involved are mostly scholars and educators in the area of special education. As we know, inclusion has its origins in special education, especially for children with disabilities and students who experience difficulties in learning. Reaffirming the right for education for every individual, as enshrined in the 1948 Universal Declaration of Human Rights, and renewing the pledge made by the world community at the 1990 World Conference on Education for All to ensure that right for all regardless of individual differences, The Salamanca Statement on Principles, Policy and Practice in Special Needs Education (UNESCO, 1994) is greatly valued by Chinese scholars and special educators (Huang, 2001; Peng & Deng, 2011; Yan & Fang, 2008).

From 1980s, more special schools were set up in China, in addition, over half of the children with disabilities were enrolled in the regular schools and classrooms. By 2014, there were 2000 special schools with 48,100 teachers, and 70,700 freshmen and 394,900 students at school, among whom 34,100 were students with vision disability, 88,500 with hearing disability, 205,700 with intelligence disability, and 66,700 with other disabilities. Meanwhile, there were 247,100 students with disabilities learning in regular schools instead of special schools (MOE, 2015b). In China, special school is the institution for the implementation of compulsory education for disabled children. Choices of these two options were determined based on the kinds and status of disabilities with these individuals. In Shenzhen City, the case city this chapter focuses on, by 2015, there were 669 schools at the elementary, junior and senior high school levels with 1,250,100 students, and one special education school with 873 students (Shenzhen

867

Education Bureau, 2015). The special education school was named Yuanping Special Education School. By 2016, it had 79 classrooms for 870 disabled students, and 224 teachers. On May 6, 2016, Shenzhen government distributed two policies about supporting the disabled children learning in regular schools and supporting the family with severely disabled children. The policies included guidance for further strengthening the disabled children's learning in regular classes and guidance for the severely disabled school-age children's "home delivery" teaching in Shenzhen (Shenzhen Education Bureau, 2016).

The policy makers have paid more attention to special education. The National Outline for Medium and Long-term Education Reform and Development (2010-2020) highlighted special education and requested different levels of government to develop special education, enhance the quality of education for students with disabilities, integrate more students into regular schools and classrooms, and support the teachers' professional development (MOE, 2010). *The Professional Standard for Elementary School Teacher* published in 2012 called all teachers to "respect the young children's personality, guarantee the student's rights, and treat students equally", and "understand the children's developmental needs at different ages, and ensure the capacities of protecting and cultivating children's physical and psychological development" (MOE, 2012a). Similarly, *The Professional Standard for High School Teacher* demands all teachers to "respect every student's personality, guarantee the student's rights, and treat students equally" (MOE, 2012b). In 2015, *The Professional Standard for Special Education Teacher* was distributed with the aim of developing the quality of special education (MOE, 2015c).

With rapid development of special education, there are still some problems. Deng (2004) investigated the local government leaders and principals and found that the development of special education was greatly affected by the value of the senior leaders, the financial resource, the social culture and environment, and the examination systems. Zhou (2008) argued that there were at least seven areas that need to be developed, including the inclusion of children with disabilities, persons infected with HIV, minorities, etc.

Inclusive Education as Education Reform for Diversity

The second step of Chinese inclusive education has been the systematic reform for diversity. With the research on inclusive education, Scholars and educators realized that the inclusive education needed a new philosophy and belief. Just as UNESCO focused, regular schools with this inclusive orientation are the most effective means of combating discriminatory attitudes, creating welcoming communities, building an inclusive society and achieving education for all. Moreover, they provide an effective education to the majority of children and improve the efficiency and ultimately the cost-effectiveness of the entire education system (UNESCO, 1994).

Huang (2003) argued that inclusive education is not only about special education, but also about human rights, equality, democracy, value, and curriculum and teaching. He regarded inclusive education as a new education beliefs and process, which respect all children, focus more on children engagement and collaboration, and try to meet the diverse needs from Children. Some scholars related inclusive education to social development and called for more social support (Peng & Deng, 2013).

Inclusive education is definitely about us, about everyday life for ordinary people (Booth & Ainscow, 1998; Zimbardo, Breckenridge, & Moghaddam, 2013). By the new understanding of inclusive education, Chinese scholars and educators found the necessity of a system reform, including the beliefs, institution, and leadership. The topics included the rural education and left behind students development (Chen, 2003), the migrant student education in urban areas (Li, 2009), the balance of key schools and struggled schools (Tan, 2012), the democracy education (Li & Chen, 2013), and school-family partnership (Li, Wang & Chen, 2013).

For example, the scale of urbanization in China in the early twenty-first century has been unprecedented. In East Asia, more than two-thirds of the region's total urban land as well as more than 80 percent of the new urban land added between 2000 and 2010 are located in China (International Bank for Reconstruction and Development, 2015). By 2014, at the compulsory education level, there are 12,947,300 migrant students, including 9,555,900 elementary students and 3,391,400 junior high school students. On the other hand, there are 20,754,200 left-behind students in rural areas, including 14,095,300 elementary students and 6,658,900 junior high school students (MOE, 2015b). The segregation among the children has been severe. A survey on 2,157 migrant students and 102 teachers in Beijing showed that 58.3% of the migrant students disliked Beijing kids, and the reasons were that they bullied the migrant children (26.2%), they looked down upon the migrant children (37.1%). The survey showed that even 3.1% migrant students had never gotten in touch with Beijing children (Han, 2002).

As one of the most important aims of urbanization, the concept of inclusive urban including inclusive education, has been developed by Chinese government. It is believed that "Inclusive urbanization provides all people access to equal opportunity to benefit from urbanization—to use their labor where they are most productive, to accumulate assets and savings, and to use public services of similar quality across China" (The World Bank and the Development Research Center of the State Council, P. R. China, 2014).

At the province level, Tan (2012) comments Shanghai education like this:

The Shanghai authorities have implemented a number of measures to help rural and weak schools under the ideologies of educational equity [jiaoyu junheng] and fair development [gongping fazhan]. ...The Chinese vision of 'education for all' - to provide equal learning opportunities for all students - explains, to a large extent, why Shanghai has the world's high percentage of resilient students in PISA 2009.

Such perspective and reform relate the inclusive education to the systematic education reforms in Chinese society, and the reforms lasts. In such a new framework and context, scholars and educators found that the education process is the key for the quality of inclusive education. This leads to the third step of understanding and practice of inclusive education.

Inclusive Education as Education Process for Equality and Quality

The third step of Chinese inclusive education development is the education process, or the quality education for all. Education is a fundamental human right and an enabling right. To fulfill this right, countries must ensure universal equal access to inclusive and equitable quality education and learning, which should be free and compulsory, leaving no one left behind. Education shall aim at the full development of the human personality and promote mutual understanding, tolerance, friendship and peace (UNESCO, 2015).

Even for those with special needs, they "must have access to regular schools which should accommodate them within a child-centred pedagogy capable of meeting these needs" (UNESCO, 1994). Therefore, the inclusive model should be implemented in the education process, and within the system reform. It is related to the reform of regular schools or general education. It is the action of Education for All, and "This implies creating an environment in schools and in basic education programs in which children are both able and enabled to learn. Such an environment must be inclusive, effective, friendly and welcoming to children, healthy and protective for children and gender sensitivity. The development of such child-friendly learning environments is an essential part of the overall efforts by countries around the world to increase access to, and improve the quality of, their schools" (UNESCO, 2005).

In Chinese context, especially at the compulsory education level, all public schools are neighborhood schools, and the students are grouped into classroom regardless of gender, ethnic, social economic status, nor academic achievement. Taking the two case classrooms from Guangming District of Shenzhen City as examples, all children were from the community, and the demographics were as below (see Table 1):

There were five students with disabilities including one student who has mental obstacles and four students with learning disabilities in Ms. Ying Huang's class. There was one student with learning disabilities in Ms. Liujuan Huang's class. In such classrooms, the inclusive education demanded quality life and *banzhuren*'s work.

New Basic Education Project in Chinese Education Reform

Among the available resources, this chapter utilized more information from the New Basic Education Project (NBEP). It was a large-scale and long-term education reform project, and conducted by principals, teachers and professors from 1994 till now (Ye, 1994). During 1994 to 1999, five Shanghai schools and one university were involved in it (Ye, 1999); from 1999 to 2004, 19 professors and doctoral candidates, 2,000 teachers and principals, 56 schools and five districts participated (Ye, 2004); from 2004 to 2009, ten schools, 976 teachers, 13,000 students, three districts and over 17 professors participated (Year 1999, 2004, 2009c, 2010). From 2009, 100 schools were involved (Ye, 2009).

NBEP focused greatly on the student involvement in the education process, and opened the door of *classrooming* reform from 1994 (Ye, 1994). It emphasized the importance of life, and regarded education as a career that embodies the concern with life in a civilized society (Ye, 2006). The intrinsic value of education in school is to improve the quality of people's life and realize the concerns for human life (Li, 2006). The NBEP argued that the students achieve quality development by active participation, healthy relationship with others, and self-awareness (Li, 2015), and this turns classroom into education space, and turns classroom life into education resources. So the NBEP declared that students' holistic development in the life world is reflected in the reform of teaching and learning, as well as in the everyday classroom life (Li, 2009).

Many efforts have been made by NBEP in the study of *classrooming* with *banzhurens*. As classroom life is related to the well-round development of students, and children can be fully involved in all kinds of activities regardless of abilities, it is fundamental for inclusive education. On the other hand, comparing with instruction, *classrooming* is a developing education area in China, so the experiments and experi-

Table 1. Demographics of two case classes

	Ms. Ying Huang's Class	Ms. Liujuan Huang's Class
Number of students	47	54
Male/Female	25/22	34/20
Living with both parents/ single parent	45/2	47/7
Local students/migrant students	3/44	20/34
Students with disabilities	5	1

Creating Inclusive Classroom

ences are very important. In the context of inclusive education, *banzhuren* should develop the inclusive classroom, and involve every student into the *classrooming* (Li, 2016).

METHODOLOGY

The authors have rich experience of the NBEP. The lead author has been in this project from 2000 till now, and the third and fourth authors are the experimental *banzhuren*s from 2014 till now. From September 2014 to August 2015, they worked together trying to improve the classroom life in Guangming, Shenzhen. Totally 5 schools involved into the NBEP. During one-year's collaboration, in order to solve the difficulties in the process, the authors met together and discussed every two months, attended and did the onsite observation during the class meetings, reflected and renewed the action strategies in the real context. During the year, and lead, third and fourth authors had been working together for over eighteen days in the authentic school context, and kept very close relationship by information tools. The relationship between professor and teachers made the data collection process a very smooth one.

The study took two case classes among the thirteen classrooms in five schools. Among the five schools, there were two schools with more students with high SES (always the local children), and three schools were for students with low SES (one school is mainly for migrant children from Vietnam, and two for migrant children from rural China). The two case schools in the chapter were typical in the five schools. Meanwhile, the thirteen experimental *banzhuren*s can be distinguished into two groups (see Table 2). The lead author talked with the third author, who has only two years' experience by June 2015 and was one of the youngest banzhurens, and the fourth author, who had eight years' experience, and achieved the agreement with them to finish this research collaboratively.

In the research, three forms of data and information were collected and analyzed: onsite-observation at school, interviews with *banzhuren*s and student's using questionnaire. By June 2015, the authors had done the onsite-observation, collected 9 videos of case-class meetings involving all students. Observations were documented with the authors' notes. In order to ensure the accuracy and consistency of the observation, authors analyzed the video and compared to the notes.

The lead author interviewed thirteen *banzhurens*, including the third and fourth authors, and the items included their understanding, value, practice and expectation with inclusive education. This helped

Table 2. The experimental banzhurens in Guangming District

	Below 3 Years' *Banzhuren* **Experience**	**Over 8 Years'** *Banzhuren* **Experience**
Guangming Experimental School	Ms. Ye	Ms. Huang
Changzhen School	Ms. Huang	Ms. Li Ms. Wu
Yulv School	Ms. Liu Ms. Xu	
Guangming Elementary School		Ms. Lin Ms. Chen Ms. Ding Ms. Yang
Aihua Elementary School	Ms. Wang	Ms. Tian

the authors understand the achievement of the experiment. The content of interviews was recorded and transcribed verbatim by authors.

From early-June to mid-June 2015, the authors designed and discussed the framework of the student's questionnaire by email and phone calls, and then put forward the final draft. The framework of the survey includes: a. Areas of student involvement in the classroom, b. The process of student involvement, c. The initiation of student involvement, d. The student development, and e. The future directions. The questionnaires consist of single-choice questions and open-ended questions. The questionnaires were anonymous, and no individual could be identified.

On July 1 and July 3, the two case classroom *banzhurens*, Ms. Ying Huang and Ms. Liujuan Huang distributed the questionnaire to all students during the class meeting time, and collected the questionnaire on the same day. During the summer break, 10th July to 5th August, the two authors used a number of analytical strategies and functions, such as frequency and percentage in EXCELL, to measure and interpret different types of data, and then shared the data with all authors of the chapter.

MAIN FOCUS OF THE CHAPTER

Contents of Chinese *Banzhuren's* Work

Based on the data and the experience the authors had in the experiments, the inclusive education was a great challenge because of the large class size, the lack of time and energy of the educators, and the little awareness of equity in the classroom. With the school reform projects conducted by different stakeholders, especially in the NBEP, *banzhuren*s always value the inclusive education very much, and include the following points into their professional activities (Li, 2015):

The first task is to develop the classroom culture. The *banzhuren* and students can develop the classroom slogan, song, flag as well as the rules that everybody in the classroom should respect. Inclusive education believes are always in the activities, that call for the involvement of everybody in the classroom and promote friendship, trust and collaboration among peers.

The second task is to develop classroom organizations. The *banzhuren* and students can develop quite a few groups, such as classroom clubs, committees, classroom NGOs, project teams, etc. These make it possible that everybody can involve into one or more groups with roles as leaders. Requirements for the roles were not based on academic achievement scores, but on the different types of interests, capacities and responsibilities.

The third task is classroom based activities. These include the class meetings every week, and the projects conducted by students and *banzhuren* in the school days. With student participation some topics of activities may cover the issues of inclusive involvement of students.

The fourth task is to participate in school-level activities inclusively, including the Sports Meeting, the Science and Technology Festival, the School Anniversary, the Field Trip, etc. *Banzhuren* is always asked by the school leaders to organize and evaluate the students during the process.

The fifth task is to promote parental involvement and children's family/community lives. In today's Chinese education, parents are deeply involved in instruction, leadership and student management. This provides students with more opportunities to be engaged in the activities in and out of school. *Banzhuren* is always the key person whose responsibility is to connect the classroom to families and communities.

Creating Inclusive Classroom

With such educational endeavors, the Chinese *banzhurens* make inclusive education possible. They create more educational moments, space, resources, and activities, and have achieved the experience of educating the youths with the belief of democracy, respect and harmony.

Reflection on the Former Work of *Banzhuren*

Classrooming is not a hot area in Chinese education, and the *banzhurens* can get very limited pre-service and in-service training. As one case *banzhuren*, Ms. Ying Huang, said that the in-service training always took the shape of lecturing, and the *banzhurens* always sat and listen without dialogue and critical thinking (Ying Huang, 2015). Before involving into the NBEP, the case classes are typical in China with the *banzhuren* focusing more on hierarchic leadership, the discipline training, and the service to the instruction.

Ms. Ying Huang reflected that the classroom was exclusive for the students as follow:

With the first and second grades, there were eight formal student leaders in the classroom as monitors, leaders for PE, leaders for discipline, and group leaders. A very interesting thing was that there was one student who took the roles of monitor, leader for PE course, and leader of one group of students. This made more students being excluded from the classroom leadership.

The classroom activities or self-organized activities were quite limited, except for the opportunities when the activities were organized by the school. The students always obeyed the rules designed by the school, prepared for the shows, and at last performed themselves in the Festival of Chinese Language, Talents Festival, Science and Technology Show, and PE and Culture Festival. Most of the students were audiences instead of the performers on stage.

The classroom culture development has the potential of engaging most of the students. Unfortunately, only several students were identified to be responsible for the material providing, and most of the decorating were finished by the banzhuren and volunteer parents.

As for the student organizations, there were only learning groups organized by the teachers, with the work of collecting the homework and group dialogue during teaching and learning sessions. (Ying Huang, 2015)

From the perspective of another case *banzhuren*, Ms. Liujuan Huang, the situation was very similar:

From September 2013 to September 2014, the classroom was diverse with some children from single-parent families or the parents working and living in other cities. The girls in the classroom did not care about the classroom activities and had little interest in the classroom development. Boys had the interest, but they had limited methods and patience to finish the tasks.

Before involving into the NBEP, the banzhuren had the belief that the work was to prevent the problems, but not to develop the classroom community. In the district, the model classroom community was the disciplined classroom which could fulfill the task distributed by the school, and the evaluation from the school and district was very important for banzhurens. To guarantee the quality of tasks, only talented students had the opportunities to be engaged in classrooming. The banzhuren's work always covered three areas: classroom culture, classroom management, and school level activity involvement.

The classroom culture development included the decoration of the walls and the blackboard newspaper. The banzhuren always chose some students who were good at drawing to do the work, and the process was always conducted by the direct and strong leadership from banzhuren. Among fifty-four students, only six to eight students had the opportunities for such activities.

In Grade Four, the banzhuren did encourage the students to be volunteer managers, but most of the girls had no interest, and the boys could not fulfill the task. At last, some students were chose to be classroom managers, and they always manage the classroom with punishment. Below is the organizational structure of the classroom.

As for the school-level activities, they were always stable in every year, and included the Arts Festival, Sports Meeting, and Science and Technology Festival. All of these activities were assessed by the school, and the collected scores would determine the performance status of the class. The *banzhuren*s always tried their best to get some students, not all students, to participate. It was reasonable that most of the students were audience who watched the performance of chosen representatives.

Figure 1. The organization of classroom

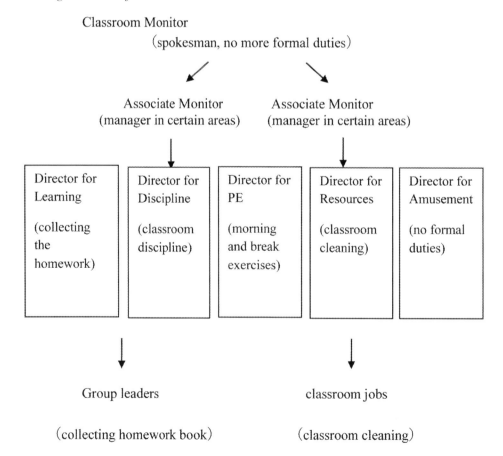

All of these led to the exclusion classroom community. In Grade Four, only eight students were engaged into the classroom culture development, seven students were responsible for the classroom management, and twenty students were actively involved in the school activities.

The students had little interest in the classroom affairs, and their potentials had not been fulfilled, especially in terms of creativity. *Banzhuren* acted as a final decision maker or boss, and the classroom life was organized by *banzhuren* with up-down management.

Challenges for Chinese *Banzhurens*

With onsite observation and interviewing with other eleven experimental *banzhuren*s in Guangming, Shenzhen, the authors found that the quality of *classrooming* could not meet the development of students, especially in the context of diverse students. Then come the idea: Could the former classroom be transformed based on inclusive education?

From 2014 to 2015, NBEPers tried to meet the demands of inclusive education and involved every student into the *classrooming*. The two case *banzhuren*s worked in the NBEP with other eleven *banzhuren*s from five schools in Guangming, Shenzhen. They reported that the inclusive classroom had been in shape, and more outcomes had been achieved.

The chapter aims at discussing the inclusive education with the evidence from experimental *banzhuren*s in NBEP. Two research questions will be answered:

1. How do the *banzhurens* create an inclusive classroom?
2. How do the students evaluate the inclusive community?

SOLUTIONS AND RECOMMENDATIONS

After joining in the NBEP, *banzhurens* had full understanding of the situation and new direction of *classrooming*. There are a lot of related books about the NBEP, from which the *banzhurens* learned and summarized the research direction and research method to get more theoretical knowledge. Meanwhile, *banzhurens* participated in classrooming based on research and organized a variety of student activities, so that they could find the problems with their experience. NBEP supplied *banzhurens* with many opportunities to contribute to communicate with experts from universities and master *banzhurens* from other districts. During the process, *banzhurens* got development by school's support, university's cooperation and their own diligence. In return the *banzhuren's* development helped every student gain suitable education and contributed to building inclusive classroom. In fact, in the process of building inclusive classroom, *banzhurens* played a significant role by encouraging children, communicating with parents, involving in activities, positive appraisal and summarizing experiences.

Case One, Ying's Class, Grade Three

Ms. Ying Huang is a novice *banzhuren* who began her teaching career from 2013. When she stepped into the NBEP, she had only one year's experience. Just during the year from 2014 to 2015, the class experienced dramatic change.

A New Picture of the Classroom Community

During the year, the classroom culture development, such as the decoration of the classroom walls, the publishing of blackboard newspaper, the election of classroom name, etc., made more students' involvement possible. The survey shows that 100 percent of the students agreed that they had been involved in such activities, and 19 percent of the students experienced the whole process of designing, organization, renewal, and reflection. By 2016, the classroom has its own name of "Family of Rainbow", the class song named "Song of Seven-Color", and the classroom slogan. All these were conducted by the students inclusively.

Every student had a voice and could be involved in the classroom management. 87 percent of the students said that they participated in the decision of classroom rules. 100 percent of the students took part in the volunteer work, the typical Chinese students' service learning in the classroom, and 94 percent of the students took different jobs during the year, and over 90 percent of students experienced the whole process. By now, the classroom has been organized and managed by all students, and there are totally three types of class jobs including management, service, and learning, which provided totally 24 positions for 44 students at the same time.

To provide more opportunities, the *banzhuren* and students developed eight groups, and students could work as a group with different classroom issues. By this way, all students could be included, and 70 percent of students had participated in the whole process of group designing, organization of group work, group assessments, and the continuing group activities.

More classroom based activities besides the school level activities had provided many opportunities for student involvement. During the schooling year, the students had the class meeting every week and noon meeting every school day, and participated in the following activities (see Table 3).

With the experience, students developed their positive emotion, interest, and creativity. The students of this class valued the activities very much, and were excited to be one part for the development of such an inclusive classroom with their *banzhuren*.

Table 3. The activity you have tried by now

	Frequency	Percentage
Classroom workers	20	43%
Noon Meeting of the Class	25	53%
Talent Festival	35	74%
PE and Culture Festival	29	62%
Series of classroom meetings of "Run, the Rainbow student"	39	83%
Decoration of the "Family of Rainbow"	29	62%
Student Flea Market	39	83%
Planning of the Father/Mother's Day	14	30%

N=47

Banzhuren's Solution of Developing Inclusive Classroom

How could the banzhuren and students achieve it? Comparing to the situation of Grade One or Two, it was a surprising achievement. There were several aspects of experience from the *banzhuren*.

Firstly, developing the students by their involvement was practicable, so students' involvement was the premise. In fact there were always some students who were not willing to participate in classroom based activities, even though the activities appeared to be more interesting for them. By interviewing these students, the *banzhuren* understood that the reason why they didn't involve in the activities: 1), the activity wasn't interesting, so the students were not willing to attend; 2), the students didn't want to be a member of the team or group; 3), the students were naughty or the academic performance was poor, so no other students wished to be team members with them; 4), the activity was so troublesome that the students could not do a good job; and 5), the group leader failed to distribute some specific tasks to them. Some students said that the result was always the same without their involvement. Thus, it seemed to be that the students' negative attitude to the *classrooming* was affected by student's subjective understanding and lacking external coordination in the classroom based activities.

Based on the analysis, Ms. Ying Huang had token flexible combination in different activities, and at the same time made definite requirements about the involvement and development of each group, as well as taking the opportunities to praise or evaluate these students with the aim of cultivating their confidence. During the process, the *banzhuren* led all students to transform their participation methods to make the involvement easier and friendly. Moreover, the *banzhuren* led students to distribute in many areas they preferred in the classroom. Thus, every student knew what they should be responsible for.

Secondly, it broadened the community based education resources. Social environment is important for students' development, and students are inevitably influenced by everyday life and social environment. Moreover, social resources can also be used by *banzhuren*s to contribute to children's development, such as the activity of *Finding the Beauty of Changzhen Community* can make children further understand the social environment where they live. Furthermore, during the process, school-family partnership will support the students' activities. For example, in the activity of *Talent Festival*, parents sent the children's photographs and videos that reflected the children's hand practice in everyday life to the *banzhuren*, which may assist *banzhuren* to deepen the understanding of children. In addition, other resources including the places, organizations, human resources in school, can also be important educational resources for *banzhuren* and students.

Thirdly, educational time is important. Students' participate in classroom based activities needs sufficient time, which implies that the teachers should spare more time for them. The noon meeting from 2:00 pm to 2:15 pm covered a wide range of topics, even if the time was limited. The activities included the class cadre's report about the previous day's duty, the evaluation report from the supervision group of class cadres, students' discussion about the current classroom situation, *banzhuren*'s summary, and if there was extra time, inviting some students to tell stories, sing songs or tell jokes.

Besides, in order to encourage students to be actively involved in the *classrooming*, *banzhuren* and students had developed a series of rules, such as the *Bulletin of Little Rainbow Comparison* which recorded the honors and awards of the student groups and individual students. At the end of the semester, the students selected the best *Rainbow Group* by adding the personal records to the group's, which virtually makes the students experience the close relationship between individual and group. There was a special group in the class called *Supervision Group of Class Cadres*. The group evaluated all the class cadres and the director of classroom jobs by quantitative methods every day, and made the evaluation results public in weekly class meeting. These kinds of evaluation and feedback informed all students of the situation and development of the class, and encouraged more responsive and creative involvement with every student.

Student's Development With Involvement

By involving in classroom based activities, the cognition of *I am the master of the classroom* has been identified among students. It has become so regular that the students consciously manage classroom affairs, develop the classroom culture and organize classroom based activities. A girl said in the survey: "Our class song is what we choose and is also what we enjoy singing most." Another girl admitted: "The class cadres are voted by ourselves and are not chosen by the teacher." A boy proposed: "We design and arrange the classroom." These students' self-reports manifested that students enjoyed the freedom of classroom life with the attitude of ownership and experience of belonging.

In the process of participation, students actively applied their creativity into practice when they dealt with the class affairs under the guidance of *banzhuren*. Thus, it was beneficial for children to accumulate wisdom of problem solving. One student reflected: "I often sought help from parents when I had trouble. I didn't dare to ask the teacher for help. But now I become confident." Another student admitted: "Now I can positively express and share my ideas, and also can listen to others and discuss with them together." It seemed that the students knew more about themselves and could objectively evaluate their potentials with involvement in the classroom life.

In the inclusive classroom, there were more opportunities of evaluating each other among classmates, because it was easy to find students' advantages and shortcomings by involving in different kinds of activities. The students were inclined to evaluate others in an objective and tolerant attitude in all aspects of performance in the process of participation in *classrooming*. It was necessary to modify the interpersonal relationship. Meanwhile Ms. Ying Huang admitted that during this academic year, the students have gradually implanted the conception of collective and class into their ideology, and now they pay more attention to the community and collaboration.

Based on the student's self-reports in the survey, the authors could summarize the following key words to explain student's development by involvement: self-discipline, self-management, quick response to the tasks, self-reflection, collaborative ability, learning skills, creativity, evaluation, language expression, and problem solving skills. Ms. Huang reflected: "I can deeply feel that the students are becoming bolder and more generous. They have the courage to express their ideas. They also become smarter, and are inclined to do things by seeking the best method. Students are becoming more united, and have a sense of collective belonging and honor." It was obvious that students were affected by an inclusive atmosphere and contributed with the development of inclusive classroom by their engagement.

With the development of class activities and more students' participation, great degree changes have taken place in the five students with disabilities. The student who had mental obstacles opened his mind to other students in the same group and *banzhuren*. The relationships among classmates were improved. The four students with learning disabilities made progress too. One student actively participated in each activity and undertook different tasks. He improved the sense of responsibility. Another student undertook the task of collecting homework in class, and later he could finish homework on time and his learning performance was better than before. The other three students' participation impressed the *banzhuren* and their classmates by the involvement of learning too.

New Planning

Based on the one-year's experiment, the *banzhuren* had the awareness of continuing the efforts of developing the inclusive classroom. From 2015 to 2016, she had some ideas.

The first idea was seeking various types of activities according to the need of students. When the students were asked by the *banzhuren*: "For the next semester, do you have any suggestions to the classroom based activities?" Handwriting contest, chess tournament, manual section, games festival, food festival, experience of teacher role. Students' answers were beyond *banzhuren*'s expectations and mirrored their thoughts and needs. Student's advice provided *banzhuren* with more directions for enlightenment. Firstly, class meetings could be organized by more arts activities with the aim of integrating subject learning into classroom based activities and providing the students with more stage opportunities. Secondly, classroom based activities could also be activities in academic areas. These activities could increase children's knowledge, and could allow students to learn from each other. Thirdly, classroom based activities could be sports-related, especially for the collective activity. It could not only inspire the children's passion to participate in sports, but also it could make the students experience more enjoyable while collaborating in the team work and authentic competition. In addition, classroom based activities may also be emotional activities, such as sharing holiday experience, telling the funny or troublesome stories in family life, or asking questions about life. The activities made children happier, and were thoughtful and diverse.

The second was exploring various forms of activity models according to students' ability levels. Classroom based activities are multiple and the models should be diverse. *Banzhuren* should be aware of the diversity of students, and make sure that the activity model is suitable to the students' developmental needs. In the new semester, the activities can focus more on planning, reporting and reflection, or problem solving, which can be regarded as three activity-models. In all the three models, students' advocating, summarizing and evaluating should be greatly encouraged, with their roles as planners, reporters, reviewers and judgers.

The third was making specific and comprehensive summary according to the student's achievement. In fact, summary and evaluation can be key events to promote student's involvement and achievement, even though children don't understand the meaning of feedback at early ages. When Students get involved in the activity, whether they have reached the expected goals it is good for them to get feedback from teachers and peers.

Case Two, Liujuan's Class, Grade Five

New Picture

The NBEP had helped her deepen the understanding about student growth: The children are not products controlled by the teacher, and they are individuals with vitality and infinite possibilities. Huang and her class had experienced the processes of passive growth, self-growth and syntrophism (Huang, 2016).

Classroom culture was an important part of the student community. Compared with the previous situation, during 2014 to 2015, this case class had formed rich culture and all students participated in the classroom culture development (see Table 4).

The data in the table demonstrated that students could participate in multiple projects of the classroom cultural development. Students could freely choose the activity, so this inspired more students to actively participate. When students were asked: "What are you proud of in the classroom?" A student said: "The

Table 4. Student's participation in classroom cultural development

Activity	Planning Frequency	Planning Percentage	Organization Frequency	Organization Percentage	Evaluation Frequency	Evaluation Percentage	Following Activity Frequency	Following Activity Percentage
Blackboard Newspaper	3	6%	7	13%	37	69%	14	30%
News Column	11	20%	7	13%	41	76%	40	74%
Book Corner	17	32%	16	30%	17	32%	45	83%
Class Slogan	7	13%	9	17%	3	6%	8	15%
Party Decorating	11	20%	13	24%	20	37%	13	24%
Other Classroom Environment Decorating	17	32%	14	26%	15	28%	16	30%
Forming or updating of Class Name, Class Song, Class Rules	9	17%	5	9%	39	72%	13	24%

N=54

classmates are very collaborative." Another student added: "I have a lot of friends in the classroom. They are very friendly and kind." Most of students reflected that they were very harmonious and they could do many things together. They also admitted that their classroom had classroom-clubs and was the star class in the school. A few students proposed that there were a lot of impressive classmates who won many awards that they were proud of. Thus, after a year's cultural development, the students' identity with the classroom and teachers had been strengthened, and the student's community consciousness got enhanced. They also learned how to appreciate others during the process.

As for classroom management, democratic election and rotation of the classroom cadres have been widely welcome. Based on fair election, *banzhuren* led the class cadres with roles of both managers and servers. The class set up 24 classroom jobs including three categories: service jobs, learning-related jobs and administrative jobs, that could be chosen by students according to their characteristics (see Table 5.). Students proposed that they chose someone to supervise and evaluate the situation of implementation.

Nowadays, the classroom had set up three project groups to involve every student into the school activities: sports group, science and technology group, and art group. The classroom had also developed a variety of classroom theme activities, such as chess contest and making cards for Father's day, which provided students with opportunities to plan and organize activities by themselves. *Banzhuren* believed in students and gave students more freedom to develop their initiatives and creativity. By June 2015,

Table 5. The student's involvement of classroom job

Activity	Planning Frequency	Planning Percentage	Organization Frequency	Organization Percentage	Evaluation Frequency	Evaluation Percentage	Following Activity Frequency	Following Activity Percentage
The election and rotation of classroom job	30	56%	5	9%	38	70%	10	19%
Classroom service job	36	67%	34	63%	10	19%	5	9%
Learning-related job	24	44%	23	43%	13	24%	11	20%
Classroom administrative job	20	37%	28	52%	16	30%	11	20%

N=54

Creating Inclusive Classroom

the class had conducted more than ten theme activities, and five of them had very strong influence on students, respectively are *looking for the joy of science and technology, you are my superstar, running star club, propulsion of star clubs,* and *my father and I.*

It was the first time for all students to take part in the five theme-activities, and these activities impressed them deeply (see Table 6). Their creativity and sense of achievement had been developed. During the process, including planning, organizing and evaluation, the students discussed, debated, and even had conflicts, but they could reach a consensus eventually. Besides, there were nine small clubs in the class such as *hand painting* and *developmental game*, which were established by students according to their own interests and hobbies. There were some features that the activity of class club was practiced:

- All students could participate in the activities. Students understood the launching, planning and organization process, and solved problems together.
- Class club was a new form for students, so it demanded the students to make it happen by themselves.
- The class club had certain members and activity plans. Its activities were conducted by the students with everyday life.

Banzhuren's Solution for Developing Inclusive Classroom

One of the features of the inclusive classroom was that every child should have equal opportunity to develop themselves by participating in activities. There were many strategies to attract all the children to participate in the activities. The following cases described how *banzhuren* got all students involved in the activities of school level artistic performance.

First, pioneer in planning. Pioneer referred to the students who had strong organization skills, certain artistic expertise, and were willing to cooperate with *banzhuren* to plan. These students played a key role in the organizing of the activities. The activity of school level artistic performance was held on April

Table 6. The five theme activities' influence on students

Option	Looking for the Joy of Science and Technology	You Are My Superstar	Running Star Club	Propulsion of Star Club	My Father and I
	Percentage	Percentage	Percentage	Percentage	Percentage
It is the first time for you to participate in the activity.	100%	100%	100%	100%	100%
I have applied my talent in the activity.	30%	37%	69%	52%	24%
I have a sense of achievement.	22%	33%	74%	35%	32%
It is my favorite classroom based activity.	41%	44%	70%	50%	43%
I contributed a lot in the activity.	24%	30%	48%	65%	19%
I developed my creativity by the activity.	30%	39%	37%	46%	32%
There were a lot of discussion, debate, even conflict during the activity, but we reached a consensus.	17%	15%	54%	48%	17%

N=54

10, 2015. In order to improve the performance, *banzhuren* convened 8 pioneers on March 18th, 2015, then preliminarily identified four different performance forms: dancing, duet, cross talk and fashion show, and then four project groups were set up. Pioneers were the leaders of each project group who were responsible for recruiting members. Students chose to participate in the project group freely. A few days later, there were 22 students participated in and 32 students didn't participate in the activity. Then, pioneers investigated the 32 students' interests and talents (see Table 7).

The findings showed that there were 9 students who were interested and good at artistic performance, 18 students were interested but had no skills of artistic performance, 2 students were not interested but had the skills, and 3 students were not interested and had no skills of artistic performance. The reasons why students were not interested in artistic performance was that: Firstly, students thought their artistic talents were not suitable for the four programs; Secondly, some students who had no artistic talents lacked confidence; Thirdly, a few students' character was introverted; Fourthly, Some students could not join the project group they were interested.

Second, optimization of the project group. The four project groups did aim at participating in the activity of school level artistic performance. Students within the project group collaborated with each other and learned from each other. In order to involve more students, program optimization and expansion of the number of each project group was considerable concerning that 32 students had not participated in the activity: The project group of dancing increased to 12 students, the duet invited boys to join in, the cross talk recruited more students, fashion show's topic was environmental protection that meant clothes were made by waste material and as long as students were interested, they could participate in (see Table 8). The decision of optimization of the project group was made by students according to the investigation of the 32 students' interest and talent.

Some students had never participated in stage performance, so they had no confidence. The project group's advertisement, especially the example's incentive could increase their confidence. The *banzhuren* hosted a class meeting, and the outcome was more students were motivated and decided to involve into the groups.

Third, the interactive solution of all students. There were still some students who had no courage to say yes. Then, the *banzhuren* encouraged the pioneers to invite their friends. According to the special requirements of the project group, students who were good at arts discussed and found the potential of the peers, and this motivated some students at last. Then, there were only seven students left. How to deal with this situation? Could we perform as an inclusive classroom? The *banzhuren* put forward such questions, and after more discussion, the students suggested that they could develop the fifth project group: chorus! Then, the last picture was: all students performing on stage.

Table 7. The investigation of student's interest and talent

Do you have skills of artistic performance?	Yes_____	No_____
Are you interested in performance?	Yes_____	No_____
Name		
You are good at The reason why you don't participate in the artistic performance is		

Creating Inclusive Classroom

Table 8. Program optimization and expansion of the number

Performance	Optimization Program	Increasing Number of Students
Dancing	Most of the members cannot dance well. So it is intended to invite others to join in, such as the students who are members of school level dancing group, aerobics classes or who have learned professional dance in after-school training institution.	six
Duet	Singing a duet is so difficult that most of students in the class cannot meet the requirements. Nearly ten boys are members of the school drum team, so we decide to increase the members of playing drum to cooperate with the cheerful song.	four
Cross talk	Some members are good at performance, but not at cross talk. In order to show the richness of cross talk, we plan to perform cross talk by more students instead of two students.	five
Fashion show	In order to save cost and be more creative, it is decided that the fashion show's theme is environmental protection and call on students to use waste materials to make clothes. All student can participate in the performance.	No upper limit

Student's Development With Involvement

When students were asked: "What have you gained by involving in classroom based activities?" Most of them reflected that they had improved their collaborative ability, communication skills, expression ability and the ability of organization. To some extent, learning ability, evaluation ability, problem solving ability and creativity have been enhanced too. A boy said: "My parents always said my expression ability was poor. Now I think my expression ability is better by participating in activities." A girl proposed "I think dance club should dance modern dance to attract more students." Then another girl added: "I become brave and have experienced many things I had never done before."

In the process of the activities, it was possible to learn to appreciate others and get along with people. Students became optimistic and confident. For example, the student, Yu, lived in a single parent family. He was introverted and disliked communicating with others. After participating in chess contest, he said "I am very grateful to teachers and parents' support. I am very happy I can have these friends by involving in activity." What is more, the student with learning disabilities received more assistance from other students and teachers, because the student's participation in the activities made *banzhuren*, other students and teachers know more about him.

New Planning

During one year's experiment, the students participated in a series of activities. Their abilities and self-awareness have been improved and their confidence has been developed. The cohesion of the class was further strengthened. Students enjoyed the democratic and substantial campus life.

Concerning Grade Six was the last academic year of the elementary school in Shenzhen, friendship between teachers and students was a treasure. Although the student's family backgrounds differed greatly and their individual characters were diverse, they had deep friendship like brothers and sisters. In the new semester, to consolidate the sense of collective belonging would be necessary, so the *banzhuren* is planning a series of activities named *We are a Family*, which may be meaningful to improve children's sense of responsibility to the class, school, community and country. At the same time, every student should participate in diverse activities, to develop their abilities and learn to care, to love, and to be grateful. The following factors are under the *banzhuren*'s consideration.

1. Self-management of classroom. The system of class convention, a weekly schedule, class cadre campaign and classroom job rotation can make each student become the real owner of this class, and assume the responsibility of maintaining class daily life. The
2. The daily conduction of classroom-club-activities. By 2015, there were totally nine classroom clubs. They should be renewed based on students experience and developmental needs, and *banzhuren* will support them and provide more resources for them. On the other hand, the club's preparation for school level activities, such as Teacher's Day, School Sports Festival and School Science and Technology Festival, will guide the direction of student's involvement.
3. The school-family partnership. Parents committee can organize students to participate in the activities. On the other hand, parents can also participate in the school activities.
4. Activities of students' cross-grades collaboration. To strengthen cooperation and communication among students of different grades is significant in the context of modern education. Older students can mentor students of Grade One to construct classroom jobs and interact with them in sports activities, so that students can experience the roles of big brothers/sisters and involve more children in activities.
5. Practical activities in community. Students could spend their weekend or holidays participating in community based service activities, such as serving as community volunteers, which was helpful to cultivate and improve students' social skills and practice abilities.

Of course, all the activities should be participated by all students under the guidance of the banzhuren, to protect and educate them. Children's joint participation will strengthen the developmental foundation for their future life.

PRACTICAL IMPLICATIONS

Just as UNESCO (2005) stated one decade ago, inclusion is a process, is concerned with the identification and removal of barriers, is about the presence, participation and achievement of all students, and involves a particular emphasis on those groups of learners who may be at risk of marginalization, exclusion or underachievement. In Chinese context, the development of inclusive classroom, school, and education appear to be a long journey. After this case and pilot study, the authors are working with over 100 schools in different provinces, and more *banzhuren*s are getting involved in this research. With more dialogue with educators and with the development of experiments, this project is presenting the value of the Chinese education reform.

First, the research can be applied to the student development at classroom level. It may be agreed by all educators that the student development is the key of education, but how to achieve it especially in the diverse context? Is it really possible to develop all children in spite of the personality, interests, abilities and learning needs? This research shares more practical tools and methods with educators, and

Creating Inclusive Classroom

the practice is based on the inclusive education theory and relates to the 21st century skills. Considering the development for the several hundred millions of students, this kind of research is really valuable.

Second, the research outcome can be helpful for teachers' professional development. Though the importance of *banzhuren*'s work is recognized by students and parents, the school leaders and policy makers easily ignore it, and this leads to the under-professional status of classrooming and *banzhuren* development. The two case *banzhuren*s gained development from 2014 to 2015. Ms. Liujuan Huang (June, 2015) said that the practice can turn the ideas into reality, peer-learning and self-reflection can make *banzhuren* open to the development, and the self-awareness can guarantee the development sustainable. Ms. Ying Huang (June, 2015) said that the *banzhuren*' engagement in the research and dialogue, the peer learning, reading, and reflection and writing are very important for the development.

Third, the research can contribute to the society development in the diverse society. Classroom is related to the families and communities, and can impact development of the society. The practice of inclusive education can fulfill every student's potentials, and enhance the student's self-awareness. This is welcomed by parents, and can improve the relationship between families and schools. What the teachers and students have done can develop the culture of the society, especially can scale up the believes and practices of inclusive education in the environment of developing the learning community and life-long education system.

LIMITATIONS AND FUTURE RESEARCH DIRECTIONS

The conclusions drawn from this research are limited as having only two case classrooms at the elementary school level. As this pilot research was conducted in elementary schools in Shenzhen, more data from middle and high school classrooms is not provided by this research. The lead author is conducting the same project in other cities and districts, for example, Shanghai, Changzhou, Qingdao, and Xiamen, but the comparing research had not been conducted because of the limited time. As this chapter is supported by onsite observation, interview and student questionnaire, more voices of parents and school leaders are waiting to be listened to. Considering of the future research, qualitative and quantitative research methods may be applied to more *banzhurens*, student, parents, and school leaders.

As for the future research, the following topics should be addressed:

First, what are *banzhurens*', students', parents' and school leaders' understandings and perspectives of inclusive classroom? The pre-understandings are very important for the inclusive classroom development. What is the student's understanding of his or her identity in the classroom? What are the parents' experience of student development and the expectations with education? What is the teacher's believes and experience of classroom-based education in diverse environment? To address these and other related questions more data from a wider array of sources will be needed for analysis.

Second, what are the situation of inclusive classroom development in elementary through high school in China? In this chapter, the authors discussed the former situation of the classroom life, and had found many challenges from the perspective of inclusive classroom. How about other classrooms? How about the classrooms in high schools or in different districts? Are they the same as the former situation of the case classrooms? Especially for Chinese high school reform, as many senior high schools or even junior high schools are more focused on test scores, they probably have abandoned the idea of inclusive education. Marginalized students are in fact further marginalized in high schools.

Third, how to connect the inclusive classroom in regular school with special education? The inclusive education research is always based on the practice of special schools, though it has been spread into the regular schools. But how can regular school teachers learn from the expertise of special education? How to educate the students who have very special needs or how to meet the diverse developmental needs from the disabled students in regular classroom? How to develop the regular classroom with more disabled children in it? All these problems require answers from regular school teachers and the collaboration between regular schools and special schools.

Fourth, how to support the *banzhuren*'s practice of inclusive classroom? School support is important. In the experiment district of Guangming, Shenzhen, the school leaders involved in the onsite-observation and dialogue, provided valuable suggestions to the *banzhuren*, gave feedback on the classroom development, developed the research-based system for *banzhruens*, and created the inclusive atmosphere in the school. But in many districts, the school support is limited, and *banzhurens* are struggling for the quality work and professional development (Li, 2015). Besides the school leaders, as a key educator who works with families and communities, *banzhuren* requires a supportive ecology among school, family and community too, including more educational resources for more students and inclusive community.

The last is the international dialogue. Inclusive education originated in the Western countries, and there is a lot of experience that Chines educators and scholars should learn. In China, there are so many children who are in disadvantaged situation, including migrant children and mentally disabled children. On the other hand, Western scholars and educators may find rich thinking and practice from Chinese *banzhuren*, which has close relationship with Confucian tradition and Chinese flavor. The international collaboration may fulfill the potential of this area successfully.

CONCLUSION

Chinese educators and scholars are contributing to the inclusive education with new roles and efforts in schooling. With the new understanding of inclusive education, Chinese *banzhuren*s are trying to develop the inclusive classroom for every student despite of the SES, gender or ethnic. *Banzhuren* is the main planner, organizer and estimator of educational activities based on everyday classroom life, including the development of classroom culture and classroom organizations, classroom based activities, participating in the school-level activities inclusively, parental involvement and children's family/community lives. Nowadays, *banzhuren* is encouraging every student to plan, organize and evaluate activities inclusively. The practice is meaningful to inclusive education, especially inclusive classroom.

This chapter took two case classrooms from Guangming District of Shenzhen City, and found *banzhuren* playing a significant role in developing inclusive classroom. *Banzhuren*'s guidance has been important premise that each student can participate in classroom life. More students have achieved the development with their involvement and enjoyed the process. *Banzhuren* has long-term activities planning to prompt every student's development by their involvement too, which will lead to new initiatives of future inclusive classroom. To achieve the goal, more support is needed from school leaders, policy makers, and international and national scholars, with the focus of *banzhuren*'s professional development.

ACKNOWLEDGMENT

The paper is sponsored by Peak Discipline Construction Project of Education at East China Normal University (ECNU). The authors are grateful for the funding support from Shanghai Municipal Education Commission (Funding Grant: A1306 and 13SG27), Shanghai Pujiang Program (Funding Grant: 14PJC029), and the help from the Center of New Basic Education of ECNU, Institute of Schooling Reform and Development of ECNU, Mr. Dehua Xie and all experimental *banzhuren*s from Guangming, Shenzhen.

REFERENCES

Booth, T., & Ainscow, M. (1998). *From them to us: an international study of inclusion in education.* London: Routledge.

Bu, Y., & Li, J. (2013). The New Basic Education and whole school reform: A Chinese experience. *Frontiers of Education in China*, 8(4), 576–595.

Chen, J., & Wang, Y. (2016). Challenges and responses: The practical dilemmas and countermeasures of inclusive education. *Journal of Northeast Normal University*, 2, 198–202.

Chen, Y. (2003). About the rural education development in view of inclusive education. *Educational Research*, 8, 13–15.

Deng, M. (2004). On the inclusive education in the eyes of special education administrators: Execution research of the policy of learning in regular class in China. *Educational Research and Experiment*, 4, 41–47.

Gu, L., Chen, J., & Li, J. (2015). The Leadership of banzhuren in Chinese school: Based on the sample survey in Changzhou City of China. *Journal of Education and Human Development*, 4(4), 102–114.

Han, L. (2002). About the question of the migrant children education: A case study of beijing. *Chinese Cadres Tribune*, 7, 25–27.

Huang, C. (2003). Outlook of inclusive education: Thinking the development of inclusive education in nearly 10 years. *Global Education*, 5, 29–33.

Huang, L. (2016). Passive growth, self-growth and syntrophism: Class growth based on the the education concept of life practice. *Banzhuren*, 5, 9–14.

Huang, Z. (2001). Inclusive education: Global education research new topic in the 21st century. *Global Education Prospects, 1*, 51-54.

International Bank for Reconstruction and Development. (2015). *East Asia's changing urban landscape: measuring a decade of spatial growth.* Washington, DC: The World Bank.

Li, F. (2009). Research of migrant children's education problem: from the perspective of inclusive education. *Chinese Journal of Education*, 4, 26-28, 57.

Li, F. (2013). *High quality education for children with special needs.* Nanjing: Nanjing Normal University Press.

Li, J. (2006). *Care for life: School education value orientation*. Beijing, China: Education Science Press.

Li, J. (2009). Efforts in reconstructing student's daily education life: The soul of students work in the new basic education. *Journal of the Chinese Society of Education*, 9, 17–21.

Li, J. (2014). Locker vs. classroom: Everyday life based leadership and policy in U.S. and China. *US-China Education Review B*, 4(6), 368–380.

Li, J. (2015). On student's development in classrooming: Based on the perspective of relationship between students and other students in the class. *Journal of Sichuan Normal University*, 42(1), 89–93.

Li, J. (2015). *Student development in everyday classroom life*. Fuzhou, China: Fujian Education Press.

Li, J. (2016). Improve the quality of banzhurens and students' life by classrooming. *People's Education*, 3-4, 56–59.

Li, J., & Chen, J. (2013). Banzhuren and classrooming: Democracy in the Chinese classroom. *International Journal of Progressive Education*, 9(3), 89–106.

Li, J., & Ni, M. (2015). Renewing the Confucian tradition: kindness and respect in children's everyday schooling. In Pedagogies of kindness and respect: on the lives and education of children. New York: Peter Lang Publishing.

Li, J., Wang, P., & Chen, Z. (2013). Student developmental needs based parent partnership: A case study of Qilun elementary school in Minhang district, Shanghai. *International Journal of Parents in Education*, 7(2), 31–41.

MOE. (2009). *Rules for elementary and secondary school banzhuren's work*. Retrieved from http://www.moe.edu.cn /publicfiles/ business/ htmlfiles /moe/ s3 325/201001/81878.html

MOE. (2010). *The national outline for medium and long-term education reform and development (2010-2020)*. Retrieved from http://www.mo e.edu.cn/publicfiles/business/htmlfiles/moe/moe_838/201008/93704.html

MOE. (2012a). *Elementary school teachers' professional standard (trial)*. Retrieved from http://www.moe.edu.cn/publicfiles/business/htmlfiles/moe/s6991/201212/xx gk _145603.html

MOE. (2012b). *Middle school teachers' professional standard (trial)*. Retrieved from http://www.moe.edu.cn/publicfiles/business/htmlfiles/moe/s6991/201212/xxgk_145603.html

MOE. (2015a). *China education situation: the national education career development in 2013*. Retrieved from http://www.moe.edu.cn/jyb _sjzl/s5990/201 503/t20150 331 _186797.html

MOE. (2015b). *The ministry of education issued national education career statistical bulletin in 2014*, Retrieved from http://edu.ifeng.com/a/20150730/41406904_0.shtml

MOE. (2015c). *Special education teachers' professional standard (trial)*. Retrieved from http://www.moe.edu.cn/srcsite/A10/s6991/201509/t20150901_204894.html

Morgan, L. (2016). Examining the Role of Banzhuren in the Development of Students in China. *Proceedings of the International Conference on Classroom, School, Society and Student*.

OECD. (2010). *Strong performers and successful reformers in education: lessons from PISA for the United States*. Paris: OECD Publishing.

Peng, X. (2011). On the challenges facing China in the promotion of inclusive education and relevant suggestions. *Chinese Journal of Special Education.*, *11*, 15–20.

Peng, X. & Deng, M. (2011). On the theory of inclusive education and the special children's education rights. *Journal of Huazhong Normal University (Humanities and Social Sciences)*, *2*, 142-146.

Peng, X., & Deng, M. (2013). The game theory and inclusion: Study on inclusive education under the background of social stratification. *Studies in Foreign Education*, *8*, 45–53.

Shenzhen Education Bureau. (2015). *The basic situation of Shenzhen education development in 2015*. Retrieved from http://www.szeb.edu.cn/xxgk/flzy/tjsj/ 201605/ t2016 052 5_3655164.htm

Shenzhen Education Bureau. (2016). *The guidance on further strengthening the disabled children's learning in regular class in Shenzhen and the guidance about the severely disabled school-age children's "home delivery" teaching in Shenzhen*. Retrieved from http://www.szeb.edu.cn/bsfw/f wxxkz_jy/ywjy 2/tsjy/ttzgg/201 605 /t 20160511_3621862.htm

Tan, C. (2012). *Learning from Shanghai: Lessons on achieving educational success*. Singapore: Springer.

The World Bank and the Development Research Center of the State Council. (2014). *Urban China: toward efficient, inclusive, and sustainable urbanization*. The World Bank.

Tucker, M. (2011). *Surpassing Shanghai: an agenda for American education built on the World's leading systems*. Cambridge, MA: Harvard Education Press.

UNESCO. (1994). *The Salamanca world conference on special needs education: access and quality. UNESCO and the Ministry of Education, Spain*. Paris: UNES CO.

UNESCO. (2005). *Guideline for inclusion: ensuring access to education for all*. Paris: UNESCO.

UNESCO. (2015). *Incheon Declaration and framework for action—towards inclusive and equitable quality education and lifelong learning for all*. UNESCO.

Xiao, F. (2005). Mainstreaming in China: History, actuality, and perspectives. *Chinese Journal of Special Education.*, *3*, 3–7.

Yan, S., & Fang, J. (2008). Implications of Manchester inclusion standard for Chinese inclusive education. *Chinese Journal of Special Education*, *8*, 21–26.

Ye, L. (1994). The spirit of the times and the developing of a new educational ideal. *Education Research*, *10*, 3–8.

Ye, L. (Ed.). (1999). *Reports on "New Basic Education" (1994-1999)*. Shanghai: Shanghai Sanlian Books.

Ye, L. (Ed.). (2004). *Reports on "New Basic Education" (1999-2004)*. Beijing: Chinese Light Industry Press.

Ye, L. (2006). *On "New Basic Education"*. Beijing, China: Education Science Press.

Ye, L. (Ed.). (2009). *Reports on "New Basic Education" (2004-2009)*. Guilin: Guangxi Normal University Press.

Yu, Y., & Zhu, Y. (2012). On the construction of the supporting and security system for disabled children's learning in regular classes. *Chinese Journal of Special Education, 8*, 3–8.

Zhou, M. (2008). Inclusive education: Concept and main issues. *Education Research, 7*, 16–20.

Zimbardo, P. G., Breckenridge, J. N., & Moghaddam, F. M. (2013). Exclusive and inclusive visions of heroism and democracy. *Current Psychology (New Brunswick, N.J.), 32*(3), 221–233. doi:10.100712144-013-9178-1

KEY TERMS AND DEFINITIONS

Banzhuren: A special role in Chinese education, very similar to the role of principal at school level. He or she teaches one or several subjects, but holds the key responsibility for the whole group of children, the collaboration among teachers, and the communication with parents.

Chinese Education: Education in the Chinese context, and based and for the Chinese student. It covers the preschool education, elementary and secondary education, higher education, and adult education.

Educational Creativity: The innovative thinking and practice by educators in education.

Inclusive Classroom: Classroom based education, and educating all students in spite of the personality, interests, abilities and learning needs.

Inclusive Education: Education for all students in spite of the personality, interests, abilities and learning needs. There is no exclusion, no discrimination, and no classification in education.

Innovative Practice: The practice with the new mindset or new way with value in it. In education context, it is referred to the creative teaching by teacher.

Special Education: Education for blind, deaf, mute, mental retardation and other physical and mental defects children, and is always conducted by special schools and teachers.

Student Development: The process that students achieve knowledge, skills, ability, civic awareness, and so on.

This research was previously published in the Handbook of Research on Classroom Diversity and Inclusive Education Practice edited by Christina M. Curran and Amy J. Petersen; pages 399-424, copyright year 2017 by Information Science Reference (an imprint of IGI Global).

Chapter 44
Equity and Inclusion in Today's Diverse and Inclusive 21st Century Classroom:
Fostering Culturally Responsive Pre-Service Teachers with the Tools to Provide Culturally Responsive Instruction

Tiece Ruffin
University of North Carolina – Asheville, USA

ABSTRACT

This chapter shares the odyssey of one African-American teacher educator at a predominately white institution in a diverse learner's course fostering culturally responsive pre-service teachers with the tools to provide culturally responsive instruction for today's diverse and inclusive 21st century classroom. Early on in this journey, the instructor found that resistance, fear, and anxiety often ruled student perception of diverse learners in the inclusive classroom. Therefore, through action research the African-American teacher educator collected data, and subsequently planned, implemented, and monitored various actions designed to lessen pre-service teacher resistance, anxiety, and fear of student diversities in the classroom while fostering culturally responsive teachers for the diverse and inclusive 21st century classroom. Ultimately, these experiences mitigated the fears and concerns of preservice teachers around the enormity of diversities in the classroom and equipped them with tools for success.

INTRODUCTION

The United States continues to become increasingly diverse. This diversity is reflected in today's public schools. Today, diverse learners make up a significant portion of public school enrollment. According to the Public Education Primer (Kober & Usher, 2012) and Condition of Education (2014), 46% of public school students are non white, 6% are gifted, 9% are English language learners, and 13% have a disability and receive special education services.

In contrast, the teaching force is less diverse. The Public Education Primer (2012) states, "Public School teachers are a far less diverse group in terms of gender, race, and ethnicity than the students they teach." (p.66). Their profile of public school teachers culled from National Center for Education Statistics (NCES), Condition of Education 2011 indicates: 75% female, 25% male, 83% white, 7% African-American, 7% Latino, 2% other, and 1% Asian-American. Therefore, today's pre-service teachers must be prepared for the realities of today's inclusive general education classroom. A typical classroom in today's public school will contain a variety of students such as multicultural students, students from a variety of socioeconomic statuses, gifted students, students with very limited English proficiency, students with disabilities such as autism or emotional disturbance, and it is the role of the teacher to create a positive learning environment in an equitable manner for these diverse learners.

Historically, teacher education programs have been cited as having an overwhelming presence of whiteness (Cochran-Smith, 1995, 2000; Sleeter, 2001). Whiteness is generally described in terms of W.E.B. DuBois' and Theodore Allen's writings on the social construction of white identity and Allen's multi-decade writings on white privilege and white supremacy. Sleeter (2001), an eminent multicultural scholar in education, intimated the following, "The great bulk of the research has examined how to help young White preservice students (mainly women) develop the awareness, in-sights, and skills for effective teaching in multi-cultural contexts." (p. 101). Recently, another education scholar, Heather Hackman, posited at the 2015 National Conference on Race and Ethnicity in American Higher Education (NCORE) that whiteness undergirds the core of teacher education and denies teacher education a racially just pedagogy.

These diversities exist in the inclusive 21 century classroom, so what are the implications for practice? What do these diversities mean for the 21st century classroom? What should teachers be mindful of? What are teachers going to do in order to address these diversities in an era of inclusion? If instruction solely focuses on the practices of the dominant culture, then other students are excluded and denied opportunities of learning. This exclusion exacerbates the opportunity gap and lessens the possibility of closing the achievement gap.

CONTEXT: LIBERAL ARTS AND TEACHER EDUCATION

Imagine walking in to a teacher preparation program at a liberal arts university where the introduction to education course and subsequent diverse learners' courses are both university designated diversity intensive courses, thus diversity centered. According to the university's website, diversity-intensive courses are defined as:

Diversity intensive courses are diversity-centered, rather than diversity-inclusive or enhanced. DI courses focus on the meaning and experience of diversity and difference and the implications of living in a diverse society whether one is advantaged or oppressed. DI courses emphasize the complex and problematic processes of identity formation. These courses encourage awareness of the relationships between self and social institutions, both of which rest upon as well as reify difference and hierarchy.

Successful engagement with others in a multicultural and pluralistic society requires an understanding of how social forces shape our sense of identity as individuals and as part of a culture. In order to acquire this understanding, students must go beyond exposure to the perspectives of others to a consideration of the ways in which social institutions impact identity formation.

Diversity intensive courses offer and encourage opportunities for transformative experiences for all participants. They do this by engaging the heart and the mind, demanding serious consideration of pedagogy, and requiring participants to reflect upon and critically engage in analysis of power, privilege, and hegemonic ideology. Such goals require faculty to be aware of their own position relative to power and privilege, be sensitive to the potential range of student reactions, and be prepared to constructively confront difficult issues in the classroom. (retrieved from: http://registrar.unca.edu/diversity-intensives-information-faculty)

Why is a liberal arts university a great place for fostering culturally responsive teachers? A liberal arts curriculum encourages students to free the mind through critical thinking, reading, writing, and discussion with multiple and alternate perspectives (challenging the mind to take control of its own thoughts); encourages students to move out of self-absorption towards intercultural competence, global perspectives, and world citizenship; lays the foundation for social justice; emphasizes the acquisition of intellectual capacities, such as analytical skills, creativity, and reasoning and judgment; and calls on students to act as bold visionaries to problem solve and advocate for social change.

METHODOLOGY

Research Questions

What if some students aren't ready to grapple with issues of culture, diversity, equity, race, class, and disability in teaching? Are pre-service teachers ready to grapple with culture, diversity, equity, and diverse learners for teaching in the diverse 21st century classroom? Some say we live in a post-racial society! My experience of student resistance in curricula cultivating and promoting culturally responsive teachers at a predominately White institution in the South illuminates the fact that we do not live in a post-racial society. Through action research, course curricula, instruction, resources, assignments, teaching practices, and student learning were investigated. Ultimately, my goal was to lessen the students' resistance, anxiety, and fears of the diversities that exist in inclusive 21st century classrooms, to a favorable reception of diverse 21st century classrooms and culturally responsive/relevant pedagogy.

The Researcher

I began my time with UNC Asheville in August 2010 after successful experiences as a public school teacher, public school administrator, and assistant professor. Before my arrival to UNC Asheville I taught high school as a special education teacher, acted as a local education agency representative for a large urban school district monitoring services for students with disabilities, and designed and facilitated courses for post-baccalaureate and Master's degree students seeking teacher licensure in Special Education or Reading Education at institutions of higher education. My professional experiences prior to

UNC Asheville were deeply rooted in human services, diversity, social justice, cultural responsiveness, equity, and inclusion. As an advocate for excellence in education for students with differences in ability (commonly known as disabilities), I worked as a social reconstructionist significantly engaged in social responsibility. My work in education as a teacher, advocate for children and youth with disabilities, and teacher educator promoted a just society, challenged injustice, and valued diversity. I sought to truly make a difference in our world and society by ensuring access and equal opportunity in education for children often marginalized in our society.

My prior knowledge and experiences prepared me to teach at a public liberal arts institution of higher education. A liberal arts curriculum encourages students to acquire intellectual capacities, such as reasoning and judgment, and to act as bold visionaries to problem-solve and advocate for social change. This aligns perfectly with my vision of preparing pre-service teachers to teach in the diverse 21st century classroom. Through my courses in the Department of Education I challenge students to consider primary axes of difference in our exploration of schooling experiences. Students consider master statuses such as race, sexual orientation, sex, gender, social class, and disability and how they're socially constructed through political, economic, legal, religious, and scientific processes. We also consider institutions, historical and contemporary, that continue to perpetuate inequalities in the U.S. educational system for diverse learners and learners with special needs. Students are not only compelled to consider the dimensions of diversity, but are encouraged and challenged to think about how individuals experience difference and how to bridge difference. We discuss the experience of difference through privilege, stigma, racism, sexism, prejudice, bigotry, and colorblindness, among others. Furthermore, as social reconstructionists who transform and advocate rather than accept the status quo, we discuss how to bridge differences by embracing culturally responsive pedagogy and by challenging the constructions of difference.

However, this is no easy task or framework for my students, but an important one for a just society and a teaching force committed to all learners in the 21st century classroom. At the end of my first year, some students were not receptive to a diversity-intensive course focused on diverse learners taught by an African-American teacher educator. After reviewing and seriously reflecting upon student information forms gauging student fears, concerns, and comments on teaching diverse learners in an inclusive class; reflection papers; and student course evaluations, it was clear to me that grave challenges abound for me in teaching a diverse learners course. For instance, I was blatantly called a racist and biased on evaluations anonymously. Several microaggressions were also hurled throughout the year regarding my articulation of speech. I contributed this idiocy and covert racism as a reaction to the complex nature of diversity-intensity courses that grapple with race, sex, class, gender, sexual orientation, and disabilities with the majority of White students still in Bennett's (1993) ethnocentric stages of denial, defense, and minimization. Additionally, I inferred from several conversations that many of them presumed me incompetent (as defined in the landmark work by Muhs, Niemann, Gonzalez, & Harris, 2012) and struggled with the fact that I was their teacher, an African-American educator in authority. For instance, many questioned my background, credentials, and experiences incessantly (although shared on the University's webpage and shared by me in class) and several shared that I was the first African-American educator they had encountered as their instructor of record. In order to minimize these challenges and foster culturally responsive pre-service teachers, I had to find an innovative approach with persuasive practices and strategies to appeal to students.

Action Research: Method of Inquiry, Data Collection, and Analysis

Method of Inquiry

According to Sagor (2000), action research is defined as "a disciplined process of inquiry conducted *by* and *for* those taking the action. The primary reason for engaging in action research is to assist the "actor" in improving and/or refining his or her actions" (Chapter 1, ¶). Furthermore, Irvine (2009) states the following about action research:

Action research is inquiry conducted by teachers for teachers for the purpose of higher student achievement. Action research requires teachers to identify an area of concern, develop a plan for improvement, implement the plan, observe its effects, and reflect on the procedures and consequences. (Irvine, 2009, Education Guesses section, ¶ 8)

Action research was well-suited for my dilemma and my solution. Its method of inquiry allowed me to collect, analyze, and reflect upon existing practice and pursue changes. Data collection involved triangulation and included student pre and post responses from beginning of semester and end of semester questions via the brief open-ended questionnaire and cultural event reflection papers.

Open-Ended Questionnaire and Data Collection

I have a deep commitment to students, their aptitudes, passions, and intellectual interests. I begin the teaching experience by assessing student opinion and interest in course concepts, their learning profile, and readiness for course topics. Students submit a student information form on the second day of class and complete a pre-assessment based on course concepts during the first week of class. The student information form includes a) brief open-ended questionnaire on students with diverse learning needs; b) learning styles inventory and multiple intelligence inventory; and c) an interest questionnaire on course topics.

These assessments provide data on students' perceptions and opinions on the topic of diverse learners, their perceived interest in the topic of the course and its related topics, along with their preferred learning styles and multiple intelligences.

The principal section of the student information form salient to this research was the brief open-ended questionnaire. The open-ended questionnaire was a catalyst of change at the beginning of the course for informed action and an indicator of change at the end of the course showing allayed fears and concerns regarding diverse learners. The open-ended questionnaire on the student information form asked the following questions:

- After reading the course syllabus and participating in the first class session what do you hope to learn from this course? (your learning expectations)
- As you prepare to work in an inclusive classroom, what hopes, comments, concerns, issues, or fears do you have about working with diverse learners?

Overall, the open-ended questionnaire provided rich and explanatory responses and a diversity of responses in the respondents' own words, which allowed the researcher to gain an understanding of student perceptions and opinions in regard to diverse learners. This is congruent to the Pew Research Center's (n.d.) viewpoint that open-ended questions provide opportunities to *discover* opinions, experiences, and behaviors of the targeted group. Traditionally, survey reports typically permit respondents to be reflective in their responses and allow respondents the opportunity to share their true feelings on an issue.

Ultimately, action research refined my practice and enhanced student learning on diverse learners and culturally responsive/relevant pedagogy. Course changes provided multiple and different types of experiences to mitigate the fears and concerns of preservice teachers around the enormity of diversities in the classroom and equipped them with tools for success as culturally responsive teachers.

Data Analysis: The Catalyst for a Solution and Indicator of Change

Content analysis was used to analyze the brief beginning-of-class and end-of-class questionnaire on diverse learners and cultural event reflection papers. According to Patton (2002),

Content analysis usually refers to analyzing text rather than observation-based field notes. More generally, however, content analysis is used to refer to any qualitative data reduction and sense-making effort that takes a volume of qualitative material and attempts to identify core consistencies and meanings. . . . . The Core meanings found through content analysis are often called patterns or themes (p.453).

Inductive analysis was employed to code and discover themes in the data. The following themes emerged through inductive analysis: students repeatedly intimated **concerns and fears** on their student information forms. Underscoring their fears and concerns were sentiments of ineptness in meeting the needs of diverse learners, incompetence, preconceived notions about student ability, and diverse classrooms as too daunting and overwhelming. Most of the commentary emphasized "inexperience, anxiety, and being overwhelmed" about the daunting task of meeting the needs of so many different types of learners in the inclusive classroom. For instance, a student declared the following:

My biggest concern about working in an inclusive classroom would be my obliviousness to that world. I'm more worried about my capabilities as an educator to meet the specific needs of my students. I really have no idea about student diversities. How can I meet the needs of students I know nothing about? I know I can read up on the topic(s), but there's a difference between having the information and having the life experience.

Another student proclaimed:

I wouldn't exactly call them fears because I feel like a little nerves is good for a teacher. A new teacher for that matter. It is healthy to have fears and nerves, it encourages us to find a way to help those fears and to work on them. A little stage fright, as we say in theatre, is good for the soul. With that being said I do have the concern of making my class equal for everyone that is participating. Teaching creates many obstacles that you have to work around and I believe in that is where lies my fear. I don't know what to expect or how to go about it. But I do know that as a future educator along side my peers we will find ways to work around and to mold a classroom that is designed for everyone involved. I will take those fears and make them into a blessing and reality. I just have the fear and nerves of the unknown.

And, another student asserted:

One of my biggest fears is that I won't be able to motivate or engage my diverse students. I am afraid that my love and enthusiasm for my material will not be enough to interest or inspire them to keep trying and to push themselves. I want to provide the right balance of challenging and accessible lessons so that my students can get the most out of my class, but I am afraid I won't be successful in reaching the individual needs of all my students, and that no matter what I try, I will leave some behind.

Finding a Solution Part I: A Precursor to the Plan

Student diversity raised fears and concerns for some pre-service teachers. This data and similar experiences of departmental colleagues warranted a re-visioning of the Department of Education's introduction to education course. Colleagues were similarly astounded by some students' anxiety and fears of diversity and resistance to anti-racist and anti-hegemonic ideals; thus, there was a call by instructors of the introductory course to redesign the course with diversity as the praxis of the course. As an instructor of the introductory course for two years, I collaborated with several Education colleagues in the summer of 2012 to obtain a university grant to redesign the course. The redesign of this course lays the foundation and is a pre-requisite to the diverse learners' course.

Introduction to Education Course (Pre Diverse-Learners Course) Snapshot

The Department of Education offers an introductory diversity-centered education course as its first course in teacher preparation. In order to address student diversity in an inclusive class, pre-service teachers must examine, contemplate, and analyze information to develop the knowledge and skills needed to effectively address student diversity in a culturally responsive manner. The Department's introduction to education course, which this author taught for three years and co-developed as a diversity-centered course, requires teachers to examine social constructions of difference, culture, identity, their cultural and personal identity, and its intersection and impact as a teacher among the study of contemporary issues in education and the institution of the K-12 education system in the U.S (see Table 1).

The introductory course laid the foundation and exposed students to basic concepts. However, students must be required to move beyond foundational knowledge to higher levels of comprehension, analysis, and application. Remember, my goal was to lessen the resistance, anxiety, and fears of the diversities that exist in inclusive 21st century classrooms, to a favorable reception of diverse 21st century classrooms and culturally responsive/relevant pedagogy.

Finding a Solution Part II: The Plan of Informed Action

"I was very uncomfortable at this event, I felt as though I were surrounded by hostile people. I felt vulnerable and like all eyes were on me because I didn't belong. I am clearly not black and have good girl written all over me. I do not have dreadlocks and I have never smoked anything. I thought people would come up to me at any moment and harass me because I was different. This experience was so uncomfortable for me that I would not go anywhere alone. Despite the feeling that I would be a victim of violence, this experience was very useful to me. I was not robbed, beaten, or abused and I began to understand how other people might feel in situations as equally unlike their own culture." ~ excerpt

Table 1. Sampling from modules on identity, culture, diversity, and culturally responsive teaching

Topic	Discussion	Readings/Films/Resources	Reflection & Dialogue
Social Constructions of Difference	Differences are connected to master statuses; master statuses matter; Primary axes of difference in American Society; How is difference constructed? (naming, creating categories of people, aggregating and disaggregating, dichotomizing, stigmatized); How do people experience difference? (The experience of privilege, The experience of stigma)	*Rosenblum, K.E. & Travis, T.C. (Eds.) (2011).The Meaning of Difference: American Constructions of Race, Sex and Gender, Social Class, Sexual Orientation, and Disability (5th Edition); *Thirty Minute Blue-Eyed by Jane Elliott; *Race: The Power of an Illusion (Episode, 1: The Difference Between Us)	Look at the primary axes of difference/master statuses . . . . -What is the experience of groups in privileged and marginalized statuses? -How do we make sense of people's experience of privilege and stigma? -How do individuals and groups experience the statuses? -How do students who occupy these statuses? experience difference in schools? data sources? Personal observation?; Discipline data? As other?, privileged?, honored?, stigmatized?, stereotyped?, devalued?
Examination of Culture & its impact	What is culture?; Definition of culture. Examining culture through your cultural lens; Why does culture and identity matter in teaching?	*Culture Excerise on cultural relativism and ethnocentrism – Reading, Critical thinking, and analysis of Horace Miner's *Body of the Nacirema* -- http://www.sfu.ca/~palys/Miner-1956-BodyRitualAmongTheNacirema.pdf	My culture, your culture! Is it all relative? How do you view a culture without judging that culture negatively through your cultural lens? Discussion on the following concepts: cultural relativism, ethnocentrism, cultural imperialism, and cultural competence
Initial Self-Examination	Identity & Cultural Identity projects> a) think of self as a cultural being by exploring your values, beliefs, and ideas and writing an autobiography of your life; b) Who am I collage, c) Who I am Poem, and d) Merry Merryfield's (1996) Tree of Life	*The National Institute for Urban School Improvement's *Cultural Identity and Teaching*: http://www.urbanschools.org/pdf/cultural.identity.LETTER.pdf?v_document_name=Cultural%20Identity%20and%20Teaching	a) Contemplate and reflect on how these values, beliefs, and ideas emerged; did they emerge from various historical, social, political, economic, religious, geographical, or familial circumstances (reflect on the social processes); b) explore and subsequently design a collage on your family's cultural roots and identity; c) design a poem with regional, ethnic, religious, family traditions and customs, mottos, and credes (an EdChange project by Paul Gorski); d) Use the analogy of a tree to conceptually map what you have learned about people different from you and about the world, from your childhood to the present.

from a white female teacher licensure student's reflection paper after assisting Department of Education faculty and staff in hosting a community outreach table at a regional festival on Africans in the diaspora

Based on student pre and post responses from beginning-of-semester and end-of-semester questions and cultural event reflection papers, I redesigned my diverse learners' course for fall 2012 as an anti-racist, social justice course focused on meeting the needs of diverse learners in the inclusive classroom. My research questions, data collection, and data analysis led to actions of developing, implementing, and monitoring a course with relevant content, current thinking and resources, responsive pedagogical practices, field experiences, culturally responsive co-curricular activities, reflection, experiential learning, collaboration with local school partners, and service learning to enhance and foster student learning.

Diverse Learner's Course: The Model

Student resistance, concerns, fears, and anxiety about diversity in the classroom along with national data highlight the importance of explicitly addressing student diversity in the pursuit of excellence through equity in education. For example, racial and ethnic disparities have become more pervasive in our educational landscape. The Civil Rights Data Collection of the U.S. Department of Education's Civil

Rights Office highlights discipline disparities, retention disparities, underrepresentation of Black and Latino students in gifted programs, and the lack of teacher equity (as minority schools often have less experienced teachers), as disparities ensconced along racial and ethnic lines. Furthermore, the school-to-prison pipeline is alive and well in schools. Data indicate that "Black and Hispanic students represent more than 70 percent of those involved in school-related arrests or referrals to law enforcement." Our schools are not exempt or immune from structural/institutional racism or covert racism, so we must be proactive and empowered to enact change.

Since schools are a microcosm of society, race-based unconscious bias, racial microaggressions, colorblindness, color muteness, and institutional/structural racism are very present in schools — public, charter and private. An article by Justin Grinage in *White Teachers, Diverse Classrooms* (2012) and a 2013 article on racial microaggressions in urban schools by researchers A. Allen, L. Scott and C. Lewis at UNC Charlotte explain how schools may use race-based assumptions to judge and discriminate against students (race-based unconscious bias). Teacher perception of student ability may be based upon racialized and stereotyped assumptions of intelligence or deviance (racial microaggression). Schools and pedagogy may be blind to racial and cultural identities in teaching and learning (color blindness). As a result, there may be a lack of culturally responsive and culturally affirming education available to Black students. Additionally, schools may avoid talking about race in any context (color mute), and there are inequities and disparities built within the structural components of the education system (structural/institutional racism).

The diverse learner's course is designed in modules and it addresses different dimensions of diversity. It fulfills the criteria for the University's designation as a diversity intensive course as it a) examines multiple dimensions of diversity, b) examines inequalities and disparities in the educational system for students with differences in ability (disability), racial/ethnic backgrounds, gender, and class, c) addresses the intersectionalities between and among dimensions of diversity, and d) is a transformative experience with a sixteen-hour field experience. Additionally, it is centered on two N.C. Professional Teaching Standards for K-12 teachers:

- Teachers Establish a Respectful Environment for a Diverse Population of Students
- Teachers Facilitate Learning for their Students

The course addresses ethnic, cultural, economic, linguistic, ability, gender, and racial differences. Diverse learners in today's schools tend to be marginalized groups in the education system. Disparities are discussed and students are expected to think about underlying causes and formulate changes to lessen disparities in educating students with special needs. After a discussion of marginalized groups and inequities faced by such groups in the education system, the course emphasizes the institutions, historical and contemporary, that continue to perpetuate inequalities, and how to engage and dismantle them. Students are encouraged to challenge their own assumptions about privilege and power as the first step in deconstructing issues around inequities and marginalized learners in today's school system. Also, students learn to meet the needs of diverse learners in today's classrooms by using proactive classroom management strategies and effective research-based strategies, accommodations, supports, and modifications (see Tables 2 and 3).

Reviewing and discussing current thinking and resources on Culturally Responsive teaching:

- Diversity & Today's Classroom –The Call for Culturally Responsive Pedagogy
- Strategies & Action Steps for Culturally Responsive Pedagogy

Table 2. Summation of course topics -- A Foundation for Teaching and Learning in the Diverse 21st Century Classroom!

Topics	North Carolina Professional Teaching Standards (NCPTS)
• Responsive Teaching (Culturally Responsive Teaching, Differentiated Instruction, and Universal Design for Learning) • An opportunity to develop the knowledge base and skills necessary for teaching learners with special and/or diverse needs in the general education classroom (laws, definitions, characteristics, prevalence, special issues, non-discriminatory evaluation, evidence-based practices, instructional strategies, and accommodations) • Populations and their plans> Multicultural learners, Gifted (DEP), English language learners (LEP plan), At Risk for Academic Failure (PEP), Disability (504 plan or IEP), English language learner with Learning disability (LEP plan and IEP), Twice-Exceptional-2e (DEP and IEP)	• **Standard 2**: Teachers Establish a Respectful Environment for a Diverse Population of Students • **Standard 4**: Teachers facilitate learning for their students http://www.ncpublicschools.org/docs/effectiveness-model/ncees/standards/prof-teach-standards.pdf

Table 3.

Topic	Readings	Concepts/terms
Diversity & Today's Classroom –The Call for Culturally Responsive Pedagogy	Why the need for culturally responsive pedagogy? (mediates and mitigates in the diverse classroom) • Lack of cultural synchronization > Monroe & Obidah's 2004 article: *The Influence of cultural synchronization on a teacher's perceptions of disruption* ; Source: http://drcarlamonroe.com/uploads/JTE.pdf • Gloria Ladson-Billings', *Yes, But how do we do it*, in White Teachers, Diverse Classrooms (2012) • *Color Blindness, Unconscious Bias, and Student Achievement in Suburban Schools* by Justin Grinage (2012) in White Teachers, Diverse Classrooms; and • *Racial Microaggressions and African American and Hispanic Students in Urban Schools: A Call for Culturally Affirming Education* by Ayana Allen, Lakia M. Scott, and Chance W. Lewis (2013)	• Culturally Responsive Teaching • Cultural relativism • Cultural synchronization • Ethnocentrism • Cultural imperialism • Colorblindness • Race-based unconscious bias • Colormute • Structural and institutional racism • Young's Metaphor of the birdcage • Embedded stereotypes • Internalized racism • Stereotype threat • Racial microaggressions
Strategies & Action Steps for Culturally Responsive Pedagogy	• Suggestions for Educators -- How to identify and reduce prejudice and stereotyping > Justin Grinage's *Colorblindness, Unconscious bias, and Student Achievement insuburban schools* article (p.133-134); • *Relevant: Beyond the basics* article by Jacqueline Jordan Irvin; Source: http://www.tolerance.org/magazine/number-36-fall-2009/feature/relevant-beyond-basics • Five Components for Delivering Culturally Responsive Instruction by Garderen, D. & Whittaker, C. (2006) Planning Differentiated, Multicultural Instruction for Secondary Inclusive Classrooms. Teaching Exceptional Children, Vol. 38, 12-20; • Addressing Diversity in Schools: Culturally Responsive Pedagogy> http://www.nccrest.org/Briefs/Diversity_Brief.pdf	Concepts/terms: • Culturally relevant pedagogy • Myths and misperceptions of culturally relevant pedagogy • Cultural mismatch/cultural incompatibility • 5 components for delivering culturally responsive instruction: o -Content integration, The knowledge construction process, An equity pedagogy, Prejudice reduction, An empowering school culture and social structure • 3 dimensions of culturally responsive pedagogy – institutional, personal, and instructional

Field Experience

All teacher licensure students spend a total of sixteen hours in an observation-only field experience with a general educator, special educator, English as a Second language (ESL) educator, and academically or intellectually gifted (AIG) specialist. This field experience builds upon and expands students' knowledge from the Introduction to Education course where students completed observations (two hour field trips)

Equity and Inclusion in Today's Diverse and Inclusive 21st Century Classroom

in each of the typical three levels of schooling (i.e. elementary, middle, and high school) and a focused visit in a school setting for an entire school day.

Culturally Responsive Co-Curricular Activities in the University and Greater Community

In addition to a sixteen-hour field experience, students are required to attend two Department of Education, local community, and/or university sponsored events approved by the instructor related to culturally congruent critical pedagogy and culturally responsive educator experience. Students attend, engage, and write a reflection on the events.

A sampling of events over the years: a) Engagement with eminent scholars in education through book discussions, workshops, and public lectures: Dr. Gloria Ladson-Billings (2011-2-12 SY), Dr. James Loewen (2012-2013 SY), Dr. Lisa Delpit (2013-2014 SY), and Dr. Pedro Noguera (2014-2015 SY); b) Houses of Worship Tour with the University's Center for Diversity Education; c) Community outreach and engagement events by hosting and staffing Kid-friendly activity booths: Walk/Run for Autism, Very Special Arts Festival, Goombay Festival celebrating the African diaspora, and Latina Festival; d) Lunch and Learns: Racial Microgaggressions, Cultural appropriation vs Cultural appreciation, The Role of Race in the Trayvon Martin decision, K-12 Education and Teacher Preparation in Nigeria (in collaboration with Sister Cities); e) Film screenings: Lee Mun Wah's *If These Halls Could Talk*, Jacob Kornbluth's *Inequality for All*, Brewster & Stephenson's *American Promise*, McQueen's *12 Years a Slave*, Guggenheim's *Waiting for Superman*; Steve James and Alex Kotlowitz's *Interrupters*, Christopher Wong's *Whatever It Takes;* f) University Speakers: Native American Speaker Paul Chaat Smith, Principal Chief Michell Hicks of the Eastern Band of Cherokee Indians, and Dr. Cornel West; g) Other events such as a Freedom Seder, CORE Ensemble's *Ain't I a Woman;* Chamber Music Theatre Performance on the life and times of four African-American women, Lee Anne Bell's lecture on anti-racist education and social justice, and Damali Ayo's *Are you Ready to Fix Racism* lecture (see Table 4).

Table 4. Reflection assignment

Increasing your Knowledge and Experience of Other Cultures
Attend an approved event. Write a two-page summary and reflection regarding the experience.
The summary must include the following:
• topic -what is it about?
• aim/purpose?
• main idea?
• conclusion?
The reflection must include the following:
• Reactions/Conclusions regarding this event for yourself:
o Was the event useful to you? Why?
▪ How has it helped you increase your knowledge and experience of other cultures? (or other dimension of diversity)
o Has it changed how you think about a culture? Or dimension of diversity?
o New ideas or insights gained (anything new to you)?
o Any implications for practice?
▪ How can this experience assist you in delivering culturally responsive instruction?
o Any other comments (response to the event)?

Other Carefully Selected Course Activities

Experiential learning. Students complete a field experience every semester for a tangential experience of theory and real-life practice. Since the field experience does not address English language learners with low levels of English proficiency who are taught in a separate setting (Newcomer Center), I organize a course field trip to a local Newcomer Center every semester. There, students have the opportunity to learn directly from an experience. They visit the Intake Center and learn about assessments used for identifying English Language Learners (ELL) for English as a Second Language (ESL) services, observed teachers and students in classrooms, interacted with students, toured the school, and meet the administrator of Federal Programs (i.e. Title III/ESL, Migrant Education, Title I).

Guest Speakers from local schools. I invite licensed accomplished practitioners in the field to present and dialogue with pre-service teachers as an intentional effort to connect theory to real-life practice with licensure candidates. Guest speakers emphasize the importance of collaborating with various professionals when meeting the needs of diverse learners within the general education classroom. I believe that guest speakers from local schools are essential. I intentionally link and share with students the importance of collaboration. As a teacher in the 21st century we must collaborate with various professionals in order to meet the unique and individual needs of our students. Academically/intellectually gifted (AIG) specialists and ESL/SIOP Coaches from local school systems present and dialogue with students in my courses every semester.

Service-learning & parent panel. Students are given the option to engage in service-learning with children with special needs at a local hospital through a local Family Support Network. Every month the Family Support Network has a Family Group Night. During the Family Group Night, UNC Asheville pre-service teachers, along with other volunteers and staff, engage with culturally and linguistically diverse children with special needs, while parents and siblings of the children attend a support group. For the past two consecutive years, UNC Asheville licensure students spent two hours engaged in the following: eating dinner with the children, interacting with children by playing games, reading books, dancing, and conversing. In-service learning, mutual benefit and reciprocity are important; therefore, I asked the Family Support Network to organize a parent panel for the diverse learners' course. The parent panel at the end of the semester included a select group of parent leaders from the Family Support Network. They focused on their personal experiences of parenting children with special needs, offered tips and strategies for pre-service teachers working with children with special needs, and tips for communicating with parents of children with special needs. A great innovation as school – family collaboration skills are integral for teacher success in an inclusive classroom.

CONCLUSION

Ultimately, the redesign of the Introduction to Education course and subsequent redesign of the diverse learners' course collectively provided opportunities and experiences that diminished the resistance, fear, and anxiety of student diversities in the classroom for pre-service teachers and equipped them with tools for success as culturally responsive educators. Student pre and post responses from beginning and end of the semester questions, cultural event reflection papers, and student evaluations consistently revealed allayed student fears and anxiety and an acute understanding of the importance and value of student diversities in the diverse and inclusive 21st century classroom.

For example, responses from the questionnaire and cultural event reflection papers illustrate a change or transformation in reduced fears and concerns regarding diverse learners:

It is doable though. I have found that as long as I give my students several different opportunities to understand a concept, they will usually catch on to at least one of them. Just be willing to adjust at any time during a lesson and be open-minded.

The best strategy that I would use in my classroom is UDL. UDL encompasses so many different techniques and options for how to teach in a diverse classroom. I can use multi-media, technology based applications, allow my students to interact and produce things either in hard copy or on the internet. Every component of UDL is broken into types of learning associated with a response from the brain. I can switch up my lesson outlines by teaching to different parts of the brain and in different styles. The way that UDL is set up is very simple. It outlines a style and then gives specific examples of what sort of language is associated with that style. It is really important to be able to differentiate to students and UDL is a great strategy to have for that. Working with diverse students and students who have special needs, already suggests that those students are going to need a different kind of lesson than the rest of the class. Rather than singling those students out, UDL teaches to the entire class at once. I got it! I can do this. I can teach in the diverse and inclusive classroom.

I also got the opportunity to observe to ESL classes at the Newcomer Center—one for students enrolled in middle level courses and one for high school students. Our group had the opportunity to introduce ourselves and to learn the names and countries of origin of the students enrolled at the center. I was surprised by how many students had emigrated from Guatemala! For many North Americans, Latino immigrants enter the U.S. from Mexico, but this simply isn't always the case. In fact, students at this center had immigrated from El Salvador, Honduras, Guatemala, Mexico, and Ukraine (to name a few)! For this reason, I think it's very important for teachers to learn as much as possible about who their students are and where they come from, rather than make assumptions based on perceptions of ethnic or linguistic background.

This anecdote demonstrates that schools treat their most difficult, highest needs students as criminals by criminalizing the students' behavior—removing them from mainstream society and placing them in a separate, "rehabilitative" environment. This cannot be the solution. In fact, treating students as mere problems to be done away with may in fact be the problem. For me, I think the key is to remain critical of the dominant power structure's treatment of less privileged groups of people. I think it is necessary to always be questioning how the dominant power structure tends to treat marginalized groups, and to consistently ask whose best interest is at stake here? I think it is important to be a leader in the schools, and to be an ally for marginalized groups who struggle for equitable access to power, privilege, and opportunity. Most importantly, I think schools and teachers need to be consistently reminded that all students have the right to a free public education, and that it is our responsibility as public educators to ensure that these students get the education they deserve, rather than be shuttled off to ISS or some other holding cell for students whose behavior is difficult to manage.

Additionally, exit surveys from the 2014-2015 academic year revealed that licensure completers highlighted my diverse learners' course as the second most useful course in preparing them for clinical practice (student teaching). I'm elated that program completers considered my course as so important in teacher licensure preparation before their clinical practice experience. This additional evidence suggests to me that a shift has occurred and the majority of pre-service teachers now understand and value the importance and richness of student diversities in the inclusive classroom and are more apt to embrace, accept, and be culturally responsive educators.

All in all, this chapter shared the journey of one African-American teacher educator at a predominately white institution fostering culturally responsive pre-service teachers with the tools to provide culturally responsive instruction for today's diverse and inclusive 21st century classroom in a diverse learner's course. Challenges proliferated under the auspices of student resistance, fear, and anxiety, but through action research, the appropriate actions were implemented, monitored, and found to be viable solutions in fostering culturally responsive pre-service teachers.

REFERENCES

Allen, A., Scott, L. M., & Lewis, C. W. (2013) Racial Microaggressions and African American and Hispanic Students in Urban Schools: A Call for Culturally Affirming Education. *Interdisciplinary Journal of Teaching and Learning, 3*(2), 117-129. Retrieved April 16, 2015 from http://www3.subr.edu/coeijtl/files/Download/IJTL-V3-N2-Summer%202013-Allen-Scott-Lewis-pp117-129.pdf

Aud, S., Hussar, W., Kena, G., Bianco, K., Frohlich, L., Kemp, J., & Tahan, K. (2011). *The Condition of Education 2011* (NCES 2011-033). U.S. Department of Education, National Center for Education Statistics. Washington, DC: U.S. Government Printing Office. Retrieved April 16, 2015 from http://nces.ed.gov/pubs2011/2011033.pdf

Bennett, M. J. (1993). Towards Ethnorelativism: A developmental model of intercultural sensitivity. In R. M. Paige (Ed.), *Education for the intercultural experience*. Yarmouth, ME: Intercultural Press.

Cochran-Smith, M. (1995). Uncertain allies: Understanding the boundaries of race and teaching. *Harvard Educational Review, 65*(4), 541–570. doi:10.17763/haer.65.4.m77263886583326v

Cochran-Smith, M. (2000). Blind vision: Unlearning racism in teacher education. *Harvard Educational Review, 70*(2), 157–190. doi:10.17763/haer.70.2.e77x215054558564

Grinage, J. (2012). Color blindness, unconscious bias, and student achievement in suburban school. In White teachers, diverse classrooms: Creating inclusive schools, building on students' diversity, and providing true educational equity. Sterling, VA: Stylus Publishing.

Hackman, H. (2015). *Calling out the wizard behind the curtain: Critically addressing the corrosive effects of whiteness in teacher education* [Abstract]. Retrieved from the 2015 National Conference on Race & Ethnicity in American Higher Education: https://www.ncore.ou.edu/en/schedule/abstracts/1366/

Irvine, J. J. (2009). Relevant: Beyond the Basics. *Teaching Tolerance, 45*(36). Retrieved from http://www.tolerance.org/magazine/number-36-fall-2009/feature/relevant-beyond-basics

Kena, G., Aud, S., Johnson, F., Wang, X., Zhang, J., Rathbun, A., . . . Kristapovich, P. (2014). *The Condition of Education 2014* (NCES 2014-083). U.S. Department of Education, National Center for Education Statistics. Retrieved April 16, 2015 from http://nces.ed.gov/pubs2014/2014083.pdf

Kober, N., & Usher, A. (2012). *A Public Education Primer: Basic (and sometimes surprising) facts about the U.S. Education System, 2012 revised edition*. Retrieved May 18, 2015 from http://www.cepdc.org/displayDocument.cfm?DocumentID=390

Merryfield, M. (2006). A framework for teacher education in global perspectives. In Preparing teachers to teach global perspectives. Thousand Oaks, CA: Corwin.

Muhs, G., Niemann, Y. F., Gonzalez, C. G., & Harris, A. P. (2012). *Presumed incompetent: The intersections of race and class for women in academia*. Logan, UT: Utah State University Press.

Patton, M. Q. (2002). *Qualitative research and evaluation methods*. Thousand Oaks, CA: Sage Publications.

Pew Research Center. (n.d). Questionnaire design section. In *US Survey Research*. Retrieved on October 15, 2015 from: http://www.pewresearch.org/methodology/u-s-survey-research/questionnaire-design/

Sagor, H. (2000). *Guiding School Improvement with Action Research*. Alexandria, VA: Association for Supervision and Curriculum Development (ASCD). Retrieved June 26, 2015 from http://www.ascd.org/publications/books/100047/chapters/What-Is-Action-Research%C2%A2.aspx

Sleeter, C. (2001). Preparing teachers for culturally diverse schools: Research and the overwhelming presence of whiteness. *Journal of Teacher Education*, 52(2), 94–106. doi:10.1177/0022487101052002002

University of North Carolina Asheville. (2015). *Diversity intensives: Information for faculty*. Retrieved June 11, 2015 from https://registrar.unca.edu/diversity-intensives-information-faculty

This research was previously published in the Handbook of Research on Effective Communication in Culturally Diverse Classrooms edited by Katia González and Rhoda Frumkin; pages 269-283, copyright year 2016 by Information Science Reference (an imprint of IGI Global).

Chapter 45
Cultivating Communities of Inclusive Practice:
Professional Development for Educators – Research and Practice

Christina M. Curran
University of Northern Iowa, USA

Becky Wilson Hawbaker
University of Northern Iowa, USA

ABSTRACT

Significant disparities in educational outcome, opportunity, and achievement endure for students with disabilities and those from culturally and linguistically diverse groups. A need for effective, responsive, and inclusive practices in schools is imperative. Educators are at the heart of providing the challenging, responsive education that each child and adolescent deserves. Professional development is the lever of change, but can or help or hinder educators in improving instructional and school practices that result in improved outcomes for all students. This chapter examines the evidence base surrounding professional development and inclusive practice. Four approaches to professional development supporting more transformative professional learning and change are featured: inquiry groups (teacher study groups and lesson study); coaching, Professional Learning Communities; and Professional Development Schools. Snapshots to practice are included with each approach to provide integrated descriptive examples of varied inclusive professional development practices.

INTRODUCTION

Teachers, I believe, are the most responsible and important members of society because their professional efforts affect the fate of the earth... (Helen Caldicott, n. d.)

DOI: 10.4018/978-1-7998-1213-5.ch045

Widespread concerns endure regarding achievement disparities in educational opportunity, access, and outcomes for students from culturally and linguistically diverse groups, including students from minority racial groups, English Learners (ELs) and students with disabilities (Blanchett, Klingner & Harry, 2009). Educators are at the heart of providing the challenging, responsive education that each child and adolescent deserves. Effective teaching requires educators to individually and collectively assume responsibility for the educational outcomes of all students. Their effectiveness is impacted by multiple factors including attitudes, dispositions, self-efficacy, developmental and contextual knowledge of learners, knowledge of content and effective pedagogy, and facility with collaborative and advocacy skills (Herring, Curran, Stone, Davidson, Ahrabi-Fard & Zhabnova, 2015). Thus, as Shulman (2005) conceptualized, effective professional learning must involve an apprenticeship of the head (knowledge), hand (skills), and heart (attitudes). When teachers are weak in one or more of these areas, their ability to be effective with inclusive teaching is limited. General and special educators have identified a need to receive ongoing education and experience in inclusive practices addressing effective teaching strategies and collaborative practices (Narian & Oyler, 2014; Royster, Reglin & Losike-Sedimo, 2014; Shady, Luther & Richman, 2013). Educators have demonstrated more positive attitudes and self-efficacy toward inclusive practices (Panscsofar & Petroff, 2013) as well as implementation of effective instructional practices and services supporting inclusion (Brusca-Vega, Alexander, & Kamin, 2014, Causton-Theoharis, Theoharis, Bull, Cosier, & Dempf-Aldrich, 2011) following professional development experiences centered on inclusion. Thus, effective professional development is a key lever for inclusion.

The complex learning needed, however is not easy nor naturally occurring. Traditional models of professional development (PD) that focus on one-shot workshops to implement top-down change are not successful (Klingner, 2004). Effective teacher PD requires ongoing, sustained, and supportive connections that include teachers' voices and address their needs in collegial networks that provide opportunities (1) to collaborate and reflect on both theory and practice, and (2) to examine evidence of impact on student learning (Darling-Hammond & Richardson, 2009). Structures adopted to support effective PD include inquiry groups, coaching, Professional Learning Communities (PLCs), school-university partnerships and Professional Development Schools (PDS), to name a few.

This chapter will examine the inclusive implications of PD in each of the above areas through a (n):

- Review of evidence-based practices in PD;
- Illustration of PD models and how they support inclusion in practice; and
- Synthesis of recommendations and implications for research and school-wide practices

PROFESSIONAL LEARNING AND DEVELOPMENT

An education system is only as good as its teachers. Unlocking their potential is essential to enhancing the quality of learning (UNESCO, 2014, p. 1)

The knowledge, skills and dispositions educators require to positively impact the learning of their students is neither static nor isolated. Traditional practices supporting educator learning have focused on a more individualistic view of teacher growth, centered on discrete skills and behaviors (Little, 2006). However, more contemporary views of what constitutes professional learning and development recognize a more complex view of teacher thinking and learning situated within professional community and rooted within practice (Little, 2006). Klingner (2004) noted that historic PD opportunities often resulted in marginal success in the improvement of student learning. Little (2006) and others (Darling-Hammond & McLaughlin, 2011; Darling-Hammond, Wei, Andree, Richardson & Orphanos, 2009) have summarized the disconnected nature of traditional PD in addressing teachers' needs, interests, and teaching contexts.

How Are Professional Development and Learning Defined?

Professional development has often been referred to as planned and facilitated activities or structures which support teacher learning (e.g. Steiner, 2004). Leko & Roberts (2014) defined PD as "a set of coordinated, comprehensive, and intensive activities designed to enhance educators' knowledge, belief, skills and practices for the purpose of improving student outcomes" (p. 43). Traditional models of PD have relied on episodic, external workshops, conferences or seminars of short-duration disconnects from the school or classroom context. The direct impact of these efforts on student learning outcomes was rarely examined. (Darling-Hammond, et al., 2009; Guskey & Yoon, 2009)

Effective professional development is viewed as "that which leads to improvements in teacher knowledge or practice, or in student learning outcomes" (Jacquith, Mindich, Wei & Darling-Hammond, 2010, p. 2). Desimone (2009) posited that effective PD can result in increases in teacher learning and changes in their attitudes and beliefs leading to altered teaching practices; these changes can result in increased student achievement. *Job embedded professional development* is a specific type of PD increasingly addressed in policy and practice. Croft and colleagues (2010) defined job-embedded professional development (JEPD) as "teacher learning that is grounded in the day-to-day teaching practices with the intent of improving student learning" (p. 2). Efforts to improve school schools through reform and renewal rely on teacher JEPD (Byrk, 2010).

What Does the Research Say About Effective Professional Development?

In order to understand the status and impact of PD on teacher and student outcomes, researchers at the Stanford Center for Opportunity Policy in Education (SCOPE) and the National Staff Development Council in Education (NSDC) undertook a three-phase study (Darling-Hammond, et al., 2009). In the first phase research findings from the past two decades on professional learning in the United States were summarized. Major findings from this project and other research are depicted in Table 1.

In the second phase, data from the 2008 data Schools and Staffing Survey (SASS) from the National Center for Education Statistics was examined to look at changes in the professional learning and development of teachers from the prior survey results in 2004 (Darling-Hammond, Wei & Adamson, 2010). In comparing data from the previous results the following changes were noted: fewer opportunities for sustained PD; less reported engagement in collaborative efforts; and increased participation in induction programs. Unfortunately, teachers reported less support for teaching students with special needs. For example, 42% of responding teachers reported available PD on teaching students with disabilities and only 27% teaching English Language Learners (ELLs). Teaching students with special needs was identified as a continued priority need in PD by teachers.

In the third phase of their research, SCOPE researchers examined state policies and practices in professional learning in the United States in case studies of four states (Jaquith, et al., 2010). Through this analysis key features of policies supporting effective PD were compiled. These are also included in Table 1.

Cultivating Communities of Inclusive Practice

Table 1. Qualities of professional development

Traditional Professional Development	Contemporary Professional Learning
Provides information often of short duration lacking follow-up during implementation	Provides continuous, ongoing, intensive, and sustained learning opportunities
Situates learning primarily in external settings, separate from practice (workshops, courses, conferences or seminar learning)	Situates active teacher learning within authentic practice and feedback in classrooms/schools (job-embedded)
Presents content with variable/weak/without connection to teaching context	Develops knowledge of content and pedagogy related to instructional roles & responsibilities applied to practice
Display disconnects to daily instructional practices and school improvement goals	Exhibits cohesion and alignment to relevant standards, assessments and school improvement goals
Engages individual & groups of educators frequently isolated from school context/community	Creates community through collaborative, collegial, reflective professional learning and action
Demonstrates inconsistent impact on improved teaching when provided in isolation	Generates local and school-based knowledge and capacity, including the use of data to inform teaching and learning
Prompts for passive reception of information, rote application of predetermined strategies	Prompts for critical inquiry and collaborative problem-solving into equitable, effective teaching and school practices for learning
Utilizes fixed formats and activities for all participants (e.g., large-group presentation or demonstration)	Provides multiple and dynamic opportunities, formats and activities for professional learning, including coaching, mentoring, observation and feedback
Has little impact on student achievement	Sustains, long term collective efforts that can demonstrate powerful impacts on student achievement and/or outcomes
Limits teacher agency	Engenders teacher agency
Archibald, Coggshall, Cochran-Smith, 2011; Blank & de las Alas, 2009; Croft, Coggshall, Dolan, Powers, Killion, 2010; Darling-Hammond, Wei, Andree, Richardson & Orphanos,2009; Darling-Hammond & Richardson, 2009; Easton, 2008; Guskey & Yoon, 2009; Lieberman & Mace, 2008	
Features of Strong District and State Policy Supporting Professional Development	
• A common and clear articulation of a vision for professional development across policy and practice • The effective monitoring of professional development efforts • A cohesive linkage of mentoring and induction requirements in a professional learning framework • An established infrastructure of organizations available for facilitating professional development • The stability of resources over time Jacquith, Mindich, Wei, & Darling-Hammond, 2010	

Taken together, these reports recognize there are principal features of PD that can lead to more powerful outcomes for teachers and students. However, it is the content, context and professional culture in which PD is designed, aligned, delivered and evaluated that can galvanize or obstruct professional learning.

What Are the Barriers to Implementing Effective Professional Development?

Despite identification of a number of critical elements in the design and implementation of PD, well-designed, effective professional development is not always the norm. Klingner (2004) reported the most common barriers for teachers are a lack of time to implement the practice/program targeted from PD, and inadequate support from administrators. Other barriers include the insufficiency of materials for implementing the PD practice, a lack of in-depth understanding of the practice, inadequate planning time for teachers, competing school-based initiatives, teacher perceptions of the relevance of the PD, costs associated with the PD, and conflicts with work schedule (Klingner, 2004; OCED, 2009; Penuel, Fishman, Yamaguchi & Gallagher, 2007).

Identifying solutions to these barriers is critical if PD is to fulfill its intent. Klingner (2004) noted that collaborative relationships between researchers and schools are one means to support sustainability of research-based practices. These partnerships can enhance the availability of support networks, address technical and/or conceptual principles of practice, and support change in useful and applicable ways. Additional considerations in breaking down barriers include: (1) addressing an understanding of the significance of the new practice; (2) establishing a clear relationship between teaching practices and student outcomes; (3) ensuring technical aspects of the practice are addressed through ongoing feedback and support; and (4) ensuring supportive school, district and state policies are in place (Jaquith, et al., 2010).

Why Should We Leverage Professional Development for Diversity and Inclusion?

Classrooms and schools are diverse places. In order to be effective, teachers and education professionals must construct responsive, effective schools and teaching practices that honor and respond to a diversity of students (Banks, 2004; Howard, 2007). In the United States, as elsewhere in the world, the representation of students from varying cultural linguistic, racial, income, and other identity or socially designated groups is changing (Aud, Fox, & KewalRammani, 2010; Banks, 2004). Moreover, the achievement and school outcomes for diverse students is often disparate. Lower expectations for these students, a concentration of less experienced or qualified teachers in high poverty and urban schools; and the continued disproportionate representation of students of color in special education are some of the factors which have contributed to the manifestation of educational social inequalities (Blanchett, et al., 2009; Darling-Hammond, & McLaughlin, 2011).

Effective PD thus must address these enduring achievement and opportunity gaps. Without the advantage of effective teachers, many students will continue to remain behind (Dwyer, 2007) and be excluded from the education that enables upward social mobility, thus reinforcing the status quo of inequity.

What Do We Know About Effective Professional Development for Inclusion?

Leko and Roberts (2014) synthesized the limited research available on PD related to improved teacher practice in inclusive schools in two areas: (1) educator beliefs and attitudes toward inclusive education, and (2) instructional practices and strategies supporting students in inclusive classrooms. In the area of educator beliefs and attitudes, the researchers concluded that PD can result in the adoption of more favorable beliefs about inclusion, and improvements in teachers' self-efficacy and confidence to support students with disabilities. In the area of instructional practices, positive teacher perceptions towards the selected practice and partial or full implementation of the strategies resulted from PD. Additional conclusions parallel broader research in PD, including:

- Ongoing support (coaching, consultation, peer support) is crucial for implementation;
- School wide implementation with appropriate infrastructure leads to greater success;
- Collaborative practices support a greater likelihood of sustainability; and
- Teacher commitment and the duration of the PD influence the outcomes.

Waitoller and Artiles (2013) conducted a systematic review of the international research literature from 2000 to 2009 on PD for inclusive education. Inclusive education was defined in the identified studies in three primary ways:

1. Ability differences of students with diverse abilities (disabilities, at-risk and learning difficulties), represented 70% of the studies. This included studies addressing instructional access of diverse learners to the general education curriculum and those addressing barriers to participation and learning for students with diverse abilities;
2. Differences related to race, class, gender or culture, represented 10% of the studies. These studies did not address students with disabilities; and
3. Inclusive education through participation and learning for all students, represented 20% of the studies. These studies addressed a broader, systemic process of overcoming barriers to learning and participation though professional development involving school-wide efforts.

Most of the studies on PD for inclusive practice used qualitative methodology, were focused at the primary levels, and did not include subject specific focus (Waitoller & Artiles, 2013). Six types of PD activities were present in the studies reviewed: action research, onsite training, university classes, PD schools, and newsletters. Further, studies on PD were classified as outcomes based (focused on the end result for teachers and/or students), or process based (focused on understanding the community of practice) and were equally represented.

A primary finding from this synthesis was the need to address improvements in the research-base in PD for inclusive education in both process and outcomes. PD for inclusion is primarily founded on unitary constructs of differences (ability, race/ethnicity, language, gender, social class) which historically support deficit thinking and exclusion. Waitoller and Artiles (2013) urged that research is needed to "shed light on how teachers learn to address the needs of students that live with complex and intersecting forms of exclusion" (p 338). Without such focus, fragmented and partial solutions are likely. They concluded that the design and examination of PD efforts should use "an intersectional approach in which teachers identify and dismantle interesting and multiple barriers to learning and participation for all students" (p. 347). Thus, this research underscores a need for collaborative, sustained, high-quality professional development addressing inclusion that is centered within the context of schools focused on enhancing educational opportunities and achievement for all students.

Overall, scant research exits on PD focused on inclusion. That which exists is often conducted separate from efforts addressing content knowledge, hindering development of a deeper ability to address diversity within content teaching.

Leveraging Professional Development Approaches for Inclusive Practice

In summary, research has identified general characteristics of effective PD and supporting policies and practices. Research on PD outcomes has concentrated on teacher impacts (beliefs, self-efficacy, and implementation). With an effective design and structures, notable changes in inclusive practice occur for teachers and schools. Research linking PD efforts to student outcomes and achievement is emerging. However, less is known about inclusive PD given the relatively fewer number of systematic studies, varied definitions and goals for inclusion and inclusive PD, and varying contexts surrounding student diversity, and school communities.

Four PD approaches support contextual, collaborative professional leaning aimed at sustained change: inquiry groups, coaching, Professional Learning Communities, and Professional Development Schools. We examine each of these in subsequent sections to explore their relevance for inclusive education. Table 2 summarizes these approaches as well as other common types of professional learning.

INQUIRY GROUPS: TEACHER STUDY GROUPS AND LESSON STUDY

Teaching is a process involving continual inquiry and renewal, and a teacher among other things is first and foremost a questioner (Stemmel, 2007, p. 1)

Teacher research is "systematic, intentional inquiry by teachers about their own school and classroom work" (Lytle & Cochran-Smith, 1992, p. 450). Inquiry plants roots for teacher ownership in professional learning and affords teachers stewardship of their learning. Traditionally, professional development practices have tried to solve problems for teachers by defining what they need to think or do in particular situations in order to effectively teach and to improve student learning (Randi & Zeichner, 2004). Inquiry moves the notion of teaching beyond that of technician. Critical interrogation can center on questions and invite action on practices of inclusivity in policy, practice and pedagogy (Schlessinger & Oyler, 2015). Two professional development approaches founded on inquiry include *teacher study groups* and *lesson study*.

What Are Teacher Study Groups?

Study groups are organized, collaborative groups of teachers who have an identified common goal to strengthen their professional learning (Cramer, Hurst, & Wilson, 1996). Gersten et al. (2010) clarified that teacher study group "has referred to a rather loose conglomerate of PD approaches that have little in common except for comprising small groups of teachers working together toward a specific goal" (p. 696). Murphy (1992) described three primary purposes of study groups: (1) to promote curricular and instructional innovations, (2) to support the study of research-based practices, and (3) to collaboratively plan for school improvement.

The success of a study group is "grounded in the principles of collaboration" (Cramer et al., 1996 p. 37). Murphy (1992) recommended groups of no more than 6 so that engagement, commitment, and discourse, are maintained. A study group may or may not have a facilitator.

Study group activities take a variety of formats and topics. Resources including books, media, articles, digital archives, or even periodic outside experts may serve as some of the grist for inquiry Study groups, among other topics, may research:

- A classroom or instructional practice,
- A new curriculum,
- The context and impact of a district or state policy,
- The historic and changing needs of the surrounding community, or
- Equity and/or deficit-founded practices.

Cultivating Communities of Inclusive Practice

Table 2. Approaches to professional learning

(Teacher) Study Groups	Lesson Study	Action Research
Description Study groups involve groups of teachers (or other professionals) who engage in collaborative meaningful learning. Members identify a shared goal for inquiry, collaborate, and work together towards the goal, Dialogue, reflection, and shared voice are essential elements. Study groups may be school-based or occur across schools, districts, or with other professional partners (e.g., universities). A study group may be used with other professional development activities such as institutes or workshops. **Inclusive Connections:** •Study groups may focus inquiry on changes impacting school-wide change for equity and inclusion through examination of theories, recent research and its applications, effective inclusive teaching practices, and culturally relevant pedagogy.	**Description** Lesson study involves a team of teachers who regularly engage in collaborative inquiry focused on curriculum planning and instruction. During lesson study a group of teachers collaboratively design, implement, and refine model *"research" lessons*. The inquiry improvement cycle includes: 1) collaborative planning of the research lesson; 2) implementation of the research lesson by a designated member and observation of the lesson; 3) post lesson discussion and analysis of pedagogy and; 4) lesson refinement and consolidation of learning. **Inclusive Connections:** •Lesson study deepens teachers' understanding of classroom practices through examining the outcomes, as well as the needs and strengths of individual students. •Enhanced pedagogy in differentiation of instruction, student engagement, research-based lesson accommodations, and culturally responsive teaching practices is collaboratively examined and supported.	**Description:** Action research is a dynamic, systematic, change-oriented inquiry process conducted by and with teachers. Teachers (individually or as a group) identify a goal for improved practice or problem solving at the classroom or school level Through a cycle of disciplined, iterative research, data collection, and reflection, collaborative understanding for informed action is fostered. Action research is also called *participatory action research*. *Collaborative action research* involves other stakeholders in the enquiry process with educators. **Inclusive Connections**: •Action research transforms individual and collective teacher dispositions and understandings of personal, school-wide and other systemic practices related to diversity and inclusion. •Meaningful, reflective practice and dialogue applied to action at the classroom and school level can support more equitable, accessible, and culturally sensitive practices.
Coaching	***Professional Learning Communities (PLC)***	***Professional Development Schools (PDS)***
Description Coaching is an arrangement of relational, collaborative learning facilitated by a coach supporting improvements in teacher and school capacity and change. Coaches observe instruction, provide non-evaluative feedback, model teaching practices, identify curricular and other resources, provide professional development, assist teachers and principals in goal-setting, and facilitate discourse around data analysis. Different approaches to coaching include: peer coaching, cognitive coaching; peer coaching; content coaching (e.g., literacy coaching, mathematics coaching); and instructional coaching. **Inclusive Connections:** •Coaching can support professional learning through modeling, resources, feedback, and information analysis that addresses supportive beliefs, dispositions and teaching practices valuing equity and inclusive practices/pedagogy at the individual teacher as well as systems level. •Transformational professional development and systems change may be supported through the intentional individual and collective efforts of coaches.	**Description** PLCs are structured groups of educators working collaboratively in ongoing and sustained cycles of inquiry to improve their own practice and their students' learning. PLCs often develop shared assessments, examine student data, and develop systems of interventions for students who are meeting learning goals as well as plans for students who have met the goals and are in need of additional challenge. **Inclusive Connections:** •PLCs focus on both collective and individual student learning, developing both learning supports or interventions and enrichment activities, and begin with the premise that all students can learn. •PLCs can provide a safe space to raise and confront difficult questions about equity and inclusion and focus on solutions. •PLCs can disrupt divisions between general education, special education, English-Language Learning, Title 1, TAG and other special areas.	**Description** PDSs are formalized partnerships between schools and universities. A PDS leverages the resources of both institutions around four main goals: 1) improving student learning, 2) ensuring quality preparation of new teachers, 3) enhancing professional development of educators, and 4) engaging in collaborative research and inquiry **Inclusive Connections:** •School-university partnerships bring new sources of human, economic, and political capital to support inclusive initiatives in school. This includes supports for PreK-12 student learning, professional development, and collaborative research. •Mentoring preservice teachers is a form of professional development and often leads to questions and reflections on inclusion. •Extended, sustained, and embedded experiences in schools, especially those modeling effective inclusive practices, better prepare new teachers for the challenges of inclusion in their future schools and classrooms •PDS partnerships have led to restructured preparation or degree programs that support inclusion and can help minimize research-to-practice gaps regarding inclusive practices.

Four common stages in the design and implementation of study groups include: (1) goal identification, (2) exploration, (3) synthesis and application, and (4) evaluation (Cramer et al. 1996). It is recommended that study group participation is voluntary and that the needs of individual members, as well as the collective group, are met through the inquiry activities. Study groups should also set explicit goals, foster trust, require commitment and confidentiality of participants, and focus on productive goal-oriented dialogue (Cramer et al. 1996; Stanley, 2011; Tichenor & Heins, 2000).

What Does the Research Say About Outcomes of Teacher Study Groups?

Teacher Study Groups have been used for over two decades, yet, research beyond design and description is scarce. Arbaugh (2003) examined the impact of a five-month teacher based study group for seven secondary mathematics teachers to address curricular reforms in mathematics for a more inquiry and student-centered geometry curriculum. The self-efficacy of the participating teachers was enhanced through participation in the study groups. Four areas of support and change occurred, including: (1) networking with other educators to build community, (2) strengthening connections across theory and practice, (3) aligning curriculum with reforms, and (4) supporting a sense of professionalism.

Vaughn (2016) described a qualitative study of a year-long inquiry project of six elementary teachers who examined literacy learning and culturally sensitive practices in a Native American context. The group's purpose was to address incongruences with the mandated curriculum and the social, cultural and linguistic needs of the school population through ongoing inquiry of pedagogical and curricular practices. A "re-envisioning" took place over time as the teachers positioned themselves as advocates and "cultural visionaries" in order to adapt instruction built upon the social and cultural interests and backgrounds of students to frame literacy instruction and support students as competent literacy learners. The inquiry group served as a catalyst for changes.

In a randomized control group study, Gersten, et al. (2010) investigated the impact of Teacher Study Group (TSG) professional development on the knowledge and implementation of vocabulary and comprehension practices of 81 first grade teachers from 19 Reading First schools. The impact of the TGT model on student achievement in vocabulary and comprehension was also studied. Observational data revealed significant improvements in the use of the instructional practices by teachers in the TGT group. In one measure of knowledge the TGT teachers also exceeded the comparison teachers. Student improvement data showed only a marginal improvement in oral vocabulary. A replication study (Gersten, Dimino, Jayanthi, Newman-Gonchar & Tahlor, 2013) also found similar impacts at the teacher level, but did not demonstrate the same student level effects. The researchers speculated that the knowledge or skills of study group facilitators may have been a contributing factor.

How Do Study Groups Support Equity and Inclusive Practices?

Study groups can be used to enhance collaboration across special and general educators in order to promote access to the general education curriculum and inclusive practices (Herner-Patnode, 2009). Herner-Patnode noted that a large barrier to inclusive pedagogy and practices is teacher knowledge of appropriate adaptations. Study groups also support school-based efforts in Response-to-Intervention (RTI) models addressing problem-solving solutions in providing appropriate, accessible and research-based solutions (Gersten, et al., 2010). Eick & McCormick (2009/10) found that study groups provide a means for novice teachers to critically examine culturally responsive pedagogy fostering changes in thinking and skills.

What Is Lesson Study?

Lesson study (LS) is a collaborative professional learning practice originating in Japan over a century ago (Takahashi & Yoshida, 2004). Lesson study involves small groups of teachers who engage in an ongoing collective cycle of inquiry through the creation, implementation, and analysis of Research Lessons (RL) in order to improve pedagogical practices (Rock & Wilson, 2005). This collaboration results in improvements in the "design of specific lessons and for teaching and learning more broadly" (Lewis, Perry, Hurd & O'Connell, 2006, p. 273). The aim of LS is for teachers to improve their understanding of how students' learning can be improved rather than in constructing a perfect lesson (Ylonen & Norwich, 2012). LS has been used to examine pedagogy in mathematics, literacy, science and history in elementary and secondary settings (Doig & Groves, 2011; Rock & Wilson, 2005). Teachers have improved their skills in instructional differentiation through the use of LS (Rock & Wilson, 2005).

The process of LS involves groups of teachers who meet regularly over time to design, implement and improve one or more RL. Research lessons are taught in the classroom of one of the participating teachers. According to Rock & Wilson (2005), RLs focus on a specifically selected problem goal or area of pedagogical practice; are carefully and collaboratively planned with LS group members; are observed by other teachers in the LS group; and are further analyzed and discussed by LS group members.

Benedict and colleagues (2013) outlined specific phases in the LS cycle: (1) Get started - develop norms, goals, processes and agenda; (2) Analyze data and study curriculum; (3) Create aligned goals; (4) Design aligned lessons; and (5) Teach RL and analyze with peers. Lewis et al. (2006) noted that deep knowledge of learning and teaching is an important component of the LS cycle conclusion.

What Does the Research Say About Outcomes of Lesson Study?

The use of LS has produced sustainable instructional improvements across teachers (Lewis, Perry, Foster, Hurd & Fisher, 2011). Hart (2008/2009) analyzed the use of LS in mathematics with eight 3rd grade teachers across a small district following four LS cycles. Notably, teachers reframed their lens on curriculum from a focus on management to an understanding of the supports and obstructions to student learning. In addition to enhanced pedagogy, Rock & Wilson (2005) found teachers reported greater professional confidence and collaboration when using LS. Lesson study has supported long-term improvements in content knowledge and the use of research-based literacy practices (Hurd & Licciardo-Musso, 2005).

Research has also documented the use of LS to support professional learning in inclusive pedagogical practices. For example, Mutch-Jones, Puttick & Minner (2012) described a middle school science project involving general and special educators addressing accessible science instruction through LS. Outcomes included an increase in teachers' ability to generate more accommodations, and adapt instructional plans for diverse learning needs in inclusive science classrooms. Ylonen & Norwich (2012) also found a shift in focus from teacher and teaching to students and their supported learning occurred through LS.

Lesson study can also enhance differentiated pedagogy through improved understanding of student needs. Norwich, Dudley & Ylonen (2014) described LS outcomes in a design-based study targeted at improving pedagogical strategies and practices for students with moderate learning difficulties (MLD). The LS process was adapted to include the use of a case student (with MLD) included within the planning, observation and analysis phases of LS. Teachers reported gains in the knowledge and awareness of student needs, as well as a broadened understanding of students.

How Does Lesson Study Support Equity and Inclusive Practice?

Lesson study can influence inclusive practices through collective efforts that improve conviction, communication and cohesion of curricular and instructional practices that support all learners. Teaching practices become public through LS with opportunities to critically examine practices in a collegial trusting and focused process. Conviction to ongoing improvements in instruction that benefit the learning of all students – especially those at the margins is fostered. LS is also founded on communication and dialogue that clarifies instructional practice, supports excellence in pedagogy, examines alternative perspectives on students, learning and teaching, and broadens understanding of the junctures between pedagogical practices, learner and learning diversity, and outcomes. A Snapshot of Practice example which describes a composite approach of study groups and lesson study used with teacher-leader coaches and school-university partnerships to support systems change follows (Table 3).

Table 3. Snapshot of practice: Supporting professional inquiry at the Richard O Jacobsen Center for Comprehensive Literacy, University of Northern Iowa

Located at the University of Northern Iowa, the Richard O. Jacobsen Center for Comprehensive Literacy (JCCL) supports Iowa schools in improving literacy for all students. Two primary goals of the JCCL are (1) closing the achievement gap between diverse groups while increasing literacy proficiency for all students, and (2) increasing teachers' knowledge and expertise through university supported professional development.
One of the projects supported by the Center is the Partnerships in Comprehensive Literacy (PCL), a school-reform model developed by Dr. Linda Dorn that uses literacy as a lever to address school change in student learning, teacher knowledge, school culture and processes. In this project the JCCL partners with other universities and schools in preparing literacy coaches to support transformative change in schools through improved literacy practices and outcomes. Coaching and mentoring are featured and collaborative learning teams within authentic contexts use study groups, book clubs, and demonstrations/observations of teaching and lessons.
The PCL coaches undertake a year-long program of coursework and learning, coupled with the observation of teaching demonstrations in model schools and field-based "learning by doing." Ongoing support is provided to the schools, coaches, administrators and teachers during this long-term association. "Literacy coaches are seen as key leaders positioned to guide, facilitate and monitor the school change process," shares Dr. Debra Rich, Assistant Director of the JCCL.
Coaches in the PCL program are "expected to maintain credibility and skill, and are required to teach a small literacy intervention group of students using the theories and practices studied during the year." Rich states, "this keeps them real and grounded in practice so that they carry some authenticity."
Coaches engage in continuous learning supported through collective inquiry and reflection of literacy practices in context. One practice includes literacy lesson observation, reflection and analysis. Demonstration lessons tied to theory and collective learning merge elements of teacher study group and Lesson Study practices.
Rich explained, "we encourage schools to network with one another." PCL literacy coaches not only network in Iowa, but are also part of a larger group of universities and participating schools using the PCL model. Rich described an example of lesson observation and analysis where a live model lesson taught in Missouri is viewed by PCL coaches in Iowa and in other state, providing "an opportunity to revisit theory and to look at underpinnings of work that align theory to practice. There is an opportunity to critique… not in a personal critical way but in a close look at the lesson in refining our work as it relates to intentional teaching."
During the year of training, coaches meet monthly for two days at the university for ongoing coursework, learning and support. Each month, two coaches present digitally recorded lessons of their small group instruction. Each lesson is introduced by the coach-teacher who communicates information about the small group, assessment data, lesson focus, areas of student growth, concerns for the students, and a personal goal for feedback. While cohort members view the lesson together, the coach-teacher leaves the room to view and reflect on her lesson simultaneously in another location. Rich notes that over time this process was more supportive to open discussion and was favored by the coaches. As the cohort views the demonstration lesson and later dialogues with the coach-teacher they "can go back and refer to theory, texts, or practice protocols to clarify, ask questions or connect things that went well."
The JCCL has developed inquiry supported professional learning melding the study of literacy practice with shared texts, intentional dialogue, and authentic study of the application of theory and practice through lesson demonstration and dialogue.

COACHING

Coaching aims to support the development of students, teachers, school leaders and the educational institutions of which they are part of... (Devine, Meyers & Houssemand, 2013, p. 1383)

Coaching is not a new practice, however, school-based coaching has grown in popularity and is now one of the fastest growing forms of PD (Darling-Hammond, et al., 2009). A primary aim of coaching is to address individual teacher learning, yet coaching is also framed as *"a lever for systemic reform"* at the school or district level (Mangnin & Dunsmore, 2015, p. 175). Moreover, *"coaching programs can be powerful tools for increasing equity in schools and building cultural proficiency in teachers"* (Chiarello, 2015, p. 23).

What Is Coaching?

Broadly speaking, coaching provides a framework for professional learning and change through collegial support, information and empowerment. Coaching is viewed as a partnership between a coach and one or more other education professionals in order to address purposeful improvement goals. (Knight, 2007). Robbins (2015) defined coaching as a form of professional learning that "fosters meaningful, personalized, professional growth opportunities for staff, increases the influence of exemplary teaching, and magnifies the collective propensity of schools to be able to provide responsive, high-quality learning experiences to ensure that every student succeeds" (p. 8). Through coaching, teachers improve their practice while constructing new meanings and understandings (Costa & Garmston, 2002).

Coaching supports teacher learning through in situ practice supported by collegial relationships. Coaching practices commonly address one or more of these three areas of change: (1) improved teacher beliefs, self-efficacy and/or implementation of new and high quality practices; (2) improved school climate for collaboration and toward shared goals and school improvement; and (3) improved student performance and achievement (Darling Hammond, et al., 2009; Kohler, Crilley, Shearer & Good, 1997; Knight, 2007; Showers & Joyce, 1996).

At the individual teacher level, there are many purposes for coaching. Some of the aims of coaching at the teacher level include promoting reflective teaching practice and problem solving, improving teacher self-efficacy, addressing beliefs and assumptions surrounding instruction and students, implementing of effective teaching practices, and differentiating of instruction. At the school and district level coaching may have goals of supporting the study of teaching and content through shared language, knowledge and skills; providing a problem solving forum for solving curricular, instruction and equity issues; or facilitating system-wide change and shared responsibility for school improvement (Annenberg Institute, 2004; Denton & Hasbruock, 2009; Robbins, 2015; Showers, 1985)

Coaching is founded on the relationship of a trusted partnership between a coach and teacher (Knight, 2007). In coaching, relationships may be hierarchical – involving an expert with less experienced or knowledgeable peers or juniors, or may be mutual with peers of equal status (Murray, Ma & Mazur, 2008). Coaching relationships may be voluntary, such as those involving peers learning new curriculum and strategies together, or may involve instructional support and learning provided by an assigned expert.

Most coaching efforts include sustained routines which include a process of observations of classroom teaching. Observational routines may include demonstrations of model practices, and pre-and post-conferences supporting reflective practice and problem solving. Further, the use of active learning, listening, inquiry, appropriate challenge and support are also viewed as core elements to coaching approaches that support personal and collective change through active engagement in reflection (Devine, et al., 2013). Perhaps the most essential element of coaching is its design and fit with the unique needs of particular schools, teachers, and students (Steiner & Kowal, 2007).

There are numerous approaches and models of coaching schools and districts employ. Denton and Hasbrouck (2009) classified coaching approaches addressing professional learning processes and change purposes including: (1) technical, (2) problem solving, (3) reflective practice, (4) collegial/team building, and (5) reform models. Cornett & Knight (2008) completed a narrative review of the research on coaching, recognizing four major models of coaching including: (1) peer coaching, (2) cognitive coaching, (3) literacy coaching, and (4) instructional coaching. Coaching approaches are not mutually exclusive (Steiner & Kowal, 2007) with overlap in purposes and processes.

What coaching looks like in practice varies widely depending on the purpose of the coaching and skills and styles of the coach. Coaching is not a single event or activity, but should provide an array of professional learning opportunities to support educators in acquiring, using, and adapting knowledge and, skills, to improve their effectiveness and impact their students (Moran, 2007). Coaching can address improved understandings and proficiency of instructional content, pedagogy and practices, as well as positive impact in the contexts in which they teach, addressing inclusive schooling, pedagogy and culturally responsive practices (Knight, 2007; Nishimura, 2014; Teemant, Wink & Tyra, 2011; West & Cameron, 2013).

Most coaching models, once implemented, employ a-three-phase cyclical process including: (1) a preconference to set goals and contexts for observation and learning; (2) a classroom observation; and (3) a post observation conference (Denton & Hasbrouck, 2009; Showers & Joyce, 1996). Throughout these activities reflective dialogue and analysis are supported through coaching conversations in order to facilitate meaningful learning and improvements in teaching knowledge, skills and/or beliefs (Costa & Garmston, 2002). Coaches may also demonstrate, model or co-teach lessons (Knight, 2007).

Coaches are skillful, experienced educators who take on additional leadership responsibilities through coaching roles. Knight (2007) delineated eight functions or roles of instructional coaches. These roles include: (1) supporting a broad repertoire of practices for teachers including behavior, content knowledge, direct instruction and formative assessment; (2) building emotional connections with teachers; (3) encouraging implementation of instructional practices; (4) creating and sustaining collaborative opportunities for reflection and dialogue; (5) modeling practices; (6) observing and providing feedback; (7) providing supporting resources; and (8) partnering with principals and other professional networks.

Coaches must be culturally competent, able to "provide feedback" and assist teachers in understanding "how culture operates in their own classrooms and schools." (Guerra & Nelson, 2012, p. 65). Additionally, they should have the dispositions, beliefs, knowledge and skills to foster inclusive practices within their schools (Alberta Teachers Association, 2011). Coaches have multifaceted roles supporting individual teachers, groups of teachers, and school wide change (Poglinco & Bach, 2004).

What Does the Research Say About Coaching Outcomes?

Research on the specific impacts of coaching programs is evolving. (Denton & Hasbrouck, 2009). There are mixed results surrounding coaching outcomes given the varied contexts, purposes, models, roles, duration, and implementation activities of coaching (Cornett & Knight, 2008). Overall, coaching has positively impacted of teacher instruction and curriculum (Showers & Joyce, 1996; Knight, 2007). Teacher effectiveness impacts include improved teacher satisfaction, reported confidence and self-efficacy, and knowledge and implementation of teaching practices when coaching programs are effectively implemented (Cornett & Knight, 2008; Showers & Joyce, 1996; Tschannen-Moran & McMaster, 2009). Most research in coaching is descriptive and efficacy studies are beginning to emerge.

Coaching research addressing impacts on student outcomes and achievement are not always reported in the literature, (Borman & Feger, 2006; Cornett & Knight, 2008). It may take a longer time of teacher refinement of newly acquired strategies or may take coaches time to prioritize support activities in order to realize a greater impact on student achievement measures or impact school culture (Biancarosa, Byrk & Dexter, 2010; Campbell & Malkus, 2011; Elish-Piper & L'Allier, 2011). Byrd-Blake & Hundley (2012) found coaching could support school improvement goals related to diversity.

Some researchers have studied the impact of coaching practices on instructional practices supporting inclusive pedagogy. Kretlow, Cooke & Wood (2012) described a combined in-service workshop and coaching model which addressed the accurate use of three first grade teachers' use of evidence-based mathematics strategies. High levels of teacher satisfaction and fidelity of implementation were found across the general and special educators. Duchaine and colleagues (2011) utilized coaching along with written performance feedback in high school inclusion classrooms to increase the use of positive praise statements and positive behavioral supports. All teachers increased their use of the practice. Reinke et al (2014) utilized coaching to provide ongoing support and feedback to teachers for universal classroom management intervention. Teachers receiving more feedback had higher levels of implementation. Finally, Kohler et al (1997) studied the impact of peer coaching on the use of an integrated instructional approach comprised of four instructional strategies used by four elementary educators. The researchers found that peer coaching impacted the refinement and continued use of these effective instructional practices, even after formal coaching support ceased.

How Does Coaching Support Equity and Inclusive Practices?

Coaching is well situated to support school-based inclusive practices. First, coaching can address the school culture itself and the "prevailing beliefs about teaching and learning and professional norms of interaction" (Allen, Nichols, & Ancess, 2004, p. 1). Using cognitive coaching and other related coaching activities, educators, coaches, and school leaders can examine personal and collective beliefs, practices, consequences, and conflicts surrounding diversity through critical conversations (Teemant et al., 2011). Increased awareness and understanding of diversity can support more thoughtful problem-solving and decision making that support inclusive school practices and policies. Aguilar noted that in coaching for equity there must be focused attention on the "social and historic forces which create and maintain systems in which children are treated differently based on who they are" (cited in Chiarello, 2015, p. 23).

Next, coaching can increase the competence of teachers to implement learning and instructional practices that support students with diverse learning needs and inclusion in the classroom. For example, to address the challenges and opportunities of inclusive education, schools in Alberta Canada utilize learning coaches, who are viewed as supporting learning outcomes for all students regardless of their educational needs (Alberta Teacher's Association, 2011). Learning coaches support teacher practices and school change in inclusive education as cohesive agents of support and advocacy. They enhance relationships among members in the school community, focus on the strengths of students, and increase the capacity of the educators and the system to address a diversity of student need through (1) the design and implementation of curriculum and assessment, (2) support in accessible and culturally relevant educational materials and assistive technologies, and (3) behavioral support and student engagement supports.

Finally, through an equity lens coaching can support a breadth of ongoing activities and interactions that undergird and actualize inclusive practices. For example, coaches can support teachers in examining curricular materials for their representation for diversity; can increase commitment and visibility of improvement goals related to vulnerable students and groups; can organize and analyze data about student outcomes such as restrictive instructional services or placements in co-teaching; can provide resources on academic language support for second language and other learners; and can facilitate the use of inclusive pedagogy practices such as differentiated instruction or universal design for learning (Alberta Teacher's Association, 2011; Wlodarczyk, Somma, Bennet & Gallagher, 2015).

In the following Snapshot of Practice, challenges and solutions to implementing a new coaching program are highlighted (Table 4).

Table 4. Snapshot of practice: Launching coaching at Kingsley Elementary, Waterloo Community Schools

Kingsley Elementary is one of 16 elementary schools in a school-district with approximately 6,300 elementary students in a community of approximately 68,000 individuals. At Kingsley there are 486 students grades K-5 with 69% of the school students identifying as white, 8% as English Language Learners, 11.1% of students supported by Individualized Education Programs, and 50% of the students receive free or reduced lunch. There are 19 full time classroom teachers at the school as well as varied support staff including para-educators, coaches and other specialist teachers. At the end of the past school year, 78.6% of Kingsley Elementary students were identified as proficient in math and 78.6% in reading.
Principal Amber Dietz is in her third year at as principal at Kingsley and is a veteran educator and leader of 18 years. Kingsley Elementary is implementing the second year of a district-supported coaching program at Kingsley Elementary School which blends district and school-based coaches to support teachers in growing their skills to meet student and school improvement goals.
During the 2014-2015 academic year, the district received state funds to expand the teacher leadership and coaching programs. In addition to two school based leadership and coaching positions (literacy and mathematics building leaders), three additional district-based coaches were also assigned to Kingsley Elementary part-time in the areas of mathematics, special needs, and induction/mentorship. As the coaching project began, explained Principal Dietz, "teacher leaders were in new roles... they were in an out of the building and it seemed there were too many coaches and a feeling it wasn't very helpful." The roles and supervision of district coaches rested with district administration. Staff were overwhelmed by the number of coaches, unsure of what they were to do and disconcerted when despite short staffing on days when substitute teachers were unavailable, coaches were not able to assist in instruction" We learned coaching is not good unless teachers buy in and feel they can influence what is happening," shared Dietz.
Midyear, Principal Dietz, proposed changes to the district for a better fit and function of coaching with the needs of Kingsley's teachers and students. Defining and connecting coaching roles to specific teacher needs and goals was a primary first step. Linking coaching activities and goals to the school improvement plan (SIP) and ensuring coaches communicated and connected with one another in strengthening a united approach to professional learning also occurred.
Some of the changes that occurred to shape this transformation in coaching came from the collective efforts of the principal, coaches and teachers themselves. A coaching PLC (professional learning community) for the five coaches and principal was established to "collaborate and communicate frequently, to reflect, set goals and take action to support teachers to positively impact student learning (socially, emotionally and academically). We will also support each other as we move our coaching forward." Coaching cycles in year 2 identified major trimester responsibilities for each of the coaches within their primary coaching role which might include working with specific grade or content level teams; co-teachers, or an individual teacher or para-educator.
Coaching roles were also redefined to better address teacher interests, needs and priority goals within Kingsley's school improvement plan. A coaching cycle in year 2 was established at the beginning of the year. A "coach menu" was created to both define and communicate areas of support and learning that were available to support teaching practices.
Choice was central to Kingsley's revision of their coaching program. All building teachers and other staff were surveyed on areas of interest for coaching. This information supported the coaching PLC in organizing specific coaching activities and opportunities One target of Kingsley's SIP was that "All staff will feel supported by instructional coaches in order to improve their practice (special needs coach, mentor coach, math coach, literacy coach, para-educator coach)."
It was necessary, shared Principal Dietz, that teachers understood that coaches were there to "support and not evaluate." "Relationship trumps content expertise" so that trust and personalized learning can occur. Where it might be easier at the district level to view coaches by the area of expertise provided, at the school level it's about the "fit" of professional learning. One of biggest successes to date of the Kingsley coaching program is – teacher empowerment and buy-in. "When the focus of teachers is in owning their own pd, they buy into their own growth. Success is that we are all growing and seeing ourselves as needing to grow," explained Dietz.
Coaching at Kingsley supports inclusive practice by empowering teachers individually and collectively to impact learning more powerfully through improvements in content-specific instruction for all students, differentiation of core instruction to address student diversity and needs and co-teaching, Principal Dietz observed, "When I came to Kingsley the primary model of supporting students who had special needs was a 30 minute pull-out. We are shifting towards supporting a true LRE, really looking at individual needs and what fits the needs of kids versus what fits in with the schedule."
Coaching at Kingsley, is a work in progress, and it's expected that each year coaching may look a little different depending on the needs of the teachers and students. Dietz summarized that coaching "is an exciting shift" that supports teacher growth and in turn school and student outcomes. "It's flexible, adaptable, and lets us think outside of the box."

PROFESSIONAL LEARNING COMMUNITIES

The working relationships that teachers have with other adults are closely connected to and deeply consequential for the teaching and learning relationships they in turn have with their students. (Fullan & Hargreaves, 1992, p. 41)

The concept of Professional Learning Communities (PLC) bridges individual teacher inquiry to sustained collaborative teacher teamwork and to systemic school improvement. With historical roots in school reform and organizational learning and change theory of the 1980s and 1990s (Fullan, 1993; Senge 1990, 2000), the most prominent PLC researchers in American schools today are the DuFours (DuFour & Eaker, 1998; DuFour, DuFour, Eaker, & Many, 2006); Newmann, (1996); and Hord (1997; Hord & Sommers, 2008). Closely related concepts include Critical Friends Groups and Community of Learners (Wenger, 1998). PLCs are often used in concert with other PD models such as coaching and inquiry.

Although there are different definitions of PLCs, each shares a broad conception of educators working collaboratively in ongoing and sustained cycles of inquiry to improve practice and student learning. PLC advocates stress that effective PLCs differ from informal groups of teachers working together on a shared task. Dufour and colleagues (2006) include six essential characteristics that differentiate effective PLCs from other such groups while Newmann (1996) Hord (1997) include five. Table 5 compares these definitions.

The DuFour and Eaker model uses four main questions to frame all PLC work: (1) What do we want students to learn? (2) How will we know they have learned it? (3) How will we respond when they have not learned it? (4) How will we respond if they already know it? PLCs typically result in shared collaboration time, agreement of essential concepts and skills, common assessments, collaborative examination of student work and data, critical reflections about teaching practices, and new supports for students.

What Does the Research Say About the Outcomes of PLCs?

Although PLCs are becoming a common feature of school improvement, relatively few empirical studies have been published on their use. A review of the PLC literature (Vescio, Ross, & Adams, 2008) found eleven empirical studies, all of which reported evidence of positive impact on teaching practices in general, and 5 of the studies identified an increased use of specific practices including student-centered or authentic pedagogy, increased variety of strategies, and a strategic focus on literacy. All 11 of the studies found evidence of a shift in school culture, especially regarding an increased value on collaboration, a

Table 5. Essential characteristics of professional learning communities

DuFour & Eaker (1998)	Newmann & Associates (1996)	Hord (1997)
• Shared mission, values, goals • Focused on learning and results • Collective inquiry • Action orientation and experimentation • Commitment to continuous improvement • Unrelenting focus on results	• Shared views and values • Clear focus on ensuring that students are not simply taught, but that they learn. • Reflective conversations about curriculum, instruction, and student development • Making practice public • Focus on collaboration	• Shared beliefs, values and vision • Supportive, shared leadership • Collective creativity and learning • Supportive conditions • Shared personal Practice

central focus on student learning, and an increase in teacher efficacy and learning. Eight of the studies found evidence of impact on student achievement, especially for learners who struggled the most. Further, four of the studies linked the most robust gains in student achievement to schools with the strongest PLCs. A meta-analysis of studies examining PLCs and their impact on student achievement found a small but significant effect (d=.25, p<.05) (Lomos, Hofman, & Bosker, 2011).

How Do PLCs Support Equity and Inclusive Practices?

A number of PLC practices support a framework of equity including: a focus on student learning, student data, and student work at the center of PLC work; rigorous expectations and shared responsibility for teaching the essentials to all students; prompts to create learning supports for students who have not learned and enrichment opportunities for those who have learned the essentials. This is especially true when the shared values and norms of a PLC include an explicit commitment to equity and inclusion.

One example of a PLC rooted in equity and inclusion resulted from a collaboration between the Bay-Area Coalition for Equitable Schools, the Bay Area Writing Project, the Coalition of Essential Schools, and the National Writing Project (Friedrich, Tateisis, Malarkey, Simons, & Williams, 2005). This three-year project used ongoing collaborative inquiry focused on equity, improving student learning, and developing resources for other educators. In contrast to protocols used by other PLC models, this project began with the following assumptions from the start:

- There are inequities in our schools that we, as teachers and educational leaders, are well-situated to investigate and address.
- All students can learn, are capable of learning and achieving to high standards of excellence.
- As teachers and educators, we have the right and a responsibility to pursue this social project of fighting for equity.
- As teachers and educational leaders, we can learn how to do this and so can other teachers. We want to debate strategy, theories, and the best ways to approach this work, but not whether or not it is possible. We will continue to talk about the whys and hows and in what ways we might work. We can discuss what constitutes successful inquiry, asking ourselves, 'successful for whom?' (Friedrich et al., 2005, p. 2)

Framing inquiry in this way and problematizing equity from the start, helped teams to push past defensiveness and create a safe space to discuss issues that others might avoid as too political, allowing collaboration around solutions. As McKamey (2005) and Freidman (2005) described, the insights teachers reached were deeply personal and powerful, and they led to confronting hidden assumptions and beliefs, changing teaching practices, and developing a more complete understanding of their students using strengths to inform support. The impact of the teams, however, was limited to the circle of participants, who then encountered obstacles and conflict when they tried to expand their team to educators who did not necessarily share the same beliefs about equity. While an equity-focused inquiry can certainly work well within the frameworks of PLCs, the PLC protocols and questions depend on members to answer in ways that confront tensions or inequities that may be uncomfortable for teams in early stages of development.

PLCs can also support inclusion by disrupting divisions between special and general education teachers. In many schools, special education teachers are assigned to grade-level or content-area PLC teams rather than special education teams, ending isolation. This resulted in a shared sense of responsibility for all students, increased opportunities for teachers to contribute specialized knowledge, and for teachers to learn from each other in ways that were not possible before. With an increased focus on struggling learners in PLCs, the expertise of the special education teacher becomes more central, but is amplified by the efforts of everyone on the team. Also, the special education teacher can be better versed in the general education curriculum and may recognize important differences in the special education curriculum that lead to inequity (Blanton & Perez, 2011; Grossman, Wineburg, & Woolworth, 2001). An example is Kildeer Countryside CCSD in Texas: *If done poorly, separate and specialized curriculum developed in isolation...can actually lower expectations... we learned that when regular and special educators work together, special education teachers no longer have to work in a chaotic curricular jungle* (Many & Schmidt, 2013, p. 2).

Although PLCs can support inclusion and equity, Wenger (1998) notes that PLCs are not "intrinsically benevolent." PLC is a social construction like disability, race, class, gender and justice. Thus, a PLC "should not be romanticized; they can reproduce counter-productive patterns, injustices, prejudices, racism, sexism, and abuses of all kinds. In fact, I would argue they are the very locus of such reproduction." (p. 132). Individual PLCs may pursue strategies to support some learners that may have unintended consequences for other learners. For example, the pursuit of providing supports to struggling learners and enrichment for those who have already mastered a concept can lead to an overuse of ability grouping feeding into increasingly inflexible tracks within a school, and in turn to inequalities in society (Goodlad & Oakes, 1988; Rubin, 2006; Slavin 1995).

PLC studies found that conflicts and tensions, especially surrounding issues of inclusion, are a natural and inherent part of the PLC process. The degree to which a PLC acknowledges rather than avoids these tensions is a marker of whether the PLC is truly a learning community and a safe place to negotiate differences or merely a group of people going through the motions. The strength of the PLC in turn impacts its success in terms of learning by the teachers and their students. (Achinstein, 2002; Blanton & Perez, 2011).

In summary, PLCs are a promising strategy to focus collaborative educational efforts to support inclusive practices, yet will not inherently do so without making inclusion and equity an explicit focus or intention as a shared goal or mission by the community.

PROFESSIONAL DEVELOPMENT SCHOOLS AND OTHER SCHOOL-UNIVERSITY PARTNERSHIPS

Ideally, you're in a setting where lots of beginning teachers are being trained together and where veteran teachers are engaged in a lot of professional development and peer coaching and continual learning themselves. And that's one of the goals of PD schools -- that the whole environment is organized around teacher learning as much as it's organized around student learning (Darling-Hammond, 2001)

Successful models of school reform and PD emphasize the importance of collaboration, but usually refer to collaborations within school systems. However, school reform movements in the 1980s and 1990s including the Holmes Group (1986, 1990, 1991) and the National Network for Educational Renewal (NNER) (Goodlad, 1990) and prominent researchers (Darling-Hammond, 1994, 2005) stressed the importance of external partnerships, especially with universities. The construct of a highly-evolved,

Table 6. Snapshot of practice: PLCs in the Cedar Falls Community School District (CFSCD)

The Cedar Falls Community School District (CFCSD) is a relatively large Midwestern suburban district of about 5500 students enrolled K-12. Diversity in the district is somewhat limited: 85% of students identify their race as White, 21% qualify for free or reduced lunch, 11% have Individualized Education Plans, and less than 2% are English Language Learners. Achievement gaps with these groups is a challenge for CFCSD, like many other districts, and a PLC model was adopted as the primary professional development model as one strategy to improve student learning.
In January 2015, CFCSD was recognized by Solution Tree as a Model PLC. At the time, they were one of only three districts in Iowa and 22 in the nation to receive the honor. The award was the culmination of five years of work using the DuFour PLC model process and framework to alter practices, structures, and culture to commit to the ideal of all students achieving at high levels. The district restructured its professional development model around PLC framework and its school board formally adopted the PLC process in 2012. In the fall of 2013, the district created designated PLC collaboration time for all teachers. PLCs used this time to ask and answer the four critical questions about student learning, coming to consensus on defining essential skills and concepts and common assessments, and using data and student work to reflect on teaching and new supports. As a result, student learning is monitored closely and more regularly. Multi-tiered systems of supports and interventions have been created for students with additional learning needs, including scheduled intervention and enrichment time during the school day.
District administrators interviewed attribute many inclusion-related successes to the PLC structure, including increases in graduation rate, improvements standardized achievement test performance, a decreases in the percentage of students with an IEP and the amount of time students with IEPs are served outside of the general education classroom, and a decrease in the number of students with failing grades. In addition, the district was twice awarded the Iowa Department of Education's *Breaking Barriers Award* for improvements in proficiency by African-American students.
Special education teachers in the district serve on either grade-level or content-area PLC teams, often with general education teachers with whom they co-teach. Both administrators and teachers say that this structure has led to a strong sense of shared responsibility for all students and increased opportunity for teachers to learn from each other and improve their practice. One secondary special education teacher explained, "I've been in special education for more than twenty years, but before [PLCs], it was always like I was an island. I've learned so much from my colleagues in the English Department and feel like PLCs helped me to know more about what content and skills matter most and to raise my expectations. We are now on the same page about what all students need to learn, whether it is in our co-taught classrooms or in the self-contained classes I also teach. That is making it easier for students to transition out of special education or into less restrictive environments." Her English teacher colleague added, "And it has helped us to really understand that all of the students are 'our kids' and that we are all responsible for helping all students to learn at high levels. We said that before, but now we are acting on it more. During intervention time, we are bringing in more students to work with us rather than handing them off to the special education teacher, and we are all working together more to develop new supports for struggling learners."
PLCs have not been a complete panacea, however. Despite improvements, the district continues to fall short of the No Child Left Behind reading and math achievement goals for many of the defined subgroups (racial minorities, students in special education, English Language Learners, and low-income students). Teachers acknowledged that there remain some issues related to inclusion that PLCs have not yet solved. For example, while essential skills and concepts have been developed for all sections of courses, some question whether there is an equivalent level of challenge, high expectations, and opportunities in a tracked "fundamentals" version of a course compared to the standard course or an honors course. While many classes are co-taught by general and special education teachers, it is sometimes true that most of the students in the class have an IEP or 504 Plan, begging the question 'is this really an inclusive setting?'
"In terms of having some of these tough conversations, we aren't really there yet, but as our PLCs grow stronger and as we continue meeting across buildings, I think we can get there if we work together," concluded one teacher. In the 2016-2017 school year, CFCSD will add new teacher leadership roles of mentors and coaches to the district professional learning model, bringing new opportunities for a synergy of complimentary strategies.

school-university partnership that resulted in mutual benefit and "simultaneously renewal" (Goodlad, 1990) of both partners became known as a Professional Development School (PDS), an alternative and parallel to laboratory schools.

What Is a Professional Development School?

Many definitions of PDS exist, from nine essential elements described by the National Association of Professional Development Schools (NAPDS) to five standards first defined by NCATE to evaluate PDSs (including a standard for equity and diversity). Teitel (2003) identified convergence around four goals for a PDS: (1) improvement in student learning, (2) preparation of educators, (3) professional development of educators, and (4) research and inquiry into improving practice. When these goals are applied to specifically to the improvement of inclusion and equity, powerful new synergies can emerge (Yssel, Koch, & Merbler, 2002).

Partnerships with schools offer universities the opportunity to immerse teacher preparation and research around the challenges of inclusion in real schools. Much of the rhetoric surrounding the mission of a PDS proposed these partnerships as a promising strategy to promote equity and social justice, although several reviews of the PDS literature questioned the impact on equitable pedagogy and empowerment of students or community (Brenault & Lack, 2009). However, PD, teaching and learning, and joint inquiry were some of the most common areas explored in the PDS research literature (Valli, Cooper, & Frankes, 1997), and these areas can support equity.

What Does the Research Say About PDS Outcomes?

Much of the PDS literature is descriptive rather than empirical. However, studies have found a positive impact on teachers, university faculty, school principals, parents and community members (Nolan, Grow, Leftwhich, Mark & Peters, 2011Table 3

The in-text citation "In January 2015" is not in the reference list. Please correct the citation, add the reference to the list, or delete th

), as well as improvements in PreK-12 student learning (Wong & Glass, 2011). PDS models are diverse and context-specific, and difficult to generalize from. However, the following aspects of PDSs have been linked to positive outcomes in professional development: (1) the shared PD inherent in mentoring pre-service teachers, (2) sharing human resources and developing new roles, (3) sharing expertise in research and inquiry, (4) sharing university-based incentives, and (5) targeting student achievement.

Mentoring as Professional Development

In the beginning stages, the PDS focus is often around developing new structures to support extended internships and residencies for preservice teachers. One of the signature pedagogies of a PDS is a year-long residency with on-site courses, a professor embedded in the school, and teachers becoming more active mentors and co-teachers for university courses. The research on the benefits of PDS residencies for teacher candidates is beyond the scope of this chapter, but shows clear benefits for the preservice teachers (Castle, Fox, & Souder, 2006; Rice, Ihrig, Merves, & Brown, 2011). Even when the learning of preservice teachers in prioritized, however, there is rich and authentic PD inherent in mentoring, including sharing and reflecting on one's practice, participating in action research led by the professor and the preservice teachers, and answering many questions posed can all result in teacher development and support a culture of collaboration and continuous improvement critical for teacher learning and preservice teacher preparation (Hagger & McIntyre, 2006; Lopez-Real & Kwan, 2005).

Sharing Human Resources and Developing New Roles

PDS partnerships often create of new hybrid roles for university faculty and teachers that support PD. In some PDSs, teachers become a formal part of the teacher education program of the university. For example, at Minnesota State-Mankato, master teachers are chosen to serve as Teachers On Special Assignment (TOSA) and are released from their classroom for three years to serve the university and school, replaced by a Mankato Graduate Teaching Fellow. The cost is shared between the institutions. The TOSA has responsibilities to their school to mentor new teachers, to lead improvement and PD initiatives, and to coach the Teaching Fellow who is assigned to teach in his/her previous classroom. The TOSA also has responsibilities to the university to teach on-site courses and supervise preservice teachers placed at the school. Hoffman, Dahlman, and Zierdt (2009) described how this reallocation of human resources enabled a school-university Professional Learning Community focused on critical needs such as early childhood readiness, the achievement of English Language Learners, and stronger family-school-community partnerships.

In other models, a university faculty member is embedded in the school as a professor-in-residence. The Special Education program at the University of South Florida created many PDS partnerships with university faculty assigned part-time to schools to teach courses, supervise student teachers, support school restructuring initiatives in inclusion, and participate in school governance (Christensen, Epanchin, Harris, Roselli, Smith, & Stoddard, 1996; Roselli, Perez, & Claggett, 1995). The USF PDS model also included school-university collaborative inquiry for mutual PD and joint governance structures to pursue shared goals (Epanchin & Colucci, 2002; Stoddard & Danforth, 1999). Gaining entree into a school naturally led to opportunities for authentic, just-in-time PD (Klingner, Arguelles, Hughes, & Vaughn, 2001).

Finally, the presence of a cadre of pre-service teachers is another source of human resources that can be marshalled to support school initiatives and to provide more individualized support to PreK-12 students. For example, Maheady, Jabot, Rey, and Micheielli-Pendel (2007) redesigned an early field experience with high-need schools. Pre-service teachers taught lessons, vetted for quality by their professors, that incorporated one or more given strategies with fidelity (e.g., think-pair-share, numbered heads together) as well as an authentic assessment strategy (e.g., quick write, performance assessment). In four semesters, the preservice teachers provided 844 formal lessons that resulted in demonstrable improvements in student learning and a total of 16,880 hours of classroom assistance.

Sharing Expertise in Research and Inquiry

Universities offer schools unique resources to pursue intellectual growth and complex skills rather than simplistic training. As Nehring and O'Brien note, "Amidst a sea of 'venders' and 'providers' that 'deliver' and 'implement' 'trainings,' the university, quite possibly alone, stands for scholarship, the quality most needed for meaningful and sustainable school improvement" (2012, p. 473). In many cases, a PDS begins with a school or district seeking technical support related to inclusion or other needs. For example, Klingner, Ahwee, van Garderen, and Hernandez (2004) described a PDS with a high-need urban school, initiated by the school's request for support with a more inclusive service delivery model. That beginning ultimately led to a multiple-year intensive partnership and the development of many mutually-beneficial initiatives.

Sharing the Incentive of Course Credit, Certificates, or Degrees

Universities offer incentives such as course credit or co-created certificate or degree programs that are both attractive to teachers for advancement and formally recognize the hard work and sustained effort of the PD. For example, King-Sears (1995) described a graduate degree in inclusion, collaboratively created with a district for practicing teachers. Six core competencies were identified by the school and university as central to the degree and key to supporting inclusion in the school. Courses were offered

Cultivating Communities of Inclusive Practice

around the school day and used applied projects to assess progress and learning, resulting in observable changes in teaching practices and dissemination to other non-participating teachers through workshops and a monograph.

Focusing on PreK-12 Student Learning and Equity

PDS models that claim an impact on PreK-12 student learning are more developed and incorporate many of the structures outlined above. However, few studies have included clear evidence of impact on student learning. One enduring example is the Juniper Gardens Children's Project, which originated in the early 1960s as a partnership between Kansas University and low-income communities in the Kansas City area and developed into a multifaceted array of initiatives involving grants, curriculum development, research, PD, and collaboration with schools, homes, and neighborhoods. Inclusion, PD, and research-to-practice were always prominent topics of inquiry for the project. (Greenwood, 1999; Hall, Scheifelbusch, Hoyt, & Greenwood, 1989).

One example of a JGCP initiative demonstrates the power of research-to-practice models examined a multi-faceted "blueprint for closing the gap in local schools" through collaboration in which university personnel provided extensive PD in evidence-based practices (e.g., Classwide Peer Tutoring, Reciprocal Teaching, and Writer's Workshop) as well as implementation supports such as modeling, coaching, co-teaching, and ongoing collaboration and consultation. There was strong evidence of impact of the school-university partnership and collaboration and positive changes in teaching practices, increases in student achievement, and increased teacher satisfaction (Abbott, Walton, Tapia, & Greenwood, 1999).

Another example of a partnership that resulted in improvements in student achievement is a low-performing, poor, rural school district and Michigan State University. This PDS created a unified system of teacher education and a collaborative site of practice and inquiry around improving student achievement (Mariage & Garmon, 2003). The school-university collaboration resulted in creation of teacher study groups, new summer school and mentoring programs, home-school partnerships, a PD center, curriculum standards alignment, and new initiatives in reading, math, and writing.

How Can PDSs Support Equity and Inclusive Practices?

While many of the examples above demonstrate an impact on equity and inclusion, one final set of examples from the long-standing PDS partnership in special education developed by the Department of Special Education at the University of South Florida exemplifies the complexity and diversity of PDS models in pursuit of inclusion and how these must evolve over time. Harris and Evans (1995) described the Florida Uniting Students in Education (FUSE) initiative to implement inclusion strategies in districts by leveraging the PDS partnership to provide PD in co-teaching and collaborative instructional strategies and new teams identified and supported students with disabilities for placement in general education classes. Roselli, Perez, and Claggett (1995) outlined a partnership with a middle school to restructure the preparation program by embedding courses and additional experiences into the school and supporting the PD of the teachers in inclusive practices and successful collaboration. Stoddard and Danforth (1995) described how assigning a university faculty member to the school one day each week with a student-teaching cohort using a new model of general education/special education collaboration resulted in new program initiatives and teacher-initiated projects.

With so many promising outcomes, one might wonder why every school and university does not have a PDS or other intensive partnership. However, Prater and Sileo (2002), in their survey of universities providing special education teacher preparation programs, found only 4 of the 115 respondents reporting a PDS partnership. There are many reasons why establishing and maintaining PDS partnerships can be difficult. PDSs are built on relationships thats take time to build and are vulnerable to changes in personnel or emerging differences or conflicts in philosophy or pedagogy. PDSs must also continue to evolve to ensure benefit for all stakeholders, and sometimes the direction or kind of change needed by one partner is not shared by the other. Finally, when resources grow scarce, the practice of sharing of them with external partners may become difficult to sustain. However, examples of partnerships that have overcome these challenges are found in the above examples and should inspire educators in schools and universities to attempt new models. Each year, the National Association for Professional Development Schools recognizes Exemplary PDSs, and its journal, *School-University Partnerships*, gives a full description from each of the awardees in the fall issue, providing ongoing examples for practitioners seeking new solutions for enduring problems.

Table 7. Snapshot of practice: Clarke University PDS at Table Mound School, Dubuque, IA

Clarke University, a small Catholic liberal arts and sciences university located in Dubuque, IA, established its first PDS in 1999. The model embedded a block of four elementary methods courses into a local elementary school, taught by a team of two professors who integrated the course curriculum and assignments as well as their own service and research agendas around the needs of the school. Clarke led in the development of the National Association for Professional Development Schools, with one of its professors serving on the founding organizational committee that created the NAPDS organization. Clarke now has four PDSs in both private and public schools. One of these, the PDS at Table Mound School, is the home of a block of special education endorsement courses. Table Mound was chosen as the site for this PDS in recognition of its inclusive practices and in particular the high percentage of students with IEPs who were in general education classes more than 80% of their day.
The Clarke students and professors meet in a classroom at Table Mound Monday-Thursday morning. Their courses include many of the aspects typical in other university courses such as textbooks, reflective journals, book studies, case studies, article reviews, and group projects. What is unique, however, is the immediacy of the application of learning from theory to practice, with Clarke students leading small group and individual enrichment and interventions in classrooms every day, all semester long. They contribute directly to the school's Response to Intervention system by collecting and sharing data with the school's Instructional Coaches and using the data to develop and implement the small group and individual instruction. Their professors ensure quality planning and are there to give lots of constructive feedback on performance for continuous improvement. Teachers and Coaches credit the Clarke PDS as a key part of the school's support system and often comment on what they learn along the way as they collaborate with Clarke students and professors.
What is also unique is the integration of the professors into the school and the school district. They are not only in-residence to support Clarke students, but also to serve the teachers and school community. Clarke professors serve on the School Improvement Leadership Team for the district or Site Council for the school. They are often asked to provide formal professional development workshops, in addition to the multitude of informal PD opportunities that occur as an inherent part of the partnership. Signs posted outside the PDS classroom proclaim a "Collaborative Community of Teachers and Learners" and outlines how Clarke candidates learn to be teachers through active teaching of Table Mound students and working with its teachers and how Clarke students and the professors-in-residence support school needs.
Interestingly, when teachers are asked about "professional development", their responses gravitate towards an association with the formal, district-provided, late-start Friday sessions that focus on initiatives such as Positive Behavioral Instructional Support and other initiatives. When asked about 'learning new things about teaching' however, they are quick to cite examples related to the PDS. The collaborative, sustained, job-embedded nature of the PDS results in learning for Clarke candidates and professors as well as Table Mound teachers, coaches, and administrators.
That is not to say that all is absolutely ideal. A more perfect alignment between the Clarke curriculum and school professional development areas as well as some aspects of special education service delivery would unlock new synergies but would require frank conversations about areas of philosophical differences. At the end of the day, the trusting relationship is the key driver in determining when and how to raise difficult issues, but in the meantime, the PDS continues to support differentiation and student support in inclusion at Table Mound as it prepares candidates for the challenge of teaching.

CONCLUSION

Every teacher is on a journey and in order to effectively reach teachers in providing inclusive practices in their classrooms, we as educators, mentors, researchers, and scholars must meet them on their journey (Nishimura, 2012, p. 37).

Effective models of comprehensive, collaborative, job-embedded PD are emerging in the literature. Each of these holds promise for developing educator capacity in inclusive practice, but to bear fruit they seem to require the community to commit to equity and inclusion as a shared goal or outcome and with willingness to critically examine ways in which the system falls short of that goal. In other words, although each of the four PD models reviewed *can* support equity and inclusion, they don't always actually *do* so, and may at times even work against inclusive aims.

Meanwhile, every school and/or district is its own laboratory of innovation and application, mixing and matching PD models to fit local needs, with varying results. Far more research is needed to describe and evaluate flexible combinations and permutations of PD models, especially those that focus explicitly on equity and inclusion and remove barriers that impede learning and participation for all children and youth. This research must include attention to teacher beliefs and values about inclusion and diversity as well as the actual practices or models and outcome measures that seek impact on teacher thinking and action, student learning, and more global measures of educational equity.

It may be that action research on the ground will be the best source for schools to learn from and with each other in real time. Technology can easily support the development of networks of study groups, coaches, PLCs or PDSs across districts, states, and nations to amplify and share successful practices. Opportunities for research and inquiry partnerships between districts, with universities, or with research centers are everywhere but are too infrequently embraced.

Finally, the impact of the Every Student Succeeds Act (ESSA) on professional development for inclusive practices is unclear. With student performance targets moving to states, it is unclear if the attention to subgroup achievement required by No Child Left Behind will continue in ways will ensure a focus on these groups in PD models. Also unclear is how new teacher evaluation systems will be based on the learning of all students and how well ESSA funds will support professional development for culturally responsive pedagogies and inclusion. In addition, its support for alternative routes for state certification of teachers may simply increase the need for professional development on the job.

As the student demographics become more diverse, the need for effective professional development in inclusion and equity will continue to become more and more critical.

REFERENCES

Abbott, M., Walton, C., Tapia, Y., & Greenwood, C. R. (1999). Research to practice: A blueprint" for closing the gap in local schools. *Exceptional Children, 65*(3), 339–340.

Abdal-Haqq, I. (1996). *Making time for professional development. ERIC Digest (ED 400259)*. Washington, DC: ERIC Clearinghouse on Teaching and Teacher Education.

Achinstein, B. (2002). Conflict amid community: The micropolitics of teacher collaboration. *Teachers College Record, 104*(3), 421–455. doi:10.1111/1467-9620.00168

Alberta's Teacher Association. (2011). *Discussion paper on learning coaches – Support for the inclusive classroom*. Edmunton, AB: Author. Retrieved from http://www.teachers.ab.ca

Allen, D., Nichols, P., & Ancess, J. (2004). *Coaching as inquiry: Interpreting culture and leveraging change*. Paper presented at American Educational Research Association, San Diego, CA.

Annenberg Institute for School Reform. (2004). *Instructional coaching*. Providence, RI: Brown University.

Arbaugh, F. (2003). Study groups as a form of professional development for secondary mathematics teachers. *Journal of Mathematics Teacher Education*, 6(2), 139–163. doi:10.1023/A:1023928410992

Archibald, S., Coggshall, J. G., Croft, A., & Goe, L. (2011). *High-quality professional development for all teachers: Effectively allocating resources*. Washington, DC: National Comprehensive Center for Teacher Quality.

Aud, S., Fox, M., & KewalRamani, A. (2010). *Status and trends in the education of racial and ethnic groups* (NCES 2010-015). U.S. Department of Education, National Center for Education Statics.

Banks, J. A. (2004). Teaching for social justice, diversity, and citizenship in a global world. *The Educational Forum*, 68(4), 289–298. doi:10.1080/00131720408984645

Benedict, A. E., Park, Y., Brownell, M. T., Lauterbach, A. A., & Kiely, M. T. (2013). Using lesson study to align elementary literacy instruction within the RTI Framework. *Teaching Exceptional Children*, 45(5), 21–30. doi:10.1177/004005991304500503

Biancarosa, G., Bryk, A. S., & Dexter, E. R. (2010). Assessing the value-added effects of literacy collaborative professional development on student learning. *The Elementary School Journal*, 111(1), 7–34. doi:10.1086/653468

Blanchett, W. J., Klingner, J. K., & Harry, B. (2009). The intersections of culture, language and disability: Implications for urban education. *Urban Education*, 44(4), 389–409. doi:10.1177/0042085909338686

Blank, R. K., & de las Alas, N. (2008). *Current models for evaluating the effectiveness of teacher professional development. Recommendations to state leaders from leading experts*. Washington, DC: Council of Chief State School Officers.

Blanton, L. P., & Perez, Y. (2011). Exploring the relationship between special education teachers and professional learning communities: Implications of research for administrators. *Journal of Special Education Leadership*, 24(1), 6–16.

Borman, J., & Feger, S. (2006). *Instructional coaching: Key themes from the literature*. Providence, RI: The Education Alliance, Brown University.

Brenault, R. A., & Lack, B. (2009). Equity and empowerment in PDS work: A review of literature (19992006). *Equity & Excellence in Education*, 4(2), 152–168. doi:10.1080/10665680902758303

Brusca-Vega, R., Alexander, J., & Kambin, C. (2014). In support of access and inclusion: Joint professional development for science and special education. *Global Education Review*, 1(4), 37–52.

Byrd-Blake, M., & Hundley, E. (2012). Promoting teacher development in a racially/ethnically, socioeconomically, linguistically and academically diverse school: A US case study. *Professional Development in Education*, *38*(4), 551–570. doi:10.1080/19415257.2012.669392

Byrk, A. S. (2010). Organizing schools for improvement. *Phi Delta Kappan*, *91*(7), 23–30. doi:10.1177/003172171009100705

CaldicottH. (n.d.). *AZ quotes*. Retrieved from: http://www.azquotes.com/quote/541744

Campbell, P. F., & Malkus, N. N. (2013). Elementary mathematics specialists influencing student achievement. *Teaching Children Mathematics*, *20*(3), 198–205. doi:10.5951/teacchilmath.20.3.0198

Castle, S., Fox, R. K., & Souder, K. O. H. (2006). Do professional development schools (PDSs) make a difference? A comparative study of PDS and non-PDS teacher candidates. *Journal of Teacher Education*, *57*(1), 65–80. doi:10.1177/0022487105284211

Causton-Theoharis, J., Theoharis, G., Bull, T., Cosier, M., & Dempf-Aldreich, K. (2011). Schools of promise: A school district partnership centered on inclusive school reform. *Remedial and Special Education*, *32*(3), 192–205. doi:10.1177/0741932510366163

Chiariello, E. (2015, Fall). Two heads are better than one. *Teaching Tolerance*, *51*, 23–25.

Christensen, L., Epanchin, B., Harris, D., Roselli, H., Smith, R. L., & Stoddard, K. (1996). Anatomy of six public school-university partnerships. *Teacher Education and Special Education*, *19*(2), 169–179. doi:10.1177/088840649601900208

Cornett, K., & Knight, J. (2008). Research on coaching. In J. Knight (Ed.), *Coaching: Approaches and perspectives* (pp. 192–216). Thousand Oaks, CA: Corwin.

Costa, A. L., & Garmston, R. J. (2002). *Cognitive coaching: A foundation for renaissance schools*. Norwood, MA: Christopher-Gordon Publishers, Inc.

Cramer, G., Hurst, B., & Wilson, C. (1996). *Teacher study groups for professional development. Fastback*. Bloomington, IN: Phi Delta Kappa.

Croft, Coggshall, Dolan, Powers, & Killion. (2010). *Job-embedded professional development: What it is, who is responsible, and how to get it done well*. Issue Brief. Washington, DC: National Comprehensive Center for Teacher Quality.

Darling-Hammond, L. (1994). *Professional Development Schools: Schools for developing a profession*. New York: Teachers College Press.

Darling-Hammond, L. (2001, September 1). *Linda Darling-Hammond: Thoughts on teacher preparation*. Retrieved from https://www.edutopia.org/linda-darling-hammond-teacher-preparation

Darling-Hammond, L. (Ed.). (2005). *Professional development schools: Schools for developing a profession*. New York: Teacher's College Press.

Darling-Hammond, L., & McLaughlin, M. W. (2011). Policies that support professional development in an era of reform. *Phi Delta Kappan*, *92*(6), 81–92. doi:10.1177/003172171109200622

Darling-Hammond, L., & Richardson, N. (2009). Teacher learning: What matters? *Educational Leadership*, *66*(4), 46–53.

Darling-Hammond, L., Wei, R. C., Andree, A., Richardson, N., & Orphanos, S. (2009). Professional learning in the learning profession. A status report on teacher development in the United States and abroad. Oxford, OH: National Staff Development Council.

Darling-Hammond, L., Wei, R. C., & Adamson, F. (2010). *Professional learning in the United States: Trends and challenges. Part II of a three-phase study. Executive summary*. Oxford, OH: National Staff Development Council.

Denton, C. A., & Hasbrouck, J. (2009). A description of instructional coaching and its relationship to consultation. *Journal of Educational & Psychological Consultation*, *19*(2), 150–175. doi:10.1080/10474410802463296

Desimone, L. M. (2009). Improving impact studies of teachers' professional development: Toward better conceptualizations and measures. *Educational Researcher*, *38*(3), 181–199. doi:10.3102/0013189X08331140

Devine, M., Meyers, R., & Houssemand, C. (2013). How can coaching make a positive impact within educational settings? *Procedia: Social and Behavioral Sciences*, *93*, 1382–1389. doi:10.1016/j.sbspro.2013.10.048

Doig, B., & Groves, S. (2011). Japanese lesson study: Teacher professional development through communities of inquiry. *Mathematics Teacher Education and Development*, *13*(1), 77–93.

Duchaine, E. L., Jolivette, K., & Fredrick, L. D. (2011). The effect of teacher coaching with performance feedback on behavior-specific praise in inclusion classrooms. *Education & Treatment of Children*, *34*(2), 209–227. doi:10.1353/etc.2011.0009

Dufour, R., Dufour, R., Eaker, R., & Many, T. (2006). *Learning by doing: A handbook for professional learning communities at work*. Bloomington, IN: Solution Tree Press.

Dufour, R., & Eaker, R. (1998). *Professional learning communities at work: Best practices for enhancing student achievement*. Alexandra, VA: ASCD.

Dwyer, C. A. (2007). Introduction. In C. A. Dwyer (Ed.), *America's challenge: Effective teachers for at-risk schools and students*. Washington, DC: National Comprehensive Center for Teacher Quality. Retrieved from http://www.gtlcenter.org/tools-publications/publications

Easton, L. B. (2008). From professional development to professional learning. *Phi Delta Kappan*, *89*(10), 755–759. doi:10.1177/003172170808901014

Eick, C. J., & McCormick, T. M. (2009/10). Beginning to think critically about culturally responsive pedagogy in practice: An elementary education book study in student teaching. *SRATE Journal*, *19*(1), 52–60.

Elish-Piper, L., & LAllier, S. K. (2011). Examining the relationship between literacy coaching and student reading gains in grades K-3. *The Elementary School Journal*, *112*(1), 83–106. doi:10.1086/660685

Epanchin, B., & Colucci, K. (2002). The professional development school without walls: A partnership between a university and two school districts. *Remedial and Special Education, 23*(6), 349–358. doi:10.1177/074193250020230060501

Friedman, T. (2005). Developing a culture of inquiry for equity: One school's story. In L. Friedrich, C. Tateishi, T. Malarkey, E. R. Simons, & M. Williams (Eds.), *Working toward equity: Writings and resources from the Teacher Research Collaborative* (pp. 129–143). Berkeley, CA: National Writing Project.

Friedrich, L., Tateisi, C., Malarkey, T., Simons, E. R., & Williams, M. (2005). *Working toward equity: Writings and resources from the Teacher Research Collaborative.* Berkeley, CA: National Writing Project.

Fullan, M. (1993). *Change forces: Probing the depths of educational reform.* London: Falmer Press.

Fullan, M., & Hargreaves, A. (1992). *Teacher development and educational change.* London: Falmer Press.

Gersten, R., Dimino, J., Jayanthi, M., Kim, J. S., & Santoro, L. E. (2010). Teacher study group: Impact of professional development model on reading instruction and student outcomes in first grade classrooms. *American Educational Research Journal, 47*(3), 694–739. doi:10.3102/0002831209361208

Gersten, R., Dimino, J., Jayanthi, M., Newmann-Gonchar, R., & Taylor, M. J. (2013). *Impact of the teacher study group professional development program on student vocabulary and observed teaching practice: A replication in a first grade classroom.* Paper presented at The Society for Research on Educational Effectiveness Conference.

Goodlad, J. (1990). *Teachers for our nation's schools.* San Francisco, CA: Jossey-Bass.

Goodlad, J., & Oakes, J. (1988). We must offer equal access to knowledge. *Educational Leadership, 45*(5), 16–22.

Greenwood, C. R. (1999). Reflections on a research career: Perspective on 35 years of research at the Juniper Gardens Childrens Project. *Exceptional Children, 66*(1), 7–21. doi:10.1177/001440299906600101

Grossman, P., Wineburg, S., & Woolworth, S. (2001). Toward a theory of teacher community. *Teachers College Record, 103*(6), 942–1012. doi:10.1111/0161-4681.00140

Guerra, P. L., & Nelson, S. W. (2012). Culture's influence on behavior doesn't stop at the classroom door. *Journal of Staff Development, 33*(6), 65–66.

Guskey, T. R., & Yoon, K. S. (2009). What works in professional development? *Phi Delta Kappan, 90*(7), 495–500. doi:10.1177/003172170909000709

Hagger, H., & McIntyre, D. (2006). *Learning teaching from teachers: Realizing the potential of school-based teacher education.* Maidenhead: Open University Press.

Hall, R. V., Schiefelbusch, R. L., Hoyt, R. K. Jr, & Greenwood, C. R. (1989). History, mission, and organization of the Juniper Gardens Children's Project. *Education & Treatment of Children, 12*, 301–329.

Harris, D., & Evans, D. (1995). Restructuring for Inclusion. In J. L. Paul, H. Roselli, & D. Evans (Eds.), *Integrating school restructuring and special education reform* (pp. 322–334). Fort Worth, TX: Harcourt Brace College Publishers.

Hart, L. (2008/2009). A study of Japanese lesson study with third grade mathematics teachers in a small school district. *SRATE Journal, 17*(1), 32–43.

Herner-Patnode, L. (2009). Educator study groups: A professional development tool to enhance inclusion. *Intervention in School and Clinic, 45*(1), 24–30. doi:10.1177/1053451209338397

Herring, M., Curran, C., Stone, J., Davidson, N., Ahrabi-Farge, I., & Zhbanova, K. (2015). Emerging qualities of effective teaching: Embracing new literacies. *The Educational Forum, 79*(2), 163–179. doi:10.1080/00131725.2015.1006405

Hoffman, P., Dahlman, A., & Zierdt, G. (2009). Professional learning communities in partnership: A 3-year journey of action and advocacy to bridge the achievement gap. *School-University Partnerships, 3*(1), 28–42.

Holmes Group. (1986). *Tomorrow's teachers: A report of the Holmes Group*. East Lansing, MI: Holmes Group, Inc.

Holmes Group. (1990). *Tomorrow's schools: Principles for the design of professional development schools*. East Lansing, MI: Holmes Group, Inc.

Holmes Group. (1991). *Tomorrow's schools of education: A report of the Holmes Group*. East Lansing, MI: Holmes Group, Inc.

Hord, S. M. (1997). *Professional Learning Communities: Communities of continuous inquiry and improvement*. Austin, TX: Southwest Educational Development Laboratory.

Hord, S. M., & Sommers, W. A. (2008). *Leading professional learning communities: Voices from research and practice*. Thousand Oaks, CA: Corwin Press.

Howard, G. R. (2007). As diversity grows, so must we. *Educational Leadership, 64*(6), 16–22.

Hurd, J., & Licciardo-Musso, L. (2005). Lesson study: Teacher-led professional development in literacy instruction. *Language Arts, 82*(5), 388–395.

Jaquith, A., Mindich, D., Wei, R. C., & Darling-Hammond, L. (2010). *Teacher professional learning in the United States. Case studies of state policies and strategies*. Oxford, OH: Leaning Forward.

King-Sears, M. E. (1995). Teamwork toward inclusion: A school system and university partnership for practicing educators. *Action in Teacher Education, 17*(3), 54–66. doi:10.1080/01626620.1995.10463256

Klingner, J. K. (2004). The science of professional development. *Journal of Learning Disabilities, 37*(3), 248–255. doi:10.1177/00222194040370031001 PMID:15495665

Klingner, J. K., Ahwee, S., van Garderen, D., & Hernandez, C. (2004). Closing the gap: Enhancing student outcomes in an urban professional development school. *Teacher Education and Special Education, 27*(3), 292–306. doi:10.1177/088840640402700308

Klingner, J. K., Arguelles, M. E., Hughes, M. T., & Vaughn, S. (2001). Examining the school wide spread of research-based practices. *Learning Disability Quarterly, 24*(4), 221–225. doi:10.2307/1511112

Knight, J. (2007). *Instructional coaching: A partnership approach to improving instruction.* Thousand Oaks, CA: Corwin Press.

Kohler, F. W., Crilley, K. M., Shearer, D. D., & Good, G. (1997). Effects of peer coaching on teacher and student outcomes. *The Journal of Educational Research, 90*(4), 240–250. doi:10.1080/00220671.1997.10544578

Kretlow, A. G., Cooke, N. L., & Wood, C. L. (2012). Using in-service and coaching to increase teachers accurate use of research-based strategies. *Remedial and Special Education, 33*(6), 348–361. doi:10.1177/0741932510395397

Leko, M. M., & Roberts, C. A. (2014). How does professional development improve teacher practice in schools? In J. McLeskey, N. L. Waldron F. Spooner, & B. Algozzine (Eds.), Handbook of effective inclusive schools: Research and practice (pp. 43-54). New York: Routledge. doi:10.4324/9780203102930.ch4

Lewis, C., Perry, R., Foster, D., Hurd, J., & Fisher, L. (2011). Lesson study beyond coaching. *Educational Leadership, 69*(2), 64–68.

Lewis, C., Perry, R., Hurd, J., & OConnell, M. P. (2006). Lesson study comes of age in North America. *Phi Delta Kappan, 88*(4), 273–281. doi:10.1177/003172170608800406

Lieberman, A., & Mace, D. H. P. (2008). Teacher learning: The key to education reform. *Journal of Teacher Education, 49*(3), 226–234. doi:10.1177/0022487108317020

Little, J. W. (2006). *Professional community and professional development in the learning-centered school.* Washington, DC: National Education Association.

Lomos, C., Hofman, R. H., & Bosker, R. J. (2011). Professional communities and student achievement: A meta-analysis. *School Effectiveness and School Improvement, 22*(2), 121–148. doi:10.1080/09243453.2010.550467

Lopez-Real, F., & Kwan, T. (2005). Mentors perceptions of their own professional development during mentoring. *Journal of Education for Teaching, 31*(1), 15–24. doi:10.1080/02607470500043532

Lytle, S. L., & Cochran-Smith, M. (1992). Teacher research as a way of knowing. *Harvard Educational Review, 62*(4), 447–474. doi:10.17763/haer.62.4.4lm3811r1033431n

Maheady, L., Jabot, M., Rey, J., & Micheielli-Pendel, J. (2007). An early field-based experience and its impact on pre-service candidates teaching practice and their pupils outcomes. *Teacher Education and Special Education, 30*(1), 24–33. doi:10.1177/088840640703000103

Mangin, M. M., & Dunsmore, K. (2015). 1 How the framing of instructional coaching as a lever for systemic or individual reform influences the enactment of coaching. *Educational Administration Quarterly, 51*(2), 179–213. doi:10.1177/0013161X14522814

Many, T. W., & Schmidt, J. (2013). All together now: Special and regular educators prosper in PLCs. *Texas Elementary Principals and Supervisors Association News, 70*(2), 1–21.

Mariage, T. V., & Garmon, M. A. (2003). A case of educational change: Improving student achievement through a school university partnership. *Remedial and Special Education*, *24*(4), 215–234. doi:10.1177/074193250302400040501

McKamey, P. (2005). Building on success: Changing our practice to better serve African-American students. In L. Friedrich, C. Tateishi, T. Malarkey, E. R. Simons, & M. Williams (Eds.), *Working toward equity: Writings and resources from the Teacher Research Collaborative* (pp. 45–58). Berkeley, CA: National Writing Project.

Moran, M. C. (2007). *Differentiated literacy coaching: Scaffolding for student and teacher success*. Alexandria, VA: ASCD.

Murphy, C. (1992). study groups foster schoolwide learning. *Educational Leadership*, *50*(3), 71–74.

Murray, S., Ma, X., & Mazur, J. (2008). The effects of peer coaching on teachers collaborative interactions and students mathematics achievement. *The Journal of Educational Research*, *102*(3), 203–212. doi:10.3200/JOER.102.3.203-212

Mutch-Jones, K., Puttick, G., & Minner, D. (2012). Lesson study for accessible science: Building expertise to improve practice in inclusive science classrooms. *Journal of Research in Science Teaching*, *49*(8), 1012–1034. doi:10.1002/tea.21034

Naraian, S., & Oyler, C. (2014). Professional development for special education reform: Rearticulating experiences of urban special educators. *Urban Education*, *49*(5), 499–527. doi:10.1177/0042085913478623

Nehring, J. H., & OBrien, E. J. (2012). Strong agents and weak systems: University support for school level improvement. *Journal of Educational Change*, *13*(4), 449–485. doi:10.100710833-012-9187-0

Newmann, F. M., & ... (1996). *Authentic achievement: Restructuring schools for intellectual quality*. San Francisco: Jossey-Bass.

Nishimura, T. (2014). Effective professional development of teachers: A guide to actualizing inclusive schooling. *International Journal of Whole Schooling*, *10*(1), 19–42.

Nolan, J., Grove, D., Leftwich, H., Mark, K., & Peters, B. (2011). Impact on professional development. In J. E. Neopolitan (Ed.), *Taking stock of Professional Development Schools: What's needed now* (pp. 403–431). National Society for the Study of Education, Teachers College, Columbia University.

Norwich, B., Dudley, P., & Ylonen, A. (2014). Using lesson study to assess pupils learning difficulties. *International Journal for Lesson and Learning Studies*, *3*(2), 192–207. doi:10.1108/IJLLS-12-2013-0059

Organisation for Economic Co-operation and Development (OCED). (2009). *Creating effective teaching and learning environments: First results from TALIS. Executive summary*. Paris: Author. Retrieved from https://www.oecd.org/edu/school/43044074.pdf

Pancsofar, N., & Petroff, J. G. (2013). Professional development experiences in co-teaching: Associations with teacher confidence, interests, and attitudes. *Teacher Education and Special Education*, *36*(2), 83–96. doi:10.1177/0888406412474996

Penuel, W. R., Fishman, B. J., Yamaguchi, R., & Gallagher, L. P. (2007). What makes professional development effective? Strategies that foster curriculum implementation. *American Educational Research Journal, 44*(4), 921–958. doi:10.3102/0002831207308221

Poglinco & Bach. (2004). The heart of the matter: Coaching as a vehicle for professional development model. *Phi Delta Kappan, 85*(5), 398-402.

Prater, M. A., & Sileo, T. W. (2002). School university partnerships in special education field experiences: A national descriptive study. *Remedial and Special Education, 23*(6), 325–335. doi:10.1177/07419325020230060301

Randi, J., & Zeichner, K. M. (2004). New visions of teacher professional development. *Yearbook of the National Society for the Study of Education, 103*(1), 180–227. doi:10.1111/j.1744-7984.2004.tb00034.x

Reineke, W. M., Stormont, M., Hermann, K. C., & Newcomer, L. (2014). Using coaching to support teacher implementation of classroom-based interventions. *Journal of Behavioral Education, 23*(1), 150–167. doi:10.100710864-013-9186-0

Rice, E., Ihrig, K., Merves, E., & Brown, M. (2011). Preservice special educators: Graduate census results support PDS preparation. In J. Nath, I. Guadarrrama, & J. Ramsey (Eds.), Investigating University-school partnerships, (pp. 75-94). Information Age Publishing.

Robbins, P. (2015). *Peer coaching to enrich professional practice, school culture and student learning.* Alexandria, VA: ASCD.

Rock, T. C., & Wilson, C. (2005). Improving teaching through lesson study. *Teacher Education Quarterly, 32*(1), 77–92.

Rosselli, H., Perez, S., & Claggett, K. (1995). Becoming a teacher for all children in a professional development school. In J. L. Paul, H. Roselli, & D. Evans (Eds.), *Integrating school restructuring and special education reform* (pp. 335–352). Fort Worth, TX: Harcourt Brace College Publishers.

Royster, O., Reglin, G. L., & Losike-Sedimo, N. (2014). Inclusion professional development model and regular middle school educators. *Journal of At-Risk Issues, 18*(1), 1–10.

Rubin, B. C. (2006). Tracking and detracking: Debates, evidence and best practices for a heterogeneous world. *Theory into Practice, 45*(1), 4–14. doi:10.120715430421tip4501_2

Schlessinger, S., & Oyler, C. (2015). Inquiry based teacher learning for inclusivity: Professional development for action and change. *Learning Landscapes, 8*(2), 39–47.

Senge, P. M. (1990). *The fifth discipline: The art and practice of the learning organization.* New York: Doubleday/Currency.

Senge, P. M. (2000). *Schools that learn: A fifth discipline fieldbook for educators, parents, and everyone who cares about education.* New York: Doubleday.

Shady, S. A., Luther, V. L., & Richman, L. J. (2013). Teaching the teachers: A study of perceived professional development needs of educators to enhance positive attitudes toward inclusive practice. *Education Research and Perspectives, 40*, 169–191.

Showers, B. (1985). Teachers coaching teachers. *Educational Leadership*, *42*(7), 43–48.

Showers, B., & Joyce, B. R. (1996). The evolution of peer coaching. *Educational Leadership*, *53*(6), 12–17.

Shulman, L. S. (2005). Signature pedagogies in the professions. *Daedaulus*, *134*(3), 52–59. doi:10.1162/0011526054622015

Slavin, R. (1995). Detracking and its detractors: Flawed evidence, flawed values. *Phi Delta Kappan*, *77*, 220–221.

Stanley, A. M. (2011). Professional development within collaborative teacher study groups: Pitfalls and promises. *Arts Education Policy Review*, *112*(2), 71–78. doi:10.1080/10632913.2011.546692

Steiner, L. (2004). *Designing effective professional development experiences: What do we know?* (2nd ed.). Naperville, IL: Learning Point Associates.

Steiner, L., & Kowal, J. (2007, September). *Principal as instructional leader: Designing a coaching program that fits.* Naperville, IL: Learning Point Associates. The Center for Comprehensive School Reform and Improvement.

Stemmel, A. J. (2007). The value of teacher research: Nurturing professional and personal growth through inquiry. *Voices of Practitioners*, *2*(3), 1–9.

Stoddard, K., & Danforth, S. (1995). Empowering teachers to be responsive to individual differences. In J. L. Paul, H. Roselli, & D. Evans (Eds.), *Integrating school restructuring and special education reform* (pp. 322–334). Fort Worth, TX: Harcourt Brace College Publishers.

Takahashi, A., & Yoshida, M. (2004). Ideas for establishing lesson-study communities. *Teaching Children Mathematics*, *10*(9), 436–443.

Teemant, A., Wink, J., & Tyra, S. (2011). Effects of coaching on teacher use of sociocultural instructional practices. *Teaching and Teacher Education*, *27*(4), 683–693. doi:10.1016/j.tate.2010.11.006

Teitel, L. (2003). *The professional development schools handbook: Starting, sustaining, and assessing partnerships that improve student learning.* Thousand Oaks, CA: Corwin Press.

Tichenor, M. S., & Heins, E. (2000). Study groups: An inquiry-based approach to improving schools. *The Clearing House: A Journal of Educational Strategies, Issues and Ideas*, *73*(6), 316–319. doi:10.1080/00098650009599434

Tschannen-Moran, M., & McMaster, P. (2009). Sources of self-efficacy: Four professional development formats and their relationship to self-efficacy and implementation of a new teaching strategy. *The Elementary School Journal*, *110*(2), 228–245. doi:10.1086/605771

UNESCO. (2014). *Teaching and learning: Achieving quality for all.* Education for All Global Monitoring Report 2013/14. Retrieved from https://www.oecd.org/edu/school/43044074.pdf

Valli, L., Cooper, D., & Frankes, L. (1997). Professional development schools and equity: A critical analysis of rhetoric and research. In M. W. Apple (Ed.), *Review of research in education* (pp. 251–304). Washington, DC: American Educational Research Association. doi:10.2307/1167377

Vaughn, M. (2016). Re-envisioning literacy in a teacher inquiry group in a Native American context. *Literacy Research and Instruction*, *55*(1), 24–47. doi:10.1080/19388071.2015.1105888

Vescio, V., Ross, D., & Adams, A. (2008). A review of research on the impact of professional learning communities on teaching practice and student learning. *Teaching and Teacher Education*, *24*(1), 80–91. doi:10.1016/j.tate.2007.01.004

Waitoller, F. R., & Artiles, A. (2013). A decade of professional development research for inclusive education: A critical review and notes for a research program. *Review of Educational Research*, *83*(3), 319–356. doi:10.3102/0034654313483905

Wenger, E. (1998). *Communities of practice: Learning, meaning, and identity*. Cambridge, UK: Cambridge University Press. doi:10.1017/CBO9780511803932

West, L., & Cameron, A. (2013). *Agents of change: How content coaching transforms teaching and learning*. Portsmouth, NH: Heinemann.

Wlodarczyk, K., Somma, M., Bennett, S., & Gallagher, T. L. (2015). Moving toward inclusion: Inclusion coaches' reflections and discussions in supporting educators in practice. *Exceptionality Education International*, *25*, 55–73.

Wong, P. L., & Glass, R. D. (2011). Professional development schools and student learning and achievement. In J. E. Neopolitan (Ed.), *Taking stock of Professional Development Schools: What's needed now* (pp. 403–431). National Society for the Study of Education, Teachers College, Columbia University.

Ylonen, A., & Norwich, B. (2012). Using Lesson Study to develop teaching approaches for secondary school pupils with moderate learning difficulties: Teachers concepts, attitudes and pedagogic strategies. *European Journal of Special Needs Education*, *27*(3), 301–317. doi:10.1080/08856257.2012.678664

Yssel, N., Koch, K., & Merbler, J. B. (2002). Professional development schools and special education: A promising partnership? *Teacher Educator*, *38*(2), 14. doi:10.1080/08878730209555313

This research was previously published in the Handbook of Research on Classroom Diversity and Inclusive Education Practice edited by Christina M. Curran and Amy J. Petersen; pages 120-153, copyright year 2017 by Information Science Reference (an imprint of IGI Global).

Chapter 46
Supporting Secondary Students with Disabilities in an Inclusive Environment

Pam Epler
Grand Canyon University, USA

ABSTRACT

This chapter is designed to inform and educate secondary (Grades 6–12) pre-service teachers on how to provide content and design assignments for students within the special education continuum. The chapter is divided into 12 sections, one for each IDEA disability category. Each section includes the definition and characteristics of the specific category as well as how it impacts learning. The prevalence of the exceptionality occurring in the secondary classroom is also discussed, thus informing pre-service teacher candidates about which disability categories they are most likely to encounter while teaching. Also included in each section is a discussion and examples of various research-based instructional strategies and assignments as well as resources such as websites or illustrations that can be utilized.

INTRODUCTION

With the introduction of the No Child Left Behind Act and the requirement that all students, regardless of ability, must be taught using the state's curriculum, more and more students with exceptionalities are being placed in the general education classroom, and all teachers, pre-service through veterans, must educate them. For this reason, it is essential that the secondary pre-service teacher be knowledgeable about the different categories of disabilities listed in the Individuals with Disabilities Education Improvement Act (IDEA, 2004) and understand how to develop their instruction and assignments to properly educate students in their classrooms who fall into one or more of the categories. Secondary students with a disability come in all shapes and sizes and have a variety of needs. This chapter will assist the pre-service teacher in being prepared to provide the very best educational experience for these students.

The following main sections of this chapter focus on the 12 IDEA disability categories. Each section includes the definition and characteristics of a specific category as well as how it impacts learning. The

DOI: 10.4018/978-1-7998-1213-5.ch046

prevalence of the exceptionality occurring in the secondary classroom is also discussed so that pre-service teachers will know which disability categories they are most likely to encounter while teaching. Also included in each section is a discussion and examples of various research-based instructional strategies and assignments as well as resources such as websites or illustrations that can be utilized.

AUTISM SPECTRUM DISORDER (ASD)

Definition

ASD is "a developmental disability significantly affecting verbal and nonverbal communication and social interaction, generally evident before age three, that adversely affects educational performance. Characteristics often associated with autism are engaging in repetitive activities and stereotyped movements, resistance to changes in daily routines or the environment, and unusual responses to sensory experiences" (34 IDEA §300.8 [c] [1], 2004).

Prevalence

Approximately 7% of children receiving special education services are receiving services for autism (Kena et al., 2014). This exceptionality is considered a high-risk disability, meaning a secondary teacher will probably see this type of disability in his or her classroom.

ASD covers a spectrum of disorders. Of these disorders, probably the most prevalent, and the one that will most likely be encountered in the general education classroom, is Asperger's Syndrome. Students with Asperger's tend to have very high IQs and can verbalize. An example of this type of student is the character Dustin Hoffman played in the movie *Rain Man*.

Characteristics

Students who qualify for special educational services under ASD typically have difficulties with social skills, engage in repetitive behaviors, and have communication difficulties. The term "spectrum" is used with this type of disability because it embraces a wide range of students, from students who may be high functioning and will probably be in an inclusive general education classroom to students with severe needs who are non-communicative and engage in repetitive behavior like flapping their hands in front of their face. Teachers will more likely see the former in the classroom as opposed to the latter because severe-needs students require a specialized, trained teacher (Autism Speaks, 2015).

Social Ineptness

Social skills that most people take for granted are a challenge for students with ASD. Something as simple as the general education teacher smiling at the student with ASD can be bewildering because of his or her inability to comprehend facial expressions. Students with ASD may also respond inappropriately to gestures such as extending a hand for a handshake because these students have difficulties understanding and predicting other people's actions (Autism Speaks, 2015). ASD students like routine and predictable situations. If they are taken outside their comfort zone, they may become disruptive and physically aggressive (Autism Speaks, 2015). These students typically are unable to maintain eye contact and often invade the personal space of others with whom they are "interacting."

Communication Difficulties

As mentioned previously, ASD covers a large spectrum. A student with ASD who has communication difficulties will use either sign language or some type of electronic device that speaks for the student (Autism Speaks, 2015). The teacher needs to speak and interact with this student just like he or she would with any other student but must give the student additional time to respond.

An ASD student on the high-functioning side of the spectrum may have no difficulties with communication and may even use vocabulary similar to a well-educated college professor. These students may also simply talk continuously since they have little understanding about the rules of conversation (e.g., one person speaks while the other listens, and then the roles are reversed; Autism Speaks, 2015).

Students with ASD are very literal and take a teacher's words to heart. For example, if a teacher sees an ASD student in the hallway after the tardy bell rings and asks them what they are doing, the ASD student may state something like, "I'm walking to class," as opposed to answering the intent of the question, which is "Why aren't you already in class?" The important thing to remember when working with ASD students is to be literal when asking questions in order to derive the information needed. This will save the teacher and the student time and frustration. These students do not do well with sarcasm, so it should be avoided. "That's just wonderful" stated in a sarcastic voice for ASD students means that something great or fantastic is happening; they will not interpret it as a sign of frustration.

Repetitive Behaviors

Some students with ASD display repetitive behaviors such as flapping their hands, repeating sounds or words, aligning objects in a specific manner, or following a very specific daily routine. Teachers with an ASD student who does the latter should allow them this courtesy. If not, the student may experience extreme stress that could lead to verbal or physical outbursts (Autism Speaks, 2015).

Impact on Learning

A secondary educational learning environment can be a challenge for any student, but it is especially difficult for a student who has a diagnosis of ASD for several reasons. First, there are at least five different teachers with many different personalities to learn and understand, plus all the rules and regulations that come with each classroom. In addition, these students tend to be disorganized and struggle with multiple-step directions, so it is important that teachers make all directives short and simple. Furthermore, ASD students crave consistency and routine, so if for any reason the daily class routine is going to change or be disrupted (e.g., a monthly fire drill), the teacher should let the ASD student know ahead of time. Also, sometimes students with ASD will fixate on a specific topic, which can be a challenge for teachers since they must cover a certain amount of information in each lesson. In order to counteract this fixation, teachers should highlight or isolate the key points of what will be taught during that lesson so that the ASD student will focus on those points and nothing else. By doing this, teachers will be able to teach the intended lesson for that class (Autism Speaks, 2015).

Supporting Secondary Students with Disabilities in an Inclusive Environment

Instructional Strategies

Secondary students with a diagnosis of ASD need to be taught the same concept several different times using different instructional strategies in order to grasp and understand the content being taught (Project IDEAL, 2013a). These students are typically visual learners, so every lesson must contain visual cues of some nature. For example, if in a social studies class the teacher is explaining a battle, he or she should also show a video of it so the ASD student can associate what the teacher is saying with what he or she is seeing. It should be noted here that some students with ASD are sensitive to loud noises (Autism Speaks, 2015). Hence, prior to showing the video, it would be a good idea to speak with the ASD student's parents and explain the activity. The decision on whether or not to show the video should be based on the parents' response.

In addition, these students need to be able to prepare for any changes in the classroom routine, so informing them 5 minutes before class will end or that a visitor will be in the classroom will give them great emotional support (Project IDEAL, 2013a).

Finally, forging relationships with parents of secondary students can sometimes be a challenge, but for students with ASD, this connection is critical for the student to be successful at school. Students with ASD may need additional practice at home in order to learn the concepts taught at school, and this is where parents can assist the teacher. Constant communication with the parents is essential in order for the ASD student to succeed academically and socially. One way to do this is to establish a website that parents can access to get assignment directions, resources (e.g., Khan Academy), and examples.

Blended learning is another great tool to provide both visual and auditory instructional support for students with ASD. Since these students struggle with communication, especially within a large group setting like a general education classroom, the digital/online platforms utilized in blended learning may provide a better way for them to express themselves (Tucker, 2013).

Assignments

Students with ASD need clear and explicit instruction when completing classroom or homework assignments (Project IDEAL, 2013a). The teacher needs to be aware that this student has difficulties making generalizations; hence, the student may only be able to give facts on a topic and may not be able to go more in depth. Thus, assignments that ask the student to compare and contrast topics may be a challenge for the ASD student.

Since ASD students are typically focused on one topic or concept, teachers should use this to their advantage and develop homework and classroom assignments around it (Project IDEAL, 2013a). When the teacher sees that the ASD student is struggling to understand an assignment, he or she should provide direct instruction to assist the student in comprehending the task.

Resources

1. Teacher's guide for developing well-structured, predictable classrooms and schedules: http://csesa.fpg.unc.edu/sites/csesa.fpg.unc.edu/files/UnderstandingAutismSecondaryTeachersGuide.pdf
2. Teaching tips: http://www.iidc.indiana.edu/pages/Tips-for-Teaching-High-Functioning-People-with-Autism

3. Teaching strategies (although this website is devoted specifically to science teachers, the teaching strategies can be used in any content area): http://www.nsta.org/disabilities/autism.aspx
4. General information. https://www.naset.org/autism2.0.html
5. Characteristics and strategies: Deaf-Blindness (DB)

Definition

DB is "concomitant [simultaneous] hearing and visual impairments, the combination of which causes such severe communication and other developmental and educational needs that they cannot be accommodated in special education programs solely for children with deafness or children with blindness" (34 IDEA §300.8 [c] [2], 2004).

Prevalence

Approximately <1% of children receiving special education services receive services for deaf-blindness (Kena et al., 2014). This exceptionality is considered a low-risk disability, meaning a secondary teacher will probably not see this type of disability in his or her classroom.

Characteristics

Like many of the IDEA disability categories, there is a range of deaf-blindness. Some of these students do have some vision or hearing and, as such, can "move about in their environments, recognize familiar people, see sign language at close distances, and perhaps read large print. Others have sufficient hearing to recognize familiar sounds, understand some speech, or develop speech themselves" (National Center on Deaf-Blindness, 2008, p. 1934). However, other students are totally deaf and blind and cannot hear or see anything. Helen Keller serves as an example of this type of student (for more information about Helen Keller, see http://www.afb.org/info/about-us/helen-keller/biography-and-chronology/biography/1235). These students' concepts of the world "depend upon what or whom they have had the opportunity to physically contact" (National Center on Deaf-Blindness, 2008, p. 1934).

Impact on Learning

Eighty percent of what one learns in school and in the world is through vision, although one communicates via hearing and speaking. Students with an IDEA diagnosis of deaf-blindness need to obtain their information about school and the world through "movement and motor development, cognitive development and the ability to learn, and through social and emotional development" (National Center on Deaf-Blindness, 2008, p. 1934).

Students who are deaf-blind may exhibit inappropriate behavioral and emotional difficulties due to their inability to comprehend and interact with the world around them (National Center on Deaf-Blindness, 2008). They may also have difficulties with movement, motor development, body image, and self-concept (Project IDEAL, 2013b).

Teachers who have a deaf-blind student in the classroom will need to communicate with the student through an interpreter or through one of the following communication devices: touch cues, gestures, symbols (either pictures or objects), sign language or finger spelling, braille writing and reading, large print reading and writing, or lip reading (National Center on Deaf-Blindness, 2008).

If these students are going to be able to live independently, they must have a sound educational background and good communication skills. In order to make this happen, teachers must be conscientious to include these students in the classroom activities.

Instructional Strategies

There are several instructional strategies a teacher can employ if he or she has a deaf-blind student in the classroom. The teacher should:

1. Pause after each concept is taught in order to allow for response time.
2. Name the object that the student is touching and be sure to repeat the word numerous times until the student has understood the concept.
3. Follow a consistent routine daily to ease the stress and anxiety associated with limited sensory information.
4. Ensure that communication with the student is meaningful and allow the student to feel control over the lesson.

Also, there are numerous technological devices, such as a braille reader and translator, that a deaf-blind student can use in order to enhance his or her educational experience (National Center on Deaf-Blindness, 2008).

Assignments

When working with a student with DB, teachers should be aware of the student's strengths. If the student has some residual hearing or sight, the teacher should use that mode to educate the child. If the student has some vision, the teacher should make the print on the classroom or homework assignment bigger or use colored paper to make the font stand out. If the student has some hearing, the teacher should have the student use a book on tape to do the reading assignment. The following two websites provide books for people who have vision difficulties:

1. The National Library Service for the Blind and Physically Handicapped (http://www.loc.gov/nls/), and
2. The American Association for the Blind Talking Books (http://www.afb.org/info/living-with-vision-loss/using-technology/reading-and-writing/talking-books-933/1235).

Simply because a student may have limited or no vision does not mean that he or she should be ignored during classroom activities. The teacher must remember to include the deaf-blind student in every part of the classroom activities.

Resources

1. Considerations when teaching students who are deaf-blind:
2. Tactile learning strategies for children who are deaf-blind:

3. Teaching strategies and more:
4. General information. https://nationaldb.org/library/list/43

DEAFNESS (D) AND HEARING IMPAIRMENT (HI)

Definition (D)

Deafness is "a hearing impairment so severe that a child is impaired in processing linguistic information through hearing, with or without amplification, and that adversely affects a child's educational performance" (IDEA §300.8 [3], 2004).

Definition (HI)

A hearing impairment is "an impairment in hearing, whether permanent or fluctuating, that adversely affects a child's educational performance but is not included under the definition of 'deafness'" (34 IDEA §300.8 [c] [5], 2004).

Prevalence

Approximately 1% of children receiving special education services receive services for speech and language disorders (Kena et al., 2014). This exceptionality is considered a low-risk disability, meaning a secondary teacher will probably not see this type of disability in his or her classroom.

Characteristics

Like the previously mentioned IDEA categories, there is a range within these two categories: "Deafness may be viewed as a condition that prevents an individual from receiving sound in all or most of its forms. In contrast, a child with hearing loss can generally respond to auditory stimuli, including speech" (Project IDEAL, 2013d, para. 2–3). Within these two categories, there are three subcategories of deafness/hearing impairment. The first is conductive hearing loss, wherein the person has been born without an ear or has lost an ear in an accident. This condition can be fixed medically and probably will not affect the person's language. The second type is a sensorineural hearing loss and involves the inner ear. This type of hearing loss will probably affect the person's language development. Last, a central hearing disorder affects the auditory nerve; hence, sound cannot get to the brain, rendering the person with no hearing at all, which will definitely affect language development. The teacher should be aware of the type of hearing loss a student has so that proper instructional strategies are used.

Impact on Learning

The severity of the hearing loss will determine the impact of the student's learning and academic achievement. Since hearing and speaking is the main way that people communicate with one another, students with a hearing loss or deafness may be impacted socially and emotionally because they may communicate differently than their grade- or age-level peers and thus feel isolated and lack friends, especially in a secondary educational arena.

These students typically have average to above-average intelligence but may struggle with speech, both written (e.g., grammar, word order, vocabulary, and idioms) and oral due to their inability to hear sounds and the spoken word. They may also struggle in reading. Educational environments where classes are taught primarily using the spoken or written word are not the ideal learning environment for a hearing impaired or deaf child (Project IDEAL, 2013d). Teachers providing visual clues and literally facing the student when speaking can greatly enhance these students' chances of academic success.

Instructional Strategies

A teacher can employ several strategies to enhance the chances of success in a general education classroom for the student who has a hearing loss or is deaf. The teacher should:

1. Provide visual clues and literally face the student when speaking.
2. Utilize the school's amplification system (if it has one). The student's hearing aid can be connected into the system, and with the amplification, the student can hear what the teacher is saying.
3. Show films or videos that have closed captioning (words scrolling on the bottom of the screen) so the student can read what is happening in the movie.
4. Learn some sign language or finger spelling to communicate with the student.
5. Remember to not shout at the student but talk normally both in pitch and pace. This will help the student who reads lips understand what the teacher is trying to say.

Assignments

When a teacher is getting ready to assign classroom work or homework assignments, certain things must be kept in mind. First, the teacher should provide the HI or D student with a written form of the assignment/homework, goals, and directions, making sure all written instructions for completing the task are written simply. Second, if going over an assignment, the teacher should make sure the answers are not only spoken aloud but also written on the whiteboard for the D or HI student to see. Next, when speaking to the D or HI student, the teacher should keep sentences short and simple and avoid the use of idioms. Finally, the teacher should write instructions based on the D or HI student's reading ability level and not on the grade level being taught. For example, if the D or HI student is in 10th grade but reads on a fifth-grade level, the instructions should be written on a fifth-grade level. The teacher may want to seek assistance from the special education teacher with this task (Project IDEAL, 2013d).

Resources

1. Tips for teaching students who are deaf and hard of hearing:
2. Guidelines for working with students who are deaf or hearing impaired: http://www.doe.virginia.gov/special_ed/disabilities/sensory_disabilities/hearing_impairment/guidelines_working_with_deaf.pdf
3. Teaching strategies (although this website is devoted specifically to science teachers, the teaching strategies can be used in any content area): http://www.nsta.org/disabilities/hearing.aspx

4. General information on hearing impairment: https://www.naset.org/hearingimpairments2.0.html
5. General information on deafness: Emotional Disturbance (ED)

Definition

ED is "a condition exhibiting one or more of the following characteristics over a long period of time and to a marked degree that adversely affects a child's educational performance:

1. An inability to learn that cannot be explained by intellectual, sensory, or health factors.
2. An inability to build or maintain satisfactory interpersonal relationships with peers and teachers.
3. Inappropriate types of behavior or feelings under normal circumstances.
4. A general pervasive mood of unhappiness or depression.
5. A tendency to develop physical symptoms or fears associated with personal or school problems.
6. Schizophrenia" (34 IDEA §300.8 [c] [4], 2004).

Prevalence

Approximately 6% of children receiving special education services are receiving services for an ED (Kena et al., 2014). This exceptionality is considered a high-risk disability, meaning a secondary teacher will probably see this type of disability in his or her classroom.

Characteristics

Like the aforementioned disabilities, students who have an IDEA diagnosis of ED have a wide range of characteristics that include but are not limited to long-term unhappiness, depression, behavioral issues, and physical aggression. Teachers will find students in this category typically have normal intelligence; however, their behavior gets in the way of their academic success. They may also have expressive (talking) and receptive (listening) language disorders that make comprehending and communicating with others a challenge. Students with an ED also have trust issues, so it is essential that the teacher build mutual trust with these students. When this is accomplished, the teacher may find that behavioral issues decrease because the student has found someone who shows him or her empathy.

Impact on Learning

Although some students with an ED have average or above-average intelligence, others struggle in specific academic areas like math and spelling. Students with an ED diagnosis must have some type of behavioral support plan that all faculty and staff in the school follow in order for the student to be successful. The teacher should check with the special education teacher to see what plan is in place and how to implement it in the classroom. Consistency is essential when working with this type of student.

It is important for the teacher to understand which triggers may cause a student with ED to have a behavioral meltdown or act inappropriately, as well as to recognize that these triggers can result from a wide range of things, from being abused to heredity (Project IDEAL, 2013c). Some triggers can be assessed by watching the student and his/her interactions with peers and the environment, but a quicker way to discover this information would be by speaking directly with the student, talking to the student's parents, or reading the student's school file. Once the triggers are known, they should be avoided if possible.

Instructional Strategies

A simple instructional strategy that the teacher can use when working with the ED student is to allow the student to choose between doing two things. Giving these students a choice allows them to be responsible for their own learning. In addition, the teacher should provide the student with ED the option to work with a peer or small group if he or she desires. If the student does not have the social skills to work cohesively in a group, then those skills will need to be taught (Henley & Long, 2003).

Another strategy is to chunk the information that the student is expected to learn. Instead of providing the entire section of a history lesson to the student, the teacher should give him or her only half or perhaps even a third of the lesson to learn. Over time, hopefully the student can learn more material, but in the beginning, it is better to start out small and increase slowly. This way the student will feel successful in his or her schoolwork. Also, making the lesson relevant to the learner's own life will assist with increasing the ED student's academic success (Henley & Long, 2003).

A third strategy is to give the student frequent breaks. On the secondary level, students are expected to learn a lot of facts and content. For the ED student, this may feel overwhelming, so giving him or her frequent breaks to relax prior to learning more information assists in lowering the stress of having to learn a lot at one time (Henley & Long, 2003).

Last, the teacher must be willing and able to provide positive affirmations to the student with an ED. The teacher should be sincere in his or her praise and give it often. The teacher should not wait until the student with an ED does something amazing; instead, praise all the small successes along the way.

Assignments

Teachers who have a student with an ED in their classroom need to remember that typically these students can work on their grade level in regards to reading, writing, and mathematics. There are, however, some guidelines that need to be followed when working with ED students. The teacher should:

1. Only have a few (three to five) simple classroom rules to follow (e.g., be respectful of others, raise your hand before speaking, and be on time to class).
2. Make sure learning activities are simple and do not include complicated directions. If the task is multiple-stepped, break it down into smaller sections for the student with an ED.
3. Provide positive affirmations and encouragement when the student is demonstrating good behavior, and when not, reprimand quietly and with respect. Work with either the behaviorist specialist or the special education teacher to learn the student behavioral plan.
4. Provide the student with short breaks and additional time to complete any class work or homework assignments. This student may also simply need a few minutes to place his or her head on the desk or even remove him or herself from the classroom to avoid feeling overwhelmed.
5. Treat all students in the classroom in the same manner. If a student with the ED breaks a rule, he or she needs to suffer the same consequence as the student without a disability (Concordia Online Education, 2015).

Resources

1. Teaching strategies (although this website is devoted specifically to science teachers, the teaching strategies can be used in any content area): http://www.nsta.org/disabilities/behavioral.aspx
2. Teaching tips: http://www.myschoolpsychology.com/wp-content/uploads/2014/02/nichcy.org-Teaching_Students_with_Emotional_Disturbances_8_Tips_for_Teachers.pdf
3. Best practices: http://schools.nyc.gov/NR/rdonlyres/6AA00136-AE40-4976-947C-CF10EB-3D5C20/0/InterventionGuide.pdf
4. Characteristics and strategies:
5. Case study:
6. General information. https://www.naset.org/emotionaldisturbance2.0.html

INTELLECTUAL DISABILITY (ID)

Definition

ID is defined as "significantly sub-average general intellectual functioning, existing concurrently [at the same time] with deficits in adaptive behavior and manifested during the developmental period, that adversely affects a child's educational performance" (34 IDEA §300.8 [c] [6], 2004).

Prevalence

Approximately 7% of children receiving special education services receive services for intellectual disabilities (Kena et al., 2014). This exceptionality is considered a high-risk disability, meaning a secondary teacher will probably see this type of disability in his or her classroom.

If the teacher does have a student with an ID in his or her classroom, this student will likely have Down syndrome (for more information, see the National Down Syndrome Society: www.ndss.org/).

Characteristics

A student with an ID has deficits in two areas—cognitive functioning (the ability to learn) and adaptive functioning (ability to survive in the world). These students have an IQ less than 70 (average IQ is between 90–120). They also will have problems with memory recall, task and skill generalization, "[and have] a tendency towards low motivation and learned helplessness" (Project IDEAL, 2013e, para. 5). Finally, they will have difficulties in "choice making, problem solving, and goal setting, as well as conceptual, social and practical skills" (Project IDEAL, 2013e, para. 5).

Impact on Learning

Students with a diagnosis of an ID must have the general education curriculum modified and adapted to meet their individual needs. For example, in the secondary educational environment, the ID student's peers may be working on Algebra II while the ID student is learning how to make change for a dollar in the same room. Often, because these students are significantly behind their grade-level peers both

Supporting Secondary Students with Disabilities in an Inclusive Environment

academically and socially, they are educated by a special education teacher trained in working with this population. Occasionally, the ID student will go into the general education classroom with an aide or paraprofessional for socialization in order to assist with developing appropriate social skills. According to Vaughn, Shay Schumm, and Forgan (1998), "Social benefits from full inclusion for students with disabilities are sufficient reason to place students in the general education classroom, even if academically they are working substantially below the level of the other students" (p. 5).

Instructional Strategies

If a student with an ID is placed in the general education classroom, the teacher can use some or all of the following strategies:

1. Divide the task or concept to be learned into very small steps or ideas, and teach each step or concept repeatedly until the student has mastered it (usually 8–10 times or about 80% of the time is a good measure of mastery).
2. Teach the concept in a one-on-one setting or in a very small group, perhaps no more than three students.
3. Once a skill is introduced, provide the student with many different opportunities to practice it.
4. Provide positive affirmations to the student. Giving praise for completing a small task goes a long way with this student (Project IDEAL, 2013e).
5. Use manipulatives. These students learn very well if they can see and touch the concept they are learning. For example, when doing a math problem, have the student use a calculator or watch a video related to the math lesson.
6. Since the student with an ID is using an adaptive curriculum that is very different from his or her grade-level peers, find out what interests the student and build the lesson around that topic. Please note that although the student with an ID may be interested in juvenile things due to the lower IQ, the materials used in the secondary classroom need to be age appropriate. If a student is interested in cooking, he or she should not be watching something on Sesame Street about the Swedish Chef; perhaps the Master Chef Junior would be more appropriate. Questions about the appropriateness of materials can be directed to the special education teacher.

Assignments

As with any student, the teacher should find out what motivates and interests the student with an ID and use that to teach him or her. In addition, the teacher should be sure that all classroom and homework assignments are broken into small tasks or steps, and after each is completed, should provide verbal praise for a job well done. Last, the teacher should both explain orally and provide a visual representation of the assignment that the student is to complete (Center for Parent Information and Resources, 2015). This way the student can see and hear what is expected of him or her.

Resources

1. Teaching strategies (although this website is devoted specifically to science teachers, the teaching strategies can be used in any content area): http://www.nsta.org/disabilities/intellectual.aspx

2. Teaching tips:
3. Characteristics and strategies:
4. General information. https://www.naset.org/mentalretardation2.0.html

MULTIPLE DISABILITIES (MD)

Definition

MD is defined as "concomitant [simultaneous] impairments (such as ID-blindness, ID-orthopedic impairment, etc.), the combination of which causes such severe educational needs that they cannot be accommodated in a special education program solely for one of the impairments. The term does not include deaf-blindness" (34 IDEA §300.8 [c] [7], 2004).

Prevalence

Approximately 2% of children receiving special education services receive services for multiple disabilities (Kena et al., 2014). This exceptionality is considered a low-risk disability, meaning a secondary teacher will probably not see this type of disability in his or her classroom.

Characteristics

Students with MD typically have average intelligence but need extensive assistance across multiple areas. This disability is such that the ability to learn and achieve in an academic setting must be done in a specialized educational environment. Students with more than one type of disability are placed in this category, as well as students with severe disabilities (below 50 IQ).

Students with MD are typically deficit in five areas of development: (a) intellectual functioning (typically functioning on a pre-school to early elementary level even as adults); (b) adaptive skills (some can take care of their own personal needs, and others will need full-time assistance); (c) motor skills (due to poor muscle tone, many need physical and/or occupational therapy); (d) sensory functioning (e.g., a student who is blind and has cerebral palsy); and (e) communication skills (some may use a communication device or use sign language).

Impact on Learning

Like their ID counterparts, students with MD need to have an adaptive general education curriculum and should learn self-help skills. These students may also need additional services like physical therapy (PT), occupational therapy (OT), and speech services. If these are necessary, the teacher should always inquire if there is anything in the general education classroom that the physical, occupational, or speech therapist wants reinforced and then do it. Some students have communication difficulties and may need to depend on technology to communicate. If that is the case, the teacher should speak to the student with MD as he or she would any other student. However, the teacher must be sure to give the student additional time to respond.

Instructional Strategies

Some students with MD will use assistive technology, like the devices that ASD students use, to communicate. Others need more intensive devices, called augmentative and alternative communication. These are primarily used with students who have motor-functioning difficulties. By using these devices, students with MD can express their wants and needs. Examples include "tangible and tactile symbol systems, choice boards, object prompts and symbols, physical modeling and prompting, and any number of techniques reliant on computer or microswitch technology" (Project IDEAL, 2013f, para. 15).

Peer tutoring is also another instructional strategy that can be used with students having this type of disability. However, the teacher must ensure that the tutoring is reciprocal and not one-sided.

Assignments

When teachers discover that they have a student with MD in their classroom, they should first learn about the student's strengths and about what motivates them. This information can be used to develop classwork and homework assignments. Also, the teacher needs to be aware that a student with MD should be fully included in all planned activities. However, the student may not be able to fully participate, and therefore modifications may need to be made (Project IDEAL, 2013f). The teacher should obtain the services of the special educator to develop these modifications. The teacher also needs to be aware that the student with MD may be using some type of technology to read, write, or speak for him or her (Center for Parent Information and Resources, 2015). If a student with MD uses these devices, assignments must be developed to include them.

Resources

1. Tips for teachers:
   a. http://www.flpda.org/independent/courses/TSWD/content/unit02/docs/Multiple_Disabilities_in_Your_Classroom_10_Tips_for_Teachers.pdf
   b. http://kc.vanderbilt.edu/kennedy_pdfs/TipSheets/tipsheet_ClassroomInclusion.pdf
2. Promising practices: http://cirrie.buffalo.edu/encyclopedia/en/article/114/
3. Classroom strategies: Orthopedic Impairment (OI)

Definition

A student with OI has "a severe orthopedic impairment that adversely affects a child's educational performance. The term includes impairments caused by a congenital anomaly (e.g., clubfoot, absence of some bodily member), impairments caused by disease (e.g., poliomyelitis, bone tuberculosis), and impairments from other causes (e.g., cerebral palsy, amputations, and fractures or burns that cause contractures)" (34 IDEA §300.8 [c] [8], 2004).

Prevalence

Approximately 1% of children receiving special education services are receiving services for OIs (Kena et al., 2014). This exceptionality is considered a low-risk disability, meaning a secondary teacher will probably not see this type of disability in his or her classroom.

Characteristics

Like the other types of disabilities, OI covers a wide range and has three subcategories. The first subgroup is called neuromotor impairment and includes students with cerebral palsy and spina bifida. This type of disability occurs prior to birth and involves damage to the brain or nervous system, which controls one's muscles. The result of this damage is a limitation in the use of one's limbs as well as other bodily functions. The second subcategory is called degenerative disease, which affects motor development. Muscular dystrophy is an example of this disability. The last category, musculoskeletal disorder, causes various types of physical limitations; juvenile rheumatoid arthritis and limb deficiency are examples of this disorder.

Impact on Learning

The type of OI will determine the impact on the student's academic achievement. Students with only an orthopedic disability probably will not have any issues with cognitive, language, or sensory functioning. These students typically have an average IQ, and the only special service they may need is PT or OT. The teacher will probably have to rearrange the classroom for easier wheelchair access.

The other students in this category, the ones with neuromotor impairments, will need more assistance from the teacher. These students may have issues with cognitive, language, or sensory functioning, and the teacher will have to adapt his or her teaching strategies to accommodate the student's needs.

Instructional Strategies

Students with a diagnosis of OI, depending on their specific disability, may need to use assistive technology in order to communicate with their peers and the teacher. They may need to use a speech recognition program like Dragon Speaks (https://en.wikipedia.org/wiki/Dragon_NaturallySpeaking) for their writing and a communication board for expressing language.

The teacher may want to speak with both the physical therapist and occupational therapist about the student since they can provide suggestions such as special seating arrangements and any fine or gross motor skills that may need to be practiced in the general education classroom. The teacher may also want to speak with the school nurse in regards to the student's medical condition and how it will affect the student academically.

Assignments

Depending on the severity of the disability, the teacher may only have to provide extra time for the OI student to complete his or her work, provide a scribe if the student has difficulty writing, or allow the student to complete written assignments orally. Also, the teacher needs to be aware that the student is "in charge." This means that if the teacher asks the student if he or she needs help or assistance and the student responds, "No," the teacher should respect the student's wishes. In a secondary educational environment, students with an OI should be able to tell the teacher their educational needs and have them addressed (Project IDEAL, 2013g).

Resources

1. Teaching strategies (although this website is devoted specifically to science teachers, the teaching strategies can be used in any content area): http://www.nsta.org/disabilities/motor.aspx
2. Classroom strategies:
3. General information on orthopedic impairments:
    a. https://www.naset.org/orthopedicimpairment2.0.html
    b. http://orthopedicimpairments.weebly.com/for-teachers.html

OTHER HEALTH IMPAIRMENT (OHI)

Definition

OHI means "having limited strength, vitality, or alertness, including a heightened alertness to environmental stimuli, that results in limited alertness with respect to the educational environment, that:

1. Is due to chronic or acute health problems such as asthma, attention deficit disorder or attention deficit hyperactivity disorder, diabetes, epilepsy, a heart condition, hemophilia, lead poisoning, leukemia, nephritis, rheumatic fever, sickle cell anemia, and Tourette syndrome; and
2. Adversely affects a child's educational performance" (34 IDEA §300.8 [c] [9], 2004).

Prevalence

Approximately 12% of children receiving special education services receive services for other health impairments (Kena et al., 2014). This exceptionality is considered a high-risk disability, meaning a secondary teacher will probably see this type of disability in his or her classroom.

Characteristics

This IDEA category encompasses a wide variety of chronic and acute health conditions. However, under medical care, and with the correct medication, these conditions have little if any impact on the affected student's academic achievement. Because there are many different disabilities in this category, it would benefit the teacher to research which one is associated with the student he or she is teaching (see a detailed list in the Resources section below).

The most common disability in this IDEA category is attention deficit disorder (ADD) or attention deficit hyperactivity disorder (ADHD), and it is the one that a teacher most likely will experience in the general education classroom. According to the DSM-IV, ADHD is a "persistent pattern of inattention and/or hyperactivity-impulsivity that is more frequently displayed and severe than is typically observed in individuals at a comparable level of development" (as cited in ADHD Institute, 2015, para. 1).

Impact on Learning

Students diagnosed with ADD or ADHD may exhibit any or all of the following behaviors:

1. Inattentiveness to details or activities they are expected to complete.
2. Disorganization, such as difficulty locating important papers like homework and losing necessary school materials needed to complete an assignment.
3. Fidgeting, including the need to get up and walk around during class.
4. Interruptive actions, such as blurting out the answer, having difficulty waiting for his/her turn, and interrupting others (Project IDEAL, 2013h).

Some students with ADHD have average intelligence, but others will struggle with executive, intellectual, and social/emotional functioning (Project IDEAL, 2013h). These students do not learn from a mistake they made previously, and, hence, will tend to repeat the same mistake again and again. These students also struggle with self-regulation and as such do not take into account the consequences of their actions, which can lead to severe disciplinary action at school and home.

Some students with ADHD struggle with academics, such as reading and math, and some have high anxiety issues. These issues can manifest themselves in "low self-esteem; difficulty making social connections; and higher rates of alcohol and substance abuse" (Project IDEAL, 2013h, para. 13).

Instructional Strategies

A teacher can use numerous instructional strategies with a student who has an ADD or ADHD diagnosis. such as the following (Project IDEAL, 2013h, para. 14):

1. Allow extra time to shift from one activity or environment to the next.
2. Teach specific techniques for organizing their thoughts and materials. Organize the classroom accordingly, and keep all materials in permanent locations for easy access.
3. Allow extra time for finishing assignments or for testing.
4. For more complex activities, simplify steps to make them more manageable.
5. Seat the student close to the teacher and away from any peers who might be distracting.
6. Post a daily and weekly schedule that clearly delineates each activity. These schedules can then be used as prompts to direct the student back on task.
7. Keep these schedules as consistent as possible, and keep unstructured time at a minimum.
8. Clearly define goals.
9. Develop objectives to achieve these goals.
10. Define the actions necessary to achieve the desired outcome.

Assignments

Depending on the type of OHI, the teacher may not have to provide any accommodations or modifications for the student. However, a student with ADD or ADHD may need one-on-one assistance to complete the task, may need the classwork or assignment divided into smaller sections, and may need to take a break in between each part (Project IDEAL, 2013h). The student with ADD/ADHD may need to use the computer to complete his or her work or even have a timer set to tell him/her to move on to another assignment. Since the ADD/ADHD student is disorganized, the teacher may want to give extra time to submit finished work and must be sure to provide positive affirmation when the student does turn in assignments. The teacher may also need to list all the steps required to complete an assignment and have the student check them off as they are completed. Highlighting or color coding important vocabulary or concepts in an assignment will help the ADD/ADHD student, as well as give him or her a choice of which assignment to complete (Project IDEAL, 2013h). If notetaking is part of the assignment requirements, the teacher may need to give the student guided notes (e.g., see http://www.interventioncentral.org/academic-interventions/study-organization/guided-notes-increasing-student-engagement-during-lecture-) so he or she is successful with this task.

Resources

1. Teaching strategies (although this website is devoted specifically to science teachers, the teaching strategies can be used in any content area): http://www.nsta.org/disabilities/other.aspx
2. Characteristics and strategies:
3. General information on ADHD. https://www.naset.org/adhd3.0.html
4. General information on OHI. https://www.naset.org/otherimpairments2.0.html

To learn more about the other specific disabilities included in the OHI category, please visit the following websites:

1. Diabetes: http://www.diabetes.org/diabetes-basics/?loc=db-slabnav
2. Epilepsy: http://www.epilepsyinfo.org/
3. Heart condition: http://www.childrensheartfoundation.org/about-chf
4. Hemophilia: http://www.nhlbi.nih.gov/health/health-topics/topics/hemophilia
5. Lead poisoning: http://www.cdc.gov/nceh/lead/
6. Leukemia: http://www.cancer.org/cancer/leukemiainchildren/
7. Nephritis: http://www.kidney.org.uk/help-and-information/kids/kids-nephritis-nephritis/
8. Rheumatic fever: http://www.kidshealth.org.nz/rheumatic-fever
9. Sickle cell anemia: http://www.nhlbi.nih.gov/health/health-topics/topics/sca/signs
10. Tourette syndrome: http://tourette.org

SPECIFIC LEARNING DISABILITY (SLD or LD)

Definition

An SLD or LD is "a disorder in one or more of the basic psychological processes involved in understanding or in using language, spoken or written, that may manifest itself in an imperfect ability to listen, think, speak, read, write, spell, or to do mathematical calculations. The term includes such conditions as perceptual disabilities, brain injury, minimal brain dysfunction, dyslexia, and developmental aphasia. The term does not include learning problems that are primarily the result of visual, hearing, or motor disabilities; of intellectual disability; of ED; or of environmental, cultural, or economic disadvantage" (34 IDEA §300.8 [c] [11], 2004).

Prevalence

Approximately 36% of children receiving special education services receive services for an SLD (Kena et al., 2014). This exceptionality is considered a high-risk disability, meaning a secondary teacher will probably see this type of disability in his or her classroom.

Characteristics

IDEA's SLD category encompasses many different subcategories. Students with this disability have difficulties in one or more of the following areas (Project IDEAL, 2013i, para. 15):

1. Disorders of attention.
2. Poor motor abilities.
3. Psychological process deficits and information-processing problems.
4. Lack of cognitive strategies needed for efficient learning.
5. Oral language difficulties.
6. Reading difficulties.
7. Written language problems.
8. Mathematical disorders.
9. Social skill deficits.

This disability is probably the one that teachers will encounter the most in the general education classroom. Some students with an SLD can get their special education services by the teacher co-teaching with the special educator. Other students with an SLD will be removed from the general education classroom and go to a resource room with the special education teacher to receive their services. The teacher needs to read each student's individual educational plan (IEP) to determine where he or she will be serviced.

Impact on Learning

Students with an SLD will have their learning and academic success impacted in one or more ways. They are impacted by "psychological processes, academic achievement, and social/emotional development" (Project IDEAL, 2013i, para. 16).

Psychological Processes

Psychological processes are how students learn and process information; within this area, there are five subcategories that include "perception, attention, memory, metacognition, and organization" (Project IDEAL, 2013i, para. 16):

- **Perception**: Perception is the ability to organize, interpret, recognize, compare, and discriminate information through the eyes and ears. Students with learning disabilities may "reverse letters, words, or whole passages during reading or writing" (Project IDEAL, 2013i, para. 17).
- **Attention**: Students with an SLD may have difficulty paying attention in the general education classroom due to too many external stimuli. Students with this type of disability tend to pay atten-

tion or focus better in a small group setting. Teachers need to be aware of this fact and adjust their teaching strategies accordingly.
- **Memory**: SLD students struggle with the memory process. They may experience "deficits in working memory which affects their ability to store new information and to retrieve previously processed information from long-term memory" (Project IDEAL, 2013i, para. 19). Teachers need to know that it is not uncommon for a student with an SLD to know and understand a concept taught on one day and completely forget all about it by the next day.
- **Metacognition**: Another area of difficulty for SLD students is metacognition, which "supplies many of the keys to learning from experience, generalizing information and strategies, and applying what you have learned" (Project IDEAL, 2013i, para. 20). Due to poor memory skills, students with an SLD have a difficult time applying what they learned in a previous lesson to the current task. The teacher needs to continuously repeat what was previously taught in order to assist the SLD student with remembering the concept.

Organization

Students with an SLD are typically very disorganized. They will have completed their homework but will not remember where they put it. The teacher will need to teach these students strategies (like having a set of books at home and another at school so the books do not get lost in transit) in order to be successful.

Academic Achievement

Students with an SLD diagnosis struggle in at least one of the academic areas discussed below. However, it is not uncommon for them to face challenges in more than one. The teacher needs to read the student's IEP and become aware of which area will require the most assistance for the student:

- **Reading**: Most students with a diagnosis of SLD struggle with some part of reading. Some students can read an entire passage out of a book either to themselves or aloud flawlessly, but when asked comprehension questions about it, they have no understanding of what they just read. Other students with an SLD have a difficult time sounding out the words they do not know. This affects their fluency, which in turn affects their comprehension.
- **Language Arts**: Some students with an SLD have difficulties spelling words or writing a simple sentence. If the teacher asks them what they want to write about, students with an SLD can *tell* them exactly, but they simply cannot place the words accurately on paper.
- **Mathematics**: Although not as common as having difficulties in reading, some students with an SLD do find math to be a challenge. Some cannot do simple math calculations (e.g., 5 x 6), while others struggle with spatial relationships or completing a multi-step word problem. While it is common for students in general to struggle in math class, for some students with an SLD, math is an almost impossible task.
- **Social and Emotional Development**: Some students with an SLD have social skill challenges. They may act impulsively without regard to the consequences of their behavior to either themselves or others (Project IDEAL, 2013i). They may also not recognize or notice social cues like their grade-level peers do. Students with an SLD also do not typically do well with idiomatic phrases or jokes.

Instructional Strategies

Students with an SLD typically are educated in the general education classroom; hence, teachers will find themselves working most often with this type of disability. Often, the teacher will be co-teaching with the special education teacher and may or may not lead the class, depending on the model. Because of the high possibility that a student with an SLD will be placed in the general classroom, following is a direct instruction strategy that teachers can use.

Step 1: Decide on the skill or concept to be taught, and since some students with an SLD are visual learners, remember to include visuals with the instruction.
Step 2: Provide examples to the SLD student of the skill or concept and have them practice with you and the rest of the class (guided practice).
Step 3: Give the students some practice to do on their own (independent practice) as you and the special education teacher walk around the classroom and assist as needed.
Step 4: Allow the student with an SLD to work independently on the concepts so that he or she can demonstrate mastery of the concept.

The following subsections discuss some specific instructional strategies that can be used to assist SLD students, depending on the area(s) in which they are struggling.

Perception

For the student with an SLD struggling with perception difficulties, the teacher should use a highlighter or bold font to emphasize important words (like vocabulary) or concepts. Also, the teacher should not teach similar concepts at the same time (e.g., adding fractions with the same denominator and ones with different denominators) because this will confuse the SLD student (Project IDEAL, 2013i).

Attention

Students with an SLD typically have a short attention span; therefore, the teacher should present the information in small segments or chunks and provide visual cues (like a manipulative in math or a picture of the story when reading). The teacher can also either ask the student to repeat the instructions (Project IDEAL, 2013i). Other strategies include:

1. Providing breaks (e.g., after working for a certain amount of time, give the student a 5-minute mental break; Reeves, 2015).
2. Removing any visual distractions like extra books on the desk or work table, or perhaps even moving the student to another area in the classroom to work on his/her own (Reeves, 2015).
3. Allowing physical activity such as standing or lying on the floor while completing a task (Reeves, 2015).
4. Asking the student to rate the difficulty of the task at hand from 1 to 10. If the task earns an 8 or higher, discuss with the student how it can be moved to a lower difficulty level, perhaps by using chunking, for example (Reeves, 2015).

5. Teaching students to self-regulate their own behavior in regards to paying attention. If necessary, give them a chart to assist them in monitoring how well they pay attention to the task at hand (Brooke Publishing, 2012).

Memory

Students with an SLD tend to have poor memories. The teacher can assist the SLD student with this deficit by chunking the information being taught into smaller segments or sections and repeating the concepts numerous times (e.g., provide many examples when doing guided practice) and incorporating the concept into other content areas if possible (Project IDEAL, 2013i).

Academic Areas

Reading. Reading is a challenge for most students with an SLD. The teacher can assist these students by providing them with a graphic organizer that has highlighted information. This allows the student with an SLD to see what the important concepts are and focus on them. The teacher can also provide the student with questions and any vocabulary words prior to reading a selection so the student will know what to look for when reading. The teacher should also have the student look at any pictures or graphs to assist them in comprehending what they are reading (Project IDEAL, 2013i). Finally, the teacher should look into providing a book that is on the student's reading ability level. Books, especially in social studies and science, are often written on a collegiate level, and some SLD students will not be able to read this material. Book companies typically will have a book on the same topic but written on a variety of reading levels. By being provided a reading-level-appropriate text, the student will learn the same information as his or her grade-level peers but at his or her comprehension level. Examples of such books can be found at High Noon Books (http://www.highnoonbooks.com/index-hnb.tpl), Hi-Lo Books (http://learningabledkids.com/home_school_info/specialty_curriculum.htm), and Benchmark Education (http://www.benchmarkeducation.com/teachers).

Language Arts. Besides needing assistance with their reading, some students with an SLD will also need assistance from the teacher with their writing. The teacher should allow students with an SLD whatever technology tools they need to accomplish the writing task. Some students will need to speak into the computer and have the computer write for them; others will need only grammar and spelling checks. Some students with an SLD may need some type of graphic organizer to organize their thoughts prior to writing, and the teacher needs to provide explicit instructions in regards to how long the written assignment is to be in terms of paragraphs or pages (Project IDEAL, 2013i). The teacher should also be willing to review students' written drafts frequently in order to ensure they are doing what is being asked of them.

Mathematics. Although rare, some students with an SLD will only struggle in understanding mathematical concepts. For these students, the teacher should start with explaining the concept very concretely and using things like manipulatives that allow the student to actually move objects. Once the student understands the concept in a concrete form, the teacher should move on to the representational task, which involves drawing the concept—like using a matrix to solve an equation. After the teacher feels that the student with an SLD truly understands the concept, the teacher can move to the abstract level, which involves completing the problems on a worksheet or page in the math book. Examples of this procedure can be found at http://fcit.usf.edu/mathvids/strategies/cra.html#. It should be noted that this research-based strategy can be used at any level of mathematical instruction.

Assignments

Students with SLDs benefit greatly from differentiated instruction (see http://differentiationcentral.com/); hence, teachers need to be aware of and able to use differentiated instruction with these students. When developing assignments and classwork for a student with an SLD, the teacher should think outside the box and try to avoid only assigning worksheets and written assignments. Students with an SLD are frequently talented in areas such as the arts and music. They also tend to be very good with their hands, so hands-on activities are usually effective with these students. Like with any student, the teacher needs to find out what interests an SLD student and what the student's strengths are and then build assignments and classwork around those things.

Resources

1. General information on specific learning disabilities:
2. Best practices: http://www.ncld.org/wp-ontent/uploads/2014/11/aacte_ncld_recommendation.pdf
3. Characteristics and strategies: a. http://do2learn.com/disabilities/CharacteristicsAndStrategies/SpecificLearningDisability_Strategies.html b. http://ldaamerica.org/successful-strategies-for-teaching-students-with-learning-disabilities/ c. http://www.nsta.org/disabilities/learning.aspx
4. Additional instructional strategies: a. Spelling: http://www.ldonline.org/article/6192 b. Study Skills. http://www.ldonline.org/article/c656 c. Reading: http://www.ncset.org/publications/viewdesc.asp?id=274 d. Math: http://educationnorthwest.org/resources/mathematics-interventions-what-strategies-work-struggling-learners-or-students-learning e. Memory: http://www.ldonline.org/article/5736 f. Organization: http://www.ldonline.org/article/5884
5. Strategies for students with dysgraphia: http://www.ldonline.org/article/5890
6. Strategies for students with dyslexia:
7. Classroom accommodations: http://www.ldonline.org/article/8022
8. Case study: http://www.ldonline.org/article/5678
9. Computerized/recorded textbooks: https://www.learningally.org/

SPEECH AND LANGUAGE IMPAIRMENT (S/LI)

Definition

An S/LI is "a communication disorder such as stuttering, impaired articulation, a language impairment, or a voice impairment that adversely affects a child's educational performance" (34 IDEA §300.8[c] [12], 2004).

Prevalence

Approximately 21% of children receiving special education services receive services for speech and language disorders (Kena et al., 2014). This exceptionality is considered a high-risk disability, meaning a secondary teacher will probably see this type of disability in his or her classroom. It is important to note that "this estimate does not include children who receive services for speech and language disorders that are secondary to other conditions such as deafness" (Texas Council for Development Disabilities, n.d., para. 2) or any of the other IDEA disabilities.

Characteristics

The S/LI IDEA category is divided into two groups: speech impairment and language impairment. These are then further divided into smaller specific categories, three under speech and five under language. These subgroups are devised according to the type of difficulty the student is experiencing. A description of how each category is set up follows.

Speech

The following are speech impairments:

- **Fluency Impairment**: Fluency impairment is a type of speech disorder in which the student may have "difficulties with the rhythm and timing of speech characterized by hesitations, repetitions, or prolongations of sounds, syllables, words, or phrases" (NICHCY, 2012, para. 2). The most common type of fluency speech disorder is stuttering, which is the "rapid-fire repetitions of consonant or vowel sounds especially at the beginning of words, prolongations, hesitations, interjections, and complete verbal blocks" (NICHCY, 2012, para. 2).
- **Articulation Impairment**: Articulation impairment is when a student mispronounces a word either by omitting a vowel or consonant, substitutes one consonant for another, or distorts the word by adding a consonant.
- **Voice Disorder**: Voice disorders are when the student speaks too loudly or the quality of the voice is abnormal.

Language Impairments

The following are language impairments:

- **Phonological Disorders**: A teacher may have difficulty understanding a student with a phonological disorder because he or she does not pronounce words correctly (Project IDEAL, 2013j).
- **Morphological Disorders**: A student with a morphological disorder has "difficulties with morphological inflections (inflections on nouns, verbs, and adjectives that signal different kinds of meanings)" (Project IDEAL, 2013j, para. 8).
- **Semantic Disorders**: A student with a semantic disorder has difficulty with vocabulary. He or she has a limited vernacular and struggles with learning new words and their meanings (Project IDEAL, 2013j).

- **Syntactical Deficits**: Students with syntactical deficits struggle with grammatical issues. The teacher will find that this student lacks the correct verb-noun agreement and uses short sentences that lack descriptive words (Project IDEAL, 2013j).
- **Pragmatic Difficulties**: Students with pragmatic difficulties struggle in social situations. They "may lack an understanding of the rules for making eye contact, respecting personal space, requesting information, and introducing topics" (Project IDEAL, 2013j, para. 11).

Impact on Learning

Because speech and language disorders are problems in communication and oral motor function, the effect on learning from this type of exceptionality can range from "the inability to produce speech or to understand and use language" to "little or no impact on daily living and socialization" (NICHCY, 2012, para. 4). However, whether the impact is mild or intensive, the secondary teacher needs to be aware that this disability can isolate a student from his or her peers and can affect the student's educational performance in ways such as avoiding collaborating with peers or doing a presentation in front of the class.

Instructional Strategies

Most students with an S/LI disability in Grades 6–12 will be provided special education services by a licensed speech pathologist outside of the general education classroom. Despite where the services are conducted, it is important for teachers to be aware of them and collaborate with the speech pathologist in order to ensure that the student is getting all of the services required by his or her IEP and is able to practice these skills in the general educational classroom. Teachers may need to provide such services as "corrective measures, helping with speech and language exercises, and providing the student with immediate feedback when the speech-language pathologist is not present" (NICHCY, 2012, para. 5).

Assignments

Depending on the S/LI disability, the student may simply need an accommodation, such as being placed at the front of the class so he or she is able to listen better, be more engaged in the lesson, and have easier access to the teacher if needing assistance. If the student with an S/LI has difficulty speaking, he or she may need to use some type of technology. The teacher will also need to provide the student with additional time to respond to questions, and instead of asking the student with an S/LI to respond orally to a directive, the teacher can have him or her write down any questions or responses. Finally, the teacher should encourage group interaction but honor the student's request to work individually or only work with specific students since some may be more tolerant than others.

Frequently in middle and high school classrooms, students are expected, either individually or as a group, and informally or formally, to present information that they have gleaned from a lesson. Students with a specific S/LI such as stuttering can still participate in this type of activity if the teacher collaborates with the speech pathologist and has the student practice a technique called "pausing" (Reitzes, 2006). This is a technique whereby the teacher instructs the speaker "to pause briefly between words to reduce the frequency of overt stuttering behaviors. By doing so, speaking rate is reduced but articulation is not modified or distorted" (Reitzes, 2006, p. 68).

Supporting Secondary Students with Disabilities in an Inclusive Environment

Before using this research-based strategy in front of the entire class, the teacher and the student should sit down together and read over the speech, placing pauses "after the first word of an utterance and every two, three or four words thereafter" (Schneider, 1995, p. 335). Reitzes (2006) provided an example with the pause lasting between a fraction of a second to a full second at each comma: "Using, pausing, helps the speaker, to reduce, the frequency of stuttering, by slowing, the rate of speech. Pausing, is a tool, to help people, stutter, less often" (p. 66). By using this technique, the student with a stuttering disability can still partake in the classroom assignment like his or her grade-level peers.

Resources

1. The pausing technique: http://www.journalofstuttering.com/1-2/Reitzes.2006.JSTAR.1.64-78.pdf
2. Teaching strategies:
   a. http://images.pcmac.org/SiSFiles/Schools/AL/BaldwinCounty/FoleyElementary/Uploads/Forms/classroomstrategies.pdf
   b. http://www.nsta.org/disabilities/communication.aspx c. http://do2learn.com/disabilities/CharacteristicsAndStrategies/SpeechLanguageImpairment_Strategies.html
3. General information on speech and language impairment: https://www.naset.org/speechandlanguage2.0.html
4. Research-based practices: http://www.speech-language-therapy.com/pdf/aPatchellHand1993.pdf

TRAUMATIC BRAIN INJURY (TBI)

Definition

A TBI is "an acquired injury to the brain caused by an external physical force, resulting in total or partial functional disability or psychosocial impairment, or both, that adversely affects a child's educational performance. The term applies to open or closed head injuries resulting in impairments in one or more areas, such as cognition; language; memory; attention; reasoning; abstract thinking; judgment; problem solving; sensory, perceptual, and motor abilities; psychosocial behavior; physical functions; information processing; and speech. The term does not include brain injuries that are congenital or degenerative, or brain injuries induced by birth trauma" (34 IDEA §300.8 (c) (13), 2004).

Approximately <1% of children receiving special education services receive services for a TBI (Kena et al., 2014). This exceptionality is considered a low-risk disability, meaning a secondary teacher will probably not see this type of disability in his or her classroom.

Characteristics

Students who have been diagnosed with a TBI have a variety of symptoms that may be temporary or permanent, mild or severe, depending on the injury. Some of the challenges they experience include difficulties with attention, memory, language processing (receptive and expressive), reading and writing, partial or total loss of one's physical senses, seizures, lack of executive functions, sleep disorders, loss of stamina, depression, and lack of motivation. The complete list of challenges a student with a TBI faces can be found at http://www.traumaticbraininjury.com/symptoms-of-tbi/severe-tbi-symptoms/, and pre-service teachers are encouraged to review these in case they ever have a student with this type of disability in their classroom.

Impact on Learning

Often, students with a TBI are misdiagnosed with an SLD, an ED, or an ID. However, the difference between the TBI category and the others previously mentioned is that the student with a TBI can remember what he or she was like before the injury (Project IDEAL, 2013k). This memory can impact the student's academic and home life, as well as affect those people associated with the student (e.g., parents, family, and friends). Teachers need to be aware of the emotional toll this disability can have on the student.

Instructional Strategies

The teacher, when educating a student with a TBI, needs to develop a consistent routine so that the student can anticipate what is going to happen. If for any reason this routine will change, the student should be informed ahead of time. When teaching a lesson, the teacher should not only present the material orally but also demonstrate it with visual cues and actual objects. Any directions the student with a TBI may need to complete the assignment should be given in small increments and repeated numerous times. The teacher should avoid figurative language when speaking to students with a TBI because this may confuse them, and the teacher should attempt to keep the classroom as stimulus-free as possible. Some students with a TBI may also use some form of technology to complete their assignment or even to speak. Patience and flexibility are important when working with students with a TBI so that their full academic potential can be reached (Project IDEAL, 2013k).

Assignments

When developing assignments for the student with a TBI, the teacher should consider placing him or her with a peer or in a small collaborative group if the student is willing. The teacher should be sure to pick a partner who is patient and encouraging to the TBI student. By doing this, the teacher reduces the amount of work the TBI student has to do individually and assists the student with developing his or her social skills. The teacher should also provide the TBI student opportunities to solve problems within the assignment because this will assist with improving executive functioning.

Resources

1. Characteristics and strategies:
2. Classroom accommodations:
3. TBI guidebook for educators: http://www.p12.nysed.gov/specialed/tbi/guidebook.pdf
4. General information on traumatic brain injury:
    a. http://www.traumaticbraininjury.com/symptoms-of-tbi/severe-tbi-symptoms/
    b. https://www.naset.org/traumaticbraininj2.0.html

Supporting Secondary Students with Disabilities in an Inclusive Environment

VISUAL IMPAIRMENT (VI) INCLUDING BLINDNESS

Definition

A VI is "an impairment in vision that, even with correction, adversely affects a child's educational performance. The term includes both partial sight and blindness" (34 IDEA §300.8 (c) (14), 2004).

Prevalence

Approximately <1% of children receiving special education services receive services for visual impairments (Kena et al., 2014). This exceptionality is considered a low-risk disability, meaning a secondary teacher will probably not see this type of disability in his or her classroom.

Characteristics

Like other IDEA disability categories, the VI group has three subcategories. Teachers need to know which subcategory their student is in so that they can plan their instructional strategy according to the student's individual needs. The subcategories are:

1. **Low Vision**: Students use their vision as their primary sensory channel.
2. **Functionally Blind**: Students can use limited vision for functional tasks but need their tactile and auditory channels for learning.
3. **Totally Blind**: Students use tactile and auditory channels for learning and functional tasks (Project IDEAL, 2013l, para. 3).

Impact on Learning

It has been said that when one sense is removed, the others compensate for it. However, this may not be the case with all students suffering from VI (Project IDEAL, 2013l). Some students with VI need visual cues (see discussion under the "Deaf-Blind" section), while others can use touch and hearing to assist them in an academic setting. The teacher needs to speak with the student and ask how he or she best learns in order to plan lessons accordingly.

Because students with VI do not share the same visual experiences as their grade- and age-level peers, these students may lack motivation, may have poor self-esteem and social skills, and may lag behind their grade-level peers intellectually. Students with VI will also need to work with a teacher specially trained to help with mobility training, learning braille, independent living, social skills, and the use of technology. The general education teacher can assist the specialized teacher by reinforcing in the general education classroom what the student is taught in these specialty classes (Project IDEAL, 2013l).

Instructional Strategies

Students who have VI can primarily be taught in the same manner as a student without a disability, but with a few notable exceptions. The teacher needs to ensure that the classroom is set up for easy mobility for the student with VI, and the student will probably want to be placed near or at the front of the class

(Project IDEAL, 2013l). The teacher should contact the student's mobility specialist if assistance is needed in this area. The teacher should also use visual and/or physical cues when instructing the class, and either the teacher or any other student speaking should identify him or herself prior to answering a question because this will assist the VI student in the learning process (Project IDEAL, 2013l).

In regards to technology, the teacher may have to provide books or materials in braille or larger print. In a math class, the student with VI may need the assistance of a talking calculator or manipulatives with Braille on them to fully participate in class. Finally, when showing a video, the teacher may need to enlarge the screen in order for the student with VI to see it (Project IDEAL, 2013l). It would behoove the teacher to ask the student with VI his or her preference and instruct accordingly.

Assignments

Depending on the severity of the student's blindness, the teacher may need to simply increase the font size of the assignment or place the assignment on a colored piece of paper. If the student has no vision, then the teacher may need to convert the assignment to braille or perhaps place it on the computer or audio tape. In regards to a written assignment or classwork, students with VI can either orally tell the teacher or a classmate what they want to say and this person will write it for them, or they can speak into the computer, and it will write for them. The teacher needs to allow the student with VI to be as independent as possible because this will assist him or her later in life (Project IDEAL, 2013l).

Resources

1. Guidelines for working with students who are blind or visually impaired: http://www.doe.virginia.gov/special_ed/disabilities/sensory_disabilities/visually_impaired_blind/visually_impaired_guidelines.pdf
2. General resources for working with students with visual impairments: http://www.perkinselearning.org/scout/resources-general-education-teachers-students-visual-impairments
3. Teaching strategies: a. http://www.ferris.edu/htmls/colleges/university/disability/faculty-staff/classroom-issues/vision/vision-strategy.htm b. https://www.tsbvi.edu/instructional-resources/1911-classroom-strategies-for-regular-education-teachers-who-have-students-with-visual-impairments c. http://www.nsta.org/disabilities/visual.aspx d. http://www.pathstoliteracy.org/sites/pathstoliteracy.perkinsdev1.org/files/uploaded-files/Effective%20Classroom%20Adaptations_CEC_2001.pdf
4. General information on visual impairments: https://www.naset.org/visualimpairments2.0.html

CONCLUSION

All teachers will more than likely have a student diagnosed with one or more of the IDEA disability categories in their classrooms. Thus, it is important that pre-service teachers learn about these disabilities and how they can employ specific strategies to help make these students' educational experience the best it can be.

It is the responsibility of teacher education programs to ensure that pre-service teachers are properly prepared to educate all students, and because of the unique needs of students with a diagnosed disability, special attention should be paid to preparing future teachers to meet the educational needs of those students. Following are some specific ways the information in this chapter can be used to help prepare middle and high school pre-service teachers to make accommodations within their subject areas.

1. Develop case studies for each IDEA disability category based on the definitions and symptoms provided herein and have pre-service teachers plan activities and accommodations accordingly.
2. Have pre-service teachers develop a "toolkit" of instructional strategies (including but not limited to the ones provided here) that they will be able to use in their content area.
3. Have pre-service teachers design a unit within their subject area using the Universal Design for Learning (see http://www.udlcenter.org/advocacy/faq_guides/general) or the Differentiation of Instruction (see http://www.diffcentral.com/model.html) models. Have them include at least four different IDEA categories in their plan and detail the instructional strategies they will use to educate these students.
4. Have pre-service teachers individually tutor or work in a small group with student(s) with disabilities and try some of the instructional strategies developed for their toolkit. Ask them to write a brief description of their experience, explaining if the strategy was successful and, if not, what other strategy could be used.

Students with exceptionalities want to be educated just like any other student, and it is hoped that the background information, strategies, and resources provided in this chapter can help prepare pre-service teachers to provide a fair and equitable educational experience for these students.

REFERENCES

ADHD Institute. (2015). *ADHD: DSM-IV*. Retrieved from http://www.adhd-institute.com/assessment-diagnosis/diagnosis/dsm-iv/

Autism Speaks. (2015). *Autism vision: Creating classroom connections*. Retrieved from https://www.autismspeaks.org/what-autism/symptoms

Brookes Publishing. (2012). *5 tips to get all your students engaged in learning*. Retrieved from http://archive.brookespublishing.com/articles/ed-article-0212.htm#choices

Center for Parent Information and Resources. (2015). *Down syndrome*. Retrieved from http://www.parentcenterhub.org/repository/downsyndrome/#hs

Concordia Online Education. (2015). *5 tips for handling EBD kids (emotional behavior disorder) in an inclusive classroom*. Retrieved from http://education.cu-portland.edu/blog/teaching-strategies/5-tips-for-handling-ebd-kids-emotional-behavior-disorder-in-an-inclusive-classroom/

Henley, M., & Long, N. (2003). Helping students with emotional problems succeed. *Educational Leadership*, 7(3). Retrieved from http://www.ascd.org/publications/classroom-leadership/nov2003/Helping-Students-with-Emotional-Problems-Succeed.aspx

Individuals with Disabilities Education Improvement Act, 20 U.S.C. § 1400 (2004). Retrieved from http://idea.ed.gov/download/statute.html

Kena, G., Aud, S., Johnson, F., Wang, X., Zhang, J., Rathbun, A., & Kristapovich, P. (2014). *The condition of education 2014 (NCES 2014-083)*. Washington, DC: U.S. Department of Education, National Center for Education Statistics.

National Center on Deaf-Blindness. (2008). *Overview on deaf-blindness*. Retrieved from https://nationaldb.org/library/page/1934

National Dissemination Center for Children with Disabilities (NICHCY). (2012). *Categories of disability under IDEA*. Author.

Project IDEAL. (2013k). *Traumatic brain injury*. Author.

ProjectI. D. E. A. L. (2013a). *Autism*. Retrieved from http://www.projectidealonline.org/v/autism/

Project, I. D. E. A. L. (2013c). *Emotional disturbance*. Author.

Project, I. D. E. A. L. (2013d). *Hearing impairments*. Author.

Project, I. D. E. A. L. (2013e). *Intellectual disabilities*. Author.

Project, I. D. E. A. L. (2013f). *Multiple disabilities*. Author.

Project, I. D. E. A. L. (2013g). *Orthopedic impairments*. Author.

Project, I. D. E. A. L. (2013h). *Other health impairments*. Author.

Project, I. D. E. A. L. (2013i). *Specific learning disabilities*. Author.

Project, I. D. E. A. L. (2013j). *Speech or language impairments*. Author.

Project IDEAL. (2013b). *Deaf-blindness*. Retrieved from http://www.projectidealonline.org/v/visual-impairments/

Project IDEAL. (2013l). *Visual impairments*. Retrieved from http://www.projectidealonline.org/v/visual-impairments/

Reeves, D. (2015). *7 ways to increase a student's attention span*. Academic Press.

Reitzes, P. (2006). Pausing: Reducing the frequency of stuttering. *Journal of Stuttering Therapy, Advocacy and Research, 1*, 64-78. Retrieved from http://www.journalofstuttering.com/1-2/Reitzes.2006.JSTAR.1.64-78.pdf

Schneider, P. (1995). A self-adjustment approach to fluency enhancement. In C. W. Starkweather, & H. F. M. Peters (Eds.), *Stuttering:* Vol. I: *Proceedings of the First World Congress on Fluency Disorders* (pp. 334-337). Nijmegen, The Netherlands: International Fluency Association.

Texas Council for Development Disabilities. (n.d.). *Speech or language impairments*. Retrieved from http://www.projectidealonline.org/v/speech-language-impairments/

Tucker, C. (2013). The basics of blended instruction. *Educational Leadership, 70*(6), 57–60.

Vaughn, S., Shay Schumm, J., & Forgan, J. W. (1998). *Curriculum handbook: Instructing students with high incident disabilities in the general education classroom*. Alexandria, VA: Association of Supervision and Curriculum Development.

Supporting Secondary Students with Disabilities in an Inclusive Environment

KEY TERMS AND DEFINITIONS

Ability Level: What a student is able to din an educational setting; it may be above or below the actual grade level.

Adaptive Behavior: Skills people need to function in our daily lives.

Co-Teaching Model: Typically a special and general education teacher working together in the same classroom using a variety of instructional strategies to teach all the students. See http://www.asdk12.org/depts/hr/student_teaching/PDF/The_Power_of_2.pdf.

Cognitive Functioning: Ability to process, speech, memories and thoughts.

Exceptionality: A student with an identified disability under the Individuals with Disabilities Education Act (IDEA).

Grade Level: The actual grade a student with a disability is in but they may not be learning the information taught at this level.

High Incident Disability: Typically found in an inclusive general education classroom and include the following disabilities: ED, SLD, and S/LI.

Low Incident Disability: May or may not be found in an inclusive general education classroom and include the following disabilities: ID, D/HI, OI, VI, D/B, TBI, ASD and MD.

Prevalence: A group of the overall population who have a specific disability.

This research was previously published in Preparing Pre-Service Teachers for the Inclusive Classroom edited by Jennifer Courduff, Patricia Dickenson, and Penelope Keough; pages 75-106, copyright year 2017 by Information Science Reference (an imprint of IGI Global).

Chapter 47
Assessing the Functions of Behavior for Students with Autism in the Inclusive Classroom Environment

Lina Gilic
St. John's University, USA

Michelle Chamblin
Molloy College, USA

ABSTRACT

Over the last decade, there has been a significant increase in the identification of students with Autism. According to research and the laws that guide Special Education, inclusive settings benefit both students with and without disabilities. However, teaching students with Autism in inclusive settings can bring about challenges, as teachers are responsible to effectively manage academic and social behaviors. Years of research support the evidence that behaviors do not occur in isolation and behaviors serve a function, even those that are deemed as socially maladaptive. Today's classroom teachers need the tools necessary to identify the function of the student behavior so that appropriate strategies can be applied. Based on the evidence, these strategies can be used to target and transform socially significant behaviors required for successful inclusion and optimized independence.

INTRODUCTION

For the past ten decades, there have been notable increases in the number of students diagnosed with Autism (Geneva Centre for Autism, 2010). Students with Autism display various characteristics such as problems communicating, delays in social development, ritualistic behaviors, and adverse reactions to changes in the environment (American Psychiatric Association, 2012). As the number of students identified as having Autism increases, so does their representation in mainstream and inclusive settings

DOI: 10.4018/978-1-7998-1213-5.ch047

Assessing the Functions of Behavior for Students with Autism in the Inclusive Classroom Environment

(Loiacono & Valenti, 2010). Teachers are expected to meet the needs of these students and find ways to include them, although they may not have specific guidelines or strategies to accomplish these tasks (Horrocks, White, & Roberts, 2008). Students with Autism display challenging behaviors and require a systematic approach for the assessment of behaviors, as well as the implementation of interventions, that differs from other students with disabilities. Legislation that guides the practice of Special Education, such as placing the student into the least restrictive environment, speaks to the ethics of what should be done for all students with disabilities without connection to specific classifications or characteristics of the student (Wright & Wright, 2007). It is the goal that all students with special needs be included to the maximum extent possible. Now that more students with Autism are being included, teachers need an inventory of skills and strategies, which address the unique needs of this student population, despite the challenges that may arise in the process (Lindsay, Proulx, Thomson, & Scott, 2013)

There are two most frequently cited issues or barriers to including students with Autism in mainstream or inclusive settings. Teachers report that they are not equipped with the knowledge or skills to address the needs of these students (Rodríguez, Saldaña, & Moreno, 2012). Teachers are not certain on how to effectively respond to student behavior (Brown & McIntosh, 2012; Hart & Whalon, 2013). The two issues are tightly knitted. In order for teachers to effectively work with student behaviors, they must have the knowledge and understanding of evidenced based practices that can be used to understand and change behavior. In fact, studies show strong connections between students' behaviors and the participation of those students in inclusive settings (Ervasti, Kivimäki, Kawachi, Subramanian, Pentti, Ahola, & Virtanen, 2012). Additionally, behavior impacts student to teacher relationships, and the perceptions of teachers, students, and families to the effectiveness of the student success in the inclusive classroom (Gao & Mager, 2011; Sari, Celikoz, & Secer, 2009). Therefore understanding the function of behavior is imperative. Understanding behavior is not just limited to behavior that is maladaptive. Behavior encompasses all actions that occur daily in the classroom, for example, speaking, walking, writing, looking at a computer screen, sitting and countless other academic and non-academic actions.

In a review of research-based interventions for students with Autism, Spencer, Evmenova, Boon, and Hayes-Harris (2014) listed several strategies used to teach students academic skills. Although the strategies were based on various theoretical perspectives with various targeted outcomes, the one common denominator for all classroom strategies was that the evaluator ultimately relied on measuring an observable behavior. Measurements should include what the students do, say or produce (Alberto & Troutman, 2012; Cooper, Heron & Heward, 2007). Measurement is required to evaluate the effectiveness of the strategy. Therefore, skills in observing and analyzing behavior are a must-have classroom skill.

The study of behavior in relation to students with Autism has grown tremendously and this chapter will highlight components of behavior analysis which have been made "classroom ready". The essential ways in which teachers can use data for decision-making is presented in a succinct and meaningful way. 'Classroom ready' refers to the features and aspects of these strategies as presented for immediate use. In addition, the strategies presented are compact but carefully selected with an intentional focus on classroom application for teachers in inclusive settings working with students diagnosed with Autism. National research indicates that training in the area of data-based solutions, including behavior intervention, needs to be more accessible (Couvillon, Bullock & Gable, 2009). The complexity of the information and variation among classroom implementation of data collection and analysis may present as a barrier (Chitiyo & Wheeler, 2009). This information is presented in the "classroom ready" manner which streamlines the information into the main skills that every teacher should have as a part of their teaching toolkit.

WHAT IS BEHAVIOR?

Behavior is what we do, how we respond, and how we act. Observable behavior is an individual's response to their environment. This interaction is observable as well as measurable (Cooper, Heron & Heward, 2007; Johnston & Pennypacker, 2008). Reading this chapter is behavior, writing of what you will do with this information for your Monday morning class is behavior, and even tapping your highlighter as you read is behavior.

Examples of Behavior and Non-Behavior

Examples of behavior can include: drinking, playing soccer, reading, listening, getting out of a seat, brushing hair, looking at others, holding a pencil.

Examples of non-behavior can include: being silent, laying down, being still, not eating or drinking.

As we observe students in the classroom we can only target observable behaviors. Students emit many behaviors and deciding where to begin may be difficult. In deciding what behaviors should be addressed first, it is those behaviors which are of social significance to the individual such as behaviors which are related to increasing one's quality of life. This may be connected to decreasing self injurious behaviors or threatening behaviors to others, or increasing academic performance, social skills, or self-regulation behaviors.

How is Behavior Measured?

Over the years researchers have observed increases in the use of classroom data to improve student and teacher performance as a result of the Comprehensive School Reform Demonstration legislation in 1997, No Child Left Behind Act, and the Individuals with Disabilities Education Improvement Act (Zirkel, 2013). Several studies have examined the ways in which teachers assess student data to increase the effectiveness of their instruction (Anderson, Leithwood, & Strauss, 2010; Marsh, McCombs & Martorell, 2010; Wayman, Cho, Jimerson, & Spikes, 2012). Academic engagement could be observed and measured through reading, writing, asking for information, replying to questions, raising one's hand, or sharing information. Being able to measure these behaviors is a key component of determining if, when and how often the behavior occurs.

Teacher observation of student's behavior identifies trends in the behavior and variables connected to the behavior such as the classroom setting, peers, educational material, and educational task which may evoke the behavior (National Research Council, 2001). This information identifies under what conditions the behavior will occur again, which is not only informative but also guides teachers in decision making for effective instruction (Osborne & Reed, 2011). Often teachers will use student data in the classroom to group students academically as well as to modify instruction as needed. Less emphasis is placed on non academic behavior that may interfere with student learning (Brown & McIntosh 2012; Hart & Whalon, 2013; Rodríguez, Saldaña, & Moreno, 2012). Research has presented information on the use of data to improve student education in the classroom (Supovitz, 2010; Wayman et al, 2012). While the variables may vary, a common outcome among the research is that data provides information to improve teaching practices.

How is Behavior Influenced?

Behavior is influenced by the consequence which follows the response (Alberto & Troutman, 2012; Cooper, Heron, & Heward, 2007). The consequence that follows behavior can be pleasant or unpleasant depending on the point of view of the individual. For example a parent may send their child to his room as a consequence for hitting a sibling. If going to his room is a pleasant consequence, the odds are that the behavior would occur again. But on the other hand, if going to his room is an unpleasant consequence, it will decrease the behavior. Consequences that increased the future occurrence of the behavior are called reinforcement.

Reinforcement can be positive or negative. Positive reinforcement occurs when something is added to increase the future occurrence of the behavior. An example of such is adding computer time for behaviors in the classroom to have those behaviors occur again. Negative reinforcement occurs when something is taken away to increase the future occurrence of the behavior. Such as taking away homework for the night to reinforce a behavior you want the student to increase in your class. Consequences which decrease the future occurrence of a behavior are called punishment. Punishment can be positive or negative punishment. Positive punishment would be adding something to decrease the future behavior, such as adding a surprise quiz in class as a way to decrease the students calling out behavior in the classroom. Additionally, negative punishment is taking something away to decrease the future occurrence of the behaviors, such as taking away computer time when the student is calling out (Alberto & Troutman, 2012; Cooper, Heron & Heward, 2012).

Reinforcement and punishment are both consequences that follow a behavior and result in the future occurrence or nonoccurrence of the behavior. Immediate consequences have the greatest effect on the reoccurrence of behavior. A delay of even 5 seconds, although minor in duration, may miss the opportunity to reinforce for the behavior. Observing the antecedent, behavior, and consequence chain in the classroom could identify what consequence is reinforcing or punishing the behavior.

Defining Behavior from Student Data

The usage of the term target behavior may cause confusion and may require further clarification. Defining behavior from data collected is critical for clear communication and evaluation. The importance in operationally defining a target behavior is repeatedly shown in the research (Chafouleas, Christ, Riley-Tillman, Briesch & Chanese, 2007). Subjective targets allow for misrepresentation and limited analysis of progress and intervention effectiveness. Precise definitions eliminate variation in the observations and allows for the target behavior to be easily identified. Observing a student "completing his math work sheet" is clear and precise. Observing a student "being cooperative" is open to interpretation. Interpretation allows for inconsistency in observers' data collection. Defining a target behavior that is clear, specific, observable, and measurable allows for the ongoing evaluation of the target behavior and data collection from the classroom teacher (Batsche, Elliott, Graden, Grimes, Kovaleski, Prasse, & Tilly, 2005).

How Do We Measure Behavior?

There is a saying that anything that is important to us, we measure it! Think about all the things we measure like our weight, our age and even the weather. This next section presents an overview of observational recording systems. Observational recording systems are used to record behaviors as they occur

(Alberto & Troutman, 2013). It is not feasible to record behavior all day so measuring a sample of the behavior can provide an indication of how often, how long, or how intense a behavior may be. In our classroom ready model, Table 1 displays questions that are asked about a behavior and the best way to measure the behavior.

Event Recording

Recording a behavior each time it occurs is event recording. Behaviors measured must be discrete, meaning that they have a definite beginning and ending (Alberto & Troutman, 2012; Cooper, Heron & Heward, 2012). This may also be referred to as frequency recording. Examples of event recording of academic behaviors include how many times the student asked a question, how many times a student provided a correct response, or how many social interactions with peers. Examples of event recordings of non-academic behaviors include how many times a student called out, how many times a student got out of her seat, or how many times a student touched a peer. Rate of occurrence can be calculated when a specific period of time is noted, or data is taken during a standardized period of time.

Rate= number of occurrences / time period

Event recording is selected when the objective is to increase or decrease the frequency of a behavior. Table 2 below shows the frequency of the behavior throughout the school day from period 1 through 7. Information can be analyzed by noticing differences in the behavior. For example, during periods 3 and

Table 1. Questions to ask when choosing a data collection procedure

Question to Ask	Dimension to Measure
How often the behavior occurs?	Each event (frequency, rate, or percentage)
How long the behavior lasts?	Duration
How strong? Intense?	Magnitude
How the behavior looks?	Topography
How long until the behavior starts?	Latency

Table 2. Event recording sample data

Observation Periods	Occurrence of behavior
1	I
2	II
3	IIII
4	IIII
5	III
6	I
7	

Assessing the Functions of Behavior for Students with Autism in the Inclusive Classroom Environment

4 the occurrence of the behavior is higher than other periods. This would lead a teacher to investigate those periods to identify what variables are influencing the behavior.

Interval Recording

Interval recording is a way of recording approximations of behavior over a period of time, (Alberto & Troutman, 2012; Cooper, Heron & Heward, 2012). Observations are conducted during an interval of time. The size of each interval could range from 5 seconds to 30 seconds. Alberto and Troutman (2013) recommend each interval should not be longer than 30 second, and the shorter the size of the interval, the more accurate the data collection. Interval recording can be implemented as partial interval recording, whole interval recording, or momentary time sampling. Observations during partial interval recording assess to see if the target behavior occurs at any time during the specified interval (i.e., record if the target behavior occurred any time during the 10 second interval). Whole interval recording observes for the target behavior to occur during the entire interval (i.e., record if the target behavior occurred for the entire interval time during the 10 second interval). Momentary time sampling however, observes the target behavior to occur at the end of the specific interval and uses longer intervals of time (i.e., record if the target behavior occurred at the end of the 5 minute interval during a 60 minute period).

Procedures for interval recording include defining a specific period of time, dividing the time period into equal intervals, and collecting data on whether or not the behavior occurred in the specific time interval. To quantify the data that is being recorded count the number of intervals the behavior occurs during the time frame for the observation. This data collection procedure is used with behaviors that are continuous and high in frequency. Table 3 shows the occurrence of calling out behavior.

An X was marked in the interval if the target behavior was observed during the 6 minute observation period. Each interval represents 30 seconds. The target behavior occurred 5 times during the 6 minute observation period. This method requires an independent observer if the classroom teacher is unable to observe without interruption.

Duration Recording

Duration recording is used when the target behavior of concern is observed as an amount or length of time rather than just an event or frequency of occurrence (Alberto & Troutman, 2012; Cooper, Heron & Heward, 2012). This recording system is best used for behaviors that have identifiable start and finish, which is easily observed by individuals in the environment. Baseline data are collected across multiple times of the school week, such as homeroom, academic and non academic classes, and other environments of the school environments. Teachers can take the average duration across a school day or total duration data for each occurrence of the target behavior. The primary concern when using duration recording is

Table 3. Interval recording sample data

	Target Behavior: Calling Out
	Start Time: 9:30AM Stop Time: 9:36AM
1	2	3	4	5	6	7	8	9	10	11	12
	X		X		X		X		X		

the length of engagement in the target behavior. Teachers can time behavior using a clock, stop watch, or cellular phone timing apps. Determining the baseline, or pre-intervention aspects of the behavior, will answer the question, "How long did the behavior last?" The duration of the behavior will lead to an appropriate target objective being determined with the intention of successfully changing the inappropriate behavior. The inappropriate behavior will not automatically become eliminated, but with an appropriate intervention the duration of the behavior can decrease as it is replaced with an appropriate behavior.

Event recording is best used for behaviors which need to increase or decrease the amount of time the student was engaged in the target behavior. Event recording or interval recording would not be appropriate as they would not identify how long the behavior was lasting. Academic behavior examples can include how long the student writes in a journal or how long the student reads from the text. Non-academic behavior examples can include, how long a student walks around, or how long a student bites his nails. Table 4 below shows the duration of the students screaming behavior.

Latency Recording

Latency recording involves how long a student takes to begin a behavior once the request has been made (Alberto & Troutman, 2012; Cooper, Heron & Heward, 2012). This has to do with how long it takes for a student to start a behavior in the classroom. If a teacher request was presented, the teacher would record the time the request was made and the time the student began the task. Additional information may be helpful such as the task, the success of completion, and the response rate of peers to the same task. The additional information can inform the teacher if the request was appropriate and if the request was within the student's current repertoire to complete the request independently. Academic behavior examples can include how long it takes the student to write their heading, or how long it takes the student to collect their notebook. Non-academic behavior examples can include, how long it takes a student to walk to the teacher's desk or how long it takes a student to obtain his lunch box.

Aside from collecting data on the target student, collecting data from the classroom peers gives information as to what would be acceptable as a target objective to meet the expectations in the classroom. When collecting data from a peer, the teacher would identify appropriate expectations.

Table 4. Duration recording sample data

Student: Mary Beth		
Target Behavior: Screaming		
Start Time	End Time	Duration of Behavior
8:32 AM	8:43 AM	11 minutes
8:44 AM	8:50 AM	6 minutes
8:57 AM	9:05 AM	8 minutes
9:24 AM	9:31 AM	7 minutes
9:51 AM	9:57 AM	6 minutes
10:33 AM	10:43 AM	10 minutes
10:38 AM	10:41 AM	3 minutes
10:52 AM	11:02 AM	4 minutes

The expectation is not for the student to respond quicker than anyone else, but to address the academic needs of the target student.

Table 5 shows the latency of a target student in math class. Data was also collected for two typical students (Peer 1 and Peer 2). Comparisons between the targeted student and peers can be used to create a behavioral goal for the targeted student's latency behaviors.

Data as a Decision Making Tool

The classroom teacher has a surplus of data to help assess student learning. With direct teacher observation, student pretest and posttest measures, and peer comparisons, assessment data is readily available to teachers to identify needs and strength of the target student (Marsh, 2012). Data supported interventions identify effectiveness for students learning. The surplus of data in the classroom including formative assessment, diagnostic assessment, curriculum based assessments, teacher made exams, and student work, are all useful as a decision making tool. This information presents the student's academic strengths, as well as weaknesses, and allows the teacher to identify skill deficits.

FUNCTIONS OF BEHAVIOR

The functions of student behavior refers to the purpose and reasons for why the student is engaging in the behavior. The function identifies what the student received or avoided from exhibiting the behavior. A functional behavioral assessment is essential as a system that collects information from various sources involving the student in a way to develop a hypothesis as to why the student engaged in the behavior (Alberto & Troutman, 2012; Cooper, Heron, & Heward, 2007).

Types of Functions of Behavior

The functions of behavior refer to what the student will obtain as a result of the behavior presented. The most common functions of behavior are escape, attention, tangible, sensory and medical (Cooper, Heron and Heward, 2007; Medeiros, Rojahn, Moore & Ingen, 2014). Medical functions of behavior refer to where a student attempts to relieve discomfort or pain. This automatic reinforcement could be attributed to a pre-existing condition, seasonal condition, or recurring medical conditions. As this is outside of the realm of the classroom teacher and the school environment, this function will not be discussed in the chapter. The remaining functions are the focus of this chapter, because these functions of behavior will be presented in the inclusive classroom. Classroom teachers will need to know how to identify and respond to these functions of behavior.

Table 5. Latency recording sample data

Instruction Takes Math	Target Student	Peer 1	Peer 2
Books out take pencil	145 seconds	20 seconds	5 seconds
Paper begins Math	90 seconds	15 seconds	12 seconds
Questions	120 seconds	18 seconds	10 seconds

To respond to student behavior effectively, a teacher must present an intervention based on the function of the student's behavior rather than the form of behavior. This analysis will help change the student's behavior with an alternative or replacement behavior. Replacing inappropriate behavior and increasing socially acceptable behaviors may correlate to academic or social success; reactive interventions are avoided. The goal is to systematically replace inappropriate behavior with appropriate behavior rather than reduce behavior problems as they occur. Function-based classroom interventions focus on teaching behaviors for long lasting change by targeting changes in student behavior, which is not person or environment specific.

Function: Attention

When attention is the function for a student's behavior, the exhibited behavior occurs to get someone's attention. This can be attention from peers, attention from the teacher or classroom assistant, or access to an item or activity that requires someone's assistance. When attention is the function of a student's behavior, that attention needs to be removed to change the problem behavior and replace it with what the student needs to be successful in the classroom. Once the classroom teacher has identified that the student's behavior occurs as a function to receive attention, the first response from the teacher would be to provide attention to the student for appropriate behavior.

Function: Escape

Escape is another function of behavior. Students may engage in behaviors to avoid something which is unpleasant in their environment. The emphasis would be placed on what the student finds unpleasant. This is from the student's perspective and will include great variability. In the classroom a student may engage in behaviors to escape academic tasks, peer interactions or teacher demands.

Function: Tangible

When tangible items are the function for a student's behavior, a student will engage in behavior to obtain the tangible item. If a student engages in maladaptive behaviors and tangibles are given then the maladaptive behavior is reinforced, and the probability of the student engaging in that behavior will increase. Teachers can provide students with a replacement behavior. Once the student has demonstrated the replacement behavior the tangible can be provided. This will reinforce the replacement behavior and over time if the maladaptive behavior is no longer reinforced, it will eventually decrease.

Function: Automatic Reinforcement/Sensory Based

Automatic reinforcement is another function for a student's behavior. The student engages in behavior to gain automatic sensory stimulation. This is specific to each individual and therefore behavior will vary. This behavior occurs to receive a pleasurable response or to escape a discomforting situation. The occurrence of this behavior does not depend on another person or object for the reinforcement. The behavior provides automatic reinforcement.

Evidence-Based Strategies and Promising Practice for the Classroom Teacher for Functions of Behavior

Escape, Tangible, Attention or Sensory Functions

- Implement an extinction procedure by removing any positive reinforcement maintaining the behavior. When a student exhibits a behavior that does not obtain the desired function, the behavior will decrease. The teacher would remove any reinforcement for the inappropriate behavior. For example, if a student raises her hand constantly to gain attention, then ignore the student's hand raising.
- Provide Differential Reinforcement of an Alternative Behavior (DRA) by reinforcing an alternate behavior. For example, to decrease calling out behaviors in the classroom, reinforce a student for raising her hand to answer a question. This behavior is an alternative to calling out.
- Provide Differential Reinforcement of an Incompatible behavior (DRI) by reinforcing an incompatible behavior. An incompatible behavior to standing is sitting. To decrease a student's standing behavior reinforces each time the student is sitting as it is incompatible to standing.
- Provide Differential Reinforcement of Other behaviors (DRO) by reinforcing more desirable behaviors. For example, a student usually off task may appropriately put away his books and materials. Reinforcing putting away books and materials removes reinforcement from the off task and reinforces the other behavior. The other behaviors will have a higher probability of occurring.
- Provide noncontingent reinforcement (NCR) in the absence of the target behavior. This allows access to a reinforcer without the occurrence of the disruptive behavior. For example, stand next to the student who interrupts for attention and reinforce the student with your attention in the absence of the target behavior.

Attention Functions

- Remove all attention or ignore the problem behavior.
- Teach an alternative behavior for the student to obtain the same function.
- Prompt the alternative behavior frequently for the student to obtain the function.
- Reinforce alternate behaviors immediately and intensely.
- Fade out prompts as appropriate behaviors increase.
- Replacement behavior should provide attention quicker than the problem behavior
- Withhold attention until student requests appropriately or terminates the behavior
- Provide attention throughout the day on a higher schedule then presented currently.

Escape Functions

- Demand should continue if within the student's repertoire.
- Provide the student with options for an alternative behavior.
- Teach the student to request breaks or help when needed.
- Teach the student to select a socially acceptable escape behavior.
- Teach the student to work for a period of time before requesting a break.
- Teach student to complete a set of demands prior to a break.

- Teach the use of demand coupons which may be traded when needed.
- Provide instructional strategies and supports to assist student to complete task.
- Create a task analysis to teach student to make an appropriate verbal request
- Create a reward system to shape student behavior.
- Use signal responses to signal the student to use an alternative behavior
- Provide accommodations or modifications for successfully completion of demand.
- Reinforce the initiation of task with positive attention and teacher assistance

Tangible Functions

- Withdraw the object for at least 30 seconds since last occurrence of the problem behavior before representing.
- Teach an alternative behavior to allow the student access to the object.
- Teach the alternative behavior frequently to shape the replacement behavior.
- Reinforce immediately to increase the occurrence of the replacement behavior
- Fade prompts to increase student's independence
- Teach and provide reinforcement for appropriate requests.
- Be consistent in reinforcing the appropriate behavior.
- Eliminate access to reinforcement following inappropriate behavior.

Sensory Functions

- Complete a preference assessment to identify potential reinforcers.
- Implement extinction to remove any positive reinforcement maintaining the behavior.
- Choose reinforcement to maintain appropriate behavior.
- Teach other forms of automatically reinforced appropriate behaviors.
- Provide less intrusive alternatives for replacement behaviors.
- Reinforce appropriate behavior in absence of the problem behavior
- Teach a replacement behavior which would be socially acceptable
- Response block to intervene as soon as student begins to emit a problem behavior
- Redirect towards an activity different from what caused the challenging behavior.
- Alter the environment to remove the desired sensory reinforcement.

FUNCTION VS. FORM

Function of the behavior refers to the purpose whereas the form of the behavior is what the behavior looks like as it is being observed, or the topography of the behavior. Different behaviors can look very different from each other when observed by the classroom teacher, but these behaviors can provide the same function for the student. Additionally, behavior which may have the same form, or topography, could provide different functions the students. (Alberto & Troutman, 2012; Cooper, Heron, & Heward, 2007). Functional classes of behavior may have many forms which serve the same function. On task behavior is a vague term that can mean the student is writing in a journal, completing math computations, or silently reading a novel. These examples will all look very differently as they are observed but they

Assessing the Functions of Behavior for Students with Autism in the Inclusive Classroom Environment

could have the same function, for example, gaining the teacher's attention as she reinforces the student for the specific on task behavior observed.

If we are observing a student looking in her desk, a student staring out the window, or a student passing a note to a peer, we would all agree these are different forms of behavior. All the behaviors would look different and not have the same form. Although the forms of the behavior may look different as the teacher is observing them, the functions of the behavior could be the same. For example, the student looking in her desk, the student staring out the window and the student passing a note could all be engaging in these behaviors to escape a task; three different behaviors, different forms but the same function. Additionally, one form of behavior may serve several functions. Tapping a classmate's shoulder could function to escape the class activity, or gain attention from the classmate, or obtain access to a tangible the classmate is holding. Herein lies the difference between the form of a behavior and the function of a behavior.

What are Data Based Supports that Can Help Students with Autism in Inclusive Settings?

Positive Behavioral Supports

As a part of the response to intervention initiative (RTI), academic and non-academic behavior requires a school wide proactive approach to support all learners. Using a Three Tier approach, Tier 1 includes primary prevention effective for 80 percent of the population, Tier 2 secondary prevention effective for 10 to 15 percent of the population that did not respond to Tier 1 intervention. and Tier 3, which is more intense and addresses the individual needs of approximately 7 percent of students who did not respond well to the Tier 1 and Tier 2 interventions (Batsche,Elliott, Graden, Grimes Kovaleski,Prasse, & Tilly 2005).

Not all students are the same in their behavior and therefore, multi layers of intervention should be available in the school environment. According to The National Autism Center's 2009 National Standards Report, strategies such as providing the student with choices, graphic organizers, prompts, visual cues and modifying tasks can serve well for Tier 1. In addition, the use of school wide token economies, a school wide code of conduct and consistency are elements required for students to be successful. These primary strategies can benefit a variety of students, not only students with Autism, and are simple to implement.

For Tier 2 interventions, students may benefit from working in smaller groups or 1:1 direct instruction during the lesson. Use of a buddy or a peer helper as well as instruction in self-management or self-monitoring strategies may be useful. In Tier 2 interventions, teachers may use simple behavioral modification charts followed by a positive consequence to manage a behavior. For example, Mr. Smith is a third grade teacher and Nigel is a student who has the repetitive behavior of asking, "What are we doing next?" This is a significant behavior because when Nigel's question is not dealt with, he becomes anxious, distracted and at times his behaviors becomes aggressive towards other students in the class.

Mr. Smith has posted a schedule of the day which was a part of his Tier 1 intervention. Although Nigel can see the schedule, he still asks and then disrupts the class. Nigel loses his focus and becomes off tasks. Nigel doesn't do well with the concept of time or knowing how long an activity will be. To say the activity will be a half hour is not reassuring for him. These interventions are too abstract for him and he needs more support.

As a Tier 2 intervention, Mr. Smith is working with Nigel on self-monitoring. Mr. Smith's plan is to make Nigel aware of his behavior and also provide visual representation of time Mr. Smith has color coded the schedule and tapes to the wall a corresponding color card. During the reading block, the color code is red. Mr. Smith takes a red colored card and tapes it to the wall. When the class moves on to math which is written in blue, Mr. Smith removes the red card and replaces it with a blue card. The color coded schedule and visual card which is displayed during the period of time in which the activity provided immediate visual feedback. Additionally, Mr. Smith has implemented a self-monitoring strategy

On Nigel's desk an index card reads:

1. Did I look at the schedule on the board?
2. Did I look at the color posted?
3. Am I following directions?

Mr. Smith has instructed Nigel to self-monitor before asking, "What are we doing next?" Mr. Smith taps the card periodically as a physical cue to remind Nigel to use the index card.

For students requiring Tier 3 interventions, Fisher (2012) suggests that the school form a professional learning community to address behavior issues. In this communities, often referred to as Behavioral Support Teams, information regarding the student, needs and goals can be discussed with other professionals in the school community. During meetings, various professionals share their insights to understand the student from other perspectives. Gathering these perspectives provides a wealth of information and insight to the who, what, when, why and where of student behavior.

Fisher (2012) recommends developing a behavior plan which includes collecting data and developing a positive relationship with the student. Behavior Intervention is about understanding behavior, its function and the strategies that will result in sustainable changes. Fisher (2012) cautions that when implementing strategies for students with Autism, each student should be treated as an individual. Strategies that are effective for one student with Autism may not work for every student with Autism. Therefore, a move toward more intensive support requires a very individualized plan. One evidenced based strategy which is highly individualized is conducting a Functional Behavioral Assessment (FBA) to determine environmental factors that contribute to the behavior. This is followed by a Behavior Intervention Plan (BIP) to change problematic or socially significant behaviors. In the next section Functional Behavioral Assessments and Behavior Intervention plans will be discussed. This highly individualized method of addressing behavior aids in understanding behavior and intervention.

Functional Behavioral Assessments and Behavior Intervention Plans

In previous sections of this chapter you have learned how to operationalize the term behavior, the functions of behavior and how to collect and quantify observations of the occurrence or absence of behavior. The Functional Behavioral Assessment and Behavior Intervention Plan process pulls together these concepts. To begin, you must have the FBA before the BIP (Scott, Anderson & Spaulding 2008). It is also important that the teacher (or team) conduct both the FBA and BIP because it is an interconnected process. All too often the research indicates that behavior intervention plans are created without a functional assessment or functional assessments that are not conducted by the same person (O'Neil & Stephenson, 2009). Constructing a BIP without the process of determining the function of the behavior is like building a house on sand. Mayer (1996) stated that functional assessments can improve the efficiency of interventions. The FBA is a method to organize observations to better understand the contributing

Assessing the Functions of Behavior for Students with Autism in the Inclusive Classroom Environment

factors to a behavior in a particular environment. Once understood, we can hypothesize reasons for the behavior (Shippen, Simpson, & Crites, 2003).

In the next section there are two different ways to construct Behavior Intervention Plans. The first, the classroom ready model, can be applied to the context of the classroom. This model uses the A-B-C observation and analysis as a means to hypothesize the function of a target behavior. By flipping the A-B-C observation the teacher can create an A-B-C Behavior Support Plan. The second, the Behavior Intervention Plan, reflects a building wide organizational and communication tool. Often when a behavior is extremely problematic and exhibited across settings in the school environment, a team approach is used. The Behavior Intervention Plan, form, serves as a tool to organize, plan, communicate and coordinate the efforts to address the behavior.

CLASSROOM READY FBA

ABC Observations-ABC Analysis-ABC Behavior Intervention.

Step 1: A-B-C Observations

The ABC method for conducting FBA is one of the most classroom ready models. The ABC model descriptive analysis examines which factors occasion a behavior, or maintains a behavior. In a classroom situation where the teacher is the primary investigator, this model may be more helpful than a team-based Behavior Intervention Plan .Observation, analysis and the creation of the plan is done by the classroom teacher or personnel who is responsible for the student in the setting where the behavior occurs. For example, a classroom teacher could have the A-B-C Behavior Intervention Plan operating to address a specific classroom behavior and concurrently, there may be a school wide Behavior Intervention Plan operating to address other behaviors exhibited in and out of the classroom. The classroom teacher may be working on increasing appropriate verbal communication and the school wide Behavior Intervention Plan might be addressing the student's escaping behaviors of running out of class and attempting to run out of the building. There may be circumstances where a classroom teacher requests a Behavior Intervention Plan because the behavior is far too serious and complex for one professional to analyze.

The classroom FBA/BIP model presented is an effective way to target a behavior, examine the antecedents and consequences, collect and analyze data to create an intervention. In this model the antecedents, consequences, or reinforcers, are used to maintain the replacement behavior. Progress monitoring data is used to determine the effectiveness of the plan. In the A-B-C model, A is antecedent, B is Behavior and C is consequence. In this model we begin with behavior. What is the targeted behavior? Is it operationalized? Targeted behaviors are those which can be observed and measured.

Clara was a student in Ms. King's 5th period 8th grade English Language Arts class. Ms. King noticed almost every day that Clara is very disruptive in the beginning of the class period. Due to Clara's behaviors, she fell behind the class and often seemed lost. She did not hand in her assignments although she had them in her messy binder. She was unorganized and frustrated. Although there are many problematic behaviors, Ms. King needed to target the behavior which is most concerning and at the crux of the situation. Ms. King decided that if Clara could be on task at the beginning of the period, then she may stay on task and not be lost or frustrated. Ms. King described the behavior she sees at the beginning of the period:

Clara fumbled with her books, dropped pencils on the floor and talked to herself while making paper balls in the beginning of class. It took her 10 minutes to begin the class assignments.

Ms. King had a clear idea of what she was going to observe: Clara took 10 minutes to begin her work (active participation in class).

Ms. King's next step was to write down what happens immediately before the the behavior. On the first day of conducting the ABC observation, this is what she recorded (see Table 6).

Step 2: Use a Data Collection Procedure to Count the Behavior

The A-B-C observation provides qualitative information about the targeted behavior. To further proceed in the data collection efforts, quantitative data can be obtained. A measure of the behavior can be taken to get the full scope on the who, what, when, why and where of the targeted behavior. There are various ways to measure behavior but selecting a measurement system depends upon the targeted behaviors' topography, and questions about the behavior as mentioned earlier in the chapter. In this case Ms. King was more concerned about Clara engagement in the class at the beginning of the period. The frequency of her off task behaviors was not primary so she did not conduct a frequency count, which is one of the most common data collection procedures. Ms. King's observed and targeted Clara's time to respond after directions, which is a latency measure.

During this phase of data collection, Ms. King collected baseline data. She did not implement an intervention. She did not make any changes at this point. She is collecting Clara's behavior as it usually occurs. Ms. King's goal was to determine what may have contributed to the behavior. Ms. King collected A-B-C observation, which is qualitative and also the latency data collection procedure, which is quantitative. Both of these are necessary during the baseline phase to hypothesize the function of the targeted behavior. This data clarifies what you feel is occurring versus the reality of what is occurring. For example, Ms. King thought it took Clara ten minutes every day to settle down and begin her assignments. Ms. King had instructed the students that when the second bell rings, the bell and written directions on the board are the directions to begin their work. Ms. King thought that each day Clara took ten minutes to begin her work after the bell, but her measurement of the behavior tells a different story. Two days out of week 1 data collection, Ms. King noted that Clara began her work immediately. Ms. King collected data for a second week.

Table 6. ABC observation data sample

Antecedents	Behavior	Consequence
Bell rings Teacher: "Begin Do Now, hand in Homework"	Clara sitting in seat flipping through binder	Teacher walks around classroom
Teacher: "Let's go over the questions".	Clara looking out the window, then drops pencils, balls up paper, puts head on desk	Teacher asks student with raised hand to answer first question
Teachers calls on other students	Clara sits up. Takes bathroom pass, exits room	Teacher continues with lesson
Teacher begins lecture on poetry	Clara is back, writing notes from the Smart Board	Teacher compliments class

Step 3: Collect Data Unique to the Student

The third step in the baseline phase is to collect data to create a student profile. This step is to provide additional insights by gathering information to to gain a better understanding of the student. A meeting with the PBIS team at this point can be instrumental in providing information regarding issues connected to the targeted behavior including medical, communication or social concerns which can be problematic factors for students with Autism. In addition, parents, teachers, teacher's aides and other professionals in the building may have pertinent information necessary before making a hypothesis about the function of the behavior. Collaborating with others to collect data unique to the student is necessary before moving to step 4.

Step 4: Analyze and Hypothesize

After collecting various data, Ms. King was ready to analyze the data to see if there were patterns or hints about the targeted behavior. When collecting baseline observations, Ms. King was in the process of conducting an A-B-C observation. Now that she has the observation and data, she is going to make an analysis of the information she has. This process is the A-B-C analysis.

Ms. King immediately noticed that three out of the ten days for data collection, Clara spent less that two minutes to settle down. Her A-B-C analysis also showed that the consequences following Clara's behaviors were that the teacher ignored Clara's behavior. Ms. King did not want to embarrass Clara and did not call on her during the beginning part of the class. During the ten days, seven lessons contained Do Nows at the beginning of the period, followed by students answering the questions. On the three days that Clara began her work in less than three minutes, the Do Now was a silent reading passage and a written reflection. Ms. King also noted that she did not collect homework on those days; rather, the homework assignment was to be posted onto the class web account system. Based on the information Mrs. King received from her grade level team, consisting of other teachers who also taught Clara, she hypothesized that the function of her behavior was to escape from the task of orally answering questions in class and large group discussions. Moving forward, Ms. King thought deeply about the Behavior Intervention. Oral communication was an academic behavior in which Clara struggled, but an area which she needed to practice.

BEHAVIOR INTERVENTION PLAN

In some cases, students have behaviors that need to be addressed across settings and in other cases students have behaviors that are occasioned by particular antecedents or consequences. For this cause, a BIP must be connected to the FBA and a hypothesized function (Moreno, G.& Bullock, L.M.,2011; Mayer, G.R. 1996). If a behavior is emitted to escape unstructured time and antecedents related to those settings, such as outdoor recess, then the BIP addressing the needs in that environment may not be suitable for the same student who is displaying attention seeking behaviors in the classroom during structured times. A classroom ready way to construct a BIP is to return to the ABC plan and flip it. Now instead of the problematic target behavior listed under "Behavior", we provide a replacement behavior. Instead of observing the antecedents and consequences that were related to the problematic targeted behavior, we think of ways to provide antecedents, consequences, or reinforcers that will support the replacement behavior.

Remember the case of Clara (see Table 7).

After engaging in the A-B-C analysis, Ms. King makes the following hypothesis:

The function of Clara's behavior is to escape from the task of speaking during the full class discussion. The discussions were forums for students to share their opinions and feelings about written selections. Ms. King also realized from the data collection, unique to Clara, that she has extreme difficulty with abstract literary concepts. She does better with facts and citing evidence than expressing her feelings about a poem.

Ms. King is now ready to flip the A-B-C observation into an A-B-C Behavior Intervention Plan (see Table 8).

Step 5: Create, Describe and Model a Replacement Behavior

Replacement behaviors are a more appropriate form of the targeted behavior that will result in the same function. In this classroom ready model, replacement behaviors will receive reinforcement and over time the schedule of reinforcement will gradually change so that the behavior will become generalized. A replacement behavior should be modeled by the teacher. By directly modeling the behavior for the

Table 7. Clara's case

Antecedents	Behavior	Consequence
Bell rings Teacher: "Begin Do Now, hand in Homework"	Clara sitting in seat flipping through binder	Teacher walks around classroom
Teacher: "Let's go over the questions."	Clara looking out the window, then drops pencils, balls up paper, puts head on desk	Teacher asks student with raised hand to answer first question
Teachers calls on other students	Clara sits up, takes bathroom pass, exits room	Teacher continues with lesson
Teacher begins lecture on poetry	Clara is back, writing notes from the Smart Board	Teacher compliments class

Table 8. A-B-C Behavior Intervention Plan sample

Antecedents	Behavior	Consequences
Events, changes or actions that can be implemented to support the onset of the target behavior	Create, describe and model the replacement behavior for the student	Reinforcement that can be used to support and maintain the replacement
Ms. King will touch her ear and give Clara a cue that the factual question is coming next	Clara will follow the success routine modeled by Ms. King upon entering the class and will answer the one factual question during the full class discussion	Ms. King will verbally praise Clara and during the discussion Clara will use a finger signal of 1 when she is extremely uncomfortable and doesn't want to be called on and two if she is willing to take a risk and be called on

student, she would understand what the replacement behavior should look like as words alone may not be enough. In addition, the description of the replacement behavior should be measureable, observable and precise. A replacement behavior of, "being good" during story time is neither measurable, observable nor precise. "Being good" is too elusive and subjective. A clear replacement behavior of sitting on the carpet during story time for four minutes with quiet hands, quiet feet and mouths modeled by the teacher is more likely to be understood.

In the case of Clara who wants to escape the discussion, Mrs. King could give her a behavior as a cue between Clara and Mrs. King to indicate Clara's level of comfort or discomfort during the discussion portion of the lesson. Another scenario is that Ms. King could provide a factual question during the discussion that Clara will be able to answer when called on. This type of replacement behavior is important because it serves as the same function but provides Clara practice in the large group discussion. Further intervention can hinge on the goal of getting her to speak more and more so that the skill of speaking in class is scaffolded.

Step 6: Manipulate the Antecedents and Consequences to Support the Replacement Behavior

In order to support the replacement behavior, the antecedents in the classroom can be manipulated to occasion or bring forth the replacement behavior. The antecedent could be a cue, the arrangement of students in the class or as in the case of Ms. King and Clara, the factual prepared questioned that Clara knows the answer to respond successfully. As a cue, Ms. King told Clara that she will know the question is coming when the teacher touches her ear. The consequences can also be used to manipulate and support the replacement behavior. For example, positive reinforcement can be used as a consequence immediately following the replacement behavior.

Step 7: Collect Data for the Replacement Behavior

During the A-B-C Observation and Analysis the targeted behavior was measured. This baseline data helped form a hypothesis about the targeted behavior and how the antecedents and consequences related to the targeted behavior. During the A-B-C Behavior Intervention Phase, data is needed to continue the process to assess changes and monitor the progress of the replacement behavior. By collecting data on the occurrence of the replacement behavior further manipulation of the consequences and antecedents can be planned. For example, teachers can adjust the consequences of the replacement behavior if it is not supporting the behavior or, reduce a reinforcer that is no longer needed. Progress monitoring data for the replacement behavior is essential to determine if the A-B-C Behavior Intervention is effective or ineffective.

It is suggested that the teacher and student sign the Behavior Intervention Plan when appropriate. Why? The teacher's signature ensures to the student that the teacher remains committed to the plan. The student's signature indicates that she is also committed to participate. Presenting the data to the student can be effective to show how often she is engaging in the behavior. Progress monitoring data on behavior should be shared just as academic progress is shared. Using this method can help build trust between the teacher and the student one behavior at a time.

Assessing the Functions of Behavior for Students with Autism in the Inclusive Classroom Environment

TEAM-BASED BEHAVIOR INTERVENTION PLAN

A team-based intervention plan is important to use when there is a school wide effort to address behaviors which occur across settings within the school environment. The difficulty is when the function of the behavior may t be different across settings and the reinforcement may be different. The goal of this type of plan is to find patterns in the behavior and the means to change the behavior. A second goal is to ensure safety and productivity in the school environment. This plan is essential for communicating the information and organizing the coordinated efforts by clarifying the role and responsibilities of each member of the team. Table 9 below is an example of a team-based Behavior Intervention Plan. The

Table 9. Sample behavior intervention plan

Behavior Intervention Plan
STUDENT INFORMATION
Name of Student:
D.O.B.
Grade:
Does the student have an I.E.P.?
Does the student have a 504 plan?
Is the student being referred for services?
Tell us about the student (*ex: what are his/her likes, dislikes, strengths, weakness, special interests, etc.*)
Is there any other information about the student that may be relevant (*home issues, medication or medical concerns, major events, etc.*)
OBSERVATIONS
Describe the information from the IEP/504 that relates to this intervention, if any.
Describe the behavioral issue.
From your observations and data, when, where and with whom does the behavior most often occur? Are there antecedents and/or predictors of the behavior?
What occurs after the behavior?
Based on your observations and/or data collection what happens after the behavior that may reinforce the behavior?
HYPOTHESIS - ANALYSIS
Why do you think the student is engaging in this behavior?
What is the function of the behavior? Select one or more and explain
_____ Escape a task
_____ Escape Attention or Social Interaction
_____ Escape Sensory Stimulation
_____ Gain Attention
_____ Gain a Tangible
_____ Gain Sensory Stimulation
Explanation:
REPLACEMENT BEHAVIOR
Generate the replacement behavior that will serve the same function.
Student will:
What are some environmental conditions and arrangements needed to make sure the replacement behavior can occur? What needs to happen in the school setting to occasion the replacement behavior? What antecedents can be arranged?
What are some consequences that can be used to support the behavior? What can the school do to positively reinforce the replacement behavior?
What other strategies can be employed to support the student so that he/she will engage in the replacement behavior?
MANAGEMENT
Who will teach, explain and or model the replacement behavior for the student?
Who will deliver the reinforcement of the replacement behavior? When, how often? Discuss how the reinforcement will be delivered with consistency if more than one person is delivering reinforcement.
How will success and usage of the replacement behavior be measured? By who, how often and will this be communicated to the team, the student, the family?
Explain and describe the role of other teachers or school personnel in this plan. What is their role? How should they handle the behavior problem? By whom and how will this information be communicated to them?
What will be the consequences if the student does not use the replacement behavior?
How will this be communicated to the student, school personnel and family?
Date of next meeting to review plan:

questions are used for the team to gather information about the behavior and determine what strategies should be used to address the behavior and how team will be coordinated to carry out the plan.

CONCLUSION

The focus of this chapter was to provide information for teachers and school personnel working with individuals with Autism Spectrum Disorders. Understanding the functions of behavior and responding effectively to student's behavior is critical to shape acceptable behavior for the inclusive setting. The inclusive setting presents the opportunity for students with and without disabilities to foster meaningful relationships and social, emotional and cognitive development. The rationale for this chapter was to bring awareness to the importance of observing student behavior, and how to properly assess student data specific for the student with Autistic Spectrum Disorder. Problem behaviors can negatively affect a person's ability to participate in family and community life, and to access educational opportunities (Crozer & Tincani, 2005). In order for students to be fully engaged in their community or school, they need to learn replacement behaviors to be productive participants in their environments. This chapter identified the function of behavior, which can be used to teach replacement behaviors for successful inclusion and increased independence. This is a goal for all students, especially students with special needs who require the successful intervention of their classroom teacher.

REFERENCES

Alberto, P. A., & Troutman, A. C. (2012). *Applied behavior analysis for teachers*. Upper Saddle River, NJ: Pearson.

American Psychiatric Association. (2012). *Autism spectrum disorders*. Retrieved from www.psychiatry.org.autism

Anderson, S., Leithwood, K., & Strauss, T. (2010). Leading data use in schools: Organizational conditions and practices at the school and district levels. *Leadership and Policy in Schools*, 9(3), 292–327. doi:10.1080/15700761003731492

Batsche, G., Elliott, J., Graden, J. L., Grimes, J., Kovaleski, J. F., Prasse, D., & Tilly, W. D. III. (2005). *Response to intervention*. Alexandria, VA: National Association of State Directors of Special Education.

Boe, E. E., Cook, L. H., & Sunderland, R. J. (2007). *Trends in the turnover of teachers from 1991 to 2004: Attrition, teaching area transfer, and school migration*. Philadelphia, PA: University of Pennsylvania.

Brown, J., & McIntosh, K. (2012). Training, inclusion and behaviour: Effect on student-teacher and student-sea relationships for students with autism spectrum disorders. *Exceptionality Education International*, 22(2), 77–88.

Chafouleas, S. M., Christ, T. J., Riley-Tillman, T. C., Briesch, A. M., & Chanese, J. A. (2007). Generalizability and dependability of direct behavior ratings to assess social behavior of preschoolers. *School Psychology Review*, 36(1), 63.

Chitiyo, M., & Wheeler, J. J. (2009). Challenges faced by school teachers in implementing positive behavior support in their school systems. *Remedial and Special Education*, *30*(1), 58–63. doi:10.1177/0741932508315049

Cooper, J. O., Heron, T. E., & Heward, W. L. (2007). *Applied behavior analysis*. Upper Saddle River, NJ: Pearson.

Couvillon, M. A., Bullock, L. M., & Gable, R. A. (2009). Tracking behavior assessment methodology and support strategies: A national survey of how schools utilize functional behavioral assessments and behavior intervention plans. *Emotional & Behavioural Difficulties*, *14*(3), 215–228. doi:10.1080/13632750903073459

Crozier, S., & Tincani, M. J. (2005). Using a modified social story to decrease disruptive behavior of a child with autism. *Focus on Autism and Other Developmental Disabilities*, *20*(3), 150–157. doi:10.1177/10883576050200030301

Ervasti, J., Kivimäki, M., Kawachi, I., Subramanian, S. V., Pentti, J., Ahola, K., ... Virtanen, M. (2012). Pupils with special educational needs in basic education schools and teachers' sickness absences- a register-linkage study. *Scandinavian Journal of Work, Environment & Health*, *38*(3), 209–217. doi:10.5271jweh.3281 PMID:22344461

FisherJ. (2012). *Positive behavioral supports for students with autism*. Retrieved from http://www.naesp.org/sites/default/files/Fisher_ND11-10.pdf

Gao, W., & Mager, G. (2011). Enhancing preservice teachers' sense of efficacy and attitudes toward school diversity through preparation: A case of one U.S. inclusive teacher education program. *International Journal of Special Education*, *26*(2), 92–107.

Geneva Centre for Autism. (2010). *Fact sheet on autism*. Retrieved from http://www.autism.net/resources/about-autism/44-fact-sheet-autism.html

Hart, J. E., & Whalon, K. (2013). Misbehavior or missed opportunity? Challenges in interpreting the behavior of young children with autism spectrum disorder. *Early Childhood Education Journal*, *41*(4), 257–263. doi:10.100710643-012-0527-8

Horrocks, J. L., White, G., & Roberts, L. (2008). Principals' attitudes regarding inclusion of children with autism in Pennsylvania public schools. *Journal of Autism and Developmental Disorders*, *38*(8), 1462–1473. doi:10.100710803-007-0522-x PMID:18256916

Johnston, J. M., & Pennypacker, H. S. (2008). *Strategies and tactics of scientific research*. New York, NY: Routledge.

Lindsay, S., Proulx, M., Thomson, N., & Scott, H. (2013). Educators' challenges of including children with autism spectrum disorder in mainstream classrooms. *International Journal of Disability Development and Education*, *60*(4), 347–362. doi:10.1080/1034912X.2013.846470

Lindsley, O. R. (1991). From technical jargon to plain English for application. *Journal of Applied Behavior Analysis*, *24*(3), 449–458. doi:10.1901/jaba.1991.24-449 PMID:1752836

Loiacono, V., & Valenti, V. (2010). General Education Teachers Need to Be Prepared to Co-Teach the Increasing Number of Children with Autism in Inclusive Settings. *International Journal of Special Education, 25*(3), 24–32.

Marsh, J. A., McCombs, J. S., & Martorell, P. (2010). How instructional coaches support data-driven decision making policy implementation and effects in Florida middle schools. *Educational Policy, 24*(6), 872–907. doi:10.1177/0895904809341467

Mayer, G. R. (1996). Why must intervention plans be based on functional assessments? *California School Psychologist, 1*(1), 29–34. doi:10.1007/BF03341090

Medeiros, K., Rojahn, J., Moore, L. L., & Ingen, D. J. (2014). Functional properties of behaviour problems depending on level of intellectual disability. *Journal of Intellectual Disability Research, 58*(2), 151–161. doi:10.1111/jir.12025 PMID:23464786

Moreno, G., & Bullock, L. M. (2011). Principles of positive behavior supports: Using the fba as a problem-solving approach to address challenging behaviors beyond special populations. *Emotional & Behavioural Difficulties, 1*(2), 117–127. doi:10.1080/13632752.2011.569394

O'Neil, S., & Stephenson, J. (2009). Teacher involvement in the development of function-based behavior intervention plans for students with challenging behavior. *Australasian Journal of Special Education, 1*(1), 6–25. doi:10.1375/ajse.33.1.6

Osborne, L. A., & Reed, P. (2011). School factors associated with mainstream progress in secondary education for included pupils with Autism Spectrum Disorders. *Research in Autism Spectrum Disorders, 5*(3), 1253–1263. doi:10.1016/j.rasd.2011.01.016

Rodríguez, I. R., Saldaña, D., & Moreno, F. J. (2012). Support, inclusion, and special education teachers' attitudes toward the education of students with autism spectrum disorders. *Autism Research and Treatment*. PMID:22934171

Ryan, J. B., Hughes, E. M., Katsiyannis, A., McDaniel, M., & Sprinkle, C. (2011). Research-based educational practices for students with autism spectrum disorders. *Teaching Exceptional Children, 43*(3), 56–64. doi:10.1177/004005991104300307

Sari, H., Celikoz, N., & Secer, Z. (2009). An analysis of pre-school teachers' and student teachers' attitudes to inclusion and their self-efficacy. *International Journal of Special Education, 24*(3), 29–44.

Scott, T., Anderson, C., & Spaulding, S. (2008). Strategies for developing and carrying out functional assessment and behavior intervention planning. *Preventing School Failure: Alternative Education for Children and Youth, 52*(3), 39–50. doi:10.3200/PSFL.52.3.39-50

Shippen, M., Simpson, R., & Crites, S. (2003). A practical guide to functional behavioral assessment. *Teaching Exceptional Children, 35*(5), 36–44. doi:10.1177/004005990303500505

Spencer, V. G., Evmenova, A. S., & Boon, R. T. (2014). Review of research-based interventions for students with autism spectrum disorders in content area instruction:implications and considerations for classroom practice. *Education and Training in Autism and Developmental Disabilities, 49*(3), 331–353.

Supovitz, J. (2010). Knowledge-Based organizational learning for instructional Improvement. In Second International Handbook of Educational Change (pp. 707-723). New York, NY: Springer. doi:10.1007/978-90-481-2660-6_40

Turton, A. M., Umbreit, J., & Mathur, S. R. (2011). Systematic function-based intervention for adolescents with emotional and behavioral disorders in an alternative setting: Broadening the context. *Behavioral Disorders*, *36*(2), 117–128.

Wayman, J. C., Cho, V., Jimerson, J. B., & Spikes, D. D. (2012). District-wide effects on data use in the classroom. *Education Policy Analysis Archives*, *20*(25). Retrieved from http://epaa.asu.edu/ojs/article/view/979

Wright, P. W., & Wright, P. D. (2007). *Special education law*. Hartfield, VA: Harbor House Law Press.

Zirkel, P. A. (2013). Recent legal developments of interest to special educators. *Intervention in School and Clinic*, *48*(5), 319–322. doi:10.1177/1053451212472234

This research was previously published in Supporting the Education of Children with Autism Spectrum Disorders edited by Yefim Kats; pages 116-138, copyright year 2017 by Information Science Reference (an imprint of IGI Global).

Chapter 48
An Integral Analysis of Labeling, Inclusion, and the Impact of the K–12 School Experience on Gifted Boys

Laurie Alisat
University of Calgary, Canada

Veronika Bohac Clarke
University of Calgary, Canada

ABSTRACT

Gifted learners are frequently marginalized in community classrooms, as they are placed in competition for special education support, with the students who struggle to meet the minimal curricular demands. In this chapter, we describe the practices of identifying and labelling gifted boys, from the perspective of gifted boys attending high school and from the perspectives of a school system. The case discussed is a large urban public school system, which endeavours to effectively identify gifted students and provide them with learner-centred learning environments. We use Wilber's (2000, 2006) Integral model as a conceptual framework to analyze the findings from an empirical study of gifted boys' school experiences (Alisat, 2013). These findings are also supported by our critical praxis, observing and conversing with gifted young people. The Integral Model is a useful framework for understanding the multiple factors impacting gifted students' daily experiences, engagement and achievement.

INTRODUCTION

Imagine you are a child attending school, being in class everyday and already knowing and understanding what is being taught to you. The gifted students, who are the subjects of this chapter, discussed this daily drudgery of boredom, repetition and lack of appropriate challenge. They described being told to "wait for the class to catch up" or to "go around the class and see who could use your help," or they were

DOI: 10.4018/978-1-7998-1213-5.ch048

given extra work (worksheets or more questions), or an extra project, because they finished early. Some gifted students would withdraw, while others would create a distraction to change up the monotony. These student experiences reflect some of the widely held societal attitudes toward gifted students: gifted students are advantaged, gifted students have a moral obligation to society to work hard and apply their gift toward the common good, gifted students are the undeserving beneficiaries of genetic recombination, and gifted students are gifted at everything. Parents sometimes exhibit these attitudes, pushing their children to excel at school as well as at numerous extracurricular studies. Schools that consciously or unconsciously act on these attitudes suppress opportunities for the optimal unfolding of these students' potential, which may ultimately inhibit their future success.

Teachers' attitudes toward the needs of gifted learners have a significant impact on the self-esteem and achievement of gifted learners. The gifted learners in this study described teaching practices that supported their performance in classrooms, whether through community engagement, or through alternative or specialized programming. They also shared experiences of teaching practices that did not support their growth and development intellectually, socially or emotionally. In fact, those negative teaching approaches may have contributed to placing some of them at risk for mental illness. Teachers who believe gifted learners 'have it all,' and therefore do not need teacher support and guidance, do not understand gifted learners. It is a matter of social justice, when the needs of other learners in the classroom are continuously placed before the needs of gifted learners. Gifted learners, formally identified or not, have the right to an education that is appropriately challenging to support their growth and development, just as all other learners in classrooms do.

The education of gifted students is also affected by a larger context, beyond the classroom and the school. In school districts, students who are not meeting minimum curricular demands are generally given priority for special support over gifted learners, as evidenced by teachers' and administrators' comments and actions regarding the lack of assessment and programming for gifted learners. However, the provincial and district mandates and policies for personalization of learning are intended to include gifted learners. Provincial funding for Special Education identifies gifted learners as those in need of special provisions. Each district decides what resources each special education area will have and how the resources will be deployed. To this end, the district in this study has developed a variety of programming options. These include cluster-grouping gifted learners within community classes, periodic pull-out classes and full-time congregated settings. The district also employs a system specialist to support gifted learners in all settings.

BACKGROUND

Selected Review of the Literature

The literature identifies contradictions in the conceptions of giftedness, from labeling giftedness and determining effective provisions for gifted learners (Brulles, Saunders, & Cohn, 2010; Brulles & Winebrenner, 2011; Freeman, 2006; Gentry, 1999; Gentry & MacDougall, 2007; Perrone, Wright, Ksiazak, Crane, & Vannatter, 2010; Renzulli & Reis, 2002), to assessing the gifted individual's function in society (Persson, 2009). The relationship that gifted individuals have with those in their world is complex. Contextual characteristics, cultural beliefs, values, organization, etc., play a significant role in their experiences and satisfaction. The interactions and influences of these different factors need to be acknowledged and understood in order to promote a greater understanding of gifted boys' experiences of schooling and the role of alternative programs in supporting them.

So who are the gifted learners? In a review of clinical data from a private practice of over 30 years, Silverman (2009) identified what has been learned about gifted learners. Some of her findings included:

- Half of children tested with high IQ scores were referred for behavioral issues;
- The ideal age for testing for giftedness is between five and eight years, after which social conditioning may interfere with the results;
- There are levels and types of giftedness, as in other learning conditions, that require different provision;
- Development of gifted learners is asynchronous; they may be advanced in some areas and demonstrate relative weakness in another;
- Gifted children are better socially adjusted when with intellectual mates;
- Perfectionism, sensitivity, and intensity are characteristics consistently associated with giftedness;
- Gifted boys are often considered "immature" and may be held back in school if they struggle to socialize with age mates with whom they have no common interests.

Teachers' Attitudes towards Gifted Learners

If we espouse the principle that all students deserve to be appropriately challenged, then gifted learners need to be included in the planning for learning in regular classrooms. As those closest to students who have control over the opportunities for appropriate challenge, teachers are influenced by their attitudes towards giftedness. The opportunities for appropriate challenge they design exemplify the social justice that gifted learners experience in the classroom. A review of the frequently cited research provides evidence of the likelihood of such provision.

McCoach and Siegle (2007) studied predictors of teachers' attitudes toward the gifted. They focused on how regular education teachers felt about providing specialized services for gifted students, whether teachers who had training or experience in gifted education were more supportive of gifted students and gifted education, if teachers who had training or experience in gifted education were more likely to perceive themselves as gifted, and if there were differences between special education teachers and non-special-education teachers in terms of their attitudes toward the gifted.

Of the 262 teachers from across the USA who responded, most were white females. Slightly more than half the teachers in the sample had some training in gifted education, with 126 teachers having no training in gifted education. Both groups held fairly neutral attitudes toward gifted education. Their attitudes toward acceleration were mixed, with 67% of teachers being ambivalent about acceleration. Also, they were neutral, neither agreeing nor disagreeing with the notion that gifted education was elitist. Some, however, had very positive attitudes regarding gifted education programs, while others had particularly negative attitudes. They found special education teachers had more negative attitudes toward the gifted. In particular, they had lower support for gifted education and were less supportive toward acceleration.

Teachers who received training in gifted education had significantly higher self-perceptions as being gifted themselves, however, these perceptions were completely unrelated to their attitudes toward gifted education. They were not more likely to display positive attitudes toward gifted education than those teachers who did not consider themselves gifted. McCoach and Siegle (2007) ask, if it is possible, that by "broadening the notion of giftedness, we are less able to make a compelling argument for the necessity of specialized service for gifted students?"

Geake and Gross (2008) looked at teachers' negative effect on academically gifted students, disputing McCoach and Siegle's (2007) findings. Their main concerns include: Why is the development of young people who may become sports stars or popular entertainers fostered, while opportunities for young educational superstars seem far more limited? Why is there resistance to identify those with high intellectual potential and to support them in our regular classrooms? Is there a key element of the human condition to harbour a suspicion of those who are highly intelligent—especially those who exhibit precocious intelligence?

To answer these questions, 377 teachers in England, Scotland, and Australia who were engaged in professional development around gifted education were surveyed about their subconscious feelings toward gifted children. Target statements were responded to as rapidly as possible, in an impulsive rather than in a considered manner, to prevent deliberation over their responses.

Geake and Gross' findings showed that teachers who had completed gifted education professional development, whether it was their choice to participate or not, were more positive about both the intellectual and social leadership characteristics of gifted children and were less negative about their potential social noncompliance. However, these teachers also expressed a negative perception of high intelligence centred on the stereotype of madness associated with genius. Thus, teachers trained in gifted education can also have a sub-conscious negative effect on students who typify nonconformist socializing.

Interestingly, when negative loaded terms were presented (such as labelling a student an articulate social misfit) participants were more negative towards gifted learners. The researchers explain this in terms of evolutionary psychology, where there is a psychological suspicion of outsiders. This could explain why the most cited reason by teachers for not accelerating a gifted child was that the child was not fitting in socially. This is in complete contrast to how precocity in sport or music is supported in schools. Superiority in physical or musical attributes is seen as social compliance, contributing to society in terms of entertainment and social bonding, whereas academic superiority is seen as an individualistic gift associated with social isolation and noncompliance, without benefit to social unity. A study by Preckel, Baudson, Krolak-Schwerdt, and Glock (2015) confirmed the negative stereotyping of social maladjustment associated with giftedness, but only in males and not females.

Moon and Brighton (2008) investigated primary teachers' beliefs and conceptions of giftedness and classroom practices related to the talent development of gifted and potentially gifted children. 434 randomly selected primary education teachers from across the USA, predominantly white female, completed the survey. 39% taught in suburban settings, 34% taught in rural settings, and 28% taught in urban settings. Slightly over one third of the participating schools offered programs for primary gifted learners.

The findings suggested that teachers generally could more easily identify positive and traditional characteristics associated with gifted behaviours than negative characteristics or non-traditional characteristics. Overwhelmingly these include: "high social intelligence resulting in a strong connection to their community," learns quickly and easily, has advanced vocabulary, is highly imaginative, offers unusual, unique, clever responses to questions and problems, has a large amount of general information, enjoys playing with words, uses details in stories and pictures and is able to see cause and effect relationships. They also believed gifted students had more social and emotional issues, and that gifted students could "be shy" and "misbehave in school." They were generally less likely to consider identifying a student as gifted if that student was well liked by classmates, made other students laugh, gave unexpected, sometimes 'smart-aleck' answers, had a lot of energy, had difficulty remaining seated, had difficulty moving onto another topic, and liked to work in small groups. Also, they had difficulty conceptualizing a student as gifted if the student did not possess strong early reading skills, had a limited vocabulary, was unable to work independently, or lacked internal motivation and persistence—characteristics frequently used to describe children from impoverished family backgrounds or having other learning needs along with giftedness.

Most participants believed the potential for academic giftedness was present in equal proportions in all racial/cultural/ethnic groups in society. However, 27% of respondents disagreed that the potential for academic giftedness was present in all socioeconomic groups in our society, believing that socioeconomic status was a major determinant in possessing some kind of academic giftedness. Most agreed that giftedness manifested itself differently among different cultural, racial, or ethnic groups, and they believed that boys were more likely to show their giftedness through spatial ability while girls were more likely to show their giftedness through verbal ability.

Teachers tended to hold deficit-oriented framework when considering programming for giftedness: students must first overcome their deficit in areas such as spelling, grammar, homework neglect, or patience before being considered for gifted program benefits. Teachers believed gifted services were most appropriate for students who demonstrated all the traditional signals of giftedness and had no observable deficits.

Siegle, Moore, Mann, and Wilson (2010) wanted to understand the factors that influenced teachers' nominations of students for gifted and talented programs. They developed eleven student profiles, with varied personal characteristics including gender, interests and skill sets, in order to measure the attitudes of 290 pre-service and 95 in-service teachers (those enrolled in a gifted education conference) and how those attitudes determined student recommendation to district gifted education programs. The majority of participants were female, and approximately half were elementary certified.

Their findings, similar to others (McCoach & Siegle, 2007; Geake & Gross, 2008; Moon & Brighton, 2008), found that in-service teachers tended to rate students higher than pre-service teachers. Students who were interested in math, had unusual or passionate interests, were voracious readers, were curious, were empathic, were from low SES, had identified gifted siblings, were rated higher. Students less willing to help other students with their learning were rated lower. Pre-service teachers thought gifted students should help tutor other students in the class, even though they may not enjoy it and may not support their learning.

Carman (2011) explored whether teachers held stereotypical thoughts about gifted students and whether there was a difference in the thoughts held by pre-service versus in-service teachers. Participants, primarily female, were university students in graduate and under-graduate education classes, having had very little exposure to the gifted in their coursework and no required courses on gifted learners at either level. Participants were 91 undergraduate pre-education majors (pre-service) and 20 graduate students (in-service) with current teaching experience.

Participants were asked to picture and describe an imaginary gifted person. 81% of pre-service teachers compared with 70% of in-service teachers held stereotypical thoughts. 60% of the participants visualized common physical stereotypes of clean-cut, brown or dark hair color, geeky/dorky, and pale males. They were four times as likely to describe their imaginary gifted person as thin, lanky, or non-athletic build. More than half of the participants mentioned free time activity of their imaginary gifted person as studying/reading, followed by playing a musical instrument, listening to classical music, playing chess, and taking college courses at a young age. Personality and interpersonal relationships were mentioned fewer than any other category, as quiet/shy/silent or witty/good sense of humour, serious, observant, eccentric/different, and show-off/snobby. Participants were almost twice as likely to report that their imaginary gifted person was not popular among their peers. In-service teachers in this sample with greater experience held fewer stereotypical thoughts, suggesting that as teachers gain experience they may shed their stereotypical thoughts.

Based on these studies on how teachers viewed and identified gifted learners and their needs, it might be suggested that both unusual students and well socialized, compliant students can be identified as gifted and in need of gifted educational programming. As researchers found (Berlin, 2009; Freeman, 2006; Perrone et al., 2010), being labeled as "gifted" has complex social implications. Some students thrive and flourish when offered different learning experiences and challenges and are invited to work with others of similar ability. Other students feel an overwhelming pressure, whether self-imposed or inflicted by others, to perform as "gifted." Meanwhile, students who were not identified as gifted until later in life, bore the negative consequences of the lack of identification and programming provision, and the memory of being held back and bored (Persson, 2009; Persson, 2010).

Educational Programming for Giftedness

There are many approaches to supporting learners identified as "gifted," including differentiation, ability grouping, and interest grouping in inclusive and congregated educational settings. Most of these approaches focus on strategies for providing appropriate challenge through learning environments of enrichment and/or acceleration.

Differentiation

One of the predominant practices used to support gifted learners is differentiation, which includes a variety of strategies to meet the diverse needs of learners. Inherent in the term differentiation is the acknowledgment of difference. In educational settings, differentiation recognizes the diversity of students' abilities, interests, and the worthiness of each student to be appropriately challenged in meaningful work (Alberta Education, 2010, 2012; Tomlinson, 2000). The teacher and students work together in flexible learning environments that are responsive to students' needs, based on authentic assessments as students actively engage in learning (Kanevsky, 2011; Tomlinson, 1995).

Tomlinson (1995) suggested differentiation as a way of supporting gifted learners in inclusive settings. It provides multiple access points to the curriculum through multiple means of exploring and understanding concepts, and encourages learning that is connected to the learners' profiles, which includes their learning preferences, interests, abilities, and readiness. Driven by interest and/or ability, students are able to push beyond the prescribed program of studies when flexibly grouped according to their learner profiles, and teachers can focus on different aspects depending on the desired outcomes.

According to Winebrenner (2001), the group of students that learned the least in mixed ability classrooms was the most able students; gifted learners became the neglected learners in the class. The learning tasks were easily completed or conversely ignored because they lacked challenge and relevance. When taken up, differentiation for gifted learners provided activities in such a way that lead to meaningful learning connected to the world beyond school (Winebrenner, 2001). There were five elements of differentiation referred to: content, process, product, environment, and assessment. Within these elements, choice, complexity, abstractness, relevance, and support were seen as foundational to the experience (Winebrenner, 2001). These elements, though semantically different, are similar to Pyryt's 5 P's (2004) for working with gifted learners: pace, product, process, passion, and peers. Students are more engaged when their learning is personalized to their particular needs and interests, with varying levels of complexity, abstractness, and relevance.

Betts (2004) developed a multilevel model for differentiation, which focused on developing autonomous learners. At tier I, all learners in the classroom were involved focusing on the mandated programs of study. In tier II, the teacher differentiated the curriculum by providing different content, process, and product opportunities. Students exercised choice and were more involved in their learning. Tier III was learner differentiated: the teacher acted as a facilitator, supporting skill, concept, and attitude development in service to student-directed content, process, and products.

These differentiation strategies have the potential to provide more challenging, personalized opportunities for all students, including those identified as gifted. The approach works from a strength-based perspective, which allows gifted learners to excel in their area of interest and/or strength. Teachers using this approach worked more collaboratively with students instead of directing the learning in a similar manner for all students in the class (Betts, 2004; Kanevsky, 2011; Pyryt, 2004; Tomlinson, 1995, 2000; Winebrenner, 2001).

Ability Grouping within Mixed Ability Classrooms

Several methods and models have been used to group students according to their ability, either generally or domain specifically. Groupings can be flexible across classrooms, whereby students are re-grouped based on frequent assessments around their understandings of specific concepts. Or, groups can be fixed across a school, with flexible grouping within each classroom.

Cluster grouping, as a strategy, initially focused on grouping gifted learners as a class within a school. Hoover, Sayler, and Feldhusen (1993) found gifted students benefited from the specialized support provided beyond just grouping. Teachers reported a positive classroom environment between clustered and non-clustered students. However, the teacher's workload increased considerably and teachers with non-clustered students were somewhat negative about losing their top students to the cluster.

As the approach became more widespread, modifications emerged. School-wide cluster grouping (Gentry & Owen, 1999) looked to group all students of the same grade into like ability and placed them in one classroom instead of into several. Each classroom had heterogeneous groups within. The notion was that clustering provided like-minded, like-ability peers for support and encouragement. Clustering also identified specific learning needs for the teacher to be able to focus on more readily. Studies reported student achievement was higher in cluster-grouped schools, which cited success as a result of teachers being better able to address individual student needs (Gentry & MacDougall, 2007; Gentry & Owen, 1999).

Significant benefits were realized when multiple strategies were employed along with the cluster grouping, according to research (Brulles, Saunders, & Cohn, 2010; Biddick, 2009; Pierce, Cassady, Adams, Speirs Neumeister, Dixon, & Cross, 2011). The benefits included: increased achievement of all students, opportunity for high ability students in non-gifted clustered classes to be leaders, full time support for gifted learners, and cost savings when all students were included in regular community schools. As identified by Gentry (1999) and reaffirmed by Biddick (2009), greater overall success was observed "when a high level of differentiation was offered, a positive classroom environment existed, with high expectations for all students, including a wide variety of strategies used to cater to individual needs" (p. 85).

Brulles et al, (2010) conducted a study comparing gifted student achievement for clustered and non-clustered gifted students. Students in cluster groups in one school were compared to those in regular heterogeneous classes in another equivalent school within the district. They found clustered gifted students achieved at statistically higher levels with greater growth than their non-clustered peers, regardless of demographics. The researchers (Brulles et al, 2010) explained these findings as a result of teacher professional development in gifted education and differentiation strategies employed in the clustered classes. Students benefited from the teachers' development and informed support.

The School-wide Cluster Grouping Model (Brulles & Winebrenner, 2011) provided a systematic approach to administratively design classrooms to reduce the range of learner needs, yet provided enough diversity to enrich the learning opportunities in classrooms. With this model students were clustered by ability across each grade or multiple grades. Then, specific clusters were combined to form particular classes.

Teachers' interests, skill sets, and knowledge were matched with particular class clusters. Professional development was targeted to particular teachers of particular clusters as well as addressing the diverse needs of the class through differentiation strategies.

Opposition to cluster grouping has been around the notion of tracking (Fiedler, Lange, & Winebrenner, 2002). With tracking, all students are assessed and then divided into class-sized groups, which are typically fixed for the school year. Little movement between levels is experienced, short term or long term. The classes are taught a uni-level program, providing little differentiation for individual skills or interests.

Enrichment as Pull-Out Support

Enrichment was frequently identified as a strategy to provide for gifted students. Identified gifted learners were bought together and met as a group to explore areas of interest. Depending on the school and school district policy, this would happen on a regular basis (daily, weekly, biweekly, etc.) or on an ad hoc basis, according to staff availability and interest.

A more systematic approach to enrichment was Renzulli's (1977) Enrichment Triad Model. It was incorporated in the School-wide Enrichment Model (Renzulli & Reis, 2002), which worked with the top 15-20% of the student population, as determined by academic achievement, teacher nominations, potential for creativity, and demonstrated task commitment. Once identified, the "talent pool" at Type I was exposed to a wide variety of topics and experiences not ordinarily covered in the program of studies.

Type II enrichment activities, at times, overlapped general classes as thinking and feeling processes were developed in both. This was similar to Betts (2004) Type II where particular skills and attitudes were acquired to support students' interests within enrichment. For Type III enrichment, students selected specific interests, gaining an advanced understanding by developing an authentic product for a specific audience. In the process, students developed numerous skills (resource management organization, decision-making, and self-evaluation) through these self-directed learning activities (Renzulli & Reis, 2002).

Differentiation as a practice offers several strategies that support learners with diverse abilities and interests. In mixed ability classrooms, differentiated practice has the potential to provide appropriate challenge and choice for all students. The challenge is providing effective support for teachers through professional development, strategic class development, and matching of teachers' interests and skill sets to their group of learners.

Congregated Programs for Gifted Learners

Enrichment

In some enrichment programs, the whole school is focused
on a particular interest, such as the arts, sports, languages, or an ideology (Montessori, 2013; traditional learning, religion, culture), that is threaded through the program of studies. These focused themes have the potential to provide rich, intensely situated learning. Students are exposed to the particular knowledge, skills, and methodology of the focus represented in the program. For some programs, a minimum level of ability is required for enrolment in the program, for others a declared interest is sufficient. This type of programming can support more intense student interests and provide motivation for advanced learning that may not exist within regular community schools. Examples of these types of program are described in Chapter 4. Citations are intentionally not provided to protect the confidentiality of study participants, as required by the school district.

Acceleration

Congregated learning settings targeting more able learners provide more advanced content at an accelerated pace. The International Baccalaureate (2013) program, the Advanced Placement (2013) courses, and specialized gifted education classes are examples of three such settings. These classes exist as separate programs within a larger school setting.

Matthews and Kitchen (2007) reported that tensions frequently existed between the mainstream students and the special program students. Elitism and special privileges were cited as points of conflict from mainstream students regarding the 'special' program students. Disrespect and lack of acceptance for their interests and abilities exacerbated these points of conflict. Students in the special program, regardless of which one they were enrolled in, appreciated having the opportunity to learn in an environment where they could be with like-minded peers to engage enthusiastically in their learning in a more challenging and comprehensive way.

Hertberg-Davis and Callahan (2008) found similar results. Gifted students found International Baccalaureate and Advanced Placement classes to be far superior than regular high school classes in terms of challenge, learning environment, and teacher engagement. In fact, student saw the program "as an opportunity to escape the drudgery of less challenging courses" and "busywork" (p.202). Though they appreciated the challenge, they were frustrated with the heavy workload and the sacrifice of their sleep and social life. Students suggested the challenge came from the workload and the pressure to complete and write the next test.

In both studies, students described their relationships with their teachers as being significant to their positive learning experience in the program (Hertberg-Davis & Callahan, 2008; Matthews & Kitchen, 2007). They liked the more adult-like nature of the relationship. As well, they felt as though their teachers had a strong grasp of their subject and really cared about their students' experience of it.

Gifted students who dropped out of the International Baccalaureate program and Advanced Placement courses cited the lack of flexibility, both in content exploration and demonstration of learning, as reasons for leaving (Hertberg-Davis & Callahan, 2008; Matthews & Kitchen, 2007). This further exemplifies the diversity of learning needs of gifted learners, as well as the complexity of providing appropriate provision for these learners.

THEORETICAL PERSPECTIVES

Integral Theory

Ken Wilber's Integral Theory (2000, 2006) is a metatheory, which provides an organizing framework or a map for viewing and coherently integrating fundamental perspectives on human development. This map has the capacity to coherently represent the complex interactions between perspectives, and the theories behind those perspectives. It is one of the few existing integrating frameworks that are available to cutting edge transdisciplinary researchers.

The Integral model is the visual representation of the metatheory. The model, which is also referred to by the acronym AQAL (all quadrants, all levels), has 5 components: quadrants, levels, lines, states and types. The quadrant map is the basic infrastructure of the model, as it represents an intersection of two basic approaches for viewing the world: inside/outside and singular/plural. The intersection of these approaches gave rise to the four quadrants –worldviews or human perspectives on the world around them.

The quadrants are:

- **Upper Left:** *The interior individual* –the subjective view, focusing on the self and consciousness, and individual experience;
- **Lower Left:** *The interior collective* –the intersubjective view, focusing on the shared understanding between individuals within a culture or a group;
- **Upper Right:** *The exterior individual* –the objective view, focusing on examination of the individual as an organism, and the observation of behavior; and
- **Lower Right:** *The exterior collective* –the interobjective view, focusing on social systems and the environment.

Figure 1 shows the four quadrants. It should be noted that the quadrants are represented this way for ease of "mapping" and understanding situations and contexts – in real life these quadrants represent four interacting perspectives for viewing the world. These are not 4 separate containers.

The next component of the model is "the levels" of development. These levels, and their mental perspectives or habits, run through whole populations or cultures, as well as through individuals. Individual humans are defined as holons – being simultaneously independent units and parts of greater units (such as family, tribe, nation, etc.). There are a number of reliable instruments for measuring these developmental levels (Loevinger, 1985, Cook-Greuter, 2004). These levels should be understood as levels of complexity at which individuals or groups operate. The more control that is required for functioning, the less complexity is possible. A very brief, simplified extract of Wilber's (2006, p. 69) conceptual map, showing three of the developmental levels of consciousness that are evident in the gifted boys' stories, is outlined below. It should be noted, that for ease of use by practitioners, Wilber assigned color labels to each level as follows:

- **Level 6-Green – Meta-systemic/Pluralistic:** Worldcentric, informational, relativistic, individualistic, sensitive self, human rights, pluralism, tolerance.
- **Level 5-Orange – Formal operational/Rational:** Sociocentric, multiplistic, conscientious, democracy, science, capitalism, strive-drive, achiever self, competition, reason.

An Integral Analysis of Labeling, Inclusion, and the Impact of the K-12 School Experience on Gifted Boys

Figure 1. The Integral Model (Adapted from Wilber, 2000, 2006). The phenomenon 'in context', when viewed through the quadrant perspectives and developmental levels.

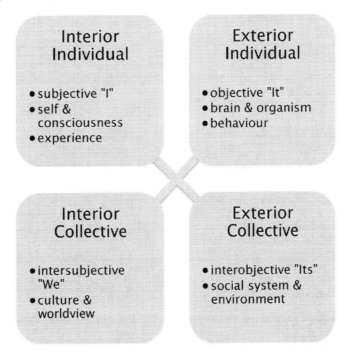

- **Level 4-Amber – Concrete operational/Mythic:** Ethnocentric, absolutistic, conformist rule/role, truth force, monarchies, authoritarian religion, discipline.

The third component is the developmental "line". Lines could be simply described as abilities or talents in particular areas, such as cognitive, interpersonal, emotional, moral, and psychosexual. The lines are also on the developmental spectrum and therefore also have levels. This component is very relevant in the case of the gifted boys, as their giftedness is generally not uniform across all abilities. The last two components are "states" (waking, sleeping, altered), and "types" (blood types, gender, etc.).

The complexity of the model is at once its strength and a source of criticism. The fact that it is hierarchical, as the levels represent increasing capacities for complexity, has also been criticised. Some of these criticisms stem from an incomplete understanding of the model. In-depth critiques of the model are offered by experts who have been working with Integral theory for decades, such as Edwards (2010) and McIntosh (2007). The integralists, such as Sean Esbjörn-Hargens, who work at developing the model further, point to the need to refine the definition of ontological pluralism, as well as to gain a better understanding of the interactions between the individual and collective holons.

Wilber (2000, 2006) suggests that all things are interconnected and interacting, and that his AQAL (all quadrants, all levels) model allows for a holistic understanding of issues, events, and phenomena. If, as Gagné (1985, 2003, 2004, 2008) suggests, environmental and intrapersonal characteristics and conditions determine talent development, then Integral theory provides the larger framework to examine and discuss the multiple perspectives and influences involved in the complex relationship of giftedness and schooling.

METHODS

The Overall Research Problem

How do identified gifted boys in alternative programs in public high schools experience giftedness?

The Research Questions

- How do identified gifted boys understand themselves as gifted people?
- How do gifted boys experience schooling socially and academically?
- How do alternative settings meet the needs of identified gifted boys?

To investigate the lived experience of giftedness, a qualitative, multi-site, embedded case study approach was used. According to Creswell (2007), qualitative research methods can provide a detailed understanding of the social world and the phenomena that exist in everyday life. These types of approaches allow for a view from the inside. The researcher has a connection to the phenomenon under investigation and can bring insights to the conversation and meaning making, allowing for more depth into the investigation of the phenomenon (Miller & Glassner, 2004).

In this case study, multiple perspectives and data sources about the phenomenon were examined. Through in-depth semi-structured interviews, the participating "identified gifted" boys described their experiences of giftedness and schooling, providing rich descriptions of the phenomenon of giftedness. The participants' cumulative school records, as well as publically available district and provincial program and policy documents and student data, were reviewed to provide a context to the participants' experiences of public schooling.

This study was conducted within a large urban public school district in Alberta, Canada. The district student population in 2015 was over 114,000. The district represented the case, with the same programs and policies applying to all the research participants. The seven embedded cases in this study provided another contextual layer for understanding the phenomenon of giftedness by allowing an examination of different alternative programs available as chosen by the participants (or their parents), and the relationship of these choices to their experience of schooling.

The participants in this study were seven high school boys, identified as gifted by means of standardized cognitive testing, as recognized and coded by provincial and district criteria. Given the number of years they had been in school, the boys had experienced considerable diversity of learning environments and were able to provide a reflective view of their experiences with multiple school settings and educators. In their reflections, though dependent on their recollections, they compared and contrasted their experiences of giftedness in particular sites with particular teachers and teaching styles.

Data analysis consisted of several strategies: a coding of the interview content to identify and examine the emerging themes from within each case as well as across cases; artifact and document analysis to develop a context to understand participant experiences; a comparison and contrast to the existing literature; and an examination of the differences and similarities in the participants' experiences of giftedness to the documentation contained in their cumulative school records.

An Integral Analysis of Labeling, Inclusion, and the Impact of the K-12 School Experience on Gifted Boys

Limitations and Delimitations

This study focused on identified gifted boys' experience of giftedness in public school alternative settings. As such, the findings speak specifically to these particular identified gifted boys' experience in a large urban school district at a particular time in provincial educational history. It was assumed that the boys spoke authentically of their experiences allowing for analysis and interpretation.

Analysis of Findings

In this chapter, we discuss three of the seven participants who were involved in this study. To familiarize the readers with the three participants, an excerpt from each boy's self description, as given in their interviews, is quoted below:

Ian

Not many people know that I am gifted. I don't really think of myself as gifted, I think it comes down to work ethic, if you work harder than kid B you will succeed, you will get to a higher level or better situation.

I can see myself delving into medicine, counselling, helping people where I can see the results with physical or emotional problems. It is probably my father's influence that has brought me to medicine and helping, though it is not a big thing that we talk about; it is not a family expectation. You can be whatever you want and you are happy with.

I always carry who I am, my giftedness, and my schooling, with me.

Martin

I go to school, do wushu [Chinese martial arts] four times a week, work, do Chinese School, and play piano. I do not like piano or Chinese school; I am doing them for the credits. I love wushu, it is my passion; I used to do air cadets, I hated that.

By Grade 12, I want to have enriched classes for all my core subjects. They are at a university level and I am trying my best to get high marks in everything.

It is recommended that even though you achieve a four or five on the Advanced Placement course, you should still do first year [university courses]; it just helps with self-accomplishment. Also, I don't know what I want to be when I grow up so I will take everything and go where I want to go.

Evan

I am anti-social, unless I am comfortable in the environment and the people I am with; in most situations, I am more anti-social, cautious. Although I observe everything on every level, sometimes I have trouble with social stuff. I don't think about it, it doesn't matter, but I don't really care for it. Sometimes I am creative and sometimes I am very literal and rudimentary, like very technical. It is hard to have that critical analytical mind - you are always questioning stuff.

I am interested in technology, computers, music, producing music using computers, making movies, and watching foreign films.

I was just a kid that did really, what I wanted to do. I really enjoyed it, had friends, got picked on; fought back. I was a bigger kid back then; the bullying was bad, but I could do something about that. It wasn't too bad; I had friends. It was normal. It wasn't until I moved here, in Grade 5, that I could see how gross people are. When you are the new kid, people won't let you into their circle; really protective and jealous, keeping you at bay.

As a kid, I was smart enough to see that side of people and realize that being social and being popular is not something that you would want.

As the cases were examined, there was much uniqueness in the participants' individual experiences. However, all of the boys described a level of ability beyond their average classmates in a particular area, coupled with an intense interest where their high ability was applied or where their ability was intensely applied. Most boys spoke of feeling different from others, depending on their setting, as well as not fitting in. They described giftedness as "thinking differently" or "looking at things differently," and particular learning and/or tasks "coming more easily" to them, rather than being better than others. Ian was the only person that suggested that effort was involved, that being gifted involved "working harder than others," but also discussed how some really gifted students did not put forth much effort into school tasks. The congruencies among the themes from individual participants formed the common understandings that were used to reflect on and analyze the participants' experiences of giftedness and schooling.

EXPLORING THE ISSUES

Discussion of Themes

Ambivalence about Giftedness

All of the boys were able to discuss the general concept of giftedness with relative ease. However, all of them without exception also hesitated to discuss and acknowledge their own academic giftedness. While they did acknowledge that they had above average abilities in some areas, they pointed out that they were not necessarily gifted in all curricular areas, even though that was the expectation from teachers and peers. The fact that one still had to work hard at some subjects created pressure, which led to such coping strategies as working much harder than their peers, procrastination and perfectionism. This was similar to Carman (2011) and Freeman's (2006) findings that identified gifted learners were expected to engage in particular activities and perform at high levels universally. Some of the boys in the study were impeded by such expectations either through elevated self-criticism (Martin), inability to engage in tasks (Martin, Evan) or complete tasks (Evan), or suffering great angst in making decisions (Martin). They were caught up in self-evaluation and prediction of others' assessment of them.

Relationships in School

It was quite apparent from the boys' stories that their relationships with their teachers greatly impacted their experience of schooling. First and foremost was the establishment of mutual respect. Teachers that demonstrated caring seemed to motivate them to learn and complete tasks that would not have otherwise engaged them. Conversely, if a positive relationship was not established with a teacher, the quantity and quality of work and engagement, for all of the boys except

Ian, suffered significantly. Other researchers (Hertberg-Davis & Callahan, 2008; Libbey, 2004; Kanevsky & Keighley, 2003) came to similar conclusions: students who believed their teachers cared about them and treated them with respect felt a greater sense of belonging, thereby engaging and achieving at higher levels.

Most of the participants' parents were positively involved in their schooling. They supported their sons' choices in programming and post secondary planning. As well, they seemed to have reasonable expectations that were appropriate to their sons' interests and abilities.

All the boys spoke at length about their relationships with the other students in the class and school. They experienced challenges finding intellectual peers, finding friends, and finding safe and acceptable social groups in the school. Bullying and social isolation were mentioned by some of the boys. All the boys consciously strategized or reflected on having control over their lives in school.

Learning: Need for Challenge and Relevance

Throughout the interviews, all of the boys commented on the need for having a deep, driving interest in the topic they were studying. "Why was it important? What does it connect to? When there are so many important things going on in the world, why do we have to study that?" Further, they reported that what they were learning was boring and simplistic: "there was so much more" that they could be taking up instead. By more, they clarified: it was not more work of the same thing they desired, but rather more complex work that required deeper thinking and connection to the world.

If the work did not provide enough challenge, they wanted the latitude to make it more multifaceted, typically through more advanced content and/or a more complex product. If the work was too easy, they struggled to engage. If they already knew what was being asked of them, why should they have to do it again? Other researchers (Cunningham, 2003; Hébert & Schreiber, 2010; Kanevsky & Keighley, 2003) also found that students wanted challenging and meaningful work and when they did not get it, they either engaged minimally or disengaged entirely.

The Integral Model: An Analysis of Perspectives

Using Integral Theory, insights into the experience of giftedness can be gained, when all the impinging perspectives are examined. An individual operates at a particular level of consciousness; simultaneously he exists as a biological organism and interacts with his environment in adaptive ways; he exists and finds meaning within a cultural context; and his life is organized through greater social and natural systems.

Interior Individual: Personality Development

From their individual perspective, the gifted boys in this study wanted to connect to the world in a meaningful way and make a positive contribution. They were critically looking at what they could do. The conflicts the participants experienced were exacerbated when the individuals and the structures they interacted with, were operating at a lower developmental level (level 5 or 4), and conforming to the social conventions and the way things were. The boys realized the "possibility of the higher" (more complex) and the contrast with the lower (more controlling) levels.

Exterior Individual: Brain Development

Neuroscience and the studies of brain development provide another perspective for understanding the boys' experiences of giftedness in schooling. The concept of genetic determinism is being questioned, as many scientists now agree that biology and environment influence the development of the brain. Controversy exists in the degree each plays and the way each can be manipulated to meet desired outcomes. Davidson, Dunne, Eccles, Engle, Greenberg, Jennings, Jha, Jinpa, Lantieri, Meyer, Roeser, & Vago (2012) suggest specifically, that contemplative practices and mental training result in identifiable differences in the brain structure. These practices have been deliberately used to strengthen positive qualities and dispositions, "which induce plastic changes in brain function and structure, supporting prosocial behavior and academic success in young people." (Davidson et al, 2012, p.146).

Interior Collective: Cultural Development

Human beings live in the world in relation to others. We interact with others through shared language meanings; we are influenced by their response to us, and visa versa. Gifted boys, like other identifiable groups, experience the overlapping values and beliefs of the different cultures in which they reside. Family dynamics, the roles people in the family play, members' cognitive functioning, and their beliefs about education and gender roles, all impact how gifted boys see themselves. Layered upon that are the cultural values of the greater society around these same issues (the societal developmental level). Frequently, these beliefs and values are played out in schools as young people try out different values and live them to extremes. In particular, gender roles and identity are continually tested in an effort to find out who they are, and how they fit with the rest of society.

Exterior Collective: Social Systems Development

Societies develop social systems to organize and manage their citizenry.

Particular beliefs and values influence the systems that are developed and implemented as well as the provisions provided within. Systems can position individuals or groups of individuals in particular ways. How they are positioned can influence the provisions received – in this case, requirements for funding and support for programs for gifted students may be competing with requirements for the funding of special education programs.

Integral View of the Gifted Boys and Their Contexts

Martin- Amber: Level 4 Rule/Role Self, Concrete Operational

Martin operated at the conformist rule level 4, very aware of the expectations, participating unquestioningly. He may have procrastinated, in fear of not being able to perform well enough to the perceived standard, and he hated taking piano and Chinese classes, but he eventually did what was required of him in all aspects of his life. He did not question the "why", rather, he complied with the demands.

Ian – Orange: Level 5 Rational Self, Formal Operational

Ian operated at the scientific achievement "orange" level 5, mastering the laws of schooling in his orange level district. He was aware of the cultural values and social systems and used them to achieve his goals in a very rational, systematic and strategic way. He knew what he needed to do to be successful within each and pursued his goals on their terms. He knew how to maximize his skills and the energy that he put into investing them.

Evan – Green: Level 6 Sensitive Self, Meta-Systematic

Evan seemed to experience the most dissatisfaction and frustration, being focused on a more relational, caring, egalitarian way of being. Evan operated at the pluralistic "green" level 6, perhaps even beginning to make forays into the "teal" level 7, the Integral Self. Living in a culture that was operating in the more scientific-rational way at the "orange" level 5, attending schools that often operated two levels lower at the conformist "amber" level 4, Evan's ideology was incongruent with where he was, and he had to withdraw (both figuratively, into drugs, and literally, in grade 8) in order to resolve the conflict.

Their Cultural Context

The cultural level of development in the schools is predominantly at the scientific rational level 5, valuing the objective measureable achievements, giving a superficial voice to a more pluralistic existence of value and acceptance of all peoples, within an objective rational corporate state system. This was determined by the boys' accounts about what they perceived was important in their setting, as well as the documents describing the various program cultures as "rigorous" and "competitive".

Their Social Systems Context

The social systems, which include the school district's and province's policies around special education would suggest a range of developmental levels, between the scientific rational "orange" level 5 and level 4 corporate state "amber", levels of complexity. These systems and their behaviors are highly structured and organized with clearly defined, objectively measured processes and protocols, in service of the beliefs, values, and ideals of the prevailing culture (Alberta Education, 2004).

Application of the Model to Three Participants

In the following three summary tables, brief descriptions of three of the boys are given in the quadrants of the integral model, to provide a map of the perspectives that are interacting with, and acting on the boys.

In addition to utilizing the quadrants and the levels, it would also be helpful to plot a psychograph of the boys' developmental lines (intelligences), particularly given that the likelihood is very high that the boys would not be developing at the same level of giftedness across the board. This combined information would provide a detailed and contextualized map of the boys' learning needs on which teachers could build appropriate teaching strategies and learning activities.

Table 1. Martin

UL: Interior Individual – Subjective- What I Experience, What I Feel	UR: Exterior Individual – Objective – What One (It) Does
• *I am trying my best to get high marks in everything* • *I don't know what I want to be when I grow up so I will take everything [classes]* • *I do not like piano or Chinese school; I am doing them for the credits* • *I love wushu, it is my passion*	• His verbal comprehension index on the Wechsler Intelligence Scale for Children IV was 'very superior', with this psychologist note: Martin is a big picture thinker; when encountering difficulty, his thinking became inflexible, he kept trying the same unsuccessful strategies; his need to have the correct answer, may underlie reluctance complete work. Martin needs to keep his anxiety down to improve his performance, as such, relaxation strategies are recommended • *Labs don't teach me much, usually I fail and I end up copying off other people, so I don't really learn much. Sitting there learning is better for me.*
LL: Interior Collective-Intersubjective What "We"(You and I) Experience	**LR: Exterior Collective–Interobjective What Systems (its) Do**
How he is seen by others in the classroom: Great effort, well behaved, quiet, hard working, pleasure to have in class, collaborating to advance learning, consistent, excellent work ethic, conscientious, sense of humor and friendliness make you an excellent member of the class team,	*The purpose of school is to prepare students for the future, to get a job, to be more successful in life and to help understand how the world works. One way to make school better would be for principals to organize a way for students to rate their teachers, for kids who want to rate their teachers. It needs to be in-depth, like an essay not a checklist. Sometimes principals can't really see what teachers are really like, some interview well and they are not really good with the kids. The purpose of this is if they are bad, they will get fired.*

Table 2. Ian

UL: Interior Individual – Subjective- What I Experience, What I Feel	UR: Exterior Individual – Objective – What One (It) Does
• *If you work harder than kid B you will succeed* • *It was my goal to keep my marks in the A-range* • *I can see myself delving into medicine, counselling - where I can see the results with physical or emotional problems* • *- I always carry who I am, my giftedness, and my schooling, with me*	• *I prefer to read instructions, so I can go over them instead of hearing them.* • *Raw information is the easiest way; I can make the connections* • *Written assignments teach me more than in a group setting talking about things. It prepares me better for tests.*
LL: Interior Collective-Intersubjective What "We"(You and I) Experience	**LR: Exterior Collective–Interobjective What Systems (its) Do**
How he is seen by others in the classroom: Demonstrates confidence and autonomy in learning; superior effort, perseverance and achievement; energetic, great sense of humour, strong work ethic, polite and respectful, conscientious and responsible, insightful, exceptional effort, loves to learn, and self-motivated.	Preparation in the high school program in relation to entering the higher education system: *The discussions in the program were not a direct reflection of the testing we did. In English, we did discussions, a lot of talking, but the final exam was written. We should have done a lot more writing, instead of the oral* part.

IMPLICATIONS AND CONCLUSION

The study revealed diverse experiences of these identified gifted boys.

However, all the boys included the following elements in their description of giftedness: an above average ability in a particular area or areas and an intense drive to understand something important to the individual. The main findings indicate the following themes.

Table 3. Evan

UL: Interior Individual – Subjective- What I Experience, What I Feel	UR: Exterior Individual – Objective – What One (It) Does
• Although I observe everything on every level, sometimes I have trouble with social stuff • As a kid, I was smart enough to see that side of people • That was kind of bad, not being there for the whole year. I kept isolating myself more and more. I was heavily into drugs too. That was the toughest point in my life. • After that year [grade 8] I realized, I always kind of cared about my schooling, like I am not stupid. It has just been really hard to try; it is so boring. It is so crap here. It is so hurtful to me, I know I could have a better education and I don't.	• He scored 'very superior' on verbal comprehension and processing speed on the Wechsler Intelligence Scale for Children IV. Scored in the at-risk for attention and adaptive behaviour on the Behaviour Assessment System for Children IV. • It is really easy for me to memorize. I read a lot of stuff, so I just know it; it is not hard. • In math, I would rather learn the theory behind it, I don't need the equation; I can figure it out.
LL: Interior Collective-Intersubjective **What "We"(You and I) Experience**	**LR: Exterior Collective–Interobjective** **What Systems (its) Do**
How he is seen by others in the classroom: Makes valuable contributions to class, mature sense of humour, creativity in writing, when engaged produces amazing pieces, wit and excellent understanding, however missing assignments negatively affected marks, does not appear to be working to potential, has a great deal of ability but was not very interested in our program	*They pay five times more for military, why can't they pay for education? If society cared about education, there wouldn't be this big of a problem. Large class sizes make it horrible for the teacher. With the overcrowding, you can't get the type of help students need. You can't get enough help to feel like you are there. You can't establish relationships, teacher/student or within the class. Your relationship with school as a child determines your relationship as adults.*

The Gifted Boys' Self-Concept: Meaningful Challenge and Overwhelming Pressure

These students indicated a driving need for meaningful and challenging learning tasks. They became unmotivated by repeated teaching of material that they already knew and mastered. The boys generally underplayed their giftedness in public, describing it in terms of skills and knowledge in particular domains. At the same time, they were aware that the label "gifted" carried with it high performance expectations. This created a significant amount of stress for the students, as indicated by the drawing by one gifted boy, in Figure 2.

Relationships with Teachers and Peers: Challenge Was within the Teacher's Control

The significance of respectful and caring relationships with teachers could not be understated. For several boys, including Martin, and Evan, that was the determining factor for their effort and participation in classes. On the other hand, teachers who held misconceptions of all around giftedness placed undue pressure on students to perform at high levels in all tasks.

Program and Curriculum: The Program Structure Influenced Learning as Well as the Social Interactions and Relationships with Other Students

Based on all the boys' comments and their continuous enrolment in alternative programs, the alternative settings seemed to better meet their learning needs than their community schools.

Figure 2. Gifted anxiety

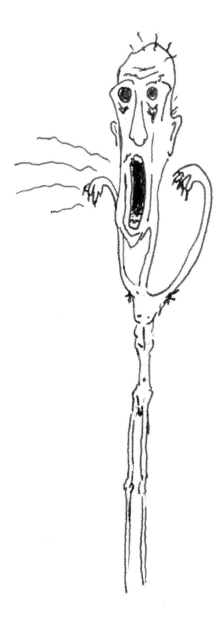

None of the boys returned to a community school setting. Ian enrolled in several alternative programs, before settling for his current setting. Those that remained in a single program over their schooling, said they were satisfied with their choice as being the best from the selection that was available to them. They noted, however, that the good intentions of a program could be sabotaged by poor teaching strategies. Finally, it was evident that the structures of the programs also influenced the students' social relationships with other students, as these structures effectively defined the gifted students' peer group. For some students, this was a haven, as evidenced by the slam poem, below, about the "GiftEd" (pseudonym for the education for gifted students) program.

An Integral Analysis of Labeling, Inclusion, and the Impact of the K-12 School Experience on Gifted Boys

On Being Gifted: An Open Letter to the Non-Gifted People in My Life

by A
I don't see myself as gifted,
maybe because it's all I've ever known.
It's how I've grown.
When I'm with others and when I am alone,
I see and hear things that no one else does
and none of that is in any way remarkable to me.
Because I have nothing to compare it to,
I often take my gift for granted.
I don't know what it's like to have an average IQ.
I don't know what it's like not to have spent half my childhood in speech therapy
so I can tell you about it
now,
you might be surprised to learn that but it is true.
It's a similar story with other gifted kids too.
You have no way of knowing what we went through,
just as we can't tell what happened to you.
Although we may not like to admit it,
most of us could just as easily have been
in a special needs class in Oregon.
It is a vibrant rose covered in thorns.
It's our biggest secret.
We don't get giftedness handed to us on a silver platter.
Most of us had to struggle in some way or another for it.
Maybe you don't notice it but you can't ignore it:
No one is perfect,
no gift is free
and I paid for mine
with a childhood spent muted,
spent with a mind glowing with fantastic thoughts and beautiful questions,
and spent not being able to share that with anyone.
Do you know how frustrating that is?
And then came "GiftEd".
All of a sudden, I was surrounded with people just like me.
I had never thought I would see another.
After finishing speech therapy, I could finally talk to people
and have them understand me!
Like a prisoner in a jailbreak,
I found myself suddenly free to take
my words and ideas to the public sphere
and I went for it.
I dove right in,

here was a place to wear my own skin.
I am very lucky to be where I am now.
Some gifted people never get to learn how
to communicate with other people,
let alone other gifted people.
We're not in different classes to keep us apart from you,
but to keep us together
so we can learn at our best.
These years in "GiftEd" have been the best years of my still-short life.
I would not have missed them for anything.
I'm not telling you this to make your experience seem like less than it is,
but to tell what mine was,
to clear the air
and show that there
is more to being gifted than being smart.

RECOMMENDATIONS FOR PRACTICE

The identified gifted boys from this study would have benefited from a classroom culture that accepted and encouraged active learning and intense educational curiosities, such that they would not be socially disdained for their scholarly pursuits. From our continued classroom observations, discussions with teachers and gifted students, as well as our ongoing reflections and integral analysis, we conclude that in order to create the appropriate challenge in learning tasks, as well as more appropriate expectations of performance and achievement, teachers need to have specific subjective as well as objective knowledge of the gifted students' learning needs and their personal experience of the classroom. This knowledge is gained through reflective practice and critical reflection with colleagues, which may be an unattainable luxury in many public school system classrooms.

As the school districts begin to implement the provincial government policy direction toward inclusive education, specific learner needs will no longer be labeled. This could actually be a problem for many gifted students. As the experience of these gifted boys indicates, in spite of the labeling issues, they still thrived better in congregated programs than in integrated contexts. For these students to continue thriving, rich learning environments would need to be developed, that would create curiosity and desire for learning, while at the same time developing resiliency and autonomy. Such an environment would, in theory be beneficial for all students, however, teachers would need to be supported in the process of getting to know their learners as individuals. Assuming that "inclusion" does not become an economical way of treating unequals equally, testing the gifted students' as well as their teachers' developmental levels would help the teachers understand the students' needs from a subjective, rather than just the usual objective Upper Right perspective. The teachers would thus be in a better position to determine appropriate growth opportunities for these students, and to thoughtfully manage their integration into the inclusive classroom.

Integral theory could be used as a framework for planning and assessing this complex endeavor. Proactively using the four quadrants, desired educational outcomes could be identified with associated action plans. For example, desired educational experiences could be determined, identifying desired educational behaviors including the characteristics required of the culture and system policies and programs that would be needed to support the desired outcomes. Each of these could contain varying levels of complexity, with multiple forms of engagement (Esbjörn-Hargens, 2007). The Integral framework could also be used to identify and resolve roadblocks, contradictions, and discrepancies within the four quadrants in order to meet the desired outcomes.

REFERENCES

Alberta Education. (2010). *Making a difference*. Retrieved from http://education.alberta.ca/teachers/resources/cross/making-a-difference.aspx

Alberta Education. (2012). *Instructional considerations for students who are gifted*. Retrieved from http://www.learnalberta.ca/content/iept2/library/documents/instructional_cons iderations.pdf

Alisat, L. (2013). *Identified Gifted Boys' Experience Of Giftedness In Alternative High School Settings: Implications For Practice And Programming*. (Unpublished PhD thesis). University of Calgary.

Berlin, J. E. (2009). It's all a matter of perspective: Student perceptions on the impact of being labeled gifted and talented. *Roeper Review*, *31*(4), 217–223. doi:10.1080/02783190903177580

Betts, G. T. (2004). Fostering autonomous learners through levels of differentiation. *Roeper Review*, *26*(4), 190–191. doi:10.1080/02783190409554269

Biddick, M. (2009). Cluster grouping for the gifted and talented: It works! *Apex*, *15*(4), 78–86. Retrieved from http://www.giftedchildren.org.nz/apex/

Brulles, D., Saunders, R., & Cohn, S. J. (2010). Improving performance for gifted students in a cluster grouping model. *Journal for the Education of the Gifted*, *34*(2), 327–350.

Brulles, D., & Winebrenner, S. (2011). The schoolwide cluster grouping model: Restructuring gifted education services for the 21st century. *Gifted Child Today*, *34*(4), 35–46.

Carman, C. A. (2011). Stereotypes of giftedness in current and future educators. *Journal for the Education of the Gifted*, *34*(5), 790–812. doi:10.1177/0162353211417340

Cook-Greuter, S. R. (2004). Making the case for a developmental perspective. *Industrial and Commercial Training*, *36*(7), 275–281.

Creswell, J. W. (2007). *Qualitative inquiry and research design: Choosing among five approaches*. Thousand Oaks, CA: Sage.

Cunningham, B. L. (2003). *The Phenomenon of intellectually gifted underachievers and education: Listening to the male adolescent voice*. (Unpublished dissertation). University of Montana.

Davidson, R. J., Dunne, J., Eccles, J. S., Engle, A., Greenberg, M., Jennings, P., ... Vago, D. (2012). Contemplative practices and mental training: Prospects for American education. *Child Development Perspectives*, *6*(2), 146–153. doi:10.1111/j.1750-8606.2012.00240.x PMID:22905038

Edwards, M. (2010). *Organizational Transformation for Sustainability: An Integral Metatheory*. New York, NY: Routledge.

Esbjörn-Hargens, S. (2007). Integral Teacher, Integral Students, Integral Classroom: Applying Integral Theory to Education. *AQAL: Journal of Integral Theory and Practice, 2*(2), 72–103.

Fiedler, E. D., Lange, R. E., & Winebrenner, S. (2002). In search of reality: Unraveling the myths about tracking, ability grouping, and the gifted. *Roeper Review, 24*(3), 108–111. doi:10.1080/02783190209554142

Freeman, J. (2006). Giftedness in the long term. *Journal for the Education of the Gifted, 29*(4), 384–404.

Gagné, F. (1985). Giftedness and talent: Reexamining a reexamination of the definitions. *Gifted Child Quarterly, 29*(3), 103–112. doi:10.1177/001698628502900302

Gagné, F. (2003). Transforming gifts into talents: The DMGT as a developmental theory. In N. Colangelo & G. Davis (Eds.), *Handbook of gifted education* (3rd ed.; pp. 60–74). Boston, MA: Allyn & Bacon.

Gagné, F. (2004). *A differentiated model of giftedness and talent*. Retrieved from http://nswagtc.org.au/images/stories/infocentre/gagne_a_differentiated_model_of_giftedness_and_talent.pdf

Gagné, F. (2008). *Building gifts into talents: Overview of the DMGT*. Retrieved from http://www.templetonfellows.org/program/FrancoysGagne.pdf

Geake, J. G., & Gross, M. U. M. (2008). Teachers' negative affect toward academically gifted students: An evolutionary psychological study. *Gifted Child Quarterly, 52*(3), 217–231. doi:10.1177/0016986208319704

Gentry, M. L. (1999). *Promoting student achievement and exemplary classroom practices through cluster grouping: A research-based alternative to heterogeneous elementary classrooms*. The National Research Center On the Gifted And Talented.

Gentry, M. L., & MacDougall, J. (2007). *Total school cluster grouping: Model, research, and practice*. Retrieved from http://geri.education.purdue.edu/PDF%20Files/Gentry_Publications/2007._Gentry,_MacDou.pdf

Gentry, M. L., & Owen, S. V. (1999). An investigation of the effects of total school flexible cluster grouping on identification, achievement, and classroom practices. *Gifted Child Quarterly, 43*(4), 224–243. doi:10.1177/001698629904300402

Hébert, T. P., & Schreiber, C. A. (2010). An examination of selective achievement in gifted males. *Journal for the Education of the Gifted, 33*(4), 570–605. doi:10.1177/016235321003300406

Hertberg-Davis, H., & Callahan, C. M. (2008). A narrow escape: Gifted students' perceptions of advanced placement and international baccalaureate programs. *Gifted Child Quarterly, 52*(3), 199–216. doi:10.1177/0016986208319705

Hoover, S. M., Sayler, M., & Feldhusen, J. F. (1993). Cluster grouping of gifted students at the elementary level. *Roeper Review, 16*(1), 13–15. doi:10.1080/02783199309553527

Kanevsky, L. (2011). *Curriculum differentiation and differentiation strategies for highly able learners*. Retrieved from http://www.sfu.ca/~kanevsky/TK/Differentiation%20Strategies%2004.11.pdf

Kanevsky, L., & Keighley, T. (2003). To produce or not to produce? Understanding boredom and honour in underachievement. *Roeper Review, 26*(1), 20–29. doi:10.1080/02783190309554235

Loevinger, J. (1985). Revision of the sentence completion test for ego Development. *Journal of Personality and Social Psychology, 48*(2), 420–427. doi:10.1037/0022-3514.48.2.420 PMID:3981402

Matthews, D., & Kitchen, J. (2007). School-within-a-school gifted programs: Perceptions of students and teachers in public secondary schools. *Gifted Child Quarterly, 51*(3), 256–271. doi:10.1177/0016986207302720

McCoach, D. B., & Siegle, D. (2007). What predicts teachers' attitudes toward the gifted? *Gifted Child Quarterly, 51*(3), 246–255. doi:10.1177/0016986207302719

McIntosh, S. (2007). *Integral Consciousness and the Future of Evolution: How the Integral Worldview Is Transforming Politics, Culture and Spirituality*. Paragon House.

Miller, J., & Glassner, B. (2004). The "inside" and "outside": Finding realities in interviews. In D. Silverman (Ed.), *Qualitative research: Theory, method and practice* (2nd ed.; pp. 125–139). Thousand Oaks, CA: Sage.

Montessori: The international Montessori Index. (2013). Retrieved from http://www.montessori.edu

Moon, T. R., & Brighton, C. M. (2008). Primary teacher's conceptions of giftedness. *Journal for the Education of the Gifted, 31*(4), 447–480.

Perrone, K. M., Wright, S. L., Ksiazak, T. M., Crane, A. L., & Vannatter, A. (2010). Looking back on lessons learned: Gifted adults reflect on their experiences in advanced classes. *Roeper Review, 32*(2), 127–139. doi:10.1080/02783191003587918

Persson, R. S. (2009). The unwanted gifted and talented: A sociobiological perspective of the social functions of giftedness. In L. Shavinina (Ed.), *International handbook of giftedness* (pp. 913–924). Dordrecht, NL: Springer-Science. doi:10.1007/978-1-4020-6162-2_46

Persson, R. S. (2010). Experiences of intellectually gifted students in an egalitarian and inclusive educational system: A survey study. *Journal for the Education of the Gifted, 33*(4), 536–569. doi:10.1177/016235321003300405

Pierce, R. L., Cassady, J. C., Adams, C. M., Speirs Neumeister, K. L., Dixon, F. A., & Cross, T. L. (2011). The effects of clustering and curriculum on the development of gifted learners' math achievement. *Journal for the Education of the Gifted, 34*(4), 569–594. doi:10.1177/016235321103400403

Preckel, F., Baudson, T., Krolak-Schwerdt, S., & Glock, S. (2015). Gifted and maladjusted? Implicit attitudes and automatic associations related to gifted children. *American Educational Research Journal, 52*(6), 1160–1184. doi:10.3102/0002831215596413

Pyryt, M. (2004). *Pyryt Enrichment Matrix*. Retrieved from http://www.gatecalgary.ca/pyrytsps.aspx

Renzulli, J. S. (1977). The enrichment triad model: A plan for developing defensible programs for the gifted and talented. *Gifted Child Quarterly, 20*(3), 303–306.

Renzulli, J. S., & Reis, S. M. (2002). *The schoolwide enrichment model: Executive summary*. Retrieved from http://www.gifted.uconn.edu/sem/semexec.html

Siegle, D., Moore, M., Mann, R. L., & Wilson, H. E. (2010). Factors that influence in-service and pre-service teachers' nomination of students for gifted and talented programs. *Journal for the Education of the Gifted, 33*(3), 337–360.

Silverman, L. K. (2009). *What have we learned about gifted children: 30th Anniversary 1979-2009*. Retrieved from http://www.gifteddevelopment.com/What_is_Gifted/learned.htm

Tomlinson, C. A. (1995). *Differentiating instruction for advanced learners in the mixed ability middle school classroom*. Retrieved from http://63.238.109.122/education-summit/archive/2010-education-summit/handouts-presentations/session-6-gifted-education/Differentiating%20Instruction.pdf

Tomlinson, C. A. (2000). Reconcilable differences? Standards-based teaching and differentiation. *Educational Leadership, 58*(1), 6–11.

Wilber, K. (2000). *Integral psychology: Consciousness, spirit, psychology, therapy*. Boston, MA: Shambhala Publications, Inc.

Wilber, K. (2006). *Integral spirituality*. Boston, MA: Integral Books.

Winebrenner, S. (2001). *Teaching gifted kids in the regular classroom: Strategies and techniques every teacher can use to meet the academic needs of the gifted and talented*. Minneapolis, MN: Free Spirit.

ADDITIONAL READING

Esbjörn-Hargens, S. (2009). An overview of Integral Theory. *IntegralPost*. Retrieved from https://integrallife.com/integral-post/overview-integral-theory

KEY TERMS AND DEFINITIONS

Alberta Education: The provincial government department responsible for K to 12 education in the province. The Minister of Education delegates his authority to run schools, to the elected school boards, through The School Act legislation and through the provision of funding to schools. Alternative Program: Referred to programs or classroom settings that had a specific focus in addition to the regular program of studies. This included: mental health support, addiction recovery support, behavior support, self-paced or advanced paced learning classes, congregated ability settings (gifted learners) and congregated interest settings (arts, language, sports, science, etc.).

Giftedness: For the purpose of identifying potential study participants, was determined using Alberta Education's definition of giftedness: "Giftedness is exceptional potential and/or performance across a wide range of abilities in one or more of the following areas: general intellectual, specific academic, creative thinking, social, musical, artistic, kinesthetic." (Alberta Education, 2010).

Identification of Giftedness: In the district included in the study, was by a registered psychologist using standardized IQ and achievement tests. Giftedness was diagnosed, by a minimum full-scale IQ score of 130 points (+/- 5 points) or a percentile ranking of 95 or greater. As a special education learning condition, giftedness required specialized accommodations and strategies in the learning setting supporting enrichment and/or acceleration in the area of the individual's strength or strengths.

Labeling: Referred to the learning diagnosis provided by the psycho-educational assessment completed by a registered psychologist. A learning code was connected to the diagnosis, provision, and additional funding from Alberta Education to support the student's complex learning needs in the classroom.

This research was previously published in the Handbook of Research on Promoting Cross-Cultural Competence and Social Justice in Teacher Education edited by Jared Keengwe; pages 355-381, copyright year 2017 by Information Science Reference (an imprint of IGI Global).

Chapter 49
A Comparison of "Inclusiveness" in Two Liberal Arts Catholic Universities:
What Nurtures an Inclusive Campus Climate?

Theron N. Ford
John Carroll University, USA

Blanche Jackson Glimps
Tennessee State University, USA

ABSTRACT

The Catholic Church has been a major player in the field of education, both nationally and internationally. Numerous religious orders, such as the Jesuits, Felicians, created higher education institutions. Such institutions afforded college education to first-generation students and were a ladder for upward mobility. A perception lingers of Catholic institutions being an exemplar of Christian values of love, acceptance and social justice. In reality, some institutions are far more successful in actualizing those values. This chapter looks retrospectively at Madonna University and compares it to John Carroll University to highlight differences in how each has dealt with the issue of inclusiveness. While each of the institutions is a single instance within the Catholic higher education community, there are still lessons we may take from this examination that intersect with issues related to religion, gender and inclusiveness.

INTRODUCTION

The authors, both African American female professors, recount the experiences one encountered during employment at two different Catholic liberal arts universities. The perspective taken in this chapter is to highlight the differences between the occurrences the professor encountered at Madonna University, in Michigan in the early 1990s and occurrences encountered by the same professor at John Carroll

DOI: 10.4018/978-1-7998-1213-5.ch049

A Comparison of "Inclusiveness" in Two Liberal Arts Catholic Universities

University, in Ohio, beginning in 2004. By contrasting and comparing the two experiences at each respective university, the authors will provide a starting point for reflection, self-discovery and deeply engaged conversation that other universities, specifically Catholic institutions should consider if they seek to build an inclusive campus climate. Lastly, specific actions that promote an inclusive campus climate are presented

The chapter utilizes an ethnographic method that is ground in the research of Patricia Hill Collins (1990) who is credited with establishing the Black feminist epistemological framework. According to Hill-Collins there are two types of knowing. The first is *knowledge* and it is adequate for the powerful or those with position. Then there is *wisdom* and it is necessary for survival of the subordinates. Personal experience equals good evidence. For African American women knowledge comes from experience and thus, "knowledge validation processes reflect this groups interest (248)."

BACKGROUND

This chapter reports research that is based on reflexivity qualitative research. Lambert, Jomeen and McSherry (2010) indicate, "qualitative research traditions consider that knowledge is based upon theory of assumption and examination of such phenomena is from a subjective position" (321). Accordingly, therefore the researchers own views and personal experiences are legitimately employed in interpretation of knowledge. Researchers are urged to talk about themselves, "their presuppositions, choices, experiences, and actions during the research process" (Mruck & Breuer, 2003, p. 3) to allow others to understand their thoughts and actions. Through the use of reflexive methodology, the author examines the elements of campus chemistry (e.g., climate, administration, etc.) on two Catholic college campuses.

Perhaps, the best illustration of campus climate can be made by reviewing, documented examples of glaringly toxic climates. Hamilton (2006) noted the death threat e-mails directed at Hispanic and African American athletes and female student leaders, to dissuade them from seeking positions in student government at Boulder, Colorado. White students, at University of Chicago wore chains, baggy pants, and partied to 50 Cent and Notorious B.I.G. at a "straight thugging party" (Hamilton, 2006). Such incidents are not unusual and often leave administrators bewildered, caught off guard. Faculty like-wise may not know what if anything should be done. For the targets of such behaviors what is apparent to them is the campus is not a welcoming respectful environment. The authors conceptualize campus climate as the feelings one has when immersed in the atmosphere of the institution. Is the atmosphere open and welcoming of people who are easily distinguishable visually? Are females respected on par with male colleagues? Do staff personnel afford persons of color the same respect given white faculty? Does the atmosphere make all people feel like they belong—if so, an inclusive campus climate would seem to exist.

Bryant (2006) describes the importance of climate for populations that have faced discrimination. As such, she studied the climate for women in campus religious settings in a campus-based religious organization. Observational data were collected from 25 interviewees. The researcher attended the "weekly large group meetings over a four month period, three small-group Bible studies, a semiformal and a women's dinner event" (p. 618). Qualitative analysis of data was conducted with an analysis of findings. Bryant found that the "gender-related attitudes expressed by the evangelical segment of the population were common in evangelical circles on college campuses" (p. 629). Women in this study were found to be socialized to accept their role as the submissive sex and encouraged to be independent from men. Beliefs about women's role, according to Bryant, can severely limit life goals and expectations. Similar socialization frequently is evident within the Catholic Church as women are excluded from ever attaining certain positions within the church hierarchy.

In a recent interview, the Presiding Bishop of the Episcopal Church, Katharine Jefferts-Schori, the recent US ambassador for Religious Freedom, the Rev. Dr. Suzan Johnson Cook, the President of Union Theological Seminary, the Rev. Dr. Serene Jones, and Sister Joan Chittister gathered to discuss the ongoing issue of sexism in the Christian Church. The determination that the Church's original sin of sexism is a palpable force in religious institutions, makes it necessary that the four women speak to the centuries long practice of discriminating against females. (Sexism: The Original Sin Of The Church, 2015). Given the life each has committed to service to her specific religious organization and traditions lends credibility to their assertions and gives an urgency to their work.

For the authors, the gender bias is compounded by race---in effect providing a double –whammy. Not only must women professors cope with an institutional environment that typically reflects the society's sexism, an African American woman must also confront racial attitudes not dissimilar to what is encountered on a daily basis in the "real-world." What is often encountered in higher education institutions is institutional racism. Hughes (2014) cites 10 signs of potential institutional racism with universities through a set of questions.

1. Have you lived in the United States (US) and never or rarely associated with people of color?
2. Are the buildings erected in the name of someone never in the name of a person of color?
3. Are the pictures of presidents, board members, award-winners not reflecting the demographics of the nation, the state, or your city?
4. Is the upper level of the organizational nearly all white and lower level positions mostly people of color?
5. Are new hires in most departments all or predominately white people?
6. Does the administration routinely have one or two people of color that serve on committees?
7. Why are the same one or two people serving on committees—lack of people of color or the administration's "comfort" with those individuals?
8. Who receives highly honored awards within the institution?
9. Is there the notion of finding people who are the "right fit"----and all of the people who are the right fit look like the majority of the people already in the institution?
10. Are opportunities to hire a person of color lost because someone on the hiring committee or an administrator intervenes to contact someone they think is the "right fit?"

Such behaviors place a burden on people of color as they strive to belong to the institution and become a contributing member to their department and the university. Taken in tandem, sexism and racism may create a sense of precariousness even within a religious university if the institution does not attend to the campus climate.

The climate at any institution can function to establish a sense of belonging with an accompanying desire to participate for the good of the institution, or the climate may actually contribute to a sense of being marginalized, undervalued, or always under scrutiny (Strayhorn, 2012). The later feelings do little to instill in the person who experiences them a sense of loyalty to peers or the institution. For example the University of California (2014) conducted workplace studies that included faculty members, administrators, and staff members and determined that those stakeholder were significantly impacted by campus climate. Further the research suggested a healthy inclusive campus climate promotes feeling of being

A Comparison of "Inclusiveness" in Two Liberal Arts Catholic Universities

personally and professionally supported among the faculty. Additionally, a direct relationship between workplace discrimination and negative job attitudes was indicated by the survey.

The fact that some institutions are better at the creation of inclusive campus climates is not an accident, but a result of a process, dedication, and ongoing assessment to establish inclusive excellence. A report by the Association of American Colleges and Universities (AACU) (2005) suggested that higher education institutions had the imperative to attend to external and internal factors that contribute to campus climate. External factors include society's persistent inequities, the nation's shifting demographics, political and legal imperatives, and workforce imperatives. By presenting occurrences from two Catholic liberal arts universities it may be possible to identify what each has done to create an inclusive campus climate and highlight areas that may need attention.

Overview Madonna University

The author's successful hire at Madonna University (MU) was greatly due to an identified need within the Teacher Education Program. Specifically, while the university was located approximately 25 minutes from Detroit, a city with the highest proportion of African Americans in the nation, there was a lack of African American faculty and little interaction with the Detroit Public Schools or the inner ring suburbs of the metropolitan Detroit area. Consequently, student teachers rarely had experiences in schools with any sizable number of minority students with the exception of Southfield and Dearborn schools. As is often the case, the national accrediting body for teacher education programs, National Council for Accreditation of Teacher Education (NCATE) cited the program for its lack of diversity within the faculty and within field experience sites. Further, faculty within the education department perceived a need to develop a systematic approach to the concept of multiculturalism and diversity. Fortunately, several top administrators in the university shared that perspective.

MU, originally an all-female institution founded in 1937, has approximately 3400 undergraduate and 1000 graduate students, with 110 faculty members. (Madonna University, n. d.) Like her predecessors, President Sister (Sr.) K., is a member of the Felician Sisters, *a religious institute of pontifical right whose members profess public vows of chastity, poverty and obedience and follow the evangelical way of life in common. It is officially known as the Congregation of Sisters of St. Felix of Cantalice Third Order Regular of St. Francis of Assisi (CSSF)* (Madonna University, n. d.). There is a dynamic order that has many ministries and is known for its joy.

The university accepts approximately 64 percent of applicants and has a faculty to student ratio of 12:1 (Madonna University, n.d.). Major administrative positions were traditionally held by the Felician Sisters, who as noted were action oriented. That action orientation became actualized on various occasions, most notably within the context of campus climate. Madonna University created a sense of connection among its faculty and staff, referred to by some as a "Madonna family." Like any family there are parents or guardians who strive to give its members a sense of wellbeing by meeting crucial needs, and maintaining a nurturing environment. The sense of family at Madonna was highly important for two specific reasons. Firstly, that concept was a match with the religious tenets of the Felician Sisters, whose mission was to live life with enthusiasm and a sense of joy. Equally important the sisters had vows of poverty and obedience. Within the context of the author's own family, there was a sense of joy merely for being together despite low family income. Each of the seven children felt cherished and was instilled with an obligation to be obedient. Children were taught to look after each other with a deeply ingrained sense of charity for each other. Further, the author's parents though poor, always seem to have a place for one more person at the table.

Secondly, the salaries at the institution were quite modest overall, and of course in keeping with their vow of poverty the sisters donated their salaries to their religious order and the university. Therefore, it was important to attempt to mediate the issue of modest salaries by other means. One such act was the annual Christmas dinner. Every faculty and staff member and guests received an invitation to this event. The atmosphere was much like a family gathering during the holiday season, as the room would be filled with family members of all ages. There were choirs, Christmas decorations, and individual gifts for each faculty and staff member. A sit-down dinner culminated the evening.

The Madonna family seemed to be inclusive of persons of color, various ethnic groups and members of non-Christian religions, as well as persons from the Gay, Lesbian, Bisexual, Transgender, and Queer (GLBTQ) community. Though the author's perceptions suggested there was a Madonna family, only individuals from each of the aforementioned groups could validate or negate those perceptions for themselves.

Overview John Carroll University

Located in an inner ring suburb of Cleveland, another city with a high proportion of African Americans, John Carroll University (JCU) like MU began as a single-sex institution, in this instance, males. Founded in 1886 in the Jesuit tradition inspired by the vision of Saint Ignatius Loyola the hallmarks of which,

... include the esteem for the individual as a unique person, training in discerning choice, openness to change, and a quest for God's greater glory in the use of this world's goods. Commitment to the values that inspired the Spiritual Exercises promotes justice by affirming the equal dignity of all persons and seeks balance between reliance on divine assistance and natural capacities. The effort to combine faith and culture takes on different forms at different times in Jesuit colleges and universities. Innovation, experiment, and training for social leadership are essential to the Jesuit tradition (John Carroll University, n. d.).

Now a co-educational university enrolling 3,001 undergraduate students and 708 postgraduates, the university takes pride in its repeated recognition on the top ten list of the US News & World Reports' annual guide, *"America's Best Colleges."* Like MU, JCU's school colors are blue and gold.

The acceptance rate at JCU is approximately 83 percent and has a faculty to student ratio of 13:1 (John Carroll University, n.d.). JCU has a strong commitment to service and social justice and the Center for Service and Social Action is nationally recognized for an outstanding record of student outreach and faculty support of service learning (John Carroll University, n.d.). Many JCU students exhibit a strong altruism much in keeping with the Jesuit ideal of being men and women for others. Some students embraced fair trade and worked to ensure that the consumables marketed on campus are under official fair trade oversight. In addition, it is not uncommon for JCU graduates to spend their first year after graduation volunteering in a developing nation, on a Native American reservation, or working for a non-profit organization. In keeping with Jesuit tradition the president is a Jesuit. Not unexpectedly, JCU is an institution in which male dominance is pervasive given it original structure.

A Comparison of "Inclusiveness" in Two Liberal Arts Catholic Universities

INCLUSIVE ENVIRONMENT

There are multiple ways by which to characterize an environment that is inclusive. Primarily, within such an environment all groups of people would feel safe, valued, respected, and most notably, a sense of *"belonging" (Strayhorn, 2012)*. If individuals belong within an institution they can negotiate the terrain fairly easily because they know and understand the unwritten rules and ways of being. Additionally, within the inclusive environment, there can be open honest discussions among members of the institution. There is also responsiveness to concerns of all members and a willingness to view change as progress (Bennett, 2011). Educators have known for some time the importance of creating and maintaining an inclusive environment for all learners (Bennett, 2011). Ford and Glimps (2014) citing Ruvolo (2007) suggests that a "faculty that is integrated and cohesive has many advantages that can impact the quality of the education it provides" (p. 200). In many work place settings, there is also a desire to accommodate differing needs and preferences and to ensure unwritten rules of the community, are understood by all members (Creating an Inclusive Environment, n. d.).

Data from the American Council on Education's Minorities in Higher Education status report, suggest the student body in higher education has become increasingly diverse (Kim, 2011). Many institutions have come to recognize the benefits of diversity on university campuses both for majority white students and minorities in terms of academic excellences and preparation for life in the work place (Prieto, 2011). Yet, it must be understood that a diverse student body does not ensure an inclusive campus environment. Equally important, the degree to which a campus creates an inclusive environment for its students and faculty of color plays a large role in determining which faculty becomes tenured: who chooses to remain at the institution, and how much they contribute to the vitality of the day-to-day operations (Hausmann, Schoflied, & Woods, 2007). As much as the historically underrepresented students of color may feel a dislocation being in a predominately white university, so too do many faculty of color. The dissonance created by being a person of color within predominately white religious institutions is further amplified by being female (Ford & Glimps, 2014).

Getting to understand the existing culture of a university campus is sometimes a difficult task for a female faculty of color because there may be unspoken rules. Resentment may emanate from white students who are unaccustomed to having a person of color, particularly an African American female, call into question their academic abilities. During the tenure track period is a particularly delicate time for females of color as some students deliberately rate the professors at the lowest end of the scale based on gender and perceived race (Reid, 2010; Lazos, 2011). Moreover, if the professor is a foreign-born Asian or African for example, student comments often entail remarks about the need for the professor to "learn to speak English." Such remarks may occur even if the foreign-born professor is fluent in English. Another frequent reaction that may emanate from a lack of respect for the professors' authority and scholarly expertise is to question why the individual is allowed to teach at the university (Pittman, 2010). The subtext of such comments is a feeling that persons of color do not belong on the predominately white university campus. While it is true one is a lonely number, so is two, three, or 10 within the context of some 200 full-time instructional staff at institutions such as Madonna and John Carroll Universities. With such limited diversity among faculty it becomes urgently important for higher education institutions to create and sustain inclusive campus environments.

INSTITUTIONAL COMPARISON: MADONNA UNIVERSITY

Administration

How did the author come to experience MU as a place that gave a sense of belonging? Reflection on time at MU suggests there were numerous factors that contributed to sense of belonging. The first of these was the administration, which as previously noted was comprised primarily of Felicians. Then President Sr. Franciline seemed inspired to create an environment in which all, students, faculty and administration, could experience personal and spiritual growth as well as acceptance. It was her presence that filled the university with a true Christian love that became actualized daily. She seemed to know every faculty and staff member by name and a good many of the students as well.

It was not out of the ordinary to see her attend student fund-raisers and make purchases, while talking with the students. The author's first encounter with Sr. Franciline shortly after being hired greatly lessened apprehension about embarking on a higher education career and relocating to the metropolitan Detroit area. While that meeting may have been a routine part of the hire process, it was not perfunctory. Sr. Franciline was actively learning about the author and in doing so projected a welcoming image. The author also recalled a first meeting with the vice president during the hire process at which time the issues of personal beliefs and political views arose. The event was memorable because most of the author's personal and political views were in direct opposition to many of the Catholic Church's doctrines. Without hesitation the vice president replied, as long as *"you don't proselytize you are free to teach and share your beliefs."* That commitment was honored during the author's employment.

During four years at MU the author became well acquainted with Sr. Franciline and the other Felician sisters. Other members of the administration, also Felicians, created a sense of being welcomed and part of the campus community through the various programs they instituted. The Felicians being action oriented sought to ensure that faculty embraced diversity as whole-heartedly as they strove to do. That desire resulted in the creation of a team lead by Sr. L. that included the author that successfully won a Kresge Foundations grant to improve campus climate. The central rationale of the grant proposal was the need to provide guidance to instructors in order to develop course syllabi that incorporated multicultural materials and instructional practices. In a series of work sessions, 10 to 12 instructors attended a session, reviewed their current course syllabi and received guidance to transform the documents. A good portion of each session involved discussions about what constituted multicultural instructional practices and why they should be routinely used. Additionally, there was the objection by some instructors that their discipline focused only on the "facts" therefore embedding multiculturalism was not important or possible. Overcoming such resistance is never easy, but with the backing of top administrators and stipends from the grant, many instructors who normally might never have modified their syllabi did so. In the process, they were exposed to inclusive instructional practices, and learned of sources for multicultural materials to incorporate. The Kresge Foundation grant also provided for the hire of a diversity trainer to facilitate anti-racism sessions. All of these actions strongly suggested an evangelical approach to developing and maintaining an inclusive campus climate.

The director of the Office of Multicultural Affairs (OMA) was also a Felician. A more committed individual to the Christian tenants of acceptance of all people would be difficult to identify than Sr. M. Together, Sr. M. and the author and others endeavored to create a club for students, faculty and staff dedicated to building cross-cultural experiences and combatting bias on the campus. The OMA sponsored a series of daylong cultural events with local performers, food vendors, handcrafts and mini lectures about

A Comparison of "Inclusiveness" in Two Liberal Arts Catholic Universities

the featured culture. Sr. M. and the author ventured to other Catholic colleges in the metropolitan Detroit area to conduct anti-bias workshops. All of these activities initiated by the administration did much to support an inclusive campus climate and sent a strong message to departments across the institution.

In any institution there are individuals who may resist such efforts for any number of reasons. Such was the case when a male faculty member sent an e-mail message specifically to the author but made it available to the entire MU community. He openly challenged the ongoing efforts to broaden and support the university's commitment to inclusiveness. For nearly two weeks the male faculty member and author exchanged open emails debating the intent, benefit and other issues related to the diversity work. During that period other members of the community felt moved to join the conversation. They contributed timely comments and observations; they acknowledged or minimized the benefits, and a few even posed embarrassingly racist questions. The exchanges and community discussion abruptly ended when the male faculty member who had initiated the emails resorted to a personal attack and one of the administrators immediately intervened. He was rebuked and his misperceptions about how and why the author came to be engaged in the university's efforts to foster multiculturalism dispelled. The administrator left no doubt that the university was not merely tolerating the new initiatives, but had literally gone forth to obtain money to initiate and support the current efforts.

One of the outcomes of that frank and open exchange among faculty and staff was the ongoing discussion. Two of the most racially naïve members of the university began to engage in conversation with the author in an attempt to begin to *know* beyond their narrow mono-cultural existent. A male noted for his lack of diversity in his personal life and his often questionable remarks, quietly admitted that he had looked forward to the email exchanges and had begun to have new perspectives on some of the issues.

Perhaps the greatest honor and action that conveyed to the author the message that she belonged was the president's invitation to be the mace-bearer at commencement. The tradition of mace-bearer goes many hundreds of years as part of Parliamentary procedures in Great Britain. The person chosen to serve as the mace-bearer was often a man of great importance---someone befitting such a prestigious honor. Within the higher education community, the mace-bearer may be a person elected to the position or appointed by the president. Again, being selected to carry the mace, a symbol of the authority of the institution, is an exceptional honor.

Department of Education

Prior to her employ at MU the institution had terminated the tenure process thereby affording the author the freedom to focus efforts on teaching and coordinator duties. The tenure process can be notorious for making the lives of those seeking to gain a permanent place at the table, unnecessarily anxious and laborious. With tenure gone, the MU faculty devised a plan that gave new hires yearly contracts for the first three years, followed by five-year contracts thereon should the hire prove satisfactory. This plan was progressive in its time and reflected MU faculty's desire to prevent *nesting,* the tendency of some tenured faculty to disengage from the university. Such a model also interrupts the practices associated with the tenure process that traditionally disadvantages females and minorities. Given this freedom, the author devoted a great deal of efforts to fulfilling the stated goals of the Department of Education; the diversification of field experience sites and systematizing actions to promote multiculturalism and diversity within the education program.

The chair of the department was a man who promoted inclusiveness for faculty, staff and students enrolled in the department through his accessibility, openness, and willingness to listen and learn. The author particularly enjoyed the weekly department lunches the chair fostered. Once a week all members of the department if they chose to do so, shared lunch at a local restaurant. It is unusual to find members of a department so collegial. The fact that the department administrative assistant also joined the lunch outings further attests to the climate within the department as being one that promoted inclusiveness for all members and broke artificially imposed hierarchies. Carrying out one's duties in such a climate facilitated the author's efforts, because of the support of the chair and department members.

The department, much like the MU administration, was action oriented particularly with regard to addressing items cited by the National Council for Accreditation of Teacher Education (NCATE) that called for more faculty of color and diversity of field experiences. Therefore diversification of field sites consumed a major portion of the author's time and energy. The author systematically identified schools in various districts that were economically, racially, religiously, and ethnically diverse. In one school for example, the student population was predominately white children from low social economic status. Conversely, students in another district were primarily Chaldean immigrants. More important than the obvious diversity, the principals and faculty at selected schools seemed to celebrate their diversity and had a commitment to the academic success of all students. Often when entering these schools, the author noted the friendly greeting extended by the office personnel, which at the least indicated that the author was recognized as someone who required assistance and was also a person who should be made to feel welcomed.

With the selection of new field sites, the department instituted a policy that required all teacher education students to complete one of their field experiences in one of the newly established schools prior to their student teaching placement. There was to be expected resistance on the part of some students. On occasion a parent would contact the author in an effort to have the requirement waived for his or her child, usually based on fear for the safety the student. Without exception the department observed the requirement. Such firm commitment to providing the students with meaningful diverse field experiences speaks well for the department.

With the chair's and department's backing the author also diversified the ranks of the university field supervisors with the hiring of two African American former principals. Being supervised by an African American educator was for some student teachers the first time they had ever had such an interaction. Interactions of that kind served to communicate to students that members of diverse groups could provide expert guidance that could prove effective in supporting the students as they fulfilled their student teaching requirement. On occasion the author travelled to small, remote school districts in which there was little to no racial diversity. Entering some of those schools was like walking into a tomb. Clearly, the office administrative team was astonished by the author's presence. After an initial bewilderment, and the delayed greeting, the author could request direction to the room in which the MU student teacher was teaching. Additional dissonance occurred when the office administrative team read the author's business card and leaned the author held a doctorate. Those encounters served to remind the author of the difference felt while being on the campus at MU and being in school buildings that clearly were not expecting diversity to walk in the door in the person of an African American female with an advanced education degrees.

Years after the author departed MU a connection continued. For example, the author received an invitation to conduct a diversity training session for a group of new nuns. It was during that return to MU that the author was invited to spend the night in the Mother House with the sisters. In the morning the author and sisters cooked breakfast and ate together. That memory was incredible --- an African American agnostic, sharing the living quarters with nuns, most of whom were of Polish or Flemish ancestry. An exploration of the Mother House allowed the author to see the sisters' inner-sanctum, view numerous religious paintings and a few nearly life size statues of various saints. Opening one's home and sharing a meal is the most intimate expression of inclusiveness. Those affirming experiences at MU that did so much to foster an inclusive climate and conveyed to the author that she belonged there, have not dimmed with the passage of many years.

Student Body

Given the absence of the tenure system, the ability of students to use course evaluations to punish the author and perhaps make obtaining difficult, students at MU usually rated the author positively. However, one incident is still suggestive of students' implicit bias. The department routinely compiled each faculty person's student evaluation scores and compared them to the university averages for all faculty. On every indicator except one, the author was rated higher than the university faculty averages. When it came to the final indicator that asked the students to rate the author compared to other instructors the students deemed the author was not quite as "good" as other professors. The results gave the author cause to contemplate the meaning of the data. How was it possible to out perform other faculty with very high scores for such things as; *the instructor is helpful, the instructor is approachable, the instructor explains the material, the instructor is respectful, the instructor is knowledgeable,* and yet, on the final item determine that author was not as good as other faculty. Speculating, the author posits that the students may have been appreciative of the quality of instruction given, yet, the final item calls for the students to judge the author in comparison to other faculty, all of whom were white. Having an African American female professor makes some white students uncomfortable, and being uncomfortable is something that is not normal for them. Where the white students make personal connections easily with professors who "look like them" persons of color such as the author, recognize that a personal connection with the students is not easily built.

Yet, the MU students were generally respectful and acknowledged the author's professional ability to instruct them, assess their performance, and give corrective guidance.

INSTITUTIONAL COMPARISON: JOHN CARROLL UNIVERSITY

Administration

The author's office is in the Administration Building as is the office of the president of JCU. After 10 years at the institution the author has had a single occasion to enter that space. For much of that time the author often observed that the office was dark and closed, with no hint of the president or the administrative staff. Evidently, for some JCU students the perceived absence of the president was palpable and precipitated the "game" in which some students engaged that reflects their sense that the president was largely an absent figure from the daily life of the institution. A student confessed that it common to snap the president's his image and "Tweeting" it to others with the tag "Presidential Sighting."

The rationale for the president's limited presence on the campus is the ongoing major efforts to strengthen and expand ties with alumni. Toward that end, it had been judged that the president has had major success in those endeavors, with a resulting increase of financial support for the institution and alumni participation. While the president pursues his goals he left in his stead numerous provosts, vice presidents and assistant vice presidents. These figures seem to serve as an insulation that filters distractions, thus allowing the president to focus on his prime goals. In such a situation the insulation can prevent an individual from being aware of campus events, ascertaining the climate of the campus, and knowing members of the faculty and staff. For the author the greatest lost opportunity for the president to promote a sense of his engagement with faculty has occurred during the Open House events held across the street from the JCU campus in what is often called the Jesuit House. The few Jesuits who reside in the house go to some effort to share their living space periodically with the JCU community by providing excellent conversation, canapés and wine. The president however, has not been present at any of the events the author attended at the Jesuit House. Such absences have created for the author a perception of the president as rather distant figure. The president's limited presence creates a disconnect between him and the author. Additionally, the author posits that a great deal of the information the president receives appears to be obtained through the filter of the administrative staff. If true, such an arrangement would make difficult in the extreme the president's ability to ascertain first hand perceptions of the campus' lack of inclusiveness as experienced by diverse members of the student body and faculty.

In response to ongoing problems with incidents of bias and hate graffiti the administration made an effort to track data through a centralized reporting system that tracked incidences of racial, sexual, homophobic, and religious intolerance. Through the system the institution is able to collect detailed data from students, faculty, and staff. Ideally, the data can be used to provide appropriate interventions and facilitate face-to-face dialogue between the perpetrators and the injured parties. The bias incident reporting system has been quite effective in some instances, specifically when student-to-student incidents occur. Members of the Office for Diversity and Inclusion seem to be diligent in their follow-up on reported incidents and then providing timely resolutions.

The author's personal experience with the bias reporting system clearly illustrated the break down in the system when faculty is involved. The Associate Academic Vice President for Student Success Initiatives and Faculty Diversity received the bias report the author filed in February 2013. Subsequently, the administrator and the author met with the director of the Human Services Office (HSO) and the author expressed a desire to have a face-to-face with the offending staff person. Additionally, the author requested that the staff person receive retraining and have a written report included in the permanent record. Months went by with numerous emails exchanges between the director of HSO and the author. There always seemed to be some unforeseen meeting or emergency that prevented the HSO director from facilitating a face-to-face meeting. An entire year after filing the bias incident report, no follow up session had been scheduled. That prompted the author to begin to share the "confidential" incident report, as well as noting the failure of HSO to arrange a face-to-face meeting. The information was disseminated to an official campus advocacy organization as well as a standing faculty council committee, both of which are devoted to ensuring female and diverse faculty are not marginalized within the campus community. Only after the author began to make public the incident that had transpired was the three-way meeting finally arranged. That lack of urgency or attention to the incident suggested a lack of importance had been attached to the complaint. That perception was confirmed when the director of HSO explained his failure to arrange a three way meeting among the parties was because he assumed the author was making the arrangements. Such an assumption seemed to the author similar to asking a victim of a robbery to apprehend the thief and bring him in for questioning. For the author the seeming indifference to the incident and the failure to validate the author's psychological injuries served to continue the sense of alienation that had begun during the first few years at JCU.

A Comparison of "Inclusiveness" in Two Liberal Arts Catholic Universities

Those early years at JCU were difficult, largely due to the demands of being a tenure track faculty member. There are two vivid memories associated with the author's tenure track travails. The actions of a former dean serve to illustrate the kinds of actions that do little to engender a sense of belonging while also remaining rather nebulous even today. The author was on medical leave during a spring semester and was contacted by the dean three days before the scheduled annual tenure review presentation. The dean suggested a postponement of the review until the fall academic semester. She reasoned the delay would result in more publications and a better dossier. Superficially, one could perceive that the offer was a supportive gesture. However, the subtext of the offer presented a different scenario. Firstly, the dean had not received the dossier for review therefore she had no idea of the quality of the document; her suggestion that it might somehow be improved was premature. Moreover, should the offer be accepted, it would have placed the author in a precarious situation. If the dossier and tenure review presentation went poorly, the dean and the tenure committee could site the additional time the author had, and legitimately note the author still failed to meet the standards. Conversely, a successful review might fall victim to the familiar "affirmative action" rhetoric that posits any success by a minor is somehow not because of the individual's ability, but the result of special treatment. The author declined the offer and when on to have a successful review two days later and emerged with a vote for continuance. Three years later the author earned tenure, by which time the dean had gained a more prestigious post at a different institution. Only then did the author learn that the dean had not consulted with either the department chair nor the Tenure and Promotion Committee before extending the offer to delay the tenure review. It was an action she unilaterally initiated, the intent of which is still unclear.

Subsequent to the aforementioned incident, an equally puzzling episode involving the dean transpired two days before an annual spring break. She contacted the author "asking" the author to attend a national conference of Jesuit institutions. Further, the dean indicated that she was unable to get faculty to attend because they had vacation plans for the break. The author's plans for the break were to work on the tenure dossier and practice the presentation for the tenure committee. As an untenured faculty, an individual is placed in a position of diminished power, making it difficult to decline invitations from tenured faculty to participate on committees and in this instance a request from the dean. Aside from the dean's need to have representatives from JCU at the conference, the author also suspects the request was motivated by a desire to show that the institution had an African American faculty person. That motive may have stemmed from the fact that the hosting institution was a predominantly African American Jesuit higher education institution. Whatever the motivation, after returning from the conference, the author had only a weekend in which to try to perfect the dossier. The lack of adequate preparation was evident in the tenure dossier submitted to the committee. The committee was not made aware of the circumstances, because to do so would suggest the author was not accepting responsibility for the rather poor quality of the dossier.

Events such as those presented by the author highlight the need for the top administrators to be present and engaged, in a manner similar to the sisters at MU. Additionally, administrators should at the very least be perceived as a neutral force by minority faculty when they are in the highly vulnerable position of being on the tenure track. The aforementioned actions by the administrators at MU stand in sharp contrast to what transpired at JCU. For the author, the events at JCU did little to create a perception of being wanted at the institution but succeeded in making the author highly suspicious and ever watchful.

In recognition of ongoing problematic events on the campus the university hired an Assistant Provost for Diversity and Chief Diversity Officer in August 2014. Female faculty, faculty of color and other members of the campus community welcomed this addition and had great hopes that the creation of this position would do much to begin to develop a sense of belonging at JCU. If the new provost is successful it will boost morale as well.

Department of Education

A major complaint expressed by many higher educational institutions is difficulty finding qualified faculty of color. The dearth of faculty of color was highly noticeable in the education department at JCU, there being none. Several years before the author's hire as a tenure track faculty member, the chair of the education department became aware of the author's professional and educational background. When a position became available, the chair initiated contact with the author, giving encouragement to apply. Those actions were a fulfillment of the chair's promise to notify the author when a tenure track position posted. Such support did not end with the author's hire. The author's first three years on the tenure track were filled with painful health issues, the death of a most beloved sister, and the demands of being the guardian of a young grandniece. Medication for the health issues created a zombie-like state, dulling the senses and fostered sleeplessness, all of which greatly interfered with the discharge of the author's responsibilities. In despair, the author finally candidly confessed to the chair the inability to continue.

Without hesitation the chair contacted HSO and quickly made arrangements for the author to take a medical leave. As supportive as that action was, what the author remembers most were the comments the chair made. She indicated she had observed the author's efforts to continue to honor all responsibilities despite physical pain and personal tragedies. That compassion and support created a sense that the chair felt the author was an asset to the department. There were other members of the department who were also openly supportive of the author. A most remarkable demonstration of that support occurred when a male colleague entered the author's office one afternoon, sat down and succinctly announced. "I'm here to help you get tenure."

Having such a mentor while on tenure track is essential to supporting faculty. Support is even more important for females and minorities as they attempt to transverse the path to tenure, and learn the unwritten rules within the department and the greater campus. Providing insights as to what the tenure committee expects during a presentation can be invaluable information. Moreover, mentors can help the untenured faculty member avoid becoming a pawn in the political power struggles that may exist within a department. The department had not established a formal mentoring process, but relies on individual tenured faculty to serve in that capacity as suits them. Formalizing this function would do much to support any tenure track faculty and certainly aid in creating a sense that members of the department are making a sincere effort to see the new hire successfully earn tenure. Absence such a structure, new tenure track hires, especially minorities; are often left adrift within a seemingly alien and indifferent environment.

A highly challenging reality of the education department has often been the lack of common servility. In a relatively small department, having one or two tenured faculty members who never speak when passing in the corridors creates a chilling and hostile climate within the department. For the author such behavior is in marked contrast to professed Jesuit values and fails to promote solidarity within the department. Further, the author is unclear if such behavior served to accentuate a distinct power hierarchy, *we are tenured and you are not,* or if race was the primary factor. Again the author is reminded of the weekly lunches with members of the education department at MU, that minimized emphasis on hierarchy and the ensuing sense of belonging that emanates from an inclusive community, something that remains elusive at JCU.

A Comparison of "Inclusiveness" in Two Liberal Arts Catholic Universities

Student Body

One of the most evident indicators of how well minority faculty may fare in an institution is the degree to which students perceive the faculty person is "qualified" to assess their academic abilities. As noted earlier, white students frequently evaluate minority faculty less favorably than they do white faculty—this is particularly so when the minority faculty is on the tenure track. The author experienced this during much of the time as an untenured faculty person. A great deal of the course content within the courses the author teaches is specifically related to issues of racial inequalities, topics many white students are not comfortable with and some often refute outright. As such, for five years the author devoted a great deal of effort to ensuring student evaluations of teaching were in the top range of scores. Even so, student comments stated the author was *racist, talked too much about race, was unfair*, and *did not grade fairly*.

Many of the students at JCU spend their entire K-12 experience in parochial schools. Frequently, indications are the author is the first instructor of color the students have ever encountered. That situation is often difficult for some students because they are not accustomed to an African American female in a position of authority. Moreover, they are greatly distressed when such a figure draws attention to their inadequacies in written expression. One student went so far as to demand to know *"Where do you get off telling me my writing is weak?"* The author feels certain the student would not approach the issue in the same disrespectful manner had the author been a white male.

If some students feel empowered to interact with an African American faculty member in such a manner, it is not unusual to find that some JCU students openly work to create a hostile campus climate for their fellow JCU students of color or those with different sexual orientation. There have been numerous incidents of racist graffiti within the dormitories and public spheres. The level of racial hostility was best illustrated when President Obama was first elected. Some students were heard to say it was time to get their guns. These are primarily good Catholic students who have chosen to attend a Jesuit institution because of its tenets of service to others. Yet, their Christianity and specifically their Catholic faith are not sufficient to overcome their deep-seated racial prejudices.

Reflecting on the students at MU, the author was not subjected to such experiences, though it is impossible to know how MU students might have reacted had an African American president been elected at point in time. Perhaps the students at MU felt their student evaluations carried less import because there was no tenure process. Perhaps, the MU students had recognized the strong advocacy for diversity by the administration and the education department and had simply followed those examples.

Conversely, given the frequent absences of the JCU president and his low visibility, the author posits that circumstance maybe a contributory factor in JCU students' behaviors that are decidedly un-Jesuit like. A strong, visible leader who speaks frequently to and aids in the creation of an inclusive campus is essential to any institution. The president's limited engagement supports an atmosphere that has lead to what some would claim are discriminatory practices directed towards female faculty. Additionally students and faculty of color, and members of the GLBTQ community would no doubt claim the campus climate at JCU has a way to go before one could claim it is one of inclusiveness.

PRACTICES AND BEHAVIORS THAT PROMOTE INCLUSIVENESS

The author's recollections of MU might be colored by the distance of time when juxtaposed to the realities of the teaching environment in which the author is now immersed. Yet, it is possible to articulate a few essential practices that must occur if there is to be an inclusive environment within a predominately white Catholic intuition of higher education. The comparison of MU and JCU suggests having top administrative posts filled with mostly nuns may indeed have promoted inclusiveness. Within that context there was no legacy of male dominance to overcome and it empowered females to aspire to any administrative post they felt qualified to hold. JCU must understand the legacy of its males only history, a replica of the Catholic Church hierarchy, and the struggles it is still experiencing as it grabbles with what it means to be a co-education Jesuit university in an increasingly diverse nation in the 21st century.

The high visibility of the top administrator, the president, is important. That visibility should manifest in the president's interaction with faculty, staff and students on a regular basis. The institution's top administrator should not be perceived as missing-in-action. It is the responsibility of the president to create the tone and direction of the institution by supporting diversity initiatives with participation, money and pronouncements. Open, earnest discussions of issues of race, gender, sexual orientation and other human diversity must take place and the JCU administrators should be in the forefront of these efforts. Only when top administrators are highly visible supporters of efforts to improve the campus climate will some faculty, staff and students begin to behave in an improved manner. Administrators must support on-going training for staff and faculty as well as for themselves. All involved must remember that it takes sustained consciousness to maintain an inclusive institutional environment. Top leadership shapes the direction of the organization and the tone set at the top does "trickle down."

JCU should consider emulating MU in seeking grants to support a variety of campus-wide activities aimed at developing ongoing practices that potentially could enhance the campus climate. For example, learning groups to examine and understand white culture and all of its inherent manifestations and privilege within the political, economic, educational, medical and religious institutional settings could be an excellent means by which to facilitate substantive discussions self examination. As envisioned these groups could be the impetus for removing the silence surrounding race talk and stripping away the colorblind lens many whites use to avoid when confronted with racial issues. JCU persistently seeks to have "good citizens" of the institution and recognizes them with merit pay. Recognizing the participation of JCU faculty in the learning groups by linking it to merit pay would be a strong statement of JCU's commitment to improving the campus climate.

The administration could also urge departments and schools to create a mentoring process to aid tenure track faculty, especially for females and people of color. There are currently new strategies in development to identify and recruit a diverse pool of potential faculty members. Equally vital to the proposed new recruitment strategies are the retention efforts the university should implement if recruitment is successful in hiring diverse clients. That would entail identifying which institutions are most successful in retaining diverse hires and then seek to implement the most promising practices at JCU. In the past other institutions raided the JCU faculty for some of its diverse professors. Is this a strategy JCU could also use to increase diversity? Can the institution identify leading members of Cleveland's Latino/a, African American and Asian American communities and develop ways to use their talent, expertise and unique life experiences to education JCU's faculty and students?

JCU's bias incident reporting system must be vigilant and timely in its handling of complaints, particularly with regard to faculty and staff. Establishing a diverse slate of faculty to serve on a bias incident committee would have the effect of letting the community know that these events are a serious matter, make events transparent, and ensure timely resolutions. Having knowledge of the nature and frequency of the microaggressions that occur on the campus might actually cause some faculty to reflect on their own behaviors and attitudes. That reflection might also precipitate other changes in behavior related to pedagogy and course content.

Monthly town hall meetings should be instituted during which faculty, staff and students examine campus, city, national or international events indicative of intolerance. Having an historic context for many of current events we witness can foster a more accurate understanding and promote informed and reasoned discussion.

Lastly, JCU could become a partner university to Spring Hill, the historically African American Jesuit institution. Faculty exchanges should be encouraged. Distance learning communities that provide interaction between JCU students and Spring Hill students could be established. Indeed, JCU should expand it vision and even partner with one of the nation's historically black higher education institutions. There are also a number of co-educational universities such as MU that were historically woman only institutions that could provide JCU with a new operational paradigm. Links with universities in nations such as Jamaica, Cuba, Ghana, Brazil, Senegal, and China could increase awareness of diversity and aid in the development of the skills required to create an inclusive campus climate.

REFERENCES

Bennett, C. (2011). *Comprehensive multicultural education: theory and practice* (7th ed.). Boston: Pearson.

Bryant, A. (2006). Assessing the gender climate of an evangelical student subculture in the United States. *Gender and Education, 18*(6), 613–634. doi:10.1080/09540250600980170

Calef, S. (2009). Charting new territory: religion and "the gender-critical turn." *Journal of Religion and Society Supplement 5*. Creating an Inclusive Environment, retrieved http://www.afsaadmin.org/wp-content/uploads/2012/02/Creating-an-Inclusive-Environment-handout.pdf

Ford, T., & Glimps, B. (2014). African American women, education, and self-actualization: Confronting gender and racial barriers in religious institutions. In P. Breen (Ed.), *Cases on Teacher Identity, Diversity, and Cognition in Higher Education*. Hersey, PA: IGI Global. doi:10.4018/978-1-4666-5990-2.ch008

Hausmann, L., Schoflied, J., & Woods, R. (2007, November). Sense of belonging as a predictor of intentions to persist among African American and white first-year college students. *Research in Higher Education, 48*(7), 803–839. doi:10.100711162-007-9052-9

Hill Collins, P. (1990). *Black feminist thought: knowledge, consciousness, and the politics of empowerment*. New York, NY: Routledge.

History and Traditions. (n. d.) Retrieved from http://www.barnet.gov.uk/info/930234/history_and_traditions/250/history_and_traditions

Hopflinger, A., Lavanchy, A., & Dahinden, J. (2012). Introduction: Linking gender and religion. *Women's Studies, 41*(6), 615–638. doi:10.1080/00497878.2012.691401

Jakobsen, J., & Bernstein, E. (2009). Religion, Politics and Gender Equality: Country Report USA. Retrieved from http://www.unrisd.org/80256B3C005BCCF9/httpNetITFramePDF?ReadForm&parent unid=460E91A405DA36328025790D004F95CA&parentdoctype=paper&netitpath=80256B3C005BC CF9/(httpAuxPages)/460E91A405DA36328025790D004F95CA/$file/WEBFinalUSA.pdf

John Carroll University (n. d.) Retrieved from http://sites.jcu.edu/mission/pages/university-mission-statement/

Kim, Y. (2011). Minorities in Higher Education: 24th Status Report 2011 Supplement. Retrieved from http://diversity.ucsc.edu/resources/images/ace_report.pdf

King, U. (2005). General Introduction: Gender critical turns in the study of religion. In King, U. & Beattie (Ed.). Gender, Religion and Diversity: Cross-Cultural Perspectives. New York: Continuum International Publishing Group.

Lazos, S. (2011). Are student teaching evaluations holding back women and minorities? The perils of "doing" gender and race in the classroom. In Guitierrez y Muhs, Gabriella et al. (Eds.), Presumed incompetent: the intersections of race and class for women in academia Chapter 1. Boulder, CO: University Press of Colorado.

Madonna University. (n. d.) retrieved http://www.madonna.edu/about/felician-sisters

Ndlazi, T. (2004). Men in church institutions and religious organizations: The role of Christian men in transforming gender relations and ensuring gender equality. Agenda: Empowering Women for Gender Equity. *Religion & Spirituality*, 61, 62-65.

Pittman, C. (2010). Race and gender oppression in the classroom: The experiences of women faculty of color with white male students. *Teaching Sociology*, 38(3), 183–196. doi:10.1177/0092055X10370120

Prieto, L. (2011). Initial factor analysis and cross-validation of the Multicultural Teaching Competencies Inventory. *Journal of Diversity in Higher Education*, 5(1), 50–62. doi:10.1037/a0026199

Reid, L. (2010). The role of perceived race and gender in the evaluation of college teaching on RateMyProfessors.com. *Journal of Diversity in Higher Education*, 3(3), 137–152. doi:10.1037/a0019865

Religion and sexuality: An introduction to the issues from the interfaith working group (n. d.). Retrieved from http://www.iwgonine.org/sexuality/

Salzbrunn, M. (2012). Performing gender and religion: The veil's impa11 (1), ct on boundary-making processes in France. *Women's Studies*, 41(6), 682–705. doi:10.1080/00497878.2012.691823

Scott, H. (2014). Perceptions of Christian women leaders in church-related organizations. *Christian Education Journal* Series 3, 52-70.

Stewart-Thomas, M. (2010). Gendered congregations, gendered service: The impact of clergy gender on congregational social service participation. *Gender, Work and Organization*, 17(4), 406–432.

Strayhorn, L. (2012). *College students' sense of belonging: a key to educational success for all students*. New York, NY: Routledge.

Religion, politics and gender equality. (n. d.). United Nations Research Institute on Social Development. Retrieved from http://www.unrisd.org/research.gd/religionandgender

ADDITIONAL READING

Delpit, L. (2006). *Other people's children: cultural conflict in the classroom*. New York, NY: The New Press.

Desimone, L., Hochberg, E., Porter, A., Polikoff, M., Schwartz, R., & Johnson, L. (2014). Formal and informal Mentoring: Complementary, Compensatory or Consistent? *Journal of Teacher Education*, 65(2), 88–110. doi:10.1177/0022487113511643

DiAngelo, R. (2012). *What does it mean to be white?: developing white racial literacy*. New York, NY: Peter Lang.

Ford, T., & Glimps, B. (2009). We live to Create Dissonance: Can you be Racist and a Christian? *Journal of Beliefs & Values*, 30(2), 103–111. doi:10.1080/13617670903174975

Harley, D. (2008). Maids of academe: African American women faculty at predominately white institutions. *Journal of African American Studies* (12), 19-36.

Hinton, D. (2010). Creating community on the margins: The successful black female academician. *The Urban Review*, 42(5), 394–402. doi:10.100711256-009-0140-3

Holmes, S. (2008). Narrated voices of African American women in academe. *Journal of Thought*, 43(3/4), 101–124.

Hornbeck, P. (2013). Heterosexism: An Ethnical Challenge. *Conversations*. Fall 2013, No. 44.

Madeloni, B. (2014). The movement we make is the community we become: on being an activist in the academy. *Multicultural Perspectives*, 16(1), 12–15. doi:10.1080/15210960.2013.867238

Patton, T. (2004). Reflections of a black woman professor: Racism and sexism in academia. *The Howard Journal of Communications*, 15(3), 185–200. doi:10.1080/10646170490483629

Reyes, R., & Case, K. (2011). National Profile on Ethnic/Racial Diversity of Enrollment, Graduation Rates, Faculty, and Administrator among the Council for Christian Colleges & Universities: 2nd Report. Retrieved from http://www.cccu.org/~/media/filefolder/CCCU-Diversity-Report-2011-1-25-11

Suzuki, D., & Mayorga, E. (2014). Scholar-Activism: A Twice Told Tale. *Multicultural Perspectives*, 16(1), 16–20. doi:10.1080/15210960.2013.867405

View, J., & Frederick, R. (2011). Sneaking out of the big house? Perceptions of African American mentees in a graduate-level teacher education program on a white campus. *The Journal of Negro Education*, 80(2), 134–148.

Wellin, C. (2009). Telling tales out of school: Dilemmas of race and inclusiveness in the liberal academy. *The American Behavioral Scientist*, 51(5), 686–708. doi:10.1177/0002764207307750

KEY TERMS AND DEFINITIONS

Diversity: The variety that exists among humans including gender, ethnicity, race, age, social class, sexual orientation, and primary language.

Inclusive Environment: Refers to the perceived atmosphere within an institution that affirms all members of the community.

Intersectionality: The convergence of multiple identities, such as race-gender; SES-sexual orientation.

Microaggression: Refers to the routine verbal and behavioral slights, whether intentional or unintentional, endured by persons of color that communicate hostile negative racial attitudes.

Racial Identity: The affinity group to which a people or an individual prefer to share that is based on physical characteristics and/or shared history.

Religious Tenets: The strongly held beliefs of a religious group.

Sense of Belonging: An affirming feeling people experience when immersed within an inclusive social setting.

Social Justice: The concept of a society that promotes fairness for all citizens resulting in members of the society actively working to address social inequities arising from human diversity.

This research was previously published in Gender and Diversity Issues in Religious-Based Institutions and Organizations edited by Blanche Jackson Glimps and Theron Ford; pages 159-183, copyright year 2016 by Information Science Reference (an imprint of IGI Global).

Index

A

ability level 295, 947, 961, 971
ableism 41, 43, 397, 514, 525, 534, 738, 740
accessibility needs 10, 52, 55, 58, 60-64, 68, 74, 499
Accommodation or Modification 238
Accommodations/Services 403
action research 437, 891, 893, 895-896, 904, 911, 925, 929
ADA 3-5, 11, 19-20, 22-23, 25, 28-30, 35-36, 220, 223, 225, 238-239, 395, 510, 513-518, 521, 523-526, 595
adaptive behavior 413, 432, 556, 578, 950, 971
adolescents 357, 369, 371-373, 375, 449
African Americans 652, 685, 689, 691, 695, 713-714, 716-718, 723, 747, 807, 1025-1026
Alberta Education 1000, 1011, 1020-1021
Americans with Disabilities Act 4-5, 19-20, 35, 37, 223, 395, 510, 513, 551, 579, 595
anxiety 108, 190, 363, 368-369, 372, 376, 391, 405, 410-411, 415, 564, 633, 673, 695, 891, 893, 896-898, 902, 904, 956, 1014
apps 19-20, 30, 446-447, 449-456, 458-459, 462, 498-499, 501, 503-505, 523, 667, 672, 675, 978
Arnold Chiari II Malformation 410, 429
Asperger syndrome 409, 581, 595-596
assistive technology (AT) 513, 526, 549
Assistive Technology Device 432, 444
Assistive Technology Services 433, 444
ATAG 58, 69, 78
auditory processing 336-337
autism spectrum disorder 446, 585, 595, 941
Aversive Racism 688, 699, 711

B

backward design 761, 766, 780
banzhuren 865-867, 870-886, 890
barrier-free 293, 312-313, 315, 509-510, 512, 517-522, 534

Barrier-Free (BF) concepts 510, 517, 534
behavior management 126, 171, 456, 771
Behavioral Consultation 167, 177
bilingualism 632, 636
blind users 63-65, 535-536, 541-543, 547
blindness 27, 73, 142, 435, 499, 540, 549, 553-554, 691-692, 899, 944, 967-968
Bloom's Taxonomy 180, 183, 185-186, 195
Braille 25, 53, 208, 500, 504, 507, 513-514, 521, 523, 549, 945, 967-968
bullying 108-109, 368-378, 621, 782, 790, 1008-1009

C

campus climate 693, 699, 712, 714-715, 719-725, 1022-1025, 1028-1029, 1035-1037
Card Sorting 280, 290, 341
Chinese education 203, 866-867, 870, 872-873, 884, 890
chronic disabilities 557, 560-561, 567-568, 570, 573, 575
Classroom Communities 102
coaching 147-148, 150, 155, 230, 520, 770, 906-907, 912, 917-921, 923, 927
cognitive functioning 950, 971, 1010
College Entrance Examination 198, 204-205
colorblindness 690-691, 696, 894, 899
Common Core State Standards 152, 179, 182, 185-186, 188, 190-191, 195, 243, 320, 591, 846
community partnerships 13, 757, 762, 816
Constructivism 183-184, 195
Control in E-Learning 295
coordinated instruction 143, 153-156
coping strategies 356-359, 361-363, 373-374, 397, 1008
co-teacher-educators 767, 773-774, 780
Co-Teaching Model 971
critical literacy 629, 782, 791-792
critical reflection 613, 615, 617-618, 636, 1016
critical theory 738-741, 750, 753, 756
Crockett 122, 124, 126, 142, 784

Index

Cross-Cultural Dissonance 821
cultural border crossing 613
cultural diversity 398, 631, 635-636, 644, 651-652, 657, 659, 787, 807, 823, 840
Cultural Mismatch 808, 821
culturally affirming education 899
culturally competent 649, 655-656, 791, 821, 918
culturally diverse 630, 632, 635-636, 638, 640, 644, 655-658, 686, 768, 806, 814, 821
culturally relevant pedagogy 629, 651
culturally responsive pedagogy 614-616, 623-624, 629, 786-787, 894, 915
culturally responsive teaching 613, 620-621, 649, 651, 653, 659, 666, 668-671, 673, 782, 806, 809, 817, 899
culture of learning 822-837, 840
Curbcuts or Curbramps 534

D

data analysis 144, 171, 360, 617, 630, 827, 846, 848-849, 851, 853-856, 896, 898, 1006
data collection 144, 226, 239, 250, 276, 373, 376, 453, 617, 637, 668, 826-827, 871, 895, 898, 973, 975, 977, 986-988
data system 8, 846-849, 853, 856, 862-863
data use 843, 845-849, 856-858
data-based 126, 130, 165, 170, 177, 244, 757, 771, 973
data-based decision making 130, 170, 177, 244, 771
Data-driven decision-making 862
data-informed decision-making 844, 847, 856, 862
Deficit vs. Difference 238
depression 62, 106, 108-109, 368-369, 372, 375-376, 391, 410, 415, 695, 948, 965
Didactic Method 295
disability disclosure 226-227, 230, 239
disability discrimination 21-22, 220, 510, 514-515, 525, 534
Disability Prevalence 239
disability services office 230, 416, 429
disclosure 35, 226-227, 230, 239, 415, 738, 742, 744, 750, 753
discrimination 4-6, 21-22, 25, 35-36, 53, 83, 92, 199-200, 219-220, 223, 238, 246, 336, 338, 393-396, 509-510, 512, 514-515, 525, 534, 566-567, 572, 582, 595, 615, 624, 658, 684, 686, 688-689, 691, 693, 695, 711, 721-723, 739, 784, 786, 788, 811-812, 890, 1023, 1025
disproportionate representation 718, 812, 821, 910
diverse learners 35, 37-38, 52, 55, 60, 74, 153, 498, 614, 622, 660, 762, 810, 818, 891-899, 902-903
diversity and equity 613-614, 644, 757, 762-763

dot code 464-466, 468-469, 471, 477, 479-480, 486, 488, 492-493
dysgraphia 274, 320, 323, 333-334, 406
dyslexia 62, 64-65, 70, 72, 272-287, 290, 320, 322-324, 334, 336, 339, 406, 498, 500, 591, 957
dysorthographia 320, 323, 331-332

E

Education Technology 6, 318
educational attainment 197-198, 200, 210-211, 816
Educational Creativity 890
educational rights 3, 199, 208, 550-551, 574, 784
effective leadership 126, 141
elderly 52, 54-55, 60, 62, 276, 676
elementary school 373, 436, 630-631, 633, 771, 818, 868, 883, 885
emotional segregation 684-685, 699
empathy 109, 228, 630, 632-636, 640-644, 667, 684-685, 744, 793, 822, 825, 948
English language learners 40, 151, 596, 620, 892, 902, 908, 926
English Learner 342, 780, 843, 845, 856
essentialist 822, 824-825, 827, 829, 834, 836-837, 840
evidence-based practices 123, 144-145, 153, 165, 241, 244-245, 251, 262, 342, 449, 774, 927
exceptionality 808, 940-941, 944, 946, 948, 950, 952-953, 955, 958, 963-965, 967, 971
executive functions 39, 184, 189, 341, 965
expressive language disability 473
Eye-Gaze Technology 523, 534

F

field experiences 660, 757, 759, 761, 763, 898, 1030
field-based teacher education 757-760, 762, 765, 767-768, 773, 776-777, 781
field-experiences 763, 768
finance 1, 7, 12, 18, 95, 208
footer 850, 852, 862
foreign students 52, 55, 60, 725, 831
Forensic psychology 697
Free and Appropriate Education (FAPE) 596
Fullan 124, 132, 134-136, 141, 921
Fullan's Framework for Leadership 135, 141

G

giftedness 408, 996-1000, 1005-1013, 1020-1021
grade level 127, 180, 186, 241, 244, 247-248, 262, 430, 564, 587-588, 623, 649-650, 653-654, 947, 949, 971, 987

Index

M

magical sheet 469, 493
Making Action Plans (MAP) 421, 430
mathematics 144-146, 148, 150-153, 156, 182, 240-257, 261-262, 321-322, 437, 496, 588, 590, 596, 652, 772, 783, 785, 844-845, 914-915, 919, 949, 961
media representations 712-714, 716-718, 721, 723-725
medical model 198, 200-202, 211, 251, 393-394, 403, 436
mental retardation 142, 322, 432, 552-554, 890
Microaggression 691-693, 699, 711, 899, 1040
micro-aggressions 740, 746, 750, 752-753, 756
mobile technologies 437, 449, 505, 666-668, 671-673, 675-677
Model Minority 693-694
Moderator Avatar 318
MOOCs 6-7, 20, 52, 54-55, 57, 59-60, 62-63, 65, 67, 72-74, 535-537, 544
motor impairment 62, 495
multicultural education 43, 632, 643, 657, 660, 782, 786-788, 806-808, 818, 821
Multi-Disciplinary Team (MDT) 178
Multi-Tiered System of Support 105, 240-241, 244
Mutually Beneficial Partnership 772, 781

N

narrative 11, 146, 149, 616-618, 629, 676, 738-739, 741-742, 744, 747-748, 750-753, 756, 918
Narrative Pedagogy 617, 629, 747
National Universities Commission 84
Nemeth Code 496, 500, 507
Nigeria 80-86, 88-96, 901
No Child Left Behind (NCLB) Act 123, 165, 552, 579, 596, 940, 974
No Tech/Low Tech 462
non-essentialist 822-827, 834, 840

O

Online and Blended Learning of Adults 295
organizational culture 392, 680, 683, 687, 689, 698, 711
overrepresentation 103, 717, 821
Over-the-Counter Data 856, 862

P

peaple/person with disabilities 2, 10, 14, 22, 41-42, 52, 60, 86, 197-205, 207-208, 210-211, 216-224, 226, 228, 231, 233, 393, 421, 432, 439, 496, 508, 510, 520, 548, 567, 595

pedagogy 35, 38, 43, 152-155, 277, 279, 287, 342, 450-451, 458, 498, 600, 602, 605, 608, 614-618, 623-625, 629, 631, 651, 653, 657, 671, 698, 711, 714, 738-739, 744, 746-748, 784, 786-788, 793-794, 817-818, 869, 892-894, 896-897, 899, 901, 907, 912, 914-916, 918-921, 925, 928, 1037
peer rejection 369, 375
Personas 273, 276, 290
Planning Alternative Tomorrows with Hope (PATH) 421, 430
postsecondary 3-9, 12-15, 18, 34-38, 42-47, 210, 219, 229, 241, 397-398, 404-405, 415, 421-422, 425, 427, 430, 496, 499
pre-service teachers 163, 171, 182, 188, 343, 630-632, 641, 644, 657-659, 661, 760, 789-790, 793, 795, 891-894, 897, 902, 904, 925-926, 940-941, 966, 968-969, 999
Prevalence 103, 127-128, 216-217, 239, 274, 322, 371, 373-374, 432, 511, 562, 940-941, 944, 946, 948, 950, 952-953, 955, 958, 963, 967, 971
problem based learning 631, 634-636, 643-644, 666, 668, 670-671, 673, 676
problem-solving 62, 124, 128-129, 163, 165, 167-171, 321, 337, 362, 653, 656, 667, 759, 914, 919
professional development (PD) 143, 145, 847, 862, 907
Professional Development Schools (PDS) 907
professional education 200, 291-293, 296-315
professional learning 148-151, 155-156, 622-623, 761, 772, 906-909, 912, 915, 917-918, 921, 926, 984
Professional Learning Communities (PLCs) 761, 907

Q

quality of life 54, 320, 364, 431-432, 439-440, 444, 514, 974
quota system 81, 84-85, 89, 93-94, 692

R

Racial Identity 1040
racism 43, 601, 656-657, 675, 680-693, 695-699, 711, 713, 716, 721-725, 738-744, 746, 748-753, 756, 782, 788, 894, 899, 901, 923, 1024
racist ideology 739-740, 745
reading disorder 323
reference guide 848, 862
reference sheet 848, 850, 862
Rehabilitation 2, 4, 7, 20, 22, 36, 217, 223, 294, 358, 363, 393, 395, 411, 432, 509-510, 512-513, 520, 550-552, 554, 559, 566-567, 572, 579, 582, 589, 595

Rehabilitation Act 4, 20, 22, 36, 223, 395, 509-510, 512-513, 550-552, 554, 566-567, 572, 579, 582, 589, 595
Religious Tenets 1025, 1040
Repressive Tolerance 741, 753, 756
Researcher Avatar 318
Response to Intervention 105, 121-123, 126-129, 133, 142-144, 164-165, 181, 244, 983
Response-to-Intervention (RTI) 105, 121-123, 126-129, 133, 142-144, 163-165, 178, 181, 244, 323, 914, 983

S

scanner pen 466, 469, 493
Scholarly Personal Narrative 747, 756
school activity 473, 479, 482-483, 487, 489, 493
screen design 275, 277, 279-281, 290, 450
screen reader 5, 9, 500, 502, 504-507, 549
SEL 102
self-advocacy 43, 391-392, 403, 591
self-determination 249, 306, 309, 391-392, 403
self-esteem 109, 362, 374-375, 579, 657, 695, 699, 807, 956, 967, 996
self-study 309, 765-767, 773, 776, 829-831
sense of belonging 54, 106, 392, 721, 1009, 1024, 1028, 1033-1034, 1040
social and emotional learning 102-112
social inclusion 275, 284, 287, 290, 599, 607-608
social justice 10, 12, 14, 18, 41-43, 46-47, 201, 392-394, 403, 515, 519, 619, 632, 655, 666-667, 670, 672, 697, 724, 726, 784-788, 790-793, 893-894, 898, 901, 925, 996-997, 1022, 1026, 1040
social justice model 393-394, 403
social skills 107, 109-111, 357, 362-363, 374, 376, 430, 449-451, 453, 564, 941, 949, 951, 966-967, 974
Social stories 411, 430
sound pen 465-466, 468-470, 473, 475-486, 489, 493
special education 13, 22, 103-105, 107, 121-130, 132-133, 136, 142-148, 150-151, 153-154, 156-157, 163-167, 169-170, 179-185, 190-191, 195-196, 198, 201-202, 208-210, 240-245, 251-256, 262, 284, 286, 322, 342-343, 369, 375, 406, 411, 427, 436, 446-447, 450, 453, 457-458, 463, 496, 522, 550-560, 562-565, 568, 572, 574-575, 578-579, 582-584, 586, 590-593, 596, 607, 654, 763, 766-767, 770, 806-808, 811-815, 821, 847, 853, 862, 866-868, 886, 890, 892-893, 910, 922-923, 926-928, 940-941, 944, 946-948, 950-953, 955, 958, 960, 963-965, 967, 972-973, 995-997, 1010-1011, 1021

Special Education Administrator 142
special education collaboration 927
Special Education Setting 163, 463
specially-designed instruction 245
specific learning disabilities 36, 242, 320, 356, 358, 406, 552, 585
speech therapy 446-447, 449, 451-452, 454-455, 458-459, 463, 560
Speech Therapy Setting 463
Spelling Disorder 323, 331
spina bifida (SB) 404-405, 430
stereotype 688, 694-695, 711, 998
struggling learners 123, 144-145, 149, 151-156, 923
Stuart Hall 712
student development 390, 751, 865, 872, 884-885, 890
student identity 41
student mobility 822-827, 832, 834-837, 840
Student Study Team (SST) 164, 166, 169, 178
student with a disability 25, 47, 142, 534, 554, 560, 570, 575, 583-584, 596, 971
study groups 40, 150, 906, 912, 914, 916, 927, 929
Switch Access 495, 507
Switch Interface 501, 507

T

task analysis 273, 276, 290, 436
teacher candidate 657, 762, 781
teacher education 146, 171, 630-632, 634, 636, 638, 642-644, 651, 656-657, 660-661, 690, 696, 698, 757-760, 762, 765-768, 771, 773-777, 781, 785-786, 790, 795, 847-849, 854, 892, 925, 927, 968, 1025, 1030
teacher knowledge 146, 148-150, 156, 908, 914
teacher learning 147-148, 150-151, 153, 155-156, 657, 761, 908, 917, 923, 925
teacher practice 910
teacher preparation programs 44, 217, 658, 775, 847, 928
team teaching 738, 748-749, 751-753, 756
Techies 549
technology devices 5, 62, 431-433, 435, 454, 456, 462, 513
Technology Services 15, 433, 444
transition planning 404
transitioning 230, 261, 341, 390, 396, 404, 417, 425, 673, 770
Triple H-AVATAR Technology 318

Index

U

UAAG 58, 79
unconscious racism 680, 683, 689, 699
underrepresentation 211, 694, 815, 821, 899
Universal Design (UD) 35, 517, 521, 534
Universal Design for Learning (UDL) 38, 179-181, 186, 495, 497, 508, 522
university culture 392, 398, 403
urban education 656, 782-783, 789
User analysis 290
User-Centered Design (UCD) 508

V

victimization 106, 109, 369, 372-376, 378, 654
Virtual Assistant 295
Virtual Research Environment 318
Visual Impaired 537-539, 549

W

WAI 23, 58, 79
WCAG 19-20, 23-27, 29-30, 58, 60-61, 72, 79
Web Accessibility 20-21, 23, 58, 73, 79, 275-276
White supremacy 690, 716, 721, 739-744, 750, 753, 756, 892
Whitten 122-123, 128-129
work experience 484-487, 493
workforce development 215-226, 229-233
Writing Disorder 323, 333

Purchase Print, E-Book, or Print + E-Book

IGI Global's reference books are available in three unique pricing formats:
Print Only, E-Book Only, or Print + E-Book.
Shipping fees may apply.

www.igi-global.com

Recommended Reference Books

Handbook of Research on Assessment Practices and Pedagogical Models for Immigrant Students

ISBN: 978-1-5225-9348-5
© 2019; 454 pp.
List Price: $255

Preparing the Higher Education Space for Gen Z

ISBN: 978-1-5225-7763-8
© 2019; 253 pp.
List Price: $175

Prevention and Detection of Academic Misconduct in Higher Education

ISBN: 978-1-5225-7531-3
© 2019; 324 pp.
List Price: $185

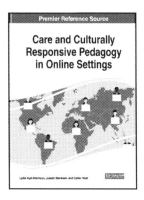

Care and Culturally Responsive Pedagogy in Online Settings

ISBN: 978-1-5225-7802-4
© 2019; 423 pp.
List Price: $195

Handbook of Research on School Violence in American K-12 Education

ISBN: 978-1-5225-6246-7
© 2019; 610 pp.
List Price: $275

Critical Assessment and Strategies for Increased Student Retention

ISBN: 978-1-5225-2998-9
© 2018; 352 pp.
List Price: $195

Do you want to stay current on the latest research trends, product announcements, news and special offers?
Join IGI Global's mailing list today and start enjoying exclusive perks sent only to IGI Global members.
Add your name to the list at **www.igi-global.com/newsletters**.

Publisher of Peer-Reviewed, Timely, and Innovative Academic Research

IGI Global
DISSEMINATOR of KNOWLEDGE

www.igi-global.com Sign up at www.igi-global.com/newsletters facebook.com/igiglobal twitter.com/igiglobal linkedin.com/igiglobal

Ensure Quality Research is Introduced to the Academic Community

Become an IGI Global Reviewer for Authored Book Projects

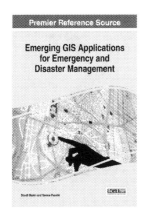
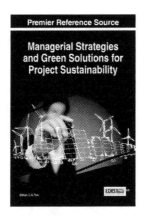

The overall success of an authored book project is dependent on quality and timely reviews.

In this competitive age of scholarly publishing, constructive and timely feedback significantly expedites the turnaround time of manuscripts from submission to acceptance, allowing the publication and discovery of forward-thinking research at a much more expeditious rate. Several IGI Global authored book projects are currently seeking highly-qualified experts in the field to fill vacancies on their respective editorial review boards:

Applications and Inquiries may be sent to:
development@igi-global.com

Applicants must have a doctorate (or an equivalent degree) as well as publishing and reviewing experience. Reviewers are asked to complete the open-ended evaluation questions with as much detail as possible in a timely, collegial, and constructive manner. All reviewers' tenures run for one-year terms on the editorial review boards and are expected to complete at least three reviews per term. Upon successful completion of this term, reviewers can be considered for an additional term.

If you have a colleague that may be interested in this opportunity,
we encourage you to share this information with them.

IGI Global Proudly Partners With eContent Pro International

Receive a 25% Discount on all Editorial Services

Editorial Services

IGI Global expects all final manuscripts submitted for publication to be in their final form. This means they must be reviewed, revised, and professionally copy edited prior to their final submission. Not only does this support with accelerating the publication process, but it also ensures that the highest quality scholarly work can be disseminated.

English Language Copy Editing

Let eContent Pro International's expert copy editors perform edits on your manuscript to resolve spelling, punctuaion, grammar, syntax, flow, formatting issues and more.

Scientific and Scholarly Editing

Allow colleagues in your research area to examine the content of your manuscript and provide you with valuable feedback and suggestions before submission.

Figure, Table, Chart & Equation Conversions

Do you have poor quality figures? Do you need visual elements in your manuscript created or converted? A design expert can help!

Translation

Need your documjent translated into English? eContent Pro International's expert translators are fluent in English and more than 40 different languages.

Hear What Your Colleagues are Saying About Editorial Services Supported by IGI Global

"The service was very fast, very thorough, and very helpful in ensuring our chapter meets the criteria and requirements of the book's editors. I was quite impressed and happy with your service."

– Prof. Tom Brinthaupt,
Middle Tennessee State University, USA

"I found the work actually spectacular. The editing, formatting, and other checks were very thorough. The turnaround time was great as well. I will definitely use eContent Pro in the future."

– Nickanor Amwata, Lecturer,
University of Kurdistan Hawler, Iraq

"I was impressed that it was done timely, and wherever the content was not clear for the reader, the paper was improved with better readability for the audience."

– Prof. James Chilembwe,
Mzuzu University, Malawi

Email: customerservice@econtentpro.com   www.igi-global.com/editorial-service-partners

H

handmade content 464, 479-480, 483-485, 488, 492
handmade teaching material 466
Hargreaves 132-133, 921
HCI 57, 78
Health Impaired 550-551, 553, 563
help system 848, 862
High Incident Disability 971
High Tech Innovative 462
High Tech Traditional 462
higher education 1-15, 18, 28-29, 34-37, 44-47, 53, 80-86, 88-92, 94-96, 126, 190-191, 197-201, 203-211, 215, 219, 221, 223, 225, 227-233, 238, 291, 297, 299, 302, 390-398, 495, 505, 509-511, 513, 517, 534, 593, 599, 649, 653-658, 660-662, 683, 686, 690-693, 695, 697, 699, 713, 719-720, 723, 726, 741, 748, 751, 753, 822, 890, 892-894, 1022, 1024-1025, 1027-1029, 1033, 1036-1037
higher education institutions 3-7, 10, 12-14, 53, 199-200, 204-206, 208-209, 211, 221, 390-395, 397-398, 649, 653-658, 660-662, 741, 1022, 1024-1025, 1027, 1037
holistic approach 9, 23, 46, 457, 462
Human-Centered-Design 290
hydrocephalus 406, 408, 410, 430

I

Identification of Giftedness 1021
IEP Goal 186, 195
inclusion 34-35, 42, 46-47, 52, 54, 60, 74, 107-108, 147, 201, 215, 218, 221-222, 231, 233, 238, 240, 254, 256, 272-277, 280, 284-287, 290, 304, 308, 313, 315, 368-369, 495, 509, 511-513, 515, 517-518, 520, 524-526, 534, 552, 558-559, 565, 574, 599-600, 602-603, 607-608, 653, 655-656, 697, 787, 867-868, 884, 891-892, 894, 907, 910-911, 919, 922-923, 925-927, 929, 951, 972, 991, 995, 1016, 1032
inclusive classroom 102-103, 190-191, 240, 865-867, 871, 875-879, 881-882, 884-886, 890-891, 896, 898, 902-904, 972-973, 979, 1016
inclusive education 45, 106, 198, 200-201, 208, 369, 509, 514, 579, 584, 600-601, 606, 865-873, 875, 885-886, 890, 910-912, 919, 1016
inclusive environment 103, 107, 109, 111, 211, 940, 1027, 1036, 1040
inclusive practices 123, 526, 599, 608, 785, 906-907, 914, 916, 918-920, 922-923, 927, 929
independent living 2, 444, 510, 519, 554, 814, 967

Indicator of Sliding Mode 318
Individual Education Plan (IEP) 179, 191, 958
Individualized Education Plan (IEP) 411, 565, 581, 596
Individuals with Disabilities Education Act (IDEA) 4, 22, 126-127, 142, 144, 195, 241, 406, 496, 551-552, 589, 596, 812, 821, 971
Individuals with Disabilities Education Improvement Act (IDEIA) 177, 322
Innovative Practice 866, 890
innovative technology 448-449, 456-457, 462
institutes of higher education 510
institutional racism 680, 683-684, 691, 693, 695-697, 699, 711, 899, 1024
Institutions of Higher Education (IHE) 510, 534
International Baccalaureate 772, 781, 1003
international students 37, 712-715, 719-720, 723, 725, 822-823, 832
internationalisation 822, 824-825, 834, 836, 840
intersectionality 42, 394, 1040
IT for inclusion 290

L

language and literacy 629, 771
Language Disorder 821
law 1, 3-7, 18-19, 21-22, 25, 44, 127, 142, 180, 198, 200-202, 207-208, 220, 224, 300, 322, 375, 391, 406, 512-514, 551-554, 557-560, 566, 579, 582-585, 595-596, 666, 675, 689, 697-698, 717-718, 721, 740, 821, 825, 899
leadership 11, 13, 121-126, 130, 134-135, 141, 182-183, 397-398, 457, 618, 621, 651, 680-683, 686-688, 690, 697, 699, 711, 724, 746-748, 762, 765-766, 768, 771, 790, 866, 868, 872-874, 918, 998, 1026, 1036
learning disability 36, 38, 40, 126-127, 142, 144, 165, 227, 229, 242, 248, 320-323, 356-358, 361, 390-398, 403-410, 514, 552-554, 567, 574, 582, 585, 870, 878, 883, 957
learning goals 295, 649, 668, 672-673, 766
learning management system 20, 25, 862
learning objectives 454, 748
lesson study 151, 153, 906, 912, 915-916
linguistic diversity 600, 630-631, 637, 640, 758
linguistically diverse 396, 614, 630-631, 638, 640, 644, 653, 659, 758-759, 770-771, 808-809, 811-818, 821, 902, 906-907
Local Educational Agency 596
loneliness 368-369, 372, 375-376, 676
Low-Incident Disability 971

Printed in the United States
By Bookmasters

Celebrating Over 30 Years of Scholarly Knowledge Creation & Dissemination

www.igi-global.com

InfoSci®-Books

A Database of Over 5,300+ Reference Books Containing Over 100,000+ Chapters Focusing on Emerging Research

GAIN ACCESS TO **THOUSANDS** OF REFERENCE BOOKS AT **A FRACTION** OF THEIR INDIVIDUAL LIST **PRICE**.

InfoSci®-Books Database

The **InfoSci®-Books** database is a collection of over 5,300+ IGI Global single and multi-volume reference books, handbooks of research, and encyclopedias, encompassing groundbreaking research from prominent experts worldwide that span over 350+ topics in 11 core subject areas including business, computer science, education, science and engineering, social sciences and more.

Open Access Fee Waiver (Offset Model) Initiative

For any library that invests in IGI Global's InfoSci-Journals and/or InfoSci-Books databases, IGI Global will match the library's investment with a fund of equal value to go toward **subsidizing the OA article processing charges (APCs) for their students, faculty, and staff** at that institution when their work is submitted and accepted under OA into an IGI Global journal.*

INFOSCI® PLATFORM FEATURES

- No DRM
- No Set-Up or Maintenance Fees
- A Guarantee of No More Than a 5% Annual Increase
- Full-Text HTML and PDF Viewing Options
- Downloadable MARC Records
- Unlimited Simultaneous Access
- COUNTER 5 Compliant Reports
- Formatted Citations With Ability to Export to RefWorks and EasyBib
- No Embargo of Content (Research is Available Months in Advance of the Print Release)

*The fund will be offered on an annual basis and expire at the end of the subscription period. The fund would renew as the subscription is renewed for each year thereafter. The open access fees will be waived after the student, faculty, or staff's paper has been vetted and accepted into an IGI Global journal and the fund can only be used toward publishing OA in an IGI Global journal. Libraries in developing countries will have the match on their investment doubled.

To Learn More or To Purchase This Database:
www.igi-global.com/infosci-books

eresources@igi-global.com • Toll Free: 1-866-342-6657 ext. 100 • Phone: 717-533-8845 x100